Financing Universal Access to Healthcare

A Comparative Review of Landmark Legislative Health Reforms in the OECD

World Scientific Series in Health Investment and Financing

ISSN: 2591-7315

Series Editor: Alexander S. Preker *(Columbia University, USA and Health Investment & Financing Corp, USA)*

Most western developed countries offer universal access to healthcare through mechanisms that provide financial protection against its high cost, either through insurance or government subsidy programs.

In most middle- and low-income countries, financing is often at the center of reforms in the healthcare sector. Success or failure of these reforms can have major impact on the political survival of governments that get involved, and major implications for the dynamics of the healthcare industry and overall economy.

With this series, World Scientific will contribute knowledge about a policy area which is still poorly-understood. The series merges policy and practice, exploring the economic underpinnings of real trends in health investment and financing.

The series will appeal and be accessible to investors, the health insurance industry, healthcare actuaries, business schools with healthcare tracts, healthcare management programs, researchers, graduate students, policy makers and practitioners working in the health sector worldwide.

Vol. 1 *Financing Universal Access to Healthcare: A Comparative Review of Landmark Legislative Health Reforms in the OECD*
by Alexander S. Preker

Forthcoming

Financing Universal Access to Healthcare: A Comparative Review of Incremental Health Insurance Reforms in the OECD
Alexander S. Preker

Financing Micro Health Insurance: Theory, Methods and Evidence
David M. Dror

Role of Private Financing in the Education of Health Workers: Gaining the Competitive Edge
Alexander S. Preker, Hortenzia Beciu and Eric Keuffel

Capital Finance in the Health Industry: A User Manual for Investors and Companies
Alexander S. Preker and Les Funtleyder

Handbook on Health System Financing and Organization
Dov Chernichovsky

World Scientific Series in Health Investment and Financing – Vol. 1

Financing Universal Access to Healthcare

A Comparative Review of Landmark Legislative Health Reforms in the OECD

Alexander S. Preker

Columbia University, USA

Health Investment & Financing Corporation, USA

World Scientific

NEW JERSEY • LONDON • SINGAPORE • BEIJING • SHANGHAI • HONG KONG • TAIPEI • CHENNAI • TOKYO

Published by

World Scientific Publishing Co. Pte. Ltd.
5 Toh Tuck Link, Singapore 596224
USA office: 27 Warren Street, Suite 401-402, Hackensack, NJ 07601
UK office: 57 Shelton Street, Covent Garden, London WC2H 9HE

Library of Congress Cataloging-in-Publication Data
Names: Preker, Alexander S., 1951– author.
Title: Financing universal access to healthcare : a comparative review of landmark legislative health reforms in the OECD / by Alexander S Preker (Columbia University, USA).
Other titles: World Scientific series in health investment and financing ; v. 1.
Description: New Jersey : World Scientific, 2018. | Series: World Scientific series in health investment and financing ; volume 1 | Includes bibliographical references.
Identifiers: LCCN 2017035131 | ISBN 9789813227163 (hc : alk. paper)
Subjects: | MESH: Organisation for Economic Co-operation and Development. | Health Services Accessibility--economics | Healthcare Financing | Universal Coverage--legislation & jurisprudence | Health Care Reform--legislation & jurisprudence | Health Expenditures
Classification: LCC RA971.3 | NLM W 76.1 | DDC 362.1068/1--dc23
LC record available at https://lccn.loc.gov/2017035131

British Library Cataloguing-in-Publication Data
A catalogue record for this book is available from the British Library.

For any available supplementary material, please visit
http://www.worldscientific.com/worldscibooks/10.1142/10629#t=suppl

Desk Editors: Herbert Moses/Shreya Gopi

Typeset by Stallion Press
Email: enquiries@stallionpress.com

Printed in Singapore

DEDICATION

This volume is dedicated to all those who will continue the struggle of achieving "Health for All" so that the dream of a world with "Universal Health Care Coverage" will be achieved in the twenty-first century. The "giants among giants" of the past, like the late Professor Brian Able-Smith, have passed the baton for this agenda to the next generations of leaders.

FOREWORD

This year, as we commemorate the 40th Anniversary of the *Alma-Ata Declaration* of "Health for All" on October 25–26 in Almaty, Kazakhstan, as well as the 70th Anniversary of the UK National Health Service, we also celebrate the great achievements in bringing affordable access to quality health services for billions of people across the world over the past decades.

This book provides a seminal review of the political process, the economic underpinnings and implementation challenges involved in achieving Universal Health Coverage (UHC). The creation of the UK National Health Service out of the ashes of the bombs dropped on London during the Second World War was a stark reminder of the important role that hospitals and emergency services played in complementing primary care under UHC. Although this volume focusses on OECD countries that provide access to comprehensive health service based on clinical need, available to all — not on the ability to pay — through major legislative reforms, other European countries like Germany, France, Switzerland and the Netherlands achieved similar coverage through a more gradual incremental legislative process. How these latter countries also achieved UHC for their populations and similar stories in low- and middle-income countries will be the focus of a forthcoming volume by Professor Alexander S. Preker.

During his 25 year career at the World Bank and International Finance Corporation, the author was an influential voice on UHC in the Bank, the International Labor Organization, and the World Health Organization. His international work during these past three decades emphasized the need to underpin worthy aspirations and declarations with needed funding, human resources and implementation capacity at the country level. As a member of the World Bank team which wrote the World Development Report 1993 on "Investing in Health" and the WHO team which wrote the World Health Report 2000 on "Health Systems: Improving Performance", and throughout his career, the author has emphasized that good health is part of economic development and that "investing in health" is a worthy economic goal, not just a lofty social aspiration. The comparative health systems framework and country case studies reviewed in this volume reflect this philosophy. During this period, it was an honor to have had a chance to work with Professor Preker and to have benefited from his insights on and innovative approaches to health care financing and service delivery.

The International Hospital Federation (IHF) is committed to advancing the UHC agenda throughout the world, giving billions of people better access to critical hospital care and basic health services when needed, irrespective of their income or geographic location in the world. Since its establishment in 1929, the IHF recognizes the essential role of hospitals and health care organizations in providing health care, supporting health services and offering education to health care providers as a critical partner during the drive for UHC throughout the world.

This pragmatic philosophy underpins the Almaty Declaration 2.0, which will reflect the changing expectations of health care providers, the needs of patients, and the challenges posed by the Sustainable Development Goals 2030. I am optimistic that the renewed approach to both primary and more advanced health care will respond to the health needs and aspirations of people throughout the world through better access and more effective use of all available health services and their associated technologies. The conditions are now present to move to a real health systems approach in which all players from front-line workers to higher levels of the referral system in both the public and private sectors can contribute effectively to all the dimensions of the UHC agenda.

This volume is a tribute to this renewed effort in achieving "Health for All".

Eric de Roodenbeke
Executive Director
International Hospital Federation
Geneva

PREFACE

Financing Health for All. What is the most practicable system of charging people for health care ....

... Thirteen years after the Health-for-All programme [Alma Ata 1978] was launched, the availability of the necessary finance remains a formidable obstacle to future progress in many developing countries. The hope that governments would increase spending on health care to 5% of the national income is in most cases unlikely to realize. Nor is there evidence that donors are willing to increase their aid to developing countries or to divert more of it to the health sector. Ministries of health are being left to find their own solution. Is the way forward to be found in user charges, community financing, private insurance, or some system of formal compulsory insurance? How does one decide which are the more promising options for a particular country? What has been learned from the experience of countries which have tried to go down particular roads?

Brian Able-Smith (1991)
"Financing Health-for-All"
World Health Forum, Vol 12

The public sector of all western developed countries has become increasingly involved in financing health care during the past century. Today, 13 OECD countries have passed landmark legislative reforms that call for compulsory prepayment and universal entitlement to comprehensive services, while most of the others achieve similar coverage through a mixture of public and private voluntary arrangements. This study carried out a detailed analysis of *why, how* and *to what effect* governments became involved in health care financing in eight of these countries.

During the early phase of this evolution, reliance on direct out-of-pocket payment and an unregulated market mechanism for the financing, production and delivery of health care led to many unsatisfactory outcomes in the allocation of scarce resources, redistribution of the financial burden of illness and stabilization of health care activities. This forced the state to intervene through regulations, subsidies and direct provision of services. Expansion in prepayment of health care gradually occurred through private insurance, social insurance and general revenues in response to different socio-economic, political and bureaucratic forces. Although improving health may have been the ultimate goal, offering universal access to affordable health care was the way the countries examined achieved this objective.

Universal comprehensive coverage was associated with a decade of stable public expenditure on health care compared with GDP, total government expenditure and government consumption expenditure. There were no disproportionate increases in health care expenditure or displacement of public funds away from social programs that depended on cash transfer payments. Nor do the countries that offer such social protection have higher public debt or poorer economic performance compared with the rest of the OECD. Measures of health status are unfortunately still not sufficiently developed or standardized to permit a detailed analysis of this aspect of outcome through cross-national comparisons. Furthermore, the countries examined may be more vulnerable to political backlash because of the high visibility of their government involvement in health care financing.

ABOUT THE AUTHOR

Professor Alexander S. Preker is a globally recognized expert on the economics of investing and financing health systems, health care policy, governance and health care reform. He has been an advisor to Ministers of Health and senior policy makers throughout the world on capital investment in the health sector, health financing, health insurance, public–private partnerships and the political process of health care reform. And he is on the executive board of several private health care companies.

Professor Preker is a Commissioner with the Global Commission on Pollution, Health and Development. He is an Honorary Member of the International Hospital Federation, a Member of the Board of the USA Health Care Alliance and several other organizations that deal with health policy and health reform.

Professor Preker is an Adjunct Associate Professor for Health Care Management at the Mailman School of Public Health at Columbia University in New York. He is an Adjunct Associate Professor of Public Policy at New York University's Robert F. Wagner Graduate School of Public Policy and he is an Executive Scholar at the Icahn School of Medicine at Mount Sinai in New York.

In addition to his health policy and academic work, Professor Preker is also active in the private health sector. He is President and CEO of Health

Investment & Financing Corporation, a New York based firm that specializes in investment and advisory services for small and medium size health care businesses. He is one of the founding members of the New York Chapter of the Keiretsu Forum, a crowd funding platform with over US$800 million in investments, and a LLP with Keiretsu Capital, a US$10 million early stage investment fund. He is an active investor in the OurCrowd Health and Life Sciences Portfolio and Landmark Angels and he manages the New York Due Diligence Fellowship program for the Keiretsu Forum at Columbia University.

Prior to his current work, Professor Preker had a distinguished career, working at different times for International Bank of Reconstruction and Development (IBRD), International Development Association (IDA), International Finance Corporation (IFC) and World Health Organization (WHO). From 2007 to 2012, he was head of the Health Industry Group and Investment Policy for the International Finance Corporation (IFC). In this position, he and his team set up a US$1 billion investment facility for health to support expansion of small and medium size business in the Africa. Prior to his work at the IFC, Professor Preker was the Chief Economist for the health sector in the World Bank Group at a time that the annual lending pipeline was about US$3 billion and a total portfolio value in the range of US$15 billion.

While at the World Bank career, Professor Preker worked with both Lawrence Summers (former Director of the National Economic Council under the Obama Administration) and Joseph Stiglitz (recipient of the Nobel Memorial Prize in Economic Sciences) during their respective tenures as Chief Economist for the World Bank Group as well as many Ministers of Health, Finance Economic Development and other senior officials in the client countries he served.

Professor Preker is a prolific writer and has published extensively, having authored and co-authored over 20 books, many scientific articles and has been the primary author of a wide range of institutional reports and policy briefs. While at the World Bank, he was a member of the Editorial Board for the World Bank's External Operations Publication Department and Editor in Chief of its health care publications.

Professor Preker's training includes a Ph.D. in Economics from the London School of Economics and Political Science, a Fellowship in Medicine from University College London, a Diploma in Medical Law and Ethics from King's College London, and a M.D from University of British Columbia.

ACKNOWLEDGMENTS

Guidance and wisdom from late Professor Brian Abel-Smith, London School of Economics and Political Science, provided the main inspiration for looking in detail at the political economy of health care reforms leading to successful implementation of universal access to affordable health coverage. Special recognition is given to Professor Rudolf Klein, University of Bath, whose constructive comments led to a critical revision of the original draft manuscript and more rigorous comparative and social policy analysis.

Countless others contributed insights over the years on the application of the original work to developing countries and elaboration of a comprehensive analytical framework for cross-country comparative studies and performance evaluation in health care policy and financing reforms.

Notably Professors Dov Chernichovsky (Ben Gurion University), André-Pierre Contandriopoulos (University of Montreal), Alain Enthoven (Stanford), Robert Evans (University of British Columbia), Mark V. Pauly (Wharton School, University of Pennsylvania), Uwe Reinhardt (Princeton), Richard M. Scheffler (Berkeley), Joseph E. Stiglitz (Columbia University), Wynand P.M.M. van de Ven (Erasmus University), and Peter Zweifel (University of Zurich) provided the intellectual underpinnings for exploring the economics of private and public approaches to health insurance.

Over the past 30 years, deep insights were gained on the topic of universal health coverage from the global and country level collaboration among the World Bank Group, the International Labour Organization

(ILO), and the World Health Organization (WHO). Notable bilateral players committed to improving health financing include the Australian Agency for International Development (AusAid), the British Department for International Development (DFID), Canadian International Development Agency (CIDA), the Danish International Development Agency (DANIDA), the Dutch Government, the French Agence Française de Développement (AFD), the German Deutsche Gesellschaft für Internationale Zusammenarbeit (GIZ), the Japanese International Cooperation Agency (JICA), the Norwegian Agency for Development Cooperation (NORAD), the Swedish International Development Cooperation Association (SIDA), and the US Agency for International Development (USAID).

The International Federation of Health Plans (iFHP), countless other bilateral, non-governmental and academic organizations, and national governments carrying out health financing reforms contributed valuable insights.

Appreciation is expressed for the collaboration and deeper understanding on the approaches to universal health care gained insights over the years from: Olusoji O. Adeyi, Chris Atim, Ladi Awosika, Cristian Baeza, Enis Baris, Nicholas Barr, Mark C. Bassett, Hortenzia Beciu, Paolo Belli, Peter A. Berman, Ricardo Bitrán, Reinhard Busse, Guy Carrin, Mukesh Chawla, Michael Cichon, Jorge A. Coarasa, Catherine Connor, Rafael Cortez, Daniel Cotlear, Agnes Couffinhal, Diana Dennett, François Diop, Richard G.D. Feachem, David M. Dror, Yohana Dukhan, Bjorn O. Ekman, Guy Ellena, Maria Louisa Escobar, David B. Evans, Scott D. Featherston, David de Ferranti, Julio Frenk, Hernán L. Fuenzalida-Puelma, Jacques van der Gaag, Sherry Glied, Pablo Gottret, Ian Grant-Whyte, Charles C. Griffin, Ralph Harbison, April Harding, Loraine Hawkins, Richard Hinz, Peter S. Heller, Jürgen Hohmann, William C. Hsiao, Melitta Jakab, Dean Jamison, Vijayasekar Kalavakonda, Daniel Kress, Gerald M. La Forgia, Gina Lagomarsino, John C. Langenbrunner, Rodney Lester, Maureen Lewis, Marianne E. Lindner, James Christopher Lovelace, Caroline Ly, Hans Maarse, Marty Makinen, Theodore R. Marmor, Anne Mills, Henry Mintzberg, Philip Musgrove, Somil Nagpal, Stefan Nachuk, Allyala Nandakumar, Charles Normand, Kieke Okma, Nathaniel Otoo, Mead Over, Ariel Pablos-Mendez, Ok Pannenborg, Oscar Picazo, Jean-Pierre Poullier, Khama Rogo, Eric de Roodenbeke, Aaltje de

Roos, Jeffrey Sachs, Thomas Sackville, Xenia Scheil-Adlung, Onno P. Schellekens, George Schieber, Agnes Soucat, Michael S. Sparer, Nicole Tapay, Robert Taylor, Edit V. Velenyi, Adam Wagstaff, Hong Wang, Marie-Odile Waty, Alan Williams and Ke Xu.

Appreciation is expressed to Herbert Moses, Shreya Gopi, Anthony Alexander, Nisha Rahul and Ranjana Rajan at World Scientific for their diligence during the editorial process in preparing the manuscript and to Kathleen A. Lynch, independent consultant and developmental editor, and to members of the World Bank publication department for the editorial support provided over the years. I am also very grateful to my family, friends, and feline companions for their unconditional love, support and wise counsel.

CONTENTS

LIST OF FIGURES AND TABLES

Figures in Text

Figures in Appendix

Tables in Text

Tables in Appendix

PART I

INTRODUCTION

The introductory section of the book provides a summary of analytical frameworks used in comparative studies, with a special focus on health care financing studies on universal coverage. This section will also provide a detailed discussion on research methodologies for such studies and the methodology used for the review summarized in this book.

CHAPTER 1

ANALYTICAL FRAMEWORK

This chapter of the book will provide a review of analytical frameworks for understanding health care financing reforms. It will review historical approaches to balancing the role of the state and private sector in social policy and health care, including known determinants of public policy, normative functions of modern governments, outcomes from health policy and policy processes.

Health systems are a complex integral part of society. To fully understand a health system and health policy, it is necessary to look beyond the health system itself to the environment in which it exists. For the purpose of the cross-national comparisons that will be made in this volume the following broad framework will be used. The country context will include an analysis of the countries' history, politics, institutions, its socio-economic and demographic aspects and its business environment and investment climate. The evolution of the countries' health systems will include both their history and reform processes. The structure of the countries' health systems will include their organization, ownership and resources. And the function of the countries' health systems will include the roles of government and the public sector, the roles of markets and the private sector and areas where the public and private sector work in collaboration or competition with each other. See Table 1.1.

Table 1.1 A Comparative Health Systems Analysis Framework

Key Domain	Components of Analysis
Country context	Historical, political & institutional context Socio-economic, demographic context & cultural context Business environment & investment climate
Evolution	History Reform Process
Characteristics	Structural features *Organization (organogram & health pyramid)* *Ownership (public/private structure, concentration & de-concentration)* *Resources (input level, range & quality)* Functions *Roles of governments & public sector* Stewardship Policy making process Governance *Roles of markets & private sector* Manufacturing (goods & services) Distribution (wholesale & retail) Trade (import & export) *Roles of partnerships between public & private sectors* Management and M&E (monitoring & evaluation) Financing (revenue collection, risk pooling & purchasing/allocation) Service delivery (preventive, diagnostics, curative, rehabilitation, & palliative) Medical education, research & development Performance *Inputs, outputs & process* *Proxy measures* *Impact*

Source: Author.

A. HISTORICAL ROLE OF THE STATE

For centuries, political philosophers have debated the nature of the relationship between the state[1] and its citizens, "*why, how* and *to what effect* different governments pursue a particular course of action or inaction."[2] In recent times, social scientists have carried out extensive investigation on the **determinants** (why), **normative functions and instruments** (how or what) and **outcome** (effects) of policies that define the normative function of modern governments. The following brief historical sketch draws attention to the perennial dilemma between individualist and collectivist concerns about the role of the state, which has a significant impact on the issues and policy options that will be explored in the study. "In dilemmatic situations, the reasons on each side of a problem are weighty ones, and none is in any obvious way the right set of reasons."[3] This debate can be extended to health care, which is one of the many complex expressions of modern welfare states — the content of specific health policies, the reasons they were introduced and their impact on both the health sector and society in general.

Religious and natural law theories on the role of the state in western societies are deeply rooted in antiquity[4] by the scriptures[5] and classical thought.[6] Plato was an elitist who believed that knowledge was a virtue and ignorance, a vice. The privileged few were entrusted to govern the ignorant masses.[7] Health systems are not only an integral subset of the state but often microcosms of their socio-economic, political and administrative systems. The *papyri*, dating to the second millennium B.C., give fascinating evidence that Imhotep, an archetypal physician, priest and court official in ancient Egypt, introduced collective services with healers who were paid by the community.[8] This early experiment in organized health care did not survive the test of time. The *Code of Hammurabi* (1792–1750 BC) laid down, *inter alia*, a system of direct fee-for-service payment based on the nature of services rendered and the ability of the patient to pay.[9] For the next 3,000 years, the involvement of the state in health care revolved mainly around enforcing the rules of compensation for personal injury and protection of the self-governing medical guild.[10] At best, financing, organization and provision of health care was limited to the royal courts of kings, emperors and other nobility who might have a physician for their personal use and troops at the time of battle. The masses got by with local healers, midwives, natural remedies, apothecaries and quacks.

The Dark Ages, Renaissance and Reformation enshrined the twin sources of European civilization — religious and state absolutism.[11]

Supported by the scourge of recurrent bouts of plague, superstition spread its poison across the continent through burning at the stake and executions. King Henry VIII gave sweeping powers to the College of Commonalty of the Faculty of Medicine of London in 1518 to punish quacks and pretenders, but did little else to change the *status quo*.[12] These events fostered an individualist backlash that eventually led to the transfer of political power from absolute monarchies and feudal states to the rising property-owning classes. Hobbes believed that individuals entered into a social contract by which they mutually agreed to form a sovereign state (Leviathan) that would limit its role to providing peace, protection and justice: "the liberty each man, hath, to use his own power, as he will."[13] Locke believed that the only valid state restriction on the innate right to liberty and freedom was to preserve "life, liberty, health, limb or goods of another."[14] Organized care for the sick, disabled and poor, who according to natural law had brought their destiny upon themselves, was left to local parishes.[15] The transition from Catholicism to Protestantism in northern Europe undermined these early efforts as sequestration of ecclesiastical properties left many reform movements without resources to carry out even minimal custodial care.[16]

The emergence of scientific thought during the Enlightenment of the eighteenth century confronted the tyranny of divine right and abuses of state sovereignty with critical reasoning.[17] Kant stressed the responsibility of individuals to be autonomous and choose their own fate as free and rational beings: "autonomy of the will ... the supreme principle."[18] As was characteristic of the individualism of the times, he believed that freedom and liberty would protect civil and political rights. In contrast, Rousseau and other early defenders of collectivism favored a social contract to protect economic and social rights.[19] Adam Smith was specific in his description of appropriate limitations in the function of the *laissez-faire* capitalist state: protecting society from violence and invasion; protecting individuals from injustice and oppression of others; and maintaining necessary public works and institutions that are of no personal interest to individuals.[20] The first two functions are carried out by all organized societies in the form of defense, police, justice and administration. The third, which anticipates a role in the allocation of resources, is more complex because it leaves scope for interpretation. Poor law relief brought on by industrialization and urbanization, unintentional as it may have been, became one of the earliest expressions of secular involvement by the state in health care.[21] The criteria for admission were "less concerned with the alleviation of poverty than with preventing public subsidy of the idle."[22]

By the nineteenth century, utilitarian theories on the role of the state formally challenged the supremacy of religious and natural law philosophies.[23] "Utilitarianism is a maximising and collectivising principle that requires governments to maximise the total net sum of the happiness of all their subjects ... in contrast to natural rights theory which is a distributive and individualizing principle that assigns priority to specific basic interests of each individual subject."[24] Appealing to "reasonable men", Bentham felt that natural rights were "simple nonsense ... nonsense upon stilts."[25] Mill believed that individuals should be free in their actions "to carry these out in their lives without hindrance, either physical or moral, from their fellow men, so long as it is at their own risk and peril."[26] Intended to liberate individuals from state intervention, his *laisser-faire* "invisible hand" left urban populations vulnerable to all sorts of social injustices in early industrial societies. This gave rise to Marx's collectivist vision of the socialist state: "Mankind must first of all eat, drink, have shelter and clothing, before it can pursue politics, science, art, religion, etc."[27] His philosophy on equity transcended the political rejection that it evoked in many western societies: "From each according to his ability, to each according to his need."[28] Poor law infirmaries,[29] the sanitary movement[30] and social insurance[31] during the latter part of the nineteenth century paved the way for health care as one of the legitimate functions of the state.

A first step beyond minimal provision would be to allow the state to carry out unanimously approved activities that lead to Pareto improvements.[32] Pareto efficiency, or the point at which no further action could be taken without worsening the position of others, would define the acceptable limit to state involvement. An individualistic social welfare utility function can be written as $\Gamma(U^1, U^2, U^3, \ldots, Uh)$, where U^h is the utility of individual h.[33] To go beyond this simple Pareto criterion, gains and losses could be optimized.[34] Benthamites would maximize each individual utility ($\Gamma = U^1, U^2, U^3, \ldots, U^h$), while Rawlsians would maximize the welfare of the least well-off ($\Gamma = \min(U^h)$).[35] Egalitarian preferences would depart from both of these by aiming to decrease the "distance" between individual utilities ($U^2 > U^1$).[36] Most western countries go beyond these approaches to include non-individualistic, collective social preferences[37] through *welfarism*[38] in the case of social security benefits and *extra-welfarism*[39] in the case of health care. These theories have been extensively discussed in the literature on the development, evolution and future of the welfare state. Governments do this through paternalist social preferences that fix "not a strictly equal distribution but an assured universal minimum."[40] Decisions to tax alcohol and tobacco while spending public funds on food, education, housing and health care follow this logic.

The dichotomy between individual and collectivist rights split the developed world into two political blocks during most of the twentieth century.[41] Theories on the modern state have remained as divergent as ever, ranging from the "minimal" state,[42] through states that ensure Pareto efficiency and justice[43] to maximization of social welfare and communism.[44] Nozick's "night-watchman" is at one extreme of this spectrum: "a minimal state limited to the narrow functions of protection against force, theft, fraud, enforcement of contracts, and so on is justified [to prevent anarchy]."[45] This hypothetical state, which does not exist anywhere, draws heavily on the earlier writings of Hobbes and Locke. At the opposite extreme are those who insist that the state should control all economic activities in an Orwellian centrally planned state to protect the collective interests of society. The traditional communist model, which draws heavily on Marx, Engles and Rousseau, was introduced as a tool of rapid industrialization by socialist states in response to the economic crisis of 1931–1933.[46] The rigid interventionist communist model has now been rejected by most of the Eastern European countries that introduced it,[47] just as the "invisible hand" has been supplemented by extensive social security provisions in most Western European countries.[48] Positivist theories, based on observable legal and social infrastructures, have replaced religious, natural law and utilitarian theories on the role of the modern state.[49]

B. DETERMINANTS OF PUBLIC POLICY

The links between the extensive body of literature of comparative studies on the determinants of public and social policy and the emerging body of literature on health policy are weak. There are three dominant schools of thought on *why* governments try to influence public and social policy: level of socio-economic development such as industrialization, urbanization and accumulation of wealth; political processes such as ideology, democratization and political party formation; and bureaucratic structures such as the age of institutions and style of administration. In addition to these mainstream theories on the determinants of the welfare effort, a significant body of literature is emerging from a totally different source on the determinants of health policy — economic theory about market failure. Although health policy cannot be analyzed in isolation from the developments that have occurred in the welfare state, an overemphasis of the latter risks distorting issues and policy options that are unique to health care as a specific program feature of the welfare effort.

Transferability of phenomena observed in the broader sphere of public and social policy should therefore not be taken for granted when addressing problems in health policy. Many investigations of the determinants of the welfare state are highly aggregate, using data that is easy to quantify. Furthermore, they characteristically focus on cash benefits offered through social security programs during times of occupational injury, illness, unemployment, disability and old age. Health care, on the other hand, is usually offered as a benefit in kind with financing coming from many sources, private and public, often making it difficult to identify the total aggregate expenditure. Early studies of the welfare effort that included health care therefore tended to concentrate on descriptive, non-theoretical and non-comparative aspects. They ignored chronological sequencing of events, intrinsic program features and the impact of health policy on other developments in the evolving welfare state. Theoretical issues were rarely validated through systematic cross-national comparisons. The closest analogous public service provided as a benefit in kind is social services. In education, the issues and debates on policy options are very different from those confronted in the health sector.[50]

1. Level of Socio-economic Development

The dominant school of thought in cross-national analyses claims that the level of socio-economic development along with its bureaucratic and demographic correlates — the number of years that social security systems have been in existence and the age structure of the population — are the most significant determinant factors in the formation of the welfare state.[51] Researchers have tried to prove this claim through multi-variant regression analysis of both cross-sectional and longitudinal time series for a variety of variables, such as the level of socio-economic development, stage of evolution of social security infrastructures and degree of affluence. Commonly used measures of the welfare effort, or the degree to which a state is involved in the provision of social security benefits, include public expenditure on social security in relation to national wealth measured as by GDP, levels of energy consumption, urbanization and literacy rates.[52] These studies consistently indicate that there is a strong correlation between the development of social insurance programs and the level of socio-economic development and growth.[53] Similar observations have been made about health care expenditure and health status as measured by life expectancy and infant mortality rates in relation to GDP. [54]

Scholars have found it more difficult to unravel the interplay between potential social determinants (historical, cultural and demographic) and socio-economic determinants (industrialization, urbanization and accumulation of wealth). Industrialization and urbanization lead to declining birth rates, ageing of populations, unemployment, industrial accidents and massive health and social problems associated with urban living. Changes in lifestyle and demographic shifts in populations lead to a loss of the traditional security offered by the land, families and local communities. Vulnerable populations gain some protection when industrialization and urbanization provide the state with the economic means to create social security programs.[55] Social transformation is therefore necessary for industrialization and economic growth itself, but by itself this is not sufficient to be a dominant factor for the formation of a welfare state.

Proponents of the importance of socio-economic development also claim that among affluent societies, an interplay of other factors such as political ideologies, mass pressures and bureaucratic structures may enhance differences among developed democracies, but fail to act as key determinant factors to explain observed variations: "Much useless controversy is generated by researchers who focus on program structure and administration and complain that researchers who study aggregate spending and taxing are wasting their time."[56] A country's affluence may have a stronger and more direct impact on social spending per capita than on its welfare effort because "a small effort by a very rich country such as the United States generally means more cash for each person than a large effort by a 'rich' country farther down the economic scale such as Austria."[57]

Although the occasional study may show a negative relationship between socio-economic level of development and welfare effort, these contradictions can largely be explained by differences in methodology, samples, indicators, cross-sectional sample and time series of the data used.[58] "These findings stand up with or without the inclusion of measures of political systems."[59] Comparing communist, authoritarian and liberal democratic societies, other investigators have concluded that system age was a more significant indicator of health, welfare and education spending than political orientation.[60] The public policies of both communist and democratic regimes have "converged" in adopting the same seven or eight basic programs, extending coverage over time and experiencing rapid increases in public expenditure. When the analysis is controlled for the level of socio-economic development, regime type was of no consequence in determining public expenditure on social programs. Although the duration of the existence of a program may also be significant, when age is controlled over time, the level of socio-economic development remains the key determinant factor.[61]

Studies that use multi-variant regression analysis to establish determinant relationships potentially have a serious flaw. A high correlation between two observations does not establish causal relationships unless accompanied by path analysis, which authors of these studies rarely carry out. The social policy literature is filled with studies that claim to establish that *X* causes *Y* because there is a high correlation between the two variables. The high correlation that exists between socio-economic development and health care expenditure therefore does not prove that one causes the other. When the number of possible causal factors is very large, special techniques are necessary to ensure that the observed correlations do not represent mere coincidences.[62]

2. Political Processes

Proponents of a second school of thought believe that the welfare state developed not only because of socio-economic level of development but also because of a more complex interplay of political processes.[63] These authors claim that, over the past 50 years, political determinants have been equally, if not more, significant in explaining growth trends in some aspects of the welfare state than the level of socio-economic development.[64] Because the scope and complexity of comparative public policy is "sometimes as broad as three-quarters of what governments do", investigators who limit their research to macro-analysis at the national level risk missing many of the subtleties that would appear at a more disaggregate level.[65] Furthermore, determinant factors that appear true for social policy and the welfare state do not necessarily apply to specific program and sub-program features such as health policy and phenomena that occur at the sub-national level.

(a) Ideology

Both meritocratic and egalitarian values exist in most modern societies. Taxes, social spending and their political effects reflect complex mixes of individualism and collectivism. The political impact of *elite* ideology as expressed through official rhetoric and mass ideology through public opinion may be self-canceling over time.[66] "People love pensions and are only a shade less enamored of national health insurance. ... Citizens in Denmark, the United Kingdom, Canada and United States alike have serious reservations about unemployment compensation and are quite doubtful, if not downright hostile, to public assistance; they think the benefits too often go to the undeserving."[67] Studies that lump these factors under a single measure or indicator will miss subtleties of individual sub-components. Although some authors claim that opposing abstract ideologies, such as the policies of ruling parties or dominant coalitions, have little impact on the welfare effort in terms of the level of social security expenditure,[68] their analysis fails to eliminate the possibility that political processes have other significant impacts on the welfare state.

Some investigators have observed that political parties promote different programs based on their underlying ideological orientation. When liberal ideologies dominate, governments are more likely to introduce subsidized voluntary schemes as was done in Denmark, whereas when socialist ideologies dominate, they are more likely to introduce compulsory plans such as was done in Norway and Sweden.[69] Unfortunately, when liberalism is inferred from the level of industrialization and urbanization, as it was in these studies, it becomes a superfluous variable of the level of socio-economic development. This demonstrates the importance of careful attention to methodological design and the selection of indicators or units-of-measurement that are representative of the issues that are being examined.

Proponents of the importance of more subtle political processes claim that studies on socio-economic development are misleading because they rely too heavily on aggregate indicators that hide the true determinants of the welfare effort. More complex indicators, such as a mixed index of per capita GDP, current general government revenues/GDP, education expenditure and infant mortality, are needed to illustrate society's welfare effort. When such composite indicators are used, the importance of ideology as a variable increases, while that of socio-economic development disappears.[70] Aggregate expenditure also fails to reflect intent and effect. Subtle indirect redistribution may occur through restrictions on private education, private medical care, private transportation, tax deductions and so on without being directly portrayed as social expenditure. "The evidence, imprecise and incomplete as it is, suggests that in countries where left-wing parties have had powerful ruling positions over many years, as in Scandinavia and Austria, policies have reflected a conscious and generally successful effort to redistribute and restrain the privileges of private wealth by measures that fall outside of the social security catchment."[71] Social democratic strategies focus on social reforms and income redistribution through taxation in mixed-market economies, while communist strategies emphasize government ownership through an elimination of the reward system of capitalism.

Similar arguments have led some investigators to conclude that countries whose constitutions are based on parliamentary monarchies as a national political culture lean toward paternalistic ideologies and are therefore more likely introduce social security programs earlier.[72] "Monarchial regimes, experiencing neither the legitimation nor the ideological constraint of liberalism, had a greater need for and ability to institute the programs of the welfare state."[73] The expansionary pressures of ageing systems soon effected the social security systems of the pre-war monarchies of Germany, Austria, Sweden and Denmark. Federal states such as Canada and Australia may be slower than central states to introduce such programs because squabbles between provinces/states and central governments compound traditional party differences. Unfortunately, the small sample size of federal states among western developed countries makes evidence for this theory Impressionistic.[74]

The influence of ideology on health policy has been the subject of heated debate in the literature for a number of years.[75] Conflicts between the medical profession and other health professionals, and between generalists and specialists, often reflect underlying class struggles that are much more complex than the issues presented.[76] Whether or not public hospitals allow pay beds to exist may represent much deeper issues such as "near-State monopoly of health care in a pluralistic, liberal democracy."[77] The battle between trade unions and the medical profession sometimes reflects political conflicts between a Labor Party and Conservative Party as much as it does labor disputes within the profession itself. Inequality in health care between different classes of the population has been the focus of much of the debate in the United Kingdom.[78] Higher education, which is often regarded as meritocratic, may lead to complex trade-offs against other welfare provisions and be associated with a heavy political price. The associated increased employment opportunity leads to not only upward mobility but also erosion of working-class solidarity. Public expenditure on education offers greater equity in opportunity while that on health care offers greater equity in results.[79] Health care systems are vulnerable to such political developments that occur outside their direct realm.

(b) Democratization

The importance of democratization as a determinant of the evolution of social policy is equally marked by contradictory evidence. In one sample of industrial societies, researchers found that differences in constitutional arrangements strongly predicted the timing of the introduction of new social security programs at the turn of the twentieth century.[80] Dualist-constitutional monarchies such as Austria, Denmark, Germany and Sweden had a 63 percent success rate in enacting proposed legislation, while parliamentary democracies such as Belgium, France, Great Britain, the Netherlands, Switzerland and Italy had only a 21 percent success rate.[81]

Although political enfranchisement did not seem to be a significant factor by 1900, social insurance legislation appeared to flourish more rapidly once a "suffrage threshold" of 50 percent of the male population has been reached. By contrast, neither the level of socio-economic development, measured by the labor force in secondary sector industry and populations in cities, nor left-wing politics, measured by the percentage of the population voting for working-class parties, had a significant effect on progressive social policy in this study.[82] Political continuity, which increases the likelihood of successful enactment of legislation and fiscal commitment seems, however, to be associated with early introduction of progressive reforms.[83]

The late democratization of the Nordic monarchical regimes and the multi-party system of proportional representation weakened the bourgeois parties of a divided right-wing opposition (conservative, agrarian, Christian and liberal parties) in face of the emerging working classes in Denmark, Norway, Sweden and Finland (Germany and Austria). This cohesion of the left wing and disunity of the right wing provided a fertile political arena for progressive social reform.[84] By contrast, early democratizers such as Australia, New Zealand, Canada and the United States brought on strong anti-government bureaucracy sentiments.

The experience of Australia and New Zealand, which became welfare state pioneers during the 1930s, contradicts these theories. Unfortunately, the lack of quantitative demographic data prevents a more detailed analysis of the importance of the ageing of the population, urbanization, political mobilization and socio-economic correlates. These and other shortcomings in the arguments fuel the challenge from critics who claim that democratization cannot be associated with the timing of the adoption of social security programs.[85]

The literature on democratization has not been linked to health policy in the same way as that on other political processes, level of socio-economic development or bureaucratic infrastructures.

(c) Political Party Formation

Some authors maintain the most significant aspect of the peaceful introduction of social reforms was the formation of modern political party systems. It has been suggested that the high levels of welfare effort in the Nordic countries is associated with a united left-wing dominance at the expense of a divided right wing in the party system. To demonstrate this point, proponents of this theory have tried to use complex composite indices as measures of welfare effort, with left dominance being defined as socialist, social democratic and labor parties. When left-wing majorities defined in this way dominate in coalition governments, they weaken non-socialist resistance to welfare policies. In contrast, based on a 15-country sample between 1945 and 1972, when right-wing parties dominate the political scene, welfare efforts have a much harder time taking hold.[86] "The most satisfactory explanation for the exceptionally high levels of welfare effort in the Scandinavian countries is the ascendency of social democratic parties."[87] This occurred largely through the significant size of the working class, the large middle class and socio-economic growth. Other authors have found similar positive associations between left-wing political power and income redistribution policies.[88]

Countries that were late to democratize had small right-wing political parties that were divided among traditional conservatives, agrarians, Christians and liberals. This led to weak support for free-market political policies. At the same time, disunity of the bourgeois parties created a fertile context for the evolution of working-class welfare ideologies. In Denmark, Norway, Sweden and Finland, the impact of an ageing social security infrastructure was enhanced by this political trend. In contrast, countries that were earlier to democratize also had more time for nineteenth-century liberal and right-wing *laissez-faire* ideologies to take hold. They were later in introducing welfare state institutions and therefore later to experience the expansionary pressures of ageing social security infrastructures. These countries — the US, Canada, Ireland and Switzerland — remained welfare state "laggards" well after other western countries had introduced sophisticated social security infrastructures.

Critics of this school of thought, however, point out that political structures and electoral procedures may lead to ambiguities when the resulting governments in power do not represent the majority political tendency: the Netherlands has enjoyed a rich history of social policies despite its weak social democratic politics, whereas Belgium, Switzerland and Luxembourg have been relatively slow to introduce social reforms despite their weak right-wing governments.[89] They also point out that the proponents of theories on party formations have omitted other determinants in their analysis. By including traditional measures of welfare effort — social security expenditure/GNP — the impact of political party formation appears less conclusive. Right-wing parliamentary strength inhibited public expenditure on education in the 1960s and 1970s, and public expenditure on health, income maintenance and total welfare in the 1970s. By contrast, social democratic rule was only associated with increased public expenditure in the 1960s, but inversely related to all other expenditure.[90]

For political ideology and political parties to have a significant effect on social reforms, the electorate must be offered distinct platforms, voters must make identified informed choices and governments must have the mandate to implement these choices.[91] "There is no empirical basis for this 'rational' image of voting behavior. Students of political behaviour have shown that there are more compelling explanations of voting behaviour such as party identification, class, values, and increasingly the influence of mass movements, the mass media, and single issue groups."[92] Parties offer generalities, voters respond to distorted images of platforms and the media creates its own political agenda.[93] Election promises are easily forgotten in the face of new economic and political environments.

Other investigators found that there is no causal relationship between left-wing power and welfare effort. They claim that left-wing dominance promotes a "tax-welfare backlash" through their support of highly visible progressive income and proper taxes, and "political backlash" when they include communist parties in their coalitions. They broadly defined left-wing power as governments committed to income redistribution and equality (economic, political and social) for the lower social strata of society. This included communist, socialist, social democratic, labor and liberal (American Democrat) party formations in power between 1919 and 1976.[94] In contrast, Catholic parties that had anti-communist/socialist/labor/social democratic/liberal sentiments were found to support corporatism and boost a balanced tax structure through indirect taxation. This prevented the tax and political backlash. The debate on the importance of political parties is therefore unresolved as are those of the importance of other political processes such as ideology and democratization. None have been convincingly linked in the literature to health policy.

3. Bureaucratic Structures

A third school of thought remains convinced that it is the bureaucratic process and administrators that act as central agents in the development of a welfare state.[95] They concede that socio-economic development provides the physical resources, interest groups the human initiative, ideologies the reasons and political parties the instruments for reform. These investigators claim that it was corporatism — the interplay of highly organized and centralized interest groups (labor, employers and professional associations) and centralized governments leading to political economies with a consensus-making machine — that was principally responsible for the flourishing of social security provisions such as health care, pensions, unemployment, sickness, accident insurance and family allowance.[96] By representing corporatism as a continuum, Norway, Sweden, Finland and Austria ranked among the most corporatist countries by the late 1970s, followed by the Netherlands, Denmark, Belgium and West Germany, and trailed by Britain, the US, Canada, Australia, New Zealand, Japan, France and Italy.

Considerable support for the importance of the bureaucratic process in influencing the timing, scope and content of social insurance legislation has come from detailed analysis of Denmark, Norway, Sweden and Finland from the 1880s onward: political setting was measured as the extent of suffrage, systems of representation and appearance of mass parties; level of socio-economic development as industrialization, urbanization and accumulation of wealth; organizational characteristics as poor-law provisions, experience with voluntary social insurance funds and trade union strength; and ideological climate as the extent of liberalism.[97]

Although the socio-economic, political and bureaucratic determinants become mixed up in this type of analysis, Denmark, the most socio-economically and politically advanced country, was ahead of the other Nordic countries in proposing reforms, passing legislation and financing such schemes with public funds. Norway followed suit, trailed by Sweden and finally Finland. Unfortunately they have the same rank-order among the Nordic countries as legislative continuity, making it impossible to distinguish the relative importance of these determinant factors.

Where liberal democratic political processes developed early, such as in Great Britain, the US, Canada, France, Switzerland, Belgium and the Netherlands, progressive social security legislation was impeded. Although their parliamentary institutions legitimized the process, their liberal ideology discouraged interference in the market economy. Monarchical regimes lacking such ideological restraints felt a more pressing need to use their control over the bureaucratic machinery to appease militant labor movements.[98] Once established, "expansionary pressures" of evolving bureaucracies lead to further proliferation of these tendencies.

Furthermore, the depolarized party system of highly corporatist countries forces planners (working groups, committees and commissions) into a long-term consensus policy process with broad comprehensive and responsible objectives, which is often respected by elected officials and bureaucrats. By contrast, the confrontational bipolar party systems of non-corporatist countries often leads planners into a short-term, narrow and ideological policy process, which is exploited or ignored by politicians and bureaucrats according to the degree of partisan ammunition it provides rather than its own merits. The latter also leads to single-policy analysis, which obscures the hard-to-measure long-term consequences of recommended policies by focusing on immediate political impact and costs, while overlooking the interdependence among social policies.

The centralized, highly disciplined and organized interest groups in the corporatist countries keep a lower political profile than the hype and banner-waving used by those in non-corporatist countries. Yet, they may be more effective in influencing reforms by successfully infiltrating the policy-making machinery. As an example, 48 percent of the administrative board posts in Norway are occupied by interest-group representatives.[99] In Norway and Sweden, a government contemplating legislation or administrative reforms that would affect a particular interest group is obliged by law to contact them at an early stage in the policy formulation process. "Groups and interest organisations are given full representation on such commissions and are thus able to use this device already at an early stage in order to reach agreement with political parties, with other groups and with administrators. The tendency is to attempt the greatest possible amount of agreement already at this stage."[100]

Under this arrangement, the parliament, government and political parties are forced to share power, not just in planning but also in implementing and administering key policies with many, often opposing, interest groups. This limits the range of radical options available to political leaders who often depend on co-operation and compromise to stay in government. Support of extreme positions will alienate groups whose support the government depends on to stay in office. Governments are forced to formulate policies through persuasion, negotiation and consensus to reconcile a wide range of competing interests, which greatly limits their political choice. Official working groups, committees and commissions that exaggerate or sensationalize issues are avoided because of the risk of being exposed by vocal opponents, "Under such circumstances, traditional political power (e.g. the number of legislative votes controlled) is devalued and persuasive power is enhanced."[101] The resulting broadly defined statutes leave much room for real policy to be defined by the administrators after the legislative phase.

The more polarized the political system, the greater the chance that stalemates, deadlocks and hung parliaments will result. Italy, having a less corporatist, more polarized system than the Nordic countries, is a case in point.[102] In a polarized political arena, where there are no corporatist pressures, executives, legislatures and regulatory agencies can introduce partisan policies that ignore the concerns of interest groups. Media presentations and mass political leverage take priority over responsible research, and the findings of working groups, committees and commissions are often rejected by oppositions and interest groups, with a resulting compromise in credibility.

The literature on health policy has not emphasized the potential role of bureaucratic infrastructures as a significant determinant of government involvement in health care.

4. Market Failure

A fourth school of thought that says that the role of market failure is a significant determinant of government intervention in the economic affairs of the state has been largely ignored by the comparative literature on public and social policy, but is at the center of much of the polemic in health policy. In a perfect market economy, governments could limit their role to a minimal range of activities such as those suggested by Adam Smith in the eighteenth century: establishing law and order and providing a few public works that would be of no interest to individuals. Unhampered competition between households and firms, free entry and interaction in a full set of markets and complete knowledge of products would allow economic activity to be self-regulating.[103] An equilibrium would be established that would require little input or interference by governments in the economic affairs of the state. The three normative functions performed by all modern governments that were described above — allocation of resources, redistribution of income and stabilization of economic activity — would be unnecessary because they would occur spontaneously in response to consumer preferences and decentralized market forces. The allocation of resources would be carried out in a way that would achieve Pareto efficiency. The collection of taxes and lump-sum transfers would be costless. Finally, the equilibrium established in the market would remove the need for internal and external stabilizing measures.

The market fails to behave in this utopian way in a number of areas. Perfect competition breaks down for several reasons.[104] Information available to consumers about products is imperfect[105] and costly to acquire.[106] Producers try to artificially influence prices by colluding with each other, forming monopolies[107] and inducing demand.[108] In the case of social goods, products lack rivalness and excludability which prevents them from being marketed efficiently and equitably.[109] Free riders[110] do not pay their fair share, but take advantage of positive externalities[111] that may result from the transaction between individual suppliers and users.[112] The market fails to distribute income or wealth in such a way that individuals have equal access and opportunity to express their true preferences in a competitive market. Finally, the market cannot regulate employment, ensure price stability or promote economic growth. Insurance, the standard market response to uncertainty by pooling risk, fails for three reasons.[113] Inflated loading charges or retention rates may occur when weak competition leads to inefficiency or monopolies. Moral hazards may lead to increased demand by consumers, supplier-induced demand and careless behavior by the insured.[114] Adverse selection leads those with higher risk to be more likely to apply for protection while concealing their risk.[115]

Health care as an economic good is especially vulnerable to many of the **market failures** that have been observed in other areas of economic activity.[116] Although it is a significant sub-component of the welfare state, health care is usually provided as a benefit in kind, whereas most other social security benefits are provided as cash reimbursements or direct transfers payments. The other most significant benefit in kind is education. Reflecting these differences, the need for government intervention and the instruments used to implement health policy are significantly different from those observed in other areas of public and social policy,[117] It requires that some of the traditional informational restrictions of welfarism, such as efficient maximization of utility and equity, be relaxed to include elements of extra-welfarism such as comfort, physical mobility, enjoyment of relationships with others and freedom to choose.[118] The subjects treated are nevertheless similar to those encountered in mainstream neoclassical economics:[119] supply, demand, competition, prices, production, firms, monopolies, efficient resource allocation, income redistribution, labor markets, employment, unemployment, inflation, stagflation, growth, general equilibrium, cyclical trends, stability, growth, risk management and insurance. But the rules of the game are different.[120] Health economics[121] is therefore not a mere extension of welfare economics,[122] public economics[123] or centralized socialist planning.[124]

First, the **supply** of health care does not have the usual characteristics of a production function and is therefore poorly regulated by market forces. Health care professionals and institutions do not react in the same way as they would in a perfect competitive market environment.[125] Professional and ethical constraints[126] oblige doctors to perform activities that are not profit-maximizing and which could be performed more cheaply by less-trained personnel.[127] They often engage in honorary and academic activities for no pay other than the prestige that they derive from the association. There is limited entry into the profession, professional control over certification of competence and exclusion of competing disciplines.[128] There are great variations in medical practice styles that cannot be explained by a response to need and demand alone.[129] Providers can artificially stimulate demand.[130] It has led to the observation that it is much easier to introduce policies that increase services, such as the number of beds in hospitals, than to reduce them.[131] The increasing cost of medical care in western countries has spurred public and private efforts to control professional autonomy.[132] The surpluses, shortages and congestion that occur reflect the market failure in the allocation of health care resources, as they become increasingly scarce compared with demand.

Second, **demand**[133] for health care is usually derived from utilization[134] statistics even though this is a poor indicator of consumer preference.[135] Utilization reflects a complex interaction between needs, demands and available services.[136] Normative needs relate to desired standards; felt needs relate to individual perceptions; expressed needs relate to demands for services; and comparative needs relate to the needs of others in society.[137] Uncertainty of illness, disability and ageing[138] prevents the individual from perceiving risks or needs for protection when young or in good health.[139] This renders him more vulnerable as he ages and faces increasing prospects of illness.[140] Insurance is the standard market response to cover such risk. Market failure due to the problems of moral hazards and adverse selection has been observed in other areas that rely on insurance to deal with uncertainty. These phenomena are accentuated in the case of health care. Asymmetry of information between consumers and providers is especially pronounced,[141] and imperfect knowledge about the nature of illness and treatment outcome make an informed choice impossible.[142] Adverse selection leads patients to hide their underlying illnesses when they know that their insurance premiums are risk-related, and insurers to try to attract clients with the least risk.[143] The existence of prepayment of health care, whether through taxation, social insurance or private insurance, influences demand and willingness to pay.[144]

Third, there is no free entry to a fully **competitive market** in health care or unrestricted interaction between consumers and suppliers.[145] Institutional and professional groups allow suppliers of medical services to manipulate prices, influence quality, stimulate demand and prevent free competition among its members by forming monopolies[146] or cartels.[147] When the Treasury or national insurance funds try to control public expenditure[148] or professional power[149] by acting as monopsonies,[150] they destroy any vestiges of a competitive market. The very concept of preferred provider organizations to constrain health care costs is contrary to the open access of a competitive market.[151] The medical profession, labor organizations and other pressure groups respond in kind to these measures by forming political lobbies to influence government policies at the national level[152] and by controlling the implementation of such policies at the local level.[153] The style of negotiation during collective bargaining may itself be a significant factor in determining the outcome of such conflicts.[154] These problems have led an increasing number of authors to question the legitimacy of competition as a valid basis for regulating the transactions that occur in the health sector.[155]

Fourth, even in highly competitive market economies, a breakdown occurs in the **pricing mechanism** of health care as an economic commodity.[156] The imperfections of the competitive market for health care make it too easy for providers of services and producers of goods such as equipment and pharmaceuticals to artificially influence what might otherwise appear to be legitimate market prices.[157] The "Gift Relationship" or charitable relationship between health care workers and their patients makes it impossible to determine the real market value of services rendered.[158] In the case of direct payment, charges may be overlooked when the patient is unable to pay. In the case of prepayment, restrictions in access due to lack of entitlement are difficult to enforce. Governments have come to realize that the public sector absorbs a significant part of the hidden cost of health care even when it is not directly involved in its financing, administration and service delivery.[159] Because a significant part of the positive and negative externalities of health care such as illness, disability and ageing falls on society as a whole, its provision has an impact which reaches far beyond the individual himself.[160]

Finally, bureaucratic rigidities prevent health care institutions from adapting to market pressures as **firms** would do in an ideal competitive environment.[161] The production function of health care in providing health has therefore been challenged by a number of authors.[162] Hospitals, doctors and other health care providers continue to operate in their traditional ways long after circumstances warrant that such behavior be changed in response to market pressures.[163] Morbidity and mortality statistics are, however, poor indicators of quality of life, [164] and the iatrogenic problems created by health care are readily dramatized by critics of health care at the expense of more subtle benefits.[165] This makes it difficult for health care firms to adapt the way they operate in response to outcome.

Governments have become increasingly active in all western countries during the twentieth century, partially as a result of market failures in the general economy.[166] At any one given point in time, most governments have nevertheless felt that public expenditure should be kept to a bare minimum to avoid excessive tax burdens and public debt. At the turn of the twentieth century, some authors considered a taxation ratio of 10 percent of national income as a serious threat to economic growth.[167] By the 1920s, these rates had doubled[168] and by the 1980s, they had more than tripled.[169] Tax revenues in the OECD today range from less than 30 percent of GDP in Japan to over 50 percent in Sweden.[170] Claims that the public sector has overstepped the limits of its expenditure capacity are as emphatic today as they were over a century ago.[171] As total health care expenditure, and more particularly, public sector expenditure per GDP on health care continues to rise, health policy is caught up in the debate on the legitimate role of the state in a mixed-market economy.[172] Authors are increasingly questioning at which point expenditure on health care has overstepped its acceptable threshold.[173] The role of market failure as a significant determinant that led to public sector involvement in health care is implied through the literature on health economics, but attempts to validate this hypothesis empirically through cross-national comparisons have been sporadic and unsystematic. See Table 1.2.

Table 1.2 Determinants of Health Policy

Extrinsic	Intrinsic
History, politics & institutions	Professionalism, advocacy, altruism
Socio-economic & demographics	Risk, uncertainty, asymmetric information
Business environment & investment climate	Demand, need, utilization, induced demand
	Rivalness, excludability, externalities
	Surpluses, shortages, congestion
	Moral hazards, adverse selection, loading
	Donations, non-profit, public/private mix
	Monopolies, monopsonies, rigidity
	Politics, ideology, class struggle
	Other

Source: Adapted from Preker (1989).

C. NORMATIVE FUNCTIONS OF MODERN GOVERNMENTS

Apart from their role in establishing law and order, the governments of all western countries have, over time, assumed three significant additional functions[174]: allocation of social goods,[175] distribution of income[176] and stabilization of economic activity.[177] The reasons they perform these functions, the instruments used and reactions to such involvement vary greatly from country to country, and has changed over the years.[178]

Whatever its accepted role, the state needs the financial means to carry out its business. This requires policies on *how* to collect public revenues, *how* to spend them and *what* to do when expenditure exceeds receipts.[179] Adam Smith described public finance as "the sources of the general or public revenue of the society … the expenses of the sovereign or commonwealth … and public debts."[180] This view remained unchanged until severe inflation and unemployment that accompanied the Great Depression and World Wars convinced western mainstream economists and legislators to consider including the regulation of employment, prices and economic growth as a legitimate stabilization function of government.[181] The economic shocks of the late 1960s and 1970s rekindled the debate about such macro-economic policies[182] which become embodied in the dialectic between Keynesianism and Monetarism.[183] One is concerned with employment, control of the business cycle and economic growth as instruments of stabilization and the other with the quantity of circulating money and control of inflation. Neither professes to address the historical tension between individualism and collectivism that remains embodied in the allocation and distribution functions.

Health care provides an instrument by which governments can, at least in part, achieve all of these objectives. The most recognized function is its role in resource allocation. Regulations, subsidies and direct provision of health care goods and services are all instruments by which governments exercise this function. The budget process and access to services are adjuncts to these mechanisms. The revenues that are collected through the prepayment of health care, whether added to the consolidated fund or social/health insurance fund, become a significant instrument of income redistribution in the form of cash reimbursements and transfer payments, or benefits in kind such as the direct provision of health services. Most of

Table 1.3 Normative Functions of Modern Governments

	Functions		
	Allocation	Distribution	Stabilization
Instruments	Regulations	Revenue collection	Employment
	Subsidies	Reimbursements	Cost Controls
	Services	Benefits in Kind	Production

Source: Adapted from Preker (1989).

the literature treats prepayment of health care as a pooling of risk to protect individuals against the uncertainty of illness rather than as part of the distributive function of government. Finally, the way public funds are spent on health care becomes an instrument of economic stabilization when it leads to employment in the public sector, when cost-containment measures influence prices and when the production of goods and services promote economic growth. Monetarists may challenge the wisdom of such activities as instruments of stabilization, but it is difficult to isolate the mechanisms of resource allocation and income redistribution from employment practices, expenditure policies and investments in the health sector, which could be considered Keynesian stabilization instruments. See Table 1.3.

D. MEASURING PERFORMANCE OF HEALTH CARE REFORMS

It is difficult to evaluate the outcome of given policy interventions in terms of health status, health services and welfare of society in general.[184] The lack of universally accepted indicators and standardized outcome measures weakens the arguments made by most of the existing studies. Authors who have examined the first issue remark that there is a lack of consensus on what constitutes outcome in terms of health and illness.[185] Even when agreement is reached at the philosophical level, it is difficult to translate the resulting abstract ideas into concrete concepts that can be measured and validated in a consistent and reliable way.[186] Yet these criteria must be met before the researcher can carry out an empirical validation of the hypothesis under investigation. There are few standard health indicators that can be used in cross-national comparisons. In developing countries, even mortality statistics are unreliable because they reflect only deaths in hospitals, while those occurring in the community remain largely unrecorded. Morbidity, quality of life and daily function indicators rely entirely on surveys that are neither designed in a standard way nor collected routinely in all countries.[187] International comparisons of such data are therefore unreliable.

In recent years, there has been an explosion of studies that attempt to measure the effects of social and health policies on health services in terms of costs, resources, performance, effectiveness, efficiency and quality.[188] The most striking conclusion that can be drawn from the work of these authors is that there is a lack of standard definitions of what is being measured and a lack of routine collection.[189] The OECD Health Database has made a significant contribution in this area by trying to define a minimum data set for health status and health services.[190]

Another group of authors have been looking beyond health status and health care by examining outcome in terms of the welfare and "happiness" of a given society, or the impact on economic growth. In technical terms, positive outcome can be viewed as those policies that result in a maximization of the social welfare utility function U over a common set of commodities ($X_{i...n}$) that would include health care (HC), health status (HS) and other factors (K). The goal of a society would be to maximize the common good for all of its citizens[191]:

$$U = U[X_{i...n}, \mathrm{HC}, \mathrm{HS}, \ldots, \mathrm{K}].$$

Once again, there are several problems associated with this approach. First, it is difficult to actually measure welfare or happiness. Second, there may be a negative interdependence between health care and health status. Affluent societies may have reached a point of diminishing and even decreasing marginal returns in the provision of health care.[192] In such a case, additional health care would lead to decreasing health status[193]:

$$d\mathrm{HC} = F(1/d\mathrm{HS}).$$

Different authors have convincingly shown a correlation between socio-economic development, welfare provisions, health care expenditure and decreasing mortality.[194] Whether or not one acts as a determinant for the others is much less clear. There are clear limits to relative growth, and the social sectors cannot continue to consume an increasing part of GDP.[195] At one point or another, the converse should logically be true, yet no study has shown that persistent economic contraction is associated with concomitant contractions in welfare programs.[196] "In Europe, as elsewhere, income per capita is the main determinant [of health care spending.] … Existing cross-sectional regression analyses do not permit any independent measure of the impact of such policies [to control health care expenditure] other than the general conclusion that centralized cash-limited budgets have a significant negative impact on the total and that public finance also reduces total expenditure."[197]

The impact of excessive health care expenditure on economic growth is equally controversial.[198] Critics of public expenditure programs claim that there is a threshold beyond which public sector expenditure has a negative effect on economic performance.[199] They argue that expenditure on social programs, such as health care, increases the cost of production, increases prices, lowers demand, displaces the productive labor force and makes industries less competitive. It may also in some unknown way "intrude" on economic growth and capital formation.[200] Social programs may lead to heavy public expenditure, and in the absence of economic growth, to mounting public debt. The impact of such debt on health and health care expenditure still needs to be clarified.[201]

Those that argue against this logic claim that expenditure on health care keeps workers healthy, increases their productivity and lowers expenditure on social benefits by creating employment. Taxes, cash transfers and indirect benefits lead to income redistribution and greater economic equality for the non-working poor — the aged, single mothers, older workers and other unemployed.[202] Left-wing rule is often associated with lower unemployment, lower inflation and growth. By using increased social benefits to counter demands for wage increases by trade unions, they may be more successful in controlling the wage bill of companies and improving profit margins, Of course, there may be little or no redistribution of wealth if the affluent segments of society succeed in re-circulating this income back into their own pockets.[203] There is no direct evidence, however, that health care expenditure leads to a displacement effect or that increased disposable income created by cutting health expenditure would lead to greater investment in productive activities. Finally, the willingness to pay taxes for the core programs of social security (health and pensions) has not significantly declined despite high taxes.[204]

Public expenditure programs lead to political backlashes with anti-tax, anti-welfare and anti-bureaucratic movements. The most significant cause of backlash is the "painfully visible" progressive income and property taxes usually advocated by left-wing political parties of the least corporatist-oriented countries.[205] A significant corollary of this observation is the possible inverse relation between universality and comprehensiveness of programs and political backlash: "programmes that extend benefits over a broad income range will be less susceptible to politically motivated protest than programmes that target the poor."[206] Among the many social security provisions that have been introduced in the twentieth century, old-age pension and health care are the most universal, most comprehensive and most popular. Means-tested public assistance for non-working, non-disabled and non-aged poor is the least popular.[207]

Paradoxically, the high visibility of direct taxes and means-tested benefits is often associated with lower tax structures and lower spending capacity of left-wing governments, due to political backlash. On the other hand, less visible but higher indirect taxes are sometimes associated with greater political acceptability and greater spending capacity of moderate centralist governments.

What is true at one level of socio-economic development may not be true at another. The impact of public expenditure for health care on economic performance may have both lower and upper thresholds in relation to GDP. In one large cross-national study, the author demonstrated that public expenditure on the health sector appeared to have no correlation to economic development (GDP) for low-income countries. For the mid-range countries, there was a weak correlation between health care expenditure and economic development. For the high-income countries, the positive correlation disappears and may even become negative.[208] Most of the other stereotype tradeoffs that are debated in the social policy literature have not been validated in cross-national reviews of health policy: the welfare state and democratic participation versus capital investment and a healthy economy; social benefits versus labor supply, productivity and economic growth; and the seemingly unlimited demand for public services versus reluctance to pay.

Cross-national studies have been largely unsuccessful in clarifying these debates for several reasons.[209] Researchers are asked to match studies focusing on different theoretical issues, different methodologies and non-comparable issues. They therefore need to be on guard constantly against the pitfalls created by artifacts from a variety of directions. Finally, there is a temptation to conclude that a determinant relationship exists when statistical analysis reveals the presence of strong correlations between different events: "To give a grotesque example, Esping-Andersen reports that the correlation between social spending levels and the number of miles a nation's capital is from Stockholm is stronger than with either economic level or left-wing party power."[210]

Despite these known constraints, comparisons was made for key indicators between the 8 countries reviewed in this volume and the full dataset of 28 OECD countries that have achieve universal access to health care by 2016.[211] It follows a value for money approach for assessing the performance of the key health care functions under universal health care, and recent methodologies developed by the OECD, the WHO and the World Bank in working with health systems across around the world.[212–217]

The basic elements of the Performance Evaluation Log-frame used in this book include:

- Inputs in terms of the financing (money), health training (people), research (information), manufacturing (drugs, medical technology, supplies and consumables), and construction (infrastructure)
- Processes in terms of the role of the state (stewardship, governance, management, monitoring and evaluation) and the role of markets (supply, demand, prices and market equilibrium);
- Outputs in terms of services provided (hospital care, rehabilitation, chronic care, primary care, diagnostic services, dental care, health promotion and prevention.
- Proxy measures in terms of efficiency, effectiveness, equity, access, productivity and quality and universal health care (population coverage, service depth and level of prepayment)
- Impact indicators in terms of health status, financial protection and patient experience

Table 1.4 Performance Evaluation Log-frame

INPUTS ➡	PROCESS ➡	OUTPUTS ➡	PROXY MEASURES ➡	IMPACT
Financing *money* **Training** *people* **Research** *knowledge* **Manufacturing** *drugs* *equipment* *supplies* **Construction** *buildings* *grounds*	**Roles of the state** *stewardship* *policy making* *governance* **Market forces** *supply* *demand* *prices* *market equilibrium*	**Public health services** *health promotion* *prevention* **Clinical services** *diagnostics* *inpatient* *rehabilitation* *palliative care* *home care* *dental care* *physiotherapy* *other allied services* **Non clinical** *management* *support services* *financing (insurance)*	**Process indicators** *efficiency* *effectiveness* *equity* *access* *productivity* *quality* **UCH indicators*** *population coverage* *prepayment* *service depth*	**Financial protection** *affordability* *impoverishment* **Health outcomes** *morbidity* *mortality* *quality of life* *functionality* **Patient experience** *patient satisfaction* *consumer quality* *waiting times*

*** Universal Health Coverage**

*** Public/Private Mix**

Source: Author (2017).

Because of the complexity of health systems, some people may argue that rigorous analysis of the performance of a health system is not much better than a "nose test." But impressions can also be misleading. Performance of the 8 country case studies has, therefore, been assessed using the Performance Evaluation Log-frame presented below. See Table 1.4.

E. POLICY PROCESSES

Cross-national studies have been used to investigate the theoretical validity of issues related to convergence, diffusion, interdependence and evolution processes in fields as diverse as history, social policy, economics, political science, etc. Phenomena observed in health policy have not been systematically related to these processes. Yet, such an extension follows naturally from their wide application to social policy.

1. Convergence

The proponents of convergence theories maintain that at the macro-aggregate level, countries have common collective responses to similar levels of socio-economic development such as industrialization, urbanization and accumulation of wealth, irrespective of differences in their historical, cultural, political or bureaucratic orientations.[218] This theory has been used to explain why social security systems of both democratic and communist countries appear to offer the same seven or eight basic programs, extend coverage over time and experience rapid increases in expenditure (decelerating recently) at similar levels of socio-economic development.[219]

Opponents to this theory claim that convergence is an artifact of statistical data that does not reflect the qualitative realities of program comprehensiveness, differentiation, entitlement, coverage, targeting, universality, accessibility and financial burden associated with benefits.[220] Such criticism is partly valid in that convergence theories have been mainly validated through statistical studies. Detailed program-by-program cross-national comparisons have not been conducted on enough of an international level to arrive at a satisfactory resolution of this debate.

2. Diffusion

In industrial societies, policy-makers imitate the time-proven polices of more advanced countries regardless of their socio-economic, political or bureaucratic contexts. Some scholars claim that the spread of social policy to neighboring countries, such as the spread of social security from Germany to its close neighbors, is due to geographic proximity.[221] Others maintain that it is a hierarchical transmission from leaders to followers, such as from Britain to its former colonies — Canada, Australia, New Zealand — despite geographic distance.[222] Threats of force, physical and economic, influence this process. These variants in diffusion are not mutually exclusive since it is possible that policies and resources be spread along historical, social, cultural, economic, political and bureaucratic as well as geographic links.[223] The vulgarization of the pure sciences and their application to solving ordinary day-to-day problems can be regarded as a diffusion of information from higher to lower levels of knowledge. The health sector depends on a successful diffusion and filtering of information from the laboratory to the bed-side. "International organisations are established with the explicit mandate of coordinating economic policies of the member countries … [with] no systematic attention to the impact of diffusion."[224]

Opponents of diffusion theories claim that countries which have reached the most advanced stage of socio-economic development are not always the first to introduce innovative reforms. Some scholars have demonstrated that lack of urbanization and low levels of industrialization preclude the introduction of social security programs.[225] Yet the United Kingdom, although more industrially developed, was later than Germany in introducing such reforms.[226] Such ambiguities have led to the conclusion that diffusion forces are necessary but insufficient as a determinant factor of social reform: other socioeconomic, political and bureaucratic factors must also be taken into consideration, since measures of the distance between societies are no longer valid as a proxy for their isolation in the present context of easy communication. Most of the studies that have examined diffusion processes have been limited to subjective observations, not statistical analysis.

3. Interdependence

It is often difficult to make a clear distinction between functional interdependence and diffusion. "If a particular trait occurred within the culture of *A*, was it because *A* contained the conditions that cause this trait or because *A* learned from other cultures."[227] Cross-sectional links may occur among different policies within the same country and there may be longitudinal influences on policies introduced at a later point in time. "Indeed, inadequate methodological attention to interdependence is the most damaging weakness of cross-national studies."[228] This neglect stems in part from the failure to operationalize methodologies for the analysis of this type of relationship. Although statistical models can distinguish internal and external correlations between particular phenomena, the increased number of variables that must be examined without changing the number of countries observed compounds the risk of overdetermination through which excessive attribution is accorded to a limited number of factors that occur in high correlation with the observed event. The intimate relationship between ability to spend and willingness to pay makes it extremely difficult to separate economic issues from political processes. Keynesian economic policies are one example of how these distinctions become obscured.

4. Evolution

Systems evolve over time due to convergence, diffusion and interdependence processes or other independent factors. If there is any interdependence among economic growth, policy commitments and the welfare state, changes in one will have an impact on the others. The literature on historical, economic and political theories has multiple references to long-term cyclical or repeating patterns that may, in themselves, evolve in a precarious way over time. Investigation limited to short time-spans will overlook such effects, giving the false impression that processes always occur in a predictable progressive direction. If the resulting oscillations were predictable, forecasting future trends would be relatively simple. Much of the current debate on the evolution of the welfare state centers around trying to predict such trends in policy.[229] Does public policy eventually double up on its historical path or do new options become available just at the moment when a return to the starting point appears inevitable? Does the welfare state face an unavoidable impending crisis due to loss of momentum in historical commitments, or self-damaging tendencies due to a negative effect of public, social and health care spending on economic growth?

One school of thought maintains that long-term trends in social policy are marked by uncertainty and are therefore difficult to predict.[230] According to these authors, the debate on the welfare state in crisis is largely written by alarmists who have a poor understanding of change and low tolerance for uncertainty, Policy inevitably evolves over time and not always in the same direction. Other authors have shown that it is possible to anticipate some trends, such as public expenditure on health care, if the forecasting time-period is kept short.[231]

Until recently, theoretical debate was almost completely absent from the comparative health policy literature. Most cross-national health care studies focused on operational aspects of service delivery such as sources of revenue collection, allocation of resources, mode of remuneration of health care providers, expenditure trends, cost controls, administrative structures and performance (efficiency, effectiveness and quality).[232] "The health literature is primarily written by and addressed to policy planners, who pay more attention to pragmatic goals: they aim to examine particular systems and abstract lessons for policy-makers rather than construct theory."[233] The lack of a solid theoretical base has been attributed to non-comparable data, problems standardizing terminologies and problems transferring policies cross-nationally.[234] There is still a widespread conviction that health policy is so complex that no two systems are alike: "One of the most striking facts about the financing and organisation of medical care is the extent to which it varies among developed countries.... I think it is premature to talk about convergence."[235]

Authors who have raised the possibility that some of these phenomena exist in health policy generally ignore its relation to the broader sphere of public and social policy.[236] "Systematic investigation is needed to establish the extent to which public commitments to the health sector reflect or diverge from commitments to other policy areas and to expansive social policy in general."[237] Only rarely are the proposed hypotheses subjected to rigorous empirical validation. Complex issues such as coverage, targeting, universality, access, equity, comprehensiveness and transferability, as well as the time sequence in which entitlement to health care was introduced in relation to other social benefits have not received rigorous treatment in the comparative literature: "The legislative initiatives as to which social groups in an industrialized society should be assured health care have been dearly the results of political choices, not merely the products of socio-economic development."[238]

ENDNOTES

1. The word "state" is generically used to connote an "organised political community under one government, commonwealth [or] nation." See J.B. Sykes, ed., *Concise Oxford Dictionary of Current English,* 7th Edition (Oxford: Clarendon Press, 1982): 1037.
2. A. J. Heidenheimer, H. Heclo, and C. T. Adams, *Comparative Public Policy: The Politics of Social Choice in Europe and America,* 2nd Edition (New York: St Martin's Press, 1983): 2–3. The expressions "comparative", "cross-national" and "international" are used interchangeably throughout the discussions which will follow.
3. T. L. Beauchamp and J. F. Childress, *Principles of Biomedical Ethics,* 2nd Edition. (Oxford: Oxford University Press, 1983): 4. See also E. J. Lemmon, "Moral dilemmas," *Philosophical Review* 71(1962): 139–52.
4. E. Brehier, *Histoire de la Philosophic: Antiquite et Moyen Age,* Volume 1, Nouvelle Edition (Paris: Presses Universitaires de France, 1938); and F. Châtelet, O. Duhamel and E. Pisier-Kouchner, *Histoire des Idees Politiques* (Paris: Presses Universitaires de France, 1982).
5. The Mishnah and Gemara of the *Talmud* still provide a basis for Jewish civil and ceremonial law. The *Bible* and *Koran* have played similar roles for Christian and Islam societies.

6. Aristotle, *Ethica Nichomachea,* Book 5, Chapters 1 and 2, in *Tile Works of Aristotle,* Volume 9, by W. D. Ross ed., (Oxford: Oxford, 1915). For early theories on democracy, see the works of Herodotus and Thucydides.
7. Plato documented the ideas on the relationship between knowledge and power that were developed by Socrates. Religious orders support a similar position as does the paternalistic medical profession.
8. *Papyri* are ancient Egyptian clay tablets. J. K. Mason and R. A. McCall Smith, *Law and Medical Ethics,* 2nd Edition (London: Butterworths, 1987): 4, quoting A. Castiglioni, *A History of Medicine,* 2nd Edition, by E.B. Krunbhaar, trans. and ed. (New York: Knopf, 1947).
9. This famous cuneiform legal code of the first Babylonian Dynasty has 9 of its 282 Statutes relating to the services of healers. Statutes 215–217 and 221–223 deal with laws governing the fees to be received for certain services; Statutes 218–220 deal with penalties to be inflicted on the healer in the case of unsatisfactory therapeutic results and death. C. B. Chapman, *Physicians, Law, and Ethics* (New York: New York University Press, 1984): 4–5.
10. Control of membership and secrecy, reflected in the *Hippocratic Oath,* was characteristic of all trades. British Medical Association (BMA), *Handbook of Medical Ethics*, (London: BMA, 1984): 6.
11. N. Machiavelli, *Le Prince,* [1513], Oeuvres (Paris: Pleiade, 1962).
12. It later became the Royal College of Physicians in England. Florence had similar powerful, guild-like organizations of physicians and apothecaries by the thirteenth century. See G. Clark, *A History of the Royal College of Physicians* (Oxford: Clarendon Press, 1964): 63; Edward Meryon, *The History of Medicine,* Volume 1 (London: Longman, Green, Longman and Roberts, 1891): 436; and England, *Statutes at Large, 14 and 15 Henry VIII,* C.5, Volume 4, pp. 155–57. The College reaffirmed its extraordinary powers by sending perceived offenders to prison in the City. England, *Statutes at Large, 1 Mary, Sec. Sess.,*C.9, 1553, Volume 6, pp. 15–16.
13. T. Hobbes, *Leviathan*, [1651], C. B. Macpherson, reprint ed. (Harmondsworth: Pelican, 1968): 189.
14. J. Locke, *Two Treatises of Government*, [1690], P. Laslett, ed., Revised Edition (New York: New American Library, 1960): 311.
15. D. Wilson, *The Welfare State in Sweden* (London: Heinemann, 1979): 1; B. Abel-Smith, *The Hospitals 1800–1948,* Heinemann Books on Sociology, by D. G. MacRae, series ed. (London: Heinemann, 1964): 1–15; and Bede, *A History of the English Church and People* (Harmondsworth: Penguin Books, 1975[1955]): 2.

16. The clergy was forbidden to study or practice medicine, which limited the care that they could give. See S. Rubin, *Medieval English Medicine* (London: David and Charles, 1974): 189–92.
17. N. Hampson, *The Enlightenment* (Harmondsworth: Penguin Books, 1968). The peaceful transfer of power that occurred in Britain exploded into a blood bath during the American [1775] and French [1789] Revolutions.
18. I. Kant, *Metaphysical Foundations of Morals* [1785], in *The Philosophy of Kant, Immanuel Kant's Moral and Political Writings* (New York: Modem Library, 1949).
19. J.-J. Rousseau, *The Social Contract and Discourse on the Origin of Inequality Among Mankind*, by L. G. Crocker, ed. (New York: Washington Square Press, 1964): 7.
20. A. Smith, *An Inquiry into the Nature and Causes of the Wealth of Nations* [1776] (Oxford: Oxford University Press Edition, 1976).
21. In Britain, unification of the Elizabethan Poor Laws took place in 1602.
22. A. W. Dilnot, J. A. Kay and C. N. Morris, *The Reform of Social Security,* The Institute of Fiscal Studies, London (Oxford: Clarendon Press, 1984): 6.
23. Utilitarian theories can be linked to the pursuit of happiness and pleasure advocated by the hedonistic philosophy of Epicurus.
24. J. J. Shestack, *The Jurisprudence of Human Rights,* in *Human Rights in International Law: Legal and Policy Issues,* Volume 1, by T. Meron ed. (Oxford: Clarendon Press, 1984): 88.
25. J. Bentham, *An Introduction to the Principles of Morals and Legislation,* in *A Fragment of Government and an Introduction to the Principles of Morals and Legislation*, by W. Harrison, ed. (Oxford: Blackwell, 1948): 78.
26. J. Stuart Mill, *On Liberty* [1859], by C. V. Shields, ed. (Indianapolis: Bobbs-Merrill, 1956): 67.
27. F. Engels, "Speech at the Graveside of Karl Marx," in *The Marx-Engels Reader*, by R. C. Tucker, ed. (New York: Norton, 1972): 603.
28. K. Marx, "Critique of the Gotha Program," in *The Marx-Engles Reader*, by R. C. Tucker, ed. (New York: Norton, 1972): 388. Marx believed that "emancipation would only be complete when capitalism had been transcended to establish a direct relationship between labour to its products." See K. Marx, *Economic and Philosophic Manuscripts* (Paris Manuscripts) in *Writings of the Young Marx on Philosophy and Society*, Anchor Books, by L. D. Easton and K. H. Guddat, eds. and trans. (Garden City: Doubleday, 1967): 291.
29. The Poor Law Amendment Act was passed in 1834 and the Poor Law Outdoor Relief Regulation Order passed in 1852. See P. Thane, *Foundations*

of the Welfare State, Social Policy in Modern Britain Series, by J. Campling, ed. (London: Longman, 1982): 4–47.

30. E. Chadwick, *Report on the Sanitary Condition of the Labouring Population of Great Britain [1842]*, by M.W. Flynn, ed. (Edinburgh: Edinburgh University Press, 1965); Clauses Consolidation and Town Improvement Acts of 1846; Nuisances Removal and Diseases Prevention Acts of 1846; Public Health Act of 1848; and Health of Towns Commission in 1848. Municipal Corporations Act of 1835.
31. O. P. von Bismarck, *Bismarck: The Man and the Statesman*, Volumes 1 and 2, by A. J. Butler, trans. (London: Smith, Elder & Company, 1898).
32. V. Pareto, *The Mind and Society,* by A. Bongiorno and A. Livingston, trans., A. Livingston, ed. (New York: Harcourt and Brace, 1935); Chapter 12; V. Pareto, *Manual of Political Economy,* A. S. Schweir, trans., A. S. Schweir and A. N. Page, eds. (New York: Kelly, 1971): Chapter 6, para. 33 and Appendix para 89; V. J. Tarascio, *Pareto's Methodological Approach to Economics* (Chapel Hill, University of North Carolina Press, 1968); and J.M. Buchanan, "A Hobbesian interpretation of the Rawlsian difference principle," *Kyklos* 2(1976): 5–25.
33. A. B. Atkinson and J. E. Stiglitz, *Lectures on Public Economics* (London: McGraw-Hill, 1980): 339. Using a positivist approach, the state is described according to *what* it does rather than *why.*
34. W. S. Vickrey, "Utility, strategy and social decision rules," *Quarterly Journal of Economics* 74(1960): 507–35; and J. C. Harsanyi, "Cardinal welfare, individualistic ethics and interpersonal comparisons of utility," *Journal of Political Economy* 73(1955): 309–21.
35. A. K. Sen, "Interpersonal aggregation and partial comparability," *Econometrica* 38(1970): 393–409.
36. J. E. Meade, *The Just Economy* (London: Alien and Unwin, 1976).
37. J. M. Buchanan and G. Tullochlk, *The Calculus of Consent* (Ann Arbor: University of Michigan Press, 1962); M. Olson, *The Logic of Collective Action* (Cambridge, M. A.: Harvard University Press, 1965).
38. R. M. Titmuss, *Essays on the 'Welfare State',* 2nd Edition (London: Allen & Unwin, 1963); B. Abel-Smith and K. Titmuss, eds., *The Philosophy of Welfare: Selected Writings of Richard Titmuss* (London: George Allen and Unwin, 1987); H. Wilensky, *The Welfare State and Equality* (Berkeley: University of California Press, 1976).
39. Extra-welfarism as applied to health care requires that some of the informational restrictions of welfarism, such as equity and utility, be relaxed to include happiness, absence of pain, freedom to choose, physical mobility,

enjoyment of relationships with others and so on. A. J. Culyer, "Demand-side socialism and health care," Second World Congress on Health Economics, University of Zurich, Switzerland, September 10–14, 1990.

40. J. Tobin, "On limiting the domain of inequality," *Journal of Law and Economics*, 13(1970): 266; J. F. Childress, *Who Should Decide? Paternalism in Health Care* (Oxford: Oxford University Press, 1982).
41. Natural law, utilitarian and positivist philosophical orientations still dominate the debate. T. Meron, ed., *Human Rights in International Law: Legal and Policy Issues,* Volumes 1 and 2 (Oxford: Clarendon Press, 1984).
42. R. Nozick, *Reading Nozick: Essays on Anarchy, State and Utopia* (Oxford: Basil Blackwell, 1974).
43. J. Rawls, *A Theory of Justice* (Oxford: Oxford University Press, 1971).
44. V. I. Lenin, *State and Revolution* [1917], in *Selected Works*, Volume 2, (Moscow, 1961): 355.
45. R. Nozick, *Reading Nozick: Essays on Anarchy, State and Utopia* (Oxford: Basil Blackwell, 1974): ix.
46. M. Ellman, *Socialist Planning,* 2nd Edition (Cambridge: Cambridge University Press, 1989).
47. C. Kessides, T. King, M. Nuti, and C. Sokil, eds., *Financial Reforms in Socialist Economies* (Washington: Economic Development Institute, 1989).
48. International Labour Office (ILO), *Social Security: Introduction to Social Security* (Geneva: International Labour Office, 1984), 9; and United States, Department of Health and Human Services (DHHS), *Social Security Programs Throughout the World — 1983*, Research Report No. 59 (Washington: Government Printing Office, 1984).
49. Developed by Auguste Comte and heavily influenced by the Jeremy Bentham, it has become the basis for twentieth-century jurisprudence. H. L. A. Hart, *The Concept of Law* (Oxford: Clarendon Press, 1961). This concept will be developed in greater detail in the section on methodology.
50. For an extensive review of this literature, see K. Hufner, J. W. Meyer and J. Naumann, "Comparative education policy research: A world society perspective," and L. C. Eliason, I. Fagerlind, R. L. Merritt, and H. N. Weiler, "Education, social science and public policy: A critique of comparative research," in *Comparative Policy Research: Learning from Experience,* by M. Dierkes, H. N. Weiler, and A. B. Antal, eds., WZB-Publications (Hants: Gower, 1987): 188–261. Also see, A. J. Heidenheimer, H. Heclo and C. T. Adams, *Comparative Public Policy: The Politics of Social Choice in Europe and America,* 2nd Edition (New York: St Martin's Press, 1983): 21–52.

51. H. L.Wilensky, G. M. Luebbert, S. R. Hahn, and A. M. Jamieson, "Comparative social policy: Theories, methods, findings," in *Comparative Policy Research: Learning from Experience*, by M. Dierkes, H. N. Weiler and A. B. Antal, eds., WZB-Publications (Hants: Gower, 1987): 384.
52. H. L. Wilensky, *The Welfare State and Equality: Structural and Ideological Roots of Public Expenditures* (Berkeley: University of California Press, 1975).
53. P. Cutright, "Political structure, economic development and national social security programs," *American Journal of Sociology*, 70(March 1965): 537–50; P. Cutright, "Income redistribution: A cross-national analysis," *Social Forces* 46(1967): 180–90; H. J. Aaron, "Social security: International comparisons," in *Studies in the Economics of Income Maintenance,* by O. Eckstein ed. (Washington, D.C.: The Brookings Institution, 1967); and J. A. Pechman, H. J. Aaron, and M. K. Taussing, *Social Security: Perspectives for Reform* (Washington, D. C.: The Brookings Institution, 1968).
54. J. P. Newhouse, "Development and allocation of medical care resources: Medico-economic approach," in *Development and Allocation of Medical Care Resources,* Proceedings of the 29th World Medical Assembly, Tokyo, Japan Medical Association, 1975; J. P. Newhouse, "Medical care expenditure: A cross-national survey," *Journal of Human Resources*, 12(1)(Winter 1977): 115–25; R. J. Maxwell, *Health and Wealth: All International Study of Health-Care Spending* (Lexington, M. A.: Lexington Books, 1981); OECD, *Measuring Health Care 1960–1983: Expenditure, Costs and Performance*, OECD Social Policy Studies. (Paris: OECD, 1985); OECD, *Financing and Delivering Health Care: A Comparative Analysis of OECD Countries*, OECD Social Policy Studies No. 2 (Paris: OECD, 1987); G. J. Schieber and J.-P. Poullier, "International health spending and utilization trends," *Health Affairs* 7(4)(1988): 105–12.
55. J. Hage and R. Hanneman, *The Growth of the Welfare State in Four Western European Societies: A Comparison of Three Paradigms* (Madison, W. I.: Institute for Research on Poverty, 1977).
56. H. L. Wilensky, G. M. Luebbert, S. R. Hahn, and A. M. Jamieson, "Comparative social policy: Theories, methods, findings," in *Comparative Policy Research: Learning from Experience,* by M. Dierkes, H. N. Weiler, and A. B. Antal, eds., WZB-Publications (Hants: Gower, 1987): footnote 2, p. 443.
57. H. L. Wilensky, *The Welfare State and Equality: Structural and Ideological Roots of Public Expenditures* (Berkeley: University of California Press, 1975): 17.

58. K. Taira and P. Kilby, "Differences in social security development in selected countries," *International Social Security Review* 22(2)(1969): 1939–53.
59. H. L. Wilensky, G. M. Luebbert, S. R. Hahn, and A. M. Jamieson, "Comparative social policy: Theories, methods, findings," in *Comparative Policy Research: Learning from Experience,* by M. Dierkes, H.N. Weiler and A.B. Antal, eds., WZB-Publications (Hants: Gower, 1987): 386.
60. F. Pryor, *Public Expenditure in Capitalist and Communist Nations* (Homewood, I. L.: Irwin, 1968): 179–80, 205, 219. A notable exception are unemployment benefits which do not exist in communist countries.
61. G. B. Peters, "Economic and political effects on the development of social expenditures in France, Sweden and the United Kingdom," *Midwest Journal of Political Science* 16(2)(1972): 225–38.
62. The section on methodological problems will discuss different techniques that can be used to minimize the chance that artifacts are misinterpreted as significant correlations.
63. J. Alber, G. Esping-Andersen, and L. Rainwater, "Studying the welfare state: Issues and queries," in *Comparative Policy Research: Learning from Experience,* by M. Dierkes, H. N. Weiler and A. B. Antal, eds., WZB-Publications (Hants: Gower, 1987): 458–68; P. Flora and J. Alber, "Modernization, democratization and the development of welfare states in Western Europe," in *The Development of Welfare States in Europe and America*, by P. Flora and A. J. Heidenheimer, eds. (New Brunswich, N.J.: Transaction Books and the HIWED Project, 1981): 37–80; and P. Flora, "The growth of mass democracies and the welfare states," in *State, Economy and Society in Western Europe 1815–1975: A Data Handbook*, Volume I (Frankfurt: Campus, 1983).
64. H. L. Wilensky, G. M. Luebbert, S. R. Hahn, and A. M. Jamieson, "Comparative social policy: Theories, methods, findings," in *Comparative Policy Research: Learning from Experience*, by M. Dierkes, H.N. Weiler and A. Berthoin Antal, eds., WZB-Publications (Hants: Gower, 1987): 392; and G. Espling-Andersen and W. Korpi, "From poor relief to institutional welfare states," in *The Scandinavian Model*, by R. Eriksson *et al.*, eds, (New York: M.E. Sharpe, 1985).
65. H. L. Wilensky, G. M. Luebbert, S. R. Hahn, and A. M. Jamieson, "Comparative social policy: Theories, methods, findings," in *Comparative Policy Research: Learning from Experience,* by M. Dierkes, H.N. Weiler and A.B. Antal, eds., WZB-Publications (Hants: Gower, 1987): 381.
66. H. L. Wilensky, *The Welfare State and Equality: Structural and Ideological Roots of Public Expenditures* (Berkeley: University of California Press, 1975).

67. R. M. Coughlin, *Ideology, Public Opinion, and Welfare Policy: Attitudes Towards Taxing and Spending in Industrialized Societies*, Monograph Series No. 42 (Berkeley: Institute of International Studies, University of California, 1980): p. xii, discussed in H. L. Wilensky, G. M. Luebbert, S. R. Hahn and A. M. Jamieson, "Comparative social policy: Theories, methods, findings," in *Comparative Policy Research: Learning from Experience*, by M. Dierkes, H. N. Weiler and A. B. Antal, eds., WZB-Publications (Hants: Gower, 1987): 393–94.
68. K. Janda, "Measuring issue orientations of parties across nations," *ICCP Reports* quoted in H. L. Wilensky, G. M. Luebbert, S. R. Hahn, and A. M. Jamieson, "Comparative social policy: Theories, methods, findings," in *Comparative Policy Research: Learning from Experience,* by M. Dierkes, H. N. Weiler, and A. B. Antal, eds., WZB-Publications (Hants: Gower, 1987): 392.
69. J. Alber, "Government responses to the challenge of unemployment: The development of unemployment insurance in Western Europe," and S. Kuhnle, "The growth of social insurance programs in Scandinavia: Outside influences and internal forces," in *The Development of Welfare States in Europe and America*, by P. Flora and A. J. Heidenheimer, eds. (New Brunswich, N. J.: Transaction Books and the HIWED Project, 1981): 125–83.
70. F. Castles, *The Social Democratic Image of Society* (London: Routledge and Kegan Paul, 1978): 55.
71. H. L. Wilensky, G. M. Luebbert, S. R. Hahn, and A. M. Jamieson, "Comparative social policy: Theories, methods, findings," in *Comparative Policy Research: Learning from Experience*, by M. Dierkes, H. N. Weiler and A. B. Antal, eds., WZB-Publications (Hants: Gower, 1987): 404; and E. Einhorn and J. Logue, *Welfare States in Hard Times: Denmark and Sweden in the 1970s* (Kent, O.H.: Kent Popular Press, 1979).
72. J. Alber, "Government responses to the challenge of unemployment: The development of unemployment insurance in Western Europe," and S. Kuhnle, "The growth of social insurance programs in Scandinavia: Outside influences and internal forces," in *The Development of Welfare States in Europe and America*, by P. Flora and A. J. Heidenheimer, eds. (New Brunswich, N.J.: Transaction Books and the HIWED Project, 1981): 125–83; and R. T. Kudrle and T. R. Marmor, "The development of welfare states in North America," in *The Development of Welfare States in Europe and America*, by P. Flora and A. J. Heidenheimer, eds. (New Brunswick, N.J.: Transaction Books and HIWED Project, 1981): 81–121.

73. H. L. Wilensky, G. M. Luebbert, S. R. Hahn, and A. M. Jamieson, "Comparative social policy: Theories, methods, findings," in *Comparative Policy Research: Learning from Experience*, by M. Dierkes, H. N. Weiler, and A. B. Antal, eds., WZB-Publications (Hants: Gower, 1987): 440.
74. Australia, Austria, Switzerland, Germany and Canada are the only federal states among the OECD group of countries.
75. K. Barnard and K. Lee, *Conflicts in the National Health Service* (London: Croom Helm, 1977); and J. Stacey, *Health and the Division of Labour* (London: Croom Helm, 1977).
76. H. Eckstein, *Pressure Group Politics: The Case of the British Medical Association* (London: Allen & Unwin, 1960); R. F. Badgley, "Health worker strikes: Social and economic bases of conflict," *International Journal of Health Services* 5(1)(1975): 9–17; B. Ehrenreich and J. H. Ehrenreich, "Hospital workers: Class conflicts in the making," *International Journal of Health Services* 5(1)(1975): 43–51; T. R. Marmor and D. Thomas, "Doctors, politics and pay disputes: 'Pressure group politics' revisited," *British Journal of Political Science* 2(4)(1972): 421–42; V. Navarro, *Class Struggle, The State and Medicine: An Historical and Contemporary Analysis of the Medical Sector in Great Britain* (London: Martin Rovertson, 1978); V. Navarro, "Social class, political power and the state and their implications in medicine," *Social Science and Medicine* 10(9/10)(1976).
77. R. Klein, *Ideology, Class and the National Health Service,* Project Paper No. RC4 (London: Kings Fund, 1980).
78. J. Le Grand, *The Strategy of Equality* (London: George Allen and Unwin, 1982); D. Black, *Inequalities in Health: Report of the Research Working Group* (London: DHSS, 1980); and R. Illsley, "Occupational class, selection and inequalities in health," *Quarterly Journal of Social Affairs* 3(3) (1987): 213–23; P. Townsend and N. Davidson, eds., *Inequalities in Health* (Harmondsworth: Penguin Books, 1982); R. Illsley and J. Le Grand, *Measurement of Inequality in Health,* Welfare State Programme Discussion Paper No. 12 (London: London School of Economics, Suntory-Toyota Centre for Economics and Related Disciplines, 1987); and M. O'Higgins, "Inequality, redistribution and recession: The British experience, 1976–82," *Journal of Social Policy* 14(3)(1985): 279.
79. H. L. Wilensky, *The Welfare State and Equality: Structural and Ideological Roots of Public Expenditures* (Berkeley: University of California Press, 1975): 3–7.
80. P. Flora and J. Alber, "Modernization, democratization and the development of welfare states in Western Europe," in *The Development of Welfare States*

in Europe and America, by P. Flora and A. J. Heidenheimer, eds. (New Brunswich, N. J.: Transaction Books and the HIWED Project, 1981): 37–80.

81. Norway and Finland were difficult to place in this series. Norway only became a parliamentary democracy in 1884 and Finland was neither a parliamentary democracy nor a constitutional monarchy, being a Grand Duchy of the absolutist Russian Tsar until it became a republic following the 1917 Revolution.
82. P. Flora and J. Alber, "Modernization, democratization and the development of welfare states in Western Europe," in *The Development of Welfare States in Europe and America*, by P. Flora and A. J. Heidenheimer, eds. (New Brunswich, N. J.: Transaction Books and the HIWED Project, 1981): 37–80.
83. J. Alber, "Government responses to the challenge of unemployment: The development of unemployment insurance in Western Europe," and S. Kuhnle, "The growth of social insurance programs in Scandinavia: Outside influences and internal forces," in *The Development of Welfare States in Europe and America*, by P. Flora and A. J. Heidenheimer, eds. (New Brunswich, N. J.: Transaction Books and the HIWED Project, 1981): 125–83.
84. F. Castles, *The Social Democratic Image of Society* (London: Routledge and Kegan Paul, 1978).
85. H. Helco, *Modern Social Politics in Britain and Sweden* (New Haven: Yale University Press, 1974).
86. F. Castles, *The Social Democratic Image of Society* (London: Routledge and Kegan Paul, 1978): 76.
87. H. L. Wilensky, G. M. Luebbert, S. R. Hahn, and A. M. Jantleson, "Comparative social policy: Theories, methods, findings," in *Comparative Policy Research: Learning from Experience*, by M. Dierkes, H. N. Weiler and A. B. Antal, eds., WZB-Publications (Hants: Gower, 1987): 397.
88. C. Hewitt, "The effects of political democracy and social democracy on equality in industrial societies: A cross-national comparison," *American Sociological Review* 42(1977): 450–64.
89. H. L. Wilensky, G. M. Luebbert, S. R. Hahn, and A. M. Jamieson, "Comparative social policy: Theories, methods, findings," in *Comparative Policy Research: Learning from Experience*, by M. Dierkes, H. N. Weiler and A. B. Antal, eds., WZB-Publications (Hants: Gower, 1987): 398.
90. F. Castles, "The impact of parties on public expenditure," in *The Impact of Parties: Politics and Policies in Democratic Capitalist States,* by F. Castles, ed., (Beverly Hills: Sage, 1982).
91. H. Helco, *Modem Social Politics in Britain and Sweden* (New Haven: Yale University Press, 1974): 228.

92. H. L. Wilensky, G. M. Luebbert, S. R. Hahn, and A. M. Jamieson, "Comparative social policy: Theories, methods, findings," in *Comparative Policy Research: Learning from Experience*, by M. Dierkes, H. N. Weiler and A. B. Antal, eds., WZB-Publications (Hants: Gower, 1987): 405.
93. N. W. Polsby, "Party realignment in the 1980 election," *Yale Review,* 72(Autumn 1982): 42–54.
94. H. L. Wilensky and G. Johannsen, eds., "Leftism, catholicism, democratic corporatism: The role of political parties in recent welfare state development," in *The Development of Welfare States in Europe and America* by P. Flora and A. J. Heidenheimer, eds. (New Brunswich, N. J.: Transaction Books and the HIWED Project, 1981): 345–82.
95. H. Helco, *Modem Social Politics in Britain and Sweden* (New Haven: Yale University Press, 1974).
96. G. Lembruch and P. C. Schmitter, eds., *Patterns of Corporatist Policy-making* (Beverly Hills: Sage, 1982); P. C. Schmitter "Interest intermediation and regime governability in contemporary Western Europe and North America," in *Organising Interests in Western Europe: Pluralism, Corporatism and the Transformation of Politics,* by S. Berger, ed. (Cambridge: Cambridge University Press, 1981); and H. L. Wilensky, G. M. Luebbert, S. R. Hahn, and A. M. Jamieson, "Comparative social policy: Theories, methods, findings," in *Comparative Policy Research: Learning from Experience,* by M. Dierkes, H. N. Weiler, and A. B. Antal, eds., WZB-Publications (Hants: Gower, 1987): 432.
97. J. Alber, "Government responses to the challenge of unemployment: The development of unemployment insurance in Western Europe," and S. Kuhnle, "The growth of social insurance programs in Scandinavia: Outside influences and internal forces," in *The Development of Welfare States in Europe and America* by P. Flora and A. J. Heidenheimer, eds. (New Brunswich, N. J.: Transaction Books and the HIWED Project, 1981): 125–83.
98. H. L. Wilensky, G. M. Luebbert, S. R. Hahn, and A. M. Jamieson, "Comparative social policy: Theories, methods, findings," in *Comparative Policy Research: Learning from Experience,* by M. Dierkes, H. N. Weiler and A. B. Antal, eds., WZB-Publications (Hants: Gower, 1987): 409.
99. F. Castles, "Scandinavia: The politics of stability," in *Modem Political Systems: Europe,* by R. C. Macridis, ed. (Englewood Cliffs, N. J.: Prentice-Hall, 1978).
100. G. Heckscher, "Interest groups in Sweden: Their political role," in *Interest Groups on Four Continents*, by H. W. Ehrmann, ed. (Pittsburgh: University of Pittsburgh Press, 1958).

101. H. L. Wilensky, G. M. Luebbert, S. R. Hahn, and A. M. Jamieson, "Comparative social policy: Theories, methods, findings," in *Comparative Policy Research: Learning from Experience*, by M. Dierkes, H. N. Weiler and A. B. Antal, eds., WZB-Publications (Hants: Gower, 1987): 436.
102. G. Pridham, *The Nature of the Italian Party System* (London: Croom Helm, 1981).
103. K. J. Arrow and F. H. Hahn, *General Competitive Analysis* (Edinburgh: Oliver and Boyd, 1971); E. Malinvaud, *Lectures on Microeconomic Theory* (Amsterdam: North-Holland, 1972); and H. R. Varian, *Microeconomic Analysis* (New York: Norton, 1978).
104. J. Robinson, *The Economics of Imperfect Competition* (London: Macmillan, 1933), Chapter 5.
105. J. D. Hey, *Uncertainty in Microeconomics* (Oxford: Martin Robertson, 1979); and J.D. Hey, "Whither uncertainty?" *Economic Journal* 92(1982): 130–39.
106. G. Stigler "The economics of information," *Journal of Political Economy* 69(1961): 213–25; J.E. Stiglitz, "Information and economic analysis," in *Current Economic Problems* by M. Parkin and A.R. Nobay, eds. (Cambridge: Cambridge University Press, 1975); S. J. Grossman and J. E. Stiglitz, "Information and competitive price systems," *American Economic Review*, Papers and Proceedings of the 88th Annual Meeting of the American Economic Association, 66(1976): 246–53; and J. E. Stiglitz, *Information and Economic Analysis* (Oxford: Oxford University Press, 1980); M. Rothschild and J. Stigliz, "Equilibrium in competitive insurance markets: An essay on the economics of imperfect information," *Quarterly Journal of Economics* 90(1976): 629–49.
107. D. J. Roberts and H. Sonnenschein, "On the foundations of the theory of monopolistic competition," *Econometrica* 45(1976): 115–28.
108. D. J. Roberts and A. Postlewaite, "The incentives for price-taking behavior in large exchange economies," *Econometrica* 44(1976): 115–28.
109. K. J. Arrow, "Political and economic evaluation of social effects and externalities," in *The Analysis of Public Output*, by J. Margolis, ed. (New York: Columbia University, National Bureau of Economic Research, 1970).
110. G. J. Stigler, "Free riders and collective action," *Bell Journal of Economics* 5(1974): 359–65; and J. Green, E. Kohlberg, and J.-J. Laffont, "Partial equilibrium approach to the free-rider problem," *Journal of Public Economics* 6(1976): 375–94.
111. J. Green and E. Sheshinski, "Direct versus indirect remedies for externalities," *Journal of Political Economy* 84(1976): 767–808; J. M. Buchanan and W. G. Stubblebine, "Externality," *Economica* (1962): 371–84; and

R. Cornes and T. Sandler, *The Theory of Externalities, Public Goods and Club Goods* (Cambridge: Cambridge University Press, 1986).

112. A. Deaton and J. Muellbauer, *Economics and Consumer Behavior* (Cambridge: Cambridge University Press, 1980).
113. F. H. Knight, *Risk, Uncertainty and Profit* (Boston: Houghton Mifflin, 1933); M. Friedman and L. J. Savage, "The utility analysis of choices involving risk," *Journal of Political Economy* 56(August 1948): 279–304.
114. K. J. Arrow, "The economics of moral hazard: Further comments," *American Economic Review* 1(1968): 537–39; and M. V. Pauly, "The economics of moral hazard: comment," *American Economic Review* 1(1968): 531–37.
115. M. Crew, "Coinsurance and the welfare economics of medical care," *American Economic Review* 59(1969) 906–08; and M. Feldstein, "The welfare loss of excess health insurance;" *Journal of Political Economy* 81(1973): 251–80.
116. A. J. Culyer, "The nature of the commodity 'Health Care' and its efficient allocation," *Oxford Economic Papers* 23(2)(July 1971): 189–211.
117. H. Aaron, "Economic aspects of the role of government in health care," in *Health, Economics and Health Economics,* by J. van der Gaag and M. Perlman, eds., (Amsterdam: North Holland, 1981).
118. A. Sen and B. Williams, eds., *Utilitarianism and Beyond* (Cambridge: Cambridge University Press, 1982). A. J. Culyer, "Demand-side socialism and health care," Second World Congress on Health Economics, University of Zurich, Switzerland, September 10–14, 1990.
119. P. A. Samuelson and A. Scott, *Economics* (London: McGraw-Hill, 1975).
120. S. Darbon and J. B. Letourmy, "La micro-economic des soins medicaux doit-elle necessairement etre d'inspiration neoclassique?" *Sciences Sociales et Sante* 2(1983): 31–75.
121. R. G. Evans, *Strained Mercy: The Economics of Canadian Health Care* (Toronto: Butterworths, 1984); A. Williams, *Health and Economics* (London: Macmillan, 1987); G. H. Mooney, *Economics, Medicine and Health Care* (New York: Harvester Wheatsheaf, 1986); A. McGuire, J. Henderson and G. Mooney, *The Economics of Health Care: An Introductory Text* (London: Routledge & Kegan Paul, 1988); J. G. Cullis and P. A. West, *The Economics of Health: An Introduction* (Oxford: Martin Robertson, 1979); P. J. Feldstein, *Health Care Economics,* 2nd Edition (New York; John Wiley & Sons, 1983); V. R. Fuchs, *The Health Economy* (Cambridge: Harvard University Press, 1986); P. Jacobs, *The Economics of Health and Medical Care,* 2nd Edition (Aspen: Aspen, 1987); M. H. Cooper and A. J. Culyer, *Health Economics* (Harmondsworth: Penguin, 1973); A. J. Culyer, J. Wiseman and A. Walker,

An Annotated Bibliography of Health Economics English Language Sources (London: Martin Robertson, 1977); M. M. Hauser, *The Economics of Health and Medical Care* (London: George Allen & Unwin, 1972); M. Perlman, *The Economics of Health and Medical Care* (London: Macmillan, 1974); J. van der Gaag and M. Perlman, eds., *Economics and Health Economics* (Amsterdam: North Holland, 1981).

122. K. J. Arrow and T. Scitovsky, *Readings in Welfare Economics* (Hannondsworth: Penguin, 1969); J. M. Buchanan, *The Demand and Supply of Public Goods* (Chicago: Rand McNally, 1968); J. Le Grand, *The Economics of Social Problems: The Market Versus the State,* 2nd Edition (London: MacMillan Press, 1984); D. M. Winch, *Analytical Welfare Economics* (Harmondsworth: Penguin, 1971); A. D. Collard, *Altruism and Economy* (Oxford: Martin Robertson, 1978); and A. J. Culyer, *The Political Economy of Social Policy* (Oxford: Martin Robertson, 1980).
123. A. B. Atkinson and J. E. Stiglitz, *Lectures on Public Economics* (London: McGraw-Hill, 1980); R. Millward, D. Parker, L. Rosenthal, M. T. Summer, and N. Topham, *Public Sector Economics* (London: Longman, 1983).
124. M. Ellman, *Socialist Planning,* 2nd Edition (Cambridge: Cambridge University Press, 1989); A. P. Lerner, *The Economics of Control* (London: Macmillan, 1944); M. Dobb, *Welfare Economics and the Economics of Socialism* (Cambridge: Cambridge University Press, 1969).
125. D. S. Lees, *Economic Consequences of the Professions,* Research Monograph (London: Institute of Economic Affairs, 1966).
126. T. L. Beauchamp and L. B. McCullough, *Medical Ethics: The Moral Responsibilities of Physicians* (Englewood Cliffs, N. J.: Prentice Hall, 1984); C. B. Chapman, *Physicians, Law, & Ethics* (New York: New York University Press, 1984); M. Cohen, T. Nagel, and T. Scanlon, eds., *Medicine and Moral Philosophy* (Princeton: Princeton University Press, 1981); C. M. Culver and B. Gert, *Philosophy in Medicine* (Oxford: Oxford University Press, 1982); I. Kennedy, *The Unmasking of Medicine: A Searching Look at Health Care Today,* Revised Edition (London: Granada, 1983); J. K. Mason and A. R. McCall Smith, *Law and Medical Ethics* (London: Butterworths, 1983); P. D. G. Skegg, *Law, Ethics, and Medicine: Studies in Medical Law* (Oxford: Clarendon Press, 1984).
127. U. E. Reinhardt, "Manpower substitution and productivity in medical practice: Review of research," *Health Services Research* 8(1973): 800–27; J. Rafferty, ed., *Health Manpower and Productivity* (Lexington, M. A.: D. C. Heath, 1974); P. Slayton and M. J. Trebilcock, *The Professions and Public Policy* (Toronto: University of Toronto Press, 1978).

128. A. Williams, "Health economics: The end of clinical freedom?" *British Medical Journal* 297(5 November): 1183–86; A. Williams, "Ethics, clinical freedom and the doctors' role," in *Competition in Health Care: Reforming the NHS,* by A. J. Culyer, A. K. Maynard, and J. W. Posnett, eds. (London: Macmillan, 1990): 178–91.
129. T. F. Andersen and G. Mooney, eds., *The Challenges of Medical Practice Variations,* (Basingstoke: Macmillan, 1990); K. McPherson, "International differences in medical care practices," Annual Supplement, *Health Care Financing Review* (1989): 9–19.
130. R. G. Evans, "Supplier induced demand: Some empirical evidence and implications," in *The Economics of Health and Medical Care,* by M. Perlman, ed., (Tokyo: Proceedings of the International Economic Association Conference, 1974): 162–73; U. E. Reinhardt, "The theory of physician induced demand: Reflexion after a decade," *Journal of Health Economics* 4(1985): 187–93; and L. Rochaix, "Academic dispute or political debate? The issue of physicians' discretionary power: A review of the theoretical literature," *Notes du G.S. Sante* (January 1986); S. Bejean, "Information asymmetries and supplier induced demand: An econometric study for the French market," Document de travail, 9005, Universite de Bourgogne, Dijon, 1990; R. D. Auster and R. L. Oaxaca, "Identification of supplier induced demand in the health care sector," *Journal of Human Resources* 16(1981): 327–42; J. Cromwell and J. B. Mitchell, "Physician-induced demand for surgery," *Journal of Health Economics* 5(1986): 293–313; V. Fuchs, "The supply of surgeons and the demand for surgical operations," *Journal of Human Resources* 13(1978): 21–34; J. R. Green, "Physician induced demand for medical care," *Journal of Human Resources* 13(1978): 21–34; C. E. Phelps, "Induced demand — can we ever know its extent?" *Journal of Health Economics* 5(1986): 355–66; G. R. Wilensky and L. F. Rossiter, "The relative importance of physician-induced demand in the demand for medical care," *Milbank Memorial Fund Quarterly* 61(1983): 252–77; and J. Richardson, "The inducement hypothesis that doctors generate demand for their own services," in *Health, Economics and Health Economics,* by J. van der Gaag and M. Perlman, eds. (Amsterdam: North Holland, 1981).
131. M. Roemer and M. Shain, *Hospital Utilisation Under Insurance* (Chicago: American Hospital Association, 1959); and B. Ginsburg, and K. M Koretz, "Bed availability and hospital utilisation: Estimates of the 'Roemer effect'," *Health Care Financing Review* 5(1983): 87–92.
132. D. Wilsford, "The fiscal imperative in health care: Responses in advanced industrial democracies to increased demand and scarcer resources," Second

World Congress on Health Economics, University of Zurich, Switzerland, September 10–14, 1990; T. R. Marmor, *The Politics of Medicare* (London: Routledge and Kegan Paul, 1970); D. A. Stone, *The Limits of Professional Power* (Chicago: University of Chicago Press, 1980).

133. P. J. Feldstein; "Research on the demand for health services," *Milbank Memorial Fund Quarterly* 44(1966): 128–62; M. Grossman, *The Demand for Health: A Theoretical and Empirical Investigation* (New York: National Bureau of Economic Research, 1972); J. Dowie, "The portfolio approach to health behaviour," *Social Science and Medicine* 9(11/12)(1975): 619–31; J.M. Muurinen, "Demand for health: A generalised Grossman model," *Journal of Health Economics* 1(1982): 5–28; J. P. Newhouse and S. E. Marquis, "The norms hypothesis and the demand for medical care," *Journal of Human Resources* 13(1978): 159–82; and J. P. Newhouse, "The demand for medical care services: A retrospective and perspective," in *The Economics of Health and Medical Care,* by M. Perlman, ed. (London: Macmillan, 1974).

134. G. L. Stoddart and M. L. Barer, "Analysis of demand and utilisation through episodes of medical services," in *Health, Economics and Health Economics* by J. van der Gaag and M. Perlman, eds., (Amsterdam: North Holland, 1981); and J. C. Hershey, H. S. Luft, and J. M. Gianaris "Making sense out of utilisation data," *Medical Care* 13(1975): 838–54.

135. A. Wagstaff, "The demand for health: Some new empirical evidence," *Journal of Health Economics* 5(1986): 195–233; A. Wagstaff, "The demand for health: A simplified Grossman model," *Journal of Epidemiology and Community Health* 40(1986): 1–11; W. G. Manning, J. P. Newhouse and J. E. Ware, "The status of health in demand estimation: Beyond excellent, good, fair and poor," in *Economic Aspects of Health*, by V. R. Fuchs, ed. (Chicago: NBBR, University of Chicago Press, 1984); R. G. Evans and A. D. Wolfson, "Faith, hope and charity: Health care in the utility function," Discussion Paper No. 80-46, Department of Economics, University of British Columbia, Vancouver 1980.

136. A. Williams, "'Need' as a demand concept, (With special reference to health)," in *Economic Policies and Social Goals: Aspects of Public Choice*, by A. J. Culyer, ed. (London: Martin Robertson, 1974); A. J. Culyer, *Need and the National Health Service* (Oxford: Martin Robertson, 1976); A. Williams, "Need — an economic exegesis," in *Economic Aspects of Health Services*, by A. J. Culyer and K. G. Wright, eds. (Oxford: Martin Robertson, 1978); D. A. Nevitt, "Demand and need," in *Foundations of Social Administration,* by H. Heisler, ed. (London: Macmillan, 1977); M. Ignatieff,

The Needs of Strangers (London: Chatto and Windus, 1984); P. Springborg, *The Problem of Human Needs and the Critique of Civilization* (London: George, Allen & Unwin, 1981); P. Chapman, *Unmet Needs and the Delivery of Care,* Series No. 61 (London: Occasional Papers on Social Administration, 1979).

137. J. Bradshaw, "A taxonomy of social need," in *Problems and Progress in Medical Care,* 7th Series, by G. McLachlan, ed. (London: Oxford University Press, 1972).
138. K. J. Arrow, "Uncertainty and the welfare economics of medical care," *American Economic Review* 53(1963): 941–73.
139. D. Kahneman and A. Tversky, "Prospect theory: An analysis of decisions under risk," *Econometrica* 47(1979): 263–91.
140. F. T. Denton and B. G. Spencer, "Health care costs when population changes," *Canadian Journal of Economics*, 8(1975): 130–35; M. L. Barer, R. G. Evans, C. Hertzman and J. Lomas, "Aging and health care utilisation: New evidence on old fallacies," *Social Science and Medicine* 24(1987): 851–62.
141. R. G. Evans and H. D Walker, "Information theory and the analysis of hospital cost structure," *Canadian Journal of Economics* 5(1972): 398–418; and J. P. Bunker and B. Brown, 'The physician-patient as an informed consumer of surgical services," *New England Journal of Medicine* 290(1974): 1051–55.
142. J. Hay and M. J. Leahy, "Physician-induced demand: An empirical analysis of the consumer information gap," *Journal of Health Economics* 1(1982): 217–309.
143. M. V. Pauly, "Is cream skimming a problem for the competitive medical market?" *Journal of Health Economics*, 3(1984): 87–95; W. P. M. M van de Ven, "How can we prevent cream skimming in a competitive health insurance market? The great challenge for the 90s," Second World Congress on Health Economics, University of Zurich, Switzerland, September 10–14, 1990; and H.S. Luft, "Compensation for biased selection in health insurance," *Milbank Quarterly* 64(1986): 566–91.
144. C. E. Phelps and J. P. Newhouse, "Effects of co-insurance: A multivariate analysis," *Social Security Bulletin* 35(1972): 20–29; C. E. Phelps and J. P. Newhouse, "Co-insurance and the demand for medical services," Santa Monica, RAND Corporation, 1974; W. G. Manning *et al.*, "A controlled trial of the effect of a prepaid group practice on use of services," *New England Journal of Medicine* 310(1984): 1505–10; R. N. Rossett, and L. F. Huang. "The effect of health insurance on the demand for medical

care," *Journal of Political Economy* 18(1973): 281–305; and M. B. Pauly, "Taxation, health insurance and market failure in medical economy," *Journal of Economic Review* 24(1986): 629–75.

145. V. R. Fuchs, "The 'Competition Revolution' in health care," *Health Affairs* 7(3)(1988): 5–24.
146. D. S. Lees *et al.*, *Monopoly or Choice in Health Services* (London: Institute of Economic Affairs, 1964); H. E. French and P.B. Ginsburg, "Imposed health insurance in monopolistic markets," *Economic Inquiry* 13(1975): 55–70; P. J. Feldstein, "The emergence of market competition in the US health care system: Its causes, likely structure and implications," *Health Policy* 6(1986): 1–20; As an example of professional restrictions, see the Hippocratic Oath and British Medical Association (BMA), *Handbook of Medical Ethics* 1984 (London: BMA, 1984).
147. W. P. M. M. van de Ven, "From regulated cartel to regulated competition in the Dutch health care system, "*European Economic Review* 34(1990): 632–45.
148. K.-D. Henke, "Cost containment in health care: Justification and consequences," to be published in *Health Economics Worldwide* by P. Zweifel and H. E. French (Kluwer, 1991); A. S. Preker, "Expenditure control through public financing in the OECD," Second World Congress on Health Economics, University of Zurich, Switzerland, September 10–14, 1990; A. J. Culyer, "Cost containment in Europe," Annual Supplement, *Health Care Financing Review* (1989): 31; B. Abel-Smith, *Cost Containment in Health Care,* Occasional Papers on Social Administration (London: Bedford Square Press, NCVO, 1984); P. Joskow, "Reimbursement policy, cost containment and non-price competition," *Journal of Health Economics* 2(1983): 167–74; and B. Abel-Smith, "Who is the odd man out? The experience of western Europe in containing the costs of health care, *Milbank Memorial Fund Quarterly* 63(1985): 1–17.
149. D. Stone, *The Limits of Professional Power. National Health Care in the Federal Republic of Germany* (Chicago: University of Chicago Press, 1980).
150. M. Pauly, "Market power, monopsony and health insurance markets," *Journal of Health Economics* 7(1988): 111–28.
151. P. Boland, *The New Healthcare Market: A Guide to PPOs for Purchasers, Payors and Providers* (Homewood, Illinois: Dow Jones Irwin, 1985); J. Gabel and D. Ermann, "Preferred provider organisations: Performance, problems and promise," *Health Affairs* 4(1)(1985): 24–40; and S. B. Jones,

"Can multiple choice be managed to constrain health care costs," *Health Affairs* (Fall, 1989): 50–9.

152. R. Klein, *Ideology, Class and the National Health Service,* Project Paper No. RC4 (London: Kings Fund, 1980); H. Eckstein, *Pressure Group Politics: The Case of the British Medical Association* (London: Allen & Unwin, 1960); and T. R. Marmor, W. L. Hoffman, and T. C. Heagy, "National health insurance: Some lessons from the Canadian experience," *Policy Sciences* 6(4)(1975): 447–66.
153. R. Klein, "Values, power and policies," in *The Welfare State in Crisis*, by OECD, ed. (Paris: OECD, 1981).
154. T. R. Marmor and D. Thomas, "Doctors, politics and pay disputes: Pressure group politics revisited," *British Journal of Political Science*, 2(October 1972): 421–42.
155. J. P. Newhouse, "Is competition the answer?" *Journal of Health Economics* 1(1982): 109–16; A. C. Enthoven, "Managed competition in health care: An unfinished agenda," Annual Supplement, *Health Care Financing Review* (1986): 105–19; A. C. Enthoven, "Managed competition of alternative delivery systems," *Journal of Health Politics, Policy and Law* 13(1988): 305–21: A. C. Enthoven, *Theory and Practice of Managed Competition in Health Care Finance* (Amsterdam: North Holland, 1988).
156. J. P. Newhouse and C. E. Phelps, "Price and income elasticities for medical care services," in *The Economics of Health and Medical Care*, by M. Perlman, ed. (London: Macmillan, 1974); and J. P. Newhouse and C. E. Phelps, "New estimates of price and income elasticities of medical services," *The Role of Health Insurance in Health Service Sector* (New York: National Bureau of Economic Research, 1976).
157. J. W. Pratt, D. A. Wise, and R. J. Zeckhauser, "Price differences in almost competitive markets," *Quarterly Journal of Economics* 93(1979): 189–211; J. P. Newhouse, "Pricing and imperfections in the medical care marketplace," Second World Congress on Health Economics, University of Zurich, Switzerland, September 10–14, 1990; M. L. Weitzman, "Prices vs quantities," *Review of Economic Studies* 41(1974): 477–91; M. L. Weitzman, "Is the price system or rationing more effective in getting a commodity to those who need it most?" *Bell Journal of Economics* 8(1977): 517–24.
158. R. M. Titmuss, *The Gift Relationship* (London: George Allen & Unwin, 1970); K. J. Arrow, "Gift and exchanges," *Philosophy and Public Affairs* 1(1974): 343–62; S. J. Grossman and O. D. Hart, "An analysis of the principal agent problem," *Econometrica*, 1(1982): 7–45; and R. S. Downie and E. Telfer, *Caring and Curing: A Philosophy of Medicine and Social Work* (London: Methuen, 1980).

159. A. J. Culyer, "The nature of the commodity 'health care' and its efficient allocation," *Oxford Economic Papers* 23(1971): 189–11.
160. Paternalistic, altruistic and self-serving externalities resulting from health care were described by A. J. Culyer and H. Simpson, "Externality models and health: A ruckblick over the last twenty years," *Economic Record* 56(1980): 222–30.
161. R. M. Cyert and J. March, *A Behavioral Theory of the Firm* (Englewood Cliffs, N.J.: Prentice Hall, 1964).
162. I. Illich, *Limits to Medicine: Medical Nemesis, the Expropriation of Health* (Harmondsworth: Pelican, 1976); T. McKeown, *Tile Role of Medicine* (Oxford: Blackwell, 1979); and A. L. Cochrane, *Effectiveness and Efficiency: Random Reflections on Health Services* (London: Nuffield Provincial Hospital Trust, 1972).
163. The same observations have been made of non-health related organizations once they reach a certain critical size. L. G. Zucker, "Institutional theories of organization," *Annual Reviews of Sociology* 13(1987): 443–64.
164. C. J. Culyer, ed., *Health Indicators* (London: Martin Robertson, 1983); R. Rosser, "A history of the development of health indicators," in *Measuring the Social Benefits of Medicine,* by G. T. Smith, ed., Proceedings of a Meeting held at Brunel University, May 16–19, 1983 (London: Office of Health Economics, 1983): 50–62; A. Carthwright, *Health Surveys in Practice and in Potential: A Critical Review of their Scope and Methods* (London: King's Fund Publishing Office, 1983); M. F. Drummond, G. L. Stoddart and G. W. Torrance, *Methods for the Economic Evaluation of Health Care Programmes* (Oxford: Oxford Medical Publications, 1987).
165. V. Navarro, "The industrialization of fetishism or the fetishism of industrialization: A critique of Ivan Illich," *International Journal of Health Services* 5(3)(1975): 351–71.
166. V. Tanzi, "Public expenditure and public debt: An international and historical perspective," in *Public Expenditure: The Key Issues,* by J. Bristow and D. McDonagh, eds. (Dublin: Institute of Public Administration 1986): 6–37.
167. P. Leroy-Beaulieu, *Traite de la Science des Finances,* Tome Premier, Des Revues Publics (Paris: Guillaumin et Cie, Librairis, 1988): 127–28.
168. E. R. A. Seligman, *Studies in Public Finance* (New York: Macmillan, 1925).
169. R. A. Musgrave and P. B. Musgrave, *Public Finance in Theory and Practice,* 4th Edition (New York McGraw-Hill, 1984); and A. R. Prest and N. A. Barr, *Public Finance: In Theory and Practice* (London: Weidenfeld and Nicolson, 1985).

170. OECD, *Revenue Statistics of OECD Member Countries, 1965–1985* (Paris: OECD, 1986).
171. J. Bristow and D. McDonagh, eds., *Public Expenditure: The Key Issues* (Dublin: Institute of Public Administration, 1986); and H. Cavanna, ed., *Public Sector Deficits in OECD Countries: Causes, Consequences and Remedies* (London: Macmillan, 1988).
172. J. P. Newhouse, "Development and allocation of medical care resources: Medico-economic approach," in *Development and Allocation of Medical Care Resources, Proceedings of the 29th World Medical Assembly* (Tokyo: Japan Medical Association, 1975); J. P. Newhouse, "Medical care expenditure: A cross-national survey," *Journal of Human Resources* 12(1)(Winter 1977): 115–25; R. J. Maxwell, *Health and Wealth: An International Study of Health-Care Spending* (Lexington, M.A.: Lexington Books, 1981); OECD, *Measuring Health Care 1960–1983: Expenditure, Costs and Performance,* OECD Social Policy Studies. (Paris: OECD, 1985); OECD, *Financing and Delivering Health Care: A Comparative Analysis of OECD Countries*, OECD Social Policy Studies No. 2 (Paris: OECD, 1987); G. J. Schieber and J.-P. Poullier, "International health spending and utilization trends," *Health Affairs* 7(4)(1988): 105–12.
173. R. Klein, ed., *Social Policy and Public Expenditure 1975: Inflation and Priorities* (London, Centre for Studies in Social Policy, 1975); and A.K. Maynard and A. Lodbrook, "Thirty years of fruitless endeavour? An analysis of government intervention in the health care market," in *Health, Economics and Health Economics,* by J. van der Gaag and M. Perlman, eds. (Amsterdam: North Holland, 1981).
174. R. A. Musgrave and P. B. Musgrave, *Public Finance in Theory and Practice,* 4th Edition (New York: McGraw-Hill, 1984): 6–19.
175. A. Smith, *An Inquiry into the Nature and Causes of the Wealth of Nations,* [1776] (Oxford: Oxford University Press Edition, 1976).
176. Although extensively written about in the socialist literature, mainstream economists and policymakers did not recognize this as a legitimate role of the state until the mid-twentieth century. See R. A. Musgrave, *The Theory of Public Finance* (New York: McGraw-Hill, 1959).
177. J. M. Keynes, *The General Theory of Employment, Interest and Money* (London: Macmillan, 1936).
178. V. Tanzi, "Public expenditure and public debt: An international and historical perspective," in *Public Expenditure: The Key Issues* by J. Bristow and D. McDonagh, eds. (Dublin: Institute of Public Administration 1986): 6–37.

179. H. Cavanna, ed., *Public Sector Deficits in OECD Countries: Causes, Consequences and Remedies* (London: Macmillan, 1988).
180. A. Smith, "The revenue of the Sovereign or Commonwealth," in *An Inquiry into the Nature and Causes of the Wealth of Nations,* [1776] (Oxford: Oxford University Press Edition, 1976), Chapter 5. See also D. Richardo, *Principles* and *Essay on the Funding System*; J. S. Smith, *Principles of Political Economy* [1848]; H. Dalton, *Public Finance* [1922]; and A. C. Pigou, *Public Finance,* 1st Edition [1928]. For a historical review see A. R. Prest and N. A. Barr, *Public Finance: In Theory and Practice* (London: Weidenfeld and Nicolson, 1985): 1–5.
181. J. M. Keynes, *The General Theory of Employment, Interest and Money* (London: Macmillan, 1936). Extensively written about in the socialist literature, this notion was first incorporated into the third edition of A. C. Pigou, *Public Finance,* 3rd Edition [1947]. See also R. A. Musgrave, *The Theory of Public Finance* (New York: McGraw-Hill, 1959).
182. M. Friedman, "The role of monetary policy," *American Economic Review*, (March 1968): 1–17; M. Friedman, *Monetary Corrections: A Proposal for Escalator Clauses to Reduce the Costs of Ending Inflation,* Series No. 41 (London: Institute of Economic Affairs, 1974); and M. Friedman, *Inflation and Unemployment: The New Dimension of Politics,* The 1976 Alfred Nobel Memorial Lecture, Series No. 51 (London: Institute of Economic Affairs, 1978).
183. Similar arguments were made as early as the sixteenth century when a rise in prices was attributed to an inflow of gold and silver to Britain from the New World. See C. P. Kindleberger, *A Financial History of Western Europe* (London: Allen & Unwin, 1984); C. P. Kindleberger, *Keynesianism vs Monetarism* (London: George, Allen & Unwin, 1985); D. Bell and I. Kristol, eds., *The Crisis in Economic Theory* (New York: Basic, 1981).
184. D. Schwefel, ed., *Indicators and Trends in Health and Health Care* (Berlin-Heidelberg:Springer Verlag, 1987).
185. R. S. Downie and E. Telfer, *Caring and Curing: A Philosophy of Medicine and Social Work* (London: Methuen, 1980): 15–21; and Constitution of the World Health Organization in 1946.
186. D. Streiner and G. R. Norman, *Health Measurement Scales: A Practical Guide to their Development and Use* (Oxford: Oxford University Press, 1989); I. McDowell and C. Newell, *Measuring Health* (Oxford: Oxford University Press, 1987); A. J. Culyer, "Need, values and health status measurement," in *Economic Aspects of Health Services,* by A. J. Culyer and K. G. Wright, eds. (London: Martin Robertson, 1978): 9–31; R. A. Carr-Hill,

"Assumptions of the QUALY procedure," *Social Science and Medicine* 29(3) (1989): 469–77; G. Loomes and L. McKenzie, "The use of QUALYs in health care decision making," *Social Science and Medicine* 28(4)(1989): 299–308; and I. McDowell and C. Newwell, *Measuring Health: A Guide to Rating Scales and Questionnaires* (New York: Oxford University Press, 1987).

187. A. Carthwright, *Health Surveys in Practice and in Potential: A Critical Review of their Scope and Methods* (London: King's Fund Publishing Office, 1983).
188. A. L. Cochrane, *Effectiveness and Efficiency: Random Reflections on Health Services* (London: Nuffield Provincial Hospitals Trust, 1972); G. T. Smith, "Measuring the social benefits of medicine," Proceedings of a Meeting held at Brunel University, May 16–19, 1983 (London: Office of Health Economics); A. F. Long and S. Harrison, eds., *Health Services Performance: Effectiveness and Efficiency* (London: Crom Helm, 1985); M. F. Drummond, G. L. Stoddart, and G. W. Torrance, *Methods for the Economic Evaluation of Health Care Programmes* (Oxford: Oxford Medical Publications, 1987).
189. F. Champagne, A.-P. Contandriopoulos, A. Lemay, and A. S. Preker, "Evaluation of health care performance in the OECD," Second World Congress on Health Economics, University of Zurich, Switzerland, September 10–14, 1990.
190. OECD, *Health Care Systems in Transition: The Search for Efficiency,* Social Policy Studies No. 7 (Paris: OECD, 1989).
191. R. G. Evans, *Strained Mercy: The Economics of Canadian Health Care* (Toronto: Butterworths, 1984): 5; G. W. Torrance "Measurement of health state utilities for economic appraisal," *Journal of Health Economics*, 5(1986): 1–30; and J. R. G. Butler, "Welfare economics and cost-utility analysis," Second World Congress on Health Economics, University of Zurich, Switzerland, September 10–14, 1990.
192. I. Ilich, *Medical Nemesis: The Expropriation of Health* (Toronto: McClelland and Stewart, 1975).
193. R. G. Evans "Faith, hope and charity: Health care in the utility function," Department of Economics Discussion Paper #80-46 (Vancouver: University of British Columbia, 1980).
194. This was described in detail on the section on correlations in social policy.
195. J. Alber, "Germany," in P. Flora, ed., *Growth to Limits: The Western European Welfare States Since World War II* (New York: de Gruyter, 1988).
196. R. Klein and M. O'Higgins, eds., *The Future of Welfare* (Oxford: Basil Blackwell, 1985).

197. A. J. Culyer, "Cost containment in Europe," Annual Supplement, *Health Care Financing Review* (1989): 31.
198. U. E. Reinhardt, "Health care in transition: Issues and options," Conference on the Economics of Health Care: Challenges for the Nineties, The Woodrow Wilson School of Public and International Affairs, Princeton University, October 28–30, 1990.
199. D. Cameron, "On the limits of the public economy," *Annals of the American Academy of Political and Social Science* 459(1982): 46–62; M. G. Schmidt, "Does corporatism matter? Economic crisis, politics and rates of unemployment in capitalist democracies in the 1970s," in *Patterns of Corporatist Policy-Making* by G. Lehmbruch and P. C. Schmitter, eds. (Beverly Hills: Sage, 1982); R. Rose, ed., *The Dynamics of Public Policy: A Comparative Analysis* (Beverly Hills: Sage, 1976); and R. Rose and G. Peters, *Can Governments Go Bankrupt?* (New York: Basic Books, 1978); and H. Cavanna, ed., *Public Sector Deficits in OECD Countries: Causes, Consequences and Remedies* (London: Macmillan, 1988).
200. D. R. Cameron, "Public expenditure and economic performance in international perspective," in *The Future of Welfare,* by R. Klein and M. O'Higgins, eds. (Oxford: Basil Blackwell, 1985): 8–21.
201. J-P. Dumont, *L'Impact de la Crise Economique sur les Systemes de Protection Sociale* (Paris: Economica, 1987); J. Bristow and D. McDonagh, eds., *Public Expenditure: the Key Issues* (Dublin: Institute of Public Administration, 1986); and L. Hakim and C. Wallich, *Deficits, Debt, and Savings Structure of OECD Countries, with Trends from* 1965 *to 1981*, World Bank Staff Working Papers, No. 727 (Washington: World Bark, 1985).
202. H. L. Wilensky, *The Welfare State and Equality: Structural and Ideological Roots of Public Expenditures* (Berkeley: University of California Press, 1975); R. Rubinson and D. Quinlam, "The world economy and the distribution of incomes within states: A cross-national study," *American Sociological Review* 41(1976): 638–39; R. Rubinson and D. Quinlam, "Democracy and social inequality: A reanalysis," *American Sociological Review* 42(1977): 611–23; and D. Cameron, "The expansion of the public economy: A comparative analysis," *American Political Science Review* 72(4)(1978): 1243–361.
203. R. W. Jackman, *Politics and Social Equality: A Comparative Analysis* (New York: Wiley, 1975); and R. W. Jackman, "Socialist parties and income inequality in Western industrial societies," *Journal of Politics* 43(1980): 135–49.
204. H. L. Wilensky, G. M. Luebbert, S. R. Hahn, and A. M. Jamieson, "Comparative social policy: Theories, methods, findings," in *Comparative*

Policy Research: Learning from Experience, by M. Dierkes, H. N. Weiler and A. B. Antal, eds., WZB-Publications (Hants: Gower, 1987): 438.

205. H. L. Wilinsky, *The 'New Corporatism', Centralization and the Welfare State* (London and Beverly Hills: Sage, 1976).
206. H. L. Wilensky, G. M. Luebbert, S. R. Hahn, and A. M. Jamieson, "Comparative social policy: Theories, methods, findings," in *Comparative Policy Research: Learning from Experience,* by M. Dierkes, H. N. Weiler and A. Berthoin Antal, eds., WZB-Publications (Hants: Gower, 1987): 412.
207. R. M. Coughlin, *Ideology, Public Opinion, and Welfare Policy: Attitudes Towards Taxing and Spending in Industrialized Societies,* Monograph Series No. 42 (Berkeley: Institute of International Studies, University of California, 1980).
208. A. Tibouti, PhD thesis, Aix-en-Province, 1982.
209. F. Kraus, "The historical development of income inequality in Western Europe and the United States," in *The Development of Welfare States in Europe and America* by P. Flora and A. J. Heidenheimer, eds. (New Brunswich, N. J.: Transaction Books and the HIWED Project, 1981): 187–236; and B. I. Page, *Who Gets What from Government* (Berkeley: University of California Press, 1983).
210. J. Alber, G. Esping-Andersen, and L. Rainwater, "Studying the welfare state: Issues and queries," in *Comparative Policy Research: Learning from Experience,* by M. Dierkes, H. N. Weiler and A. B. Antal, eds., WZB-Publications (Hants: Gower, 1987): 459.
211. OECD countries that have not achieved Universal Access such as Mexico, Turkey and the USA are not included in the rankings or comparisons made in this section, which draws h eavily from a publication by the Fraser Institute.
212. B. Barua, I. Timmermans, I. Nason, and N. Esmail, *Comparing Performance of Universal Health Care Countries, 2016,* Report (Vancouver: Fraser Institute, October 2016). https://www.fraserinstitute.org/sites/default/files/comparing-performance-of-universal-health-care-countries-2016.pdf. Accessed July 17, 2010.
213. N. Esmail and M. Walker, *How Good Is Canadian Healthcare? 2008 Report: An International Comparison of Healthcare Systems* (Vancouver: Fraser Institute, 2016). https://pdfs.semanticscholar.org/c4a0/5d20fa32a624c4072902 3292fc316662684e.pdf?_ga=2.8718645.1044595675.1499713218-4413199.1499713218. Accessed July 10.
214. M. Rovere and B. J. Skinner, *Value for Money om Health Insurance Systems in New Zealand and the OECD, 2012 edition,* Fraser Institute (Vancouver: Fraser Institute, October 2013). https://www.fraserinstitute.org/sites/

default/files/value-for-money-from-health-insurance-systems-2012.pdf. Accessed July 10, 2017.

215. B. Barua, *Provincial Healthcare Index 2013,* (Vancouver: Fraser Institute, 2013). https://www.fraserinstitute.org/sites/default/files/provincial-health-care-index-2013-rev.pdf. Accessed July 10, 2017.
216. C. J. Murray and J. Frenk, "A framework for assessing the performance of health systems". *Bulletin of the World Health Organization* 6(78) (2000): 717–731.
217. A. Onyebuchi, G. P. Westert, J. Hurst, and N. S. Klazinga (2006). A Conceptual Framework for the OECD Healthcare Quality Indicators Project. *International Journal for Quality in Healthcare* (September): 5–13.
218. H. L. Wilensky, *The Welfare State and Equality: Structural and Ideological Roots of Public Expenditures* (Berkeley: University of California Press, 1975): 41; and M. Gordon, *Tile Economics of Welfare Policies* (New York: Columbia University Press 1963): 322–5.
219. F. Pryor, *Public Expenditure in Capitalist and Communist Nations* (Homewood, I. L.: Irwin, 1968).
220. J. Alber, "Government responses to the challenge of unemployment: The development of unemployment insurance in Western Europe," in *The Development of Welfare States in Europe and America,* by P. Flora and A. J. Heidenheimer, eds. (New Brunswich, N. J.: Transaction Books and the HIWED Project, 1981): 37–80.
221. Such diffusion may apply to human and physical resources as well as to social policy. See S. Kuhnle, "The growth of social insurance programs in Scandinavia: Outside influences and internal forces," in *The Development of Welfare States in Europe and America* by P. Flora and A. J. Heidenheimer, eds. (New Brunswick, N. J.: Transaction Books and HIWED Project, 1981): 125–50; H. Helco, *Modern Social Politics in Britain and Sweden* (New Haven: Yale University Press, 1974); and K. Taira and P. Kilby, "Differences in social security development in selected countries," *International Social Security Review* 22(2)(1969): 1939–53.
222. R. Bendix, "Tradition and modernity reconsidered," *Comparative Studies in Society and History* 9(1967): 292–342.
223. D. Collier and R. Messick, "Prerequisites versus diffusion: Testing alternative explanations of social security adoption," *American Political Science Review* 69(1975): 1299–315.
224. A. Przeworski and H. Teune, *The Logic of Comparative Social Inquiry* (New York: Wiley-Interscience, 1970): 44.

225. D. Collier and R. Messick, "Prerequisites versus diffusion: Testing alternative explanations of social security adoption," *American Political Science Review* 69(1975): 1299–315.
226. P. Flora and J. Alber, "Modernization, democratization and the development of Welfare States," in *The Development of Welfare States in Europe and America*, by P. Flora and A. J. Heidenheimer, eds. (New Brunswick: Transaction Publishers, 1981): 37–47.
227. A. Przeworski and H. Teune, *The Logic of Comparative Social Inquiry* (New York: Wiley-Interscience, 1970): 44.
228. A. Przeworski and H. Teune, *The Logic of Comparative Social Inquiry* (New York: Wiley-Interscience, 1970): 44.
229. R. Erikson and R. Aberg, *Welfare in Transition: A Survey of Living Conditions in Sweden 1968–1981* (Oxford: Clarendon Press, 1987); H. Glennerster, *The Future of the Welfare State: Remaking Social Policy* (London: Heinemann, 1983); J. Creedy and R. Disney, *Social Insurance in Transition: An Economic Analysis* (Oxford: Clarendon Press, 1985); M. A. Jones, *The Australian Welfare State: Growth, Crisis and Change* (Sydney: George Allen & Unwin, 1983).
230. R. Klein and M. O'Higgins, eds., *The Future of the Welfare* (Oxford: Basil Blackweit, 1985).
231. T. E. Getzen and J.-P. Poullier, "International health spending forecasts: Concepts and evaluation," Second World Congress on Health Economics, University of Zurich, Switzerland, September 13, 1990.
232. B. Abel-Smith, "World trends in health care financing and delivery," International Symposium on Health Care Systems, Taipei, Taiwan, Republic of China, December 18–19, 1989.
233. H. L. Wilensky, G. M. Luebbert, S. R. Hahn, and A. M. Jamieson, "Comparative social policy: Theories, methods, findings," in *Comparative Policy Research: Learning from Experience,* by M. Dierkes, H. N. Weiler, and A. B. Antal, eds., WZB-Publications (Hants: Gower, 1987): 416–17; B. Abel-Smith, *Value for Money in Health Services: A Comparative Study* (London: Heinemann, 1976); B. Abel-Smith, *Cost Containment in Health Care,* Occasional Papers on Social Administration (London: Bedford Square Press, NCVO, 1984).
234. G. J. Schieber and J.-P. Poullier, "Overview of international comparisons of health care expenditures," Annual Supplement, *Health Care Financing Review* (1989): 1.
235. J. W. Hurst in response to A. C. Enthoven, "What can Europeans learn from Americans," Annual Supplement, *Health Care Financing Review* (1989): 65.

236. U. E. Reinhadt in response to B. Jonsson, "What can Americans learn from Europeans?" Annual Supplement, *Health Care Financing Review* (1989).
237. H. L. Wilensky, G. M. Luebbert, S. R. Hahn, and A. M. Jamieson, "Comparative social policy: Theories, methods, findings," in *Comparative Policy Research: Learning from Experience,* by M. Dierkes, H. N. Weiler, and A. B Antal, eds., WZB-Publications (Hants: Gower, 1987): 417.
238. A. J. Heidenheimer, H. Heclo, and C. T. Adams, *Comparative Public Policy: The Politics of Social Choice in Europe and America*, 2nd Edition (New York: St Martin's Press, 1983): 53.

CHAPTER 2

METHODOLOGY

This Chapter of the book, will provide a detailed discussion on research methodologies for comparative health studies and the specific methodology used for the review summarized in this book. It includes a review of approaches to comparative health policy as a hybrid multi-disciplinary field and the need for rigor in applying a scientific method to social policy (defining clear objectives, hypothesis, research design and data collection). And, finally it discusses different analytical techniques, ranging from descriptive to quantitative.

A. HYBRID DISCIPLINE

Cross-state comparisons, "the study of *why, how* and *to what effect* different governments pursue a particular course of action or inaction," provided the underlying framework for the research.[1] Comparative studies attempt to identify the phenomena which are true of one society at any given one point in time that are true of all societies over time.[2] They may be cross-national, cross-time within single countries, cross-level between different tiers of government, cross-policy and so on. Such studies have been carried out for centuries, but their application to health care is a recent development. The early forerunners to today's investigations were used as tools of political theorizing and analysis.[3] During the second half of the twentieth century, investigators tried to apply the knowledge gained through social science to refine the research technique used to study public policy[4] which has come to include cross-national comparisons of both social and health policy.[5] The dominant focus in recent years has been to examine the contents, determinants and effects of policy on society. It helps researchers to identify theoretical issues, develop methodologies, carry out investigations, analyze data and formulate future policy options based on validated hypothesis.[6] It helps planners, legislators and administrators to assess the acceptability, feasibility and appropriateness of policy options based on the real experiences of other national settings.

By necessity, the theoretical base for cross-national studies has become a complex hybrid that often crosses many traditional boundaries to respond to the multi-faceted dimensions of the issues and policy options that are being examined.[7] It bridges fields as diverse as philosophy, history, political science, sociology, public administration, mathematics, statistics, economics and so on. The occurrence of phenomena such as thresholds, historical breaks, conjunctures, shifts, contractions and reversals makes it impractical to adhere to the unidimensional techniques of any of these non-comparative disciplines.[8] Instead, it is often necessary to go beyond the standard research design used in the pure and applied social sciences. This has left the discipline open to harsh criticism on lacking theoretical unity.[9] Cross-disciplinary investigations have been accused of being "essentially non-comparative ... essentially descriptive ... essentially parochial ... essentially static ... [and] essentially monographic."[10] Other social sciences are equally vulnerable to such admonishment. Yet, the note of discordance heard about cross-national studies reflects variations in the orientations of universities and university departments as much as it does shortcomings in the research itself: "many universities encompass greater theoretical heterogeneity than most multi-national research teams."[11]

B. SCIENTIFIC METHOD

Although the controlled *in vitro* laboratory experiment cannot be used for most research conducted in the humanities, the same scientific principles apply to carefully planned field experiments: "cross-national research is needed and conducted because it is the closest approximation to the controlled laboratory experiment of the natural scientists which is available to social scientists..."[12] The application of the scientific method to social research is generally referred to as "quasi-experimentation."[13]

The research design for the study was therefore strategically underpinned by the scientific method of investigation. At first sight, much of the accumulated cross-national public and social policy literature gives the disheartening impression that its only commonality is an inability to come to any conclusion. Many are flawed by haphazard and inappropriate methodologies: unclear objectives, incomplete reviews of the literature, badly formulated hypotheses, poorly designed methodologies, careless experimental techniques, inadequate analysis and construction of incorrect theories. Health policy has not remained immune to these faults. Instead, a thorough preliminary review of the literature should help the investigator to formulate a clear objective for the research, recognize the relevant key issues and identify existing hypotheses. Methodological rigor then provides the basis for a solid experiment, and the possibility of making a positive contribution to knowledge or the formulation of new theories.[14] A pure experimental research design, in which the independent variable is fully controlled, is not possible in the case of the social sciences. A careful selection of countries with certain characteristics is the closest approximation. The following schematic representation of the research design tries to capture all of these elements. See Figure 2.1.

Overemphasis on rigid methodological purity can be counterproductive if it leads to the publication of time-sensitive results years after the research is relevant: "Methodologists can inform us that *all* we have done thus far is wrong and that we must begin again ... Like preachers, [they] are at times listened to, always acclaimed, but rarely followed."[15] Mapping the dynamic flux of policies with no apparent fixed landmarks does not lend itself well to the randomized double-blind prospective trials of the clinical sciences. Using a carefully designed research strategy, many hypotheses can be rejected quickly on purely empirical grounds. One good study may influence research practice more than volumes of theoretical textbooks on methodological purity.[16]

Such criticism of methodological purity should not be misconstrued as an excuse for lack of rigor, but in recent years many of the significant contributions to the knowledge of cross-national phenomena have come from empirical validation or repudiation of hypotheses, and not from

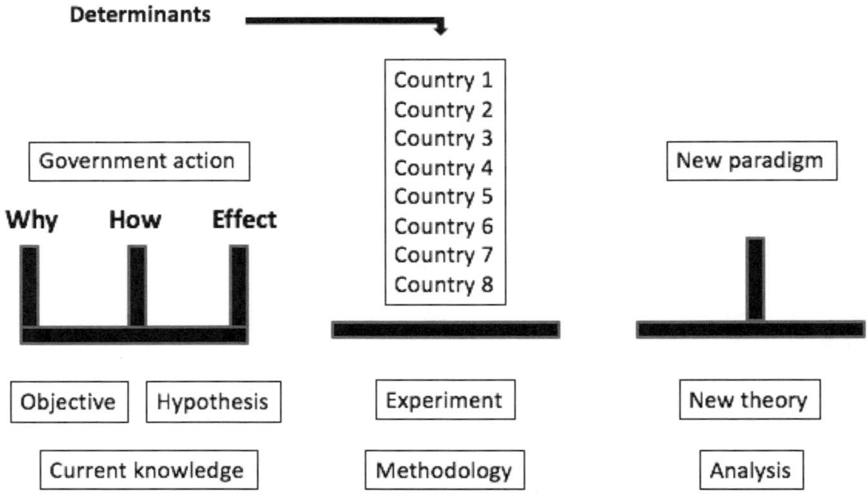

Figure 2.1 Quasi-experimental Method

Source: Adapted from Preker (1989).

methodological breakthroughs.[17] "In general, during the past decade epistemological discussions of cross-national research and the essence of the 'comparative method' have exhibited visibly diminishing returns."[18] How to accumulate knowledge through cross-national research has ceased being an area of extensive esoteric debate. "Indeed, references to manuals on comparative methodology gradually disappear from articles presenting substantive studies.... Researchers now know how to do it and no longer need to legitimate [sic] their procedures by reference to textbooks.[19] The component elements of the scientific method of investigation research as it was adopted for the study are tabulated in Table 2.1.

C. OBJECTIVES

This study involved an in-depth cross-national analysis of statutory provisions for compulsory participation and universal entitlement to comprehensive health care services.[20] The objective of the research was to explore the process that led to the introduction of such legislative provisions, to deepen our understanding of associated health financing mechanisms, to

Table 2.1 Research Design

Objective	Clarification of Issues and Policy Options in Health Care Financing
Mechanisms	*Direct charges versus prepayment*
Participation	Voluntary versus compulsory
Entitlement	Restricted versus universal
Services	Basic versus comprehensive
Linkages	Risk-rated versus open-ended
Hypotheses	*Government involvement in health care financing*
Why	Socio-economic, political, bureaucratic, market failure
How	Allocation, redistribution and stabilization
Effects	Growth, debt, opportunity, displacement, backlash, expenditure, equity
Trends	Historic, future
Processes	Convergence, diffusion, interdependence, evolution
Methodology	*Quasi-experimental research design*
Styles	Descriptive, quantitative
	Case study, statistical
	Longitudinal, cross-sectional
Elements	Contextual, spatial, temporal
Dimensions	Content, terminology, scope, boundary, units-of-measurement
Countries	All, many, few, similar, different
Timeframes	Historical, current, future, fixed, relative
Experiment	*Cross-national and national profiles*
Data collection	Written records, surveys, interviews
Analysis	*Conceptualization, explanation and validation*
Descriptive	Logic, positivist, linguistic, narrative, graphic scaling
Quantitative	Computer assisted, cluster, statistical, econometric
Theory	*New paradigms*

Source: Adapted from Preker (1989).

test specific theories about some of their effects and to propose relevant paradigms about related health policies. As the contribution that research makes to the state of current knowledge increases according to the theoretical complexity of the issues under investigation, the last element is the

Table 2.2 Issues and Policy Options Examined in Study

Issues	Policy Options
Mechanisms	Direct charges versus prepayment
Participation	Voluntary versus compulsory
Entitlement	Restricted versus universal
Services	Basic versus comprehensive
Linkages	Risk-rated versus open-ended

Source: Adapted from Preker (1989).

most difficult, but potentially also the most rewarding: specific problem-solving, descriptions of the state of the art, validation of existing theories and formulation of new theories.[21] Preferences between direct out-of-pocket charges versus prepayment through third-party financing mechanisms, voluntary versus compulsory participation, restricted versus universal entitlement, basic versus comprehensive services and various linkages between these dichotomies in health policy have significant implications in terms of equity and efficiency of both financing and delivery of services. An analysis of the choices that governments have made when faced with an option between such policies provides a powerful instrument for examining a number of empirical and theoretical questions related to the role of the state in health care financing. See Table 2.2.

D. HYPOTHESES

The conceptualization of clear hypotheses to be tested remains one of the most critical challenges in comparative studies because it influences all the other components of the research design ranging from experimental choices to data collection to analytical instruments, and ultimately to the conclusions that can be derived from the investigation. The process also influences its conceptualization. Hypotheses can only be constructed after the formulation of clear objectives and a thorough review of the literature. A thorough exploration of the arguments for and against a particular hypothesis invariably leads to a need for revision in attitudes, objectives and research designs.[22]

The final formulation of hypotheses for the study had to take place after "pilot" field trips to some of the countries that would be included. This trial-and-error process was unavoidable because a significant part of the literature review was not readily available in any one country. Financing, participation, entitlement and services are only four of a constellation of characteristics that distinguish health systems. The importance of the dichotomies presented by the issues and policy options of direct out-of-pocket charges versus prepaid third-party financing, voluntary versus compulsory participation, restricted versus universal entitlements, basic versus comprehensive services and their various linkages was more evident in the literature of the Nordic countries than in the English language literature. In the Nordic countries, identification of the landmark legislative reforms took in-depth analysis of primary sources because even well-informed scholars gave the initial impression that "things have always been as they are today."

A dominant focus of scholars in recent years has been to examine the socio-economic, political and bureaucratic determinants of public and social policy. Although much of this work is inconclusive because alleged causal correlations are at best aleatory, it has potentially important implications for health policy. Even unequivocal correlations between GDP per capita, health care expenditure per capita and health status ignore a constellation of potentially important political and bureaucratic variables. Furthermore, most past studies have focused on the independent variable — the possible determinants. Few scholars have examined the dependent variable or program features such as legislative provisions, financial burden, participation, entitlement and services. To what extent does socio-economic level of development, political choice and bureaucratic infrastructure influence these variables? Are there other significant correlations that have not been explored in the past? There is a great need for such program by program and sub-program by sub-program validation of a number of unproven hypotheses about the determinants of health policy as well as its relation to observations in the public and social policy literature.

Theories on the state offer some clues as to *why, how* and *to what effect* different governments pursue a particular course of action or inaction. The often-cited hypothesis in the health policy and health economics literature, which has escaped systematic cross-national validation, is that the governments involve in health care financing either for ideological reasons or because "market-failure" prevented individuals and private institutions from providing an adequate response to needs for health care. Although all western countries have some legislative provisions for prepayment of health care, several important questions remain unanswered. Why did some countries introduce compulsory participation while others continue to rely on voluntary participation? Why do some countries rely more on one type of prepayment, such as general revenues, social insurance or private insurance, than others? Why did some countries extend entitlement to their whole population while others still restrict it to a subgroup? Why did some countries expand benefits to include comprehensive care while others limit this to basic services? Why did some abandon risk-rated contributions and membership-dependent access? Health policy has largely escaped systematic validation of convergence, diffusion, interdependence and evolution processes that are at the center of the theoretical debate on social policy. The study tried to provide some of these missing links by answering these questions.

How governments get drawn into health care — through regulations, subsidies and direct provision of services, or simply by doing nothing — varies greatly from one state to another, but this may be as important as why they get involved. Style of governing may in itself shape the unfolding health policy. The process of policy-making has received much less attention in the cross-national health policy literature compared with the many hypotheses about possible determinants and effects.

In the absence of the ability to establish concrete causal relationships, falsifying popular myths has the advantage of exposing such distortions to policy-makers. Claims that definitive actions will lead to decisive outcomes remain at the center of many of the debates on health care reforms today. The effect of health policy on society in terms of equity, efficiency, socio-economic development, political backlash and health status is extremely difficult to prove in concrete terms. Was government involvement in health care financing the first step on the road to socialism, as the medical profession has repeatedly warned over time? Do compulsory participation and universal entitlement to health care inevitably lead to problems in economic growth, escalating national debt and opportunity

Table 2.3 Government Involvement in Health Care

Hypotheses	Factors
Why	Socio-economic, political, bureaucratic, market failure
How	Allocation, redistribution and stabilization
Effects	Growth, debt, opportunity, displacement, backlash, expenditure, equity
Trends	Historic, future
Processes	Convergence, diffusion, interdependence, evolution

Source: Adapted from Preker (1989).

costs in terms of other publicly programs? Does it displace revenues away from other social security benefits or lead to a political backlash as claimed by some critics? Did it have an impact on equity in financing? Does it lead to an explosion in public sector and health care expenditure? Is health care a luxury consumer good, public good or merit good?

Finally, to what extent do the theories on convergence and diffusion phenomena that are widely discussed in the public and social policy literature apply to health policy? Is there any evidence of less-debated interdependence and evolution processes in policies? There may be close links or an interdependence between the introduction of social security provisions and state involvement in health care. What is the relation between the two in terms of evolution? Few direct links have been made between observations in social policy and health policy. Even fewer have been systematically validated. What were the past trends? Is there any basis for future forecasting? See Table 2.3.

E. RESEARCH DESIGN

The study was designed to capture both complexities of individual policies and generalities of broad trends through a combination of research styles and elements of investigation. This made possible an exploration of constant and dynamic facets of health policies as they occurred over time and across national boundaries that would have been impossible through any single analytical framework. See Table 2.4.

Table 2.4 Quasi-experimental Research Design

Methodology	Techniques
Styles	Descriptive, quantitative Case study, statistical Longitudinal, cross-sectional
Elements	Contextual, spatial, temporal
Dimensions	Content, terminology, scope, boundary, units
Countries	All, many, few, similar, different
Timeframes	Historical, current, future, fixed, relative

Source: Adapted from Preker (1989).

1. Styles

The study used two broad research styles that are common to most cross-national investigations — descriptive and quantitative studies. A matrix of eight methodological variations can be constructed from these options. Not all provide useful information. Some should even be avoided because they will lead to distortions. There are four basic variations of descriptive studies: longitudinal case studies, longitudinal statistical studies, cross-sectional case studies and cross-sectional statistical studies. Likewise, there are four variants of quantitative studies. The possibility of combining these approaches places cross-national studies in a category by themselves, distinct from both non-experimental case studies and experimental statistical studies.[23] Vastly different facets of similar issues may surface when studies that use mismatched methodologies are compared. Some of the contradictory conclusions observed in the literature are due to inappropriate research designs. See Table 2.5.

Descriptive studies often focus in great detail on qualitative aspects of terminology, content, scope, boundaries, units-of-measurement and transformation of policy issues. These types of studies do not seek to establish causal relationships, but rather examine the subtle nuances of the substantive issue and validate hypotheses empirically about determinants that have already been established through quantitative analysis. The number of countries selected is therefore less important than in quantitative

Table 2.5 Descriptive and Quantitative Studies

	Case Study	Statistical
Descriptive		
Longitudinal		
Cross-Sectional		
Quantitative		
Longitudinal		
Cross-Sectional		

Source: Adapted from Preker (1989).

studies, although the choice remains crucial. These studies can be divided into several subgroups[24]:

Descriptive studies where causal relationships are well established[25];
Descriptive studies that impose global structures on partial data[26];
Descriptive studies of innovative policies.

By contrast, quantitative studies focus on concrete units-of-measurements which have been assigned as proxies to reflect the realities of the policies being investigated. These studies often seek to establish causal relationships through statistical analysis. The number of countries selected is crucial to the research design, and the more random the choice, the less biased the results. These studies can be divided into several subgroups[27]:

Studies that ask whether X is responsible for Y;
Studies that ask whether X is an effective measure for or against Y;
Studies that ask whether X is producing a sufficient effect upon Y;
Studies that compare the effectiveness of partial changes within complex systems.

Researchers who carry out descriptive analysis on case studies are able to explore the subtle qualitative aspects of core explanatory variables in much greater detail than is possible through statistical studies. "Comparative case histories uncover a myriad of details of social reforms, their administrative properties, coverage, financial agreements, distributive logic and so forth. In the correlational approach, the welfare state is often reduced to one or two highly aggregate indices."[28] This applies to both cross-sectional and longitudinal historical material from case studies. The reliance on the case study approach for comparative studies of health policy may reflect the conviction that the unique historical settings and the subject matter being treated is too complex to compare similarities, leaving only the contrast of differences as an option.

In-depth investigations using case studies are both time-consuming and costly. They are therefore often limited to an exploration of a few countries at a time. Although this permits a rich description of complex interacting policy issues, it also limits the possibilities for significant statistical analysis of causal relationships.[29] The fewer the countries, the greater the number of potentially competing determinant variables. The purported identification of causal relationships through statistical analysis of a large number of independent variables from a small cross-sectional or longitudinal database should be avoided because it leads to **over-determinism,** and observations that have virtually no statistical significance.[30]

Researchers using statistical studies are faced with a totally different set of possibilities and constraints. Quantitative analysis of standard longitudinal time series and cross-sectional data, such as multi-variant regression analysis, allows the investigator to pinpoint the relative importance of each of a large number of possible correlated factors.[31] Descriptive material in longitudinal time series and cross-sectional databases can also be quantified and analyzed statistically. Path analysis, in which the sequence of events is carefully mapped may even suggest determinant relationships. The substantive issue becomes the dependent variable and the possible determinant factors, the independent or intermediate variables, but there is an excessive claim of causal relationships in the literature based on correlations that merely co-exist. The random selection of a large number of countries leads to the least biased conclusions about the determinants of social policies.

Statistical studies have their disadvantages, since the subtle nuances of the substantive issues lose some of their richness and complexity through the **reductionism** inherent in aggregates. Many policy issues are not readily quantifiable; some are impossible to represent as precise unidimensional units-of-measurement. The terminology, boundaries, scope, units-of-measurement and transformation of policies vary greatly from one country to another. Sweeping generalizations and trends described in statistical studies at the national level do not necessarily reflect the realities of micro-systems at the state/regional/local levels, or the realities of the institutional features of their composing programs and sub-programs.

The investigator has recourse to one or more of four, rather than eight, effective research styles because those that lead to either over-determinism or reductionism are best avoided. The best descriptive studies use longitudinal or cross-sectional historical material. This is characteristic of the case study approach. Descriptive analysis of statistical data is best avoided because it is vulnerable to reductionism. The best quantitative studies use longitudinal or cross-sectional statistical data. This is characteristic of economic approaches. Quantitative analysis on case study material is best avoided because it is vulnerable to over-determinism. The policy issues that will be explored will largely determine the type of research style that is best suited for a given investigation. The research style will in turn determine the most appropriate group of countries and relevant time period. See Table 2.6.

Several of these research styles were combined to explore complex subjective and objective aspects of the policy issues that were being investigated in the study.[32] Issues on why and how the state became involved in legislative reforms that lead to compulsory participation and universal entitlement to health care were best explored through longitudinal descriptive case study techniques. Hypotheses about their determinants and effects are best explored though cross-sectional quantitative statistical techniques. Empirical evidence for validating or disputing many

Table 2.6 Over-determinism and Reductionism

	Case Study	Statistical
Descriptive		
Longitudinal	Over-determinism	
Cross-sectional	Over-determinism	
Quantitative		
Longitudinal		Reductionism
Cross-sectional		Reductionism

Source: Adapted from Preker (1989).

hypotheses and trends, such as convergence, diffusion, interdependence and evolution processes, came from a mixture of techniques. Descriptive analyses of statistical data were avoided, as were quantitative analyses of case study material.

2. Elements

The study integrated different elements of cross-national comparisons that can be graphically represented along three separate axes: *dimensions* (content, terminology, scope, boundary and units-of-measurement), *countries* (all versus many versus few and similar versus different) and *time-frames* (current versus historical and fixed versus relative). Dimensions of issues and policy options that were true in one setting had to be carefully matched with other settings. Some were best examined through in-depth reviews of a few countries, while others best observed through broad overviews of larger numbers of countries. Finally, some were easily confined to narrow time-frames, while others required much longer periods. The existing literature does little to put these methodological elements of cross-national research into a simple structured framework.[33] See Figure 2.2.

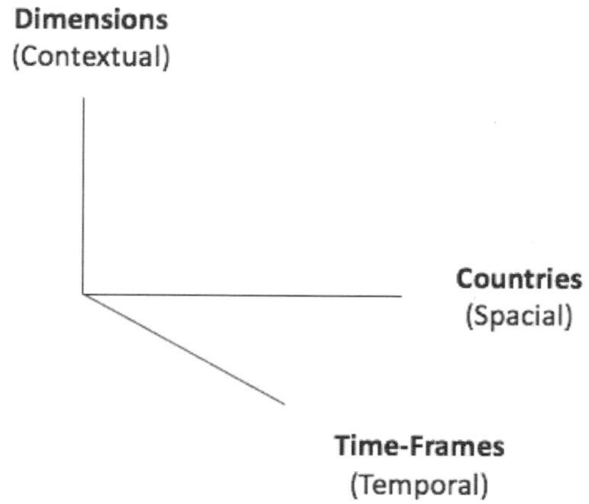

Figure 2.2 Methodological Choices

Source: Adapted from Preker (1989).

(a) Dimensions (Contextual)

The comparative literature has given little attention to **transformations** such as historical breaks, thresholds, conjunctures, shifts, contractions and reversals that occur over time in issues and policy options. "The concepts which give rise to philosophical problems should be analyzed and clarified noting their use in everyday life."[34] In longitudinal time series, static descriptions fail to capture the changes that occur over time in the terminology, content, scope, boundaries and units-of-measurement of each of the key issues that were examined in the study — compulsory participation and universal entitlement to health care. Likewise, cross-sectional analysis at any one point in time is vulnerable to mismatching transformations in meanings between disciplines. "Historically, welfare-state 'laggards' like the United States tend to be education leaders … [occurring] well before the big expansion of the rest of the welfare state."[35] Even though some errors are unavoidable when aiming at moving targets, awareness of the existence of such problems draws attention to the limits of cross-national comparability. See Table 2.7

Similar **terminology** can describe vastly incongruous concepts if their dimensions differ significantly. A classic example of this difficulty appears in the difference between the terms *policy* and *politics* in English language, which have only one equivalent in both German (*politik*) and French (*politique*). Debate about health care financing is often confused in the literature because at times it refers to activities involving revenue collection, at other times, to the allocation of financial resources and, at still other times, to the cost or expenditure on services. The terms direct

Table 2.7 Transformation in Issues and Policy Options

Original	Modified
Terminology	Terminology
Contents	Contents
Scope	Scope
Boundaries	Boundaries
Units-of-measure	Units-of-measure

Source: Adapted from Preker (1989).

payments, user charges, fees, out-of-pocket payments, co-payments, cost recovery and *ticket moderateur* are used in different ways in many countries. The notion of health insurance is extremely poorly differentiated. At times it refers to any collective prepayment, including general revenues. At other times, it refers only to earmarked social insurance or risk-related private insurance. Principles that apply to one of these aspects of health care financing do not apply to the others. The same term may have slightly different meanings in different cultural settings or when translated from one language into another. The study tried to clarify the ambiguities of such terminology through special analytical techniques that will be described later.

Comparative studies on the welfare state have often focused on the **contents** of "core programs" without validating their composition or consistency. Health care represents vastly different things in different countries or at different points in time. Similar standard provisions for ambulatory care, institutional care and public health may differ significantly in a number of qualitative aspects. Each sub-component is the peak of a pyramid of its own. The minimum standards for social security advocated by the International Labour Organization (ILO) in 1952 included medical care, sickness benefits, unemployment benefits, old-age benefits, employment injury benefits, family benefits, maternity benefits, invalidity benefits and survivors benefits, all of which have some impact on health.[36] Health care was initially meant to include treatment by generalists, specialists, essential medications, pre- and post-natal care, deliveries, hospitalization, dental care and medical prosthesis. Today, most Western and Eastern European countries offer the same seven or eight basic programs, but their content varies considerably. Some include dentistry, pharmaceutical products, prosthesis, ophthalmological equipment, social services, chronic care and health spas, while others provide none of them. These differences had to be clarified in the study. The core content of health care was much more limited in 1900 than in the 1950s and the 1980s.

The scope of health care has no clear demarcation within the broader sphere of social benefits. "The key term 'minimum standards' has proved unacceptable to some who insist on a definition based on 'adequate standards' or even 'optimal' standards. These questions are crucial to comparative research."[37] According to the World Health Organization (WHO), which advocates a more comprehensive definition than the ILO, health care must reduce differences between individuals, allow full expression of individual potential, reduce diseases and disabilities, prevent premature deaths and care for those who cannot care for themselves through all stages of the life-cycle if it hopes to improve health status.[38] Without food, water, shelter, education, employment and useful participation in society, traditional health services probably have an insignificant impact on health status. At the extreme, the medicalization of society is almost limitless since most activities can be construed to have some direct or indirect impact on health, well-being and the life-cycle.

The **boundaries** between different programs, such as health care and social services, often obscure the complexity of the issues and policy options being examined. The cleavages made to delineate their content and scope are rarely natural. The public/private debate confuses financing, production (administration and ownership) and resource allocation issues.[39] Just as public expenditure on social services is not an accurate index of total welfare effort, health care expenditure ignores important related sectors, such as education, pensions, social security, agriculture, defense and housing, as well as the informal sectors such as households.[40] At the same time, extensive disaggregation risks camouflaging phenomena such as the processes of convergence, diffusion, interdependencies and evolution that may be more apparent at the macro-aggregate level of analysis.

The assignment of appropriate **units-of-measurement** that accurately reflect the realities of the policies also poses a difficult, sometimes impossible, challenge. Mortality and morbidity statistics do not accurately reflect degree of incapacity, suffering or quality of life.[41] Macro-aggregates have the advantage of being easily available, readily quantifiable and the only statistical way to discriminate among a large number of possible determinant factors. Sweeping generalizations in macro-analyses at the national level, however, do not reflect the realities of their component programs or sub-programs at the state, regional and local levels. Traditional measures of social expenditure (social security expenditure/GDP) and health care expenditure (public expenditure/GDP) do not reflect the qualitative components such as financial burden, participation, entitlement and services. High spending may indicate unavoidable expenditure on a high incidence of social problems rather than political will. "The validity of any study depends on whether it explains what it purports to explain."[42] For example, the notion of GDP did not exist before the *1950s*. Indices were developed as proxies for measuring efficiency and outcome. Whenever possible, the study used the standard terminology, content, scope, boundaries and units-of-measurement for health care that have been developed by the OECD Health Data File.[43]

(b) Countries (Spatial)

Two opposing approaches have emerged in relation to the number of countries to include in cross-national comparisons. The best selection depends to a large extent on the hypotheses that will be tested and the research style that will be chosen to examine the issues and policy options under investigation. Selection criteria for cross-sectional statistical analysis should therefore be different from that for in-depth descriptive case study analysis because they look at different facets of health policy and use different analytical techniques.

One school of thought claims that there is no valid reason to limit countries to a specific subset.[44] On the contrary, limitations based on such constraints as the dictates of funding agencies that may have a special interest in certain countries are as damaging as an arbitrary selection on the basis of socio-economic, geo-political or other characteristics. A second school of thought claims that irrelevant *noise* should be filtered out by carefully selecting a specific subset of countries to highlight the information that will be examined in detail. In reality, these two approaches are not at odds with each other, since the proponents of the random selection approach perform mainly macro-aggregate quantitative analyses on large groups while the proponents of the limited sub-group approach perform mainly descriptive case study analyses on small groups. Pre-selection limits the quality of the quantitative analysis of statistical studies as much as haphazard selection introduces a lot of irrelevant material into case studies.

The proponents of the quantitative statistical analytical method argue that random selection of a large cohort leads to the least biased results in establishing causal relationships through techniques such as multi-variant regression analysis. Although the distinction between descriptive and explanatory is often unclear, "in explanation or evaluation research, the choice of countries becomes a crucial decision in the design of a study."[45] The most comprehensive cross-national study would include all the countries in the world. These investigators favor enlarging the sample size until purportedly universal principles observed in a handful of countries are validated in a larger group. Increasing the sample size allows a randomization of factors that will eventually uncover competing hypotheses. "A hypothesis which defends itself among 22 countries that happen to belong to the same data-collecting organisation while apparently more dubious elsewhere is suspect."[46]

Unfortunately, the greater the number of countries, the greater the chances that the data will involve the standardization of terminology, content, scope and boundaries of the substantive issues and policy options. Although statistically significant, the results may be irrelevant because the quality of the data is unreliable — garbage-in-garbage-out (GIGO). Most quantitative studies are, therefore, forced to select a sub-group of countries for which reliable data is available, the choice of which remains important to the outcome of the analysis.[47]

The proponents of the descriptive case study method argue that detailed historical reviews force the investigator to limit studies to a sub-group of countries in order to explore the complex substantive issues and policy options in sufficient depth. A number of well-known studies have demonstrated that precisely formulated hypotheses focusing on a small number of countries can give a richness of insight into specific issues that would have been impossible with the statistical approach.[48] The case study approach is best when reserved for exploration of qualitative issues, empirical validation of hypothesis or quantitative analyses of selected longitudinal historical trends, not for identifying causes and effects.

Investigators choosing the case study approach are faced with three additional choices: should the sub-group of countries be selected on the basis of a random sample, the presence of similar or contrasting characteristics? The arguments for selecting a random sample to enhance unbiased quantitative statistical analysis of macro-aggregates lose most of their power of persuasion because the potential cohort group is usually too small for significant statistical analysis from the outset. This leaves only

Table 2.8 Similar and Contrasting Characteristics

	1	2	3	4	5	6	7	8
Similar	+			+	+			
Contrasting		–	–			–	–	–

Source: Adapted from Preker (1989).

two options — the "most similar" approach and the "contrasting" approach. See Table 2.8.

Since certain policy issues are observed only within a specific context, detailed analysis should logically be limited to those countries for which such policies are relevant. For example, the legislative provisions for compulsory participation and universal entitlement to health care can only be observed in countries that have introduced or debated not to introduce such policies. The "most similar" comparative approach is most suitable in these studies.[49] This allows the investigator to focus on similarities, nuances and differences between the issues and policy options being examined without the distraction of irrelevant "noise" from countries that have neither introduced nor debated their introduction.[50] Added weight can be given to observations that bisect an otherwise homogeneous preselected group by using Bayesian analytical techniques. "Although over-determination is and will continue to be the central problem of cross-national research, some, perhaps a lot of it may be avoided by devoting more attention to research design, thinking in Bayesian terms, and overcoming institutional and cultural parochialism."[51] Only a few authors have applied the "most similar" comparative approach to health policy analysis.[52]

The debate in favor of the "contrasting" characteristics method is unconvincing. Those who criticize the "most similar approach" do so on the basis that limited sample size prevents significant statistical analysis. They often say "the most similar systems ... [design] ... is simply a bad idea ..." motivated by Eurocentrism and parochialism.[53] The choice of a few countries with contrasting features does not make the analysis statistically more valid. It still leads to over-determinism. Random selection or contrasting features of a small number of case studies increase "noise" without contributing to the analysis. Another reason for favoring the "contrasting" case study approach reflects the unsupported conviction that all health systems are unique. "By selecting only a few countries that differ greatly in the provisions they make for health care, analysts are biased toward this conclusion. A more systematic comparative approach would require an analysis of covariation: cross-national similarities (or differences) in health care systems need to be aligned with differences (or similarities) in political, economic or cultural contexts."[54] Authors of health policy have been especially prone to falling into this trap, limiting themselves to detailed case studies of a small number of countries selected purely on the basis of some contrasting policy feature, hoping to establish casual relationships in this way.[55]

Although the investigator may feel forced to make an imperfect choice between seemingly mutually exclusive approaches, all the schools of thought stress the importance of choosing a theoretical framework and a systematic research design. Many of the pitfalls described in the literature could have been avoided if investigators had used the research style and selected countries on the basis of what they were intending to do rather than on a pre-determined bias for or against any particular methodology. In one study of 50 randomly selected countries and 158 political parties, the investigator realized that three of the most interesting Anglo-Saxon cases had been omitted — the UK, US and Canada.[56]

For the purpose of the study, different groups of countries were selected for the cross-sectional quantitative analysis and in-depth descriptive case study analysis to respond to the needs of each of these techniques. The part of the study that observed causes and effects used a random selection of a large group of countries for which there was reliable standardized data. Most of the high-income countries in the world meet the reliable data criteria because of the OECD Health Data File.[57] There were two obvious, but unavoidable, weaknesses in the selection process used to choose this large group of countries. First, high-income but non-OECD member economies such as Saudi Arabia, Israel, Singapore, Hong Kong, Kuwait and the United Arab Emirates were excluded from the group because their health care expenditure databases are not standardized with those of the OECD. Second, middle-income countries such as Turkey, Portugal and Greece which belong to the OECD group were included because their data is standardized with that of the others.[58]

For the in-depth descriptive case study analysis, the main selection criteria were that the country should have passed legislation to introduce compulsory participation and universal entitlement to health care as well as belong to the group for which meaningful cross-sectional quantitative analysis could also be carried out. Of the OECD group of countries, 13 had passed such legislation and 8 had sufficient data to construct historical profiles of their health financing reforms.[59] Greece, Italy, Portugal and Spain were eliminated because insufficient historical data was available to construct meaningful profiles, and their recent reforms made post-reform analysis premature. Iceland, with its small population and remote location, was also omitted from the detailed analysis. This left the four English-speaking countries (Australia, Canada, New Zealand and the United Kingdom) and four Nordic countries (Denmark, Finland, Norway, Sweden). National profiles were created from common socio-economic, political, bureaucratic and intrinsic program features which developed over time.[60] Cross-national profiles were then created from comparable characteristics that evolved irrespective of spatial and temporal boundaries. See Figure 2.3.

The obvious, but unavoidable, weaknesses in the selection process used to choose this smaller sub-group of countries related to the countries that had to be omitted from the descriptive component of the study. Many of them have passed legislative reforms either as part of their social security legislation or through services offered by their Ministries of Health (Welfare).[61] They were primarily eliminated because they lacked comparable standardized data and therefore had to be excluded from the

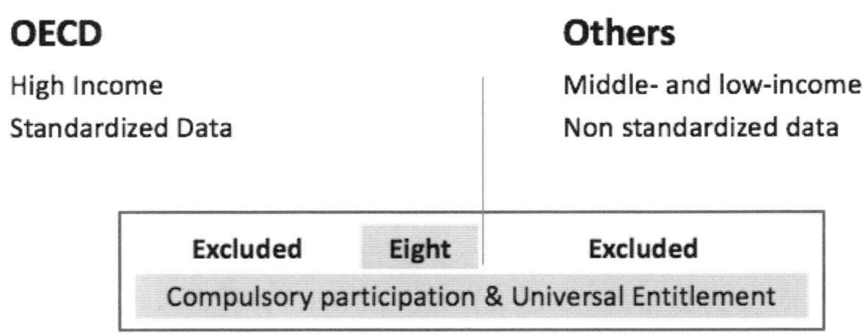

Figure 2.3 Selection Criteria for Eight Case Studies

Source: Adapted from Preker (1989).

cross-national statistical analysis. The most notable omission was many of the COMECOM member countries, most of which have universal entitlement to health care, although individuals make no direct contributions to pre-paid financing.[62]

(c) Time Period (Temporal)

Two different approaches have also emerged in relation to the time-frame examined in comparative studies. One focuses on cross-sectional data while the other focuses on longitudinal data. In both cases, the dependent and independent variables usually correspond to the substantive issue being examined and its determinants or effects, not the countries themselves or the time-frame used for the investigation. See Figure 2.4.

Most cross-sectional analyses use a single chronological date as the fixed frame-of-reference, with the substantive issue being examined as the dependent variable and the possible determinant factors as the independent variables.[63] A few studies have looked at the effects of social reform on society, its political system and the economy. In this case, the independent variable is the substantive issue and the dependent variables are the effects.[64] When using this approach, choosing a suitable time-frame becomes crucial because both the dependent and independent variables may be at different stages of evolution from one country to another at any one given point in time. Their terminology, content, scope, boundaries and transformations risk being different from one country to another, undermining the quality of any observed statistical or descriptive similarities or variations.

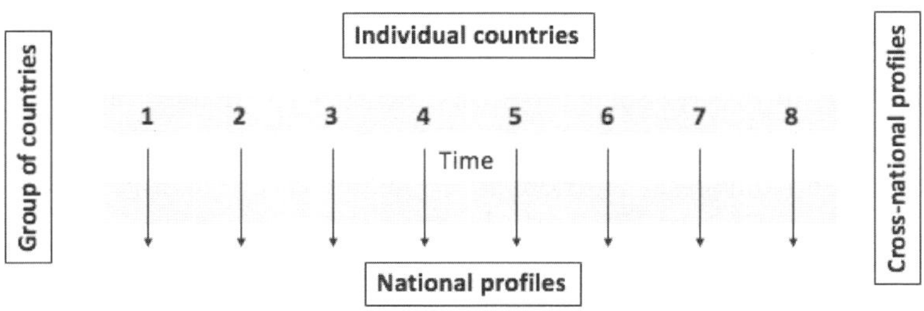

Figure 2.4 National and Cross-national Profiles

Source: Adapted from Preker (1989).

Instead of looking at the substantive policy issues for a fixed reference year in cross-sectional analysis, some investigators have tried to standardize the dependent variable by matching different stages of its development as the fixed frame of reference for their studies. For instance, the investigator might choose to compare programs at different chronological times when programs were first proposed, introduced in legislature, implemented or at a certain level of maturity. The extensive in-depth historical reviews needed to closely match the definitional boundaries of complex issues and are extremely time-consuming and costly, which may explain why this approach is largely ignored in the literature. For pragmatic reasons, such studies tend to use the case study approach, limited to a small group of countries. This limits the possibility of subsequent significant statistical analysis.

Longitudinal historical reviews, because of their in-depth nature and the complexity of the subject matter, are also often restricted to a small group of countries focusing on a limited number of variables. Although their terminology, content, scope and boundaries can be defined much more precisely, transformations over time may easily be missed. Even when the sample group is too small for cross-sectional quantitative statistical analysis, statistically significant analysis of longitudinal historical data can still reveal important trends within any one country. Hypotheses about determinants and effects need to be empirically validated through larger, statistically valid cross-sectional analysis. "Descriptive studies merely placed side by side would not be considered a suitable end product, but would be defined as raw material for further analysis."[65]

The longitudinal time-frames used for the case studies were divided into three broad historical periods that covered more than a century for most countries: the early period of involvement by the public sector in establishing the early financial infrastructures for health care; the later introduction of landmark legislative reforms leading to compulsory participation and universal entitlement to health care; and the post-reform period during which persistent barriers to full coverage remained. These time-frames were staggered because no two countries had identical profiles. See Figure 2.5.

Determinants were examined on a relative chronological time-frame based on the dates that landmark legislative reforms were introduced. This

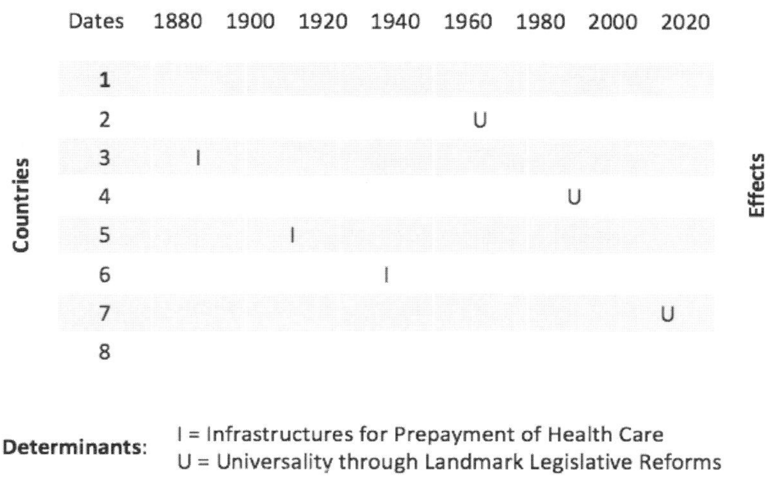

Figure 2.5 Longitudinal Time-frames

Source: Adapted from (1989).

varied from country to country. Outcome and effects were examined on a fixed chronological time-frame based on a cross-sectional cut made in 1982 for all the OECD countries. Both of these approaches had unavoidable limitations. First, it is difficult to standardize quantitative data taken from asynchronous time-frames to make it comparable for cross-national comparisons. Second, the influence of determinants acts on a continuum. Third, the countries that had no landmark legislative reforms could not be included. Finally, the time interval between passing legislative reforms and the arbitrary date chosen for the fixed cross-sectional cut varied from country to country. This inevitably had an impact on the validity of the observations. The conclusions that can be drawn from such comparisons are directly related to the quality of national data, degree of transformation in issues and ability to match asynchronous historical developments.

F. DATA COLLECTION

Access to politically sensitive data and public figures often presents a special problem in comparative research. The researcher who has privileged entry through official channels will be more successful in obtaining

Table 2.9 Data for Cross-national and National Profiles

Action	Data Source
Data collection	Written records, surveys, interviews

Source: Adapted from Preker (1989).

the needed information than the researcher who has no such access. Research carried simultaneously for the Commission of Inquiry into the Health and Social Services of Quebec greatly facilitated data collection as well as field work for this study.[66] The research styles and three axes of the elements of investigation provided the rationale for the data that was collected for the different components of the study. Textual and nominal or categorical data was gathered for the descriptive analysis. Ordinal or ranked, interval and ratio data was gathered for the quantitative analysis. See Table 2.9.

1. Descriptive

The standard tools used in social sciences to collect qualitative data — review of written records, surveys and interviews — remains central to cross-national research.[67] Descriptive data was gathered from an extensive review of written documents, visits to each country and interviews.[68] Primary sources included working documents, official reports, green papers, white papers, legislative bills, statutes and regulations, as well as journal articles and conference proceedings.[69] The work done by Commissions prior to introducing important legislation provided an invaluable source of information.[70] This data was supplemented by a review of secondary and tertiary sources such as monographs, handbooks, textbooks, statistical series and journals.[71] Whenever possible, interviews were carried out with the people who had been directly responsible for bringing about the reforms: politicians, civil servants, administrators, health professionals, economists and social scientists.[72] Finally, during visits to each country, the existing health care systems were examined directly. For the reasons described above, detailed descriptive data was collected from primary sources for eight in-depth case studies. This covered a time-frame of almost a century. Less detailed descriptive data was collected on other OECD and COMECOM countries through secondary sources.

Data on social protection such as entitlement and services is more difficult to compile and interpret. Most of the documentation is descriptive, making language barriers a significant obstacle. Legal and constitutional provisions may differ significantly from customary practices. Translating either of these into indicators that can be used in time series or cross-sectional analysis bears many risks. All-or-nothing classifications are the most reliable indicators, but these were of limited use in the project because they fail to capture the gradations that occurred in the introduction of compulsive prepayment and universal entitlement to health care.

Several key questions were asked for each of the historical time periods:

- Why did infrastructures for collective financing of health care develop? What were the key determining factors leading to a growth in these financial infrastructures? Why did the public sector get involved? What percentage of the population remained without protection prior to the introduction of legislative provisions for universal access to comprehensive health care? Who were those without protection? Who were the key health care reformers?
- Why were legislative provisions introduced to provide universal access to comprehensive health care? What were the anticipated secondary gains from the reform? Why did the public sector get involved? How developed was each country's financial infrastructure prior to the reform? What was the society's sense of civic responsibility for financing social programs through the public sector before the reform? Who were the key health care reformers?
- What were the persistent barriers to universal access following the reform? Who were the key health care reformers?

2. Quantitative

The collection of quantitative statistical data on health care expenditure presents a different set of problems. The scope of work done by early researchers was limited because of the problems in data compatibility. To overcome some of these obstacles, authors went through laborious and costly processes to compile their own data sets.[73] Later, as guidelines were established for the recording of health expenditure data,[74] some countries began to standardize their national account records.[75] Three approaches have evolved to compile official statistical data at the international level:

A single agency finances and conducts surveys in different countries based on controlled questions, concepts, definitions and processing.

A single compilation unit gathers the data provided by different agencies that work in close collaboration to provide standardized information.

A single analyst adjusts readily accessible data from different countries to comparable standards.

The first method is the most reliable way to obtain full cross-national comparability. Because of the high cost of this type of investigation, it is only conducted on rare occasions and in an episodic way which limits its usefulness as way to compile ongoing data. The second method will lead to a more solid database. It also requires extensive cooperation between many agencies, which is rarely possible and involves long studies, which is unsuitable in time-sensitive investigations. The third method is the least costly and most expedient way to collect a useful body of information for cross-national comparisons. Conveniences offset the disadvantages of having to depend on the judgment of a single compiler and the obvious limits to extracting useful data from sometimes vastly different sources. However it also limits the possibility of verification and validation of the data. This is the method that the OECD uses to collect its comprehensive Health Care Data File which, since 1985, has triggered an extensive reevaluation of accepted national accounting standards for health care.[76] The researcher must decide when the need for timely accessibility to data for cross-national comparisons justifies accepting the concomitant compromises that must be made when national data is manipulated to reflect international standards.

The OECD health care expenditure data is based on a national accounting concept that has become an international standard.[77] It presents a comprehensive series which adheres to rigorous economic classification principles in an attempt to ensure that all costs incurred are added up. Private consumption includes hospital care, physician services, pharmaceuticals, therapeutic appliances and other insurable health-care–related benefits. Public consumption includes public health services, administration, regulation, education and biomedical research. Sickness benefits paid in cash, which belong to income maintenance functions, are excluded from both public and private health care expenditure. Total health care expenditure (HCE) is the arithmetic sum of public expenditure, private expenditure, expenditure on health care in non-related fields such as education, research and other ministries and informal expenditure by households.[78] Data becomes increasingly unreliable and unavailable toward the bottom of this list.[79] The OECD and most other statistical sources on health care expenditure ignore the fourth category, give an incomplete account of the third and base the second on estimates.

In principle,

$$\text{Total HCE} = \Sigma\ \text{Public} + \Sigma\ \text{Private} + \Sigma\ \text{Other} + \Sigma\ \text{Informal}$$

But in practice,

$$\text{Total HCE} = \Sigma\ \text{Public} + \Sigma\ \text{Private}.$$

The impressive statistical health care database and accounting standards established in the OECD countries continues to expand with time. The most recent OECD health care publication includes a compendium of 67 tables from more than 400 tables presently being compiled as part of the Health Data File.[80] It includes detailed data on health care expenditure trends, prices and incomes, social protection, medical care use and personnel, medical practice variations, health status indicators and demographic and economic background data. Similar information is being compiled for developing countries by the World Bank's technical assistance division, but collection of this information is much more episodic and carried out by a team of researchers rather than a single individual.

The national accounting concept of health care expenditures used by the OECD is not without inconveniences. National aggregates fail to represent provincial, regional, local and individual realities. There are gaps in the comprehensiveness of the data series of some countries. Not all activities that contribute to health status are classified under health expenditure, especially those made by other ministries. Health expenditure made by enterprises is treated as an "intermediate" outlay rather than final consumption. Gross capital expenditures are added to the aggregate outlay. Even among OECD countries, some national accounting systems are rudimentary, leading to underreporting. Information on public sector activity is more reliable than that for private sector activity, which may be splintered and even deliberately falsified for fiscal reasons. Information on public expenditure on health care is more reliable than information on total expenditure, which relies on estimates of private expenditure. Furthermore, statistics on utilization, practice styles, health status and outcome indicators are essential to investigations that look at health care performance in terms of efficiency, effectiveness and quality of care. Even within individual countries, such data is still fragmented and at an infancy stage of development. Cross-national comparisons using the limited available standardized data remains precarious. Furthermore, OECD data dates back only to the year 1960.

The OECD Health Data File and the UN statistical records provided an important source of information for quantitative analysis that required cross-sectional comparability for comparisons of financing mechanisms, expenditure levels, coverage, efficiency and outcomes. For quantitative analysis of time series, data was required from before 1960. National statistical series were used for this purpose because internal consistency was considered more important than cross-national comparability for this phase of the study.[81] A single source was used rather than multiple time series whenever possible to minimize the introduction of artifacts. These were then compared with other sources to check for inconsistencies. Original statistical sources were preferred over secondary sources. The use of raw data from national statistical sources posed many unavoidable inconveniences. There were changes in classifications used to gather data by national authorities,[82] devaluation of currencies,[83] omitted or added data,[84] revised estimates in later volumes of statistical yearbooks[85] and data sources with conflicting information.[86] All the problems of transformation in terminology, content, scope, boundaries and units-of-measurements posed a serious problem for the use of non-standardized data. When possible, corrections were made for such inconsistencies.

Information on the sources of revenue for financing health care is much less readily available than expenditure data.[87] Total health care revenues (HCR) is the arithmetic sum of several sources: budgetary revenues (BR) may include both general revenues (GR) and social insurance (SI); extra-budgetary revenues (ER) may include public funds available to other ministries for health care, special funds, cash intake by institutions, other private sources and foreign aid in the case of many developing countries; private revenues (PR) in the form of health insurance (HI) and out-of-pocket spending (OOP). Double counting often occurs between cash intake by institutions and OOP spending. Data once again becomes increasingly unreliable and unavailable further down this list. Most official statistical reports limit their treatment of revenue collection for health care to general revenues, social insurance and estimates of private revenues.

In principle,

$$\text{Total HCR} = \Sigma\ \text{Prepayment} + \Sigma\ \text{Direct Charges}$$

But in practice,

$$\text{Total HCR} = \Sigma\ \text{GR} + \Sigma\ \text{SI} + \Sigma\ \text{PR}.$$

G. ANALYTICAL TECHNIQUES

The key issues and policy options examined in the study were analyzed using both descriptive and quantitative techniques. The purpose of the descriptive phase of the study was to identify, clarify and analyze some of the subjective aspects of the concepts being explored. Many of these relate to questions on *why* and *how* governments introduced compulsory participation and universal entitlement to health care. The purpose of the quantitative phase of the study was to recognize patterns, analyze existing hypotheses and provide an objective basis for constructing new theories. Many of these relate to explanations and predictions about the *determinants* and *effects* of government on the policies being examined. Both techniques were useful for empirical validation of existing hypotheses. See Table 2.10.

Table 2.10 Analytical Techniques

Analysis	Techniques
Descriptive	Logic, positivist, linguistic, narrative, graphic scaling
Quantitative	Computer assisted, cluster, statistical, econometric

Source: Adapted from Preker (1989).

1. Descriptive

Many aspects of health policy would lose their richness if reduced to quantifiable representations. Deductive and inductive reasoning were the most powerful analytical techniques used in the descriptive phase of the study.[88] The countries selected for the case studies[89] were submitted to *positivist analysis* of their constitutional provisions, health and social legislations, regulations, conventions, administrative infrastructures and health policies[90] and *linguistic analysis* of relevant issues and policy options.[91] These two techniques, which formed the cornerstone of the descriptive analysis, are described in greater detail in the sections below. *Multi-dimensional graphic scaling* made possible the design of a perceptual map from the three axes of the elements of investigation (contextual, spatial and temporal).[92] *Narrative accounts* of historical data were used to explore the validity of rival theories and construct national and cross-national profiles.[93] *Discriminate analysis* made possible a weighted classification of other countries according to variables that had been assigned to the key issues investigated in the case studies.[94]

The following technical developments in descriptive analysis were not applied to the eight case studies, because statistical analysis of limited cross-sectional samples leads to over-determinism. *Formal models of choice* provide for an assessment of the impact of changes in institutional structures and strategic policies on the behavior of individuals within the system being examined.[95] *Hierarchical models of organizations* provide a measure of the impact of constraints on individual units within an organization.[96] *Contextual analysis* provides an appraisal of the impact of system-level characteristics on the behavior of individuals within organizations.[97] *Factor analysis* takes a number of measurements of a particular issue and attempts to explain differences.[98] *Statistical techniques* provide a more sophisticated treatment of qualitative variables that has previously been limited to quantitative variables.[99] *Intervention analysis* provides an evaluation of the effects of policy changes, regulations and dynamic behavior on systems.[100] *Meta-analysis* makes it possible to re-evaluate a body of otherwise contradictory literature.[101]

(a) Positivist Analysis

The classic position of the positivist theory of analysis, which has come to dominate legal jurisprudence in the nineteenth and twentieth centuries, is to deny any *a priori* source of natural laws, and to recognize only positive facts or observable phenomena.[102] Interpretation of policies based on the authority of existing legal systems and established social infrastructures offers advantages over value-laden distortions of what things ought to be or might be under ideal circumstances. Public debate on the philosophical or ethical aspects of health care as an important subset of the welfare state is very different from political commitment to preparing, passing and implementing a law that offers such provisions.

Several factors made this rigorous approach possible. Legislative reforms provided useful landmarks for many of the transitions that occurred in health policy such compulsory participation and universal entitlement to health care. Both constitutional provisions[103] and legislative amendments related to health care[104] are well documented. These legislative landmarks provided the reference citation that allowed other important related works to be identified: early public debates, commissions of enquiry, related legislations and so on. This orientation was adopted as the cornerstone during the descriptive analysis of the eight case studies selected for the study and to establish chronological reference points for many of the quantitative analyses.

The positivist approach has its disadvantages. Reliable information on legislative reforms and official documents requires extensive field work. Many of the parliamentary papers that were consulted for the study were only available in the archives of the host countries. Most were not translated into English and therefore required a working knowledge of Scandinavian languages. Taken in isolation, legislative landmarks fail to capture the long preparatory time period that often precedes a new law. There may also be delays before the law is implemented and shortfalls in realizing its objectives. Legal authority is sometimes rejected by vested interest groups. The medical profession systematically tried to frustrate legal provisions with which it did not agree by refusing to implement the reforms. Transformations in issues and policies occur despite legal provision. Terms used in the laws of one country may not represent the same concepts in other countries. To overcome these problems, the positivist approach had to be supplemented by other techniques of descriptive analysis.

(b) Linguistic Analysis

The central thesis of linguistic theory of analysis is that concepts that give rise to ambiguities can be clarified by noting their everyday use.[105] Its application to the analysis of political phenomena is heavily influenced by the logical positivism described above.[106] The theory rejects the belief that policies have specific intrinsic philosophical meanings because this depends on abstract speculation rather than empirical analysis of facts, therefore, it is a powerful adjunct to other techniques used for concept formulation.[107]

This approach had a clear applicability to the descriptive component of the study. As an example, in recent times, health needs/demands/desires have come to be regarded as conferring certain rights/entitlement/claims to cure/rehabilitation/care which in turn confers a notion of duties/obligation/responsibility on the part of society/state/systems to provide rewards/benefits/privileges. This relatively short statement contains several extremely complex concepts necessary to fully understand the issues and policy options in the relationship between the state, health care systems and populations.

Case studies made it possible for constituent words such as compulsory, universal and comprehensive to be observed in a variety of contexts. Does compulsory mean mandatory or unavoidable? For whom? When does compulsory become coercive rather than protective? Can compulsory participation be enforced? If not, does the obligatory nature lose some of its authority? Does universal mean that a particular thing is everywhere or that everyone is affected similarly by it, or are some social classes different?[108] If access is limited, for example, in rural settings, does universal entitlement become a "paper right"? Does comprehensive mean availability of a heart-lung machine for everyone or humane nursing homes when people become old, weak and disabled? Answers to these questions had to be clarified to make subsequent quantitative analysis meaningful.

The initial step was to examine the range and limits of the concept by an exploration of its uses by different populations in different countries at different times. The second step was to discriminate and distinguish characteristics of the concepts from one another. The third step was to reduce the concept to broad categories of significant basic meanings. Because it is difficult to conceive of totally value-neutral concepts, an attempt was made to identify evaluative overtones. To completely dissociate interpretation from evaluation is probably impossible because judgments are themselves a reflection of the views of the society being observed. Universal and comprehensive connote one notion, while compulsory connotes another. Universality and comprehensive could be perceived to be good because they confer equity. This could be contrasted with the cynical view that they are bad because health care is useless,[109] or worse, harmful.[110] Likewise, compulsory might be seen by subgroups such as the medical profession as a threat to power and independence when juxtaposed with government control.[111] The final step was to place the resulting interpretations in their normal social setting and explain why a particular interpretation emerged at a particular point in time. These can be summarized as an exploration of the range, limits, differentiation and interpretation, followed by a reduction and valuation of the concepts under examination.

Linguistic analysis is not without criticism. Even rigorous analysis leaves some gaps in the detection of the complex dimensions of policy such as transformation in terminology, content, scope, boundaries and units-of-measurement over time and across national boundaries. First, terms are used differently in a historical context compared to the present day. The technique is susceptible to "temporal parochialism"[112] because subtle nuances evolve over time. Second, some terms such as medical or technical jargon have ambiguous usage between two segments of the same society. Finally, the same term may have different meanings in different political and cultural settings. These three limitations — historical variation, interpretive divergences and natural context — suggest that linguistic analysis is necessary but not sufficient in itself to fully understanding all the issues and health policy options. The positivist legal approach helped to fill in some of the gaps. Field work and interviews clarified others.

2. Quantitative

Just as some aspects of health policy are best analyzed by descriptive techniques, others are impossible to unravel without quantitative methods. Computer-assisted cluster analysis, statistical techniques and econometric modeling were the standard analytical tools used during the quantitative phase of the study.[113] Many early works on comparative health policy limited their treatment to a small number of descriptive case studies, making it impossible to carry out statistically significant cross-sectional analysis.[114] Time series were usually limited to reporting of unadjusted health expenditure trends. In recent years, the accumulation of detailed case studies of many individual countries has allowed a closer matching of comparable issues and more accurate mapping of similarities and differences among countries for cross-sectional analysis. The standardization of health care expenditure reporting,[115] and the accumulation of a detailed Health Data File by the OECD,[116] is permitting new and more rigorous treatment of both longitudinal and cross-sectional macro-aggregate data.[117] Comparative micro-analysis is less advanced than macro-analysis, but many authors are now looking at disaggregates indicators in an attempt to analyze complex policies.

Each country has its own unique historical setting and health care system. Among the countries that have health care systems characterized by compulsory participation and universal entitlement to health care, only some introduced all three aspects at the same time. Many had other potentially significant features such as salaried medical services, nationalized ownership, co-existence of private or para-public health insurance and so on. Computer-assisted *cluster analyses* and *pattern recognition* proved useful for classifying issues, grouping similar countries and distinguishing those that were different.[118] This analysis was carried out as part of the pre-selection for determining both the issues and countries that would be included in the case study phase of the study.

(a) Time Series

Detailed analysis of longitudinal trends is best carried out through quantitative techniques performed on *time series*.[119] Such longitudinal analysis was used to examine health care expenditure trends, opportunity costs and displacement effects. Governments often express alarm at what they describe as an explosion in public expenditure on health care. The social policy literature is full of apprehension about the opportunity cost of health care expenditure and the danger that it might draw funds away from other social programs that have equal or greater effects on health through a displacement effect.

The identification of an appropriate chronological time-frame posed a difficult methodological problem at this phase of the analysis. There was often a lag between when legislative reforms were passed, when resulting laws were implemented and when expenditures reflected the resulting impact. Positivist, linguistic and narrative analysis of the case histories was indispensable to identifying the starting point of the time series, which differed from country to country.

Nominal changes in health care expenditure ($d\text{HCE}_{\text{nominal}}$) at a given point, in time ($t + 1$) compared with expenditure during the previous year (t) are sometimes used to observe changes.[120]

Simple Macro-aggregate Approach

$$d\text{HCE}_{\text{nominal}} = (\text{HCE}_{t+1} - \text{HCE},)/\text{HCE}_t.$$

This simplified approach is misleading because it ignores a number important interacting factors that influence expenditure trends such as demographic growth (dD), health care price increases (dP) and changes in utilization patterns (dQ) per capita ($d(\text{Q/D}) = d\text{Q}_{\text{D}}$), as well as associated growth in GDP and public sector expenditures. Changes in health care prices can be disaggregated even further into a component that is due to general consumer price increases (dPc). The implicit GDP deflator ($d\text{P}_{\text{GDP}}$) has been used by some authors as an indicator of overall inflation. There are several other options such as the implicit expenditure deflator, the consumer price index and the wholesale price index. None are satisfactory substitutes for a health sector specific price index. Nominal health care expenditure can be broken down into its component parts to provide a more complex representation of annual trends[121]:

Complex Disaggregate Approach

$$d\mathrm{HCE} = d\mathrm{D} \times d\mathrm{P}_{\mathrm{H}} \times d\mathrm{P}_{\mathrm{GDP}} \times d\mathrm{Q}_{\mathrm{D}}.$$

A clear advantage of this approach is that it identifies some of the factors that influence nominal health spending. From 1975 to 1987, an analysis of the annual compound rate of growth in spending among the seven richest countries in the world indicates general inflation to be the most important extrinsic factor driving up overall health care expenditure.[122] Health-care–specific inflation was the most important intrinsic factor, followed by increases in volume-intensity activities and population growth.

Such complex decomposition of health care expenditure also has some significant shortcomings. First, the identification of relationships does not impute causality, capacity or appropriateness.[123] Second, even countries with extremely well-developed data systems have difficulty measuring utilization rates and health-specific prices indices. Most derive utilization-intensive activities from other components ($d\mathrm{Q}_{\mathrm{D}} = d_{\mathrm{HCE}}/(d\mathrm{D} \times d\mathrm{P}_{\mathrm{H}} \times d\mathrm{P}_{\mathrm{GDP}})$). In those instances where this kind of information *is* slowly becoming available due to computerized record keeping, different components are difficult to re-combine into *indices* that have cross-national comparability. Practice styles vary, the behavior of different age groups vary, the use of technology varies and so on. Third, health-care–specific price indices are still *in* an embryonic stage of development. They are often derived from GDP deflators and health care expenditure trends, *ignoring* demographic and volume-intensive factors ($dP_{\mathrm{H}} = d_{\mathrm{HCE}}/d\mathrm{P}_{\mathrm{GDP}}$). Furthermore, price indices that have been developed for overall medical consumption do not capture the differences in in-patient care, ambulatory care, pharmaceutical production and therapeutic appliances. Wage and supply components are usually mixed, so are public and private components.[124] Because almost all of this work ignores cost data, it fails to adjust performance for efficiency and cost-effectiveness.[125]

Although this technique offers promise for future analyses, it was of limited value in the historical analysis of expenditure trends date back to the 1950s and earlier. Utilization statistics and price deflators were even more unreliable during this time period than they are today. Disaggregates of complex relationships were therefore not used to follow health care expenditure trends in the study. Health care expenditure trends can be represented in two other ways.[126] Some authors have tried to adjust all values ($t + 1$) in the simple macro-aggregate approach by a price deflator (P) to arrive at a representation of expenditure trends *in* real terms[127] ($d\text{HCE}_{\text{real}} = d\text{HCE}_{\text{nominal}} \times \text{P}$). Attractive as this may seem at first sight, it still leads to distortions because the health-care–specific price deflators are unreliable. Both national and cross-national trends described *in* constant values are vulnerable to these distortions. An alternative approach *is* to represent health care expenditure as a ratio relative to other expenditures such as GDP, government total expenditure (GTE), government consumption expenditure (GCE) and government social expenditure (GSE).[128]

Ratio Approach

$$\text{R}_{\text{GDP}} = \text{HCE/GDP}$$

$$\text{R}_{\text{GTE}} = \text{HCE/Government total expenditure}$$

$$\text{R}_{\text{GCE}} = \text{HCE/Government consumption expenditure}$$

$$\text{R}_{\text{GSE}} = \text{HCE/Government social expenditure.}$$

This approach has several technical advantages over other methods of analyzing macro-aggregate expenditure trends. It avoids the problems associated with health-specific price indices and assessments of volume-intensive activities. At the same time, it broadens the scope of issues that can be examined by incorporating notions of national wealth (GDP), as well as political willingness and capacity to pay (GTE), competing demands for funds to finance public services (GCE) and various forms of cash transfer payments or social security benefits (GSE » GTE – GCE).

These factors can then be re-combined in different ways to track expenditure trends within any given country, or to provide standardized indicators for cross-sectional analysis of determinants and effects. The GTE/GDP ratio can be used as an indirect measure of government involvement in the economic activities of a country, and the GSE/GDP ratio can be used as an indirect indicator of the financial resources devoted to public services and their infrastructures. Finally, HCE/GDP ratio can be used as an indirect indicator of the financial resources devoted to the health sector and its infrastructures. Changes in R_{GTE} over time can be used as an indicator of fiscal responsibility for health care. Changes in R_{GCE} over time can be used as an indicator of opportunity costs. Changes in R_{GSE} over time can be used as an indicator of the extent which public funds are channeled away from social security cash benefits.

This technique is not without disadvantages. Straight ratios hide distortions created by disproportionate growth in GDP or government expenditure. The R_{GDP} ratio will remain stable when health care expenditure and GDP both increase or decrease at the same rate. When health care expenditure grows more quickly than GDP, the ratio will rise rapidly. Conversely, when health care expenditure grows more slowly than GDP, the ratio will fall even though there may still be some growth in real terms. Similar distortions occur in the R_{GTE}, R_{GCE} and R_{GSE} ratios because of differential growth rates. The straight ratio approach was therefore weakened to the marked differences in rates of economic growth during the 1940s, 1950s, 1960s and 1970s. This problem was partly overcome by validating the observed trends against health care expenditure per capita growth rates ($d\text{HCE}_{capita}$) relative to the per capita growth rates of the other variables ($d\text{GCE}_{capita}$ and $d\text{GSE}_{capita}$ $d\text{GCE}_{capita}$ and $d\text{GSE}_{capita}$). This calculation was carried out by using a double logarithmic regression on HCE and the variable in the denominator of the equation during a specific time-period (10 years) following the introduction of compulsory participation and universal entitlement to health care.[129]

Elasticity Approach

$$E_{HCE/GDP} = d\text{HCE}_{capita}/d\text{GDP}_{capita}$$

$$E_{HCE/GTE} = d\text{HCE}_{capita}/d\text{GTE}_{capita}$$

$$E_{\text{HCE/GCE}} = d\text{HCE}_{\text{capita}}/d\text{GCE}_{\text{capita}}$$

$$E_{\text{HCE/GSE}} = d\text{HCE}_{\text{capita}}/d\text{GSE}_{\text{capita}}$$

(b) Cross-sectional Analysis

Validation or falsification of hypotheses about determinants and effects are carried out more effectively through *multi-variant regression* techniques than through quantitative analysis of trends in time series.[130]

Two methodological problems were confronted at this point in the study. First, the key issue being investigated was not readily quantifiable. Cluster analysis was performed on scaling ratios for direct/prepaid financing mechanisms, voluntary/compulsory participation, restricted/universal entitlement and basic/comprehensive services in the OECD for data from the early 1980s. Detailed information on these variables was, however, episodic, and could therefore not be used to provide a tracer over time. The most reliable historical marker was the introduction of legislative reforms for compulsory participation and universal entitlement to health care. This was used as a chronological landmark and as a way to dichotomize countries into two groups. Those that had passed and implemented such legislation were assigned a "dummy" variable $t = 1$, while those that had not taken these steps were assigned $t = 0$. This statistical trick provided a framework for carrying out further quantitative analysis of determinants and effects. Second, there were no ideal quantitative indicators to measure many of the trends, determinants and effects. Some were based on the work of past authors, while others were developed specifically for the study. The extent to which macro-aggregates succeed in describing reality perfectly or imperfectly varies greatly. They can never capture the full richness of most complex policy issues and therefore need to be supplemented by other, more descriptive techniques.

Socio-economic level of development, political processes and administrative infrastructures are the most frequently postulated determinants of public expenditure in a welfare state. They have not been examined for their impact on health policy. Other authors have proposed quantitative indicators that can be used as measures for many of these determinants. National wealth per capita (GDP_{cap}) is often used as a standard indicator of level of socio-economic development.[131] The ratio approach was once again seen as a more reliable standard than absolute expenditures. General government total expenditure can be used as an indirect indicator of the extent of government involvement in the economic activities of a country (economic effect of political ideology).[132] Government consumption expenditure can be used as an indirect indicator of the financial resources devoted to public services and their infrastructures, while government social expenditure can be used as an indirect indicator of the financial resources devoted to social security transfer payment and their infrastructures.[133] Health care expenditure can be used as a direct indicator of the financial resources devoted to the health sector and its infrastructure.[134]

Because the countries that had introduced legislative reforms for the policies being examined did so at different chronological points in time and countries that had not introduced such legislation had no marker date at all, cross-sectional regression analysis on possible determinants was impossible. Serious errors would also have been introduced into the analysis if absolute values had been deflated over a 50-year period and converted into a single currency for cross-sectional comparison. Analysis of determinants was therefore limited to a descriptive empirical validation of different hypothesis. The ratio approach did, however, allow some comparison of trends in GTE/GDP, GCE/GDP, and GSE/GDP among the countries that had introduced the policies in question.

A cut-off date (1987) was chosen because more recent dates would have led to gaps in data. Indicators were developed to quantify a number of possible long-term effects of the reforms.[135] First, in the case of socio-economic development, GDP per capita (GDP_{cap}) and average real GDP growth rates (GDP_{gwt}) were used for economic performance; accumulated general government debt relative to GDP (GGD/GDP) for national debt; and government consumption expenditure relative to GDP (GCE/GDP) for opportunity costs. Second, in the case of political processes, government social expenditure relative to GDP (GSE/GDP) was used for displacement effects on social security; and GDP elasticity of health care expenditure (HCE_{els}) and policy reversals for backlash. Third, in the case of administrative structures, general government total expenditure relative to GDP (GTE/GDP) was used for public sector activity or the extent of government involvement in economic affairs of the state; and purchase-power-parity-adjusted health care expenditure relative to GDP per capita (HCE_{capita}/ GDP_{capita}) for total expenditure on health care. Finally, in the case of state responses to market failure, the ratio of public to total health care expenditure (Pub/Tot) was used for equity. It was felt that health status indicators were not sufficiently standardized or refined to be useful in detailed cross-national comparisons of outcome. Analysis of life expectancy and infant mortality rates would be more misleading than informative.

The standard regression equation is a straight line ($y = a + bx$), where x and y represent the independent and the dependent variable. When the principle of least squares is applied to linear regressions, the exercise is to minimize the expression $\Sigma\ (y - a - bx)^2$ for the **constant** a (intercept on the y-axis) and **X coefficient** b (slope of the line). Because it is tedious to carry out the calculations that are needed to find the "best fit" of a line through a "scatter plot," they are best performed by computer-assisted techniques. The **degrees of freedom** are the number of observations minus the number of constants. The smaller the number of observations, the less statistically significant the analysis. **The standard error coefficient** gives an indication of the reliability of the slope b. The standard error (a) of the slope b and intercept a is usually unknown. It is based on the standard deviation (SD) of the observed points about the fitted line ($S_{xy} = \surd\Sigma(y - Y)^2/(n - 2)$). Finally, R squared, which ranges from 0 to 1, indicates the predictive value or correlation between x and y; if the correlation is perfect, R Squared is 1 and if there is no correlation, R Squared is 0.

The equation is easily adapted to more than one explanation ($y = a + b_1x_1 + b_2x_2 + b_3x_3$). The greater the number of correlating factors (x_1, x_2, x_3,...x_n), the greater the R Squared and the greater the combined predictive power of the hypothesis being tested. Occasionally it is difficult to find a linear fit for complex mathematical forms ($y = ac^{bx}$).

In these cases, some manipulation of the data will help achieve a linear fit ($\log y = \log a + bx \log c$). By redefining the values ($y' = \log y$, $a' = \log a$; $b' = b \log c$) this equation becomes a linear relationship ($y' = a' + b'x$). The calculation of elasticities, where relationships were complex, required this technique.

When it is impossible to designate at least one independent variable, the relationship is more correctly described as a correlation between two mutually dependent variables. In this case, **the coefficient of the correlation** describes the extent of the relationship between x and y, also known as the **product moment correlation** or **Pearson's coefficient** of correlation. Furthermore, without concomitant *path analysis*,[136] even strong correlations fail to give unequivocal evidence of causal relationships or proof of the existence of determinants:

$$r = \frac{\Sigma(x-\overline{x})(Y-\overline{y})}{\angle\Sigma(x-\overline{x})^2\,\Sigma(y-\overline{y})^2}.$$

Many authors claim that there is a high correlation between a country's level of socio-economic development or capacity to spend and expenditure on health care, based on statistical regression analysis of income trends and health care expenditure.[137] Like other techniques, statistical regression analysis in health care is not without flaws. First, in cross-national comparisons of absolute values rather than ratios of expenditure data, exchange rates cannot be used because they are too sensitive to short-term fluctuations in capital flows and international capital markets. Researchers are still in the early stages of developing purchasing power parities (PPP) that represent average prices in specific countries relative to average international prices ($HCE_{ppp} = HCE \times PPP$).[138] Second, for cross-sectional regression analysis of income to be valid, income elasticity must be constant; in reality, it rises with income. Third, public choice or preference may vary considerably within a country. This is especially true in the case of highly decentralized systems and federations of states. National macro-aggregate indicators cannot represent such differences. Some reductionism of complex policy issues is unavoidable. Fourth, health care is not homogeneous. Similar expenditure may represent vastly different standards of health care

Table 2.11 Questions, Techniques and Indicators

Question	Techniques and Indicators
Why	Linguistic, case studies
How	Positivist policy analysis, constitutions, laws, regulation
Processes	Path analysis, national, cross-national profiles
Effects	
National wealth	Econometric, regression, ranking, GDP_{cap}
Growth	Econometric, regression, ranking, GDP_{gwt}
Debt	Econometric, regression, ranking, GGD/GDP
Opportunity cost	Econometric, regression, GCE/GDP
Displacement	Econometric, regression, GSE/GDP
Backlash	Positivist policy analysis, econometric, elasticity HCE_{ela}
Expenditure	Econometric, regression, GTE/GDP and HCE_{ppp}/ GDP_{cap}
Equity	Econometric, regression, ranking, Pub/Tot health expenditure rations
Trends	
Historic	Linguistic, case studies, econometric, statistical
Future	Positivist policy analysis, econometric, forecasting

Source: Adapted from Preker (1989).

depending on the structure, policy orientation and quality of the service delivery system. Finally, some things are simply not quantifiable. These are important areas for future research which this study did not attempt to address. See Table 2.11.

ENDNOTES

1. A. J. Heidenheimer, H. Heclo, and C. T. Adams, *Comparative Public Policy: The Politics of Social Choice in Europe and America,* 2nd Edition (New York: St Martin's Press, 1983): 2–3. The expressions "comparative", "cross-national" and "international" are used interchangeably.
2. S. Rokkan, *Comparative Research Across Cultures and Nations* (Paris: Mouton, 1968).
3. The political analysis of early Greek philosophers such as Aristotle and Plato refers extensively to foreign experiences.

4. D. Ashford, ed. *Comparing Public Policies* (Beverly Hills: Sage, 1978); T. R. Dye, *Policy Analysis: What Governments Do, Why They Do It, and What Difference It Makes* (University of Alabama: University of Alabama Press, 1976); and S. Nagel, *Contemporary Public Policy Analysis* (University of Alabama: University of Alabama Press, 1984).
5. P. Flora and A. J. Heidenheimer, eds., *The Development of Welfare States in Europe and America* (New Brunswich, N.J.: Transaction Books and the HIWED Project, 1981).
6. J. Berting, F. Geyer, and R. Jarkovich, eds., *Problems in International Comparative Research in the Social Sciences* (Oxford: Pergamon, 1979).
7. K. W. Deutsch, "Prologue: Achievements and challenges in 2000 years of comparative research," in *Comparative Policy Research: Learning from Experience,* by M. Dierkes, H. N. Weiler, and A. B. Antal, eds., WZB-Publications (Hants: Gower, 1987): 7.
8. A. Przeworski and H. Teune, *The Logic of Comparative Social Inquiry* (New York: Wiley –Interscience, 1970).
9. E. J. Feldman, "Comparative public policy: Field or method?" *Comparative Politics* 10(1978): 287–305.
10. R. C. Macridis, *The Study of Comparative Government* (New York: Doubleday, 1955): 7–12.
11. A. Przeworski, "Methods of cross-national research, 1970–1983: An overview," in *Comparative Policy Research: Learning from Experience,* by M. Dierkes, H. N. Weiler, and A. B. Antal, eds., WZB-Publications (Hants: Gower, 1987): 44.
12. E. Lisle, "Perspectives and challenges for cross-national research," in *Comparative Policy Research: Learning from Experience,* by M. Dierkes, H. N. Weller, and A. B. Antal, eds., WZB-Publications (Hants: Gower, 1987): 475.
13. D. T. Campbell and J. T. Stanley, *Experimental and Quasi-Experimental Designs for Research* (Chicago: Rand McNally, 1966); and T. D. Cook and D. T. Campbell, *Quasi Experimentation: Design and Analyses of Issues for Field Settings* (Chicago: Rand McNally, 1979).
14. R. Dubin, *Theory Building* (New York: Free Press, 1969): and B. G. Glaser and A. L. Strauss, *The Discovery Grounded Theory: Strategies for Qualitative Research* (London: Weidenfeld and Nicholson, 1967).
15. A. Przeworski, "Methods of cross-national research, 1970-83: An overview," in *Comparative Policy Research: Learning from Experience,* by M. Dierkes, H. N. Weiler, and A. B. Antal, eds., WZB-Publications (Hants: Gower, 1987): 31.

16. D. T. Campbell, "'Degrees of Freedom' and the case study," *Comparative Political Studies* 8(1975): 179–193.
17. A. Etzioni and F. L Dubow, eds., *Comparative Perspectives: Theories and Methods* (Boston: Little, Brown and Company); J. M. Armer and A. D. Grimshaw, eds., *Comparative Social Research: Methodological Problems and Strategies* (New York: Wiley, 1973); N. J. Smelser, *Comparative Methods in the Social Sciences* (Englewood Cliffs, NJ: Prentice-Hall, 1975); M. Niessen and J. Peschar, eds., *International Comparative Research: Problems of Theory, Methodology and Organisation in Eastern and Western Europe* (Oxford: Pergamon Press, 1982); A. Szalai and R. Petrella, eds., *Cross-National Comparative Survey Research: Theory and Practice* (Oxford: Pergamon Press, 1977); D. P. Warwick and S. Osheron, eds., *Comparative Research Methods* (Englewood Cliffs, NJ: Prentice-Hall, 1973); and J. Betting, F. Geyer, and R. Jurkovich, eds., *Problems in International Comparative Research in the Social Sciences* (Oxford: Pergamon Press, 1979).
18. Adam Przeworski, "Methods of cross-national research, 1970-83: An overview," in *Comparative Policy Research: Learning from Experience,* by M. Dierkes, H. N. Weiler, and A. B. Antal, eds., WZB-Publications (Hants: Gower, 1987): 34.
19. *Idem.*
20. These were the founding principles of the Canadian health care system set forth in the *Health Charter for Canadians:* "The achievement of the highest possible health standards for all our people... This objective can best be achieved through a comprehensive, universal Health Services Programme for the Canadian People, ... financed through prepayment arrangements". See Canada, "The Royal Commission on Health Services (RCHS)," Report [Chairman Emmet M. Hall] (Ottawa: Queen's Printer, 1964): 11.
21. P. H. Grinyer, *5th National Conference on Doctoral Research in Management and Industrial Relations*, University of Aston Management Centre, 6–7 April 1981.
22. Preliminary notions about concepts were analyzed further through cluster analysis and other techniques for the formulation of concepts described under the section on analysis.
23. N. J. Smeiser, "The methodology of comparative analysis," in *Comparative Research Methods,* by D. Warwick and S. Osheron, eds. (Englewood Cliffs, N.J.: Prentice-Hall, 1973); and E. Vedung, "The comparative method and its neighbours," in *Power and Political Theory: Some European Perspectives* (Chichester: Wiley, 1976).

24. A. Przeworski, "Methods of cross-national research, 1970-83: An overview," in *Comparative Policy Research: Learning from Experience,* by M. Dierkes, H. N. Weiler, and A. B. Antal, eds., WZB-Publications (Hants: Gower, 1987): 3–36.
25. B. P. Bosworth, "Capital formation and economic policy," *Brookings Papers on Economic Activity* 2(1982): 273–326.
26. M. Rein and L. Rainwater, *From Welfare State to Welfare Society: Some Unresolved Issues in Assessment,* IIVG-AP (Berlin: WZB, 1981).
27. D. G. Taylor, "Analyzing quantitative data," in *Handbook of Social Research* (New York: Academic Press, 1983); and A. Przeworski, "Methods of cross-national research, 1970-83: An overview," in *Comparative Policy Research: Learning from Experience,* by M. Dierkes, H. N. Weiler, and A.B. Antal, eds., WZB-Publications (Hants: Gower, 1987): 36–37.
28. J. Alber, G. Esping-Andersen, and L. Rainwater, "Studying the welfare state: Issues and queries," in *Comparative Policy Research: Learning from Experience,* by M. Dierkes, H. N. Weiler, and A. B. Antal, eds., WZB-Publications (Hants: Gower, 1987): 462.
29. Some causal relationships can be inferred from formal models of choice, contextual analysis, hierarchical models of organizations and intervention analysis, but their conclusions are all vulnerable to overdeterminism.
30. J. J. Wiatr, "The role of theory and methodology in cross-national research," *Polish Roundtable* (1070-1): 4.
31. S. Feinberg, *The Analysis of Cross-Classified Categorical Data* (Cambridge: MIT Press, 1977).
32. The specific techniques used arc discussed under the section on analysis.
33. The components of these axes could be quantified through multi-variant scaling.
34. One approach to analysing political ideas in this way is linguistic analysis which will be discussed under the methodology section on analysis. See D. Miller, *Social Justice* (Oxford: Clarendon Press, 1976).
35. H. L. Wilensky, G M. Luebbert, S. R. Hahn, and A. M. Jamieson, "Comparative social policy: Theories, methods, findings," in *Comparative Policy Research: Learning from Experience,* by M. Dierkes, H. N. Weiler, and A. B. Antal, eds., WZB-Publications (Hants: Gower, 1987): 402; and A. J. Heidenheimer, "Education and social security entitlement in Europe and America," in *The Development of Welfare States in Europe and America*, by P. Flora and A. J. Heidenheimer, eds. (New Brunswich, N.J.: Transaction Books and the IDWED Project, 1981): 269–304.

36. International Labour Office (ILO), Social Security (Minimum Standards) Convention, No. 102 (Geneva: ILO, 1952).
37. J. Alber, G. Esping-Andcrsen, and L. Rainwater, "Studying the welfare state: Issues and queries," in *Comparative Policy Research: Learning from Experience,* by M. Dierkes, H. N. Weiler, and A. B. Antal, eds., WZB-Publications (Hants: Gower, 1987): 460.
38. World Health Organization (WHO), Regional Office for Europe (ROE), *Targets for Health for All: Targets in Support of the European Regional Strategy for Health for All* (Copenhagen: WHO, ROE, 1985): 23.
39. M. Rein and L. Rainwater, *The Private/Public Interplay in Social Protection* (New York: M.E. Sharpe, 1985); G. McLachlan and A. Maynard, eds., *The Public/Private Mix for Health: The Relevance and Effects of Change* (London: Nuffield Provincial] Hospitals Trust, 1982); and A. J. Culyer and B. Jonson, eds., *Public and Private Health Services: Complementarities and Conflicts* (Oxford: Basil Blackwell, 1986).
40. G. Crumper, *Health Sector Financing: Estimating Health Expenditure in Developing Countries,* A Discussion Paper, EPC Publication No. 9 (London: London School of Hygiene and Tropical Medicine, 1986).
41. G. W. Torrance, "Utility approach to measuring health-related quality of life," *Journal of Chronic Diseases* 40(6) (1987): 593–603.
42. J. Alber, G. Esping-Andersen, and L. Rainwater, "Studying the welfare state: Issues and queries," in *Comparative Policy Research: Learning from Experience,* by M. Dierkes, H. N. Weiler, and A.B. Antal, eds., WZB-Publications (Hants: Gower, 1987): 462.
43. This database will be described in detail in the section on data collection.
44. A. Przeworski, "Methods of cross-national research, 1970-83: An overview," in *Comparative Policy Research: Learning from Experience,* by M. Dierkes, H. N. Weiler, and A. B. Antal, eds., WZB-Publications (Hants; Gower, 1987); 31–49.
45. A. Przeworski, "Methods of cross-national research 1970–83: An overview," in *Comparative Policy Research: Learning from Experience,* by M. Dierkes, H. N. Weiler, and A. B. Antal, eds., WZB-Publications (Hants: Gower, 1987).
46. *Op. cit*., p. 36.
47. G. J. Schieber and J.-P. Poullier, "Overview of international comparisons of health care expenditures," Annual Supplement, *Health Care Financing Review* (1989): 1–7.
48. R. T. Kudrle and T. R. Marmor, "The development of welfare states in North America," in *The Development of Welfare States in Europe and*

America, by P. Flora and A. J. Heidenheimer, eds. (New Brunswick, N.J.: Transaction Books and HIWED Project, 1981): 81–121; S. Kuhnle, "The growth of social insurance programs in Scandinavia: Outside influences and internal forces," in *The Development of Welfare States in Europe and America*, by P. Flora and A.J. Heidenheimer, eds. (New Brunswick, N.J.: Transaction Books and HIWED Project, 1981): 125–150.

49. A. Inkeles, "Cross-national research confronts the needs of the policy-maker," in *Comparative Policy Research: Learning from Experience,* by M. Dierkes, H. N. Weiler, and A. B. Antal, eds., WZB-Publications (Hants: Gower, 1987): 50–55.
50. The researcher is, nevertheless, obliged to examine some irrelevant "noise" to confirm that it does indeed lack the desired information.
51. G. E. P. Box and G. C. Tiao, *Bayesian Inference in Statistical Analysis* (San Francisco: Holden-Day, 1973).
52. T. R. Marmor, W. L. Hoffman, and T. C. Heagy, "National health insurance: Some lessons from the Canadian experience," *Policy Sciences* 6(4)(1975): 447; M.C. Brown, *National Health Insurance in Canada and Australia: A Comparative Political Economy Analysis,* Research Monograph No. 3 (Canberra: Health Economics Research Unit, 1983); and R. T. Kudrle and T. R. Marmor, "The development of welfare states in North America," in *The Development of Welfare States in Europe and America*, by P. Flora and A. J. Heidenheimer, eds. (New Brunswick, N.J.: Transaction Books and HIWED Project, 1981): 81–121.
53. A. Przeworski, "Methods of cross-national research, 1970–83: An overview," in *Comparative Policy Research: Learning from Experience,* by M. Dierkes, H. N. Weiler, and A. B. Antal, eds., WZB-Publications (Hants: Gower, 1987): 39.
54. H. L. Wilensky, G. M. Luebbert, S. R. Hahn, and A. M. Jamieson, "Comparative social policy. Theories, methods, findings," *in Comparative Policy Research: Learning from Experience,* by M. Dierkes, H. N. Weiler, and A. B. Antal, eds., WZB-Publications (Hants: Gower, 1987): 416.
55. C. Altenstetter, *Health Policy-making and Administration in West Germany and the United States* (Beverly Hills: Sage, 1974); C. Altenstetter, *Innovations in Health Policy and Service Delivery: A Cross-National Perspective* (Cambridge, M.A.: Oelgeschlager, Gunn and Hain, 1981); O. Anderson, *Health Care: Can There be Equity? The United States, Sweden, and England* (New York: Wiley, 1972); H. Leichter, *A Comparative Approach to Policy Analysis: Health Care Policy in Four Nations* (Cambridge: Cambridge University Press, 1979); W. Glaser, *Health*

Insurance Bargaining: Foreign Lessons for Americans (New York: Halsted, 1978). J. W. Hurst, *Financing Health Services in the United States, Canada and Britain* (London: King's Fund, 1985); K. Henke, "What can Americans learn from the German health insurance system?" *Social Science* 55(1980): 134–137. In recent years, the literature is filled with studies on the contrasting features between the Canadian and American health care systems that try to postulate the causes and effects of these differences based on comparisons between the two countries.

56. K. Janda, *A Conceptual Framework for the Comparative Analysis of Political Parties* (Beverly Hills: Sage, 1980).
57. Australia, Austria, Belgium, Canada, Denmark, Federal Republic of Germany, France, Finland, Greece, Iceland, Ireland, Italy, Japan, Luxembourg, Netherlands, New Zealand, Norway, Switzerland, Portugal, Turkey, United Kingdom and United States. Yugoslavia participates with special status. See J. Paxton, ed., *The Statesman's Year-Book: Statistical and Historical Annual of the States of the World for the Year 1986–1987*, 123rd Edition (London: MacMillan Press, 1986): 34.
58. The data for Turkey is still not reliable.
59. Extensive preliminary review of all the OECD countries was needed to identify these countries and eliminate those that had not passed such legislation.
60. Similar points in the evolution of the reforms under investigation were used as landmarks rather than chronological dates because the latter often differed for any given issue and policy option.
61. United States, Department of Health and Human Services (DHHS), *Social Security Programs* [sic] *Throughout the World·* 1983, Research Report No. 59 (Washington: Government Printing Office, 1984); and World Health Organization (WHO), *Health Care Legislation of the World* (Geneva: WHO, yearly publication).
62. CMEA is the acronym for Council for Mutual Economic Assistance (COMECON). The six founding members, Bulgaria, Czechoslovakia, Hungary, Poland, Romania and USSR, were later joined by Albania (1949–1961), German Democratic Republic (1950), Mongolia (1962), Cuba (1972) and Vietnam (1978). Yugoslavia, Afghanistan, Angola, Ethiopia, Laos, Mexico, Mozambique, Nicaragua and the People's Democratic Republic of Yemen attended as observers. See J. Paxton, *Statesman's Year-Book* 1986–1987: 48.
63. See the section on substantive issues.
64. R. Rubinson and D. Quinlan: "The world economy and the distribution of income within states: A cross-national study," *American Sociological*

Review 41(1976): 638–659; R. Rubinson and D. Quinlan, "Democracy and social inequality: A reanalysis," *American Sociological Review* 42(1977): 611–623; D. Cameron, "The expansion of the public economy: A comparative analysis," *American Political Science Review* 72(4) (1978): 1243–361; D. Cameron, "On the limits of the public economy," *Annals of the American Academy of Political and Social Science* 459(1982): 46–62; D. Hibbs, "Political parties and macro-economic policy," *American Political Science Review* 71(1977): 1467–1488; H. L. Wilinsky, *The Welfare State and Equality: Structural and Ideological Roots of Public Expenditures* (Berkeley: University of California Press, 1975); and R. Rose and G. Peters, *Can Governments Go Bankrupt?* (*New* York: Basic Books, 1978).

65. A. Inkeles, "Cross-national research confronts the needs of the policy-maker," in *Comparative Policy Research: Learning from Experience,* by M. Dierkes, H. N. Weiler, and M. B. Antal, eds., WZB-Publications (Hants: Gower, 1987): 52.
66. A. S. Preker, "Public finance and provision of health care services in Quebec: An international perspective," *Brief,* presented to the Commission of Inquiry into the Health and Social Services of Quebec [Chairman Jean Rochon] (London: IIHS, December 1986).
67. R. K. Som, *A Manual of Sampling Techniques* (London: Heinemann, 1973).
68. The survey technique was limited to guidelines used during open-ended interviews with selected individuals in each of the countries chosen for the case studies. It was not intended for statistical analysis.
69. M. Bulmer, ed., *Social Research and Royal Commissions* (London: George Allen & Unwin, 1980). Original documents were also examined for the Nordic countries with the exception of a few key documents for Finland, which were translated into English by Helle Satala of the Finnish Embassy in London.
70. R. A. Chapman, ed., *The Role of Commissions in Policy-Making* (London: George Allen & Unwin, 1973); G. Rhodes, *Committees of Inquiry* (London: George Allen & Unwin, 1975); T. J. Cartwright, *Royal Commissions and Departmental Committees in Britain* (London: George Allen & Unwin, 1975); M. Komarovsky, ed., *Sociology and Public Policy: The Case of the Presidential Commissions* (New York: Elsevier, 1975); and M. Bulmer, *Social Research and Royal Commissions* (London: George Allen & Unwin, 1980).
71. M. Bulmer, *The Uses of Social Research: Social Investigation in Public Policy-Making* (London: George Allen & Unwin, 1982). For more comprehensive reviews, see references in C. Lindblom and D. Cohen, *Usable*

Knowledge: Social Science and Social Problem Solving (New Haven: Yale University Press, 1979): 102–126.

72. In the Nordic countries, Australia and Canada, many of the key people involved in earlier reforms were still alive and willing to grant interviews.
73. B. Abel-Smith and R. M. Titmuss, *The Cost of the National Health Service in England and Wales* (Cambridge: Cambridge University Press, 1956).
74. B. Abel-Smith, "Paying for health services: A study of the costs and sources of finance in six countries," *World Health Organization Public Health Papers* 17(1963); and B. Abel-Smith, "An international study of health expenditure, and its relevance for health planning," *World Health Organization Public Health Papers* 32(1967).
75. J.-P. Poullier, "Health data file: Overview and methodology," Annual Supplement, *Health Care Financing Review* (1989): 111–118.
76. OECD, *Measuring Health Care 1960–1983: Expenditure, Costs and Performance,* OECD Social Policy Studies (Paris: OECD, 1985).
77. Quantitative differences among classification systems are discussed in "Structural problems of social security today and tomorrow," Proceedings of the European Institute of Social Security, Leuven, Belgium, ACCO, 1988, TableA-1.
78. G. Crumpet, *Health Sector Financing: Estimating Health Expenditure in Developing Countries,* Discussion Paper, EPC Publication No. 9 (London: London School of Hygiene and Tropical Medicine, 1986).
79. Likewise, Gross Domestic Product (GDP) underestimates real national wealth because it excludes the productivity of informal sectors such as households and "black markets."
80. OECD, *Health Care Systems in Transition: The Search for Efficiency,* Social Policy Studies No. 7 (Paris: OECD, 1989).
81. See the Select Bibliography for references for the statistical time series used for the Nordic countries, New Zealand and the United Kingdom whose time series preceded the beginning of the OECD Health Data File.
82. This happened in most countries during the late 1960s and early 1970s.
83. This happened in Finland during its time series.
84. This was a major problem in the case of New Zealand and the United Kingdom prior to the 1950s. The Nordic statistical series is issued only once every two or three years.
85. The most recent revision was considered the most reliable.
86. In recent years, the national time series differ significantly from the OECD Health Data File because the latter is standardised for international comparability.

87. The OECD Health Data File includes no information on the sources of revenue.
88. K. Popper, *The Logic of Scientific Discovery* (London: Hutchinson, 1959); A. J. Heidenheimer, H. Heclo, and C. T. Adams, *Comparative Public Policy: The Politics of Social Choice in Europe and America,* 2nd Edition (New York: St. Martin's Press, 1983); P. Flora, *State, Economy, and Society in Western Europe,* 1815–1975: *A Data Handbook in Two Volumes* (Chicago: St James, 1983); and M. Dierkes, H. N. Weiler, and A. B. Antal, eds., *Comparative Policy Research: Learning from Experience,* WZB-Publications (Hants: Gower, 1987).
89. See the section on selection of countries for the rationale behind those selected for detailed case studies: Australia, Denmark, Canada, Finland, Norway, New Zealand, Sweden and the United Kingdom.
90. H. L. A. Hart, *The Concept of Law* (Oxford: Clarendon Press, 1961).
91. D. Miller, *Social Justice* (Oxford: Clarendon Press, 1976).
92. R. N. Shepard, A. K. Romney and S. B. Nerlov, *Multidimensional Scaling: Theory and Applications in Tile Behavourial Sciences,* Volumes 1 and 2 (New York: Seminar Press, 1972); and A. H. G. S. van der Ven, *Introduction to Scaling* (New York: Wiley, 1980).
93. J. Carrier and L. Kendall, "The development of welfare states: The production of plausible accounts," *Journal Social Policy* 6(1977): 271–290.
94. P. A. Lachenbruch, *Discriminate Analysis* (London: Collier Macmillan, 1975); and M. Goldstein and W. R. Dillon, *Discrete Discriminate Analysis* (New York: Wiley, 1978).
95. D. C. Mueller, *Public Choice* (Cambridge: Cambridge University Press, 1979).
96. J. F. Padgett, "Hierarchy and ecological control in federal budgetary decision making," *American Journal of Sociology* 87(1981): 75–129.
97. L. H. Boyd, Jr. and G. R. Iversen, *Contextual Analysis: Concepts QJ1d Statistical Techniques* (Belmont, CA: Wadsworth Publishing Company, 1979).
98. H. H. Harman, *Modern Factor Analysis* (Chicago: University of Chicago, 1967); and R. J. Rummell, *Applied Factor Analysis* (Evanston: Northwestern Press, 1970).
99. S. E. Fienberg, *The Analysis of Cross-Classified Categorical Data* (Cambridge: MIT Press, 1977).
100. R. McLeary and R. A. Hay Jr., *Time Series Analysis* (Beverly Hills: Sage, 1978).
101. Editorial, "Meta-analysis: Controlled clinical trial," *Journal of Rheumatology* 16(4)(1989): 3.

102. J. Bentham, "An introduction to the principles of morals and legislation," in *A Fragment of Government and an Introduction to the Principles of Morals and Legislation,* by W. Harrison, ed. (Oxford: Blackwell, 1948): 78. See also H. L. A. Hart, *The Concept of Law* (Oxford: Clarendon Press, 1961); H. Kelsen, *General Theory of Law and State* (Cambridge: Harvard University Press, 1945); and J. Austin, *The Province of Jurisprudence Defined*, in Library of Ideas (New York: Prometheus Books, 1921).
103. A. P. Blaustein and G. Flanz, *Constitutions of the Countries of the World,* Continuous Update.
104. World Health Organization, *World Health Legislation Review Journal,* Continuous Update and Statutes of individual countries.
105. T. D. Weldon, *The Vocabulary of Politics* (Harmondsworth: Pelican, 1953).
106. D. Miller, *Social Justice* (Oxford: Clarendon Press, 1976).
107. N. Bolton, *Concept Formation* (Oxford: Pergamon, 1977).
108. P. Townsend and N. Davidson, eds., *Inequalities in Health: The Black Report* (Harmondsworth: Penguin Books, 1982).
109. T. McKeown, *The Role of Medicine* (Oxford: Blackwell, 1979).
110. I. Illich, *Limits to Medicine: Medical Nemesis, The Expropriation of Health* (Harmondsworth: Pelican, 1976).
111. For a discussion of the battle between the AMA and the US federal government during the 1950s and 1960s, see C. Chapman, *Physicians, Law, & Ethics,* (New York: New York University Press, 1984): 103–124.
112. D. Miller, *Social Justice* (Oxford: Clarendon Press, 1976): 3.
113. SPSS, *SPSS/PC + Advanced Statistics,* IBM PC Computer Module, Version 4.0 (Chicago: SPSS, 1990).
114. C. Altenstetter, *Health Policy-making and Administration in West Germany and the United States* (Beverly Hills: Sage, 1974); C. Altenstetter, *Innovations in Health Policy and Service Delivery: A Cross-National Perspective* (Cambridge, MA.: Oelgeschlager, Gunn and Hain, 1981); and O. Anderson, *Health Care: Can There be Equity? The United States, Sweden, and England* (New York, Wiley, 1972).
115. B. Abel-Smith, "The history of medical care," in *Comparative Development in Social Welfare*, by E. W. Martin, ed. (London: Allen & Unwin, 1972); H. Leichter, *A Comparative Approach to Policy Analysis: Health Care Policy in Four Nations* (Cambridge: Cambridge University Press, 1979); W. Glaser, *Health Insurance Bargaining: Foreign Lessons for Americans* (New York: Halsted, 1978); M. I. Roemer, *Comparative National Policies on Health Care* (New Haven: Yale University Press, 1977); M. I. Roemer, *Health Care Systems in World Perspective* (Ann Arbor: Health Administration

Press, 1976); B. Abel-Smith, "Paying for health services: A study of the costs and *sources* of finance in six countries," *World Health Organization Public Health Papers* 17(1963); B. Abel-Smith, "An international study of health expenditure, and its relevance for health planning," *World Health Organization Public Health Papers* 32(1967); and J.-P. Poullier, "Health data file: Overview and methodology," Annual Supplement, *Health Care Financing Review* (1989): 111–118.

116. OECD, *Measuring Health Care 1960–1983: Expenditure, Costs and Performance,* OECD Social Policy Studies (Paris: OECD, 1985); OECD, *Financing and Delivering Health Care: A Comparative Analysis of OECD Countries,* OECD Social Policy Studies No. 2, (Paris: OECD, 1987); OECD, *Social Expenditure 1960–1990: Problems of Growth and Control,* OECD Social Policy Studies (Paris: OECD, 1985); and US Department of Health and Human Services, Annual Supplement, *Health Care Financing Review* (1989).
117. T. E. Getzen and J.-P. Poullier, "International health spending forecasts: Concepts and evaluation"; U. G. Gerdtham, B. Jonsson, F. Andersson, and J. Sogaard, "The determinants of health expenditures: An econometrical analysis across the OECD countries"; A. S. Preker, "Expenditure control through public financing in the OECD"; and F. Champagne, A.-P. Contandriopoulos, A. Lemay, and A. S. Preker, "Evaluation of health care performance in the OECD," *Second World Congress on Health Economics*, University of Zurich, Switzerland, September 10–14, 1990.
118. M. R. Anderberg, *Cluster Analysis for Applications* (New York: Academic Press, 1973); B, Everitt, *Graphical Techniques for Multivariate Data* (London: Heinemann, 1978); and B. G. Batchelor, *Pattern Recognition* (New York: Plenum Press, 1978).
119. G. E. P. Box and G. M. Jenkins, *Time Series Analysis: Forecasting and Control,* Revised Edition (San Francisco: Holden-Day, 1976).
120. Nominal = Current Values.
121. Four factors were used in this model. See G. J. Schieber and J.-P. Poullier, "Overview of international comparisons of health care expenditures," Annual Supplement, *Health Care Financing Review* (1989): 1–9. Others have tried to include factors such as demand/need, economic resources, substitution of care, supplier-induced demand, public/private mix in financing and relative price on health care. See U. Gerdtham, F. Anderson, J. Sogaard and B. Jonsson, "Economic analysis of health care expenditures: A cross-sectional study of the OECD countries," in *GMT Report 1985–1989* (Linkoping: Centre for Medical Technology Assessment, 1988).

122. Based on composite values of Canada, France, Germany, Italy, Japan, United Kingdom and United States.
123. E. Kleiman, "The determinants of national outlay on health," in *The Economics of Health and Medical Care*, by M. Perlman, ed. (London: Macmillan, 1974).
124. R. R. Leu "The public-private mix and international health care costs," in *Public and Private Health Services: Complementarities and Conflicts*, by A. J. Culyer and B. Jonsson, eds. (Oxford: Basil Blackwell, 1986).
125. A. F. Long and S. Harrison, eds., *Health Services Performance: Effectiveness and Efficiency* (London: Crom Helm, 1985).
126. B. Abel-Smith and R. M. Titmuss, *The Cost of the National Health Service in England and Wales* (Cambridge: Cambridge University Press, 1956).
127. Real = Constant Values.
128. Government transfer payments (payments made through social security programmes) comprise the main difference between government total expenditure and government consumption expenditure (GSE » GTE – GCE).
129. GOP elasticity of health care expenditure is defined as the percentage change in per capita health care expenditure divided by the percentage change in per capita GOP. Similar elasticities can be developed relative to different aspects of government expenditure per capita.
130. N. R. Draper and H. Smith, *Applied Regression Analysis,* 2nd Edition (New York: Wiley, 1980); and R. J. Freund and P. D. Minton, *Regression Methods* (New York: Dekker, 1979).
131. Other indicators that have been tried include levels of energy consumption, urbanization and literacy rates. See H. L. Wilensky, *The Welfare State and Equality: Structural and Ideological Roots of Public Expenditures* (Berkeley: University of California Press, 1975).
132. H. Helco, *Modem Social Politics in Britain and Sweden* (New Haven: Yale University Press, 1974); and F. Castles, *The Social Democratic Image of Society* (London: Routledge and Kegan Paul, 1978). Most other authors have used more descriptive analysis to look at the impact of ideology, democracy and political parties. See P. Flora and A. J. Heidenheimer, eds., *The Development of Welfare States in Europe and America* (New Brunswich, N.J.: Transaction Books and the HIWED Project, 1981); F. Castles, "The impact of parties on public expenditure," in *The Impact of Parties: Politics and Policies In Democratic Capitalist States,* by F. Castles, ed. (Beverly Hills: Sage, 1982).
133. Social security spending is the standard indicator for the evolution of administrative infrastructures. See H. Heleo, *Modern Social Politics in*

Britain and Sweden (New Haven: Yale University Press, 1974); and G. Lembruch and P. C. Schmitter, eds., *Patterns of Corporatist Policy-making* (Beverly Hills: Sage, 1982).

134. This is the standard indicator used in most of the health economics literature, but there have been few attempts to relate health care expenditure to specific programme features of health policy.
135. The impact of the "dummy" variable *t* was checked against these outcome indicators.
136. H. M. Blalock, *Casual Models in the Social Sciences* (London: Macmillan, 1971); and K. G. Lockyer, *An Introduction to Critical Path Analysis,* 3rd Edition (London: Pitman, 1969).
137. L. I. Leviatan, *Consumption Patterns in Israel* (Jerusalem: Falk Project for Economic Research in Israel, 1964); E. Kleiman, "The determinants of national outlay on health," in *The Economics of Health and Medical Care*, by M. Perlman, ed. (London: Macmillan, 1974): J. P. Newhouse, "Development and allocation of medical care resources: Medico-economic approach," in *Development and Allocation of Medical Care Resources,* Proceedings of the 29th World Medical Assembly, Tokyo, Japan Medical Association, 1975; J. P. Newhouse, "Medical care expenditure: A cross-national survey," *Journal of Human* Resources, 12(1)(1977): 115–125; R. J. Maxwell, *Health and Wealth: An International Study of Health-Care Spending* (Lexington, M.A.: Lexington Books, 1981); OECD*, Financing and Delivering Health Care: A Comparative Analysis of OECD Countries,* OECD Social Policy Studies No.2 (Paris: OECD, 1987); D. Parkin, A. McGuire and B. Yule, "Aggregate health care expenditures and national income: Is health care a luxury good?" *Journal of Health Economics* 6(2) (1987): 109–128: G. J. Schieber and J.-P. Poullier, "International health spending and utilization trends," *Health Affairs* 7(4)(1988): 105–112; and A. J. Culyer, "Cost containment in Europe," Annual Supplement, *Health Care Financing Review* (1989): 31.
138. M. Ward, *Purchasing Power Parities and Real Expenditures in the OECD* (Paris: OECD, 1985).

PART II

NATIONAL PROFILES

This section of the book, provides a review of the experience of 8 countries in the OECD that introduced landmark legislative health care financing reforms to expand access to health care for their whole population. The countries reviewed in the order of their presentation are New Zealand, the United Kingdom, Canada, Australia, Denmark, Norway, Sweden and Finland.

CHAPTER 3

NEW ZEALAND

Our New Zealand National Health Service must be 'free', it must be complete, it must meet all the needs of all the people.[1]

D. G. McMillan, 1935

A. HISTORICAL CONTEXT

1. Colonial Military Outposts

Western settlers in New Zealand were young and energetic people, largely from England and Scotland, who had left the old world to better themselves. Their working-class background quickly set the pattern for the financing of health care, which developed through social-democratic ideals.[2] Unlike other English colonies where the native populations were largely exterminated, New Zealand integrated its Maori population into the health care system at an early stage.

British military outposts provided the colony with its first rudimentary medical facilities. New Zealand therefore began its colonial history with a "nationalized" health service, financed through the British treasury. As the population grew, such facilities became inappropriate for civilian needs. Since the young colony had no landed gentry and few wealthy business elite to finance charitable and voluntary organizations, the sick and needy remained largely the responsibility of the colonial government.[3]

Four agencies evolved to provide health care for the early settlers: central government institutions, private institutions, voluntary organizations and self-help groups. The sick, the socially needy and the poor were considered liabilities by most of these organizations. Although in theory the voluntary hospitals were financed through members' subscriptions, these institutions depended on public subsidies to pay their running costs.[4] The incurable, infectious, mentally ill, elderly and poor, as well as pregnant mothers and alcoholics were often denied admission.

The civilian population soon began using the public hospitals, originally established to treat the Maori people. Even those who could afford the luxury of private care at home found that such care was unavailable because of the scarcity of doctors. Furthermore, medical science remained primitive during the nineteenth century; those who could, did without health care.

2. National Insurance Plan of 1882

Britain initially tried to establish a strong central government in most of its overseas colonies. The Crown Colony of New Zealand, nevertheless, decentralized its government between 1840 and 1876. Its first constitution of 1846 established two provinces. This was increased to six by 1852, and later to nine. By 1876, when a policy of "colonial governmentalism" returned authority to the central government, considerable damage had been done: public services, including health care, had become fragmented, leaving a "hybrid system" of "residualism", "parochialism" and "adhocracy."[5]

A spirit of renewed commitment to a strong central government led Harry Atkinson, the Colonial Treasurer, to propose a compulsory national health insurance plan in 1882. His proposal called for cash support during illness, old age and infirmity due to accidents, as well as for widows and orphans. A flat-rate compulsory national insurance contribution of £40 per year from workers would finance most of the program, while a consolidated fund would finance old-age benefits, and rates on property would finance widows' and orphans' benefits.[6]

Atkinson was an unusual politician. He was the "mainstay" of the Conservative Party, but his political views were "quasi-socialistic."[7]

In a passionate speech, he defended his plan: "In accordance with the ideas of equality which we hold in this part of the world, then everybody would pay to the fund and everybody would have the right to draw from it."[8]

He maintained that this was the only way that New Zealand could "strike a fatal blow at pauperism.... [and the] inadequate remedy of the poor laws.... [which he felt were a] blight upon the social scene" in Great Britain during the nineteenth century.[9]

George Grey of the Liberal Opposition maintained that subtle evils lurked behind Atkinson's plan:

> "It will sap the independence of the people so relieved, it will sap the relations between different members of a family ... it will sap the feelings of children to their parents."[10]

The ensuing conflict between Atkinson and Grey foreshadowed events that would occur in New Zealand 50 years later. Similar conflicts would also arise in other countries that would later try to introduce public financing for universal entitlement of health care.

Although Atkinson's motion was defeated, he persisted and re-submitted his proposal a year later when he became Prime Minister. The political price was high; the Atkinson Government suffered a serious defeat in the next election, and the national insurance plan collapsed.

Over the following years, public sector involvement in the financing of health care increased slowly. The Hospitals and Charitable Aid Act of 1885 drew a reluctant Government into a compromise arrangement of joint financing for the few existing private hospitals, voluntary hospitals and public hospitals. The Government agreed to meet "a reasonable" proportion of the running costs through general revenues.[11] By 1905, 48 hospitals were operating under this Act, serving a growing proportion of the population which had no other options for affordable health care. Despite these provisions, the isolation of New Zealand from the rest of the world and the inhospitable terrain of mountains and inlets made access to existing facilities difficult.

By the late nineteenth century, public hospitals were serving patients of all classes and had long ceased to be regarded as charitable institutions. In 1900, a fear of plague led to the creation of the Department of Public Health, the first of its kind in the world. The Department of Mental Hospitals and Department of Hospitals and Charitable Institutions were established in 1907. In an attempt to regionalize care, the Department of Hospitals and Department of Public Health merged, and the number of hospital districts was reduced in 1909. Through this process, public hospitals developed a broad base of popular support, although during the early years they continued using a means-test to determine who would receive free care.[12]

Despite such efforts, institutional care continued to be fragmented, and there were virtually no collective provisions for financing ambulatory care. Not many doctors could survive on the limited income they earned in private practice. At the turn of the century, health care outside an institutional setting failed to provide adequate coverage for New Zealand's population of 815,853 spread over the country's 268,103 square kilometers of mountains, inlets and islands.[13]

3. Friendly Societies

Over the next 40 years, public financing for social security and health care increased slowly in New Zealand as it did in most European countries. Specific measures were introduced to satisfy both idealistic and pragmatic objectives.

First, Governments hoped to use public financing for social security to indirectly redistribute the wealth of society to the aged, the disabled, widows, orphans and other needy sectors of the population.[14] Miners' pensions, workers' compensation and unemployment payments offered support to victims of economic and employment hazards. Sickness, accident and disability insurance offered hope of improving the quality of life and sharing the cost of illness.

Collective measures that bridged moments of hardship in the lifecycle were also intended to prevent social unrest and improve the productivity of the workforce. Local authorities, rate-payers and doctors, who in the past had complained that it was they who carried the financial burden of charity, welcomed initiatives by the central government which offered them some relief from this legacy.

The introduction of social security in New Zealand was, however, a fragmented and incomplete process. Old-age pension, financed through general revenues, was introduced in 1898, widows' pension in 1911, pension for the blind in 1924, family allowance in 1926 and invalidity pension and pension for deserted wives in 1936. New Zealand did not use means-tested social insurance but rather general revenues to finance these programs. Membership with friendly societies, on the other hand, remained low. By the late 1930s, such societies included only 20 percent of the population.[15]

During the Great Depression of the 1930s, only the independently wealthy and better-paid workers could afford the luxury of paying fee-for-service. Using a "Robin Hood" principle, doctors often overcharged the rich, claiming that this allowed them to offer cheaper and sometimes free treatment to the poor. Doctors in their private offices and public hospitals absorbed the fees for those who could not afford to pay. Both groups were anxious to explore alternative modes of financing.

The Department of Health reviewed the official proposals for national health insurance in Australia (1927), South Africa (1928), Canada (1932) and those of the British Medical Association (1930).[16] On several occasions, the Department debated the merits of introducing a national health insurance program similar to the Lloyd George Plan in Great Britain. New Zealand's Annual Conference of the Hospital Boards supported a proposal of this kind in 1924 and 1929.[17] The New Zealand branch of the British Medical Association proposed its own plan during the late 1920s, anticipating the financial advantages for its members.[18]

However, since the rural population would receive few benefits from a Lloyd George industrial-type plan, popular support for such a program was lacking. "Conditions in New Zealand, and the outlook of our people are so different from those in overseas countries that no existing programme could be adopted in toto."[19]

Instead, a fragmented system of financing of health care was maintained well into the twentieth century in New Zealand, at a time when Great Britain and other European countries were offering extensive protection through social insurance. Major social upheavals and political reforms were necessary to change the course of history. The Great Depression and the election of New Zealand's Labour Government triggered these changes.

B. LANDMARK LEGISLATIVE REFORMS

1. General Election of 1935

The Social Democratic Party, forerunner to New Zealand's Labour Party, had called for free hospital treatment, sickness insurance and pension for orphans, the blind and the disabled in 1914.[20] The Labour Party continued this commitment to free health care, pensions and unemployment benefits. In 1921, the party slogan, created as a response to the economic hardships of the 1920s, included "free" medical attention.

By 1934, a rise in the price of wool had improved economic conditions in New Zealand.[21] Many people, however, continued to harbor a fear that the cost of health care and hospitalization would impoverish them. The poor resented their lot as recipients of handouts from doctors; the medical profession likewise begrudged the burden of involuntary charity imposed on them. Rate-payers wished to be relieved of subsidies that they paid for public hospital beds and social assistance.

Not surprisingly, every political party in the country, sensitive to an issue with immense popular support, developed proposals for some form of national health plan in anticipation of the 1935 elections. The Coalition Government of Prime Minister Joseph Gordon Coates called for a state health service as part of its election platform. The program would include a general practitioner service, specialists, dentists and maternity benefits.

Before the election, the Government established an Interdepartmental Committee on Compulsory National Superannuation and Health Insurance.[22] The committee called for a major reform and consolidation of the splintered social security system. The existing system was deemed disorganized and costly.[23] Contributions based on actuarial calculations from workers and employers as well as state subsidies would finance the proposed national program. A means-test would exclude the rich and self-employed from collecting benefits.

The Labour Party's election platform likewise called for major social reforms. If elected, the party promised to introduce guaranteed prices, a minimum wage, improved educational services and a national health and superannuation plan. Health care would include free family doctors, specialists and hospitals. The state would provide "non-contributory, universal, comprehensive and adequate" services as a civil right to all Inhabitants.[24] Although the radicals in the party wanted to "soak the rich" by forcing employers to finance the whole program, the final official platform called for financing through general revenues.

In 1935, New Zealand elected its first Labour Government. The personal popularity of Michael Joseph Savage, the new Prime Minister, had secured massive support for the party.[25] In contrast to more radical forms of socialism that had swept across Europe, Savage believed in a humanitarian socialism which rejected bloody revolution.

Peter Fraser became the Minister of Health and Education (later wartime Prime Minister), Walter Nash became the Minister of Finance and Dr. D. G. McMillan became the spokesman on health. The Labor Caucus was split between those who supported acceptance of continued colonial economic status and those advocating freedom from such dependence.[26] Savage, Fraser and Nash, known as the "Savage Trinity", believed in maintaining historical links with Britain and continuing international payments.[27] H. T. Armstrong, J. A. Lee and McMillan, members of the left wing of the Caucus, wanted to introduce a more radical socialist economy.

McMillan's social views were formed while he worked in contract practice for various unions. His ideas on a national health program were first outlined at the Labour Party Conference of 1935. The blueprint of his plan was later published in a pamphlet entitled *A National Health Service.*[28] It called for universal entitlement, free access, comprehensive services, local clinics, prevention, and income replacement during illness. Prevention would include good housing, adequate nutrition and healthy physical and emotional surroundings. A "non-contributory insurance" would finance the program.[29]

Several of McMillan's ideas were revolutionary for their time. His convictions and skill as a public speaker provided the Government's opponents with a formidable adversary. But his failure to design his plan in collaboration with the medical profession and his attachment to the Labour Party made him increasingly unpopular with the New Zealand branch of the British Medical Association, even though the Prime Minister and the left wing of the Caucus supported his proposals.[30]

Peter Fraser, Minister of Health and Education, had a gentler manner and was more compromising in nature. He shunned the more controversial debates over health care during the early years in government, letting McMillan push the party line with his colleagues. This allowed Fraser to devote his attention to improving education, particularly among the Maori people.[31] He also acted as Prime Minister during the frequent periods when Savage was indisposed due to terminal bowel cancer.

Walter Nash, Minister of Finance, believed that society had "obligations towards the old and infirm because of their work ... [and] obligations towards the young ... to make a still better world tomorrow."[32] He also supported McMillan's call for universal entitlement and free access to a national health service. Nash, however, deeply distrusted doctors. He was aggressive, "at times leaning on the doctors none too lightly" during negotiations.[33] This abrasive approach unfortunately stirred much unnecessary resentment and did little to secure the cooperation of the medical profession during the later stages of negotiations.[34]

2. International Communist and Socialist Influence

Critics of the Labour Party's health platform were quick to accuse the Government of trying to introduce a communist system of socialized medicine in New Zealand.[35] The medical profession quickly jumped on this bandwagon. Even radical socialists wanted to distance themselves from the great social upheavals occurring in Eastern Europe during the early twentieth century and were horrified by the rumors of Stalin's purges during the mid-1930s.

In reality, the health care policies of the seven European countries of the communist bloc were less progressive that those proposed in New Zealand. As was described in the introduction, a well-developed system of social insurance provided health care for urban workers long before the onset of communist rule in Eastern Europe.[36] In financing universal access through general revenues, early developments in health care in these countries following the Bolshevik revolution focused on strengthening the existing social insurance systems, transferring the administrative responsibilities to trade unions and improving services for industrial workers, thereby redistributing the existing scarce resources. Initially, those on either side of the working age, as well as farmers, housewives and the unemployed, remained without protection.

Even when free health care became recognized as a civic right in many of the communist bloc countries, limited resources prevented universal access, especially to rural populations. In practice, tipping continued and black markets thrived. None therefore offered a functioning universal entitlement that New Zealand could use as a model for its ambitious plans in 1938, although New Zealand's Minister of Finance, Walter Nash, may not have been aware of this subtlety during his visit to Moscow in 1937.

3. National Health Insurance Committee of 1935

The New Zealand branch of the British Medical Association maintained close communication with its British parent body. During the early years, most of New Zealand's doctors were trained in England and Scotland; during later years most went to Britain for advanced education. In this context, it was not surprising that the New Zealand branch quickly turned to Britain for guidance on how to deal with the Labour Government's planned legislation for creating a National Health Service.

As an early strategy, the New Zealand Association established a National Health Insurance Committee in 1935 to conduct an extensive assessment of the health needs of the country. Dr. J. P. S. Jamieson, its Chairman, was a Shetland Islander and surgeon of modest means. The personal financial price which he endured during subsequent years proved his commitment to his appointment. His "pertinacious personality" and leadership would soon pose a serious challenge to the Government.[37]

Dr. H. Guy Dain, the Chairman of the British Medical Association, visited New Zealand shortly after negotiations started between the Government and the medical profession. Dain was known as an advocate of the British panel system and was described as an "encyclopedia" of health insurance knowledge.[38] Dr. G. F. McCleary, the Chief Medical Officer for Health Insurance in the British Ministry of Health and author of a book on Britain's national health insurance, was an advocate of the Lloyd George Plan. He also visited New Zealand to advise its doctors.[39] During the more difficult stages of negotiations in 1937, Henry Brackenbury, Vice-President of the British Medical Association (later Chairman), was asked to come to New Zealand to offer his advice.

Brackenbury had played a significant role in the Lloyd George Plan in England and had worked with the old "fourpenny club," "sixpenny club" and "panel systems." As a result, he advocated a contributory national health insurance program with remuneration on a capitation basis. He regarded this as "payment proportional to the responsibility undertaken," while he accused the fee-for-service system of "reducing practice to the status of selling packets of goods over the counter."[40] The New Zealand Association, however, preferred fees-for-service. The medical profession was, therefore, unhappy about Brackenbury's recommendations and at times "had to discipline old 'Brack' a bit ... to emphasize and what not to say, even if he thought it."[41]

In June 1937, the New Zealand Association published its proposal which called for a contributory plan with a means-test dividing the population into four different groups based on income.[42] The profession wanted to introduce a system whereby those with reasonable financial means would pay while the poor and disabled would receive free treatment, financed through public funds: "To expect the medical profession to treat the unemployed and their dependents free of cost is an unjust tax upon one section of the community."[43] Their proposal sparked immediate indignation from both the population and the Labour Government: "Anything more out of touch with public opinion than a scheme of charity, when the public wanted social security, is hard to imagine."[44]

Jamieson, however, also called upon the Government to direct its efforts toward preventive medicine: "You have huge institutions which aren't necessary, huge staffs which aren't necessary, and if there was a system by which these people could secure treatment which could be given to them in their homes, it would be of benefit to everybody."[45]

The Government and the medical profession had by this time became so hostile to each other that even constructive proposals fell on deaf ears. As a result of these events, the Government, in formulating its plan, ignored both the Zealand Medical Association's self-serving demands and Jamieson's constructive recommendations for greater emphasis on ambulatory care and prevention.

4. Parliamentary Investigation Committee of 1937

In keeping with the Labour Party's 1935 election promises, Fraser appointed McMillan as Chairman of a Parliamentary Investigation Committee on National Health and Superannuation. The committee was charged with drafting the proposal for such a plan, although its terms of reference did not include a mandate to establish a national health service. Through its work, it consulted hospital boards, friendly societies, health insurance groups, doctors, medical schools, other health professionals and anyone who wanted to express an opinion on the future health plan.[46]

In September 1937, B. C. Ashwin and J. S. Reid from the Treasury Department prepared a separate inter-departmental report before Nash's Cabinet Committee had finished its work. Ashwin and Reid estimated that universal superannuation, other pensions and a non-means-tested health service would cost the country £30 million. Income from general revenues, however, added only £20 million to the Treasury in 1937.[47] Nash kept these sobering estimates confidential while looking for other options for financing the Labour Government's social security reform.

As the Government prepared the plans for the future national health service, its silence on the matter was interpreted by the doctors as a lack of consultation. This became yet another point of conflict that soured the relationship between the two parties. Negotiations were characterized by Jamieson's intransigence, McMillan's hostile campaigning and Nash's paranoid distrust for the profession. Fraser's conciliatory efforts were to no avail as relations between the medical profession and the Government deteriorated. By 1937, negotiations had all but come to a standstill.

Interest groups other than the medical profession also opposed the Government's plans. The friendly societies and the private hospitals rightfully feared that a national health service would put them out of business. Although the latter two groups were in themselves too weak and poorly organized to pose a direct challenge to the Government, they joined with the medical profession to form a powerful conservative right wing-lobby, opposing anything that could be perceived as socialized medicine.[48]

With the help of W. H. Watt, Director General of Health, McMillan submitted his Parliamentary Committee Report on September 4, 1937. His report called for universal entitlement and free access to a national health service: "Any scheme which ... divides the people into two groups, those able to pay private fees and those unable to do so ... would be foreign to ... the people of New Zealand in general."[49]

According to McMillan's proposal, the program would be introduced in two phases. During the first phase, the plan would offer general practitioner services, maternity care, anesthetics, laboratories, pharmaceutical benefits, hospital treatment, dental care and research and medical education. During the second phase, the plan would add specialist consultations, home care, physiotherapy, pre-hospital transport, additional dental care and optical benefits. A central administration would run the program through local branches.

The committee recommended that insurance contributions from those who could afford to pay should finance the future program. It upheld the principle that everyone should be eligible for full benefits regardless of their ability to contribute and that the new program should pay doctors a capitation free for their services.[50] Many of these recommendations were in direct conflict with those made by the Medical Association's National Health Insurance Committee which earlier had released its report in June 1937.

5. Select Committee on National Health and Superannuation of 1937

Shortly after McMillan released his report, the House of Representatives established a Select Committee on National Health and Superannuation to prepare the Social Security Bill. Rev. A. H. Nordmeyer, a close friend of McMillan, became Chairman of the committee, while R. S. Wogan was nominated as Secretary.[51] During the early phases of its work, the committee gathered evidence from various interest groups such as the British Medical Association, the Farmers' Union, the Federation of Labour, the Associated Chambers of Commerce, the Life Offices' Association of New Zealand and municipal associations.

The committee explored three options for the future national health service: a general practitioner services with universal entitlement; a comprehensive service with a means-tested target group; and a comprehensive service with universal entitlement, financed through general revenues. Both Nash and Fraser supported the third option. Fraser agreed, believing that such a program would be easier to finance and administer than a limited plan. It would also be consistent with the Labour Party's political platform.

The New Zealand Medical Association, however, continued to demand that the Government limit public funding to a means-tested target population which could not afford to pay for health care. Such a plan would free doctors and hospitals of their charity function to the poor, while encouraging those who could afford to pay for their own health care to do so. Although Fraser was prepared to negotiate with the doctors, Nash refused to compromise. Since Nash had the support of the Prime Minister and the left wing of the Caucus, negotiations between the Government and the medical profession reached an impasse by December 1937.

Although Nash had originally wanted to finance the full social security plan through general revenues, he had to satisfy the London financiers who controlled New Zealand's foreign borrowing as well as the critics in his own treasury department.[52] Ashwin and Reid of the Treasury Department, who earlier had submitted their pessimistic inter-departmental report on the projected cost of the future social security program, felt that contributory financing based on actuarial principles would be easier to control than a program financed exclusively through general revenues.

As early as 1936, Nash had made a diplomatic gesture by consulting Walter Kinnear, Controller of Health and Unemployment Insurance at the British Ministry of Health. He also sought the advice of Godfrey Ince, Chief Insurance Officer at the Ministry of Labour. When the British Actuary, George Maddex, was asked how the plan should be financed, Nash declined to give a direct answer: "With all respect, I think that is an unfair question to address to the actuary."[53] All three influenced the Labour Government's final choice for financing the future New Zealand social security reform.[54]

As a compromise, the National Health and Superannuation Committee suggested that the health benefits, which would cost £17,850,000, could be financed through a combined 1 percent levy on income yielding £7,500,000, a flat membership contribution of £1 per head per annum yielding £500,000 and a Consolidated Fund contribution of £9,850,000. This would represent a £2,355,000 increase in outlay to the Social Assistance Consolidated Fund above the outlay in the previous financial year 1938–1939. The committee concluded that the purpose of the "scheme [was] simply to provide a more equitable distribution of the national income."[55] The self-employed, such as farmers and owners of small businesses, would be covered under the plan, but the details of how to collect contributions from such groups were not specified.[56]

The left wing of the Caucus, which included Armstrong, Lee and McMillan, rejected the proposal: "We were prepared to make concessions regarding the levy on incomes but we were not prepared to limit our pension scheme to the interest on accumulated funds."[57] They therefore rejected Nash's "complex tables" and "beautiful material."[58] As a result of this internal conflict, the provisions for financing the program had to be modified before drafting the final Social Security Bill.

6. Social Security Act of 1938

Despite protests from the medical profession, the Government presented its White Paper in April 1938. The Social Security Bill was introduced on August 11, 1938, and the Social Security Act passed in the House of Representatives on September 8, 1938. The Pensions Department and the Employment Promotion branch of the Department of Labour would join to form a new Department of Social Security which would administer the consolidated and simplified social security program.

Part III of the Act, which dealt with the medical provisions, was revolutionary for its day. It called for public financing for universal entitlement to health care which would be introduced in two stages.[59] Phase I would be introduced on April 1, 1939, providing free access to general practitioner services, hospitals, sanatoriums, pharmaceuticals and maternity benefits for the whole population. Phase II, designed to follow when public financing became available, would provide free access to anesthetic services, laboratories, diagnostic radiology services, consultation by specialists, pre-hospital transport and dental care. The program also called for health promotion, prevention, home nursing and domestic help for the ill.[60]

Individual registration fees, charges on individual income and contributions from the newly established Social Security Fund, would finance the plan.[61] The Commissioner of Taxes would assess and collect the social security charges according to the rates applicable to those liable for payment.[62] All persons over 16 years of age were required to register, and a penalty was set for evaders. Exemptions were defined precisely, and it became an offense to employ unregistered persons.[63] Charges on salaries, wages and other income would finance the contributory part of the program.

New Zealand's social security reform captured the imagination of both the local population and people in other countries whose memories of the personal hardships suffered during the Depression were still fresh. The British playwright Bernard Shaw wrote: "[New Zealand legislators] struck me as men who knew the nature of the task that confronted them and had the ability to see it through."[64] The British Labour Party MP, Ernest Bevin, praised the reform when he visited New Zealand in 1938 and was outraged that British doctors had helped the New Zealand Association in their propaganda campaign against the reform.[65]

Believing that their reforms were popular, the Labour Government called a general election eight days after passing the Social Security Act. On October 15, 1938, the Labour Party was returned with an increased majority.[66] The Opposition National Party did not challenge any major aspects of the act during the election.[67]

The medical profession, however, was determined to fight the health care reforms: "It is our duty to oppose to the uttermost this ill-conceived measure so strongly tainted by party politics."[68] Despite the doctors' lack of cooperation, wide application of the institutional benefits became possible immediately because general hospitals and mental hospitals were already financed through public funds when the reform took place. Free treatment in mental hospitals was introduced in April 1939, free maternity services in May 1939 and free in-patient treatment in public hospitals in July 1939. Doctors in these hospitals became salaried workers rather than honorary appointees, a development which few found objectionable since it allowed them a stable additional income.

The Government, however, remained unsuccessful in its negotiations. The Medical Association's National Health Insurance Committee argued that the health and welfare of the population and the welfare of doctors were inseparable. It claimed that it was in the interest of the patient to pay his doctor because "satisfactory attendance to the sick depends upon the private and personal relationship between the patient and his doctor."[69] The medical profession, therefore, remained intransigent: "Evolution, not revolution, was what was required."[70]

Fraser warned the Medical Association that, unless it cooperated, the Government would create a state medical service.[71] With 25 percent of doctors on overseas military duty, however, no one took this threat seriously; it would have been impossible for the overworked doctors who remained in New Zealand to staff such a service. Later, protracted negotiations met with failure and the general practitioner service, called for under the Social Security Act of 1938, was never established.[72]

7. Social Security Amendment Bill of 1941

In 1940, Fraser became acting Prime Minister, replacing Savage whose health had deteriorated. The social and economic hardships created at this time by World War II were putting the Labour Government under considerable political pressure to implement the remaining provisions called for under the Social Security Act of 1938, including its health care benefits. Fraser at this point appointed H. T. Armstrong as the new Minister of Health and Education, hoping to utilize his new Minister's talents as a negotiator in dealing with the medical profession.[73]

Despite protest from McMillan, Nash, Nordmeyer and most of the Cabinet, Fraser and Armstrong proposed a general practitioner service which would allow five different options for paying doctors. The program offered the following payment choices: salaries, capitation, direct fee-for-service, refunds to patients following direct fee-for-service payments to doctors, refunds to doctors following bulk-billing for services rendered to patients and "tokens" and "tips" under the latter two.

The pressures imposed by World War II and the conciliatory approach of Fraser and Armstrong finally broke the previously deadlocked negotiations. Under these terms, the medical profession agreed to participate in the national program, and in September 1941, the Social Security Amendment Bill containing these options was introduced.[74] It passed in the House of Representatives on November 1, 1941.[75] The reform made New Zealand the first western developed country with a market economy to offer public financing for universal entitlement to comprehensive health care.

C. CONTINUED POLICY REFORM PROCESS

1. Hostages to History

New Zealand's Social Security Act of 1938 and Social Security Amendment Act of 1941 eliminated reliance on charity for the financing of health care. The provisions of the reform, however, were introduced in a piecemeal fashion. Hospital out-patient benefits, pharmaceutical benefits and partial general medical services were introduced in 1941. Physiotherapy was introduced in 1942, district nursing and domestic help in 1944, laboratory services in 1946, dental benefits and prosthesis in 1947, specialists' consultations in 1969 and accident benefits and nurse practitioner services in 1974.

The varied and complex modes of paying for the General Practitioner Services led to chaos. During the initial period of trying to implement the refund system, 30 percent of claims were inaccurately completed by patients, leading to incorrect refunds.[76] Erosion in coverage occurred because doctors charged more than the Government was willing to refund, and because they supplemented their official income with extra charges.[77] The principles behind public financing, universal entitlement and comprehensive services were quickly lost. Patients could not afford the various "tokens", "tips" and "incomplete refunds" needed to access hospitals services.

The New Zealand branch of the British Medical Association gave the unfortunate impression that doctors "were concerned solely with their own financial interests and not with the health of the community."[78] The 1,000 members of the medical profession blocked what the electorate had emphatically endorsed in 1938, thereby creating a class-structured health care system.[79] Only a few rebels broke ranks with the profession: "A cynic amongst us once said 'We are not the doctors, we are the disease.'"[80] The long-term dangers of a refund system with its inevitable erosion in coverage were not recognized in 1941.[81]

2. From the 1950s to the 1980s

By the post war period when most other countries were just beginning to experiment with universal health coverage, New Zealand already had several decades of experience and growing pains.[82,83]

In line with the right-leaning National Party Government at that time, the 1953 Consultative Committee on Health Reform ('the Barrowclough Committee') recommended that private hospital beds supplement services provided by the public sector. The Hospitals Act 1957 recommended that the Minister of Health (rather than individual hospital boards) would have ultimate responsibility for hospital and health services.

Although recommendations to restructure hospital boards and health services under a 1969 Department of Health Review of Hospital and Related Services in New Zealand were not implemented immediately due to changes in the government, elements from this review were picked up later. Likewise, the main recommendations from the 1974 White Paper on A Health Service for New Zealand, were not implemented immediately. It outlined a need for more integration of the health services, emphasis on health promotion and greater equity in access across socio-economic groups.

The right-leaning National Party which held office from 1975 to 1984 set up a Special Advisory Committee on Health Services Organization, which proposed the establishment of 14 regional "Area Health Boards" and continued active private sector engagement.

3. Major Policy Updates in New Zealand Since the 1980s

Since the 1980s, the New Zealand health system has continued to evolve. Starting with what was essentially a fully publicly funded and publicly owned national health service at the beginning of the twentieth century, several post-war reforms introduced more market-based approaches to both funding and delivery of health care, creating a mixed public–private.[84–86]

Many of the early reforms of the 1980s focused more on reshuffling the deck of the Health Boards in different configurations than on anything fundamental entitlement, coverage and funding. But later, under the 4th Labor Government that were elected in 1984–1990 (under the leadership of David Lange, later Jeoffrey Palmer and finally Mike Moore), New Zealand introduce a number of world-famous economic and public sector reforms that applied private business discipline into the public sector. Many of these reforms, originally designed for other parts of the public sector, eventually also reached the health sector during the early 1990s.

Several noteworthy reforms included: (a) the State-Owned Enterprises Act 1986 (to restructure government departments into more business-like); (b) the State Sector Act 1988 (to introduce managerial and performance benchmarks into the public sector; and (c) and the Public Finance Act 1989 (to improve the incentives used in financial management in government departments).

Two health policy reviews defined implications for the health sector. The 1986 Health Benefits Review (led by Scott, Fougere & Marwick, 1986) and the 1988 Hospital and Related Services Taskforce (led by Gibbs, Fraser & Scott, 1988), outlined five options for the government's role funding health care. Although neither of the recommendations from these reforms were enacted under the Labor government which recommended them, they sent shock waves through the world in terms of a new way of thinking about funding and delivering health care in the public sector. Like in the UK under the Margaret Thatcher reforms, they set the scene separating the purchasing and provision of health care under a national health service model.

The National Party government that was elected in 1990 finally implemented the reforms through the 1993 Health and Disability Services Act. It was during this period that New Zealand pioneered the famous "new public sector" management approaches, with a focus on greater managerial accountability, market-based economic incentives, and greater competition among providers. Four regional health authorities (RHAs) were given a budget to purchase health and disability services for their geographic regions from a mix of public and private providers. The previous 14 Area Health Boards were transformed inot 23 commercial Crown Health Enterprises (CHEs) which were to that become responsible for running hospitals, community and public health services.[87]

Innovative as they were, the reforms challenged the established way of delivering health care through the public sector and were therefore soon met with a range of resistance from providers and the population. Before clear gains could be demonstrated, concerns were raised about the cost of the reforms, purchasing practices and the role of competition rather than cooperation in delivering health care.

By 1996, when the National Party and the smaller New Zealand First party formed a new coalition government, the momentum of the market-based reforms had been lost, with a Shift back to a more national health service approach. The four Regional Health Authorities were abolished on 30 June 1997 with a transfer of their function to a Transitional Health Authority called the Health Funding Authority (HFA) on 1 January 1998. The HFA continued the split between purchase and provision but as a monopsony rather than competitive purchaser. The CHEs were transformed into 23 Hospital and Health Services (HHSs). Health care organizations became independent legal and financial entities and were required to operate as commercial business entities (i.e. balance their budget and not run deficits)

When a Labour–Alliance coalition government was elected in 1999, they enacted the New Zealand Public Health and Disability Act 2000, which led to yet another major reorganization of the health sector, with a re-establishment of 21 District Health Boards (DHBs) to replace the HHSs and the HFA. The new DHBs and Ministry of Health (MOH) once again become responsible for planning and funding of all health services

This swing of the pendulum back and forth between a greater and lesser involvement of the state and market forces in the health sector continued during the first decade of the new Millennium. Prime Minister Bill English who became the leader of the 9th National Government on December 12, 2016 is known for his conservative views on social issues. It is still too early to know if this will usher in a new era of more market-based reforms in New Zealand.

ENDNOTES

1. D. G. McMillan, *A National Health Service in the New Zealand of Tomorrow* (Wellington: New Zealand Labour Party, 1935): 7.
2. J. B. Condliffe, *The Welfare State in New Zealand* (London: George Allen & Unwin, 1959): 323; W. Brunton, "Hostages to history," *New Zealand Health Review*, (1983): 3; and W.B. Sutch, *The Quest for Security in New Zealand: 1800 to 1966* (London: Oxford University Press, 1966).
3. These included the infirm, sick, old, widowed, displaced peasants, ex-soldiers, servants without masters, abandoned children and beggars.
4. Editorial, *New Zealand Medical Journal*, December (1932); and J. B. Lovell-Smith, *The New Zealand Doctor and the Welfare State* (Auckland: Blackwood & Janet Paul, 1966): 16.
5. Brunton, "Hostages to history," p. 3
6. Lovell-Smith, *New Zealand Doctor*, p. 11.
7. J. Rutherford, *Sir George Grey, K.C.B., 1812–1898: A Study in Colonial Government* (London: Cassell & Company, 1961): ix.
8. New Zealand, "Atkinson," *Parliamentary Debates 41* (Wellington: King's Printer, 1882): 191; and Lovell-Smith, *New Zealand Doctor*, p. 11.
9. From Harry Atkinson's National Insurance Proposal of 1882. See New Zealand, "Atkinson," p. 191.
10. New Zealand, "Atkinson," p. 112; and Lovell-Smith, *New Zealand Doctor*, p. 11.
11. New Zealand, Governmental Investigation Committee into National Health Insurance (GICNHI), "Report," *Parliamentary Papers* (Wellington: King's Printer, 1935).

12. New Zealand, National Health Insurance and Superannuation Committee (NHISC), "Report [Chairman Rev. A.H. Nordmeyer],"*Parliamentary Papers* (Wellington: King's Printer, 1938): 7.
13. The population for 1901 is based on United Nations (UN), Statistics Office (SO), Department of Economic and Social Affairs (DESA), *Demographic Yearbook* 1962, 14th Edition (New York: UN, 1962): 283; and the area is based on J. Paxton, ed., *The Statesman's Year-Book: Statistical and Historical Annual of the States of the World for the Year* 1986–1987, 123rd Edition (London: MacMillan Press, 1986): 879.
14. W. B. Sutch, *The Responsible Society in New Zealand* (Christchurch: Whitcombe & Tombs, 1971): 33.
15. W. H. Oliver, "The origins and growth of the welfare state," in *Social Welfare and New Zealand Society*, by A. D. Trlin, ed. (New Zealand: Methuen, 1977): 13.
16. British Medical Journal, "British Medical Association's proposals for a general medical service for the nation," Supplement, *British Medical Journal*, 26 April (1930). The *British Medical Journal* published a similar proposal in 1938.
17. Lovell-Smith, *New Zealand Doctor*, p. 19; and Combined Hospital Boards Association, "Report," *Annual Reports* (Wellington: Combined Hospital Boards Association, 1929).
18. New Zealand Medical Journal, "National health insurance," *New Zealand Medical Journal* 34(1935): 291.
19. New Zealand, National Health Insurance Investigation Committee (NHIIC), "Report [Chairman D.G. McMillan]," *Parliamentary Papers* (Wellington: Parliament, 1937): 11.
20. The Labour Party was formed from the Social Democratic Party.
21. J. Thorn, *Peter Fraser. New Zealand's Wartime Prime Minister* (London: Odham's Press, 1952): 106.
22. The report was compiled by senior civil servants from the Public Service Commission, Treasury, the National Provident Fund and the Pensions, Actuary's and Health Departments.
23. Under the existing system, cash benefits for superannuation, sickness, invalidity, widows, orphans, children and pregnant women were all separate. New Zealand, Appendices H-30, *Journals of the House*, September (1935), quoted in Sutch, *Responsible Society*, p. 45.
24. E. A. Hanson, "The social security story: A study of the political origins of the 1938 Social Security Act," Master's Thesis (Auckland: University of Auckland, 1975): 49.

25. K. Sinclair, *Walter Nash* (Auckland: Auckland University Press, 1976): 161.
26. Sutch, *Responsible Society*, p. 41.
27. P. Fraser, Walter Nash and Paddy Webb formed the pre-election "Trinity". See J. A. Lee, *Simple on a Soap-Box* (Auckland: Collins, 1963): 32.
28. McMillan, *National Health Service.*
29. Funds for the non-contributory insurance used to finance the various social security programmes derived from general revenues. See Oliver, "Origins and growth," p. 19.
30. Sinclair, *Walter Nash*, p. 160; and Lovell-Smith, *New Zealand Doctor*, p. 38. McMillan and Dr. D. Robb believed in the public health approach, rare at the time. See D. Robb, *Medicine and Health in New Zealand: A Retrospect and A Prospect* (Christchurch: Whitcombe & Tombs, 1941); and D. Robb, *Health Reform in New Zealand* (Christchurch: Whitcombe & Tombs, 1947).
31. Thorn, *Peter Fraser*, p. 147.
32. W. Nash, *New Zealand: A Working Democracy* (London: Dent & Sons, 1943): 176.
33. Sinclair, *Walter Nash*, p. 163.
34. In his personal life, he "never said anything harsher than 'dash'." Lee, *Soap-Box*, p. 23.
35. Lovell-Smith, *New Zealand Doctor*, p. 49, 55, 74.
36. COMECON is the unofficial abbreviation for CMEA (Council for Mutual Economic Assistance). The founding members were USSR, Bulgaria, Czechoslovakia, Hungary, Poland and Romania. Later admissions were Albania (1949–1961), German Democratic Republic (1950), Mongolia (1962), Cuba (1972), Vietnam (1978), Yugoslavia, Afghanistan, Angola, Ethiopia, Laos, Mexico, Mozambique, Nicaragua and the People's Democratic Republic of Yemen attend as observers. See J. Paxton, *Statesman's Year-Book* (1986–1987): 48.
37. Lovell-Smith, *New Zealand Doctor*, p. 26; and Sinclair, *Walter Nash*, p. 161.
38. New Zealand branch of British Medical Association, National Health Insurance Committee (NHIC), "Interview with members of the British delegation to the Melbourne conference," Supplement, *New Zealand Medical Journal* October (1935): 10–15. Dain would later play a major part in the negotiations between the British Medical Association and the Government during the creation of the British National Health Service.
39. G. F. McCleary, "Report of an address on 14 February 1936," Supplement, *New Zealand Medical Journal* (June 1936): 18.
40. New Zealand branch of the British Medical Association, National Health Insurance Committee (NHIC), "Report," *New Zealand Medical Journal*, December (1937): 42–48; and Lovell-Smith, *New Zealand Doctor*, p. 60.

41. Lovell-Smith, *New Zealand Doctor*, p. 61.
42. New Zealand branch of British Medical Association, National Health Insurance Committee (NHIC) "Suggested scheme of payment for services rendered," Supplement, *New Zealand Medical Journal* (1937): 21–24.
43. C. E. Hercus, "Health insurance in New Zealand," *New Zealand Medical Journal* 34(1935): 90.
44. Sinclair, *Walter Nash*, 161.
45. Jamieson addressing the Napier to Hawkes Bay Division of the New Zealand branch of the British Medical Association on March 14, 1937, quoted in Lovell-Smith, *New Zealand Doctor*, 36.
46. The doctors were coached by the New Zealand Medical Association on how to respond to a questionnaire that was distributed by the Government.
47. Hanson, "Social security," pp. 57–58; and Sinclair, *Walter Nash*, p. 132, 160.
48. Sinclair, *Walter Nash*, p. 162.
49. New Zealand, NHIIC, "D. G. McMillan," p. 13.
50. The term "contributory" referred to a special tax in New Zealand.
51. New Zealand, Select Committee on National Health and Superannuation (SCNHS), "Report," *Parliamentary Papers* (Wellington: King's Printer, 1938). Members included the following: Atmore and Cobbe (United Party), Kyle (Reform Party), Holland (Reform Party), Nash and Savage (Labour) and others. B. C. Ashwin and J. S. Reid from Treasury Department (Conservatives), and G.H. Maddox from England joined as experts; Dr. M. H. Watt, A. D. Keisenberg, and C. E. Wynne represented the Department of Health.
52. Sutch, *Responsible Society*, p. 41.
53. New Zealand, SCNHS, "Report," Minutes, Volume 2; and Sutch, *Responsible Society*, p. 61.
54. Sinclair, *Walter Nash*, p. 164; Hanson, "Social security," p. 102. The misnomer "social insurance" to describe financing originating from general revenues in New Zealand may have been an attempt to appease critics in London.
55. New Zealand, SCNHS, "Report," p. 18.
56. New Zealand, SCNHS, "Report," Minutes, Volume 2.
57. Lee, *Soap-Box*, p. 98.
58. Lee Msss, 441/22, quoted in Sinclair, Walter Nash, p. 164.
59. New Zealand, SCNHS, "Report," p. 5.
60. New Zealand, "Social Security Act," *Statutes* (Wellington: Parliament, 1938): Part III, pp. 77–104.
61. Although the radicals in the Caucus tried to block funding superannuation through a consolidated fund, such financing was maintained as a partial

source of financing for health care. The assets of the Employment Promotion Fund would be transferred to the Social Security Fund.

62. Collection would include the issuing of a Social Security Stamp.
63. New Zealand, "Social Security Act," pp. 102–35.
64. Letter by Bernard Shaw quoted in Thorn, *Peter Fraser*, p. 159.
65. W. Beveridge would later formulate a similar comprehensive social security reform for Great Britain.
66. Elections in 1943 and 1946 returned the Labour Party with a reduced majority compared with the 1938 election results.
67. The Opposition did not challenge the act in two later general elections. See Robb, *Health Reform*, p. 25; and Sutch, *Responsible Society*, p. 60.
68. British Medical Journal, "General medical service," p. 242.
69. New Zealand branch of British Medical Association, National Health Insurance Committee (NHIC), "Minutes, 11 March 1935," Supplement, *New Zealand Medical Journal*, April (1936): 12.
70. Sinclair, *Walter Nash*, p. 162.
71. *Dominion*, 31 May (1939), quoted in Lovell-Smith, *New Zealand Doctor*, p. 103.
72. Reports opposing the reform issued by the Medical Association's National Health Insurance Committee appeared at regular intervals in the *New Zealand Medical Journal* from 1938 to 1940.
73. While Minister of Labour, Armstrong had been known as a skilful conciliator.
74. J. Thorn, *Peter Fraser*, p. 158; and Sinclair, *Walter Nash*, p. 196.
75. New Zealand, "Social Security Amendment Act," *Statutes*, November 1 (Wellington: Parliament, 1941).
76. Lovell-Smith, *New Zealand Doctor*, p. 151; and Robb, *Health Reform*, p. 20.
77. They would charge 3s from the patient and claim 7s 6d from the Social Security Fund, thereby resulting in a total payment of 10s 6d.
78. D. Stark Murray, *Health For All* (London: Victor Gallancz, 1942): 44.
79. B. Easton, *Social Policy and the Welfare State in New Zealand* (Sydney: George Allen & Unwin, 1979): 139.
80. Robb, *Medicine*, viii; and W. B. Sutch, "Introduction," in *The Future of New Zealand Medicine: A Progressive Viewpoint*, by D. W. Beaven and B. H. Easton, eds. (Christchurch: N.M. Peryer, 1974): 6.
81. Had the Labour Government examined the problems which the refund system had created for sickness funds in the Nordic countries, especially in

Norway during the 1920s, Fraser and Armstrong might have been more reluctant to introduce to such a system in New Zealand in 1941.

82. R. Gauld, *Revolving Doors: New Zealand's Health Reforms — The Continuing Saga*, 2nd ed. (Wellington:Health Services Research Centre and Institute of Policy Studies, School of Government, Victoria University of Wellington, 2009).
83. J. Cumming, J. McDonald, C. Barr, G. Martin, Z. Gerring, and J. Daubé, *New Zealand: Health System Review in Health Systems in Transition*, 2014, 4(2):1 – 272. http://www.wpro.who.int/asia_pacific_observatory/hits/series/Nez_Health_Systems_Review.pdf. Accessed July 25, 2017.
84. R. Gauld, "Beyond New Zealand's dual health reforms," *Social Policy & Administration* 33(5)(1999):567–585.
85. R. Gauld, "One step forward, one step back? Restructuring, evolving policy, and information management and technology in the New Zealand health sector," *Government Information Quarterly* 21(2)(2004):125–142.
86. R. Gauld, *Revolving Doors: New Zeland's Health Reforms — the Continuing Saga*, 2nd ed. Wellington, (2009, Wellington: Health Services Research Centre and Institute of Policy Studies, School of Government, Victoria University of Wellington).
87. G. Scott, L. McKenzie and J. Webster, "Maladjustments in the Corporatization Model: Hospital Reform in New Zealand, in A. S. Preker and A. Harding, eds. *Innovations in Health Service Delivery : The Corporatization of Public Hospitals*, (2003, Washington, DC: World Bank). https://openknowledge.worldbank.org/handle/10986/15145. Accessed August 17, 2017; pp. 205–345.

CHAPTER 4
UNITED KINGDOM

If someone discovered a universal panacea which would guarantee health for everyone throughout their lives, he would be hailed as the greatest man on earth.[1]

D. Stark Murray, 1942

A. HISTORICAL CONTEXT

1. Elizabethan Poor Laws

From the Middle Ages to the nineteenth century, care for the sick and the poor in England was largely the business of the church. Poverty, malnutrition, long hours of labor and insanitary living conditions led to "crippled and distorted forms ... widespread [accumulation] of human excreta, ... and terrifying dangers of epidemic disease."[2] The high mortality rates from recurring scourges of cholera, typhus and smallpox were recorded in the first report of the Registrar General in 1836.[3]

Two types of institutional care were available during the nineteenth century. Under the Elizabethan Poor Laws, the sick, disabled and elderly were housed either in mixed or separate workhouses.[4] The criteria for relief were "less concerned with the alleviation of poverty than with preventing public subsidy of the idle."[5] The philosophy of the Poor Laws was that able-bodied paupers would find it preferable to work than to obtain outdoor relief under the "rigor" of the workhouse, a fate more unpleasant than the worst-paid job.

The second type of institutional care was the voluntary hospitals and venerable institutions. Their progenitors and patrons were members of the social elite who had founded them after King Henry VIII dissolved the monasteries in the sixteenth century. "Worthy" patients in the voluntary hospitals excluded the incurable, hopeless and contagious; their families had to guarantee funeral expenses before hospitals would accept them as patients.[6]

The primitive state of medical science, shortage of trained nurses and inadequate physical facilities of institutions limited the quality and effectiveness of care offered through hospitals.[7] The middle and upper classes, therefore, considered home a far healthier place to recover from illness.[8]

Doctors staffed hospitals on an honorary basis, using such appointments to make professional connections. They earned their main income from private practice where they charged wealthy clients a fee-for-service. During the period before financing of health care was introduced by the friendly societies, patients who could not afford general practitioner services relied on the out-patient departments of voluntary hospitals, charitable dispensaries, family care, local healers, natural remedies, apothecaries and quacks.[9]

Nurses and other salaried hospital workers were often domestic servants of a "rough and coarse type", employed on a salaried basis.[10] The nursing profession later gained some respectability as "an outlet for the social conscience and frustrated energies of the Victorian spinster."[11] When matrons and nurses realized the value of their work, their demand for higher salaries became a financial burden to the under-financed hospitals. As a result, many hospitals established nursing schools whose trainees paid a fee for their education even though they provided a pair of free hands on the wards during their training.

Lack of adequate ambulatory care led to an overuse of hospitals which were always short of funds.[12] Poor Law infirmaries, public hospitals and fever hospitals were financed through local rate, levies, central grants-in-aid and loans.[13] Venerable institutions were financed through income from their endowments. Newer voluntary and teaching hospitals depended on a combination of current subscriptions, donations, bazaars, dinners and balls for their financing. Finally, cottage hospitals, popular among general practitioners, were financed through a mixture of contributions and charges.[14] Except for a few provincial hospitals, special hospitals and nursing homes, direct payment for beds in the voluntary hospitals was very uncommon until after World War I.[15]

When Edwin Chadwick became the first Secretary of the Poor Law Commission, established in 1834, he emphasized the inability of the existing institutions and current medical practice to deal effectively with the epidemics of infectious diseases.[16] Poor health, he claimed, was due to problems of bad drainage, inadequate water and poor ventilation.[17] Reflecting Chadwick's concern, the Municipal Corporations Act of 1835 called for public action. Under the Act, the municipalities appointed Medical Officers of Health to survey sanitary conditions.[18]

As antiseptic techniques improved, the Poor Law infirmaries built from 1867 onward became safer and more acceptable to the ordinary working class. This acceptance was advanced by the Medical Relief Disqualifications Removal Act of 1885 which eliminated the label of "pauper" from those who used these institutions. Previously, sick paupers had been disenfranchised, losing both the right of citizenship and the right to vote.[19]

At the turn of the twentieth century, poverty with its associated illnesses still remained widespread throughout the 151,118 square kilometers of England and Wales with its population of 32,527,843.[20] "The interests of human life, except against willful violence, are almost uncared-for by the law. ... I do not hesitate to say, [this] constitute[s] a national scandal, and perhaps in respect of their consequences, something not far removed from a national sin."[21]

Hoping to find solutions to the burdens placed on local rate-payers by the Poor Laws, the Conservative Government of Prime Minister G.W. Balfour appointed a Royal Commission on the Poor Laws and the Relief of Distress in 1905. Its majority report called for greater co-operation in the hospital sector but was opposed to a free national health service which it feared the growing middle-class would make too expensive.[22] Its minority report, drafted by Beatrice Webb (formerly Potter) and her husband Sidney Webb, however, called for a unified service run by health committees of the local authorities. The Webbs felt that their proposed means-tested service should aim at prevention and should be financed through general revenues.[23] Although the medical profession as a whole rejected the Webbs' recommendations, a small group of doctors supported the call for a nationalized medical profession.[24]

These two reports raised most of the controversial issues which would later be the subjects of heated debates between the Government and doctors. Should there be a universal, comprehensive and free national service or a limited, means-tested and selective service? Should doctors receive a salary, capitation fees or fees-for-service? Should the administrative structure be central or local? Should the administration of the service include or exclude medical representation? Should it have an elected or an appointed membership? Should voluntary hospitals be incorporated into a unified system or should they be allowed to maintain their independence? Finally, should the financing of the service be through general revenues, insurance, local rates or charges?

2. Lloyd George's National Insurance Plan of 1911

The 1906 election, which gave a sizable majority to the Liberal Party led by Prime Minister Herbert Henry Asquith, determined the outcome of the debate. Lloyd George, Chancellor of the Exchequer, and Winston Churchill, President of the Board of Trade, both supported a Bismarckian social insurance plan for health care.[25] This was consistent with the traditional Liberal Party *laisser-faire* philosophy.

The National Insurance Bill, introduced on May 4, 1911, called for national contributory and compulsory insurance. The preamble to the legislation described it as "an Act to provide for insurance against loss of health and the prevention and care of sickness, and for purposes incidental thereto."[26] The plan would cover all manual workers and other employed persons aged between 16 and 65 whose income was below £160 per year. Membership would also be available on a voluntary basis for those excluded from compulsory membership and members of five years' standing.

Benefits would include diagnostic services, treatment by general practitioners, sanatoria, sickness pay and maternity benefits. Of the 13.5 million who would be compulsorily insured, the friendly societies would cover 6.5 million, large insurance companies would cover 5.5 million and trade unions would cover the remainder. These "approved societies", would offer a "panel" of doctors who would provide care for members.[27] The plan would be financed through workers' and employers' contributions as well as a general revenues subsidy.

Most medical practitioners in private practice earned their income from contracts with friendly societies and private clubs. These contracts were drawn up by the doctor for his poorer patients at a small annual subscription fee. Fearing a continuation of the conflicts that doctors had experienced in their relationship with the friendly societies, the British Medical Association (BMA) demanded the following "six cardinal points" before agreeing to participate in the national insurance plan: means-testing for memberships, free choice of doctor, administrative committees, expert medical representation on these committees, increased levels of remuneration and a range of choice in the mode of remuneration. The medical profession pledged not to support the plan unless their demands were met.

The National Insurance Act was nevertheless passed on December 16, 1911, coming into effect on July 15, 1912, just before the beginning of World War I in January 1913. The Government won the cooperation of the medical profession by proposing an increase in the capitation fee, limiting the range of services offered under the program and excluding those who could not afford to pay contributions. Under these terms, most of doctors quickly joined the plan fearing they would to be left without patients if they "opted-out". The basic terms of the plan remained in force for the next 40 years. During this time, the friendly societies slowly ceased offering health care benefits, eventually providing only cash benefits.

3. World War I to the Great Depression

Elements of a national hospital service were introduced during World War I to treat casualties and to stem the spread of venereal disease.[28] When this system was disbanded following the war, enquiries and official reports continued to examine many of the issues that had already been raised by the earlier Royal Commission on the Poor Laws and the Relief of Distress in 1905. These enquiries nearly all called for reforms in the uncoordinated hospital system and extension of the health care provisions of the friendly societies.

The Report of the Local Government Committee felt that local Boards of Guardians for the Poor Law infirmaries should be abolished and their functions transferred to the county councils and county borough councils.[29] The Haldane Committee led to the creation of the Ministry of Health in 1919.[30] The Minister of Health, Dr. Christopher Addison, established a Consultative Council to review Britain's health care needs.[31] Later, the Dawson Report stated that the current organization of medicine in Britain was not serving the public well and outlined the first official proposal for a national health service.[32]

The Cave Committee on the Voluntary Hospitals recommended the establishment of a Hospital Commission to improve co-ordination between the hospitals which were all in need of financial support.[33] The Onslow Commission also stressed the need for a central body to co-ordinate hospitals.[34] The Royal Commission on National Health Insurance recommended that national insurance should be extended to cover more of the population and that insurance should be used in the financing of hospitals.[35] The Royal Commission on Local Government once again recommended that the Poor Laws' jurisdiction over hospitals should be handed over to local authorities.[36] This reform was implemented in 1929 by Neville Chamberlain, then Minister of Health (later Prime Minister).[37] Following the recommendations of the Report of the Voluntary Hospitals Commission in 1937, the country was divided into hospital regions,[38] and the Nuffield Provincial Hospitals Trust was established.[39]

By the 1930s, voluntary insurance provided an increasing share of the revenues for both doctors and hospitals.[40] Not surprisingly, the BMA called for an extension of such insurance in their proposals for a national medical service in 1930.[41] "The system of medical provision which the Ministry of Health should seek to establish is one which would give to all who need it every kind of treatment necessary for the cure or alleviation of disease and would utilise for this purpose every class of medical practitioner."[42]

The medical profession saw the family doctor as a coordinator and a unified public authority who would be responsible for the administration and financing of their program. Despite their objections to government intervention, over 90 percent of general practitioners had joined the panel system by 1938. Only 50 percent of the population, however, were covered through these provisions.[43]

Restraints in public expenditure, brought on by World War I and the early years of the Great Depression (1929–1931), hampered the implementation of previous recommendations. As World War II approached, the incomplete coverage offered by the friendly societies forced a significant portion of the population to seek medical attention through hospitals. These institutions in turn became increasingly dependent on Government funds for financing their running costs. Charitable donations, subscriptions, contributions, charges, pay beds and central block grants were no longer sufficient.[44] The call for reform came from all directions.

4. World War II

Just as World War I had led to a trial run for a national hospital service, so did World War II. The medical services of 1939 were judged unable to handle the projected massive civilian casualties resulting from German air raids, gas warfare, increased infections and neuroses.[45] The Emergency Medical Services, Public Health Laboratory Service, Hospital Laboratory Services and Civilian Blood Transfusion Services were all established to cope with potential casualties.[46] "Because war means the organization of killing and wounding it must also mean the organization of services to repair and heal."[47] Proper care of casualties was seen as a crucial means of maintaining high morale and an effective fighting force.

> "The frame and pattern of the hospital services at the end of the war were due as much — if not more — to the kind of war expected as to the kind of war that happened."[48] Forced for the first time to come into contact with the average poorly equipped local hospital, which would handle the wounded, the influential members of the medical profession reacted in horror to existing physical and manpower deficiencies, calling for a large-scale reorganization of the hospital sector.[49] "The Ministry of Health then became the department responsible for base hospitals, the cost falling entirely upon the Exchequer."[50]

At this point, all political parties were demanding increased financing for existing health care services to benefit the population on a more permanent basis. The Liberal Party developed a program based on local authority health centers offering universal entitlement, free access and comprehensive services.[51] The Communist Party published a memorandum early in 1943 which gave tacit support to an improved service, but without describing the details. Finally, the Labour Party drew up a plan for a National Health Service in 1943 in close collaboration with the Socialist Medical Association. Their plan included regional services, unified central administration, salaried doctors, sub-contracted voluntary hospitals and financing through general revenues.[52]

Preparing for what appeared to be the inevitable, the Ministry of Health considered various plans for separate hospital and general practitioner services. John Maude, the permanent secretary from 1940 to 1945, resisted these efforts. Instead, he hoped to develop a national health service which would be integrated into a comprehensive social security program. "It [was] the objective of the Government … to ensure that by means of a comprehensive hospital service appropriate treatment [would] be readily available to every person in need of it."[53] Each of three successive Ministers of Health drew up a different proposal — Brown, Willink and Bevan.

B. LANDMARK LEGISLATIVE REFORMS

1. Beveridge's Report

The first concrete official proposal for a national health service was issued under the auspices of a social security plan: "The Health Departments soon found that they could not limit their interests and activities to the emergency sector of the hospital services as they had originally intended."[54] On June 10, 1941, the war-time Conservative Coalition Government, led by Prime Minister Winston Churchill, appointed William Beveridge as Chairman of an Inter-Departmental Committee on Social Security and Allied Services.[55] Its terms of reference were as follows: "To undertake, with special reference to the inter-relation of the existing national schemes for social insurance and allied services, a survey of the existing national schemes for social insurance and allied services, including workmen's compensation."[56]

Although, critical of existing health care provisions, Beveridge felt that the British social security system was "not surpassed and hardly rivaled in any other country of the world."[57] Its medical service, on the other hand was inadequate, "both in the range of treatment which [it] provided as a right and the classes of persons for whom it [was] provided."[58] Beveridge concluded: "Want is only one of five giants on the road of reconstruction… The others are Disease, Ignorance, Squalor, and Idleness."[59]

The report went on to state that a comprehensive national health service would "ensure that for every citizen there [was] available whatever medical treatment he [required] … for prevention and cure of disease and restoration of capacity for work."[60] He hoped that an effective program of prevention, early diagnosis and treatment would reduce the number of people qualifying for sickness benefits and that a controlled general practitioner service would verify claims.

The Government's actuary, G. S. W. Epps, estimated the breakdown of public financing for the social security plan as follows: 28 percent from workers, 20 percent from employers, 2 percent from interest on existing funds, 25 percent from Exchequer revenues and 25 percent from local rates.[61] Under the new plan, he estimated an income to the treasury of £697 million, while previous arrangements would have yielded only £432 million.

Public expenditure on health care was estimated at £249 million. Treatment would account for £170 million and cash benefits for £79 million. Adjusting for other incomes and expenditures, the health care provisions were estimated to involve an additional public expenditure of £70 million or an increase of 28 percent compared with previous arrangements.

Reactions to Beveridge's National Insurance plan varied. Some acclaimed it for having invented the National Health Service (NHS). It was a war-time "best seller", capturing the public imagination.[62] "Beveridge himself promoted the plan with almost messianic fervor, addressing gatherings of all kinds all over the country."[63]

The health care provisions of the plan were, however, branded as an uninspired extension of the existing National Health Insurance program. Others described it as a "Trojan horse which the Ministry of Health [was] attempting to introduce into the camp of the medical profession."[64] Kinglsey Wood, the Chancellor of the Exchequer, worried about the eventual cost of the plan. The Beveridge Report, nevertheless, introduced two great principles which would later form the cornerstone for the National Health Service: universal entitlement and comprehensive services financed through the public sector.[65]

2. Vested-Interest Groups

A number of groups tried to protect their own interests against the threats introduced by the proposal. These included pressure groups with skills to offer (doctors, dentists, pharmacists, opticians, physiotherapists, nurses and many others), pressure groups of administrative organizations (county councils, non-county boroughs, districts, insurance organizations and others) and pressure groups with property at stake (local government and voluntary hospitals).[66] The dentists wanted independence from the medical profession. The pharmacists resented having to sell cosmetics to make a living. Finally, the opticians claimed the right to test eyes and prescribe glasses, domains which doctors claimed as their own. The general practitioners wanted independence from the friendly societies and local authorities.

Three contentious issues divided the medical profession. Some members wanted a central ministerial administration, while others wanted local control.[67] Some wanted a salaried service, citing examples from the judiciary, episcopate, civil service, teaching profession and business world to support their stance.[68] Others feared a loss of clinical freedom, loss of individual initiative and freedom of choice under salaries.[69] Group practice was desired by many, but others feared competition from health centers.

The British Medical Association, representing general practitioners, wanted a comprehensive public program with the right to private practice and remuneration on a fee-for-service or capitation basis.[70] The Medical Officers of Health wanted universal entitlement under local authority control but financing through the Exchequer. The Royal College of Physicians wanted a salaried service run by an independent central board such as the BBC.[71] The Royal College of Surgeons preferred ministerial control with a preservation of the voluntary hospital system.[72] The Socialist Medical Association wanted a service based on universal entitlement, comprehensive benefits and free access using salaried doctors working in health centers.[73] All wanted reform, but as Lord Moran explained, "it [was] difficult for a doctor who [was] nurtured in the voluntary system to speak of its extinction with detachment."[74]

In August 1940, the BMA established a Medical Planning Commission in collaboration with the Royal Colleges, the Royal Scottish Corporations and the Society of Medical Officers of Health.[75] Its only report, an interim report, called for a limited service covering the poorer 90 percent of the population. Their proposal included the following recommendations: central government control with local administrations, means-tested general practice services based on health centers (group practice), regional hospital services, free choice of doctor, basic salary supplemented by fee-for-service, prohibition of the sale of practices, extension of contributory insurance to cover treatment by consultants, laboratory services for the poorer 90 percent of the population, acceptance of generalist-specialist divisions and financing through general Exchequer funds.

The report stressed that a national plan should give equal emphasis to health promotion, prevention of disease and treatment of illness. When the general membership opposed the official BMA line by rejecting the salary option, the younger doctors formed their own Medical Planning Research Association. Their association advocated universal access to free services as part of a comprehensive social security package.[76]

During the war, however, "those who suffered … were not air raid casualties, nor were they men in uniform. They were the sick, the diseased, the old, the very young and mothers."[77] Most of the vested-interest groups reacted favorably to the call for reform. But there was considerable disagreement on how to achieve this reform. If the doctors had formed a united front, they would have been a formidable adversary; instead, their divided ranks prevented a serious challenge to the Government's plans.

3. Brown's Plan

Social reforms "do not come down inscribed on sacred tablets from some political party's research center, …they are, rather, built up in discussion and negotiations."[78] When Ernest Brown became the Coalition Government's Minister of Health on October 9, 1941, he immediately had his Permanent Secretary, John Maude, and Deputy Secretary, John

Wrigley, conduct a survey of existing hospital facilities and draft a plan for a comprehensive post-hospital service. Contributions and central subsidies would finance the plan.[79]

In a conciliatory tone, largely intended to ease the concerns of doctors, Brown stated that private arrangements would still be allowed and that patients would retain the freedom to visit the doctor of their choice. His directives, however, contained many conflicting concepts, "What was really meant by such words as safeguard, collaboration, co-operation, unification, comprehensive and ... ultimate responsibility?"[80]

In February 1943, the Lord President of the Council, John Anderson, announced that the Coalition Government had adopted a formal policy to create a National Health Service. The legislation would be introduced in three stages. First, there would be confidential and tentative negotiations with the medical profession, voluntary hospitals and local government authorities. Next, a general plan would be published as a White Paper for public discussion. Finally, the legislation would be presented to Parliament.

By March 1943, Brown's plan started to take form. It called for a unified administration with the Minister of Health advised by a Medical Advisory Committee. Medical committees, joint boards of local authorities and voluntary hospitals would together delegate administrative responsibility to Area Committees. These, in turn, would administer all services on a regional basis. A Central Medical Board would be responsible for the terms of service, appointments, inspection and discipline. Salaried comprehensive general practitioners in health centers would offer a comprehensive range of free services "Here in simple terms was the full-time salaried local government service: it included almost everything that the BMA hated most."[81]

The plan resembled earlier plans produced by the National Association of Local Government Officers and the Society of Medical Officer of Health. This was not surprising since many of the medical officers in the Ministry of Health who had drafted the program had come from the local government.

The relationship between the doctors and the Government soured when the medical profession realized they would become civil servants working in health centers. Dr. Charles Hill, Deputy Secretary of the BMA, called for the medical profession to unite and fight for their freedom.[82]

"The profession objected to salaries as a mode of remuneration, to the proposed 'subjection' to local government, and above all to 'the speed at which the Government was moving.'"[83]

The doctors accused the Government of wanting to control the medical profession in order to gain control over the certification of illness.[84] This brought violent opposition from the BMA, voluntary hospitals and local governments. By the time Henry U. Willink replaced Brown as Minister of Health in December 1943, failure of the Brown Plan was imminent.

4. White Paper

The White Paper on the National Health Service, issued in February 1944, was dubbed "many people's business but nobody's responsibility."[85] Its recommendations were much less radical than the earlier proposal by Brown: "[it] approaches the millennium somewhat indirectly."[86] The White Paper admitted its limitations: "The idea of a full health and medical service for the whole population is not a completely new one ... but should be regarded as the natural next development."[87]

The White Paper called for a central administrative body, with the Minister of Health advised by an appointed Central Health Services Council.[88] The original ideas of regionalism and a unified administrative structure were replaced by a tripartite administrative planning body. There would be a continuation of the dual hospital system, thereby safeguarding the voluntary hospitals. New joint boards of the local authorities and the voluntary hospitals would be responsible for the new Hospital Service. County councils and county borough councils would be responsible for local clinics and domiciliary services. A central medical board would oversee Local General Practitioner Committees. The consultants in hospitals would be employed on a part-time or full-time basis, while salaried doctors would work in health centers side by side with those in private practice.

An Exchequer grant, local authorities and private sources would finance voluntary hospitals.[89] The local authorities, county councils and county borough councils would finance local services, including new health centers and home nursing services. The estimated cost was £132 for

England and Wales and £16 million for Scotland. To finance this expenditure, the new Social Insurance Plan would contribute 27 percent, local rates 36.4 percent and the Exchequer 36.6 percent; under the old system, social insurance would have contributed 20 percent, local rates 74 percent and the Exchequer 6 percent.

The White Paper stimulated the discussion which it had invited.[90] Prime Minister Winston Churchill fully endorsed the plan: "Our policy is to create a national health service, in order to ensure that everybody in the country, irrespective of means, age, sex or occupation, shall have equal opportunities to benefit from the best and most up-to-date medical and allied services available."[91] Willink honored its four major principles in the Commons: comprehensiveness, freedom of the individual, democratic responsibility and professional guidance.[92] In summing up for the Opposition, Greenwood supported the White Paper; Woolton praised it in the Lords.[93]

As time progressed, however, opposition mounted from almost every sector of the population. Although the *Lancet* favored the program,[94] the *British Medical Journal* was distinctly critical.[95] Dr. H. G. Dain, the new Chairman of the BMA, caustically summed up the Association's position. "We have stated emphatically that we do not wish to be employed by local authorities, that there should be no civil direction, that there should be no whole-time salaried service for general practice and that we shall have no clinical control.... We prefer these services to proceed by evolution."[96] Despite the stance of the Association's leadership, an opinion poll showed most members were in favor of the 100 percent coverage of the population.[97] The *Lancet* commented that there was some basis for criticism, but that "opposition to the White Paper has been cultivated by zealots," leaving the medical profession open to ridicule.[98]

Other groups entered into the debate attacking the provisions which dealt with the dental, pharmaceutical, optical and nursing professions. Both the County Councils Association and the Association of Municipal Corporations wanted to limit the jurisdiction of the joint authorities to that of planning. The voluntary hospitals were afraid that granting local authorities jurisdiction over the administration of hospital funds would give them abusive powers. The British Hospital Association rejected the proposal for joint authorities, fearing that this would not promote a true partnership between voluntary and local authorities that was essential for efficient services.[99]

5. Willink's Plan

The debate over the White Paper dragged on for 15 months. Secret negotiations with the BMA led to further dilution of the contents of earlier proposals. In September 1944, while Willink was still trying to re-draft a blueprint for a National Health Service, a Social Security White Paper appeared containing many recommendations from the Beveridge Report. It aimed to "secure the general prosperity and happiness of the citizens."[100] It would include the following benefits: allowances for families, orphans, training, women, widows, dependents and death, as well as benefits during sickness, hospitalization, unemployment, accidents at work, retirement and national assistance.

The proposed Social Security Programme would be financed through a "tripartite" scheme of contributions, with 44 percent from beneficiaries and employers, 54 percent from the Exchequer and 2 percent from interest on existing funds.[101] Men would contribute 10d, women 8d and employers 1.5d toward a National Health Service. Income under the new contribution schedule was estimated £429 million, which was higher than the £411 million calculated by Beveridge.[102]

Projected public expenditure on the new Social Security Programme was estimated at £650 million; Beveridge had estimated the same expenditure at £697 million. Several reasons were given to explain this discrepancy: workers' compensation, estimated at £17 million, was treated separately[103]; savings on delayed health services were estimated at £22 million; savings on family allowances were estimated at £40 million; decreases in unemployment and sickness benefits were estimated at £10 million; and increases in retirement and widows benefits were expected to cost £45 million. Sickness benefits were distributed as follows: £55 million for sickness and invalidity benefits, £9 million for maternity benefits and £17 million for workers' compensation.[104] These estimates were close to those made by Beveridge: £57 million for sickness benefits, £7 million for maternity benefits and £15 million for worker's compensation.[105]

By 1945, the Willink Plan had undergone another revision: "However complicated it appears, it must be conceded to be a masterpiece in the art of compromise."[106] The plan offered little new. A Central Health Services Council, assisted by a Standing Advisory Committees, would advise the Minister of Health. Three tiers — a Regional Advisory body, an Area Health Authority and a local Hospital Planning Group — would serve the boroughs. In this way, the local authorities and the voluntary hospitals would remain independent administrative executive units. National Health Insurance Committees, similar to the earlier Insurance Committees, would deal with general practitioners. The plan did not address the questions of doctors' remuneration or the sale of practices. Willink promised a draft legislation by September 1945 at the latest, a "last flicker of life in the dying Government."[107]

6. Bevan's Plan

The general elections of August 1945 gave the Labour Government and Clement Attlee, the new Prime Minister, an absolute majority. On August 17, 1945, the Lord Privy Seal (Greenwood) made it clear that the new Labour Government did not intend to abide by the "muddle" of concessions made by Willink: "We must go back to the beginning. We must go back to the White Paper, which is what my Rt. Hon. Friend the Minister of Health proposes to do."[108]

Both Aneurin Bevan, the new Minister of Health, and the Labour Party's policy on health care created much apprehension. Bevan was the "young" and "vigorous" left-wing rebel that Churchill had called a "squalid nuisance" during the war.[109] The Labour Party's proposal for a National Service for Health in April 1943 called for health centers, salaried doctors, abolition of private practice and local authority administrations.[110] Its policy was influenced by the Socialist Medical Association which had also recommended a salaried service run by local authorities.[111]

The Prime Minister supported the call for the creation of a National Health Service. Wilson Jameson (Deputy Chief Medical Officer), John Charles (Deputy Chief Medical Officer), William Douglas (Permanent Secretary) Arthur Rucker (Deputy Secretary) and John Hawton (Deputy Secretary after 1947) were ready to support Bevan's plans.[112]

The Cabinet was, however, divided in its views. Chuter Ede (Home Secretary) feared that a takeover of local authority hospitals would have negative political repercussions. Herbert Morrison (Lord President of the Council), a former leader of the London County Council, was known to favor local government control over the hospitals. He therefore opposed any program under which local governments would lose power to the Ministry of Health. Winston Churchill, now in the Opposition, tried to pressure the Government into rushing its plans.[113]

As expected, the BMA immediately drew its battle-lines. Before participating in a public program, the Association demanded that seven conditions be met: remuneration without public control, professional freedom, patients' freedom to choose a doctor, doctors' right to mobility, doctors' right to participate in the service, doctors' right to medical representation in the administration of the future system and hospitals' right to be associated with universities.[114] Following the war, the medical profession also feared that the Government might use the thousands of demobilized doctors to establish a salaried national service.

Bevan and the doctors first began meeting on social occasions: "The first was a dinner party at the Cafe Royal on 25 October when Bevan was entertained by Dain, Souttar, Moran, Webb-Johnson, Miller and Hill."[115] During these early talks, Bevan tried to win the confidence of the medical profession by emphasizing the importance of clinical freedom, choice of doctor by the patient and the special nature of the doctor-patient relationship. He was not the "ranting dogmatist of political caricature" that the medical profession had expected to confront.[116]

Bevan proceeded to prepare his proposal in secrecy. Following their meetings, Hill claims to have noted, "not a sign of belligerency ... [or] inordinate affection."[117] Bevan, on the other hand, remained suspicious of the medical profession, claiming to have "detected a certain gleam in [Hill's] eye."[118] When Bevan started more formal meetings with the doctors in January 1946 he focused not on the "form" of the health service but on the "terms" of service within it.

7. National Health Service Act of 1946

On March 19, 1946, the National Health Service Bill was presented to the Commons.[119] Reactions were varied. The *Lancet* was sympathetic.[120] The

BMA saw the tripartite administrative structure as fragmented rather than unified, and the Association established a "fighting fund" to challenge the Government.[121] It objected to salaries and the prohibited sale of practices but supported the call for a comprehensive service and regionalization.[122] The British Hospital Association condemned the proposals.

As the legislation slowly made its way through the Commons, the Commons' Standing Committee and the Lords, the level of polemics increased.[123] In the Commons, Bevan and Charles Key, the Parliamentary Secretary, praised the legislation. Willink from the Opposition objected to the salaried general practitioners, abolition of voluntary hospitals, weakening of local government, the lack of proper consultation and the control of the medical profession by a tribunal without right of appeal to the High Court. He appeared bitter that Bevan would be credited with creating the National Health Service which he himself had advocated.[124]

In the Lords, Lord Moran welcomed the hospital proposals.[125] Lord Holder, his rival for the presidency of the Royal College of Physicians, was opposed to a National Health Service and called for "evolution not revolution". Bernard Docker called the reorganization of the hospital sector a "mass murder of the voluntary hospitals and their replacement with state institutions."[126]

Although the Lords demanded several amendments, two of which were rejected by the Commons, the National Health Service Bill received Royal Assent on November 6, 1946. In December 1946, Scotland presented its legislation which received Royal Assent on May 21, 1947. Northern Ireland introduced similar legislation on February 4, 1947.[127]

The new National Health Service would adopt a central administrative structure similar to that proposed by Willink. A Central Health Services Council, assisted by Standing Advisory Committees, would advise the Minister of Health, thereby vesting the power and interest of politicians and civil servants alike. There would be a tripartite administrative structure consisting of hospitals and specialists' services, local authority health and social services, and general practice services (including dental, pharmaceutical and ophthalmic services).[128]

The nationalized voluntary and local authority hospitals would form the future general and teaching hospitals. Both amenity or standard free beds and private charge beds would be available. Nursing homes, however, were excluded from the plan. New hospital regions would be based on university medical schools. General hospitals would be managed through a two-tier structure: regional hospital boards and local hospital committees. Teaching hospitals, however, would be given special treatment, having their own board of governors with direct accountability to the Minister of Health. A central Hospital Endowment Fund would pool the endowments from individual hospitals.

County councils and county borough councils, which would lose authority over their hospitals, would form the new Local Health Authorities branch of the tripartite structure. Such services would expand to offer health centers, clinics, home nursing, midwifery, home help, health visitors, ambulances, vaccination and immunization.

General Practitioner Services (including pharmaceutical, dental and ophthalmic services) would form the third branch of the tripartite executive structure. These, in turn, would be administered by local executive councils. The sale of practices for goodwill would be abolished, although some official compensation would initially be offered to those affected by this change. Regulations would determine the policy affecting doctors' remuneration and other contentious issues, although a basic salary with a superimposed capitation fee was envisaged from the onset. Mental Health Services, although formally transferred to the Ministry of Health, would be covered under a separate legislation and would have an independent Board of Control to administer the Lunacy Act and other legislations.[129]

To finance the NHS, national insurance would contribute 21 percent, local governments would contribute 6 percent, savings from discontinued grants previously financed through the Ministry of Health and Ministry of National Insurance would contribute 10 percent and Exchequer funds would contribute 63 percent. The Exchequer and local authorities would spend £152 million on the service. In the event of a deficit, "expenses incurred by the Minister in the exercise of his functions ... [would] be defrayed out of moneys provided by Parliament."[130]

Many issues had to be settled by regulation following implementation on July 5, 1948.[131] The Government had not yet secured co-operation from the medical profession.[132] New administrative structures for hospitals and general practitioner services still needed to be created.[133] The NHS Act was in a vulnerable position, reminiscent of the New Zealand

Social Security Act in 1938. The underlying principles were clear, but making them operational still required much negotiation.

A plebiscite which the BMA carried out among its members indicated that 64 percent wanted to drop negotiations with the Minister of Health, meaning that the doctors would not work in the new service.[134] Two questions had dominated professional negotiation over the years: "on the pay of the hospitals, it [was] the dread of being put under local authority, and on the part of general practitioners, it [was] the fear of this whole-time service."[135] British doctors were aware of the earlier New Zealand experience: "In New Zealand today, so confused is the situation, there are five systems under which a general practitioner may give his service [whole-time salary, capitation, fee for service, partial refund and full refund]."[136] As a result by March 1948, a representative meeting of the BMA unanimously decided not to enter the new service on Appointment Day unless substantial changes were made.

The medical profession's united front was short-lived. With considerable finesse, Bevan managed to "play on the ancient split in the medical profession ... While the negotiating committee under the aegis of the British Medical Association was awaiting a summons to Whitehall, Bevan was dining with Lord Moran (President of the Royal College of Physicians) at Prunier's restaurant in St. James's Street."[137] Moran wanted to raise the Royal College "to the standing it once held but had largely lost, that of adviser to government on matters of health and medical policy."[138] Offering the specialists a variety of attractive options, including private practice, part-time appointments and special merit awards for senior and renowned specialists, Bevan "stuffed their mouths with gold."[139]

The general practitioners, in contrast, were offered vague promises that they would not become salaried civil servants. Ambiguous messages, such as "I cannot read into the mind of any future minister ... but it is not our intention.... [and] there is all the difference in the world between plucking fruit when it is ripe and plucking it when it is green," however, lowered the credibility of such assurances.[140] Other comments, such as "I have my spies," raised the suspicions of the BMA even further.[141] As a result, Hill mounted an intensive campaign to sabotage the new service. Bevan countered by accusing Hill of being a "saboteur-in-chief" and leading a "squalid political conspiracy".[142]

Members of the BMA, nevertheless, approved the new service through a plebiscite. On June 17, 1948, Dr. Guy Dain, then Chairman of the BMA, admitted the Government's victory: "The profession will do its upmost to make the new service a resounding success."[143]

Epps had advised the Government against making precise estimates of the cost of the new service: "it is impracticable at the present time to attempt to measure with any precision the changes which may occur in the social constitution ... [and] ... the war is not yet finished ... it is impossible to assess the extent of future casualties."[144] The Beveridge Report estimated that health care would cost £132 million under the new system compared with £60 million under the previous system. It was on the basis of these projected figures that the Coalition Government committed itself to public financing for universal entitlement to health care. In 1937, PEP had made a much higher estimate of £400 million. More accurate estimates came to £305 million based on the Net Vote of the Appropriation Accounts, £388 million based on the Gross Vote and £385 million based a later economic appraisal of the British health sector.[145]

C. CONTINUED POLICY REFORM PROCESS

1. Administrative Reorganizations

The final version of the National Health Service included many compromises to meet the conflicting demands made by political groups, underlying bureaucratic realities and interest groups. Details of the final act reflected these pressures. There were no salaried service, no health clinics, no elected representation and no local government control. Instead, general practitioners would retain their independent status in private offices, the service would be administered by appointed executives' bodies and regionalism would be based on hospital districts with teaching hospitals retaining a special status. The new service did not include broad preventive measures such as environmental services, housing and nutrition, although it did offer specific measures such as vaccination and immunization.

The act derived as much from the discussions between the medical profession and the Minister of Health as it did from party politics. The decision to create a national health service stemmed from the political mood of the times, calling for a free service with comprehensive benefits and universal entitlement; the final design revealed the influence of many pressure groups. These very compromises, however, may have spared the British NHS the ill fate of New Zealand's short-lived experiment: "Critics who formerly had lamented the creation of the NHS now congratulated themselves on being its originators."[146]

Forty years and two major administrative reorganizations later, Bevan's NHS has so far stood the test of time.[147] "The most 'socialist' plan came from the Liberal National minister [Ernest Brown], whilst only a middle of the road plan came from the Labor minister [Aneurin Bevan]: an odd political paradox as a memorial to the power of the medical pressure group."[148]

2. UK Entry into the European Union

The United Kingdom joined the European Economic Community on January 1, 1973 with Denmark and Ireland. Although this did not change the fundamental character of the British NHS, the fiscal constraints on deficit funding under the Acquis, and accompanying requirements of freedom of movement of people, goods, services and financing opened up the NHS to competition in both the provision of services and the health labor market.[149]

3. Major Policy Updates in the United Kingdom Since the 1980s

Since the latter part of the 1980s, the National Health Service in the United Kingdom has continued to evolve. Starting with what was essentially a fully publicly funded and publicly owned national health service post World War II, recent reforms have introduced more market based approaches to both funding and delivery of health care, adopting the "new public sector" management approach from New Zealand, and creating a more mixed public–private system, while preserving its predominant public tax funded and public National Health Service character. [150]

Originally the main changes focused on a continued shuffling of the deck in terms of various configurations of regionalization with adjustments in the budget allocation to the regions to offset perceived inequity. By 1990s, however, the UK under the Conservative government of Prime Minister Margaret Thatcher, passed a far reaching National Health Service and Community Care Act. This reform introduced an "internal market", similar to the earlier experiments in New Zealand and based on some pilot studies in Sweden. The essence of the reforms was to separate the purchasing ("commissioning") function from the provision of health care services.[151]

Like in New Zealand, the goal was to introduce market competition into the public service in the hope of increasing the efficiency and quality of care. General practice (GP) fund-holders were set up with 11,000 or more patients with own budgets to cover the cost of staff costs, medication, outpatient care, and a few well-defined in-patient services like elective surgery. These fund-holders became "purchasers" on behalf of their patients who "commissioned" services from NHS trusts (hospitals and community and mental health services).

Under the Labor Government of Prime Minister Tony Blair, which was elected in 1997, there was a major devolution of the British NHS to national administrations in Scotland, Wales and Northern Ireland. Although each of these entities have evolved increasingly diverse ways, overall the public character of public funding and public provision has remained a highlight of the British NHS. The GP fund-holders were abolished in England and reorganized into geographic entities called primary care trusts (PCTs) covering larger patient population groups. These new entities retained the purchaser-provider split and assumed responsibility for organizing and providing primary and community health care within specific geographical boundaries.

During this period, there was a shift back to strategic planning rather than relying on competitive market forces. Under the Health Act (2006), the Secretary of State had a legal duty to promote comprehensive and free health services, providing services free of charge, except for those with charges already in place. New national standards and targets were set up to strengthen inspection and regulation, supported by bodies such as the

Commission for Health Improvement (Care Quality Commission (CQC) from 2009) and the National Institute for Health and Clinical Excellence (National Institute for Health and Care Excellence (NICE) from 2012).

Following the election of Prime Minister David Cameron on May 11, 2010, the pendulum swung back to a more market oriented approach. The Health and Social Care Act in 2012 removed some of the barriers for commissioners to purchase services from NHS trusts that had been set up during the Labor Government of Tony Blair and more scope was once again provided for the private and voluntary sector to provide NHS-funded services.

Brexit and the anticipated withdrawal from the European Union (EU) poses a whole new set of challenges for the Conservative Coalition Government of Prime Minister Theresa May who assumed office on July 11, 2016, and those parts of the NHS that had opened up to the EU.[152] But it should fundamentally change the universal access to care in the different part of the UK.

ENDNOTES

1. D. S. Murray, *Health For All* (London: Victor Gallancz, 1942): 1.
2. A. Gibbins, *Industrial History of England*, quoted in J. S. Ross, *The National Health Service in Great Britain: An Historical and Descriptive Study* (London: Oxford University Press, 1952): 26.
3. The office of the Registrar General was established in 1836. See P. Thane, *Foundations of the Welfare State,* Social Policy in Modern Britain, by J. Campling, series ed. (London: Longman, 1982): 4–47.
4. Unification of the Poor Laws took place in 1602. The Poor Law Amendment Act was passed in 1834 and the Poor Law Outdoor Relief Regulation Order passed in 1852.
5. A. W. Dilnot, J. A. Kay, and C. N. Morris, *The Reform of Social Security*, The Institute of Fiscal Studies London (Oxford: Clarendon Press, 1984): 6.
6. B. Abel-Smith, *The Hospitals 1800–1948*, Heinemann Books on Sociology, by D.G. MacRae, series ed. (London: Heinemann, 1964): 1–15 and 64.
7. Ross, *National Health Service*, p. 32.
8. Abel-Smith, *Hospitals*, p. 2.
9. Conflicts between out-patient clinics and general practitioners were reduced following introduction of the referral system. See Abel-Smith, *Hospitals*, p. 116.

10. B. Abel-Smith, *A History of the Nursing Profession*, Heineman Books on Sociology, D.G. MacRae, series ed. (London: Heineman, 1960): 1–16; and Abel-Smith, *Hospitals*, p. 8.
11. Florence Nightingale, who founded the Training School and Nurses Home at St. Thomas Hospital, helped the nursing profession gain respectability. See Abel-Smith, *Hospitals*, p. 66.
12. The underfinancing of the hospital sector and the problem of out-patient abuses were explored in detail by the Lords' Committee in 1890–1893. The work of the committee led to the establishment of the King Edward's Hospital Fund. See United Kingdom, Select Committee on Metropolitan Hospitals (SCMH), "Report of Lords Committee 1890-93," *Accounts and Papers* (London: HMSO, 1893); and Abel-Smith, *Hospitals*, p. 135.
13. Abel-Smith, *Hospitals*, pp. 4–5, 39, 101.
14. Abel-Smith, *Hospitals*, p. 107.
15. Abel-Smith, *Hospitals*, p. 103, 189.
16. E. Chadwick, *Report on the Sanitary Condition of the Labouring Population of Great Britain [1842]*, by M. W. Flynn, ed. (Edinburgh: Edinburgh University Press, 1965). Others have since supported this view: I. Illich, *Limits to Medicine, Medical Nemesis: The Expropriation of Health* (Harmondsworth: Penguin, 1976); T. McKeown, *The Role of Medicine: Dream, Mirage or Nemesis*? (Oxford: Basil Blackwell, 1979); and S. B. Halstead, J. A. Walsh and K. S. Warren, "Good health at low cost," Proceedings of a Conference held at the Bellagio Conference Center, Bellagio, Italy, April 29–May 3, 1985 (New York: Rockefeller Foundation, 1985).
17. Clauses Consolidation and Town Improvement Acts of 1846; Nuisances Removal and Diseases Prevention Acts of 1846; Public Health Act of 1848; Health of Towns Commission in 1848; and the Report of Lancet Commission. Commissioners included Charles Dickens and John Stuart Mill.
18. Medical Officers of Health were often general practitioners who also performed clinical duties. United Kingdom, "Local Government Act," *Statutes* (London: HMSO, 1929); and United Kingdom "Local Government Act," *Statutes* (London: HMSO, 1933).
19. Abel-Smith, *Hospitals*, p. 130.
20. C. Booth, *The Life and Labour of the People in London* (London: Mcmillan, 1902–1904); and B. S. Rowntree, *Poverty: A Study of Town Life* (London: Mcmillan, 1902). The population for 1901 is based on United Nations (UN), Statistics Office (SO), Department of Economic and Social Affairs (DESA), *Demographic Yearbook 1962*, 14th Edition (New York: UN,

1962): 281; and the area is based on J. Paxton, ed., *The Statesman's Year-Book: Statistical and Historical Annual of the States of the World for the Year 1986-1987*, 123rd Edition (London: MacMillan Press, 1986): 1281.

21. J. Simon, quoted in Ross, *National Health Service*, p. 29. He was the architect of the "Magna Carta" of public health, the Public Health Act of 1875, drawn up after the Royal Commission of 1871.
22. United Kingdom, Royal Commission on the Poor Laws (RCPL), "Report [Chairman G. Hamilton]," Cd. 4499, *Accounts and Papers* (London: HMSO, 1909).
23. The Webbs who were members of the Fabian Society, a forum for social reform, advocated a socialized state.
24. *British Medical Journal*, 1906: 1732 and *British Medical Journal* 1913: 529–30, discussed in Abel-Smith, *Hospitals*, p. 249.
25. H. Levy, *National Health Insurance: A Critical Study* (Cambridge: Cambridge University Press, 1944): 3; and J. E. Pater, *The Making of the National Health Service*, King's Fund Historical Series No.1 (London: King Edward's Hospital Fund, 1981): 4. Lloyd George had studied Bismarck's plan during a visit to Germany in 1908.
26. United Kingdom, "National Health Insurance Act," *Statutes* (London: HMSO, 1911).
27. Levy, *National Health Insurance*, p. 6. Institutional care, consultants, women and children were all excluded.
28. The Venereal Disease Act provided for free treatment for every citizen with a 75 percent grant to co-operating local authorities. See R. M. Titmuss, *Problems of Social Policy*, in *History of the Second World War*, by W. K. Hancock, ed., United Kingdom Civil Series [London: HMSO, 1950] Revised Edition (Nendeln: Kraus Reprint, 1976): 2–5; and Abel-Smith, *Hospitals*, pp. 252–283.
29. United Kingdom, Local Government Committee (LGC), "Report [Chairman Donald Maclean]," *Accounts and Papers* (London: HMSO, 1917).
30. United Kingdom, "Ministry of Health Bill," *Accounts and Papers* (London: HMSO, 1918); and United Kingdom, Ministry of Reconstruction (MR), Machinery of Government Committee (MGC), "Report, [Chairman Viscount Haldane]," Cd. 9230, *Accounts and Papers* (London: HMSO, 1918).
31. The Ministry of Health, which was established in 1919, became responsible for both health and local government.
32. United Kingdom, Ministry of Health (MH), Consultative Council on Medical and Allied Services (CCMAS), "Interim Report on the future provision of medical and allied services [Chairman Lord Dawson]," Cmd. 693, *Accounts and Papers* (London: HMSO, 1920).

33. United Kingdom. Ministry of Health (MH), Voluntary Hospitals Committee (VHC), "Final Report [Chairman Viscount Cave]," Cmd. 1335, *Accounts and Papers* (London: HMSO, 1921).
34. United Kingdom, "Report on voluntary hospitals accommodation in England and Wales [Chairman Earl of Onslow]," Cmd. 2486, *Accounts and Papers* (London: HMSO, 1923).
35. United Kingdom, Royal Commission on the National Health Insurance (RCNHI), "Report [Chairman Lord Lawrence]," Cmd. 2596, *Accounts and Papers* (London: HMSO, 1926).
36. United Kingdom, Royal Commission on Local Government (RCLG), "Second Report," Cmd. 343, *Accounts and Papers* (London: HMSO, 1928).
37. Chamberlain wanted to reform local governments, hospitals and services offered by general practitioners.
38. The Commission included Dr. Henry Brackenbury from the BMA and representatives from the Royal Colleges. See British Hospital Association, *Report of the Voluntary Hospitals Commission [Chairman Lord Sankey],* Monograph (London: British Hospital Association, 1937).
39. Lord Nuffield created the trust with a gift of one million shares (yielding £115,000 per year) in Morris Motors.
40. Abel-Smith, *Hospitals*, p. 404.
41. Dr. H. Guy Dain and Dr. Henry Brackenbury had been closely involved in the New Zealand experience, and the BMA's proposal was studied carefully overseas in New Zealand, Canada and Australia.
42. British Medical Journal, "British Medical Association's proposals for a general medical service for the nation," Supplement, *British Medical Journal* 26 April (1930): 1. An almost identical draft was presented in 1938.
43. J. Blanpain, L. Delesie, and H. Nys, *National Health Insurance and Health Resources: The European Experience* (Cambridge, M.A.: Harvard University Press, 1978): 59.
44. Central block grants, based on demographic, geographic, income and other epidemiological characteristics, were started in 1929.
45. Titmuss, *Problems of Social Policy*, p. 6.
46. Abel-Smith, *Hospitals*, p. 431; Ross, *National Health Service*, pp. 77–78; and Pater, *National Health Service*, p. 20.
47. Titmuss, *Problems of Social Policy*, p. 54.
48. *Ibid.*
49. The most talented doctors worked in the teaching hospitals which were all within a mile or two of Harley Street.
50. Titmuss, *Problems of Social Policy*, pp. 56–57. By June 1, 1938, the Government abolished the distinction between base and casualty hospitals.

See *Annual Report of Chief Medical Officer of the Ministry of Health*, 1938, p. 58, quoted in Titmuss, *Problems of Social Policy*, p. 58. The Government later took over responsibility for the ambulatory health services. *Ibid.*, pp. 216–32.

51. Liberal Party, "Health for the people: Proposals for a positive and active health policy for the nation," *Monograph* (London: Liberal Publications Department, 1942). The Beveridge Report appeared in late 1942.
52. Labour Party, "National service for health: The Labour Party's post-war policy," *Monograph* (London: Labour Party, 1943); Abel-Smith, *Hospitals*, p. 321; and Pater, *National Health Service*, p. 106.
53. United Kingdom, House of Commons, *Parliamentary Debates*, Volume 374 (London: HMSO, October 9, 1941): col. 1116, quoted in Titmuss, *Problems of Social Policy*, p. 504.
54. Titmuss, *Problems of Social Policy*, p. 502.
55. Arthur Greenwood, Minister without Portfolio, acted as Chairman of a committee on reconstruction problems. Committee members included various senior civil servants from the Government departments previously involved in the administration of cash benefits and pensions.
56. United Kingdom, Inter-departmental Committee on Social Insurance and Allied Services (ICSIAS) "Report [Chairman Lord William Beveridge]," Cmd. 6404, *Accounts and Papers* (London: HMSO, 1942): 2.
57. United Kingdom, ICSIAS, "Lord William Beveridge," 3.
58. *Ibid.*
59. *Ibid.*, p. 7.
60. *Ibid.*, p. 158.
61. United Kingdom, ICSIAS, "Lord William Beveridge," Appendix A.
62. A. J. Willcocks, *The Creation of the National Health Service: A Study of Pressure Groups and a Major Social Policy Decision* (London: Routledge and Kegan Paul, 1967): 23.
63. Pater, *National Health Service*, p. 45.
64. United Kingdom, "Lord Derwet," House of Lords, *Parliamentary Debates* (London: HMSO, 1 June 1943): col. 729–67.
65. United Kingdom, ICSIAS, "Lord William Beveridge," p. 201.
66. Willcocks, *Health Service*, pp. 32–33.
67. The general practitioners fought against control by both local governments and specialists.
68. Pater, *National Health Service*, p. 35.
69. The general practitioners refused to accept salaries.
70. Dr. Guy Dain would replace Dr. Henry Souttar as Chairman.

71. Lord Moran (Churchill's doctor) represented them both as President of the Royal College of Physicians and as a member of the House of Lords. He strongly advocated a regional hospital plan, opposing local government control.
72. Lord Webb-Johnson was their President.
73. The members of the association were accused by Henry Brackenbury of working "logically and assiduously" to produce a salaried health service. See Abel-Smith, *Hospitals*, p. 422; and Murray, *Health*, pp. 77–78.
74. United Kingdom, "Lord Moran," House of Lords, *Parliamentary Debates* (London: HMSO, 16 April 1946): col. 824.
75. Notable members were Lord Dawson, Lord Moran (Royal College of Physicians) and Lord Webb-Johnson (Royal College of Physicians).
76. British Medical Journal, "Medical Planning Commission," Supplement, *British Medical Journal*, 20 June (1942): 93.
77. Titmuss, *Problems of Social Policy*, p. 193.
78. Willcocks, *Health Service*, pp. 104–5.
79. United Kingdom, "National health services, future of hospitals: Health Services Bill," House of Lords, Parliamentary Debates (London: HMSO, 9 October 1941): col. 1116–9.
80. Abel-Smith, *Hospitals*, pp. 456–7.
81. Willcocks, *Health Service*, p. 77.
82. Hill became Secretary following the death of Dr. George Anderson in 1944.
83. Abel-Smith, *Hospitals*, p. 459.
84. Pater, *National Health Service*, p. 64.
85. United Kingdom, Ministry of Health and Department of Health for Scotland (MHDHS), "A National Health Service: Scotland," Cmd. 6502, *Accounts and Papers* (London: HMSO, 1944), quoted in Titmuss, *Problems of Social Policy*, p. 73. It was prepared by John Hawton. Distinguished members included Lord President Clement Attlee (war-time Labour Party leader), Herbert Morrison, Ernest Bevin and Chairman Lord Woolton, Minister for Reconstruction.
86. The *Lancet* quoted in Willcocks, *Health Service*, p. 39.
87. United Kingdom, MHDHS, "A National Health Service," p. 5.
88. United Kingdom, MHDHS, "National Health Service," pp. 12–20.
89. United Kingdom, MHDHS, "National Health Service," Appendix E.
90. Today the White Paper would have been a Green Paper. It was a consultative document, not a policy statement.
91. Winston Churchill, quoted in Ross, *National Health Service*, p. 5.
92. United Kingdom, "Henry U. Willink," House of Commons, *Parliamentary Debates* (London: HMSO, March 16, 1944): cols. 427–518.

93. United Kingdom, "Arthur Greenwood," House of Lords, *Parliamentary Debates* (London: HMSO, March 16, 1944): cols. 35–160.
94. Lancet, "Reactions to the White Paper," *Lancet*, 1(4 March 1944): 313–4.
95. British Medical Journal, "White Paper," *British Medical Journal* (26 February 1944): 293–5.
96. Dr. H. G. Dain quoted in Willcocks, *Health Service*, p. 40.
97. British Medical Journal, "Gallop poll on White Paper: Comparison with Council's Report," Supplement, *British Medical Journal* (26 February 1944): 63.
98. Lancet, "Now for negotiation," *Lancet* 2 (16 December 1944): 789–90.
99. Willcocks, *Health Service*, p. 66.
100. United Kingdom, "Social insurance, part I," Cmd. 6550, *Accounts and Papers* (London: HMSO, September 1944): 5.
101. United Kingdom, "Social insurance, part I," p. 37.
102. The difference was mainly due to changes the unemployment programme (lower unemployment and lower interest on funds). See United Kingdom, "Social insurance, part I," p. 55.
103. United Kingdom, "Social insurance, part II: Proposals for an industrial injury insurance Scheme-workmen's compensation," Cmd. 6551, *Accounts and Papers* (London: HMSO, September 1944): 53.
104. United Kingdom, "Social insurance, part I," p. 49, 53.
105. The Government actuary G.S.W. Epps had worked out the cost of both programmes. 106 Willcocks, *Health Service*, p. 68.
106. Willcocks, *Health Service*, p. 68.
107. Pater, *National Health Service*, p. 104.
108. Ross, *National Health Service*, p. 90.
109. Bevan and J. Westwood, the Secretary of State for Scotland, would prepare the future service. See Pater, *National Health Service*, p. 106.
110. Labour Party, "National service for health."
111. Abel-Smith, *Hospitals*, p. 447.
112. All had played some role in developing previous plans.
113. Pater, *National Health Service*, p. 112.
114. The Medical Practitioners' Union called them "seven futile clauses" all based on syndicalism. See Willcocks, *Health Service*, p. 42.
115. Pater, *National Health Service*, p. 107.
116. *Ibid.*
117. British Medical Journal, "Mr. Bevan's hopes for National Health Service," Supplement, *British Medical Journal* (15 September 1945): 63–65.
118. Abel-Smith, *Hospitals*, p. 476.

119. United Kingdom, Ministry of Health (MH), "National Health Service Bill," *Accounts and Papers* (London: HMSO, 19 March 1946). Unless otherwise stated, the following description of the "Bill" refers to the March issue. It was John Hawton, not Bevan, who drafted the final legislation. Hawton had also prepared the 1944 plan.
120. Lancet, "Participation," *Lancet* (23 March 1946): 421–4.
121. Lancet, "BMA opens emergency fund," *Lancet* 1(9 March 1946): 354.
122. British Medical Journal, "The BMA Council's Report," Supplement, *British Medical Journal* 1(30 March 1946): 469–74; and British Medical Journal, "The press, the Minister and the Bill," Supplement, *British Medical Journal* 1(20 April 1946): 612–3.
123. The initial reading in the House of Commons took place on April 30, 1946.
124. In reality the real architects of the NHS were Jameson and Hawton. See Pater, *National Health Service.*
125. United Kingdom, "Lord Moran," House of Lords, Parliamentary Debates (London: HMSO, 16 April 1946): cols. 822–66.
126. Docker, Chairman of the British Hospitals Association, quoted in Pater, *National Health Service*, p. 122.
127. United Kingdom, "An Act to provide for the establishment of a comprehensive health service for Scotland, and for purposes connected therewith," *Statutes* (London: HMSO, 21 May 1947); and United Kingdom, "Northern Ireland Health Services Act," *Statutes* (London: HMSO, 1948).
128. The geographic boundaries were non-conterminous.
129. United Kingdom, Ministry of Health (MH), "National Health Service Bill," *Accounts and Papers* (London: HMSO, 23 July 1946).
130. United Kingdom, Ministry of Health, "National Health Service Bill, 23 July," col. 52.
131. The issue of remuneration would be dealt with through regulations and the Spens Committee. United Kingdom, Ministry of Health and Department of Health for Scotland (MHDHS), Inter-Departmental Committee on the Remuneration of Consultants and Specialists (IDCRCS), "Report, [Chairman Will Spens]," Cmd. 7420, *Accounts and Records* (London: HMSO, 1948).
132. By then the branches of the medical profession had split, leaving a divided front to face the Government.
133. The local authorities had to expand their scope.
134. British Medical Journal, "Yes or no," Supplement, *British Medical Journal* 2(16 November 1946): 739–46.
135. United Kingdom, "Lord Moran," Col. 833.

136. British Medical Journal, "Medical planning in New Zealand," Supplement, *British Medical Journal* 2 (September 1944): 51.
137. Bevan quoted in Abel-Smith, *Hospitals*, pp. 486–7.
138. By a narrow margin he had just renewed his presidency of the Royal College of Physicians against Lord Holdan. His opponent would have made the negotiations much more difficult. See Pater, *National Health Service*, p. 139.
139. Bevan quoted in Abel-Smith, *Hospitals*, p. 48.
140. United Kingdom, "Aneurin Bevan," House of Commons, *Parliamentary Debates* (London: HMSO, 4 November 1946): Col. 1127.
141. Pater, *Health Service*, p. 172.
142. United Kingdom, "Aneurin Bevan," House of Commons, *Parliamentary Debates* (London: HMSO, 9 February 1948): cols. 35-160; and Pater, *Health Service*, p. 156, 179.
143. Dr. Guy Dain writing to the *Times*, on June 17, 1948, quoted in Ross, *National Health Service*, p. 126; and Pater, *National Health Service*, p. 163.
144. United Kingdom, "Social insurance, part II," p. 56.
145. United Kingdom, Committee of Enquiry into the Cost of the National Health Service (CECNHS), "Report [Chairman C.W. Guillebaud]," Cmd. 9663, *Accounts and Papers* (London: HMSO, 1956): 7; and B. Abel-Smith and R.M. Titmuss, *The Cost of the National Health Service in England and Wales* (Cambridge: Cambridge University Press, 1956): 24.
146. C. Webster, *The Health Services Since the War*, Volume I, *Problems of Health Care: The National Health Service Before 1957* (London: HMSO, 1988): 389.
147. The Conservative Government under Prime Minister M. Margaret Thatcher tried to alter this history of the British NHS. United Kingdom, *Working for Patients: the Health Service, Caring for the 1990s* (London: HMSO, 1989).
148. Willcocks, *National Health Service*, p. 85.
149. The term acquis is also used to describe laws adopted under the Schengen Agreement, prior to its integration into the European Union legal order by the Treaty of Amsterdam, in which case one speaks of the Schengen acquis. The term acquis has been borrowed by the World Trade Organization Appellate Body, in the case Japan — Taxes on Alcoholic Beverages, to refer to the accumulation of General Agreement on Tariffs and Trade (GATT) and WTO law ("acquis gattien"), though this usage is not well established.
150. J. Cylus, E. Richardson, L. Findley, M. Longley, C. O'Neill, and D. Steel, *United Kingdom: Health System Review in Health Systems in Transition*,

2015;17(5):1–125. http://www.euro.who.int/__data/assets/pdf_file/0006/302001/UK-HiT.pdf?ua=1. Accessed July 25, 2017.

151. C. Ham, "Betwixt and Between: Autonomization and Centralization of UK Hospitals," in A. S. Preker and A. Harding, eds. *Innovations in Health Service Delivery: The Corporatization of Public Hospitals*, (2003, Washington, DC: World Bank). https://openknowledge.worldbank.org/handle/10986/15145. Accessed August 17, 2017; pp 265–297.

152. Brexit is the popular term for the United Kingdom's intended withdrawal from the European Union.

CHAPTER 5

CANADA

The enemies we shall have to overcome will be on our own Canadian soil. They will make their presence known in the guise of sickness, unemployment and want. It is to plan for a unified campaign in Canada against these enemies of progress and human well-being that we have come together at this time.

Prime Minister Mackenzie King, 1945

A. HISTORICAL CONTEXT

1. The British North America Act of 1867

Early colonial outposts in Canada had military infirmaries staffed by commissioned naval surgeons, overseers, dispensers and untrained nurses as in other regions of the new world. Since the British Treasury financed these primitive medical facilities, Canada can be viewed as having begun its colonial history with a "nationalized" health service. Civilian needs, however, soon outgrew these primitive provisions.

Many of the settlers who had left Great Britain and France to escape the degrading aspects of the Elizabethan Poor Laws were unable to afford the care offered by the colony's few private doctors. Far from their families, the aged, destitute, disabled and sick therefore had little personal support when they needed medical attention. Instead, they sought assistance from religious groups, benevolent societies, quacks, faith healers and frauds.

Medical doctors working for parishes, charitable institutions and voluntary hospitals offered free treatment to the poor in return for the right to treat their private patients on a fee-for-service basis in the same institutions. The treasuries of public authorities were drawn into financing institutional care when many such institutions ran out of funds to finance their operations.

The British North America Act of 1867, which formed a confederation of Canada's four most populous colonies, limited the Federal Government's involvement in health care to issues of national importance such as quarantine and the maintenance of marine hospitals.[1] The Provinces were given exclusive jurisdiction over "the establishment, maintenance, and management of hospitals, asylums, charities, and eleemosynary [charitable] institutions in and for the Province, other than marine hospitals"... [and] generally all matters of a merely local or private nature in the Province.[2]

The Federal Government initially became involved indirectly in matters relating to health care through its Departments of Agriculture, Marines and Fisheries. At the turn of the century, with a population of 5,371,314 living mainly along the southern border of the country's 9,970,610 square kilometers of mountains, hinterlands and lakes, federal involvement in health care was limited as much by physical as by constitutional restraints.[3] It nevertheless established the Department of Health in 1919,[4] and a Select Standing Committee on Industrial and International Relations reported in favor of a national health program as early as 1929.[5] By 1935, the Employment and Social Insurance Act created the framework for a national health and welfare plan. Despite such progress at the federal level, infrastructures for the financing of health care first developed in a piecemeal fashion at the provincial not federal level.

2. Provincial Government Health Programs

Provincial Governments began assuming greater responsibility for health care following World War I. In British Columbia, the Legislative Commission of 1919 recommended the use of health insurance similar to that found in Europe. Saskatchewan took a different path by passing legislation allowing municipalities to levy taxes to pay for their health care services.

Three early tax-financed systems are worthy of mention: the municipal doctor system, the union hospital system and the municipal hospital care plan. The first allowed rural municipalities to offer a salary as an incentive to attract doctors into their areas. The second permitted joint municipalities to build local hospitals.[6] The third paid for the running costs of such hospitals. Although the plans were initially financed entirely though local taxes, they required provincial subsidies almost from the outset.[7]

One region, the Swift Current Health Region No.1, in Saskatchewan, formed the testing ground for the Province's future medicare program.[8] The region paid its doctors through funds collected from local taxes, supplemented by provincial grants. Doctors in the region welcomed the initiative since they could not survive on the income that they earned from fee-for-service in private practice.

Other Provinces followed Saskatchewan's lead with programs of their own. In British Columbia, the Royal Commission on State Health Insurance of 1932 recommended a Provincial Government health insurance program. Protest from the medical profession and the Manufacturer's Association, however, led to a defeat of the legislation in 1935. Alberta and Manitoba experimented with salaried municipal doctor and hospital plans during the 1930s and 1940s. In Alberta, two Commissions of Inquiry reported in favor of Provincial Government health insurance in 1929 and 1933, but the Government which came to power in 1935 dropped the Health Insurance Act. Manitoba developed a similar plan, and Ontario established the first provincial fund to provide payments for doctors.[9]

By 1937, the Great Depression had forced two-thirds of the population of Saskatchewan to depend on some form of relief. This created "a mood of rebellion against the universal risks of unemployment and sickness, disability and old age, widowhood and poverty"[10] Those needing help resented having to "crawl on [their] hands and knees to a municipal official before [they could] be admitted to hospital."[11]

Local rate-payers of municipalities, many of which were near bankruptcy, could no longer carry the financial burden for the sick and poor.[12] The limited personal resources, scattered rural populations and the economic risks of a "one-crop boom or bust grain economy" forced people to look to public financing of health care.[13]

In June 1944, the Cooperative Commonwealth Federation (CCF) took office in Saskatchewan.[14] Tommy C. Douglas, the new Premier, reserved the health portfolio for himself as a signal of the high priority that he would place on health care. He pledged that "someday ... people would be able to get health services just as they [were] able to get educational services, as an inalienable right of being a citizen."[15]

By 1946, Saskatchewan was ready to pass its Hospitalization Act despite the lack of financial support for the program from the Federal Government. It was the first provincial program to offer universal entitlement to hospital insurance in Canada.[16] That same year, the Saskatchewan Health Services Act expanded the scope of the municipal doctor plans to cover broader health regions.

Other Provinces followed the Saskatchewan example. British Columbia, which introduced its Hospital Insurance Service in 1948, had the painful experience of trying to establish a new infrastructure for collecting its premiums.[17] The oldest Canadian colony, Newfoundland, already had an operating cottage hospital system when it joined the Canadian Confederation in 1949. Alberta introduced limited hospital benefits in 1950 through provincial subsidies for municipal programs.

Most of the poorer Provinces, however, did not have the economic means to finance health care. Despite constitutional limitations, therefore, the time was ripe for a re-evaluation of federal involvement in the financing of health care.

3. Heagerty Committee Draft Bill of 1944

In 1937, the Rowell–Sirois Royal Commission on Dominion-Provincial Relations examined ways that the Federal Government could become more directly involved in areas of provincial jurisdiction.[18] The Commission warned that constitutional reforms alter the nature of the country, while cost-sharing would lead to a reduced sense of responsibility. This left grants-in-aid as the only option for the Federal Government to finance national programs that were under provincial jurisdiction.

The Commission recommended greater federal involvement in unemployment insurance and old-age pensions, while the Provinces should retain responsibility for health insurance and workmen's compensation,[19]

"In recommending [maintenance of] provincial jurisdiction over Health Insurance we are aware ... that it may result in inequalities."[20]

In 1939, Ian MacKenzie, the Minister of Health, suggested to Prime Minister Mackenzie King that the "demand for a national health system is inevitable."[21] As a result, Dr. J. J. Heagerty, the Director of Public Health, began working on the plans for a Canadian health service in 1941.[22] His report was completed in 1943.[23]

Following a review of health insurance programs in Germany, Britain, France and South Africa, the Canadian Medical Association's Advisory Committee on Health Insurance recommended similar insurance for Canada.[24] "The CMA ... stands ready to render any assistance in its power towards the solution of one of the country's most important problems, namely the safeguarding of the health of our people."[25] The Association had for some time wanted to relieve its members of the burden of providing free care to those who could not afford to pay.

Other organizations supported national involvement in the financing of health care during the 1940s. These included the Canadian Hospital Council, the Canadian Dental Association, the Canadian Life Insurance Officers Association, the Canadian Trades and Labour Congress, the Canadian Congress of Labour and the Canadian Federation of Agriculture.

By 1943, the various groups had completed the first blueprint of a Canadian health insurance plan which advanced several principles: universal entitlement, compulsory membership, prevention, national participation in financing and provincial jurisdiction over the delivery of services.[26] The Provinces would pay for the administrative cost while the Federal Government would pay for any expenses not covered by the amount collected from the insured.

W. C. Clarke, the Deputy Minister of Finance, however, advised that federal participation in social security and health insurance should be postponed until after negotiations for a complete re-ordering of the financial relationship between the Provinces and the Federal Government. As a result, the original national health insurance plan was dropped and committees continued working on alternatives throughout the duration of World War II.

MacKenzie and Heagerty nevertheless wanted to proceed with their plan. The rejection rates for preventable conditions had been unacceptably high during World War II. Infant mortality rates and maternal mortality rates were high compared with those of other developed countries; so were deaths from communicable diseases such as tuberculosis, influenza, whooping cough and measles.[27]

By May 1944, the provincial Ministers of Health and their Deputies, the House of Commons Committee, the Advisory Committee and the Finance Committee all approved a draft legislation on health insurance. The Medical Association endorsed the plan clause-by-clause. All political parties supported Federal Government financing of health care during the campaign leading up to the 11 June 1945 general elections.[28] Finding a way to extend federal jurisdiction over health care remained the only stumbling block.[29]

4. Dominion-Provincial Conference of 1945

Inspired by the work of William Beveridge in Britain, Mackenzie King, the Canadian Prime Minister, called for a Dominion-Provincial Conference on post-war reconstruction in 1945.[30] "Our lives have been given over largely to life-long study of social problems."[31] King supported what Winston Churchill called the "magic" of insurance.[32]

Leonard Marsh, who had known Beveridge at the London School of Economics and Political Science, was appointed Chairman of a Special Social Security Commission.[33] In his report of 1943, Marsh recommended federal involvement in financing of health care.

When Brooke Claxton succeeded Ian MacKenzie as Minister of the Department of Pensions and National Health, he carried out a departmental reorganization which led to the creation of the Department of National Health and Welfare in 1944. Other members of the Cabinet Committee did not share the new Minister's enthusiasm for constitutional reform to secure the necessary federal jurisdiction over health care.[34] King, nevertheless, appointed Claxton as Chairman of a Supervisory Committee of Parliamentary Assistants to oversee the work of the Dominion-Provincial Conference planned for 1945.[35]

The Green Book proposals presented at the conference were complex. The Federal Government wanted exclusive right to levy personal and corporate income taxes and succession duties. In return, the Provinces would obtain unconditional annual subsidies for a variety of social security programs, such as unemployment insurance, children's allowance, pensions, health insurance and financial assistance for the indigent, aged and physically handicapped.[36] The Provinces could finance their share through whichever means they chose, excluding those reserved for the Federal Government.

The Federal Government would finance 20 percent of the basic cost of a comprehensive social security program through a Dominion Grant. In addition, it would cover 50 percent of the running cost up to a predetermined limit. Based on the 1941 census, the estimated annual cost of such a program would be $250 million, of which the federal contribution would be $150 million.[37]

The Provinces, however, demanded large financial concessions without wanting to surrender the tax fields desired by Ottawa. Premier Drew of Ontario presented a counter-proposal that the Federal Government felt was too expensive. Premier Maurice Duplessis, as expected, accused the Federal Government of interfering with Quebec's provincial jurisdiction over health care.

The proposals for health care included grants for planning and organization, health insurance grants, health grants and financing for the construction of hospitals.[38] Health insurance would cover general practitioner services, hospital care and visiting nurses and later include consultants, specialists, nursing, dental, pharmaceutical and laboratory services.

It soon became evident, however, that to negotiate the terms of a national health insurance program at a Federal-Provincial Conference on tax reforms was a bad strategy. The Provincial Governments, many of which had already started to introduce their own plans, rejected the joint package.

5. National Hospital and Diagnostic Services Act of 1957

Ten years would pass before another Federal-Provincial Conference would address the same issues. In the intervening time, anticipating a shortage in hospital beds, Paul Martin who replaced Claxton as Minister of Health, started introducing the Green Book Health Grants in 1948.[39] "My ultimate aim was to eliminate the extremes of poverty and wealth....I proposed that government eat away at big incomes ... in favor of an economic and social program."[40]

The Provinces received grants for the construction of hospitals and to carry out health surveys (planning and organization). "The Prime Minister had seen exactly what I was trying to do — creating a demand for government action."[41] By the 1950s, many Provinces had begun increasing their institutional capacity by "milking Martin's millions".[42]

During the 1949 federal elections, all political parties advocated some form of health insurance.[43] Eighty percent of the population supported national participation.[44] During the 1953 elections, the tide had changed.[45] The Liberal Party platform by this time supported a continuation of the provincial health grants rather than a national health insurance program: "The Liberal Party is committed to support a policy of contributory health insurance to he administered by the Provinces when most of the Provinces are ready to join."[46]

During the 1955 Federal-Provincial Conference, the issue of national hospital insurance forced itself back onto the agenda in an unforeseen manner.[47] Trying to avoid a replay of the errors committed in 1945, Prime Minister Louis St. Laurent thought that the "conference [was] most likely to succeed" if the agenda was restricted to a "limited number of subjects of primary importance."[48] He therefore intended to prevent the provinces from bringing health insurance into the discussions.[49]

Leslie Frost, Ontario's new Conservative Premier, felt that the allegations that the Provinces were holding back health insurance were directed at Ontario.[50] He raised his objections to these charges at the Federal-Provincial Conference: "Since [health insurance] is one of the great objectives in the field of human betterment, it should be placed on the agenda for study."[51] Most of the other Provinces supported Ontario's proposition, forcing the reluctant Prime Minister to include health insurance in the discussions.[52]

Following the Conference, St. Laurent appointed a special Federal-Provincial Committee on Health Insurance to examine possible ways that the Federal Government could negotiate the terms of such a plan with the Provinces. He was supported by Martin who wanted "the health grants ... broken away from the fiscal and other social aspects ... [to] prepare the way for introducing health insurance at some later date."[53]

The Federal Government offered to contribute 25 percent of the national average per capita cost of hospital services plus 25 percent of the provincial average per capita cost. This would equalize benefits between the poorer and richer Provinces; the former would receive more than 50 percent, while the latter would receive less than 50 percent as a federal grant.

In return for these federal grants, the Provinces had to establish comprehensive hospital and diagnostic services, universal entitlement and out-patients departments and prohibit co-insurance. The Provinces also had to cover the full administrative cost: "The governments of the various Provinces [had] to take the initiative in working out plans adapted to local conditions."[54] Federal support would not start until a majority of the Provinces representing a majority of Canadians, entered into such an agreement with Ottawa.[55]

A variety of circumstances still worked against the establishment of a national program. First, constitutional legality of a federal-provincial contract for financing health insurance was still uncertain. Second, hospitals were distributed unevenly throughout the Provinces, making services unavailable to many. Third, other programs such as defense and pensions competed with health care for public funds. Finally, the Canadian Medical Association had abandoned its previous 1943 endorsement of public involvement in a national health insurance program in 1949.[56] By the 1950s, the medical profession was fully committed to backing voluntary insurance.[57]

But the most important stumbling block to a national health insurance program was lack of cooperation from Ontario, without which the Federal Government's demand for support from a majority of Provinces could not be achieved. Frost was determined to avoid introducing universal entitlement which would require compulsory membership and be unpopular with his conservative constituents. To avoid compulsory membership, he asked Ottawa to accept 90 percent as "universal." Following extensive negotiations and an informal promise that Ontario would "soon" offer universal entitlement on a voluntary basis, the Federal Government accepted Frost's offer.[58]

On March 28, 1957, Ontario finally passed the Hospital Services Commission Act, giving the go-ahead to the Federal Government. Later on April 10, 1957, the Federal Government passed the Hospital Insurance and Diagnostic Services Act by a unanimous vote in the House of Commons; on April 12, 1957, the Senate also gave it a unanimous vote of support.[59] Ontario introduced its Hospital Services Plan on January 1, 1959. By the end of the year, 92.3 percent of Ontario's population had joined the provincial program. This encouraged the other Provinces to enter the agreement.

In 1957, before the new Hospital Insurance and Diagnostic Services Act could be implemented at the provincial level, the Liberals lost the general election to the Progressive Conservatives. John G. Diefenbaker became the new Prime Minister. During the campaign leading up to the election Diefenbaker had supported a national hospital insurance plan: "We in the Opposition throughout the years have favoured this type of legislation."[60] Once in office, he amended the Hospital Insurance Act on June 26, 1958, advanced the date of implementation to July 1, 1958, eliminated the six-Province criterion and allowed inclusion of mental and tuberculosis services.[61]

Newfoundland, Manitoba, Saskatchewan, Alberta and British Columbia already had plans that qualified for federal cost-sharing; Nova Scotia, New Brunswick and Ontario were ready by January 1, 1959. Prince Edward Island joined on October 1, 1959. The Northwest Territories joined on April 1, 1960, and the Yukon on July 1, 1960. Finally, Quebec joined on January 1, 1961.

During the 1940s, both the Heagerty Committee and the Canadian Medical Association had advocated a parallel expansion in institutional care, ambulatory care, diagnostic test, convalescent care, chronic care and home care. The introduction of hospital insurance in isolation of other services had many shortcomings. It depended on the goodwill of hospitals, doctors, civil servants and citizens to use resources without marketplace restraints. It discouraged the use of cheaper and more appropriate ambulatory care, which had to develop independently at the Provincial Government level before federal involvement in their financing.

6. Provincial Health Insurance

The Swift Current Health Region No. 1 medical plan had tested the ground for the tax-supported approach in Saskatchewan. The new federal contribution offered under the Hospital Insurance and Diagnostic Services Act allowed the Provinces that already had provincial hospital insurance to use the new funds to extend other programs. With new $13.3 million to finance its hospital plan, Saskatchewan now introduced a provincial health plan to pay for doctors' services.[62]

The CCF had promised the electorate a comprehensive Provincial Government health service throughout its 15 years in power.[63]

T.C. Douglas renewed his commitment to this policy by promising to uphold "the dignity of the individual ... the undeniable right of every person to health, opportunity and freedom," by introducing universal entitlement to doctors' services.[64]

The Saskatchewan medical profession, led by Dr. Harold Dagleish, hired public relations experts to conduct a publicity campaign against the Provincial Government's program.[65] The doctors argued that universal entitlement and compulsory membership was a threat to their freedom; their stance echoed the arguments used earlier in New Zealand and the United Kingdom. At a general meeting of the Saskatchewan Medical Association, the medical profession voted to refuse to cooperate in carrying out the plan.[66]

After Douglas left provincial politics to lead the federal branch of the CCF, renamed the New Democratic Party (NDP) in 1961, Premier Woodrow S. Lloyd introduced Saskatchewan's health care legislation. Lloyd appointed William G. Davies, a former trade-unionist, as his Minister of Public Health. Davies adopted a strategy of non-communication with the medical profession: "Much damage was done by the failure of the two sides to talk to each other."[67]

Understanding between the Government and the doctors deteriorated rapidly. Both parties adhered to their deeply entrenched ideological beliefs and viewed each other with suspicion. Anticipating work-stoppage pressure tactics, the Government began recruiting doctors from other Provinces and the United Kingdom.

With the support of the Canadian Medical Association, which acted as sponsor for eleven voluntary insurance plans, the Saskatchewan doctors mounted a strong political lobby against the proposed legislation.[68] When Saskatchewan passed its Medical Care Law on November 17, 1961, the discussions between the medical profession and the Government had completely broken down.

The plan was nevertheless implemented on July 1, 1962, despite 23 days of doctors' strike and a leadership crisis.[69] By the time the strike ended, the medical profession was accused of having sacrificed patient care to protect its own self-interests, causing doctors to lose much prestige and public sympathy.[70]

B. LANDMARK LEGISLATIVE REFORMS

1. Royal Commission on Health Services

It was Dr. A. D Kelly, the Executive Director of the Canadian Medical Association, who approached the Diefenbaker Conservative Government to "establish a committee to study the existing and projected health needs and health resources of Canada."[71] The medical profession hoped that such a Commission, appointed by a Conservative Government, would rule in favor of voluntary insurance, thereby avoiding a repetition of Saskatchewan's unfortunate experience, The Prime Minister accepted the request by establishing the Royal Commission on Health Services.[72]

Diefenbaker appointed a lifelong friend, Chief Justice Emmett M. Hall, as Chairman of the Commission. Both came from poor families in Saskatchewan. Both graduated from the same law school in 1919.[73] Both were self-proclaimed champions of the needy and believed in the welfare provided by the state. And both came from a Province that accepted universal entitlement to health care as a necessary and just part of public policy.[74]

The reports of the Royal Commission on Health Services were published in 1964 and 1965.[75] They stressed both the humanitarian and economic grounds for a national program: "We now believe that an individual family should not have to bear alone the full cost of risks that could happen to anyone [sic] of us."[76] The Canadian Sickness Survey during the 1950s had shown that illness and utilization of health care services were both directly related to income.[77]

> "To the extent, then, that health expenditures prevent or shorten periods of sickness, reduce the extent of disability, postpone death and contribute to the productivity of citizens, then to that degree health expenditures are investments in our human resources, with the prospect of rich dividends,"[78]

The first report made an extensive analysis of the protection offered through voluntary pre-payment plans, commercial insurance and cooperatives which had all become increasingly popular during the 1950s and early 1960s.[79] Through mergers and extensions, these plans offered increasingly complex coverage (deductibles, co-insurance and interprovincial transportability).[80] The private insurance industry formed a national group, the Canadian Health Insurance Association (CHIA) in 1959. The medical profession established its own national association, the Trans-Canada Medical Plans (TCMP) in 1951.[81] By the 1960s, the TCMP aimed at offering uniform national coverage and portability across the country.[82]

Several provincial programs had likewise opted for the insurance model. On March 11, 1963, Alberta had introduced legislation to subsidize the memberships of low-income earners to encourage them to join voluntary organizations. By October of the same year, voluntary insurance covered 84 percent of Alberta's population. In April 1963, Ontario had introduced similar medicare legislation to encourage purchase of voluntary insurance, the Ontario Medical Services Insurance Plan. British Columbia followed the example of Ontario, establishing its own agency, the British Columbia Medical Plan, to insure those who could not afford to subscribe to private plans.

Voluntary insurance, however, posed many problems. It offered limited comprehensiveness, incomplete coverage and inequitable access. High premiums excluded the poor. Waivers, waiting periods and carrier cancellation privileges excluded the ill. The excluded were the segment of the population who often needed health care the most, those who sought attention through hospitals and those who received federal and provincial assistance. Finally, the private insurance organizations kept high retention rates despite their public subsidies.[83]

The commission estimated that to subsidize health insurance premiums, once expenditure rose beyond 5 percent of income, would require means-testing 10 million Canadians; raising the level to 7 percent would require means-testing of 15 million.[84] The Commission also claimed that, although, the federal financial contribution was already 80 percent of the anticipated run cost of a comprehensive service, it left the most needy unprotected. The cost of extending coverage to the additional 20 percent would amount to $466 million: "Surely a nation which spent $973 million on alcohol ... could afford half of that amount for a vastly improved health system."[85]

The Commission, therefore, recommended that Canadian health policy should correct "the paradox of our age ... the enormous gap between our scientific knowledge and skills on the one hand, and our organizational and financial arrangements to apply them to the needs of men, on the other."[86] Canadians would achieve this goal through the application of a *Health Charter for Canadians* enunciated in the report[87]:

> The achievement of· the highest possible health standards for all our people must become a primary objective of national policy and a cohesive factor contributing to national unity, involving individual and community responsibilities and actions. This objective can best be achieved through a comprehensive, universal Health Services Programme for the Canadian People,
>
> IMPLEMENTED in accordance with Canada's evolving constitutional arrangements;
>
> BASED upon freedom of choice, and upon free and self-governing professions;
>
> FINANCED through prepayment arrangements;
>
> ACCOMPLISHED through the full cooperation of the general public, the health professions, voluntary agencies, all political parties and governments, federal, provincial, and municipal;
>
> DIRECTED towards the most effective use of the nation's health resources to attain the highest possible levels of physical and mental well-being.

Universal entitlement meant "adequate health services ... available to all Canadians wherever they reside and whatever their financial resources may be, within the limitations imposed by geographic factors." Comprehensive services meant "all health services, preventive, diagnostic, curative and rehabilitative, that modern medical and other sciences can provide."[88]

To avoid a constitutional challenge, the program would maintain provincial jurisdiction over health care, allowing the Provinces to finance their share through "premiums, subsidized premiums, sales or other taxes, supplements from provincial general revenues and ... by federal grants taking into account provincial fiscal need."[89] It would also preserve the freedom of patients to choose their own doctor and the freedom of the medical profession to remain self-governing.[90]

The medical profession and members of the Conservative party who had advocated the appointment of the Commission reacted with consternation. They could not understand how a group of "establishment types, appointed by a Conservative Prime Minister" could arrive at a unanimous decision to advocate universal entitlement, comprehensive benefits, compulsory membership and public financing.[91]

By the time the Royal Commission presented its reports, however, the Conservative Party was no longer in power. During the campaign leading up to the 1963 general elections, the Liberal Party had pledged to "establish a medical care plan for all Canadians" in cooperation with the Provinces.[92] The NDP was equally committed to a national program.[93] Neither the Progressive Conservative Party nor the Social Credit Party, however, mentioned health care in their 1963 election platforms.[94]

Hall defended his recommendations by embarking "on a series of highly controversial public speeches, all urging the implementation of his report, and quickly."[95] He later defended his actions: "I think we [Hall and Douglas] can both take some satisfaction out of knowing that we have helped push back a little the shadows of fear and anxiety from the lives of many people."[96] Hall's new audience was attentive.

2. Federal-Provincial Conference of 1965

Prime Minister Lester B. Pearson, leader of the new Liberal Minority Government, signaled his party's renewed commitment to a national health plan in the Throne Speech of April 5, 1965: "My government will at an early date meet with the governments of the Provinces in order to discuss with them ways in which federal and provincial action can most effectively contribute to programs [sic] that will provide health services to Canadians on a comprehensive basis."[97] He appointed Walter L. Gordon as Minister of Finance and Judy LaMarsh as Minister of Health and Social Welfare.

A special Federal-Provincial Conference on Health, recommended by the Royal Commission, started on July 19, 1965.[98] "[It is] the responsibility of the Federal Government to cooperate with the Provinces in making Medicare financially possible for all Canadians."[99] The conference established four principles for such a service: comprehensive doctor services (general practitioners and specialists), universal entitlement, inter-provincial portability and administration by a public authority.[100] "[The] provision of health services … the item of our agenda which is most important of all ... [making it] the responsibility of the Federal Government ... [to make] medicare financially possible for all Canadians."[101]

The Liberal Minority Government needed support from the NDP, led by Douglas, to stay in power.[102] Social legislation, like the national health care program, was certain to secure this support.

Gordon, had previously been instrumental in developing the party strategy that brought the Liberals back to power; he was the first Minister of Finance with a sympathetic attitude toward a national health care program.[103] "A rich man's son from upper-class Tory Toronto who embraced relatively radical views and grew more radical with age … made Bay Street shudder."[104] He wanted "better standards of education, better provisions for our old people [and] proper medical care for everyone."[105]

LaMarsh had encountered the "shocking examples of the devastating impact of the costs of long-term medical care on meager incomes."[106] Her mother's terminal illness and depletion of her husband's lifetime savings to meet medical expenses had taught her the financial tragedies resulting from the failings of the voluntary health insurance system: "The subject matters dealt with in 'NH&W' [the Department of National Health and Welfare] are 'gut' issues — basic to the whole philosophy of the role of government in modern society."[107]

Many circumstances had changed since the 1950s. The Canadian economy had expanded, freeing the Provinces from their dependence on federal financial support. Most Canadians by then preferred voluntary insurance to compulsory insurance.[108] Six Provinces were led by new parties, and seven had new leaders.[109] "The Quiet Revolution," ushered in by the election of the provincial Liberal Party under Premier Jean Lesage in 1960, reflected Quebec's mood for greater political autonomy.[110] These changes presented new obstacles to a federal health care program, adding to the traditional constitutional ones.

3. National Medicare Program

LaMarsh, with the support of the Prime Minister and the Minister of Finance, however, created a unique and powerful advocacy for national action. The members of the new Liberal Minority Cabinet who supported the program were optimistic. "Considering the extent of Walter Gordon's commitment to [Pension and Medicare] programs as campaign chief, [the fight for money] wouldn't be too tough!"[111]

Several legislative reforms had already tested the strength of the Minority Government and increased its self-confidence. The Government had survived the long negotiations with Quebec over a Canadian Pension Plan. It had increased benefits under the Old Age Security Plan. It had introduced a Student Loan Act. It had brought in a distinctive Canadian flag, discarding the British Union Jack. Finally, it had extended family allowance benefits: "It remained for the Canada Assistance Act and Medicare to be passed ... to have a respectable social-security base."[112]

A committee of senior officials from the Department of Health and Department of Finance joined the Privy Council Office to draw up a proposal for the new Medicare program. The working committee relied extensively on recommendations from Royal Commission on Health Services.[113] To avoid a constitutional challenge, their proposal called for a 50 percent cost-sharing arrangement between the Federal Government and the Provinces.[114] To qualify, a Province had to establish comprehensive, universal, accessible and portable doctor services administered by public non-profit authorities.

Anxious about the risks facing Medicare legislation if introduced by a weak Minority Government, Walter Gordon urged the Prime Minister to hold an election in 1965: "Life as a member of a Minority Government is a most uncertain business."[115] When the election failed to give the Liberal Party a majority, Gordon resigned: "I called Mike ... and reminded him of my undertaking to resign if we did not get an over-all majority." Alan MacEachen became the new Minister of Health. Mitchell Sharp became the Minister of Finance.

Gordon represented the left and Sharp the right of the party: left stood for social security programs and human welfare above financial stability; right stood for postponement when public expenditure strained the economy. "One became uncomfortably aware that there was an undeclared war between the two men [Gordon and Sharp]."[116] LaMarsh noted that Sharp "always prefaced his arguments against proceeding with the caveat that he was really in favour of medicare himself. No one ever believed him."[117]

Sharp claimed that he only wanted to avoid "adding to the already large increases that were taking place in federal expenditures in 1966."[118]

Despite these conflicts, a draft legislation finally appeared in 1966 which called for Medicare to be implemented July 1, 1967. The legislation reflected the recommendations of the Royal Commission on Health Services, adding two new criteria: only the participating Provinces would determine the national average, and private insurance companies could act as provincial carriers, providing that they submitted to a public audit and that they remained accountable to Parliament.[119]

The summer recess interrupted the second reading, allowing time for opponents to mobilize against the legislation. "The opponents of medicare smelled an ally. They came out from their lairs again; the medical profession, the Provinces, medical care insurers, all of them."[120] While Pearson went abroad for a Commonwealth Conference in the United Kingdom, Sharp introduced a new austerity program, calling for a postponement of the Medicare legislation.[121] Later, to justify another delay, "he pulled a one-billion-dollar cost figure from the air (ignoring everything the Hall Report had meticulously documented).... It had a telling effect, coming as it did from the Minister of Finance."[122]

Everyone supporting the legislation was exasperated: "The cheque the Liberals first wrote in 1919 has been bouncing ever since."[123] MacEachen threatened to resign. Tommy Douglas warned that the Conservatives would succeed in introducing their "tin-cup medicare" program.[124] Gordon reminded the Liberals that their earlier "collective decision on medicare must be respected and not undermined."[125]

Pearson, however, defended his Minister of Finance: "It was not a question of whether one [was] for or against Medicare ... [Sharp's actions were] in fundamental sympathy with the policies Walter Gordon advocated, but [Sharp] was more careful and cautious in seeking their implementation."[126] The new date for introducing the national program was July 1, 1968: "Looking back, it may seem that the one-year delay in the introduction of medicare was hardly worth the bitter political struggle."[127]

The Medical Care Bill passed second reading on October 25, 1966, after eight days of intense debate, and the third reading on December 8 by a vote of 177 to 2. Little debate took place in the Senate and Royal Assent was given on December 21, 1966. Medicare would finally became a reality after 20 years of negotiation on July 1, 1968: "And on that date Medicare did come into operation, without undue strain on our economic capacity."[128] Among the many reforms introduced by the Liberal Minority Government, Medicare "was to be one of the crowning achievements of the Pearson administration."[129]

Although the Canadian Medical Association protested against the program throughout the negotiations and legislative process, the abortive Saskatchewan strike was still fresh in the minds of most doctors. The Saskatchewan strike had damaged their public image, prestige and pride. Many doctors were reluctant to become embroiled in a similar controversy at the national level. As a consequence, the Canadian Medical Association urged its members to accept the new Act as law. In effect, the passing of the Canadian Medical Care Act had little immediate effect on doctors; each Province first had to pass its own individual plan.

Implementing federal policies in Canada "requires the same political skills as international diplomacy; the end product is often fraught with compromises."[130] The Canada Medical Care Act only initiated the introduction of public financing for universal entitlement to health care. The economic impact would not become clear until later.[131] The Provinces still had to establish their own commissions, committees and working groups to evaluate the terms of their respective commitments.[132] MacEachen assigned his new Deputy Minister of Health, Dr. John N. Crawford, the difficult task of persuading the provincial branches of the Canadian Medical Association to accept the plan. [133]

4. Strike, Armed Insurrection and War Measures

At the time of the inaugural date on July 1, 1968, only two Provinces qualified for Federal Government funds, Saskatchewan and British Columbia. Others followed over the next four years. Newfoundland, Nova Scotia and Manitoba qualified on April 1, 1969. Alberta qualified on July 1, 1969, Ontario on October 1, 1969, Quebec on November 1, 1970, Prince Edward Island on December 1, 1970, New Brunswick on January 1, 1971, the Northwest Territories on April 1, 1971 and the Yukon on April 1, 1972.

General revenues would finance the new the federal contribution towards the Medicare program. A three percent non-earmarked social development tax was, however, introduced by the Federal Government during the same time. Although the Liberals denied that this tax was intended to finance Medicare, it provided additional funds for the federal treasury.[134] The Provinces were left to finance their contribution through combinations of provincial general revenues, premiums, user charges, indirect sales taxes, special interest-bearing funds and their share of the federal contribution.

The total cost of the health care services was $3.3 billion in 1965, $6 billion in 1970 and $11 billion in 1975. This made Finance Minister Sharp's earlier prediction of $1 billion seem conservative. The Canadian Medical Association's warning that abuse would occur if there were no deterrent charges proved invalid; doctors who provided the services controlled their use.[135] "Universal health insurance in Canada has not 'broken the bank.'"[136]

During the course of implementing the Medical Care Act, Quebec's doctors were the most vocal in their opposition. The death of Premier Maurice Duplessis in 1960 had marked the end of a long era of Quebec conservatism and traditionalism, during which time a rural, church-bound society was dominated by a rigid Provincial Government. Premier Jean Lesage and later Premier Johnson blocked all federal initiatives which they felt were a threat to Quebec's new sense of assertiveness.[137]

Premier Jean-Jacques Bertrand, leader of the Union Nationale Government, who succeeded Johnson, introduced the Quebec Health Insurance Bill 8 on March 12, 1970. When the new Provincial Liberal Government, under Premier Robert Bourassa, put the Act into effect, Quebec's medical specialists withdrew their services. The Quebec Government, less patient than Saskatchewan had been several years earlier, legislated the doctors back to work.

These events coincided with a series of terrorist incidents by small separatist cells of the "Front de la Liberation du Quebec" which kidnapped a British diplomat, James Cross, and a provincial Liberal Cabinet Minister, Pierre Laporte.[138] With the murder of Laporte, the *revolution tranquille* ceased being so "quiet." The new Federal Liberal Prime Minister, Pierre Elliott Trudeau, decided to invoke Canada's 1917 War

Measures Act, sending in troops to prevent an "apprehended insurrection" in Quebec. The ongoing power struggle between Ottawa and the Provinces over Medicare occurred against this backdrop.

C. CONTINUED POLICY REFORM PROCESS

1. Canada Health Act of 1984

Despite its general success, Hall's blueprint failed to the produce the comprehensive health service conceptualized by early Canadian reformers. The original Federal-Provincial cost-sharing arrangement covered only hospital care and doctors' services. The provision of other ambulatory services was left to the private sector. Individual Provinces eventually introduced some of these services in a piecemeal fashion, but most lacked the political initiative and financial resources to make such programs uniform across Canada. "The ultimate goal of medicare must be the task of keeping people well rather than just patching them up when they're sick."[139] This would include aspects of "human biology, environment, lifestyle and health care organization," that cannot be provided merely through hospitalization and doctors services.[140]

Furthermore, successive Federal Governments since the 1960s have tried to limit Ottawa's financial commitment to the Canadian health care system.[141] "You will never have another Medicare, I promise you that," Prime Minister Trudeau remarked in 1969.[142] In 1979, a Minority Government formed by the Progressive Conservatives once again appointed Emmett M. Hall to review the state of the Canadian health care. "Medicare as we knew it is gradually eroding. Through a cumulation of direct charges on the sick … the goal of complete insurance, fully prepaid, is being abandoned."[143] Hall continued to favor public provision of health care in Canada. Monique Begin, the Liberal Minister of Health in 1982, supported this stance. She introduced the Canada Health Act of 1984 which combined hospital care and doctors' services under one piece of legislation.

The same principles that were embodied in the 1967 Medical Care Act reappeared in the 1984 Canada Health Act: comprehensiveness, universality, portability, accessibility and public administration.[144] The new law confirmed past commitments by introducing stiff penalties for Provinces that allowed user charges and extra-billing which had increased over time and which were eroding the spirit of the original federal-provincial agreement.[145] The new Hall Report found much work left for the Federal Government to complete. "It may be that the introduction of block-funding has created, in both public and governments, the notion that the federal role in health is completed. This is not so ... without further federal action the gap between levels of service in high and low income Provinces will increase, and the goal of a comprehensive health system will never be met."[146]

The Canadian story on universal entitlement is therefore incomplete. The pluralism of the Canadian federal political system has provided an excellent experimental model for testing various modes of financing and delivering health care. Ambulatory care, other than doctors' services, now needs federal action to ensure more comprehensive coverage, Some Provinces have already taken the initiative to extend ambulatory care to services other than those offered by medical doctors. Extending such benefits to the rest of the country remains an important challenge for the Canadian Federal Government.[147]

2. Major Policy Reforms in Canada Since the 1980s

Since the latter part of the 1980s, the Canadian health system has continued to evolve. Starting with what was already a mixed public–private partnership, recent reforms have not significantly altered this approach to both funding and delivery of health care. The public character of tax funding and public/nongovernmental/private character of the service delivery system has prevailed, despite periodic constitutional challenges.[148] [149]

In 2002, the Royal Commission on the Future of Health Care in Canada, also known as the Romanow Report led by Roy Romanow, made sweeping recommendations on ways to preserve the long-term sustainability of Canada's health care system.[150] The proposed changes were outlined in the Commission's final report, *Building on Values: The Future of Health Care in Canada*, which was tabled in the House of Commons on 28 November 2002.[151]

The Report led to a significant agreement in September 2004 whereby the Government of Canada agreed strengthen ongoing federal health support provided through the Canada Health Transfer (CHT) and ways to address significant wait times for access to essential health care services. It did not alter the underlying fundamental principles of the Canadian health care system set forth in the Canada Health Act 1984, led by Health Minister Monique Bégin, which replaced the earlier Hospital Insurance and Diagnostic Services Act and the Medical Care Act.

The Royal Commission continued to discourage extra billing and user fees for physician and hospital services. It required the federal government to deduct (dollar-for-dollar) the value of all extra billing and user fees from a given provincial government's share of Established Programs Financing (EPF). Private profit-making hospitals were excluded from public funding arrangement, thus restricting the growth of such hospitals in Canada, although the municipal and non-profit-making hospitals were allowed such funding leading to a proliferation in this segment of the hospital sector. It also meant that other than mental hospitals, the public hospital sector in Canada has remained small.

Overall, for the past 40 years, the Canadian health care system has remained remarkably resistant to erosion in the basic principles established under the Canada Health Act of 1984.[152] By the 1990s, Canada already had a mixed market-based health care system that embraced quasi "new public sector" management approaches like those that were later pioneered in New Zealand, with their focus on greater managerial accountability, market-based economic incentives and greater competition among providers.[153]

As of 2017, the Federal Government continues to co-finance provincial and territorial programs, providing that the provinces and territories adhere to the original five principles of the Canada Health Act: (1) publicly administered; (2) comprehensive in coverage; (3) universal; (4) portable across provinces; and (5) accessible (i.e. without user fees).[154]

After a period fiscal restraint under the Conservative Prime Minister Stephen Harper, Justin Trudeau leading the Liberal Party, assumed office on November 4, 2015. This has once again ushered in a new era of a more favorable Federal fiscal support for health care in the Canadian provinces.

ENDNOTES

1. The Federal Government's responsibility included jurisdiction over the Yukon and Northwest Territories in cooperation with local authorities, the military services, the penitentiaries, the Royal Canadian Mounted Police, immigrants, Indians, Eskimos and some aspect of the health care of public employees.
2. United Kingdom, "British North America Act (BNA Act)," *Statutes* (29 March 1867): 30, 31 Victoria 7, sec. 92.7.
3. The population for 1901 is based on United Nations (UN), Statistics Office (SO), Department of Economic and Social Affairs (DESA), *Demographic Yearbook* 1962, 14th Edition (New York: UN, 1962): 264 and the area is based on J. Paxton, ed., *The Statesman's Year-Book: Statistical and Historical Annual of the States of the World for the Year 1986–1987*, 123rd Edition (London: MacMillan Press, 1986): 271.
4. The Department of Health, created in 1919, became the Department of Pensions and National Health in 1928 through a merger with the Department of Soldiers' Civil Re-establishment, and the Department of National Health and Welfare in 1944.
5. Canada, Select Standing Committee on Industrial and International Relations (SSCIIR), *Report* (Ottawa: King's Printer, 1929).
6. The Municipal Hospital Plan in Alberta in 1919 and the Newfoundland Cottage Hospitalisation and Medical Care Plan in 1934 offered similar provisions.
7. Dr. M. Anderson, who had known a similar plan as a boy in Norway, started the first tax-based municipal doctors' systems in Saskatchewan. See R. F. Badgley and S. Wolf, *Doctors' Strike: Medical Care and Conflict in Saskatchewan* (New York: Atherton Press, 1967): 13.
8. Other early plans included the Rural Doctor Plans of Saskatchewan in 1917 and Manitoba in 1921. See E. A. Tollefson, *Bitter Medicine: The Saskatchewan Medicare Feud*, Prairie Books (Saskatoon: Modern Press, 1964): 40.
9. M. G. Taylor, *Health Insurance and Canadian Public Policy: The Seven Decisions that Created the Canadian Health Insurance System* (Montreal: McGill-Queen's University Press, 1978): 6.
10. Taylor, *Health Insurance*, p. 2; and Personal communication with Dr. Malcolm G. Taylor, historian and professor of political science, University of York, Toronto.
11. Taylor, *Health Insurance*, p. 4.

12. The forerunners to these programmes began in Saskatchewan in 1914 in the rural municipality of Sarnia. Taylor, *Health Insurance*, p. 70.
13. Badgley and Wolf, *Doctors' Strike*, p. 3.
14. The party was the forerunner to the New Democratic Party.
15. T. Douglas on Apri1 2, 1954, quoted from the *Regina Leader Post* by Taylor, *Health Insurance*, p. 81.
16. The Saskatchewan Hospitalization Act came into effect on January 1, 1947.
17. Personal communication with L. F. Detwiller, former Commissioner of the British Columbia Hospitals Insurance Service in 1951.
18. Canada, "Employment and Social Insurance Act," *Statutes* (1935).
19. Canada, Royal Commission on Dominion-Provincial Relations (RCDPR), *Report [Chairman Rowell-Sirois]*, (Ottawa: King's Printer, 1937).
20. Canada, RCDPR, *Rowell-Sirois*, 40–41.
21. Ian Ma-ckenzie on December 27, 1939, quoted in Taylor, *Health Insurance*, p. 16.
22. He used the expertise of the Dominion Council of Health and Dominion Bureau of Statistics (Inter-Departmental Advisory Committee of Health Insurance) to help him draft his plan. The Dominion Council of Health comprised the Ministers of Health from the Provinces.
23. Canada, Special Committee on Social Security (SCSS), *Report of the Advisory Committee on Health Insurance [Chairman J.J. Heagerty]* (Ottawa: King's Printer, 1943).
24. Canadian Medical Association (CMA), Committee on Economics (CE), *Report* (Ottawa: CMA, 1943).
25. The Canadian Medical Association gave evidence to the House of Commons Special Committee on Social Security. See Canadian Medical Association, General Council (GC), *Special Meeting: Transactions*, January 18–19 (Ottawa: CMA, 1943); and Canada, House of Commons Special Committee on Social Security (HCSCSS), *Report [Chairman Cyrus MacMillan]* (Ottawa: King's Printer, 1943): 145.
26. Canada, Advisory Committee on Health Insurance (ACHI), *Report [Chairman W.C. Clarke]* (Ottawa: King's Printer, 1943): xi–xxii. Other committees supporting national programmes for social security and health reported during the same year: Canada, HCSCSS, *Cyrus MacMillan;* Canada, SCSS, *Chairman J.J. Heagerty;* and Canada, Committee on Health Insurance Finance (CHIF), "Interim report," *Brooke Claxton Papers*, 28 December (1943).
27. Canada, National Health and Welfare (NHW), *Illness and Health Care in Canada: Canadian Sickness Survey 1950–51* (Ottawa: Queens Printer, 1960).

28. The parties on the ballot consisted of the Liberal Party led by Mackenzie King, the Conservative Party led by John Bracken of Manitoba, the Cooperative Commonwealth Federation (the New Democratic Party after 1961) led by Stanley Knowles, the Social Credit Party and the Communist Party.
29. An opinion poll indicated that 80 percent of Canadians supported a national hospital and medical care insurance plan. See Taylor, *Health Insurance*, p. 48.
30. Beveridge visited Ottawa in May 1943.
31. Mackenzie King, *Industry and Humanity*, quoted in J.W. Pickersgill, *The Mackenzie King Record: 1939–1944*, Volume I (Toronto: University of Toronto Press, 1960): 546.
32. Winston Churchill, quoted in Taylor, *Health Insurance*, p. 67.
33. Canada, *Report for Social Security for Canada [Chairman Leonard Marsh]* (Ottawa: King's Printer, April 1943); and P. Martin, *A Very Public life — Far From Home*, Volume 1 (Ottawa: Deneau, 1983): 316.
34. The protest from the Minister of Justice, Louis St. Laurent, foreshadowed the stance he would take later as Prime Minister.
35. The provincial Premiers attending the Conference included Drew from Ontario, Duplessis from Quebec, Manning from Ontario and Douglas from Saskatchewan.
36. Canada, Dominion-Provincial Conference (DPC), *1945 Proceedings: Green Book Proposals* (Ottawa: King's Printer, 1945). By 1945, Canada, Australia and the United States were the only three industrialized nations to lack significant social security legislation which included health care provisions.
37. Canada, DPC, *1945 Proceedings.*
38. According to the British North America Act of 1867, the Provinces also had jurisdiction over medical education.
39. As the general manager of the Metropolitan Life Insurance Company, after a short period in the Ministry of Defence, Claxton became an ardent opponent to medicare.
40. Martin, *Public Life*, p. 317. Personal communication with Paul J.J. Martin, the Minister of Health from 1946 to 1957.
41. Martin, *Public Life*, p. 40.
42. Taylor, *Health Insurance*, p. 164.
43. D. Owen Carrigan, *Canadian Party Platforms 1867–1968* (Toronto: Copp Clark, 1968). The major parties were the Liberal Party, the Progressive Conservative Party, the Cooperative Commonwealth Federation and the Social Credit Party.

44. Results of a Gallup Poll reported in the *Toronto Daily Star* (13 July 1949) discussed in Taylor, *Health Insurance*, p. 166.
45. Only the Social Credit Party made no direct reference to health insurance in 1953.
46. The Liberal Party platform for the 1953 general election quoted in Taylor, *Health Insurance*, p. 108.
47. The term "national health insurance" is a misnomer since the intention was always to use general revenues for the Federal Government component.
48. Canada, Federal-Provincial Conference (FPC), *1955 Proceedings* (Ottawa: Queen's Printer, 1955): 2.
49. The provincial Premiers attending the Conference were Duplessis (Quebec), Frost (Ontario), Hicks (Nova Scotia), Robichaud (New Brunswick), Matheson (Prince Edward Island), Bennett Sr. (British Columbia), Smallwood (Newfoundland), Douglas (Saskatchewan), Campbell (Alberta) and Manning (Alberta).
50. Drew became the Conservative Party leader in Ottawa.
51. Canada, FPC, *1955 Proceedings*, pp. 12–15.
52. Quebec abstained.
53. Martin, *Public Life*, p. 47.
54. Canada, FPC, *1955 Proceedings*, pp. 3–4.
55. In practical terms, this meant Ontario plus five other Provinces.
56. The 1943 programme was based on a report from 1933. The General Council of the Canadian Medical Association unanimously endorsed this programme on January 18, 1943. The House of Commons Advisory Committee on Health Insurance reported these findings on July 23, 1943.
57. Canadian Medical Association, *Policy Statement* (Ottawa: CMA, 1955).
58. Other Provinces, wanting to avoid a debate over compulsory insurance, abandoned the premium system in order to comply with the "universal" clause.
59. Opposition leaders were Diefenbaker (Progressive Conservative Party), Knowles (Cooperative Commonwealth Federation) and Hansell (Social Credit Party).
60. Canada, "John G. Diefenbaker," House of Commons, *Debates* (4 April 1957).
61. No Province exercised the option of financing their psychiatric services in this way because the Federal Government would subtract from other subsidies an amount equal to the added cost of these services, Instead, most Provinces established psychiatric wards in general hospitals which were covered under the program.

62. British Columbia would use its new funds to subsidize doctors' services for low-income groups, while encouraging the rest of the population to subscribe to voluntary insurance.
63. The Saskatchewan Medical Care Advisory Planning Committee visited Australia, New Zealand, United Kingdom, Norway, Sweden, Denmark and Holland to obtain information about their health care plans.
64. Saskatchewan, "Throne speech [Premier T.C. Douglas]," *Legislative Assembly Debates* (17 April 1960).
65. They copied the tactics that the American Medical Association had used to oppose such a plan in the United States. See Badgley and Wolf, *Doctors' Strike*, p. 30.
66. Badgley and Wolf, *Doctors' Strike*, p. 40.
67. *Ibid.*,p. 44.
68. M. G. Taylor, "The role of the medical profession in the formulation and execution of public policy," *Canadian Journal of Economics and Political Science* 25(February 1960): 108–27, 108–27; and Taylor, *Health Insurance*, p. 334.
69. The Cooperative Commonwealth Federation lost the 1964 provincial election.
70. Badgley and Wolf, *Doctors' Strike*, p. xi. At the time Canada was the eighth country to introduce universal health care legislation. It was the first to have a doctors' strike over such legislation.
71. Canadian Medical Association, Committee on Economics (CE), "Transactions of the 94th annual meeting of the CMA," June 19–21 (Ottawa: CMA, 1961):29.
72. Canada, Royal Commission on Health Services (RCHS), *Report [Chairman Emmett M. Hall]* (Ottawa: Queen's Printer, 1964).
73. Other members of the Commission were Dr. David Baltzan, a surgeon; Dr. Arthur van Wart, a past president of the Canadian Medical Association; Alice Girard, Dean of University of Montreal School of Nursing; Dr. Leslie Strachan, a dentist and former president of the Ontario Dental Association; Wallace McCutcheon, an industrialist; and Dr. O. J. Firestone, an economist. Professor Bernard Blishen was research director. Dr. Pierre Jobin and M. G. Taylor were research consultants.
74. Diefenbaker's introduction of the Canadian Bill of Rights and Fundamental Freedoms was a great achievement; it makes no mention, however, of social rights or more specifically, rights to health care.
75. Personal communication with Justice Emmett M. Hall. Although there was no minority report, winning unanimous support from of all the Commissioners required much personal effort by Hall.

76. Canada, RCHS, *Emmett M. Hall*, p. 5.
77. Canada, (NHW), *Illness and Health Care.*
78. Canada, RCHS, *Emmett M. Hall*, p. 6.
79. C. Howard Shillington, *The Road to Medicare in Canada* (Toronto: Del Graphics, 1972): 44–64.
80. Shillington, *Road to Medicare*, p. 104.
81. *Ibid.*, p. 93.
82. *Ibid.*, p. 100, 143. The Canadian Medical Association participated closely in the administration of the TMCP.
83. Canada, RCHS, *Emmett M. Hall*, p. 421.
84. M. G. Taylor, quoting Hall in D. Gruending, *Emmett Hall* (Toronto: Macmillan, 1985): 90.
85. Gruending, *Emmett Hall*, p. 95.
86. Canada, RCHS, *Emmett M. Hall*, p. 10.
87. Canada, RCHS, *Emmett M. Hall*, p. 11.
88. Canada, RCHS, *Emmett M. Hall*, p. 11. The comprehensive provisions were short-sighted, leaving out most ambulatory services other than Doctor's visits.
89. Canada, RCHS, *Emmett M. Hall*, p. 12.
90. Canada, RCHS, *Emmett M. Hall*, p. 99.
91. Gruending, *Emmett Hall*, p. 99.
92. Taylor, *Health Insurance*, p. 333.
93. The NDP, formed in 1961, was the federal wing of the Saskatchewan Cooperative Commonwealth Federation.
94. Carrigan, *Party Platforms*, 1968.
95. This was an unprecedented and questionable action for a Supreme Court Judge to take. See J. LaMarsh, *Memoirs of a Bird in a Gilded Cage* (Toronto: McClelland and Stewart, 1968): 120.
96. Tommy Douglas, quoted in Gruending, *Emmett Hall*, p. 80. Personal communication with Emmett M. Hall.
97. Lester Pearson, quoted from the Throne Speech. Canada, Parliament House of Commons, *Debates* (1965): 2–3. The Liberal Party's commitment to a national health insurance programme first appeared in a policy paper in 1919. See Carrigan, *Party Platforms*; Taylor, *Health Insurance*, p. 220; and Martin, *Public Life*, p. 457.
98. Canada, "Throne speech by Prime Minister Lester B. Pearson," House of Commons, *Debates* (5 April 1965): 2–3.
99. Canada, Federal-Provincial Conference (FPC), *1965 Proceedings*, July 19–22 (Ottawa: Queen's Printer, 1965).

100. A Health Resources Fund would finance medical schools and teaching hospitals.
101. Lester Pearson, quoted in the opening address. Canada, Federal-Provincial Conference (FPC), *1965 Proceedings*, July 19–22 (Ottawa: Queen's Printer, 1965).
102. The Liberals had 129 seats, NDP 17 seats, Conservatives 95 seats and Social Credits 24 seats.
103. Gordon was the Chairman of the Policy Committee of the National Rally of the Liberal Party in 1961.
104. Christopher Young of *Southern News Services*, quoted in W. Gordon, *A Political Memoir*, [Toronto: McClelland and Stewart 1977], Paperback reprint (Halifax: Good read Biographies, 1983).
105. W. L. Gordon, *Troubled Canada: The Need for New Domestic Policies* (Toronto: McClelland and Stewart, 1961): 3; and Personal communication with Walter L. Gordon.
106. LaMarsh, *Gilded Cage*, pp. 120–1.
107. LaMarsh, *Gilded Cage*, p. 48.
108. Provincial voluntary insurance plans had already forged ahead in British Columbia in September 1965 and Ontario in January 1966.
109. The Premiers were Lesage (Quebec), Robarts (Ontario), Stanfield (Nova Scotia), Fleming (New Brunswick), Shaw (Prince Edward Island), Bennett Sr. (British Columbia), Smallwood (Newfoundland), Thatcher (Saskatchewan), Roblin (Alberta) and Manning (Alberta).
110. He had already convinced the Federal Government to accord Quebec taxation points instead of the usual conditional "grant-in-aid." See Canada, Federal-Provincial Conference (FPC), *1960 Proceedings* (Ottawa: Queen's Printer, 1960).
111. LaMarsh, *Gilded Cage*, p. 48.
112. Gordon, *Memoir*, p. 217.
113. The Deputy Minister, Dr. G.D.W. Cameron, was responsible for drawing up the early plans. Personal communication with the subsequent Minister of Health, Alan J. MacEachen, and his Deputy Minister, Dr. John N. Crawford.
114. Since distribution would be on a per capita basis, the poorer Provinces would receive nearly 80 percent, while the wealthier Provinces would receive less than 50 percent.
115. Gordon, *Memoir*, p. 219, 220.
116. LaMarsh, *Gilded Cage*, p. 323.
117. *Ibid.*

118. M. Sharp, "The role of economic advice in political decisions," in *Economic Policy Advising in Canada: Essays in Honour of John Deutsch*, by D.C. Smith, ed. (Montreal: C.D. Howe Institute, 1981): 221.
119. Canada, "Health Resources Fund Act," *Statutes* (1966). This Act was passed during the negotiations on the Medical Care Act. Under the Act, the Federal Government would pay 50 percent of approved projects for planning, construction and renovation of teaching and research facilities for health services personnel. This was an important step in securing medical man power for the future.
120. LaMarsh, *Gilded Cage*, p. 340.
121. Canada, "Mitchell Sharp," House of Commons, *Debates* (8 September 1966).
122. LaMarsh, *Gilded Cage*, p. 325.
123. Leonard Shifrin, editor of the Liberal Party newspaper, quoted in Taylor, *Health Insurance*, p. 371.
124. D. Smith, *Gentle Patriot: A Political Biography of Walter Gordon* (Edmonton: Hurting, 1973): 291; and *Taylor*, *Health Insurance*, p. 372.
125. Smith, *Gentle Patriot*, p. 336.
126. L. B. Pearson, *The Memoirs of The Right Honourable Lester B. Pearson: Mike*, Volume 3, by J. A. Munro and A. I. Inglis (Toronto: University of Toronto Press, 1975): 226.
127. Sharp, "Economic advice," p. 221. Personal communication with Mitchell Sharp, his Deputy Minister, R. B. Bryce and Assistant Deputy Minister, Dr. A. W. Johnson.
128. Pearson, *Memoirs*, p. 227.
129. LaMarsh, *Gilded Cage*, p. 122.
130. Personal communication with Malcolm G. Taylor.
131. Canada, National Health and Welfare (NHW), Task Force on the Cost of Health Services in Canada (TFCHSC), *Reports* (Ottawa: Information Canada, 1969); and Canada, National Health and Welfare (NHW), *The Community Health Centre in Canada [Chairman J.E.F.Hastings]* (Ottawa: Information Canada, 1973).
132. British Columbia, Commission on Health Security for British Columbians (CHSBC), *Report [Chairman Richard* G. *Foulkes]* (Victoria: Government of the Province of British Columbia, 1973); Quebec, Commission of Inquiry on Health and Social Welfare (CIHSW), *Report [Chairman Gerard Nepveu]* (Quebec City: Government of the Province of Quebec, 1970); and Ontario, Committee on the Healing Arts (OCRA), *Reports* (Toronto:

Government of the Province of Ontario, 1970). Other Provinces also commissioned management consultants and special studies.

133. Personal communication with Alan MacEachen.
134. The Federal Government also benefited from the delayed introduction of Medicare in Ontario and Quebec. It collected taxes without having immediately to spend the funds. Personal communication with Mitchell Sharp.
135. Lee Soderstrom, *The Canadian Health System* (London: Croom Helm, 1978): 175–185.
136. G. H Hatcher, *Universal Free Health Care in Canada*, 1947–77 (Washington: U.S. Department of Health and Human Services, 1981): 2; and M. LeClair, "The Canadian Health Care System," in *National Health Insurance: Can We Learn From Canada?* by S. Andreopoulos, ed. (New York: John Wiley and Sons, 1975): 50–51.
137. French President Charles de Gaulle encouraged the separatists movement with a tactless "*Vivre le Quebec libre*" in his speech from the balcony of Montreal's city hall during a visit to the Province of Quebec in 1967.
138. Quebec was the only Province where the doctors went on strike.
139. T. C. Douglas, "We must go forward," in *Medicare: The Decisive Year*, Conference Proceedings Series No. 3 (Ottawa: Canadian Centre for Policy Alternatives, 1982): 266.
140. M. Lalonde, *A New Perspective on the Health of Canadians: A Working Document* (Ottawa: Information Canada, 1975): 31; and Personal communication with Marc Lalonde, the Minister of Health in 1975.
141. Under the Established Programmes Financing arrangement in 1977, the Federal Government ceased matching the Provinces' health care expenditure under the guise of allowing greater flexibility to the Provinces in establishing their own priorities. See Canada, "Federal-Provincial Fiscal Arrangements and Federal Post-Secondary Education and Health Contributions Act," *Statutes* (1986).
142. Prime Minister Pierre Elliott Trudeau speaking to Quebec's Minister of Finance, Dozois. Constitutional Conference, February 1969, p. 648, quoted in Taylor, *Health Insurance*, p. 381.
143. Canada, National Health and Welfare, *Report: Preserving Universal Medicare by Monique Begin*, *Monograph* (Ottawa: MSSC, 1983): 6; and Personal communication with Monique Begin and Emmett M. Hall.
144. S. S. Lee, "Health insurance in Canada — An overview and commentary," *New England Journal of Medicine* 290 (28 March 1974): 716.

145. The Provinces must still meet the original five criteria to ensure full Federal Government contribution under the Federal-Provincial Fiscal Arrangements Act of 1977. See Canada, "Canada Health Act," *Statutes* (1986).
146. E.M. Hall, *Report, Canada's National-Provincial Health Program for the 1980s: A Commitment for Renewal [Commissioner Emmett M. Hall]* (Saskatoon: Government Printer, 1980).
147. Present plans within the Department of Health and Welfare Canada, however, exclude further Federal Government involvement in the health care field. Personal communication with David Kirkwood, the Deputy Minister of Health in 1986.
148. G. P. Marchildon. *Canada: Health System Review, Health Systems in Transition* 15(1)(2013):1–179. http://www.euro.who.int/__data/assets/pdf_file/0009/80568/E87954.pdf. Accessed July 25, 2017.
149. S. Dhillon, "Constitutional challenge against Canada's health-care system begins," The Globe and Mail, Published Tuesday, Sep. 06, 2016. https://www.theglobeandmail.com/news/british-columbia/medicare-on-trial-as-private-vancouver-clinic-challenges-coverage-rules/article31720282/. Accessed May 28, 2017.
150. Government of Canada, *Royal Commission on the Future of Health Care in Canada*, (Ottawa: Government of Canada, 2002). http://www.hc-sc.gc.ca/hcs-sss/com/fed/romanow/index-eng.php. Accessed May 28, 2017.
151. Government of Canada, *Building on Values: The Future of Health Care in Canada*, Report (Ottawa: Government of Canada, 2002). http://publications.gc.ca/site/eng/237274/publication.html. Accessed May 28, 2017.
152. Government of Canada, *The Canada Health Act 1984*. (Ottawa: Government of Canada, 1984). https://lop.parl.ca/content/lop/researchpublications/944-e.htm. Accessed May 28, 2017.
153. G. Scott, L. McKenzie, and J. Webster, Maladjustments in the corporatization model: Hospital reform in New Zealand, in A. S. Preker and A. Harding, eds., *Innovations in Health Service Delivery: The Corporatization of Public Hospitals* (2003, Washington, DC: World Bank). https://openknowledge. worldbank.org/handle/10986/15145. Accessed August 17, 2017; pp. 205–345.
154. S. Allin and D. Rudoler, *The Canadian Health Care System, 2015, Report* (New York: The Commonwealth Fund, 2015, pp. 21–30. http://www.commonwealthfund.org/~/media/files/publications/fund-report/2016/jan/1857_mossialos_intl_profiles_2015_v7.pdf?la=en. Accessed May 28, 2017.

CHAPTER 6

AUSTRALIA

The living standards of Australian families have fallen dramatically over the last six years. A major element in this decline has been Mr. Fraser's refusal to honour his unqualified commitment to maintain the universal health care scheme introduced by Bill Hayden in 1974.[1]

Australian Labor Party, 1982

A. HISTORICAL CONTEXT

1. Colonial Government Health Services

Early European settlements in Australia were established as open prisons for British convicts. The Treasury in London financed these colonies, which had infirmaries staffed by commissioned naval surgeons, overseers, dispensers and untrained nurses.[2] Australia, therefore, began its modern history with a "nationalized" health service "admittedly for practical rather than ideological reasons."[3] The primitive medical facilities of these penal colonies developed slowly and eventually formed the foundation of the Australian public hospital system.[4]

During the early colonial years, treatment at the penal hospitals was free to anyone who wished to or dared to use such facilities. As the population of free-settlers grew, however, the naval surgeons began offering the freeman private consultations on a fee-for-service basis to treat common afflictions such as scurvy and dysentery. The Colonial Government unsuccessfully contested this practice, arguing that the salaries that the surgeons already received from the Crown should cover all the services that they provided.

Reflecting a mood of professional independence, doctors in New South Wales (NSW) established the NSW Medical Board in 1838 to register and accredit new members.[5] "Governments were expected to do no more than regulate society so that all persons had opportunities to produce and acquire the commodities essential for well-being, such as food and housing. Medical care belonged in this category."[6]

Dr. William Bland, a naval surgeon sent to NSW for killing a ship's purser in 1814, became the colony's first full-time private practitioner when the Governor granted him a pardon the following year.[7] By 1839, most doctors were charging settlers such direct fees-for-service while the government infirmaries continued to treat the military staff and convicts without a charge.[8]

By the nineteenth century, "drunkenness, lawlessness and squalor prevailed ... almost as universally as dirtiness and the itch."[9] As most settlers came to Australia alone, the aged, destitute, disabled and sick freemen were usually without family support. Few could afford the fees charged by private doctors. At best, they sought medical attention from religious benevolent societies and faith healers, at worst from quacks and frauds.[10]

Voluntary groups formed a system of non-governmental agencies which offered some relief for the destitute, sick and elderly in both outdoor and indoor relief.[11] Medical doctors provided free treatment to the poor in these institutions in return for the right to treat private patients.[12]

Private subscribers financed only 20 percent of the running cost of such institutions, while the Governor and British Treasury provided the rest.[13] The paid members of the voluntary hospitals gained the right to elect the executive committee and nominate patients for treatment: "Those who could afford it saw a doctor in his rooms and were treated there rather than go into hospital."[14]

When the transport of convicts to Australia ended in 1855, the British Government ceased its direct funding of the colony. Neither the parish nor the voluntary organizations, however, had the resources to take over the financing of existing government services.[15] The Colonial Government was soon financing up to 50 percent of the capital and running cost of what became the public hospitals.

Those wanting free treatment from the public hospital out-patient departments required a ticket of entry, proving their inability to pay for services. "The individual client was assumed to be in need of correction, not the social structure. Welfare services meant that 'we' who were alright [sic] gave help to 'them' who were not."[16] Since a visit to a private doctor cost the equivalent of one-third of the average weekly minimum wage, many people who regarded the entry ticket as degrading simply did without medical attention when sick.

Toward the end of the century, doctors began establishing separate hospitals for their wealthier patients.[17]Although registration with the state governments was required by law, these institutions retained their independence, eventually developing into many of Australia's modern private hospitals. Tuberculosis and venereal diseases continued to compel the Colonial Government to provide institutional care: "Infectious diseases that strike regardless of class dampen arguments against government Intervention."[18]

The Commonwealth of Australia Constitution Act of 1900, which united the Australian states, gave individual states responsibility for most health services, while the Australian Government retained responsibility for quarantine and industrial hygiene.[19] Two non–health-related areas, placed under central Government jurisdiction, would later play an important role in the country's health policy. Section 51(xiv) empowered the Australian Government to legislate on "insurance, other than state insurance."[20] Under special circumstances, Section 96 allowed the Australian Government to grant financial help to states.

The Australian Government also had indirect authority over health-related matters through trade, commerce, imports and exports. These powers were soon exploited by providing "a wide range of physical infrastructure, such as railways, power, drainage and other public services."[21] Yet, Australia's health care system faced some difficult challenges at the turn of the twentieth century owing to the country's small population of 3,773,801 living mainly on the eastern and southeastern coastline of a continent of 7,682,300 square kilometers.[22]

2. Doctors and Pre-paid Health Care

Public interest in about pre-paid health care increased at the turn of the century. The Australian friendly societies had by then reached a membership of one million or 25 percent of the population.[23] The first societies dated back to 1831, when a group of Sydney boat builders formed a mutual aid organization. Other workers established similar societies soon afterward. Their main function was to provide cash income support during illness, and to pay the medical bills of members and their families. Some societies made special arrangements with doctors to work on a capitation basis.

The relationship between the friendly societies and doctors, however, deteriorated over time.[24]Although the societies added to the doctors' private incomes and decreased their work-load in the hospitals, the latter felt that the societies interfered with their professional freedom. The medical profession objected to the capitation payments, variations in contracts between societies, non-professional employers and the coverage of high-income families.[25]

Germany's Bismark Plan (1883) and Britain's Lloyd George Plan (1911) sparked debate on the need for compulsory national health insurance in Australia. The Australian Government statistician, George Knibbs, presented a detailed report on social insurance to Parliament in November 1910, following his review of European programs: "Inquiries are being made and material is being gathered necessary for the formulation of a comprehensive scheme of national insurance on a contributory basis, embracing sickness, accident, maternity, widowhood and unemployment."[26]

In 1902, the Australian Labor Party advocated a nationalized health care program. A few years later, in 1908, the NSW Political Labor League made the first call for universal entitlement and free access hospital care. They wanted to finance the program through municipal taxes. It was during these early years that Australia became known as a "social laboratory" because of the Labor Party's call for binding arbitration to enforce settlement of industrial disputes.[27]

The medical profession rejected these options. Their position was enhanced in January 1918 when a third of the country's doctors enrolled in the military service for World War I. The remaining 406 doctors were able to stage an effective protest in Victoria by resigning *en bloc* from the friendly societies. They refused to accept re-appointments until the friendly societies agreed to limit membership to healthy persons and exclude a variety of procedures from the covered services such as operations, anesthetics and confinement during pregnancy.[28]

Following World War I, Australia experienced a period of prosperity which created a flourishing petty bourgeoisie of self-employed tradesmen, professionals, small owners, contractors, agents, shopkeepers and farmers. The Conservative Government conducted a "relentless offensive against any kind of socialist or social democratic ideas or indeed any criticism from nationalists or scrupulous liberals."[29] This political mood strengthened the medical profession's stance against collective provisions for health care.

By 1920, these circumstances led to a marked decrease in memberships with the friendly societies.[30] In subsequent years, half the population paid doctors directly for private consultations and hospitalization. Many low-income earners, who could no longer afford the increasing contributions needed to remain a member of the friendly societies, were forced to turn to emergency departments for minor illnesses and public hospitals when seriously ill.[31]

3. Royal Commission on National Insurance of 1923

Hoping to encourage Australians to care for themselves, the Bruce–Page Liberal–Country Party (LCP) Coalition appointed a Royal Commission on National Insurance in 1923. The terms of reference of the Commission were to "inquire into national insurance to provide for sickness, invalidity, unemployment and old age."[32] Shortly afterward, carried by the impetus of Dr. J. H. L. Cumpston, the first Director-General of the Department of Health, the Government appointed a Royal Commission on Health.[33] Its terms of reference were to examine the health benefits under a national insurance plan.

Dr. Earle Page, the Treasurer, was a country doctor turned politician. He compared tax-funded public programs such as pensions to the "poorhouse or soup-kitchen."[34] Cutting public expenditures was his main concern, Cumpston, on the other hand, was deeply committed to developing Australia's health care system. He felt that the proper objective of public health was "nothing less than positive health, freedom from all illness and disability for every individual human unit in the community."[35]

The Royal Commission on Health included four conservative medical practitioners. Not surprisingly, its report of 1926 reflected the traditional view of the medical profession that the Australian Government lacked constitutional powers to provide a national health service, a recommendation which the Government welcomed.[36]

The Royal Commission on National Insurance, which reported in 1927, recommended a comprehensive compulsory social security and national health insurance plan. Following the report, Page introduced his National Insurance Bill in 1928, describing it as "the most comprehensive and progressive measure of social reform ever brought forward in any Parliament in Australia."[37] Benefits would include sickness pay, disablement benefits, widows pensions, orphans support and superannuation financed through an equal flat rate contribution from workers and employers.[38]

Opposition to the program was immediate. The state branches of the British Medical Association claimed that direct fee-for-service was the only mode of payment which safe-guarded the doctor-patient relationship.[39] The friendly societies feared that health benefits would interfere with the spirit of thrift and independence. J. H. Scullin, the new Labor Prime Minister elected in 1929, felt that social insurance added to the burden of workers: "Where practicable social benefits should be provided on a universal basis to remove from them the stigma of charity."[40]

4. National Health and Pensions Insurance Act of 1938

In 1931, J. A. Lyons, leader of the United Australia Party, formed a Coalition Government with the Country Party. Wanting to fight the Great Depression by stimulating the nation's private sector, he immediately asked R. G. Casey, the Treasurer, and Frederick Stewart, the Under-Secretary for Employment, to advise him on strategies for cutting public expenditure and stimulating private industry.[41]

In 1938, Casey presented a National Health and Pensions Insurance Bill to Parliament. A 2 percent levy on workers' incomes, with additional financing from employers and the Australian Government, would pay for the predominantly self-financing plan.[42] Dependents, small farmers, the self-employed, most women and the unemployed would be excluded. The plan would include compulsory means-tested health insurance.

All the old opponents once again protested. The unions and employers complained about the proposed levy. John Curtin, the Labor Opposition spokesman, felt that national health services "should be free to all members of the community."[43] The friendly societies feared that new agencies would infringe on their domain. Finally, state branches of the British Medical Association, which had formed a Federal Council in 1933, objected to the proposed capitation payments, free medical treatment and public funding.[44]

In response to increased intervention by the Government in health-related matters, the Federal Council for the State Branches of the British Medical Association established the Federal National Health Insurance Committee in 1938. The committee, headed by Dr. George Bell and Dr. W. F. Simmons, concluded that the Medical Association should support "a complete medical service to the nation."[45] Their proposed general practitioner service, financed on a fee-for-service basis, would focus on health and prevention. In addition, doctors would receive a capitation fee for means-tested low income earners.[46]

Although the National Health and Pensions Insurance Act was passed on July 5, 1938, the Government was unable to secure the cooperation of doctors to staff the new service before the day of enactment on January 1, 1939.[47] Furthermore, the members of a Royal Negotiation Committee, appointed to carry out further negotiations with the doctors, were killed in an airplane crash: "This tragedy was perhaps symbolic of the fate of the whole scheme."[48]

Following Lyons' death, Robert Menzies, the new Prime Minister, introduced legislation for an indefinite postponement of the program. "While impending war was a contributory cause for ending the national insurance project in 1939, there can be no doubt that the decisive factor was the determined opposition of the medical profession. … The medical profession had demonstrated that it had become a highly organized and repeatedly effective pressure group, having had its way with the friendly societies in the 1920s and the national insurance proposals in the 1930s."[49]

5. National Health Services Act of 1948

In October 1941, John Curtin was elected Prime Minister, beginning eight years of Labor Government. While in the Opposition, Curtin had expressed his views on health care. "The Labour Party believes that the time has arrived when national health services should be treated, in principle, in the same way as education. They should be free to all members of the community."[50]

Australia's involvement in World War II enhanced the Government's plans to create a national health service in two ways. First, the war mobilized a planning bureaucracy which could potentially be used for social planning after the war. Second, the war helped the public to grow accustomed to increased tax rates which, if maintained after the war, would help finance such social programs.[51]

Three groups produced independent reports during World War II, making this period a "critical historical juncture in the development of [Australian] national health policy."[52] First, in November 1941, the National Health and Medical Research Council recommended a free comprehensive National Health Service run by salaried doctors.[53]

Second, an Australian Medical Association Sub-Committee recommended a health service with minimal public interference, financed through voluntary contributory insurance and run by doctors receiving direct fee-for-service payments.[54] Finally, in October 1942, the fifth report of the Joint Parliamentary Committee on Social Security recommended a comprehensive social security plan including a health service.[55]

During the parliamentary debates in 1943, Joseph Benedict Chifley, the Minister for Post-War Reconstruction and Treasurer, announced the Government's intention to establish a comprehensive social security plan as part of the Australian post-war reconstruction.[56] To initiate the process, he established a National Welfare Fund into which the Government would deposit an annual sum of £30 million or 25 percent of individual income tax. Following the war, there would be two separate income tax levies, one of which would be set aside for the Fund.[57]

During the parliamentary debates, Opposition leader Robert Menzies advocated a non-means-tested contributory plan which he said upheld self-respect and dignity of the individual.[58] The Government, wanting to finance its proposed social security program through general revenues, argued that contributory financing put an additional burden of the cost on workers, who would indirectly pay for the Government's contribution through taxes and indirectly pay for the employer's contributions through increased prices. The Government used the theories of British economist John Maynard Keynes to support their argument: "The subsequent public expenditure programs generated out of necessity by World War II seemed to validate [Keynes'] theoretical approach."[59]

Anticipating that the states would challenge the proposals on constitutional grounds, the bill gave the Australian Government the necessary powers to introduce its post-war Social Reconstruction Program.[60] When the states refused to approve the legislation. Chifley called a national referendum in August 1944 which he lost despite Labor's substantial majority following the 1943 elections.[61]

The Government, nevertheless, pressed ahead with the Pharmaceutical Benefits Act of 1944, which offered a restricted list of free prescription drugs. The medical profession, however, boycotted the program, claiming that a limited formulary and official forms represented unconstitutional interference with doctors' clinical freedom. In 1945, the Government lost another challenge on this issue in the High Court in Victoria.[62]

A renewed attempt to alter the Constitution in 1946 was finally successful, leading to the Constitution Alteration (Social Services) Act of 1946.[63] This act allowed the Australian Government to provide maternity allowances, widows' pensions, child endowments, unemployment, pharmaceutical, sickness and hospital benefits, medical and dental services, benefits to students and family allowances. Parts of this legislation, however, greatly limited the Government's options.[64]

The Government later introduced a variety of health programs in a piecemeal fashion. Notable among these was the Hospital Benefits Act of 1946 which made public wards free of charge and increased subsidies on non-public wards.[65]Although the program eventually collapsed in all states but Queensland, it represented an early attempt at universal entitlement to institutional care.[66]

Doctors, claiming that negotiation with the Government amounted to "professional euthanasia," continued to boycott the introduction of free drugs.[67] Instead of proceeding with the implementation of the new National Service, the Government passed another Pharmaceutical Benefits Act in 1947, making it compulsory for doctors to use official prescription forms for drugs that were on the official formulary. The medical profession once again successfully challenged this legislation on constitutional grounds in October 1949.[68]

The National Health Services Act, introduced by the new Minister for Health. Senator McKenna, and later passed by Parliament in November 1948, called for universal entitlement to a National Health and Dental Service which would to be administered by the Department of Health.[69] The Act empowered the Australian Government to engage directly in the provision of services, including the establishment, take-over, and management of hospitals and other health care organizations.[70] Everyone living in Australia would qualify for medical attention without any direct charges at the time of treatment.

A delay in implementing the National Health Services Act, however, gave its opponents time to mount a publicity campaign which portrayed the legislation as being the first step towards the creation of a socialist state. This hit home because nationalization had become the symbol of "ideological purity" to the radicals in the Labor Party, rather than a commitment to practical social reform.[71] Although the Labor Party strove for popular issues, such as stability in the economy, full employment and a gradual social transformation, Chifley's Government was defeated in December 1949.[72]

6. Earle Page Voluntary Insurance of 1953

When the Liberal–Country Party Coalition under the leadership of Robert G. Menzies took office in 1949, Earle Page, Treasurer in the Bruce–Page Coalition, became the Minister for Health. During the elections, the Coalition Government had promised to introduce its own version of a comprehensive national health insurance plan. "The great danger in any government-aided health scheme is the tendency to develop a psychology of dependence and diminished personal and community responsibility. The fundamental aim of any social security scheme should be to raise the individual to a level at which he can help himself."[73]

As a member of the Australian Medical Association and founder of the Royal Australasian College of Surgeons, Page cautiously refrained from introducing any radical elements in his proposal.[74] "Indeed it is not unreasonable to describe the Earle Page health benefits program, introduced in 1953, as consisting essentially of the AMA's proposals of 1943."[75] He rapidly reached an agreement for his new plan with the Pharmacy Guild, the medical profession and the friendly societies. "The socialist policies of the Labour Party were anathema to us," Page observed.[76]

Non-profit voluntary insurance organizations would pay for the program under which the states would reintroduce a means-test to determine who would receive free treatment on public wards of hospitals and the combined Australian Commonwealth-Insurance Fund benefit could not exceed 90 percent doctors' charges.[77] Finally, there would be no attempt by the Government to control the fee-for-service charged by the doctors, and the freedom of choice by both doctors and patients would be guaranteed.

Since the Menzies Government lacked a majority in the Senate, it conveniently introduced the new program through amendments to existing provisions of the National Health Services Act of 1948, thereby avoiding having to pass new legislation. Through regulations, the Government later introduced pharmaceutical benefits (1950), pensioner health services (1951), hospital benefits (1952) and medical benefits (1953).[78] The National Health Act of 1953 consolidated these benefits.[79]

"Almost from its inception, adjustments began to be made in Earle Page's national health scheme."[80] The rise in medical fees and expensive medical procedures outstripped the refunds, leaving even insured patients with a significant portion of the bill. The patient paid the difference which steadily rose.[81] Only 11 percent of the total cost of the health services were financed through voluntary funds, whose retention rates were in the order of 24 percent.[82] Many people were under-insured, 15–17 percent were left without coverage and people had to go into debt or declare bankruptcy to pay their medical bills.[83]

The Coalition Government, however, was initially successful in "defusing health" [sic] as a political question. "An important reason for this success was the failure of the Labor Party ... to produce effective criticism of the Government's health scheme."[84] Following 15 years of Conservative Coalition Governments, critics such as Scotton and Deeble began pointing to some major flaws in the Page-inspired voluntary insurance system.[85] The arrangements were scathingly described as "private practice publicly supported."[86]

B. LANDMARK LEGISLATIVE REFORMS

1. Committee of Inquiry into Health Insurance of 1968

In April 1968, the Labor Opposition, which had a majority in the Senate appointed a Senate Select Committee, chaired by Senator Ivy Wedgwood, to examine medical and hospital costs.[87] Two weeks later, on April 18, 1968, Prime Minister John Gorton appointed a Commonwealth of Australia, Committee of Inquiry into Health Insurance to counter the mounting criticism against the Government's health insurance policy.

The three-man Commonwealth Committee of Inquiry consisted of Justice John A. Nimmo, Leslie Melville and Norman McIntosh. "The Government was opposed to a universally compulsive [sic] plan, however financed and was careful to restrict the terms of reference of our committee ... [to voluntary insurance]."[88]

In its report of March 25, 1969, the committee condemned the inadequate provisions offered under voluntary insurance: the existing system was too complex; benefits were below the costs of treatment; contributions were prohibitive for many people; rules were excessively cumbersome; insurance organizations kept high retention rates and unnecessary reserves; services were incomplete, excluding coverage of optometry, chiropractic and dentistry.[89]

The committee then made a series of recommendations that it felt would improve the system: standard hospital wards with salaried doctors should be free to everyone; insurance organizations should be regionalized; disclaimers should be eliminated; and fee schedules should be standardized.[90] It also recommended that an independent authority, a National Health Insurance Commission, should be established to run the new service with representatives from the Department of Health, the medical profession, hospitals, consumers and the financial world.

In its first report of September 1969 and final report of June 2, 1970, the Senate Select Committee followed the general lines of the Commonwealth Committee of Inquiry by calling for an expanded and subsidized voluntary insurance system: "As a programme for reforming a voluntary insurance scheme, the Nimmo Committee's proposals are comprehensive and well considered."[91] As a program for improving the health care system, however, it represented a "marginal modification, rather than fundamental reform."[92] Two Labor Senators, therefore, wrote a minority report, calling for a "universal health scheme financed by a surcharge on taxable income."[93]

2. Scotton–Deeble Compulsory Insurance Plan of 1969

During the deliberations of the Committee of Inquiry, two economists, Richard Bailey Scotton and John S. Deeble, published an independent report. They claimed that a compulsory and public-administered plan was "simply the most efficient and equitable method of achieving universally acknowledged objectives."[94] Their proposal called for free ambulatory health care services, free treatment on public hospital wards, restricted choice of doctor, curtailed private practice and centralized health planning.

A statutory Health Insurance Commission would administer a new health fund which would be financed by a 1.25 percent income-tax levy, matching Australian Government subsidy, combined workmen's compensation contribution and third-party motor insurers contribution. Even with an upper limit for the contributions, the levy would make health contributions more progressive in nature and, therefore, more equitable than in the past: "The whole plan could be seen as a very astute exercise in producing a policy with maximum political acceptability."[95]

Although doctors would be encouraged to "bulk-bill" the new Health Insurance Commission, they would still be allowed to charge patients directly. Eighty-five percent of such fees would be reimbursed based on a standard fixed fee.[96] The remaining 15 percent would act as a small deterrent charge to prevent abuse. Voluntary insurance could cover the "gap," but such expenses would no longer be tax-deductible.

The authors estimated that under their plan, doctors' incomes would rise, while patients' payments would fall. They also projected that their plan would decrease the cost of the Australian health care system through savings on administrative expenses and elimination of the high retention rates by the voluntary insurance funds. They calculated the cost of the existing system for hospital and health care in 1965–1966 as $326 million, while the projected cost under their proposed plan would be only $312 million.[97]

Deeble and Scotton presented their recommendation to the Senate Select Committee in September 1968 and privately to the Opposition Labor Party leader, Edward Gough Whitlam, who accepted the plan as the Labor Party's official platform on health care.[98] There was little formal consultation on the Deeble–Scotton proposal: "The decision to adopt this policy appears to have been taken by Mr. Whitlam, no doubt in consultation with the Labor Party's health spokesman at that time, Mr. Hayden."[99]

3. Whitlam Labor Government of 1972

Labor policies of the late 1960s represented a pragmatic compromise as part of an attempt to regain a political base following the setback of the Chifley era: "Whitlam's energetic leadership, sensitive to the strong 'middle-classing' [sic of modern Australian standards and expectations," brought success to Whitlam himself and led to a re-emergence of the Labor Party's strength in Australia.[100] During the years before the 1969 and 1972 general elections, Whitlam travelled extensively throughout the country selling the party's platform on health care: "Governments have a responsibility to ensure that health services are provided free of cost to the individual."[101]

There was less "socialism vs. free enterprise, collectivism vs. individualism, the rights of the poor vs. the privileges of the rich, anarchy vs. law and order, equality vs, freedom, the public sector vs. the private sector and so on."[102] Instead, a political convergence emerged "with Labor accepting moderate reformism [sic] within a 'mixed' economy, and the Liberals accepting high levels of welfare expenditure and various forms of government control over the economy."[103] In this context, Labor tried to play down the role of "stifling or intrusive government ... and introduce[d] a universal health insurance scheme that would be funded according to one's ability to pay."[104]

Several circumstances contributed to the development of moderate political platforms: an increasingly affluent society had shifted the political spectrum to the center; there was an increased competition for this important uncommitted center of the electorate; bureaucratic and constitutional structures made it difficult to introduce radical reforms; and vested-interest groups and limited public revenues curtailed major public expenditure programs.[105]

As a result, the Australian Labor Party's social insurance policy during the late 1960s "could hardly be regarded as radical, even in the forms in which they were originally developed."[106] Following the resignation of Robert Menzies, the Liberal Party's founder and patriarch, the Government continued to lose popular support, while the Labor Opposition gained strength.[107] Worried about losing further electoral support, non-Labor policies were equally marked by moderation.[108]

During the 1969 general elections and the 1970 Senate election, voluntary health insurance became a major political theme. John Gorton, the incumbent, campaigned in favor of increasing health care coverage through the expansion of the existing voluntary insurance system in line with the recommendations of the majority report of the earlier Commonwealth Committee of Inquiry.[109] When the Liberal–National Country Party returned to power, it introduced a Health Benefits Plan in 1970 which was based on the recommendations of the majority report of the committee.

To please the medical profession, many important recommendations were omitted from the plan. This greatly embittered some of the former committee members: "There is a history in Australia of governments ignoring the findings of commissions and committees."[110] Their outrage was in vain. When William McMahon replaced Gorton, and Senator Greenwood, the Minister for Health, replaced Forbes, the nonconciliatory approach of Forbes enraged the doctors.[111]

Taking advantage of the Liberal Party's troubles, Labor set out to defeat the Government which had held power for more than two decades, using a slogan "It's Time." To avoid a confrontation with the medical profession, Whitlam avoided the topic of financing of health care during his pre-election speeches. Instead, Bill Hayden, the Labor Shadow Minister for Health and Social Welfare, outlined the party's platform which consisted of universal entitlement to health care offering regional health services, nursing homes, domiciliary services, school dental care, national aboriginal health care, prevention, rehabilitation, integrated psychiatric services and general practitioner services.[112]

"The defeat of the Labour Government in 1949, after its unsuccessful attempts to move in the direction of a social-welfare oriented health system, made the [Australian Labour Party] cautious of pursuing radical policies in this field."[113] Unknown to the Liberals, the slick Labour political machine successfully cloaked the potentially threatening parts of the party's dogma.[114] Following Labor's success in the 1972 elections, however, "the new Government, no matter what its complexion, was headed for trouble from a disgruntled medical profession."[115]

4. Medibank I

After winning the general elections on December 2, 1972, Whitlam's Labor Government established the Hospitals and Health Services Commission to plan the health services and the Health Insurance Planning Commission to prepare the health insurance program (Medibank). Dr. Douglas Everingham became the Minister for Health, and Bill Hayden became the Minister for Social Security. When Dr. Gwen Howells replaced Dr. William D. Refshauge as Director-General of the Department of Health in 1973, the medical profession lost one of its most loyal lieutenants within the Department.[116]

Dr. Sydney Sax was later appointed Chairman of the Hospitals and Health Services Commission, which submitted its first report on a Community Health Program for Australia on May 28, 1973. His committee called for an extensive, integrated and equitably distributed primary health care network offering health care, nursing care, health outreach (education) and social advocacy (liaison between services) for the daily personal health care needs of the population.[117]

Although Parliament failed to pass the enabling legislation to finance the full Community Health Program for Australia as proposed by the Hospitals and Health Services Commission, it did approve a $10 million allocation for a more limited program intended to expand non-institutional care. The latter program intended to establish an extensive network of community health clinics as an alternative to private practice.

At Hayden's request, the responsibility for health insurance was undertaken by Department of Social Security rather than the Department of Health.[118] Hayden claimed that separation of health insurance from the Department of Health was necessary to allow him to focus fully on the financial aspects of the new plan.[119] It also permitted him to distance himself from direct contact with the medical profession.[120]

During the early planning stage, Hayden continued to rely extensively on the advice of John Deeble, who became Chairman of the Health Insurance Planning Committee, and Richard B. Scotton, who became one of its members. L. J. Daniels, the new Director-General of Social Security, was given the task of carrying out a "complete re-structuring of charges and benefits" under the new program.[121]

In April 1973, the Health Insurance Planning Committee released its Green Paper on Health Insurance.[122] A Health Insurance Fund, Medibank, would finance medical and hospital benefits under a new Australian Health Insurance Program designed to replace the amended provisions of the National Health Act of 1948. The program would cover "all residents of Australia, without payment of any premium or contribution, in respect of services received inside and outside Australia."[123] Medibank's first General Managers, Roy William and his successor C. Robert Wilcox, would face the difficult challenge of creating an efficient and workable administration for the program.[124]

Under Medibank, 85 percent of approved doctors' fees would be reimbursed. Private insurers would be allowed to cover the 15 percent "gap" up to a maximum of $5. To avoid having them stage a repeated constitutional challenge, doctors were permitted to continue billing patients directly. Those who wished to do so, however, were given various incentives to "bulk-bill" Medibank directly.[125] "The [programme] will not interfere in the doctor-patient relationship nor in the practice of private medicine."[126]

All hospital in-patient and out-patient care on standard wards would be universally available, free of charge and staffed by salaried doctors. The Australian Government would reimburse the states for any additional cost incurred through offering such services.[127] Private patients would continue to have the option to contract independently for services but they would no longer be able to use such treatment as tax-deductible expenses.

Medibank would be financed through a 1.35 percent health insurance levy on personal taxable incomes and a Government subsidy of 1.5 percent (1.28 percent in the first year) drawn from consolidated revenues.[128] A smaller contribution from workmen's compensation and automobile insurers would supplement this source of financing. Low-income earners would not make contributions, while a ceiling would exist for contributions from high-income earners.[129]

Medibank posed a direct threat to many of the vested-interest groups. Coverage by independent health insurance organization was limited to insuring the "gap" between the established schedule and the fees charged by doctors. The increase in free beds in the public wards lowered the demand for private beds and private hospitals. The medical professions feared a salaried national health service.

"The AMA refused to cooperate when it was informed that the principles of the scheme were non-negotiable."[130] To fight the plan, they established a "fighting fund" by raising $2 million to finance an extensive advertising campaign against Medibank.[131] They unilaterally increased their fees by 25–29 percent in July 1973.

Since reimbursing these fees would exceed the Government's planned financial outlay on the new program, Hayden countered with a 10 percent interim offer.[132] A medical fee tribunal under Justice Ludeke, however, came out in favor of a fee increase of 20 percent.[133] Despite this generous decision, the AMA went ahead with its earlier recommendations, letting doctors decide which fee to charge.[134]

The Liberal–Country Party won a majority in the Senate in the following mid-term elections. A Canberra lobby, established by the medical profession, private hospital and private health insurance organizations, immediately pressured the Senate to block the Government's proposed Medibank legislation: "The profession achieved a lot of success in having its view accepted."[135] Ignoring this threat, the Labor Government introduced its legislation to the House of Representatives which passed the Health Insurance Commission Bill and Health Insurance Bill on December 11, 1973. The Senate, under pressure from opponents, defeated both legislations on December 12, 1973.

The Government reintroduced its proposed bills on April 4, 1974, in the House of Representatives, but both pieces of legislation were once again defeated in the Senate on April 9, 1974.[136] "In defence of their wealthy friends and vested interests, they [the Opposition in the Senate] have rejected the democratic principle of equal electorates."[137] Finally, when Opposition leader, Snedden, threatened that he would block Supply Bills in the Senate, Whitlam asking the Governor-General, Paul Hasluck, to call a double dissolution of Parliament under Section 57 of the Constitution.

During the brief campaign leading up to the general elections of May 18, 1974, the Liberal–Country Party alliance called for a return to voluntary health insurance with free care limited to those falling below a means-tested poverty line. The Labor Party promised to reintroduce its health insurance bills.

When the Labor Government returned to power on May 18, 1974, with a majority in the House of Representatives, it still lacked control over the Senate, Both Labor and non-Labor each obtained 29 seats in the Senate, leaving control of the Parliament in the hands of two Independents. By June 1975, two unprecedented state appointments of non-Labor replacements to vacancies in the Senate and the death of a Labor Senator gave the Opposition an absolute majority in the Upper House.[138]

The Government reintroduced the two bills to Parliament for a third time on July 10, 1974, with the same result as before, By this time, the Government had also introduced two supplementary pieces of legislation: the Health Insurance Levy Bill and Health Insurance Levy Assessment Bill. These described the Australian Government's future financial obligations to Medibank. The Senate rejected both levy bills on July 31, 1974.[139]

To break the deadlock, the Government called for a joint sitting of the two Houses on August 7, 1974, when both the Health Insurance Bill and Health Insurance Commission Bill finally passed.[140] The levy bills, however, were still at the beginning of this convoluted legislative procedure.[141] "By this obstructive manoeuvre the Opposition forced the Government to finance all of its universal insurance scheme from general revenue funds. Medibank was scheduled to be implemented on 1 July 1975."[142]

"Deeble originally estimated that Medibank would cost the Government $595 million in its first year, starting 1 July 1974."[143] Because of the delaying tactics of the Opposition, "Medibank was introduced in July 1975 a year later than planned, at roughly double the original estimated cost [to the Australian Government] and with virtually no visible contribution by the public."[144] A later estimate for 1974–1975 was $898 million. In addition, the National Welfare Fund would contribute an additional $66 million for pensioners, special account deficits and other existing arrangements, and $5.7 million in transfer liabilities on outstanding arrangements not affecting the Fund.[145] The Opposition used this discrepancy between the original estimates and the actual cost of Medibank to criticize the new program.

The battle between the medical profession and the Government continued. To encourage executive management boards to eliminate the honorary system of staffing hospitals with doctors and offer free treatment on public wards, the Government agreed to pay 50 percent of their net operational deficit. During the July 1975 Premiers' Conference, Whitlam informed the four Liberal–National Country Party Premiers that unless they signed the Medicare agreement, his Government would withdraw all financial support from their hospitals. This threat proved effective in forcing the states to accept his Offer.[146] Labor-held states of South Australia and Tasmania readily signed the agreement. The conservative states of New South Wales, Victoria, Western Australia and Queensland joined soon afterwards.

The medical specialists, hoping to frustrate the program until the Opposition had a chance to defeat the Government, refused to accept their new hospital appointments. The private insurance organizations backed this strategy and refused to act as agents for the program.[147] To counter the refusal of the private insurance organizations to cooperate, the Health Insurance Commission organized a network of retail pharmacies which agreed to act as agents. Although this was an effective strategy against the private insurance organizations, it did not resolve the conflict with the medical profession or increase support from the Senate.

The Opposition leader, Malcolm Fraser, once again threatened to have the Senate block the supply bills.[148] Preempting a deadlock, which might have paralyzed the public sector, Governor-General John Kerr dismissed the Labor Government on November 11, 1975, and installed the former Opposition leader, Malcolm Fraser, as caretaker Prime Minister. The process leading to the dismissal of the Government involved a series of unprecedented consultations between the Governor-General, the Opposition and non-governmental advisors: "The Prime Minister of Australia [Malcolm Fraser], came to power through a decidedly unconservative [sic] constitutional '*coup d'etat*'."[149]

The Labor Party and Whitlam were intensely bitter about the dismissal of the Labor Government and the repeated court challenges which had frustrated Labor's health care legislation: "After the manipulation of the monarchy in 1975, I became committed to the Australian republic," Whitlam observed.[150] He later protested that the Australian Labor Party "had to devise policies which could secure not only the approval of electors but also the approval of judges."[151] Opponents of Medibank had succeeded in putting universal entitlement in peril almost immediately after it was implemented in Australia.

C. CONTINUED POLICY REFORM PROCESS

1. Earle Page Revisited

The election campaign which followed focused on high taxation and inflation, not health care. On December 13, 1975, the conservative Liberal–Country Party Coalition headed by Malcolm Fraser won a large majority in both Houses of Parliament on a platform of cutting inflation and reducing the Government deficit: "We will not dismantle Medibank," Fraser promised.[152]

The following eight years, nevertheless, witnessed a gradual return to a voluntary health insurance program similar to that which Earle Page had introduced during the 1950s. "Within a year of its introduction, Medibank had undergone a massive restructuring: it changed from a system which was providing medical insurance to the whole population to one which covered about [50] percent."[153]

The new Government introduced a series of amendments to the original Medibank legislation which encouraged people to opt-out of the national program in favor of subsidized private plans. Medibank Private, a publicly run program, would compete with the private insurance funds: "Instead of a better, brighter health insurance scheme, we appear to have a costlier, unwieldier [sic], class conscious, divisive and confusing rag bag."[154]

The Fraser Government argued that the Labor program had been too expensive because of over-utilization: "Ironically one of greatest increases in utilization took place in 1976–1977, the year following the emasculation of Medibank."[155] The Minister for Health, Ralph J. Hunt, realized this too late: "In retrospect I believe it would have been far better to have adhered to the first change or to have reverted to the original health insurance arrangements prior to the election of the Whitlam Government."[156]

Early rises in cost occurred before Medibank was fully implemented.[157] The cost in real terms to the Australian Government alone was $931 million (1973–1974), $1,271 million (1973–1974) and $2,716 million (1975–1976). The cost to the state and local government was $892 million, $1,340 million and $2,716 million for the same years. "Medibank did cost somewhat more than originally estimated but not because of mistaken estimates but primarily because of Senate refusal to pass the levy legislation and to a lesser extent because of the widening of the benefits."[158]

By 1977, 58.5 percent of the population had opted-out of Medibank in favor of private insurance.[159] The estimated savings of $170 million for 1976–1977 and $90 million for 1977–1978 were offset by an even greater decrease in revenues from persons opting-out.[160] Furthermore, by 1979, a major portion of ambulatory care was no longer financed directly by Canberra, forcing many to use costly institutional care as the only available source of free health care: "One sees in health and welfare in Australia a system out of contro1."[161]

Wishing to diminish its involvement in the provision of health care, the Government next established an inquiry into its role in financing hospitals.[162] The terms of reference of the Commission of Inquiry into the Efficiency and Administration of Hospitals were to examine the costs, resource allocations, efficiency and cost containment in hospitals, as well as related institutions and services.[163]

The resulting Health Acts Amendment Act of 1981 ignored most of the Commission's recommendations.[164] Instead, it introduced block grants to replace the previous cost-sharing arrangements. This policy intended to return the financial responsibility for health care to the states. It represented a throwback to the basic principles of the 1950 Earle Page Program.

2. Medicare of 1984

If history is said to repeat itself, then Australia has repeated its history of financing health care several times. The early colonial settlements depended entirely on public funding for health services. As middle-class free settlers, they embraced an independent pioneer self-help philosophy and rejected public intervention only to find that their levels of personal income prevented the voluntary hospital movement from remaining self-sufficient. The growing public subsidies for the voluntary hospitals represented a drift back to public funding.

Following legislation introduced in 1928 and 1938, Labor Governments refused to cooperate with contributory compulsory means-tested health insurance plans that previous politically Conservative Coalition Governments had introduced. On two other occasions, following legislation introduced in 1948 and 1973, Conservative Coalition Governments refused to cooperate with universal entitlement under national health insurance programs that previous Labor Governments had introduced. Between each of these events, interim health policy consisted of limited voluntary health insurance.

Throughout these events "the dominant characteristic of welfare action in Australia [became] its *ad hoc* nature and lack of reference to general principles of development."[165] The clear losers were the Australian people who were deprived of a universal entitlement to health care. When Labor came to power again in 1983, they were determined to repeat this history.

The Hayden Family Health Plan of 1979 and the official Hayden Health Plan of 1982 promised that, if elected in 1983, "Labor [would] return to the basic principles of the Bill Hayden's original health scheme. ... This return to Medibank principles [would] restore equity in health contribution rates, universality of cover, and simplicity and efficiency in operation."[166] All Labor had to do was win the election.[167]

After Labor did win a large majority on March 5, 1983, the new Minister for Health, Neal Blewett, quickly presented a Health Legislation Amendment Bill which reintroduced universal entitlement under a renewed medicare program.[168] Parliament passed the legislation on February 1, 1984.

The new program also aimed to promote a physical and social environment conducive to good health, encourage community participation, ensure access for all and help the less advantaged in society.[169] The Department of Health and Social Welfare formalized these ideas in a detailed proposal for an Australian *Health for All* program based on the World Health Organization's guidelines.[170] Health policy would focus on health not just health care.

The vested-interest groups in Australia are, however, equally committed to repeating rather than learning from the past. The Australian Medical Association still maintains its old position: "It is [the] Government's job to manage the economy and keep public expenditure under control."[171] The Opposition vowed to re-privatize of Medicare Mark II if given a chance to do so.

3. Major Policy Reforms in Australia Since the 1980s

Since the latter part of the 1980s, the Australian health system has continued to evolve. Starting with what was already a mixed public–private partnership, recent reforms have not significantly altered this approach to both funding and delivery of health care. The mixed public–private character of tax funding and public/non governmental/private character of the service delivery system has prevailed.[172]

As described in the previous section, under the Liberal-led Coalition Government (1975–1983 Medibank Private (the private arm of the government's health insurance program set up to provide benchmark competition with other private health insurance programs) has continued to evolve: individuals were given a choice to opt-out by purchasing private health insurance, or pay a levy of 2.5 percent of taxable income to remain in the scheme. As a result, by 1981, a significant part of the population was not fully insured. The Labor Governments that followed (1983–1996), reversed this trend by reintroducing a largely universal, tax-funded health insurance system. By the 1990s, Australia already had a mixed market-based health care system that embraced quasi "new public sector" management approaches like those that were later pioneered in New Zealand, with their focus on greater managerial accountability, market-based economic incentives and greater competition among providers.[173]

Since the turn of the Millennium, the pendulum has continued to swing back and forth in this way several times between right wing coalition governments that expand the role of private health insurance and left-wing coalition governments that roll back the role of private health insurance, favoring tax based funding. The Private Health Insurance Act 2007 regulated the private health insurance market. Complaints are referred to a Private Health Insurance Ombudsman.

Prior to the 2007 election, the right leaning Liberal-National Coalition Government under John Howard threatened that Medibank Private would be sold if they won the 2007 elections. However, they were defeated by the left leaning Australia Labor party under Kevin Rudd who pledged to keep Medibank Private under public ownership. By 2013, however, the pendulum swung the other way.

In 2016, Medicare (the public arm of the government's health insurance program) was funded by a 2 percent Medicare levy (with low-income earners being exempted). An additional 1 percent levy is imposed on high-income earners who choose to opt-out of health insurance coverage. Individuals take out private insurance to cover out-of-pocket payment and copayments (gap insurance).

Prime Minister Tony Abbott who finally took office on September 18, 2013 and was followed by Prime Minister Malcolm Turnbull who took office on September 15, 2015, have been leading right-wing Liberal-National Coalitions that once again favor a liberalization of the private health insurance market in Australia and may bring the privatization of Medibank Private back into the cross hairs of its health insurance policy reforms.

ENDNOTES

1. Australian Labor Party [sic], "Cheaper for Australians; Cheaper for Australia: The Hayden Health Plan," (1982): 1.
2. Nurses were often elderly infirm prisoners who were incapable of performing heavier duties.
3. C. Grant, *Australian Hospitals: Operation and Management*, 2nd Edition (Melbourne: Churchill Livingstone, 1985): 9.
4. Grant, *Hospitals*, p. 9.
5. R. Hicks, *Rum Regulations and Riches* (Sydney: Australian Hospital Association, 1981): 3. This was 38 years before a comparable body appeared in England.
6. S. Sax, *A Strife of Interests: Politics and Policies in Australian Health Services* (Sydney: George Allen & Unwin, 1984): 6.

7. The absence of physicians led the naval surgeons, who became the country's general practitioners, to learn the skills necessary to perform general medical duties. Bland, who founded the Australian Medical Society, served as its first president in 1859.
8. Sax, *Strife*, p. 4. Since private care was expensive, most people sought medical attention from out-patient departments of hospitals.
9. Sax, *Strife*, p. 4.
10. In 1881, only 23 percent of the medical work-force in Victoria were registered medical practitioners, many of whom lacked basic medical skills. Sax, *Strife*, p. 12.
11. C. J. Cummins, *The Development of the Benevolent (Sydney) Asylum*, 1788–1855 (Sydney: New South Wales Department of Health, 1971). By the 1850s, however, the infirmary section of these institutions housed the sick and infirm, not unlike the English workhouses.
12. This complementary relationship between voluntary organizations and the states also existed in New South Wales, Victoria and Queensland. In South Australia and Tasmania, the states played a central role. Sax, *Strife*, p. 5.
13. Hicks, *Rum Regulations*, p. 5.
14. Hicks, *Rum Regulations*, p. 3.
15. G. A. Rennison, *We Live Among Strangers* (Melbourne: University Press, 1970).
16. R. F. Henderson, ed., *The Welfare Stakes: Strategies for Australian Social Policy* (Melbourne: University of Melbourne, Institute of Applied Economic and Social Research, 1981): 3.
17. Later health insurance provided a major source of financing for these hospitals.
18. J. A. Jones, *The Australian Welfare State: Growth, Crisis and Change*, Revised Edition (Sydney: George Allen & Unwin, 1983): 7.
19. "Commonwealth" in Australia refers to the federated states of Australia. c. f. British 'Commonwealth' of Countries.
20. Australia, "Commonwealth of Australia Constitution Act," *Statutes* (9 July 1900): 63 & 64 Victoria.
21. Jones, *Welfare State*, p. 7. As in Britain, a Public Health Act was passed toward the end of the century.
22. The population for 1901 is based on United Nations (UN), Statistics Office (SO), Department of Economic and Social Affairs (DESA), *Demographic Yearbook 1962*, 14th Edition (New York: UN, 1962): 281; and the area is based on J. Paxton, ed., *The Statesman Year-Book: Statistical and Historical*

Annual of the States of the World for the Year 1986–1987, 123rd Edition (London: MacMillan Press, 1986): 94.

23. Hicks, *Rum Regulations*, p. 13.
24. T. H. Kewley, *Social Security in Australia 1900–72* (Sydney: Sydney University Press, 1973): 12.
25. Sax, *Strife*, p. 19.
26. Liberal Prime Minister Joseph Cook in 1913, quoted in J. C. H. Dewdney, *Australian Health Services* (Sydney: John Wiley and Sons, Australasia, 1972): 28.
27. E. Fry, ed., *Common Cause*, in Essays in Australian and New Zealand Labour History (Wellington: Allen & Unwin/Port Nicholson, 1986): xiii.
28. Sax, *Strife*, p. 20.
29. Fry, *Common Cause*, p. 145.
30. Sax, *Strife*, pp. 20–21.
31. Sax, *Strife*, p. 21.
32. The "Constitution Act" of 1900 gave the Australian Government the power to legislate for invalid and old-age pensions. Inquiries into compulsory social insurance began after 1910. See Australia, Royal Commission on National Insurance (RCNI), "Report," *Parliamentary Papers* (1923): 1.
33. The Department of Health was created in 1921.
34. Kewley, *Social Security*, p. 145; and Sax, *Strife*, p. 36.
35. J. H. L Cumpston, "Health of the People," MSS 613, 2/4, Canberra: National Library of Australia n.d. quoted in Australia, Senate Standing Committee on Social Welfare (SSCSW), "Through a glass, darkly: Evaluation in Australian health and welfare services," *Parliamentary Papers* (1979): 19.
36. Australia, Royal Commission on Health (RCH), "Report," *Parliamentary Papers* (1926): 1081.
37. Earle Page, quoted in Dewdney, *Health Services*, p. 29. Page's means-tested compulsory insurance of 1928, was more progressive than his later voluntary insurance model during the 1950s.
38. General revenues would finance superannuation until a fund had time to accumulate reserves.
39. C. Thame, "Health and the state: The development of collective responsibility for healthcare in the first half of the twentieth century," Ph.D. Thesis (Canberra: Australian National University, 1974): 294.
40. The Labor Party platform of 1912, quoted in Sax, *Strife*, p. 34.
41. Stewart approached Walter Kinnear in the insurance department of the British Ministry of Health for advice. See Sax, *Strife*, p. 39.

42. A National Insurance Commission would administer the plan.
43. J. Curtin, Labor Opposition spokesman and former Prime Minister during the House of Representatives parliamentary debates quoted in Dewdney, *Health Services*, p. 30.
44. The Federal Committee, established in 1911, became the Federal Council in 1933.
45. The choice of terminology, calling it a "medical" rather than a "health" service, was important. British Medical Association policy, quoted in Sax, *Strife*, p. 48.
46. The Federal Council was especially anxious to distinguish itself from a minority group of doctors who advocated a salaried service.
47. Personal communication with Professor George R. Palmer, School of Health Administration at the University of New South Wales. See G. R. Palmer, "Health," in *Public Policy in Australia*, by R. Forward, ed., (Melbourne: Cheshire, 1974): 181. A similar sequence of events had taken place in New Zealand.
48. Dewdney, *Health Services*, p. 31.
49. Sax, *Strife*, p. 42.
50. Australia, "John Curtin," House of Representatives, House of Representatives, *Parliamentary Debates* 155(1938): 1329–30.
51. Dewdney, *Health Services*, 34; and M.C. Brown, *National Health Insurance in Canada and Australia: A Comparative Political Economy Analysis*, Health Economics Research Unit, Research Monograph 3 (Canberra: Australian National University, 1983): 63–64.
52. Thelma Hunter, quoted in Palmer, "Health," (1974): 181–2.
53. Australia, National Health and Medical Research Council (NHMRC), "Recommendations on the reorganization of medical services in Australia," *Parliamentary Papers* (July 1941); Australia, National Health and Medical Research Council (NHMRC), "Outline of a possible scheme for a salaried medical service," *Parliamentary Papers* (November 1941); and Sax, *Strife*, p. 49.
54. Australian Medical Association, "A general medical service in Australia," *Medical Journal of Australia*, (November 1941): 513–26; and Australian Medical Association, "Principles which should govern a general medical service in Australia," *Medical Journal of Australia*, (March 1943): 370–1.
55. The committee, which produced nine reports, was appointed by Robert Menzies Government in July 1941. See Australia, Joint Parliamentary Committee on Social Security (JPCSS), "Fifth interim report," *Parliamentary Papers* (October 1942). Apart from a salaried health service, the sixth report

also recommended free hospital treatment on public wards and public subsidies for non-public patients. See Australia, Joint Parliamentary Committee on Social Security (JPCSS), "Sixth interim report," *Parliamentary Papers* (July 1943): Appendix C.

56. Australia, "Joseph Benedict Chifley," House of Representatives, *Parliamentary Debates* (1943): 548–9. Chifley became Prime Minister after Curtin's death on July 5, 1945. Sax, *Strife*, p. 50.
57. The seventh report recommended a graduated income tax to finance the National Welfare Fund. See Australia, Joint Parliamentary Committee on Social Security (JPCSS), "Seventh interim report," *Parliamentary Papers* (March 1944).
58. Australia, "Robert Menzies," House of Representatives, *Parliamentary Debates* (1944): 2263; and Sax, *Strife*, p. 51.
59. Brown, *Health Insurance*, pp. 63–64.
60. The states rejected the legislation in October 1942.
61. Section 128 of the "Constitution Act" of 1900 requires a referendum to approve amendments to the Act.
62. Palmer, "Health," (1974): 183.
63. Australia, "Constitution Alteration (Social Services) Act," *Statutes* (1946): Sec. 51(23A).
64. Robert G. Menzies, Leader of the Opposition, introduced a restriction prohibiting "civil conscription" of doctors. This was recommended by Dr. Henry Newland, later President of the Australian Medical Association (AMA), and accepted by the Attorney-General, Dr. H. V. Evatt.
65. Sax, *Strife*, p. 56.
66. Sax, *Strife*, p. 57. The Liberal–Country Party Coalition Government, which came to power in Queensland in 1957, retained the program. See Palmer, "Health," (1974): 180.
67. Hicks, *Rum Regulations*, p. 18.
68. Sax, *Strife*, p. 55; and R. Sackville, "Social welfare in Australia: The constitutional framework," in *Perspectives in Australian Social Policy*, by A. Graycar, ed. (Melbourne: MacMillan, 1978).
69. Australia, "National Health Services Act," *Statutes* (1948).
70. The Australian reform was more progressive than its British counterpart which did not recommend nationalization of ambulatory care.
71. E. G. Whitlam, *The Whitlam Government* 1972-1975 (Harmondsworth: Penguin Books, 1985): 335.
72. Palmer, "Health," (1974): 184. The trade unions continued to advocate more militant policies. See Fry, *Common Cause*, p. xv.

73. Australia, "Earle Page," House of Representatives, Parliamentary Debates 221(1953): 1757; and Sax, *Strife*, p. 59.
74. Sax, *Strife*, p. 59.
75. Palmer, "Health," (1974): 185.
76. Page quoted in L. F. Crisp, *Australian National Government*, 5th Edition (Melbourne: Longman Cheshire, 1983): 226.
77. The Government would subsidize these voluntary insurance organizations.
78. The doctors immediately accepted the new Government's Pharmaceutical Benefit Scheme offering 139 life-saving drugs.
79. Australia, "National Health Act," *Statutes* (1953).
80. Sax, *Strife*, p. 75.
81. This became known as the "one-third" formula: one-third finance out of pocket, one-third by health insurance organizations and one-third by the patient.
82. R. B. Scotton, "Voluntary health insurance in Australia," *Australian Economic Review*, 2nd Quarter (1967): 37–44. A retention rate of 21 percent in Canada was a major reason that the Canadian Royal Commission on Health Services advocated universal entitlement under a plan administered through public agencies.
83. The non-insured were often the segment of the population in greatest need of medical attention. See R. B. Scotton, "The Nimmo Report: A new deal for patients?" *Australian Journal of Social Issues* 4(1969): 85–87. Personal communication with Richard B. Scotton.
84. From 1951 to 1966, health insurance was an insignificant campaign issue at election time. See Palmer, "Health," (1974): 186.
85. J. S. Deeble, "The costs and sources of finance of Australian health services," *The Economic Record* 43(1967): 518–43; Scotton, Voluntary health insurance in Australia," pp. 37–44; and R. B. Scotton and J. S. Deeble, "Compulsory health insurance for Australia," *Australian Economic Review* 4th Quarter (1968): 9–16.
86. T. Fox, "Antipodes: Private practice publicly supported," *Lancet*, 1(1963): 875; and Sax, *Strife*, p. 66.
87. Australia, Senate Select Committee on Health (SSCH), "Report on medical and hospital costs [Chairman Ivy Wedgwood]," *Parliamentary Papers* (1970).
88. Personal communication with John A. Nimmo, Chairman of the committee.
89. Australia, Commonwealth Committee of Inquiry into Health Insurance (CCEHI), "Report," *Parliamentary Papers* (1969): 8.

90. When the Liberal–Country Coalition returned to power, the new Government introduced a similar health insurance plan in 1970. See Palmer, "Health," (1974): 192.
91. R. B. Scotton and John S. Deeble, "The Nimmo report," *The Economic Report* 45(June 1969): 275.
92. Scotton, "Nimmo Report," p. 85.
93. Hicks, *Rum Regulations*, p. 31.
94. Scotton and Deeble, "Compulsory health insurance," p. 14.
95. Palmer, "Health," (1974): 189.
96. To avoid another constitutional debate, the authors omitted any reference to a compulsory fee schedule.
97. Scotton and Deeble, "Compulsory health insurance," p. 13.
98. Personal communication with John S. Deeble and Richard B. Scotton.
99. Palmer, "Health," (1974): 199; and Personal communication with John S. Deeble and Richard B. Scotton.
100. Crisp, *Government*, p. 225.
101. Whitlam, *Government*, p. 333.
102. A. Patience and B. Head, eds., *From Whitlam to Fraser. Reform and Reaction in Australian Politics* (Melbourne: Oxford University Press, 1979): 1.
103. *Ibid.*, p. 2.
104. B. Hayden, "The contemporary implications of democratic socialism," in *Labour Essays 1982: Socialist Principles and Parliamentary Government*, by G. Evans and J. Reeves, eds. (Richmond, Victoria: Drummond, 1982): 3.
105. Patience and Head, *Whitlam to Fraser*, pp. 3–8.
106. G. R. Palmer, "Health," in *From Whitlam to Fraser. Reform and Reaction in Australian Politics*, by A. Patience and B. Head, eds. (Melbourne: Oxford University Press, 1979): 123.
107. S. J. Duckett, "Structural interests and Australian health policy," *Social Science and Medicine* 18 (1984): 959.
108. Crisp, *Government*, p. 229.
109. The Australian Medical Association supported this approach.
110. This style of policy-making is common in Australia. Personal communication with John A. Nimmo.
111. The Australian Medical Association had evolved out of the independent stale branches of the British Medical Association in 1963.
112. Announced at the Australian Hospital Association's National Congress in Melbourne, October 1972. See Sax, *Strife*, p. 101.
113. Palmer, "Health," (1974): 206.

114. M. Young, "The build-up to 1972," in *The Whittam Phenomenon*, by F. Papers, ed. (Ringwood, Victoria, 1986): 92.
115. Hicks, *Rum Regulations*, p. 34.
116. Personal communication with Dr. Douglas Everingham and Dr. Gwen Howells. See D. Everingham, "Towards a healthier Australia," *Parliamentary Papers* (1974); Australia, Australian Department of Health (ADH), "Annual report of the Director-General of Health 1972–73," *Parliamentary Papers* (1973); and Australia, Australian Department of Health (ADH), "Australian health expenditure 1975–76 to 1979–80: An analysis," *Parliamentary Papers* (September 1983).
117. Sax was involved only in the planning of the new program, not in its eventual administration. See Australia, Health Insurance Planning Committee (HIPC), "Report to the Minister for Social Security" *Parliamentary Papers* (1973). Personal communication with Dr. Gwen Howells, the former Director-General of the Department of Health.
118. Because of these changes, the Department of Health played a subsidiary role in the introduction of Medibank.
119. Palmer, "Health," (1974): 197.
120. Personal communication with Dr. Keith Jones, President of the Australian Medical Association during the Whitlam years, and with Dr. William D. Refshauge, Director-General of the Department of Health up until 1972.
121. Personal communication with L. J. Daniels, previously Deputy Director of the financial branch of the Department of Health.
122. Australia, "The Australian health insurance program," *Parliamentary Papers* (November 1973); and Australia, "Health program," *Parliamentary Papers* (1973).
123. Australia, Health Insurance Commission (HIC), "First annual report 1974-75," *Parliamentary Papers* (1975): 3. The old system covered 87 percent of the population. Bureau of Census and Statistics, Bulletin No, 17.7, 31 May 1973, quoted in Australia, "Health insurance program," p. 3.
124. Personal communication with Dr. Gwen Howells, the Director-General of the Department of Health after 1972, and C. Robert Wilcox, the present General Manager.
125. By the end of Medibank's 15-month existence, more than 70 percent of doctors used bulk billing.
126. Australia, "Health Insurance program," p. 2.
127. The Government's proposal simplified this arrangement: the Australian Government would pay 50 percent of the future operating cost.

128. Australia, "Health insurance program," Sec. 7.1.
129. Contributions to private health insurance organizations continued to qualify as tax-deductible.
130. Personal communication with Dr. Keith Jones. The private health insurance organizations, using reserves from their contributors, staged similar protests.
131. Whitlam, *Government*, p. 345.
132. The Medibank proposal had recommended a general increase in the order of 6 percent.
133. The committee had powers to determine the level of health insurance refunds not to set fees charged by medical practitioners. Sax, *Strife*, p. 110.
134. The conflict over the official fee schedule recurred on a yearly basis.
135. Personal communication with Keith Jones.
136. During the first year of the Labor Government, the Opposition parties which dominated the Senate, rejected 13 bills, deferred 10 bills and amended another 20. See S. J. Duckett, "Chopping and Changing Medibank, Part I," *Australian Journal of Social Issues* 14(1979): 232.
137. Prime Minister Gough Whitlam, quoted in Duckett, "Medibank, Part I," p. 232.
138. Crisp, *Government*, p. 411.
139. Under Medibank II, the Fraser Government introduced a health insurance levy of 2.5 percent, which exempted those who bought basic insurance from private organizations for making such a contribution.
140. Australia, "Health insurance levy assessment bill," *Parliamentary Papers* (1974); and Australia, "Health insurance levy bill," *Parliamentary Papers* (1974).The rules of Parliament called for such a joint sitting when a deadlock arose between the two Houses, Parliament gave assent to the Health Insurance Act on August 8, 1974. See Australia, "Health Insurance Act"; *Statutes* (1973): 187.
141. This procedure did not repeal the earlier National Health Act of 1954.
142. Sax, *Strife*, p. 117.
143. Hicks, *Rum Regulations*, p. 36; ($360 million from the levy on taxable income; $508 million from consolidated revenues; and $60 million from third-party insurers). See Australia, "Health insurance program," Sec. 7.15.
144. Hicks, *Rum Regulations*, p. 39.
145. Australia, "Health insurance program," Secs. 7.11 and 7.12.
146. The states that opted out would lose millions of dollars each week.
147. Similar tactics had been used in 1916 when the New South Wales Labor Government wanted to introduce free hospital care, in 1938 when the Casey

Government tried to introduce the National Health and Pensions Act and in 1945 when Parliament passed the Chifley Government's National Health Services Act. See Sax, *Strife*, p. 117.

148. Previous Australian convention held that the less democratically constituted Senate would approve Supply Bills recommended by the House of Representatives.
149. N. Blewett, "The challenge of the new conservatism," in *Labor* [sic] *Essays 1982*: *Socialist Principles and Parliamentary Government*, by G. Evans and J. Reeves, eds. (Richmond, Victoria: Drummond, 1982): 35. Also see Crisp, *Government*, pp. 412–4. Normally the Governor-General would first consult with the Government in power. See E.G. Whitlam, *The Troth of the Matter* (Harmondsworth: Penguin Books, 1979): xii.
150. Whiltlam, *Government*, p. 185.
151. Queen Elizabeth II refused to grant Whitlam an audience in London, deferring to her official representative Governor-General John Kerr. See Whitlam, *Government*, p. 2.
152. *Financial Review*, 17 (May 1976) quoted in Sax, *Strife*, p. 126; Whitlam, *Government*, p. 348.
153. Duckett, "Medibank, Part I," p. 230; and S. J. Duckett, "Chopping and changing Medibank, Part II," *Australian Journal of Social Issues*, 15(1980): 79–90.
154. Editorial, "Modi-gamble," *The Launceston Examiner*, 30 July (1976).
155. Whitlam, *Government*, p. 48.
156. Personal communication with Ralph J. Hunt.
157. Various authors have since criticized the Department of Health's estimates of health care costs. See R. B. Scotton, "Medibank 1976," *Australian Economic Review*, 1st Quarter (1977): 23–36; R. B. Scotton, "Costs and use of medical services," *Australian Economic Review* 2nd Quarter (1978): 72–76; J. S. Deeble, *Health Expenditures* in *Australia 1960–61 to 1975–76*, Research Report No.1 (Canberra: Australian National University, Health, 1978); and J. S. Deeble, "Financing health care in a static economy," *Social Science and Medicine* 16(1982): 713–24.
158. Neal Blewett while Shadow Minister for Health. N. Blewett, "Consistency and consensus in Labor's [sic] health policy," *Australian Health Review* 5(December 1982): 8.
159. Australia, Department of Health (CDH), "Annual report, 1976–77," *Parliamentary Papers* (1977). See Sax, *Strife*, p. 131.
160. R. B. Scotton, "The Fraser Government and social expenditures," in *Public Expenditure and Social Policy* in *Australia*, Vol. 2, by R. B. Scotton and H. Ferber (Melbourne: Longman Cheshire, 1980): 181, 205.

161. Australia, SSCSW, "Through a glass," p. 1.
162. Australia, Commission of Inquiry into the Efficiency and Administration of Hospitals (CIEAH), "J. H. Jamison," *Parliamentary Papers* (1980).
163. Its Chairman was J. H. Jamison.
164. The Minister for Health, M. J. R. MacKellar, was opposed by the Cabinet and treasury over which Recommendations to introduce. Personal communication with J. R. MacKellar and J. H. Jamison.
165. Ronald Mendelsohn, *The Condition of the People: Social Welfare in Australia 1900–1975*, Revised Edition (Sydney: George Allen & Unwin, 1982): 321.
166. Australian Labor Party [sic], "Cheaper for Australians," p. 1.
167. N. Blewett, "Australian Labor Party [sic] viewpoint," in *Perspectives in Health Policy*, by M. Tatchell, ed. (Canberra: Australian National University, Health Economics Research Unit, 1984): 252.
168. A one percent levy on personal taxable income and health insurance subsidies provided the financing for the new medicare program.
169. Australian Labor Party [sic], "Australian Labor Party [sic] platform, constitution and rules 1984," (1984): 111, 119; sec. 74.
170. Australia, Department of Health (CDH), "Advancing Australia's health: Towards national strategies and objectives for health advancement." Draft Plan, *Parliamentary Papers* (1985): 3–15. Personal communication with Bernie McKay, present Director-General of the Department of Health and Social Affairs.
171. Dr. L. Thompson, past President of the AMA. See L. Thompson, "Australian Medical Association viewpoint," in *Perspectives in Health Policy*, by M. Tatchell, ed. (Canberra: Australian National University, Health Economics Research Unit, 1984): 256.
172. J. Healy, E. Sharman, and B. Lokuge, *Australia: Health System Review in Health Systems in Transition*, 8(5)(2006): 1–158. http://www.euro.who.int/__data/assets/pdf_file/0007/96433/E89731.pdf. Accessed July 25, 2017.
173. G. Scott, L. McKenzie, and J. Webster, Maladjustments in the corporatization model: Hospital reform in New Zealand, in A. S. Preker and A. Harding, eds., *Innovations in Health Service Delivery: The Corporatization of Public Hospitals* (2003, Washington, DC: World Bank). https://openknowledge. worldbank.org/handle/10986/15145. Accessed August 17, 2017; pp. 205–345.

CHAPTER 7

DENMARK

For the revolutionary, the struggle for reform involves strategy, ... to overthrow the [class structure].... For the reformist, the reforms are goals in themselves.[1]

Jens Otto Krag, n.d.

A. HISTORICAL CONTEXT

1. Early Danish Sickness Funds

The Danish Poor Laws during the nineteenth century reflected the existing liberal self-help philosophy and therefore offered only the most basic provisions for health care. The sickness funds, on the other hand, allowed the individual to preserve his dignity, while maintaining some protection against the uncertainties of illness.

Tradesmen and industrial workers were the first to benefit from the sickness funds, the first of which was established in Sorø on October 3, 1841.[2] Similar organizations were rapidly set up throughout the country during the latter part of the nineteenth and beginning of the twentieth centuries.[3] The new sickness funds were, however, soon threatened by the proposed Trade Act which called for the elimination of all medieval trade guilds.[4]

Danish doctors immediately recognized the potential of the sickness funds as an important source of income. Not surprisingly, a key item on the agenda of the first General Assembly of the Danish Medical Association in 1857 was a defense of these organizations. The medical profession, therefore, was pleased when the sickness funds were preserved in the form of mutual aid organizations in 1861.

By 1871, 60 percent of doctors in Denmark were in private practice.[5] Under the existing arrangements, doctors treated members of the sickness funds and their families free of charge, receiving payment for their services from the organizations. This eliminated all direct financial transactions between the patient and the doctor. The capitation system developed as a norm for paying doctors, with the Medical Association negotiating the fee schedule.[6]

Over the next 40 years, four separate commissions determined the direction of the voluntary sickness fund system in Denmark, which in turn later paved the way for universal entitlement to health care. The prevailing ethos remained that the "state should pay but not say."[7]

2. Law on Recognized Sickness Funds of 1892

The early sickness funds were slow to gain official recognition. Mayor S. Linnemann of Copenhagen became the Chairman of the first Sickness Fund Commission on November 18, 1861. His Commission recommended a continuation of the existing *laisser-faire* system, without government interference or financial support. C. N. David, a former Minister for Finance, became the Chairman of the second Sickness Fund Commission on February 10, 1866. He supported a similar "hands-off" approach. Both felt that the sickness funds were an important part of the existing liberal self-help system, which should remain voluntary with minimal regulation or financial support from the state.[8]

Opposition to this liberal view increased with the gradual emergence of an organized labor movement in Denmark. As early as 1876, E. W. Klein, the Chairman of the Central Administration of the Socialist Trade Unions, proposed that the sickness funds should amalgamate to create a common fund covering all workers. He felt that the state and municipal governments should finance such a system through general revenues.[9] The Permanent Secretary of the Department of the Interior, Christian Bache, backed this approach.

When E. E. Rosenoern became the Chairman of the third Sickness Fund Commission on September 20, 1875, he favored a compromise system which would require low-income workers to become members of sickness funds.[10] Under his proposal, the state and municipal governments would subsidize the sickness funds, thereby lowering the direct cost for members.[11]

Although the Conservative Government in the Upper Chamber of Parliament opposed such a program, a new and more favorable political climate was developing in the Lower Chamber. Following the general elections of June 1884, the Left (Liberals) controlled the Lower Chamber by holding 83 seats against the Social Democratic Party's 2 seats and the Right's (Conservatives) 19 seats.[12] The two Social Democratic Party members, who were elected to Parliament for the first time in 1884, strongly advocated financing of health care through public funds.[13]

When H. C. Hansen became Chairman of the fourth Sickness Fund Commission on July 4, 1885, his Commission recommended some public financing and control over the sickness funds.[14] The new Minister for the Interior in 1885, H. P. Ingerslev, adopted these recommendations in the hope that the long-standing debate on the sickness fund would come to a conclusion. The first draft legislation for official recognition and public subsidies for the sickness funds was presented in 1887; the law passed in Parliament on April 12, 1892.[15]

Under the new law, the state gave a generous grant to the sickness funds which met certain official criteria. Approved sickness funds had to prove that they were an association of 50 people or more representing a local municipality, trade group or profession.[16] They also had to provide free medical care, free drugs, free hospitalization and limited income support for their members during periods of illness.[17]

A sickness fund Inspector, appointed by the Minister for the Interior, decided which sickness funds qualified for the program.[18] A representative from the local municipalities, a representative from the sickness funds and a doctor formed a committee which determined which workers were eligible as new members.[19] Eligible workers had to be at least 15 years old, healthy and belong to a trade group.

The voluntary sickness funds could sign on two types of members. "Active" members, usually from low-income groups, received the benefit of full health care coverage. Such benefits included free health care, drugs and hospitalization. "Passive" members, usually from higher income groups, received no direct health coverage, but their "passive" membership made them eligible for benefits from other social programs such as pensions.

As a result of these arrangements, health care by doctors rather than cash benefits was the major expense for the Danish sickness funds.[20] Cash payments of up to two-thirds of the usual wage were, however, available to members for a limited period of time. Members could also subscribe to additional cash benefits, burial benefits and old-age benefits.[21]

The workers, state and municipalities shared the financing of the new program. In addition, the municipalities contributed indirectly to the financing of health care by independently financing hospitals. As the Poor Laws still held them responsible for providing medical attention to the sick and destitute, the municipalities welcomed the sickness fund system, hoping that it would lower the need for different kinds of public assistance.

3. Danish Medical Association

It was within this historical context that the Danish Medical Association was founded on September 1, 1857. One of the original goals of the Association was to unite Danish doctors and to "serve as the body through which the medical profession's influence [might] be exercised on general social issues."[22]

The medical profession welcomed the 1892 Sickness Insurance Law: "The law guaranteed financial security to a large proportion of Danish private practitioners and has continued to be an important financial benefit to them."[23] Some of the medical profession's most prominent members had played important roles in shaping many of the early official regulations affecting the sickness funds. Their participation in official enquiries ensured that the terms affecting the organizations were favorable to doctors.[24]

Dr. L. I. Brandes, a member of the 1862 and 1866 Sickness Fund Commissions, had earlier established his own sickness fund in Copenhagen. Dr. T. M. Trautner, a member of the 1885 Labor Commission, was instrumental in formulating the 1892 Sickness Fund Law. He was also founder of a sickness fund in Odense. Trautner later served as Superintendent Medical Officer in Odense and Chairman of the Danish Medical Association.

Dr. T. Soerensen, also a member of the early Sickness Fund Commissions, became the first Sickness Fund Inspector under the new law.[25]

In 1847, the medical profession established a Health Collegiate as a central health bureaucracy. It was the forerunner of the present National Board of Health which the Government established in 1909.[26] The new law, therefore, gave official recognition to a system which the medical profession had helped nurture and supported.[27]

Following passage of the legislation, conflicts similar to those which took place in other countries nevertheless soon took place between the medical profession and sickness funds. These disagreements centered on income of doctors, their conditions of employment and protection of clinical freedom.[28] At first, an independent Arbitration Chamber settled such disputes.[29] After 1915, a public authority, the National Arbitration Board, assumed this responsibility.[30]

The rapid growth of the voluntary sickness funds gave doctors in private practice a sense of economic security, sparing Denmark from the protectionist manpower policies that were implemented in the other Nordic countries.[31] This resulted in the spontaneous growth of an extensive network of private medical practices for Denmark's population of 2,449,540, which at the turn of the century was scattered over 43,084 square kilometers of flat farm-lands and Islands.[32]

It also lessened the role of the District Medical Officers of Health, who did not have to perform clinical duties as did their counterparts in countries where the primary care network was less well developed. Reflecting this trend, the Danish Medical Officers' Association remained weak and a separate body from the Danish Medical Association.[33]

Danish legislators accurately predicted that the voluntary system would draw a large membership if generous public subsidies supported the sickness funds. The program became so popular that within a few years the entire country had local sickness funds.[34] Their membership rates grew rapidly during the early years, increasing from 10 percent of the population before the 1892 law to 35 percent by 1911.

4. Minor Social Reform of 1921

A revised Sickness Fund Law was passed in 1921 through the Minor Social Reform.[35] Yet the underlying principles of the 1892 Sickness

Insurance Law remained in force under which memberships, contributions, benefits, regulations and public subsidies increased slowly over time.

Under the Minor Social Reform, the existing sickness fund system expanded to cover all Danes in need of collective provisions to pay for health care. Public subsidies expanded, coverage increased to include those over 40 years of age, provisions were made to include the employed who were chronically ill and a separate bill was introduced to include disability insurance. The municipalities became responsible for providing medical attention for those in need who were not covered by existing programs.[36]

By 1925, as a result of these reforms, the voluntary sickness insurance system in Denmark had achieved a membership rate of 42.5 percent of the population, outstripping all other countries in Europe: "By the early 1930s, the Danish program came close to full coverage of the needy population,"[37] reaching 90 percent of those qualifying for the disability pensions program of 1921. Later, eligibility for benefits under the old-age pensions program of 1937 became conditional to being a member in a sickness fund.

Despite the success of the voluntary movement, in which "the role of government was more to support the private sector's activities rather than interfere with them," these measures became inadequate during the Great Depression.[38] The economic pressures of the 1930s provided the impetus for political change which led to further social reforms.

5. Social Insurance Law of 1933

The general elections of April 24, 1929, resulted in a Social Democratic Party–Radical Liberal Party (SDP-RLP) Coalition Government under Prime Minister Thorvald Stauning (SDP).[39] Although the Danish Social Democratic Party was founded in 1871, it was not until Stauning developed its platform and bolstered its strength during the 1920s that the party became a political reality.[40] The new Government prepared to introduce the welfare reforms that the SDP had earlier planned as part of their series of social programs called "Denmark for the People."[41]

K. K. Steincke, the new Minister for Social Affairs, quickly set about preparing an extensive social reform. Steincke had previously worked as an Inspector for the Frederiksberg Poor Law program in Copenhagen. He wanted to unify the numerous and splintered social welfare programs that had slowly evolved over the years. Provisions for public assistance alone, for example, emanated from 41 different pieces of legislation.[42] Through the reforms that he introduced, Steincke became known as the "lawyer whose greatest achievement was … the socio-political reform of 1933."[43]

A new Social Insurance Law was passed on May 20, 1933; it came into effect on October 1, 1933. The reform, known as the Major Social Reform, was timely.[44] "It was difficult to be unemployed at that time. Public assistance was low. There were long waiting periods [for unemployment benefits], and the benefits were quickly used up."[45] The new Social Insurance Law incorporated the previous sickness funds into a unified social insurance system which included public assistance, national insurance (including the sickness funds), accident insurance, disability insurance and unemployment insurance.[46]

Under the new Law, health care benefits offered through the Sickness Insurance Law were once again increased. "Passive" membership became compulsory for all persons under the age of 60 years. Greater "active" membership was encouraged through a generous 33 percent state subsidy and other associated benefits such as pensions. Previous restrictions on memberships were removed. The sickness funds could no longer impose limits on age or physical health. The maximum waiting period for new members was reduced. Finally, benefits became more comprehensive, including the cost of drugs. The 1933 Law aimed "to fill out the framework of the social reforms, and to combat the [Great Depression] and its inevitable companion, a high rate of unemployment."[47]

6. World War II

The Nazi occupation ended this golden period of social reform. The non-aggression pact concluded between Germany and Denmark was short lived. On April 9, 1940, Denmark was swiftly overrun by Hitler's forces: "In that pocket handkerchief-size country on Germany's border, the Nazis set out to create a docile fiefdom as a demonstration to the world that their occupation was benign and even welcome."[48]

During the first three years of the war, there was some political continuity despite the occupation. Thorvald Stauning, the previous Social Democratic Party Prime Minister, formed war-time Coalition Government: "We choose that way to spare the country and its people an inevitable state of war."[49] As a consequence of its rapid surrender to German forces, Denmark did not suffer the same devastating physical destruction that occurred in other occupied countries.

After five years and four Coalition Governments, the Danes emerged from World War II having passively resisted the Germans "with a high degree of effectiveness and with the subtle humor that is so much part of the Danish temperament."[50] A post-war reconstruction program was nevertheless necessary to resurrect many of the benefits introduced during the 1930s.

7. Public Sickness Insurance Law of 1960

Further social reforms were slow to develop in the post-war period. Although Jens Stroem, the Minister for Social Affairs, appointed an expert committee of civil servants to examine the sickness funds in 1946, this committee never reported.[51] During the decade which followed, the cost of health benefits to the sickness funds continued to rise without parallel increases in their revenues.

As a result of what they saw as inaction by the expert committee, the sickness funds established their own Joint Advisory Committee with Ernst Larsen as Chairman and H. C. Hansen as Administrative Director.[52] The committee, concluding that the sickness funds were underfunded, requested that Stroem constitute a formal Commission of Inquiry on Sickness Insurance.[53]

On May 28, 1954, the Minister for Social Affairs appointed P. Juhl-Christensen as Chairman of a broadly represented Sickness Fund Commission. Its terms of reference were to review the benefits offered through the sickness funds, their administrative structure and eligibility for "active" membership.[54] The Commission published its report in 1959, a document which formed the basis for the Public Sickness Insurance Law of 1960.[55] The new law was introduced by the Minister for Social Affairs, J. Bomholt, and came into effect on April 1, 1961.

The 1960 Law limited the number of sickness funds to one per municipality. Each municipalities had to appoint a representative to the executive management board of their respective sickness fund to ensure public representation. The Ministry of Social Affairs appointed a Director who would be directly responsible for overseeing and coordinating the activities of the organizations.[56]

The Law offered improved benefits for "active" members, including free medical attendance by general practitioners and specialists, free hospitalization, coverage for 75 percent of the cost of drugs, school dental services, home nursing, prosthesis, maternity benefits, funeral benefits, transport, cash allowances and sickness pay for all wage earners. It also removed many of the previous restrictions on membership. Furthermore, the sickness funds could no longer exclude groups such as the elderly, the chronically ill or those who had already used up their statutory benefits.

Workers, local municipalities and the state continued financing the program. The means-test for compulsory membership was, however, "fixed so high that 80 per cent of the population [became] A-members ["active"]."[57] Through these reforms, the voluntary sickness funds in Denmark evolved to offer near universal entitlement.[58]

The 1960 reforms increased memberships with the sickness funds and thereby strengthened the financial position of the organizations: "Even though the law did not introduce increases in contributions … this became a prosperous time for the sickness funds."[59] The evolving social democratic mood in Denmark would soon make such privileges enjoyed by one segment of society unacceptable.

B. LANDMARK LEGISLATIVE REFORMS

1. Danish Social Politics

In September 1962, when Jens Otto Krag became leader of the Social Democratic Party, replacing Viggo Kampmann as Prime Minister, he symbolically ended the period of unstable Coalition Governments which followed the war: "After tobacconist Thorvald Stauning, lithographer Hans Hedtoft and typographer H. C. Hansen, academic Social Democrat leaders entered the political arena."[60] This change would eventually have a profound effect on public involvement in the financing of health care.

Schooled in economics, Krag had acted as advisor to the Danish Ambassador in Washington during the early 1950s. He believed in peaceful social transformation, rejecting the revolutionary socialism that had swept across eastern Europe: "For the revolutionary, the struggle for reform involves strategy, … to overthrow the [class structure]…. For the reformist, the reforms are goals in themselves."[61] Danish social reforms were introduced through the latter process.[62]

Krag was responsible for formulating one of the party's early platforms, "Future Denmark 1945," which introduced a progressive income tax-system which collected contributions at source.[63] Under a later policy, the "Way Forward 1961," the party aimed "to guarantee security and to offer the opportunity for [the] development of responsibility for fellowship."[64] Putting these ideals into practice was the party's major challenge during the 1960s and early 1970s, laying the foundation for what became known as the "New Society 1969."[65]

The other major political parties each had their own platforms. The Liberals believed that freedom involved responsibility, since "individual freedom is realised in fellowship with other human beings. … Society must give support to those fellow citizens, who because of age, illness, mental or physical handicaps or failed possibilities for employment have a need for such assistance."[66] They stressed that the individual was responsible for himself and that society was only responsible for those who were unable to achieve such self-reliance.

The Radical Liberals believed that public outlay on education, research, health care and social security was necessary since demand for such benefits would increase more rapidly than private investments in these areas. They felt that careful long-term planning under public control was necessary to ensure efficient functioning of social policies.[67]

As for the Conservatives, they believed that careful long-term planning and public administration was necessary to control the cost of social programs. They therefore advocated a complete re-examination and revision of the public sector with the aim to cut public expenditure.[68]

Although their expressed aims were far apart, all the parties advocated far-reaching reforms and increased public control over social planning; some intended to cut public expenditure while others intended to increase it.[69] "The years since 1968 ... represent the most extensive administrative reforms that the local and regional administration has experienced in modern times."[70] In 1968, when the Liberals took office, Hilmar Baunsgaard (Radical Liberal) became the Prime Minister of a Coalition Government formed by Liberals, Radical Liberals and Conservatives. This allowed the Liberals and Conservatives to carry out their version of "social reorganization."[71]

2. County Councils and Municipalities

A re-organization of local government into new self-sufficient geographic and financial entities and a unification of the Danish social welfare system during the 1960s had a profound effect on the collective provisions for sickness insurance and the future of the sickness funds.[72]

The local government reforms followed the recommendations of the Local Government Reform Commission, which presented its findings in 1968. It recommended a re-structuring of the existing geographic boundaries "to provide the local governments at both levels [municipal and county] with a better foundation, population-wise and therefore also tax-wise, for providing and managing those services which, according to tradition and to the general political philosophy in Denmark, should be left to the responsibility of locally elected councils."[73]

Most of the political parties were in favor of local government reforms but for greatly varied reasons. The Social Democratic Party was deeply committed to reforms which would lead to decentralization and increase its political control over local government. The Conservative Party and Liberal Party also supported such reforms which they felt would lead to greater self-sufficiency and fiscal responsibility of local governments. They also hoped that a reorganization of local government would dislodge the Social Democratic Party from their traditional stronghold.[74]

Under the reform, local governments would continue to receive a major part of their financing from local taxation, including income taxes. The provision of health care would remain their major activity.[75] "In fact, the committee, which prepared the local government reform, based its recommendation on the idea that a population of this size [was] required to satisfy and to motivate a degree of specialization within the hospital service, which … [was] desirable, from the point of view of the patients as well as that of the medical profession."[76]

3. Parliamentary Resolution of 1964

The political motives for the reforms in the social welfare system which eventually led to universal entitlement to health care were equally diverse. It was the Liberals and Conservatives who, on April 9, 1964, presented a parliamentary resolution which prompted the Minister for Social Affairs, Kaj Bundvad, to set up a Social Reform Commission: "On behalf of the Liberals and Conservative Parties, I [P. E. Eriksen] have the honour to present a 'Proposal for a parliamentary resolution for the preparation of a Social Reform' through the appointment of a Commission to examine and prepare a new social reform."[77] The terms of reference for the Commission were to "unify [the] social security system's organizational, administrative and financial structure and to present the necessary recommendations for preparing legislation in this regard."[78]

The forced cooperation between the Social Democratic Party (Socialdemokratiet), Radical Liberals, Liberals and the Conservatives during the 1960s became even more strained than it had been in the past. The Liberals and Conservatives wanted to simplify a system which they felt had become cumbersome, excessive and difficult to control financially. The Social Democratic Party, on the other hand, wanted to unify, decentralize and expand the existing system.[79]

By being the ones to present the parliamentary resolution, the Liberals and Conservatives had stolen some of the political gains that the Social Democratic Party had hoped to reap from proposing such an inquiry. Not surprisingly, the Social Democratic Party found it hard to embrace the Government's initiative with enthusiasm even if they supported the call for reform. They therefore quietly accepted the inquiry, hoping that they could turn it to their advantage at some later stage.

4. Social Reform Commission of 1969

The Minister for Social Affairs, Kaj Bundvad, responded to the parliamentary resolution by appointing a Social Reform Commission on May 29, 1964. Its terms of reference aimed to eliminate the redundancies in the existing social security system, while retaining its base of public financing.[80] The honeymoon atmosphere that the Sickness Insurance Law of 1960 had created for the sickness funds would soon be over.

The Chairman of the Commission, H. C. Seierup, was also Chairman of the Association of Disability Organizations.[81] The Assistant Chairmen were Niels Moerk of the Social Democratic Party and Finn Nielsen, the Permanent Secretary of the Department of Social Affairs. Commissioners were drawn from a broad non-partisan representation; the five major parties, Parliament itself, the county councils and other interested parties such as the sickness funds were all represented. Rudy Schroeder and H. C. Hansen represented the sickness funds. By their own choice, however, neither the Danish Medical Association nor the Danish Board of Health participated directly in the Commission's work.[82]

The Danish Medical Association "did not wish to be represented on the Commission," hoping to remain neutral in the impending confrontation between the Government and the sickness funds.[83] It nevertheless kept up the appearance of supporting the organizations, claiming that doctors could not "see any problems in an extension in … the existing sickness funds."[84] In the same breath, however, the Association offered its full support to reforms proposed by the Government.[85]

Despite the Medical Association's claim that it wanted to maintain a neutral stance, it emphasized its preference for allowing patients freedom in choosing a doctor and doctors clinical freedom in treating patients. Doctors warned that a universal system with completely free attendance paid through taxes would lead to abuses. The Association, therefore, recommended that an income barrier be maintained for membership and that patients should contribute at least a token amount toward the cost of their treatment.

The first report produced by the Social Reform Commission appeared in October 1969. The majority report lodged a strong criticism against the established order. It felt that a new unified health care system should be completely public and available to the whole population through a truly unified public administration, the county councils. It also recommended that health care, like other public services, should be financed through general revenues.

The Commission was critical of the lack of true public representation under the existing system. Rules specifying that members of the sickness funds had a voting right in appointing representatives on the organizations' boards of administration were inadequate, since only a few members exercised this right.[86]

The slow evolution of the various health benefits available to the public under the existing system had led to poor inter-sectorial coordination.[87] Benefits such as routine health exams, disability pensions, rehabilitation, maternity help and nursing homes were offered through separate provisions. Furthermore, the protection offered through the sickness funds applied mainly to curative care not prevention.

The report made extensive reference to other proposals for combined reforms in both local government and health care which had been made in Norway, Sweden and Great Britain.[88] In particular, the Commission drew special attention to the British Seebohm Report, which recommended similar local government reforms.

The Commission considered both earmarked sickness insurance contributions and general revenues as the basis for financing the proposed reform. General revenues were favored as "simpler than a system of collection of a special sickness insurance contribution, that [would] have the character of a special tax."[89] To emphasize its preference, the Commission stressed that most other public services were financed through general revenues.

The division of patients into two groups by the sickness funds — group A and group B — did not distribute the burden of the cost of illness evenly. Families with children living at home beyond the age of 16 years had to pay contributions which often worsened their financial predicament. The Commission emphasized that, although well-to-do members enjoyed generous state subsidies, 10 percent of the population who needed health care or public assistance remained ineligible for such benefits.[90]

Various interest groups submitted dissenting opinions to the Commission. Kurt Brauer, representing the Socialist People's Party, called for a more radical arrangement in dealing with the doctors to "secure the effectiveness of the social structure in the future."[91] He recommended the creation of a salaried national health service.

Niels Moerk, representing the Social Democratic Party, also felt that the recommended reforms had not gone far enough. He advocated that the new system should include compulsory accident insurance, full compensation for lost wages during illness and financing through a single progressive income tax. Furthermore, he felt that there should be no exchange of money between doctors and patients, and that universal entitlement should include pap-tests, breast cancer screening, routine medical exams, abortions, chiropractic care and dental care. Moerk also defended the sickness funds: "The Danish sickness funds have ... solved many problems throughout the years."[92] It would be wrong, he felt, to exclude them in the new system.[93] This stance was not surprising, since the Social Democratic Party was heavily represented on the administrative boards of the sickness funds.[94]

H. C. Hansen and Rudy Schroeder, representing the sickness funds, felt that continued use of the existing organizations offered "the simplest … [and] the least expensive solution."[95] They warned that other options, such as administration through special health organizations, municipal councils, county councils or the state, would not alleviate the problems of coordinating the various services. They rejected the options of a salaried health service and a refund system as steps backward.

The Commission conceded that the existing system had already spontaneously evolved in the desired direction: "Part of the rules that earlier gave cause for criticism were changed through the Sickness Insurance Fund Law of 1960."[96] Following introduction of this law, the sickness funds could no longer exclude groups such as the elderly, the chronically ill and those who had already used up their benefits.[97] The Commission nevertheless concluded that the time was ripe for a unified system which would leave little room for the sickness funds: "Public sickness insurance should withdraw from [reliance on] the private insurance system, based on voluntary membership."[98] The report was a "death sentence" for the sickness funds.[99]

5. Sickness Funds' Publicity Campaign

The sickness funds, realizing that the proposed reforms threatened their existence, fought back in August 1969, with a major publicity campaign to inform the public of their stance.[100] They accused the Commission of advocating a "multicolored supermarket" of social benefits.[101] "One has a feeling, that from a political point of view, there was a greater interest in the administrative problems than in the improvement of social benefits."[102] The sickness funds claimed that a unified system would be too large to cope with the complexities of the many proposed benefits.[103] Furthermore, they felt that the Commission's recommendations for a unified system represented change for the sake of change rather than an effort to improve the existing system.[104]

Instead, the sickness funds recommended that the Government establish independent health organizations which would be administered through a continuation of the existing system.[105] Such health organizations would follow the lines of the existing system. Coverage would include universal compulsory membership, universal access to doctors, comprehensive benefits and a removal of all economic barriers to health care.

Finally, the sickness funds claimed that a moderate reform would avoid major additional financial outlays by the Government, since the existing system already covered more than 90 percent of the population.[106] The cost for 1967 under the existing system was estimated at 990 million Crowns for health benefits and 211 million Crowns for cash benefits. On the other hand, according to the sickness funds the Commission's reforms would lead to a 50 percent increase in cost.[107]

The sickness funds announced their campaign in all the major newspapers and through distribution of leaflets, in the hope that their members would support them.[108] The public, however, reacted with hostility to this publicity which they felt used members' contributions to protect the comfortable jobs of a few administrators.[109] Finally, after a difficult struggle "the sickness funds realised that it was impossible to change the direction of the stream."[110]

6. Social Reform Investigations

The social reforms of the 1960s had captured the imagination of the Danish intellectual community. At the request of the Social Reform Commission, Bent Rold Andersen, Kaj Westergår, Anders From and Jytte Ussing produced four volumes of data to support the need for such reforms.[111] "It is evident that the Social Reform Commission should, on the one hand, examine ways to unify and improve the effectiveness of the social administration, on the other hand, examine [its] consequences."[112]

In Volume II of the investigations, Bent Rold Andersen described the ethos of the 1960s: "The social-political debate and legislation has [in Denmark] undergone a change since the end of the Second World War."[113] Before the war, there was a focus on social insurance and welfare aimed at extending the existing provisions through compulsory membership: "The theoretical debate concerned itself especially with the demarcation between public involvement in insurance and benefits together with the financing and distribution in these connections."[114] The main problem was to find a balance between the individual's responsibility and that of the society. Excessive public intervention was seen as an unwanted intrusion.

Following the war, it became fashionable "to put added weight on service and outcome" than dogma. Debate on welfare were less about the ideology of individual and social responsibility than about relieving social hardship, improving well-being and providing better lifestyles for the population.

The previous approach had been to offer benefits after an individual had fallen below a certain unacceptable standard. The new philosophy set out to provide such assistance long before the individual reached this low point. Help would be offered in commensurate with the normal standards of different groups in society in the hope that this would allow them to regain independence and productivity before becoming completely incapacitated and dependent on public assistance: "Behind this shift in the social-political theory and practice lay a change in the understanding of the goals and aims of social benefits."[115]

Andersen recommended six major changes in the existing system: unification of the existing public assistance programs, cooperation between social and health sectors, simplification of the existing complicated system, improved benefits, increased staff to deal with clients and greater emphasis on the delivery of services than on control.[116]

This re-orientation in the approach to social welfare advocated by Andersen and his group had clear implications for health care. Offering health care only after the individual had become ill was no longer acceptable; whenever possible health promotion through education, prevention, rehabilitation and care should be aim to avoid such illness in the first place.[117]

7. Sickness Insurance Law of 1971

Hilmar Baunsgaard (Radical Liberals), Denmark's new Prime Minister, appointed. Nathalie Lind (Liberal) as Minister for Social Affairs in 1968. Lind's experience as a lawyer enabled her to oversee the myriad of legislative changes necessary to carry out the desired social security reform and to coordinate these with a decentralization in local government.

Lind announced the proposed legislation in Parliament on January 14, 1970: "A proposal for a law on the introduction of a local authority administered public sickness insurance system for the whole population will be presented to Parliament during the Parliamentary year 1970–1971."[118]

Because the conflicting points of view about the sickness funds had been thoroughly discussed in the past, Lind wanted to avoid renewing these in Parliament. She promised that the new administration would employ the staff of the sickness funds.[119] This reassurance helped limit the parliamentary debates to two days, May 12 and 13, 1970.

The formal proposal for the new Public Sickness Insurance Law was tabled on January 13, 1971. It closely followed the recommendations of the majority report of the Social Reform Commission of 1969.[120] The law passed its three readings in Parliament on May 14, 26 and 28, 1971.[121] When implemented on April 1, 1973, the new law offered residents of Denmark public financing for universal entitlement to health care.[122] A central body, the National Board of Insurance, would administer the running of the new program.

Under the new system, the population was given "equal, sufficient and free access … [to the general practitioner], the first and most essential link in the service chain … the key person and gatekeeper."[123] New County Council Committees representing various social and health care organizations would deal with all negotiations with the medical profession.

The reserves amassed by the abolished sickness funds were pooled into a new Health Fund, later used to pay for research, medical education, nursing homes and pensions for the non-employable members of the sickness funds.[124]

The new program would, however, maintain the previous two groups of beneficiaries. Those earning below a certain income, would qualify for completely free medical care; those above this yearly income would pay for visits to doctors but qualify for partial reimbursements and special treatment.

The cost of health care to the central government in Denmark in 1969 had been 1,356 million Crowns. Of this, members had financed 73 percent, the state 22 percent, and other sources 3 percent.[125] The estimated cost of the new system, in 1969 prices, was 1,096 million Crowns. Since hospitalization would be financed through the county councils under the new system, and the 7 percent administrative cost previously used for the sickness funds would be eliminated, the net cost of the reform to the central government was anticipated to decrease.[126]

"The major effect of the sickness insurance reform… [was therefore], that the expenses of health care [were] no longer shared by the population on a per capita basis but... according to income."[127] Even the sickness funds recognized the positive contribution to health care made by the new law: "A country's culture can be measured by the quality of the help and support, that benefits the society's sick and weak."[128] The reformers felt that the new law would allow the Danish health care system to begin focusing on health, not just universal entitlement to health care as it had under the old sickness insurance system.

C. CONTINUED POLICY REFORM PROCESS

1. Entry into the European Union

Denmark joined the European Economic Community on January 1, 1973 with the UK and Ireland. Although this did not change the fundamental character of the Danish health system, the fiscal constraints on deficit funding under the Acquis, and accompanying requirements of freedom of movement of people, goods, services and financing opened up the Danish health service to completion in both the provision of services and the health labor market.[129]

2. Groennegår Committee of 1986

Universal entitlement to health care in Denmark had several unique characteristics and shortcomings. First, an income-determined means-test continued to divide the population into two groups of patients: the well-to-do and those of ordinary means. According to this system, personal wealth therefore continued to determine the nature of services enjoyed by an individual.

Secondly, the reforms failed to secure improved inter-sectorial cooperation, despite the fact that this was one of the main ideological reasons for recommending that a broad social reform should include the health sector: "The collaboration between the primary health care sector and the social welfare sector needs strengthening if the objectives of developing alternative models for comprehensive health care at the grass roots level are to be achieved."[130]

Finally, raising the threshold for the welfare safety net still did not prevent a small group from persistently "falling between the cracks."[131] This small group, comprising 10 to 15 percent of cases needing public assistance, became chronically dependent on the welfare system, resisting all efforts to make them self-sufficient.[132]

In 1982, institutional care remained totally financed by public funds, while ambulatory care still offered financing through the two-group system.[133] Although in principle, universal entitlement existed for all inhabitants as a "paper right", in practice, comprehensiveness was limited by an income barrier for ambulatory care for some, and universal access was limited through poor inter-sectorial cooperation.

Dr. Joergen Fog, current Deputy Director of the National Board of Health, and Dr. Esther Ammundsen, past Director General of the Board of Health, emphasize the importance of public participation to promotion of health: "Maintaining good health is something you have to engage yourself in and fight for with the support of your community and your professional servants: the primary health workers. The responsibility for the care of those with, or in risk of, ill health in the community must be shared by the health people in solidarity,"[134] Such participation in healthy living cannot be provided through legislative reforms alone but requires a reorientation of people's approach to health and illness.[135]

To encourage such public participation, the Groennegår Committee of 1986 examined the possibility of handing over a larger share of health financing to the primary health care sector, which, in turn, would have to contract services from the hospital sector. This would encourage primary health care doctors to become more self-sufficient, avoid unnecessary use of institutional care and offer an incentive for patients to seek healthy lifestyles.[136]

3. Major Policy Updates in Denmark Since the 1980s

Since the latter part of the 1980s, the National Health Service in the Denmark has continued to evolve. Starting with what was originally a mixed insurance based system and then fully publicly funded and publicly owned national health service post World War II, recent reforms have reintroduced more market based approaches to both funding and delivery of health care, but preserving its predominantly public tax-funded and public National Health Service character.[137]

During the latter part of the 1980s, there was an increasing focus on shifting care from an acute hospital- and nursing home-based system to community services, primary care and home care. The number of GPs, home nurses and other community-based services increased substantially with increase salary levels for such staff. By the 1990s, the emphasis on non-institutional approaches such as health promotion and disease prevention (primary and secondary) continued, with major campaigns against cancer, heart disease and diabetes.

During the 1990s, Denmark also embraced the "new public sector" management approaches that were first pioneered in New Zealand, with a focus on greater managerial accountability, market-based economic incentives and greater competition among providers.[138] In 1993, patients were given the freedom to pick the hospital of their choice. Starting in 1998, diagnosis-related groups (DRGs) were introduced as the basis for paying hospitals rather than the previous historical budgets that were used up until them.

After 2000 the focus was on cutting waiting times, with a maximum two-month waiting introduced in 2002, reduced one month in 2007.

Patients that could not be treated within these time limits were allowed to go elsewhere for care within Denmark and EU.

As in the other Scandinavian countries, the consensual system of government in Denmark, avoided the ideological swings that were observed since the 1980s in Australia, Canada, New Zealand and the UK. Prime Minister Lars Løkke Rasmussen, who took office on June 28, 2015, leads a Venstre party coalition (which is considered to be center-right although the literal translation means left). As a minority party, it relies on support from its right-wing coalition partners. Having been in power for almost a decade now under different leaders, it has allowed a continuation of a mix of administrative reforms and market based approaches.

ENDNOTES

1. J. O. Krag, quoted in J. Engberg *et al.*, *Dansk Arbejderbevoegelse: Med Kritik of Jens Otto Krag, Ib Noerlund og Gen Petersen, Seks Foredrag*, No. 5 (Arhus: SFAH'S Publikationsserie, 1976): 84.
2. H. C. Hansen, *Historien om Sygekasseme* (Copenhagen: De Samvirkende Centralforeninger af Sygekasser i Denmark, 1974): 26.
3. During the reign of thirteenth century Danish monarch Queen Margrethe I, private associations and tradesmen's guilds provided some financial assistance to their members during periods of illnesses or to the families of the deceased. See Hansen, *Sygekasseme*, p. 9; and O. Rasmussen, *Sygesikringsloven med Kommentarer* (Copenhagen: Juristforbundets Forlag, 1979): 48.
4. The law passed on December 29, 1857, and came into effect in 1861. See Rasmussen, *Sygesikringsloven*, p. 48; and H. Ito, "Health insurance and medical services in Sweden and Denmark 1850–1950," in *The Shaping of the Swedish Health System*, by A. J. Heidenheimer and N. Elvander, eds. (London: Croom Helm, 1980): 50.
5. Ito, "Health insurance," p. 54.
6. Ito, "Health Insurance," p. 52.
7. Ito,"Health insurance," p. 60.
8. Hansen, *Sygekasseme*, p. 46, 49.
9. Hansen, *Sygekasseme*, p. 53.
10. His report was published on October 25, 1878. See Hansen, *Sygekasseme*, p. 55.
11. O. von Bismark, influenced by the German socialist workers' movement, introduced similar compulsory sickness and accident insurance for workers in Germany on June 15, 1883.

12. The King had absolute power as head of state. He appointed the J. Estrup of the Right, which still had a majority in the Second Chamber, to lead the Government. The position as president of the Council later became the position of Prime Minister.
13. Hansen, *Sygekasseme*, p. 58.
14. Dr. T. Soerensen (later Sickness Fund Inspector) was a member of the Commission which reported on July 31, 1885. See Hansen, *Sygekasseme*, p. 65.
15. Denmark, "Lov om Anerkendte Sygekasser," 12 April (Copenhagen: Folketinget, 1892).
16. *Ibid.*, para. 1.
17. The wives and children of working members were automatically covered by the sickness funds.
18. Denmark, "Lov om Anerkendte Sygekasser," para. 24.
19. *Ibid.*, para. 12.
20. In the other Nordic countries, cash benefits, which the individual could use to pay his health care, comprised the main expense for the sickness funds.
21. Denmark, "Lov om Anerkendte Sygekasser," para. 17. Illnesses caused by drunkenness, venereal diseases or fights were not covered.
22. Danish Medical Association statutes quoted from an Information Brochure by the Association available in 1986.
23. Ito, "Health insurance," p. 52.
24. *Ibid.*, p. 51.
25. *Ibid.*
26. *Ibid.*, p. 50.
27. In Sweden, the early state subsidies were so low that the sickness funds considered them insignificant.
28. Hansen, *Sygekasseme*, pp. 121–32.
29. The Federation of Central Sickness Funds, the Danish Medical Association and the county councils all sat on the local Administrative Board.
30. Ito, "Health insurance," p. 49.
31. *Ibid.*, p. 51.
32. At the time, the Danish economy was largely based on agriculture and the population was mainly rural. The population for 1901 is based on United Nations (UN), Statistics Office (SO), Department of Economic and Social Affairs (DESA), *Demographic Yearbook 1962*, 14th Edition (New York: UN, 1962): 277 and the area is based on J. Paxton, ed., *The Statesman's Year-Book: Statistical and Historical Annual of the States of the World for the Year 1986–1987*, 123rd Edition (London: MacMillan Press, 1986): 405.

33. Ito, "Health insurance," p. 56; and V. A. Fenger, *Den Almindelige Danske Laegeforening 1857–1957* (Copenhagen: Nordisk Forlag, 1957): 219.
34. Hansen, *Sygekasseme*, p. 90.
35. A Revised Sickness Fund Law was passed in 1915 but it offered few significant improvements over the previous law. In 1901, the sickness funds in Denmark formed a National Federation of Sickness Funds.
36. Hansen, *Sygekasseme*, p. 151.
37. Ito, "Health insurance," p. 45.
38. *Ibid.*, 49.
39. Stauning formed the first Social Democrat–Radical Left Coalition Government from 1924–1926.
40. It changed its name from the International Workers' Association to the SDP in 1878.
41. K. Tagholt, *Hvem var Minister. Dansk Politik Gennom Mere end 100 Ar* (Arhus: Forlaget Aros, 1984): 168.
42. Hansen, *Sygekasseme*, p. 166.
43. Rasmussen, *Sygesikringsloven*, p. 18.
44. Tagholt, *Hvem var Minister*, p. 168.
45. A. Joergensen, *Styrk Digeme: Artikler og Taler 1972–82 i Udvalg ved Harry Rasmussen* (Copenhagen: Socialdemokratiet Fremad, 1982): 174.
46. Denmark, "Lov om Folkeforsikring," (Copenhagen: Folketinget, 1933).
47. Rasmussen, *Sygesikringsloven*, p. 20.
48. M.W. Childs, *Sweden: The Middle Way on Trial* (New Haven: Yale University Press, 1980): 127.
49. Wartime Prime Minister Thorvald Stauning, quoted in J. Bomholt, ed., *Bogen om Stauning* (Copenhagen: Westermanns Forlag, 1950): 288.
50. Childs, *Sweden 1980*, p. 127.
51. The committee never issued a report.
52. A different H. C. Hansen was the Social Democratic Party Prime Minister at this time.
53. Hansen, *Sygekasseme*, p. 187.
54. The Commission included representatives from all the political parties. Others included Niels Moerk from the Social Democratic Party, Dr. J. Frandsen from the Board of Health, Ernst Larsen (P. F. Olsen, J. W. Joergensen and H. C. Hansen after the death of Larsen), Drs. C. Jacobsen, J. Riising and T. Krarup from the Medical Association, and representatives from a variety of labor organizations and local governments. Denmark, "Betaenkning fra Sygekassekommissionen" (Copenhagen: Folketinget, 1959).

55. Denmark, "Lov om Offentlig Sygeforsikring" (Copenhagen: Folketinget, 1960).
56. Denmark, "Lov om Offentlig Sygeforsikring," Chapter VII, para. 41.
57. J. Koch and C. Toftemark, *NHS and EEC – Denmark* (London: King Edward's Hospital Fund, 1974): 8.
58. Personal communication with A. Gersnov.
59. Hansen, *Sygekasseme*, p. 192.
60. H. Rasmussen, quoted in the forward to Joergensen, *Styrk Digeme*, p. 9.
61. J. O. Krag, quoted in Engberg *et al.*, *Dansk Arbejderbevaegelse*, p. 84.
62. Personal communication with Jacob Vedel Petersen, Director of the Danish Social Research Institute.
63. V. Kampmann, *Seks Socialdemokratiske Statsministre: Skildret af den Syvende* (Copenhagen: Fredmad, 1973): 58.
64. Social Democratic Party platform expressed at the 28 Congress of the party in June 1961, quoted in L. Bille, *Danske Partiprogrammer 1945–70: Historie og Samfund–Kilder og tal* (Copenhagen: Gyldendal, 1972): 15.
65. Bille, *Danske Partiprogrammer*, pp. 12–20.
66. Based on the Liberal Party's political platform in 1963, prior to the parliamentary resolution. See Bille, *Danske Partiprogrammer*, p. 72.
67. Based on the Radical Liberal Party's political platform in 1969, at the time of the first report of the Social Reform Commission. See Bille, *Danske Partiprogrammer*, p. 42.
68. Based on the Conservative Party's political platform in 1966. During the work of the Social Reform Commission. Bille, *Danske Partiprogrammer*, p. 53.
69. In 1963, Danes voted in favor of joining the European Economic Community (EEC).
70. P. Meyer, *Dansk Politik 1944–1984* (Copenhagen: G. E. C Gads Forslag, 1984): 119.
71. Ito, "Health insurance," p. 46.
72. Denmark, Ministry of Social Affairs (MSA), National Board of Social Welfare (NBSW), *Social and Health Planning: Administrative Organization and Decentralisation* (Copenhagen: MSA, NBSW, 1982): 1.
73. Denmark, Indenrigsministeren (I), "Kommunalreformkommissionen," (Copenhagen: Indenrigsministeren, 1968): 1; and L. H. W. Paine, "Health services in Denmark: NHS and EEC," *Health and Social Service Journal* 84(1974): 1743. The 23 county councils and the 1,300 municipalities were reorganized into 14 and 217 new natural geographical and political areas. Councils, elected every four years, would administer the new local governments.

74. Personal communication with Adam Trier, Deputy Secretary in the Ministry of Social Affairs, former Member of the Social Reform Commission.
75. This reform was similar the local government reforms following the Seebohm Report England. See Paine, "Health services," p. 1743.
76. Koch and Toftemark, *NHS and EEC*, p. 5.
77. P. E. Eriksen, quoted from parliamentary resolution. See Denmark, "Forslag til folketingsbeslutning om forberedelse af en socialreform," (Copenhagen: Folketinget, 64): 3767. E. Eriksen, leader of the Liberal Party and former Prime Minister, was a law reformer who had earlier been responsible for the constitutional reforms in 1953. Poul Sørensen from the Conservative Party proposed the reform.
78. Denmark, "Forberedelse af en socialreform," p. 1674.
79. Personal communication with Ernst Andersen who was responsible for drafting the Radical Liberals' original proposal for a Social Reform Commission.
80. Denmark, Socialministeriet (S), "Socialreformkommissionens 1, det sociale tryghedssystem: Struktur og dagpenge," Betaenkning No. 543 (Copenhagen: Statens Trykningskontor, 1969): 3. During the 1960s, a variety of laws and regulations on sickness insurance had already extended existing provisions, which had evolved into a comprehensive but unnecessarily complicated system.
81. K. Andersen, the first Chairman, resigned to accept a cabinet post.
82. Both the Danish Medical Association and the Danish Board of Health declined to offer representatives for the Commission. Personal communication with Dr. E. Ammundsen, former Director-General of the Danish Board of Health, and O. Baggesen, Director of the Danish Medical Association.
83. Denmark,, "Socialreformkommissionens 1," p. 416. Supported through personal communication with Dr. J. Larsen, President of the Danish Medical Association 1964–1970; O. Baggesen, Director of the General Practitioners' Branch of the Danish Medical Association since 1971 and member of the Secretariat of the Social Reform Commission; and Dr. J. Fog, Deputy Director General of the National Board of Health and former leader of the Danish Younger Doctors Association.
84. From the brief submitted by the Danish Medical Association to the Social Reform Commission on December 20, 1968. See Denmark, S, "Socialreformkommissionens 1," p. 425.
85. Denmark, S, "Socialreformkommissionens l," p. 425.
86. Denmark, S, "Socialreformkommissionens 1," p. 203, para. 52.

87. Supported by personal communication with O. Høeg, present Permanent Secretary in the Department of Social Affairs; and Adam Trier, present Deputy Permanent Secretary in the Ministry of Social Affairs, who were both actively involved as members of the secretariat of the Social Reform Commission.
88. Denmark, S, "Socialreformkommissionens 1," p. 377.
89. Denmark, S, "Socialreformkommissionens 1," p. 220.
90. In contrast to Norway, assistance for the excluded 10 percent was available in Denmark following the reforms of 1960.
91. Denmark, S, "Socialreformkommissionens 1," p. 319.
92. Denmark, S, "Socialreformkommissionens 1," p. 322.
93. Hansen, *Sygekasseme*, p. 217.
94. Personal communication with Adam Trier, Deputy Secretary in the Ministry of Social Affairs, former Member of the Social Reform Commission.
95. Denmark, S, "Socialreformkommissionens 1," pp. 322, 409–16.
96. Denmark, S, "Socialreformkommissionens 1," p. 203, para. 51.
97. Unlike the situation in Norway before the introduction of compulsory insurance, those most needing medical attention in Denmark did not form part of the unprotected 10 percent.
98. Denmark, S,"Socialreformkommissionens 1," p. 203, para. 50.
99. Hansen, *Sygekasseme*, 238.
100. *Ibid.*
101. *Ibid.*, p. 218.
102. *Ibid.*
103. Denmark, S, "Socialreformkommissionens 1," p. 409.
104. Brief submitted to the Social Reform Commission by the Danish Co-operative of Central Sickness Funds in August 1968. See Denmark, S, "Socialreformkommissionens 1," pp. 409–15.
105. Denmark, S, "Socialreformkommissionens 1," p. 413.
106. Hansen, *Sygekasseme*, p. 233.
107. Denmark, S, "Socialreformkommissionens 1," p. 412.
108. *Ibid.*, p. 238.
109. An opinion poll, conducted before the publicity campaign, suggested that 41 percent of the public favored a system without the sickness funds, 28 percent supported a continuation of the existing role of the sickness funds and 31 percent did not express a preference. Following the publicity campaign, those supporting a continuation of the sickness funds had dropped to 26 percent.
110. Hansen, *Sygekasseme*, p. 239.

111. They worked at the Danish National Institute of Social Research which the Commission had asked to conduct an extensive review of social reforms.
112. K. Westergård, *Socialreformundersoegelseme: De Sociale Ydelser*, Volume 2, Socialforskningsinstituttet Publication No. 53 (Copenhagen: Teknisk Forlag, 1971): 13.
113. B.R. Andersen, *Sociolreformundersoegelseme: Borgeren og Tryghedssystemet*, Volume 2, Socialforskningsinstituttet Publication No. 44 (Copenhagen: Teknisk Forlag, 1970): 13. B. R. Andersen directed the Social Reform Investigations for the Social Reform Commission.
114. Andersen, *Socialreformundersoegelseme*, p. 13.
115. *Ibid.*, 14.
116. *Ibid.*, pp. 13, 264–65.
117. *Ibid.*, pp.13, 277.
118. Nathalie Lind, presenting the Sickness Insurance Legislation to Parliament. See Denmark, "Lovforslag til Sygesikringsloven," (Copenhagen: Folketinget, 1970): 1953–84; and Denmark, "Sygesikringsloven" (Copenhagen: Folketinget, 1971): 2434.
119. Personal communication with Nathalie Lind, Minister for Social Affairs from 1968–1971 and Commissioner for the Social Reform Commission of 1969.
120. The new law would apply only to health care; sickness pay was not included under this reform.
121. The sickness funds were dissolved on March 17, 1973.
122. Denmark, "Lovforslag til Sygesikringsloven," pp. 1982–84; and Denmark, "Sygesikringsloven," p. 2434. The Faroe Islands and Greenland were not included under the law.
123. S. K. Soerensen, *Public Administration and Health Care in Denmark* (Copenhagen: National Board of Health, 1984): 7; and D. Gannik, E. Holst and M. Wagner, "The national health system in Denmark: A descriptive analysis," Department of Health, Education and Welfare (DHEW) and National Institute for Health (NIH), Monograph, Publication No. 77–673 (Washington: John E. Fogarty International Center for Advanced Study in Health Sciences, 1976): 36.
124. Expropriation would have required compensation which the Government of course wanted to avoid.
125. Denmark, "Sygesikringsloven," p. 2456.
126. Cash benefits were part of later reforms on public assistance. See Denmark, "Lov om Social Bistand," No. 333 (Copenhagen: Folketinget, 1974); and

O. Baggesen, G. Buss, and B. Frederiksen, *Bistandsloven* (Copenhagen: Juristforbundets Forlag, 1981).

127. Koch and Toftemark, *NHS and EEC*, p. 9.
128. Personal communication with H. C. Hansen, representative from the sickness funds to the Social Reform Commission.
129. The term acquis is also used to describe laws adopted under the Schengen Agreement, prior to its integration into the European Union legal order by the Treaty of Amsterdam, in which case one speaks of the Schengen acquis. The term acquis has been borrowed by the World Trade Organization Appellate Body, in the case Japan — Taxes on Alcoholic Beverages, to refer to the accumulation of General Agreement on Tariffs and Trade (GATT) and WTO law ("acquis gattien"), though this usage is not well established.
130. Personal communication with Dr. J. Fog, the present Deputy Director of the National Board of Health, who was also one of the leaders of the FayL during the late 1960s. See J. Fog, "Primary health care services in Denmark," Paper presented at National Board of Health, San Marino, Copenhagen, 11–13 October 1985, p. 12.
131. Personal communication with T. Fridberg, member of the follow-up studies to the Social Research Investigations of the 1960s at the Danish Institute of Social Research.
132. W. Joergensen and I. Thaulow, *Socialreformundersoegelseme 6: Klientemes Levekår og Problemer*, Publikation 130 (Copenhagen: Socialforskningsinstituttet, 1984); and M. Roerbech *et al.*, *Socialreformundersoegelseme 7: Hvordan Går det Klienteme*? Publikation 136 (Copenhagen: Socialforskningsinstituttet, 1985).
133. A. S. Preker, "Public finance and provision of health care services in Québec: An international perspective," Brief presented to the Commission of Inquiry into the Health and Social Services of Québec [Chairman J. Rochon] (London: IIHS, 1986): 27; and Organization for Economic Co-operation and Development (OECD), *Measuring Health Care 1960–1983: Expenditure Costs and Performance*, OECD Social Policy Studies No.2 (Paris: OECD, 1985): 68–69, 74–75.
134. Fog, "Primary health care," p. 13.
135. Personal communication with Dr. E. Ammundsen, the Director General of the National Board of Health during the period of the reforms.
136. Personal communication with Adam Trier, Deputy Secretary in the Ministry of Social Affairs, former Member of the Social Reform Commission and present member of the Groennegår Committee.

137. M. Olejaz, A. Juul Nielsen, A. Rudkjøbing, H. Okkels Birk, A. Krasnik, and C. Hernández-Quevedo. *Denmark: Health System Review in Health Systems in Transition* 14(2)(2012):1–192. http://www.euro.who.int/__data/assets/pdf_file/0004/160519/e96442.pdf. Accessed July 10, 2017.
138. G. Scott, L. McKenzie and J. Webster, "Maladjustments in the Corporatization Model: Hospital Reform in New Zealand, in A. S. Preker and A. Harding, eds. *Innovations in Health Service Delivery: The Corporatization of Public Hospitals*, (2003, Washington, DC: World Bank). https://openknowledge.worldbank.org/handle/10986/15145. Accessed August 17, 2017; pp. 205–345.

CHAPTER 8

NORWAY

Without an effectively developed health care system, our country's defences can be completely paralyzed. Such a health care system must be developed so that it not only takes into consideration the 10–15 per cent of the population who will be mobilised during war, but also the remaining 85–90 per cent.[1]

Rakel Seweriin, 1955

A. HISTORICAL CONTEXT

1. Sickness Funds

During the nineteenth century, only the rich in Norway could afford to receive treatment from private medical doctors.[2] "The introduction of prepaid medical care in Norway was not opposed by the medical profession," since doctors found it difficult to survive on the income that they earned from the well-to-do alone.[3] Private practitioners were therefore scarce, leaving a few publicly employed county officers of health and hospitals responsible for most of the medical care in the community.[4]

Private charities, religious groups and the Poor Laws likewise offered only minimal provisions for the sick and destitute. Although centuries earlier King Magnus the Law-Mender (1263–1280) had enforced a limited national social aid program for the needy, most Norwegians had to rely on the informal network of health care during the nineteenth century.[5]

Toward the latter part of the previous century, as urbanization accompanied early industrialization, working Norwegians sought other ways to finance health care than through handouts. Trade guilds and small private insurance groups, established by lodges and labor unions, provided limited financial aid to its members. Both of these were more acceptable to the ordinary working man than charity.[6] This led King Oscar II, of the joint Swedish-Norwegian Kingdom, to become interested in the Bismarckian model of sickness insurance.[7]

In December 1884, the King asked Johan Sverdrup, the Prime Minister, to examine the social benefits enjoyed by industrial workers. A. Hedin, a member of the Swedish Parliament, had proposed a motion for increasing the obligations of employers earlier that year: "The same question [concerning workmen's welfare] is posed in all of the civilized world; it can no longer be avoided.[8]

In response to the King's initiative, the Minister of the Interior established a Commission on Labour on August 19, 1885, under the Chairmanship of Christian Arneberg. Its terms of reference were to examine social insurance available to workers, including sickness insurance.[9] The Commission presented its report on sickness insurance for workers in February 1890. It called for compulsory sickness insurance for all workers earning less than 1200 Crowns per year, excluding certain groups such as farmers, forestry workers, seamen or fishermen.[10]

Gunnar Knudsen, one of the members of the Commission (later Prime Minister), felt that contributions from members should finance the entire plan.[11] According to his recommendations, there would be no state subsidies or employer contributions. The program would offer cash benefit only, not medical treatment. Sickness funds administered the plan, under the supervision of a public authority, the National Sickness Fund. The latter would in turn have its own branches in all municipalities and ensure coverage for those not holding private insurance.

The Accident Insurance Law of 1894, which passed following the Commission's study, limited coverage to industrial accidents.[12] More comprehensive sickness insurance, which had been discussed during the Commission's inquiry, was not introduced until years later. Shortly after the introduction of the new law, the Parliament established two new working groups to continue examining he many unsettled issues.

2. County Medical Officer

The Norwegian Health Act of 1860 placed the responsibility for public health on the local authorities whose jurisdiction was soon extended to include other aspects of health care.[13] Each municipality established a Board of Health to oversee hygiene and disease prevention in the community.[14] These provisions expanded to include midwives, public health nurses, home nurses, clinics for children, clinics for mothers and school health.[15]

County Medical Officers of Health, who existed in Norway since the Seventeenth century, were responsible for traditional public health duties, such as prevention, inspection, control of epidemics and administration.[16] Of necessity, they also provided clinical care for the poor and destitute.[17] The result was that primary health care — in the widest sense of the term — came to be regarded from the very start as the prerogative of a local Medical Officer with both preventive and curative duties."[18]

The national Government paid the Norwegian Medical Officers of Health a basic salary for their public health duties, while patients paid fee-for-service for medical care. This combined income allowed the doctors to enjoy a much higher standard of living and status than their medical counterparts in other Nordic countries.[19] Despite their increase, the Norwegian Medical Officers of Health nevertheless remained too few to provide adequate health care for Norway's population of 2,240,032, which at the turn of the century was scattered over 3,243,878 square kilometers of mountains, desolate fjords and northern wastelands.[20]

3. Committee Work

The Permanent Social Affairs Standing Committee, established in 1894, with Gunnar Knudsen as its Chairman, recommended the appointment of a Parliamentary Select Commission on Labour to review disability insurance and old-age pensions. W. Konow, Minister of the Interior, became its Chairman.[21]

In subsequent years, these two groups presented proposals for sickness insurance to Parliament at regular intervals. The debate became was deadlocked over two conflicting approaches: Knudsen on the Standing

Committee supported a comprehensive sickness insurance program, while Konow on the Select Commission advocated limited accident and disability insurance.[22]

As time passed, several major questions were raised. First, should the program include treatment by doctors, medications and cash benefits?[23] Second, should the state, employers and workers all contribute toward the financing of the program? Finally, should supplementary insurance be offered on a voluntary basis to those who did not qualifying for the basic program?

Both the Secretary of the Norwegian Medical Association, Dr. R. Hansson, and the Director-General of Health feared that unlimited coverage would be abused and become too expensive. They also warned that without a means-test the number of applicants for the program would quickly outstrip the capacity of the health care system to deliver the required services.[24]

In 1908, O. A. Efterstoel became Chairman of the Social Affairs Standing Committee.[25] Wishing to break the long-standing stalemate in the sickness insurance debate, Efterstoel tried to convince the Minister of Social Affairs, Johan Castberg, that a comprehensive compulsory sickness insurance program was superior to a separate accident and disability insurance.

Under Efterstoel's direction, the Committee outlined a means-tested program which would aim at select groups of workers and be administered through local sickness funds. Benefits would include sickness pay, treatment by medical doctors and various prostheses such as glasses. Four groups would contribute toward the financing of the program which would cost 6.6 million Crowns: workers (60 percent), employers (10 percent), municipalities (10 percent) and the state (20 percent).[26]

4. The Labour Party

The Norwegian Labour Party became active in the health care debate at an early stage.[27] Dr. Oscar Nissen, the Chairman of the party in 1908, supported Labour's earlier call for health care financing through general revenues.[28] "There is only one way to go: all the sick must be covered by one system. Doctors and midwives must become public employees and prohibited from accepting private cash. Only in this way can all be made equal, so that there is no reason to treat one human being differently from another."[29]

Nissen criticized the sickness insurance model which he felt would only create an added burden for workers and provide inadequate coverage for those who needed help the most. His alternative was "health care through taxation."[30] When asked how a doctor could function on a salary, Nissen replied that there was no reason that doctors paid a regular salary and guaranteed a pension could not work with the same sense of responsibility as before.

The Labour Party's proposal was presented to Parliament on February 27, 1907: "Through an insurance program, there can never be enough help for those who need it. ... As most other solutions through workers' insurance, sickness insurance is in reality experienced by workers not as a relief but as an added burden."[31] The Labour Party claimed that only taxation could justly distribute the financial burden of illness more evenly across society.

The Norwegian Medical Association initially accepted the general principles of a national program with doctors on salaries financed through general revenues.[32] At their Annual Meeting in 1909, the Association declared that, although it preferred direct fee-for service with free choice of doctor, it would co-operate with a salaried service: "The Norwegian Medical Association declares that, from a hygienic point of view, there are no objections to a transfer of doctors to a taxation system."[33]

At the insistence of one of its members, Lars O. Sæbø, the Social Affairs Standing Committee examined the Labour Party's proposal. The Committee, however, concluded that the proposal was too radical, having no parallel program in Western Europe. Furthermore, it felt that old-age pensions and disability insurance should be introduced before comprehensive sickness insurance.

Sæbø, defending the Labour Party position, sounded a note of dissent. He pointed out the absurdity of sickness insurance which offered sick pay without health care, especially when the former was inadequate.[34] He also objected to giving old-age pensions and disability insurance a higher priority than sickness insurance.[35]

The Secretary of State for Commerce and Industry, Lars Abrahamsen, presented the draft legislation for a Sickness Insurance Law to Parliament on the August 17, 1909. The proposal followed the lines of the recommendation made by the Social Affairs Standing Committee.[36] Although more conservative supporters of Konow and the socialist supporters of Sæbø immediately voiced objections, Efterstoel was able to convince the Parliament to accept his compromise plan, reminding its members that Sweden, Denmark and Germany had already introduced such Government-supported sickness insurance: "We feel ...that it is necessary to proceed in a step-wise fashion."[37] The upper house of Parliament passed the means-tested Compulsory Sickness Insurance Law on September 18, 1909, which would be implemented on July 1, 1911.

5. Compulsory Sickness Insurance Law of 1909

Workers' and employers' contributions as well as subsidies from local municipalities and the state financed the new program. To qualify for state subsidies, a sickness fund had to comply with the criteria established under the law. These rules included the public election of members to the sickness funds' administrative boards and the provision of a variety of predetermined benefits, such as free medical treatment in hospitals, and sick pay for members and their families. A later amendment allowed non-wage earners to join a supplementary voluntary program.

Several administrative changes were introduced through the reform. A public authority, the National Insurance Institute, would oversee the sickness funds which would be established in each municipality.[38] The sickness funds in turn formed a National Association of Insurance Offices. Finally, the Ministry of Social Affairs assumed the responsibility for health care from the Ministry of the Interior in 1913.

The new program was immediately contested by several groups. The National Association of Insurance Offices wanted the means-test raised. The labor unions and the Social Democratic Party objected to such means-tests, the exclusion of certain groups of workers and lack of coverage for certain categories of illnesses.[39] Konow continued to press for a postponement of the date of implementation, while Sæbø still advocated a universal salaried doctor service.

Despite such criticisms, "the programme became immediately popular: even though members paid a good share of the expenses themselves through premiums and ordinary taxes, more people constantly desired to be included."[40] The Compulsory Sickness Insurance Law of 1909 was a landmark in Norway because it created the terms of collective financing of health care which the country would follow over the next 50 years: "In my opinion, it was an ingenious thought that became law ... the family insurance principle."[41] Later reforms would expand and modify its provisions but not its basic underlying principles.[42]

6. Norwegian Medical Association

The Norwegian Medical Association, which was created in 1886, made sure that the views of the medical profession were heard by early legislators.[43] R. Hansson, General Secretary of the Association, was a member of both the Social Affairs Standing Committee and the Finance Committee which prepared the 1909 legislation.[44] This reflected the philosophy of the Association to "strive for greater influence and thus enhance its authority," an objective which was quickly fulfilled.[45]

Most doctors in private practice and County Medical Officers of Health had found it difficult to survive on the small incomes available through fee-for-service before the introduction of the 1909 law, Sickness Insurance "not only created "health security" in the field of curative medicine for the population but also provided a higher degree of financial security for the doctor."[46]

The 1909 law was therefore welcomed by most of the medical profession. Private doctors retained their full professional freedom, obtained virtually unlimited third-party payments on a fee-for-service basis in urban areas and remained free to determine their own fees. Doctors hailed the new act for making them financially more secure and freer in their work.[47] The state-salaried district doctors continued to treat patients in the less-populated rural areas. Patients continued to have a free choice of doctor. This, Hansson believed, would avoid a small group of panel doctors from gaining control of all benefits evolving out of the new law.

Despite such praise, the shortcomings of health care coverage through third-party insurance soon became apparent. "The Sickness Insurance Law has given the doctors a unique power over the district insurance funds. The law requires that the sickness funds provide its members and their families with free health care. But it does not compel the doctors to respect whatsoever the terms of such health care."[48] Since each sickness fund had to negotiate with its own doctors, there was no standard fee-schedule, and doctors were accused of "plundering" the sickness funds.[49]

A variety of unsuccessful attempts were made to settle this conflict. Professor A. Palmstrøm, an actuary familiar with the Lloyd George plan in Great Britain, suggested collective negotiations in 1912. This led to an informal agreement on a fee schedule between the Norwegian Medical Association and the National Association of Insurance Offices.[50] This and later collective agreements were, however, often ignored by many doctors who continued charging patients as they wished.

By the mid-1920s, difficult economic times in Norway forced the Government to look for ways to limit public expenditure. This led Parliament to introduce a reimbursement principle for sickness insurance in 1925, ending a golden era for the medical profession.[51] Under the revised system, doctors charged the patient directly instead of being reimbursed by the sickness funds for offering free medical treatment. It was now patients that had to claim reimbursements based on a fixed pre-established fee schedule. Any difference in the amount charged by the doctor and the official fee schedule was borne by the patient.[52]

Although the new system succeeded in stemming the growth in public subsidies for the sickness funds, a gap soon developed between the recommended fee schedule and what was charged by doctors. Everyone lost through this new policy: patients now had to pay not only health care contributions and taxes but also a fee-for-service; doctors had to handle cash transactions during patient visits; and the Government and the sickness funds still had no control over the fees charged by the medical profession or the overall and the cost of health care.

B. LANDMARK LEGISLATIVE REFORMS

1. The Great Depression

Unemployment and the Great Depression led to a collapse of the Mowinckel Government, and with it a political era ended in Norway. The Labour Party, which formed a Minority Coalition Government in 1933, would remain in power for the next 10 years and mark the beginning of 30 years of intermittent Labour rule.[53] "With Nygaardsvold's Government in March 1935, we entered a new epoch in the Norwegian people's history."[54]

Prime Minister Johan Nygaardsvold wanted to combat unemployment and the effects of the Great Depression with a program of economic and social reform.[55] Despite the lack of economic resources to finance such reforms, Oscar Torp, the Minister of Social Affairs in 1936 (later Prime Minister), "eagerly went to work implementing the social reforms that the Nygaardsvold Government had recommended."[56]

Shortly after taking office, the new Government was troubled by new developments in Europe, forcing it to take an active stance on defense. In approving the previous Government's defense budget, Nygaardsvold said with dismay: "I hope that you do not want me to go farther than Mowinckel did."[57] Despite this additional economic burden, the Labour Government pressed on with its proposed social reforms.

The Permanent Secretary of the Department of Social Affairs, Berger Ulsaker, became the Secretary of a Social Legislation Committee. The terms of reference of the Committee were to review and improve existing social security provisions.[58] Within a short period of time, Norway had introduced "old age pensions, blindness and disability insurance, insurance for fishermen and sailors, unemployment insurance and preparations for [a new] sickness insurance."[59] Gunnar Størvold, Director of the National Insurance Institute, in 1937, stressed that future reforms should include health care: "It has already been advocated that a further evolution should be ...sickness insurance for the whole population."[60] He added, "I am very interested in an evolution in that direction."[61]

At a general meeting of the National Association of Insurance Offices, the organization supported an "efficient social insurance programme covering the whole population."[62] Such a program would include sickness insurance, a stance that the Association would maintain after the report of the Social Legislation Committee was released in 1939.

Gunnar Størvold and M. Ormestad presented their proposal for a joint law on health and disability insurance in 1935.[63] Their proposal recommending that everyone between the ages of 5 and 70 years be included, continued the Labour Party's platform on universal entitlement to health care that it had first advanced in 1909. The Social Legislation Committee that finally reported to Parliament on sickness insurance on March 4, 1939, called for a new Universal Compulsory Sickness Insurance Law similar to that proposed by Størvold and Ormestad.[64] It also recommended that disability insurance be examined separately in greater detail before its inclusion.

The Committee denounced the practice of limiting social insurance to the employed, claiming that the many farmers, self-employed, artisans and other small business people had an equal right to benefits: "The main part of [the excluded] population live under economic conditions that are not better but probably rather worse than they are for a large part of those who are now covered by the compulsory insurance.[65] Such extension in coverage was justified not only as a general claim for equality of treatment between the different groups of the population but also because it was felt that a fully effective sickness insurance program warranted such measures.[66]

By 1937, the sickness funds had attained a membership of 1 million, comprising 60 percent of the population.[67] However, many had by this time run into financial difficulties, owing the National Insurance Institute over 3 million Crowns by 1939.[68] Furthermore, those who needed protection the most were often those excluded from coverage under existing provisions. Although a further extension in coverage by the sickness funds was badly needed, the outbreak of World War II forced Torp to abandon such plans. Instead, the Norwegians had to turn their full attention to the struggle for survival.

2. War Occupation and Joint Reconstruction Program

Norway was badly prepared for the war.: "The air-raid sirens and angry noises woke us up."[69] Having maintained neutrality during World War I, Norwegians had no recent experience to draw on for their mobilization. Evacuation of the sick and the numerous casualties suffered during the war exposed many of the weaknesses in the existing health care system.

During the occupation, Nazi sympathizers had appointed a National Assembly under the leadership of Vidkun Quisling: "Most Norwegians were opposed to Nazism and throughout the occupation maintained a strongly anti-Nazi front."[70] When the Nazi regime arrested the Secretary General of the Norwegian Medical Association and appointed a Nazi commissary, 80 percent of the members withdrew from the organization.[71] Norwegians were subdued physically, but never morally. Civil resistance prevailed throughout the war.

Prime Minister Nygaardsvold formed a Norwegian Government-in-exile in London. The "London-Regime" was "at times resentful and even bitter over Sweden's neutrality."[72] Nygaardsvold declared in a speech in London that a union among the Nordic states was "not part of Norway's postwar plans."[73] Despite such sentiments, those who remained in Norway often found neutral Sweden the only place where they could seek refuge.[74]

When Nazi troops invaded Norway on April 9, 1940, human fellowship and the courageous Norwegian underground provided the best protection for the fleeing refugees and those who remained prey to the Nazi "puppet regime": "In the shadows of prisons, concentration camps and execution centres, a brotherhood developed that we had been unaware of before."[75]

The post-war Joint Reconstruction Program had its origin during those difficult years. German forces began retreating from Norway in October 1944; liberation took place on May 8, 1945. On June 25, 1945, Einar Gerhardsen, who had spent most of the war in Norway and Sweden as well as in German concentration camps, became Prime Minister of the post-war Coalition Government.

All parties pledged support for a Joint Reconstruction Program which gave birth to the Norwegian universal sickness insurance system.[76] The program, "Work for All," aimed to secure freedom, rebuild the economy with employment and security for all, create solidarity between the social classes and establish a new international order to secure peace for the future.[77] This was seen as the only way "to make Norway a secure and good home for all."[78]

3. Parliamentary Decree

On November 19, 1948, the Labour Government, under the leadership of Einar Gerhardsen, announced in a parliamentary decree that the Joint

Reconstruction Program would include provisions for a comprehensive social security program.[79] Later, the Ministry of Social Affairs revealed that such a program would include universal entitlement to health care under compulsory sickness insurance. The proposal, reflecting the spirit of the national fellowship that existed immediately following the war, was supported by all political parties.[80]

Gerhardsen's years as a prisoner-of-war in German concentration camps had taught him the compassion for human suffering which the civilian population needed in the post-war period: "[He believed that] politics of social security, and especially social insurance, [was] solidarity in practice. Those who are healthy, help the sick and disabled, those who are employed, help the unemployed, those who are of working age, help the old."[81]

During the war, the sickness funds had been unable to meet the costs of health care and cash benefits, especially in the northern regions. By 1947, they had a deficit of 15 million Crowns. Although, the Department of Social Affairs had until then resisted going back to the "means-tested sickness benefits that existed before the war," the existing condition could not prevail much longer.[82]

The Members of Parliament who had been in the war-time London Shadow Cabinet believed that social insurance and a modified Beveridge Plan could provide a solution to these difficulties: "The social security legislation should evolve with a view towards making poor relief superfluous. The social insurance programmes should be consolidated in order to establish a common insurance programme for sickness, disability, unemployment and old age."[83]

Sven Oftendal, the Minister of Social Affairs who had been intimately involved with the proposed social reforms during the 1930s, became the driving force for the new social legislation. Assisting Oftendal in his task were R.G. Caspersen, Director of the National Association of Insurance Offices, and Knut Getz Wold, Permanent Secretary in the Department of Social Affairs.

There were many priorities, each seeming as important as the other: pensions, unemployment insurance, child benefits, disability insurance, accident insurance and sickness insurance. "During the war, Oftendal had helped relieve the suffering of fellow prisoners and save lives in various

German concentration camps. Now in a free Norway he had to secure his countrymen their life and health. No one could have been better suited for [the job]."[84]

When Sven Oftendal died in 1948, he had finished most of the preliminary work for the future plan. His successor Aaslaug Aasland presented a draft for a unified social insurance program to Parliament on November 19, 1948.[85] The health provisions called for compulsory sickness insurance for all Norwegians. This would include health care, hospital treatment, transportation, drugs and the usual cash benefits. Other benefits would be added later in response to local needs and initiatives.

Workers, employers, the municipalities and the state would finance the new program. It would be administered by National Insurance Institute, which would use existing sickness funds as local agents.[86] Extending the previous program to all Norwegians was estimated to cost 325 million Crowns.[87]

To avoid a conflict with the medical profession, doctors would be paid on a fee-for-service basis rather than a capitation fee or salary. Hospitalization would remain completely free of charge, financed largely through the local municipalities. There would be a charge for prescriptions, although essential medications would be available at as low a cost as possible.

Public reaction to the legislation was anticlimactic: "One cannot deny that the public reaction or rather near total lack of reaction to the announcement [was] somewhat of a disappointment for those of us who have worked on it."[88] The Norwegian Medical Association considered the parliamentary proposal an "important document" which it felt could form the basis for further efforts to develop a sickness insurance program.[89] Only the National Association of Insurance Offices, whose independence was threatened, objected to a tax-based system of financing and to the new central role of the National Insurance Institution which would collect the finances and distribute the benefits of the new program.[90]

The Social Affairs Standing Committee immediately began drafting the legislation for the social insurance reform[91] and the more specific sickness insurance reform.[92] In 1951, a committee was assigned the task of examining and unifying the existing social security system, including voluntary and means-tested compulsory sickness insurance.[93]

4. Social Insurance Committee Report No. I

Nils Hoensvald, a Member of Parliament, became the Chairman of the Social Insurance Committee. Its members included R. G. Caspersen, the Director of the National Association of Insurance Offices, and Dr. Axel Stroem, the President of the Norwegian Medical Association. Both Caspersen and Stroem felt that many people could not afford to insure themselves and that there was a strong desire for collective protection: "The first and most important task will be to ease the social needs of groups that cannot care for themselves. ...A natural consequence of solving this mentioned and most important task will be that… the cost [of social needs] will be collectively divided among the working portion of the population."[94]

The first report of the Social Insurance Committee recommended that Norway introduce universal entitlement to social security, "compulsory for the whole population, with no consideration for either contributions or income."[95] The program would provide the working population with comprehensive benefits: sickness insurance, accident insurance, workmen's compensation and old-age pensions. The report concluded that coverage for sickness insurance should be expanded to include "all the population without regard to contribution or income."[96]

Workers, employers, the state and the local municipalities would finance the new program with contributions being collected at source together with ordinary income taxes. Every capable person would contribute to the program: "It is necessary to build a security system for people that are not capable of caring for themselves and who require a collective support from the working population."[97]

The leaders of the Labour Government hoped that a contributory program which would pay for itself would avoid putting an added burden on the treasury. Based on an estimate that the social security system had cost 390 million Crowns in 1947–1948, the Committee projected that under existing separate provisions the system would cost 747 million Crowns in 1952–1953. Under the proposed integrated system, the cost would only increase to 765 million Crowns for 1952–1953.[98] Seweriin, later Minister of Social Affairs, however warned that the cost might be "considerably more."[99]

The first report emphasized that those not covered under existing provisions were often those in greatest need. The excluded group included the self-employed, unemployed, older people, pensioners, those covered under public assistance and perhaps most importantly, those who previously were in too poor health to qualify for membership with the sickness funds. All depended on the state for financial support.

Meanwhile, Norway was undergoing its "biggest and richest expansion in the history."[100] The mid-1950s (Torp years) represented a tumultuous time in Norwegian politics, marked by internal political strife and economic difficulties.[101] The Chairman of the Committee, Nils Hoensvald, recommended delaying introduction of the planned social reforms until after post-war economic recovery to avoid it becoming a financial nightmare for the State. Oscar Torp, who had replaced Gerhardsen as Prime Minister, likewise feared that his Government would have to bear the brunt of discontent if the Treasury incurred a deficit which would worsen inflation. Reforms through contributory social insurance were therefore seen as a safer route than the Labour Party's traditional call for the financing of public programs through general revenues.

Finn Alexander, later Director of the National Sickness Insurance institution, felt that if the local sickness funds took over all responsibility for social security, the program would avoid contributing to the financial burden of the state. He therefore recommended that a sickness insurance should be given priority attention, since it would provide the basis for other social reforms.[102] Seweriin supported this view.[103] "Norway is one of those countries in the world where public sickness insurance has become a truly popular institution."[104]

5. Social Insurance Committee Report No. II

The parliamentary debates on social security included discussions on sickness insurance on November 6 and 7, 1952. Over the next two years, the details of the program took form. The second report of the Social Insurance Committee, published on February 9, 1954, dealt exclusively with the sickness insurance question: "The Committee recommends that compulsory universal sickness insurance should be introduced as soon as possible."[105]

Before the reform was carried out, however, regulations had already extended the compulsory sickness insurance to include all employees and their families, irrespective of their income.[106] Anyone else could join on a voluntary basis. Life-saving and indispensable medications were covered for the first time. The time-limit for hospital treatment had been removed. Finally, midwifery and medical attention during pregnancy were a part of standard benefits. By the time the second report was presented to Parliament in 1954, extending existing provisions for universal entitlement was no longer seen as a major reform.[107] "The Committee now feels that the time has come to take the step and introduce sickness insurance for all."[108]

During the years following the war, the costs of administering the hospital sector had risen sharply. The growing hospital deficit was financed mainly through general revenues from the county councils and local municipalities. Not surprisingly, the different local authorities hoped that universal entitlement to ambulatory care might decrease the demand for hospitalization from the segment of the population that could not afford private care.

In 1950, the Department of Social Affairs even suggested that social insurance should be used to make the financing of hospitals more self-sufficient: "The Department found such an arrangement reasonable in that a significant portion of the expenses of hospital sector would be covered by insurance."[109] This proposal was unanimously approved by the Departmental Standing Committee on Social Affairs and Parliament.

Based on estimates of the financing of the existing system, the Department estimated that 25 million Crowns could be collected from employers' premiums, 45 percent from workers, 25 percent from the municipalities and 20 percent from the state. To control costs, doctors' fees would be determined through negotiations between the Norwegian Medical Association, the Department of Finance and the National Pricing Board.[110] This strategy met with immediate, though short-lived success. Both Dr. Axel Stroem, President of the Norwegian Medical Association, and Finn Alexander, Director of the National Insurance Institute, hoped that the favorable terms proposed by the reform would encourage doctors to work in rural regions.

6. Compulsory Universal Sickness Insurance Law of 1956

To finalize the reform, Seweriin appointed an expert working committee of senior civil servants to draft the new Compulsory Universal Sickness Insurance Law. F. W. Ohldieck, the Chairman, worked as Assistant Director of the National Insurance Institution. S. Amble and Hans Johnsen, also from the National Insurance Institution, helped him with this task.[111] Ottar Lund, Assistant Secretary of Social Affairs, and Per Ramholt, Government actuary, represented the Department of Social Affairs.

The expert working committee, which reported in March 1955, used the 1909 and 1930 sickness insurance laws as the basis for drafting the new legislation. Although the National Insurance Institution had originally wanted to conduct a more thorough revision of the whole sickness insurance system, the Department of Social Affairs wanted to "keep the existing law, with the changes and additions that [were] necessary to extend coverage of the Insurance."[112] They feared that a more radical reform would only lead to added costs and further delays.

A renewed estimate of existing membership under the old system showed that 90 percent of the Norwegian population was already covered in 1954.[113] Those excluded from the previous program were the self-employed, pensioners, the occupationally inactive and those receiving other forms of public assistance.[114] "There [was] no doubt that the greater part of those who [were] excluded ... [needed it], to some extent more than many of those who [were] covered by the program."[115] The proposed program, on the other hand, would cover all Norwegians: employees, self-employed, families, public servants, seamen overseas, military personnel, fishermen and prisoners.[116]

Benefits in kind would include medical treatment by doctors, dental treatment, physiotherapy, speech therapy, life-saving medications, medications necessary at the time of accidents, hospital treatment and maternity treatment. Hospitalization, however, referred only to curative medicine, not chronic nursing care.[117] Benefits in cash would include sick pay, maternity pay, cost of home help for seamen, subsidies for non-home ambulatory treatment and burial benefits.[118] Sick pay, of up to 90 percent of previous income, would be available to all contributing workers. The self-employed and others who had an income could qualify for similar cash benefits by making a special voluntary contribution.[119] Doctors would still work on a fee-for-service basis, with patients being reimbursed for the charges.

Workers, employers, municipalities and the state would finance the program.[120] Seweriin, now Minister of Social Affairs, supported this arrangement: "I feel that the proposed law will introduce a just distribution of the expenses for sickness insurance. I think that it is reasonable that workers and employees should share this burden."[121] The estimated cost of the new program was revised upward from 375 million to 470 million Crowns. Income from premiums were estimated at 470 million Crowns.[122]

Dr. Gudmund Harlem, the next Minister of Social Affairs, had the honor of presenting the sickness insurance proposals to Parliament on June 19, 1955.[123] The spokesman for the Minister of Social Affairs, Kjell Bondevik, called it "a milestone in Norwegian social legislation... the largest reform in the past lifetime."[124] Seweriin emphasized that the important contribution made by the new law was the inclusion of the final 10 percent of the population who had been without coverage.[125]

The organizations and departments that submitted opinions on the legislation all reflected the mood of national unity that prevailed following the war.[126] The Directorate of Health, represented on the expert working group by Jon Bjoernsson, supported the new law: "The extension of the existing sickness insurance system to include the whole population represents an end, and an especially happy one, to a long toil."[127] The Directorate hoped that the new system would lead to an improvement in both the standards of medicine and standards of life in Norway.

The Norwegian Medical Association, which was pleased with the existing sickness insurance system, welcomed an extension of this system.[128] "In contrast to many other countries, there has been little resistance to sickness insurance among doctors in Norway. ... Nor have the doctors had fundamental objections to the extension of the sickness insurance to cover the whole population."[129]

The Association, however, echoed the concerns expressed by doctors in other countries that such reforms should be introduced gradually, citing an eastern proverb to support their claim: "One should not march faster than the camel can follow."[130] Furthermore, the Association criticized the law for having created a sharp distinction between curative and preventive medicine, claiming that it would have been preferable to develop the two branches simultaneously.[131]

The National Insurance Institute responded to allegations of the Norwegian Medical Association by pointing out that sickness insurance was a short-term solution, with improved health as the long-term goal. It agreed that health care and prevention were both important issues that required further reform in the future.[132] The sickness funds and other insurance organizations, which would act as agents for the National Insurance Institution, supported the principles of the legislation.[133]

The parliamentary debates took place on February 14 and 17, 1956, with minimal discussion.[134] The law was passed by both Houses without amendments: "I cannot recall any opposition at all ... our sickness insurance system was accepted by all — both the public and medical [profession] wanted to extend its coverage."[135] The legislation passed into law on March 2, 1956, and as planned, universal entitlement to health care was implemented on July 2, 1956.[136]

The reform completed the incremental policy process in sickness insurance that had been in progress over the previous 50 years. It represented an important symbolic landmark in Norwegian social reform legislation: "The basis of Norwegian National Insurance is that it is a right, not a privilege granted at the discretion of someone else to receive support from society when one's welfare is impaired by disease, pregnancy, old age, unemployment or the like."[137]

Although the 1956 law did not introduce radical new ideas, in the aftermath of the Second World War, Norwegians rightly prided themselves on their "slow revolution [which] had not cost a single person his life."[138] The Compulsory Universal Sickness Insurance Law would remain in force for years. "When I look back on the developments which occurred 50 years ago, I am struck with amazement and respect for our ancestors. The framework of the law has not changed in all these years."[139]

C. CONTINUED POLICY REFORM PROCESS

1. Civil Defense Health Plan

World War II had exposed many weaknesses in the Norwegian civil defense system, including its health care systems. Determined not to get caught off-guard again, O. C. Grundersen, the Minister of Justice, asked his Department on November 11, 1946, to initiate a review of the country's preparedness should another war ever occur. The Departmental Civil Defense Legislation Standing Committee, under the Chairmanship of Judge Carl Johan Fleischer, began its work on December 16, 1949.

The Committee, which reported in 1952, recommended that the old Civil Defense Law of 1930 be replaced by new legislation.[140] "Modern warfare demands that one not only has a military but also civilian defense. The civilian part of the total defence can be said to include all citizens that must be mobilised so that a country can defend itself."[141] The resulting Norwegian Civil Defense Law was passed in 1953.[142]

The Minister of Social Affairs, Rakel Seweriin, asked the Standing Committee of the Department of Social Affairs to examine the health provisions contained in the Civil Defense Law. The Committee, then under the Chairmanship of Kjell Bondevik, presented its report in 1955.[143] Few people, however, recognized that the proposal "represented a desire for a universal and improved health care system."[144]

The legislation was presented to Parliament on March 25, 1955. It went through the two Houses of Parliament with little debate and few amendments. It was ignored by both the press and the Norwegian Medical Association.[145] The resulting Civil Defense Health Plan, which passed on December 2, 1955, contained no peace-time provisions.

A war-time program would cover institutional care, materials, public health, health care personnel and other health-related items, In particular, its provisions included hospital, infirmaries, convalescent homes, health resorts, maternity hospitals, orphanages, old-age homes, laboratories, vaccination and full health personnel (doctors, dentists, apothecaries, pharmacists, nurses, physiotherapists, masseurs, midwives, students and any other personnel in health institutions).[146] It provided for the "availability of adequate medical care and nursing facilities at the time of war."[147]

To initiate the program, the Government allocated a grant of 12 million Crowns for capital construction, In the event of war, however, "expenditure incurred through the implementation of the provisions laid down in this act, or which are a consequence of instructions or provisions issued pursuant to this act, [would] be defrayed by the Government."[148]

Seweriin, having been in London during the World War II, was well aware that Norway could have introduced a service like the British

National Health Service, rather than a mere extension of the existing sickness insurance system.[149] "In Britain ... they have a programme that is somewhat more comprehensive than the sickness insurance program that we have here at home [in Norway]"[150] A similar war-time civil defense health plan had played a significant role in the creation of the National Health Service in Great Britain.

Norwegians, anxious to put behind them the grim memories of the war, failed to realize the broader potential scope of their civil defense plan: "We hope that we will never need the law that we have dealt with today."[151] Instead, the country followed the time-tested, less comprehensive, sickness insurance approach as the basis for financing health care.[152]

2. Health for All

There were advantages and disadvantages to the slow introduction of universal health care through sickness insurance in Norway. "The fact that social insurance in Norway has developed over a period of more than 70 years has meant that the speed could be adapted to the country's economic capacity and the necessary mental adjustment could take place. It has not been necessary to make such sudden and radical changes as in other countries with the shock-effects that these have often led to. But the step-by-step development has, on the other hand, had the disadvantage that the individual insurance programs have not been well coordinated.[153]

The organizational shortcomings of the sickness insurance system of financing, the fee-for-service system of paying for doctors and the reimbursement system of offering benefits to patients soon emerged, especially in rural areas. Medical services varied considerably from one municipality to another, and there was an uneven distribution of general practitioners: "Until now too much of health service planning has been carried out separately for the different parts of the health service."[154] Patients often received treatment and care in hospitals "not because they need the highly specialized services that only the hospitals [could] provide, but because the primary health care services in many parts of the country [did] not have sufficient capacity to treat the patients outside institutions."[155]

These difficulties became more apparent during the 1960s and early 1970s. General practitioners were dwindling, and there was no system to ensure an equitable geographic distribution of doctors throughout the country.[156] Norway tried to deal with these problems through an increase in the number of Medical Officers of Health, hoping in this way to offer a better service to rural regions: "Only then can we proceed towards the stated aim of the health services of high quality on an equal basis to every citizen, irrespective of where he lives and of his financial situation and social status."[157]

Over the years, the county municipalities slowly increased their jurisdiction. These responsibilities extended to psychiatric hospitals in 1961, general hospitals in 1969, mental retardation in 1979, child welfare in 1980, comprehensive health care and prevention in 1982 and public dental services in 1984.[158]

By 1982, however, institutional care remained fully financed through public funds while ambulatory care still relied significantly on private financing.[159] Although, in principle, universal entitlement exists for all inhabitants as a "paper right," in practice, charges created an income barrier for ambulatory care, and poor distribution of resources limited access to services.

The Municipal Health Services Act of 1984 was intended to correct many of these deficiencies in the Norwegian sickness insurance system. The new Health Act, which came into effect January 1, 1984, made provisions for both salaried District Health Officers and a guaranteed wage for clinical doctors. The local Medical Officers of Health became employees on contract to the municipalities rather than appointed and paid for by the state. The improved basic wage for clinical doctors hoped to reduce the importance of previous fee-for-service payments: "With the addition of this guaranteed wage, today's fees will be dropped by about 40 percent."[160]

Norway claims that the new focus of its health policy is "Health for All" not just universal sickness insurance.[161] The complete elimination of sickness insurance from the financing of health care in 1986 opened the way for more radical reforms in this direction.

3. Decision to Remain Outside the European Union

Although the Kingdom of Norway is not a member state of the European Union (EU), it is closely associated with the Union through its membership in the European Economic Area (EEA), in the context of being a European Free Trade Association (EFTA) member. Although this did not change the fundamental character of the Norwegian health system, the fiscal constraints on deficit funding under the Acquis, and accompanying requirements of freedom of movement of people, goods, services and financing opened up the Norwegian health service to completion in both the provision of services and the health labor market through its affiliation with the other Scandinavian countries. In many areas of health policy, Norway entered into special agreements with the EU to be consistent with their policies.[162]

4. Major Policy Updates in Norway Since the 1980s

Since the latter part of the 1980s, the National Health Service in the Norway has continued to evolve. Starting with what was originally a mixed insurance-based system and then fully publicly funded and publicly owned national health service post World War II, recent reforms have preserved this predominant public tax-funded and public National Health Service character.[163]

After the Municipalities Health Services Act of 1982 made municipalities responsible for all primary care services, the previous district medical officer system disappeared. This role of the municipalities has continued to expanded to include nursing homes and environmental health services in 1988 and services for people with developmental disabilities in 1992.

During the 1990s, Norway also embraced some of the "new public sector" management approaches that were first pioneered in New Zealand, with a focus on greater managerial accountability, some market-based economic incentives and greater competition among providers.[164] But the Norwegian reforms focused more on planned changes in the delivery and organization of health care within the public sector rather opening up the health sector to full competition. For example, in 1998, a four-year action plan was introduced for local nursing and care services, and in 1999, a seven-year action plan for mental health services.

The Health Personnel Act of 1999 defined 29 health personnel groups that would be regulated. This was followed by a program that gave patients the right to choose their GP from a regular general practitioner (RGP) list. In 2002, the Norwegian Hospital Reform transferred responsibility for hospital care to the five Regional Health Authorities (RHAs). Since 2008, the focus has been on increasing coordination between the municipal level and the RHAs (coordination reform), with an increased focus on quality of care and patient safety issues. By 2012, This led to municipalities being given a larger financial responsibility for the services under their control.

As in the other Scandinavian countries, the consensual system of government in Norway, avoided the ideological swings that were observed since the 1980s in Australia, Canada, New Zealand and the UK. Furthermore, unlike their counterparts in the rest of Europe, Norwegian Prime Ministers do not have the option of advising the King to dissolve the Storting and call a snap election. The Constitution requires that the Storting serve out its full four-year term. For the past few decades there has been a rotation between the Labor Party, Conservative Party and Christian Democrats. Prime Minister Erna Solberg, from the Conservative Party, took office on October 16, 2013.

ENDNOTES

1. R. Seweriin introducing the Civil Defense Health Plan in Parliament in 1955. See Norway, "Lov om Helsemessig Beredskap," *Ot. prp.* 39(1955): 1.
2. State-employed district doctors, however, were available in Norway at an early stage.
3. S. E. Ekeid, *Health Services in Norway: Commitment to Decentralisation*, Monograph (Oslo: Directorate of Health, n.d.): 8.
4. Salaried doctors staffed hospitals.
5. On January 14, 1814, after 400 years under the Danish Crown, Denmark handed Norway over to the King of Sweden as part of a war settlement. Although never accepted by Norway, this union existed until June 7, 1905.
6. Norway, *Social Insurance in Norway* (Stockholm: National Insurance Administration, 1984): 5.
7. *Ibid*., p. 5.
8. Prime Minister Sverdrup, quoted in N. Urdal, *Syketrygden i Femti Ar. Historien om en Grunnleggende Social Reform* (Oslo: Norges Trygdekasselag, 1961): 12.

9. Urdal, *Syketrygden*, p. 17.
10. *Ibid.*, p. 20.
11. *Ibid.*, p. 22.
12. A corresponding programme for sailors and fishermen followed in 1911.
13. The District Doctor Law of July 26, 1912, required the presence of a County Medical Officer of Health in each municipality.
14. The County Medical Officer of Health acted as Chairman.
15. K. Salvesen, *Norwegian Health Administration: Past and Present*, Monograph (Oslo: Royal Norwegian Ministry of Health and Social Affairs, 1985): 5.
16. *Ex officio*, he was the Chairman of the local Board of Health and the National Health Administration Representative.
17. Ekeid, "Health services in Norway," p. 6, Much later the state appointed a County Medical Officer of Health at the level of the regional county. His duty was to supervise and enforce the health-related statutory responsibilities of the counties.
18. Ekeid, "Health services in Norway," p. 6.
19. K. Evang, "Public health services," *Den Norske Loegeforening*, 90(1970): 1141.
20. At the time the population was mainly rural, and the Norwegian economy was largely based on non-industrial activities such as fishing, forestry, mining and some agriculture in arable regions. The population for 1900 is based on United Nations (UN), Statistics Office (SO), Department of Economic and Social Affairs (DESA), *Demographic Yearbook* 1962, 14th Edition (New York: UN, 1962): 280 and the area is based on J. Paxton, ed., *The Statesman's Year-Book: Statistical and Historical Annual of the States of the World for the Year 1986–1987*, 123rd Edition (London: MacMillan Press, 1986): 929.
21. Urdal, *Syketrygden*, p. 31. A second Commission, established in 1902, reported in 1904.
22. *Ibid.*, p. 37.
23. *Ibid.*, p. 29.
24. *Ibid.*, p. 45.
25. Dr. R. Hansson became an important member of this Committee. A second parliamentary Commission had been unsuccessful in securing public and political support for its work.
26. Urdal, *Syketrygden*, p. 53.
27. The Norwegian political parties include: Party of Progress, Conservative Party, Christian Democratic Party, Centre Party, Labour Party, Social Democratic Party and Socialist Left Party.

28. Norwegian Labour Party Platform of 1893. See Urdal, *Syketrygden*, p. 56.
29. Urdal, *Syketrygden*, p. 56.
30. *Ibid.*, p. 56.
31. *Ibid.*, p. 60.
32. Most doctors would benefit from the new system; only a few doctors making unreasonably high incomes would suffer.
33. Norwegian Medical Association, quoted in Urdal, *Syketrygden*, p. 76.
34. Considering the limited effectiveness of medical science at the turn of the century, compensation for lost income during illness may in fact have been more important than medical treatment.
35. Urdal, *Sykelrygden*, p. 69.
36. The state subsidy was decreased while employer contributions were increased.
37. Efterstoel, quoted in Urdal, *Syketrygden*, p. 75.
38. T. Stroem became its director.
39. Urdal, *Syketrygden*, pp. 105–14.
40. K. Evang, *Health Services in Norway*, 4th Edition (Oslo: Universitctsforlaget, 1976): 37.
41. The Minister of Health in 1955, Dr. G. Harlem, referring to the earlier Compulsory Sickness Insurance Law of 1909. See Urdal, *Sykettygden*, p. 369.
42. H. Siem, *Choices for Health: An Introduction to the Health Services in Norway* (Oslo: Universitetsforlaget, 1985): 53. By the 1930s, access to services financed through public funds was already considered as right by the population, not as a condition of charity and poor relief. Personal communication with Dr. H. Siem, author on the Norwegian health care system.
43. A. B. Aubert, "The Norwegian Medical Association as it should be," *Tidsskrift for Den Norske Laegeforening* 10(1970):51. Today, the Norwegian Medical Association considers itself a "trade union" like its counterpart in Sweden. See H. Hauge, "The view of the Norwegian Medical Association," in *Scandinavian Health Care: Report of an Estes Park Conference*, by R. C. Bates, ed. (Englewood, Colorado: Estes Park Institute, 1983): 32.
44. O. Berg, "Verdier og interesser: Den Norske Laegeforenings fremvekst og utvikling," in *Legeme of Samfunnet*, by O. Larsen, O. Berg and F. Hodne, eds. (Oslo: Den Norske Laegeforening, 1986): 255. Personal communication with Dr. O. Berg, Associate Professor at the Institute of Political Science, University of Oslo.

45. O. Bjercke, "The Norwegian Medical Association as it is," *Tidsskrift for Den Norske Laegeforening* 10(1970): 48.
46. Evang, *Health Services*, p. 46.
47. Berg, "Verdier og interesser," p. 255.
48. Urdal, *Sykelrygden*, p. 126.
49. Dr. M. Solberg from Drangedal, quoted in Urdal, *Sykarygden*, p. 117.
50. Urdal, *Syketrygden*, p. 116.
51. Despite these conflicts, the rising membership with the sickness funds included 22 percent of the population.
52. Urdal, *Syketrygden*, p. 219.
53. V. Quisling, the fascist and Nazi sympathizer who had been appointed Minister of Defense under the Mowinckel Government, would soon haunt Norwegians.
54. E. Gerhardsen, *Unge Ar: Erindinger fra Arhundreskifter Fram til 1940* (Oslo: Tiden Norsk Forlag, 1974): 297.
55. E. Helle, *Oscar Torp: Arbeidergutt og Statsmann* (Oslo: Gyldendal Norsk Forlag, 1982): 134; and Urdal, *Syketrygden*, p. 271.
56. Helle, *Oscar Torp*, p. 134. Torp replaced Kornelius Bergsvik who took the portfolio as Minister of Finance.
57. Gerhardsen, *Unge Ar*, p. 353.
58. Norway, "Innstilling om en Lov om Syketrygd," *Innstilting*, No. 4, from Sosiallovkomiteen (March 4, 1939). The Committee began its work on sickness insurance in 1937, following its reports on old-age pensions and insurance for unemployment, blindness and disability.
59. Gerhardsen, *Unge Ar*, p. 298.
60. G. St ørvold quoted in Urdal, *Syketrygden*, p. 285.
61. *Ibid.*
62. Personal communication with O. Lund, committee member from the Department of Social Affairs to the expert working group drafting the Sickness Insurance Law of 1955.
63. Norway, "Innstilling om en Lov om Syketrygd." Størvold was then head of a division in the National Insurance Institution; Ormestad was the Chairman of the Norwegian Sickness Fund Society and Director of the Oslo Insurance Office.
64. Norway, "Innstilling om en Lov om Syketrygd"; and Norway, "Folketrygden om pliktig syketrygd for alle," *Innstilling*, No. 2 from Folketrygdkomiteen (1954): 5. Both Størvold and Ormestad were also members of the Social Legislation Committee.

65. Personal communication with O. Lund, Assistant Secretary of Social Affairs in 1955. Supported through personal communication with Hans Johnsen, committee member from the National Insurance Institution to the expert working group drafting the Sickness Insurance Law of 1955.
66. Norway, "Innstilling om en Lov om Syketrygd."
67. Urdal, *Sykelrygden*, p. 288.
68. *Ibid.*, p. 292.
69. E. Gerhardsen, *Fellesskap i Krig of Fred: Erindinger 1940–45* (Oslo: Tiden Norsk Forlag, 1970): 9.
70. A. Stroem, "Laegeforeningen under okkupasjonen," *Tidsskrift for Den Norske Laegeforening*, 11(1961): 712.
71. Stroem, "Social insurance," p. 712.
72. M. W. Childs, *Sweden: The Middle Way on Trial* (New Haven: Yale University Press, 1980): 126.
73. *Ibid.*, p. 130.
74. Gerhardsen, *Fellesskap.*
75. Gerhardsen, *Fellesskap*, p. 149.
76. Gerhardsen, *Fellesskap*, p. 161.
77. E. Gerhardsen, *Samarbeid og Strid: Erindinger* 1945–55 (Oslo: Tiden Norsk Forlag, 1971): 32.
78. G. Ousland (Labour), C. A. R. Christensen (Right), V. Gang (Left), and H. Holten (Farmers), the four "forefathers" of the joint reconstruction programme. See Gerhardsen, *Fellesskap*, p. 150.
79. The new Labour Government came to power on November 5, 1945, with a majority in Parliament. See Norway "Stortingsmeldingen om fylktrygd," *Stortingsmeldingen*, 58(1948); and Norway, "Folketrygden om pliktig syketrygd," p. 9.
80. Gerhardsen, *Fellesskap*, p. 7.
81. Gerhardsen, *Samarbeid*, p. 167.
82. Urdal, *Syketlygden*, p. 319, 324.
83. *Ibid.*, p. 325. Supported by personal communication with O. Lund and R. Seweriin.
84. Gerhardsen, *Samarbeid*, p. 165.
85. Norway, "Stortingsmeldingen om fylktrygd"; and Urdal, *Sykelrygden*, p. 325.
86. The problem of collecting contributions from the self-employed and other non-employed remained unsettled.
87. Urdal, *Syketrygden*, p. 327.
88. *Ibid.*, 333.

89. Norwegian Medical Association, quoted in Urdal, *Syketrygden*, p. 336.
90. Urdal, *Syketrygden*, p. 334.
91. The Committee was appointed on February 23, 1951. Norway, "Folketrygden," *Innstilling st.* 265(1952).
92. Norway, "Folketrygden om pliktig syketrygd."
93. The sickness funds covered 70 percent of the population in 1945 and nearly 90 percent of the population by the mid-1950s.
94. Norway, "Folketrygden," 1.
95. *Ibid.*; and Norway, "Folketrygden om pliktig syketrygd," p. 9. The terms of reference of the Committee had been to examine the principle of coordinating and developing a comprehensive social security programme for Norway.
96. Norway, "Folketrygden," quoted in Urdal, *Syketrygden*, p. 339.
97. *Ibid.*, 338.
98. Norway, "Folketrygden," quoted in Urdal, *Syketrygden*, p. 340.
99. R. Seweriin quoted in Urdal, *Syketrygden*, p. 342.
100. M. Lid, Minister of Finance in 1955, quoted in Gerhardsen, *Samarbeid*, p. 1972.
101. Helle, *Oscar Torp.*
102. Personal communication with F. Alexander, former Director General of the National Insurance Institution. See Urdal, *Syketrygden*, p. 337.
103. Seweriin replaced Aaslaug Aasland on November 2, 1953, as Minister of Social Affairs in the new Oscar Torp Labour Regime (November 19, 1951 to January 22, 1955).
104. R. Seweriin speaking to Parliament during the November 1952 parliamentary debates, quoted in Urdal, *Stetrygden*, p. 341.
105. Norway, "Folketrygden om pliktig syketrygd," Preface. Dr. A. Stroem, President of the Norwegian Medical Association, was a member of the Committee. He ensured that the views of the medical professions were heard by the reformers.
106. Norway, "Folketrygden om pliktig syketrygd," p. 9. These regulations were passed on July 17, 1953.
107. *Ibid.* Around the same time period, Sweden had only attained a membership rate of 53 percent of its population.
108. *Ibid.* p. 10.
109. Urdal, *Syketrygden*, p. 350.
110. *Ibid.*, p. 351.
111. Norway "Innstilling til Lov om Syketrygd," *Innstilling*, Sosialdepartementet (1955).
112. Norway "Lov om Syketrygd" *Forhandlinger i Stortinget* 12(1956): 1.

113. Norway, "Innstilling til Lov om Syketrygd," p. 6.
114. Personal communication with Ottar Lund.
115. Norway, "Innstilling til Lov om Syketrygd." Personal communication with Hans Johnsen.
116. Norway, "Innstilling til Lov om Syketrygd," p. 8– 9, 12, 18, 19, 82–85.
117. *Ibid.*, pp. 44–45.
118. *Ibid.*, pp. 43–44.
119. *Ibid.*, p. 45.
120. *Ibid.*, p. 61.
121. Norway, "Lov om Syketrygd og Endringer i Lov om Ufoertrygd for Militaere," *Forhandlinger i Odelstinget* 12(1956): 98.
122. Norway, "Innstilling til Lov om Syketrygd," p. 33. The estimated cost of the programme was later revised to 482 million Crowns, while the initial income under the programme was 493 million Crowns. See Urdal, *Syketrygden*, p. 360.
123. Following the return to a Gerhardsen Government in January 1955, Dr. G. Harlem became the new Minister of Social Affairs on August 1, 1955. See Norway "Instilling fra Sosialkomiteen 1) Om Lov om Syketrygd; 2) Om Lov om Endring I Lov om Ufoeretrygd for Militaerpersoner av July 19, 1953 m. fl. Lover" *Ot. Prp.* 52(June 19, 1955).
124. K. Bondevik speaking during parliamentary debates on February 14, 1956. Norway, "Lov om Syketrygd og Endringer," p. 86. Expecting no opposition to the proposed reform, the Minister of Social Affairs, Dr. G. Harlem, was busy with a North Norway Development Project and therefore did not attend the opening day of the debates on February 14, 1954. See Norway, "Lov om Syketrygdog Endringer," p. 86.
125. Norway, "Lov om Syketrygd og Endringer," p. 97.
126. *Ibid.*, p. 1.
127. Urdal, *Syketrygden*, p. 360. Personal communications with O. Lund.
128. J. Bjoerneboe, "Endringer i Lov om Syketrygd," *Tidsskrift for Den Norske Legeforening*, 1(1954).
129. Dr. A. Stroem, the President of the Norwegian Medical Association in 1948–1951. See A. Stroem, "Social insurance in Norway," *Tidsskrift for Den Norske Laegeforening*, 10(1970): 15. Supported by personal communication with Dr. J. W. R. Haffner, President of the Norwegian Medical Association from 1954–1957.
130. Bjoerneboe, "Endringer i Lov om Syketrygd," p. 19.
131. Urdal, *Syketrygden*, p. 362.

132. *Ibid.*
133. H. Asphaug, "Proposisjon om syketrygd for alle," *Social Trygd*, 10(1955): 317–18.
134. Norway, "Lov om Syketrygd og Endringer"; and Norway, "Lov om Syketrygd."
135. Personal communication with Dr. G. Harlem, Minister of Social Affairs, who introduced the act in 1955.
136. F. W. Ohldieck, I. Litlere, and H. Rygh, *Lov am Syketrygd: Av 2 Mars 1956 med Senere Endringer of Tillegg, Sist ved Low av 221 Januar 1960* (Oslo: Sem & Stenerson, 1960).
137. Harold, *Choices for Health*, p. 51.
138. O. Larssen, quoted from his book *The Slow Revolution*, by Gerhardsen, *Unge Ar*, p. 355.
139. G. Harlem, Minister of Social Affairs who introduced the act to Parliament in 1955. Quoted in Urdal, *Syketrygden*, p. 369.
140. Norway "Lev om Sivilforsvaret," *Ot. prp.* 28(1953).
141. *Ibid.*, 5.
142. Norway, "Lov om Sivilforsvaret."
143. Norway, "Innstilling fra Sosialkomiteen om Lov om Helsemessig Beredskap," *Ot. prp.* 39(1955).
144. Personal communication with R. S. Bang, Assistant Deputy General of the Directorate of Health, who worked as a lawyer in the Directorate during the 1950s.
145. Personal communication with Dr. J. W. R. Haffner, President of the Norwegian Medical Association from 1954–1957.
146. Norway, "Lov om Sivilforsvaret," pp. 1–4, para. 2–9.
147. Norway, "Lov om Slvilforsvaret," p. 1, para. 1.
148. Norway, "Lov om Sivilforsvaret," pp. 4–5, para. 12.
149. Personal communication with R. Seweriin, Minister of Social Affairs, at the time of the introduction and passing of the Civil Defense Health Legislation.
150. Norway, "Lov om Syketrygd og Endringer," p. 98.
151. Grundersen speaking in Parliament on 5 April during the debates on the Civil Defense Law, quoted in Gerhardsen, *Samarbeid*, p. 74.
152. Thirty years later, another working committee advocated a similar plan which once again "concerns defence-related action and has little or no beating upon the general national health care programme," Personal communication with K. Salvesen, Deputy Director-General, Norwegian Ministry of Social Affairs. Personal communication Dr. G. Vig, Chairman of the Civil

Defense Plan Working Group 1983. Periodic reviews have been carried out on the Norwegian civil defense plan since the 1950s. Norway, Helsedirektoratet (H), *Katastrofe-PJanlegging ved Sykehus* (Oslo: Helsedirektoratet og Norske Kommuners Sentralforbund, 1972); and Norway, Helsedirektoratet og Norske Kommuners Sentralforbund (HNKS), *Planlegging av Helsetjenesten for Katastrofer og Krig* (Oslo: Helsedirektoratet og Norske Kommuners Sentralforbund, 1980).

153. Stroem, "Social insurance," p. 14.
154. T. Mork "Health services in Norway; "Special issue of *Sykehuset* at the 21st International Hospital Congress, Oslo, June 24–29," *Journal of the Norwegian Hospital Association* 4(1979): 254.
155. Mork, "Health services," p. 253; Present Director General of the Norwegian Directorate of Health.
156. Evang, "Public Health Services," p. 1143.
157. Mork, "Health services," p. 254.
158. Salvesen, "Norwegian health administration," p. 5.
159. A. S. Preker, "Public finance and provision of health care services in Quebec: An international perspective," Brief presented to the Commission of Enquiry into the Health and Social Services of Quebec [Chairman Jean Rochon] (London: IIHS, December 1986): 27; and Organization for Economic Co-operation and Development (OECD), *Measuring Health Care* 1960–1983: *Expenditure Costs and Performance*, OECD Social Policy Studies No. 2 (Paris: OECD, 1985): 68–69, 72–73.
160. Hauge, "Norwegian Medical Association," p. 33.
161. Norway, *Health for All by the Year 2000: Norwegian Contribution to an ad hoc Meeting on Health for All in Industrialized Countries*, Geneva, May 1–2, 1980 (Oslo: Directorate of Health, 1980).
162. The term acquis is also used to describe laws adopted under the Schengen Agreement, prior to its integration into the European Union legal order by the Treaty of Amsterdam, in which case one speaks of the Schengen acquis. The term acquis has been borrowed by the World Trade Organization Appellate Body, in the case Japan — Taxes on Alcoholic Beverages, to refer to the accumulation of General Agreement on Tariffs and Trade (GATT) and WTO law ("acquis gattien"), though this usage is not well established.
163. Å. Ringard, A. Sagan, I. Sperre Saunes, and A. K. Lindahl, *Norway: Health System Review in Health Systems in Transition* 15(8)(2013): 1–162. http://www.euro.who.int/__data/assets/pdf_file/0018/237204/HiT-Norway.pdf. Accessed July 25, 2017.

164. G. Scott, L. McKenzie, and J. Webster, "Maladjustments in the Corporatization Model: Hospital Reform in New Zealand, in A. S. Preker and A. Harding, eds. *Innovations in Health Service Delivery: The Corporatization of Public Hospitals*, (2003, Washington, DC: World Bank). https://openknowledge.worldbank.org/handle/10986/15145. Accessed August 17, 2017; pp. 205–345.

CHAPTER 9

SWEDEN

All services needed by the individual should be offered free of charge at the time of treatment... the community [will] deliver this by means of an extended and regulated organization, public health, hospital care, preventive medicine on an individual basis and ambulatory medical care.[1]

Axel Höjer, 1948

A. HISTORICAL CONTEXT

1. Swedish Sickness Funds

Sweden was slow to industrialize compared with other Western countries: "At the close of the nineteenth century, Sweden ranked as one of the backward nations of Europe."[2] Although the sickness funds were equally slow to develop, local governments had a long history of financing health care. The first paragraph of the Constitution of Sweden's Parliamentary monarchy underscores the importance of such local self-government: "Swedish democracy ... shall be realized through a representative and parliamentary polity and through local self-government."[3]

In 1863, the county councils and later the municipal councils assumed substantial taxation powers, including the right to levy income taxes.[4] Their health-related responsibilities developed later.[5] These included the provision of local hospitals, small provincial hospitals, sanatoria and special hospitals for the infectious diseases. Such hospitals became public institutions at an early stage, financed through the local governments.[6]

A lack of financial security in private practice meant that there were few private practitioners even in the larger cities. Provincial doctors, who served both as medical officers of health and general practitioners in rural regions, first appeared in the 1700s but remained scarce.[7] Although a position as a district medical officer of health offered more security than fee-for-service private practice, both were less honored than work in hospitals.[8] These two groups of doctors were, therefore, unable to meet the medical needs of Sweden's population of 5,136,441, which at the turn of the century was scattered over the country's 410,929 square kilometers of northern regions.[9]

Hospitals doctors were salaried by the institutions in which they worked, but supplemented their incomes through fee-for-service consultations in out-patient departments. The county councils encouraged this practice to reduce the occupancy of hospitals, thereby saving money for their residents. This habit would later be difficult to break.

From the sixteenth century onward, tradesmen's guilds began providing limited sick pay for their members.[10] As there were few doctors in private practice, and salaried district medical officers of health were scarce, the independent sickness funds, which began appearing in the mid-eighteenth century, offered mainly cash support during illness.[11]

These circumstances lead King Oscar II of the joint Swedish-Norwegian Kingdom to encourage the Swedish Parliament to examine Bismarck's model of sickness insurance.[12] In 1884, S. A. Hedin, a Swedish Member of Parliament, asked the Government to appoint a Workers' Insurance Commission. The terms of reference of the Commission were to enquire into old-age pensions and workers' accident insurance.[13]

The combination of late industrialization, few doctors in private practice and the liberal self-help philosophy which prevailed during the nineteenth century, led the Commission to recommend voluntary sickness insurance plan when it reported in 1889.[14] The question of compulsory sickness insurance did arise for the first time during these deliberations.

The Sickness Fund Law of October 30, 1891, defined the conditions which voluntary sickness funds had to meet in order to qualify for state registration and a small public subsidy.[15] Because the subsidies contributed less than 10 percent to the sickness funds finances, most of the organizations did not bother to apply for registration. Their benefits remained unregulated, offered only limited coverage and had long initial waiting periods.[16]

Hjalmar Branting, a Member of Parliament (later Prime Minister), called for compulsory sickness insurance as early as 1900: "A country that leaves its injured workers helpless for the first two months [following an accident] will soon be forced to have compulsory sickness insurance."[17] Reforms were subsequently slowly introduced. In 1908, Edvard Wawrinsky, a Member of Parliament, presented a motion to introduce maternity benefit insurance. By 1912, such insurance was available separately through many of the voluntary sickness funds.[18]

An amended law on Registered Sickness Funds, appeared in Parliament in 1909; it passed into law on July 4, 1910, and came into effect on January 1, 1911. During the parliamentary debates, James J. Gibson, a Member of Parliament tried unsuccessfully to persuade Government to introduce a compulsory plan.

The 1911 law refined the criteria necessary for official registration and increased the subsidies offered by the state. Recognized sickness funds were required to have at least 100 members and to reimburse patients for the cost of medical treatment, hospitalization and drugs.[19] The small subsidies offered by the Government were still insufficient to act as an incentive for the sickness funds to attract a large membership.[20] Their benefits continued to consist mainly of income support during illness not treatment by doctors.

To gain greater control over the activities of the sickness funds, the Board of Social Welfare became responsible for supervising their activities in 1912, The Commercial Collegiate and the Sickness Fund Bureau had previously filled this function.[21]

In 1915, A. Lindstedt was appointed Chairman of a Social Insurance Commission.[22] The terms of reference of the Commission were to conduct a detailed examination of social insurance, including superannuation, invalidity benefits, maternity benefits, sickness insurance and accident insurance.[23] The Commission, which reported in October 1919, recommended a means-tested compulsory sickness insurance for workers. It also recommended that the Government introduce the program through a comprehensive social security package, which would include old age pensions.[24]

Although the Scandinavian countries managed to stay out of World War I, Sweden did not escape the war's economic consequences: "The depression that followed the end of the First World War affected Sweden profoundly."[25] One-third to one-half of the labor force was unemployed, In this context, the Ministry of Finance for the Conservative Government in power was unwilling to consider the expensive social reforms recommended by the Social Insurance Commission. Instead, the Minister of Social Affairs, Bernhard Eriksson, appointed an expert committee, under the Chairmanship of A. Jochnick, to explore other options, This latter committee, however, never reported.[26]

By 1928, 17 European countries had introduced compulsory sickness insurance, leaving Sweden significantly behind.[27] In March 1929, a new committee conducted yet another inquiry into sickness insurance under the Chairmanship of Lav Rydin. Its report of October 11, 1929 once again called for compulsory hospital insurance.[28]

After 50 years of voluntary sickness insurance and extensive debate, Eriksson finally had the Ministry of Social Affairs draft a law which would lead to compulsory sickness insurance in Sweden, The new Sickness Fund Law passed in Parliament on June 26, 1931, coming into effect on January 1, 1933.

The new law offered means-tested compulsory sickness insurance with improved maternity benefits and full reimbursement of the cost of medical care. It reorganized the existing sickness funds into 21 geographically-based central sickness funds that would oversee local organizations. The reform aimed to unify the Swedish sickness insurance system,

The Swedish Medical Association voiced little protest against these early reforms for several reasons. First, private doctors, the main members of the Association, supported the voluntary sickness insurance reforms which offered them an added source of income.[29] Secondly, over 60 percent of doctors held public posts which were unaffected by the sickness insurance debate and were not members of the Association. Finally, the hospital appointments of the younger doctors depended on their maintaining a good relationship with the senior doctors, a system which discouraged dissension. The Swedish Younger Doctors' Association (SYLF) formed a conservative branch of the parent Swedish Medical Association that advanced few radical policies of its own during the 1930s and 1940s.[30]

By 1930, only 21 percent of eligible adults were covered by voluntary sickness insurance.[31] Eriksson hoped that compulsory means-tested membership and increased state subsidies would overcome some of the shortcomings of the previous voluntary system.[32] The outcome was disappointing: there were few doctors in private practice, state subsidies remained low and membership with the sickness funds remained low.[33]

To fill the gap where no other care was available, legislation was passed to extend the health care responsibilities of county councils and local hospitals. By the 1930s, these responsibilities expanded to cover non-institutional care such as district nurses, midwives, maternity, pediatric care and dental care. Provision by the county councils of ambulatory clinics in hospitals, however, did not become mandatory until 1958 and ambulatory community care not until 1961.

2. Social Democratic Party

The inadequacy of the new compulsory Sickness Insurance Law of 1931 became obvious almost as soon as the law was passed. More radical reforms were needed to extend the benefits of pre-paid health care to larger segments of the population. The Social Democratic Party, which formed a Coalition Government in 1932, was committed to introducing such reforms.

Karl Hjalmar Branting founded the Swedish Social Democratic Party in 1889. Much later, he briefly led Social Democratic Governments in 1920, 1921 and 1924 by "cultivating the Liberals."[34] The 1920s and early 1930s were politically unstable times with much economic hardship in Sweden. There was a change in leadership and Government almost every year, resulting in fragile coalitions composed of right-center parties. The Social Democrats were often forced to choose "the middle way" to remain partners in these Coalition Governments.[35]

In a world polarized between fascism and communism, the Swedish Social Democratic Party followed a reformist path, rejecting a policy of revolution from the onset. Radical reform proposals such as nationalization were rarely advocated. Instead, the party allowed private enterprise to continue unhampered as long as its adherents were willing to contribute to the cost of society.

In 1932, the Social Democratic Party formed a Coalition Government with the Agrarian (Farmers) Party which would last through World War II. Per Albin Hansson, the new Prime Minister, wanted to end the 30 years of *laisser-faire* social policies of the previous Conservative, Liberal and Agrarian Governments.[36]

Hansson believed that the state should satisfy "those programmes [accident, sickness and maternity insurance], ...that one cannot do without, if one truly wants the population to have some feeling of security and comfort in its own country."[37] He became known to his fellow countrymen as the "archetype of the moderate socialist leader ... an assurance of peace and prosperity."[38]

His Minister of Finance, Ernst Wigforss, was Albin's opposite: "An intellectual, an ideologue ... witty, brilliant, with an absorbing interest in the people of every kind and class, was to become a kind of Social Democratic saint."[39] Wigforss felt that a demand for equality was normal in society that had "need side by side with plenty."[40]

Wigforss believed that free competition was an appalling squandering of resources. After 1932, he quickly put his beliefs into practice by expanding public works and introducing a progressive tax structure. His long period in office as Minister of Finance allowed him to successfully alter the economic policy of his country.

Sweden was the first industrialized nation to use such Keynesian deficit spending strategies with success. The business sector flourished, giving the Government the economic means to introduce reforms aimed at easing poverty, unemployment and social inequity. This unexpected economic growth during the 1930s was, envied by other countries that were still suffering from the Great Depression.

The country's economic prosperity allowed Gustav Moller, the Minister of Social Affairs, to lay the groundwork for a comprehensive social welfare reform, "The People's Home."[41] It introduced subsidies for housing construction and special unemployment insurance in 1934, pensions in 1935, means-tested maternal benefits in 1937 and two-week paid vacations in 1938.[42]

The Social Democrats build their political platform on a social humanism which maintained that the ills of a free society can be cured and that injustices are intolerable, "a pragmatic belief acknowledging the frail nature of the human condition."[43] To achieve this goal, their social security reform focused on two separate mechanisms: an expanded social insurance system which would pay for new benefits, including universal entitlement for sickness insurance, and an expanded public sector which would provide such services.

B. LANDMARK LEGISLATIVE REFORMS

1. Social Security Commission of 1938

Before the outbreak of World War II, the Minister of Social Affairs, Gustav Moller, appointed Bernhard Eriksson as Chairman of a Parliamentary Commission on Social Security.[44] The terms of reference of the Commission were to explore the health responsibilities of the county councils and examine how to unify their diverse functions under one administration. The war, however, soon caused a shift in priorities, and the country's attention turned to maintaining its neutrality.

The Social Democrats constituted a four-party Coalition Government on December 1, 1939, which included the Liberals, Agrarians (later Centre) and Conservatives. Hitler humiliated the Prime Minister, Per Albin Hansson, on several occasions by forcing him to make a series of concessions to Germany, which violated Sweden's pledge of neutrality. One of the more publicized events occurred in 1941 when Sweden allowed Germany to transport its armed Engelbrecht division from occupied Norway to Finland on Swedish railways, having previously refused the Allies and Finland similar advantages.[45] There were few illusions about the strains that events like these would place on the Nordic Union following the war.

Both Ernst Wigforss and Gustav Moller wanted Sweden to accept refugees seeking asylum.[46] Others, however, felt that humanitarian aid would compromise the country's economic standing with Germany: "Given the close ties in trade with Germany, the pressure from Hitler's Reich to come in on the German side was intense.... The German connection, as it had existed during the years of rearmament and then during the war, deeply troubled the Swedish conscience."[47]

The Swedish Medical Association advocated a protectionist manpower policy during the war, claiming that since Sweden had a surplus of doctors, it should refuse demands for immigration from non-Swedish refugee doctors: "As long as the present difficult conditions for young doctors persist in our country, no action should be taken which could lead to a further worsening of the chances of young doctors to earn a livelihood."[48] The Social Democrats and others critical of this stance used international standards to show that Sweden, on the contrary, had a shortage of doctors. Dr. Karl Evang of Norway, addressing the Karolinska Institute in March 1933, exclaimed that it was "absurd for the Swedes to talk about the dangers of 'overproducing' doctors."[49]

These troubled times had an important influence on the work of the Parliamentary Commission on Social Security which anticipated a period of economic hardship following the war. When the Commission finally presented its report on sickness insurance in April 1944 it recommended a complete reorganization of the Swedish social security system which would include universal entitlement to health care through sickness insurance.[50] Its report on pensions was issued in 1945, unemployment insurance in 1948 and workmen's compensation in 1951.[51]

The proposed sickness insurance program called for both medical treatment and cash benefits during incapacity due to illness.[52] Medical benefits would include visits to doctors' offices and hospitalization (365-day limit).[53] Income support would be limited to 730 days.

The new county council boundaries created by the local government that was taking place at the same time would strengthen public control over the administration of the program. Each new region would have central offices responsible to the Board of Pensions to ensure that each county had its own local insurance office.[54] The sickness funds would be allowed to continue to act as agents in administering the new sickness insurance benefits locally. Members of recognized sickness funds would automatically qualify for membership under the new system. Those who had no previous protection would be given the names of new local organizations to join. In this way, the program intended to cover all residents in Sweden.

Workers' and employers' contributions as well as a central government subsidy would finance the program. Employers would collect their employee's contributions at source. The anticipated annual cost of the program was 235 million Crowns per year, with central government subsidies financing a third of this cost.[55]

During the war there was little opposition to the proposed reform in the sickness insurance system. The sickness funds fully endorsed it in their yearly congress held in Goteborg in 1945.[56] "The [medical] profession as a whole did not seem to be aware of the trend until the late 1940s."[57] The Swedish Medical Association favored a continuation of the existing system, but raised no protest to the reform.[58] The report of the Parliamentary Commission on Social Security was accepted by most Swedes in a spirit of national unity.

2. Sickness Insurance Law of 1947

During the war, the Social Democratic Party continued to strengthen its popular base. In the 1940 general election, the Social Democrats won an absolute majority of 54 percent of the vote, the largest ever. In the 1948 election, they won 46.1 percent of the vote, while the Liberals won 16 percent and the Conservatives and Agrarians won 12 percent each. When the war-time Coalition Government dissolved in 1945, the Social Democrats were left with a majority in the Parliament. This enabled them to carry out their planned social security reforms which included universal entitlement to health care through sickness insurance.

With the sudden death of Per Albin Hansson in 1946, Tage Erlander became Prime Minister. Although Erlander was not widely known in the party or to the public, his years in the Department of Social Affairs under Gustav Möller had prepared him for implementing the recommendations of the Parliamentary Commission on Social Security. It was also largely through the support of Möller that Erlander became Prime Minister: "It was lucky for me to have had Gustav Möller as supervisor and close friend."[59]

To secure a strong Government, Erlander formed a Coalition Government with the Agrarian Party (later Centre) led by Gunnar Hedlund in 1951.[60] Hedlund became Minister of the Interior, responsible for both the Board of Health and county councils. The chairmen of the County Council Federation, Erik Fast and Fridolf Thapper, were both Social Democrats.

The Universal Compulsory Sickness Insurance Law was presented to Parliament in 1946. The law intended to extend coverage under sickness insurance to the whole population. Benefits would include reimbursement of 75 percent of the cost of medical treatment by doctors, free transport to and from hospitals and free medications. The county councils would receive a state subsidy to help them finance hospital care at a nominal charge to patients. Although it became law on January 3, 1947, without major opposition, it was never implemented in its original form.

Enactment of the law, which was planned for July 1, 1950, was postponed on several occasions. First, the date of implementation was delayed to allow for the preparation of the concomitant local government reform.[61] The latter led to the formation of larger municipalities, based on a population of 2,000 or more, which was considered a more appropriate economic unit.[62] On April 20, 1950, the Prime Minister announced another delay, fearing that Sweden was heading for a period of post-war economic depression.[63] A further indefinite delay, announced on December 8, 1950, no longer surprised anyone.

Sweden's policy of neutrality during the war spared its industry from destruction, obviating expensive physical reconstruction. The context in which the original act had been conceived, therefore, changed rapidly. Following World War II, instead of facing an economic depression as anticipated, the country entered a period of rapid growth and inflation. As a result, on December 28, 1951, the Under Secretary of State of the Ministry of Social Affairs, Per Eckerberg, headed a working group to re-examine the social security reform in light of these changes, including its sickness insurance provisions.

The terms of reference of the new investigation were to minimize the cost of sickness insurance and to integrate workmen's compensation into a comprehensive program. Relying heavily on earlier recommendations made by the Parliamentary Commission on Social Security, the group published a Social Security Report in 1951 and a Social Insurance Report on November 4, 1952, Eckerberg's working group recommended that sickness insurance and workmen's compensation be coordinated but treated under different laws.

3. Höjer Report of 1948

While pressing ahead with the new sickness insurance law, Möller also wanted to explore the possibility of more radical reforms in health care:

"Left-wingers in the party were contemptuous in the mid-1940s of what they said was merely a social insurance system that left a few wealthy families in control of industry."[64] The Universal Compulsory Sickness Insurance Law of 1947 belonged to such social insurance.

In 1943, Möller appointed Dr. Axel Höjer, the Director General of the Swedish Board of Health, to head a seemingly benign Commission to examine out-patient regulations in hospitals.[65] Following an informal meeting with the Minister, Höjer interpreted the terms of reference of the Commission as demanding an extensive review of the whole Swedish health care system.[66]

Höjer's experience as a district medical officer for deprived areas in Stockholm and Malmo had taught him the limitations of the existing system. This exposure, combined with his socialist political views, led him to favor an increased emphasis on primary care rather than a further expansion of the traditional institutional sector:

> All [health care] services needed by the individual should be offered free of charge at the time of treatment ... the community [should] deliver this by means of an extended and (comprehensively) regulated organization, [including] *public health, hospital care, preventive medicine on an* individual basis and ambulatory health care.[67]
>
> If the system develops in the projected way, there should be by 1960 or 1970, only a very few physicians employed at the hospitals who would not be willing or obliged to enter the civil service compensation system.[68]

He expressed these views in his final report.[69] First, he recommended the development of an effective primary care plan in tandem with the evolving hospital sector. Health centers would provide both preventive and curative treatment. Second, he wanted to increase the total number of doctors in Sweden, including district doctors. Finally, he envisaged a change in the status of doctors from that of independent contractors to that of public employees on salaries.

The report was revolutionary. The manpower and remuneration issues posed a direct threat to the lucrative fee-for-service practices enjoyed by a few privileged and influential consultants in hospitals. Regionalization would require extensive administrative reform in local government and the county councils.

Sweden, however, having based its welfare state on a moderate socialism rather than revolution and radical nationalization, found the Höjer Report too radical. Many years would pass before some of the principles in his proposal would be accepted and implemented.[70]

4. Swedish Medical Association

With the election of Dr. Dag Knutson as Chairman in 1947, dramatic changes took place within the Swedish Medical Association. Knutson immediately introduced new regulations for all members of the medical profession to participate in local and national organizations.[71] This policy resulted in a sharp increase in membership and a strengthening of the political influence of the Association.

Knutson and Höjer had previously engaged in heated debates on "whether doctors should continue to be members of a free profession" or become civil servants.[72] Knutson, whose support came mainly from private practitioners and senior hospital doctors, defended the free medical profession: "My main interests were education — further training ... and preservation of the freedom of physicians as professionals."[73]

The previously unassertive medical profession and other vested-interest groups reacted with horror to Höjer's report.[74] By the time the Government released the Report, Knutson had prepared doctors for the worst: "We must refuse to cooperate with the Medical Director. He is dangerous and must be removed from post as soon as possible."[75]

The Swedish Medical Association scored an early success by influencing the Government to abandon the recommendations in the report: "By defeating the reform proposals of Axel Höjer, [the Swedish Medical Association] won the first round of the postwar struggle, unlike their British colleagues who had to accept a National Health Service."[76] This early success of the Swedish Medical Association was deceptive, however, since later events would support Höjer's vision of the Swedish health care system.

5. Sickness Insurance Law of 1953

The new Minister of Social Affairs, Gunnar Sträng, accepted the revised sickness insurance reforms as proposed. The amended compulsory sickness insurance law was presented to Parliament on March 27, 1953, and passed on June 19, 1953, following a lively debate. On January 1, 1955, Sweden finally introduced universal entitlement to health care through national sickness Insurance.[77] "To a great extent ... it was Gunnar Sträng in collaboration with Per Eckerberg, then State Secretary in the Department of Social Affairs, that formulated and pushed through the new sickness insurance legislation."[78]

The amended Sickness Insurance Law called for compulsory economic protection against illness for all Swedes over 16 year of age, children being included under their parents. The program would cover 7.1 million people, all of the Swedish population.[79] A total of 31 central and 630 local registered sickness funds would administer the benefits of the program. These organizations, in turn, would be administered by the National Health Insurance Institution.

The law provided for cash benefits during illness, free hospital care financed through the county councils and reimbursement for 75 percent of doctors' fees. Hospital insurance would finance part of the cost of hospitalization and pre-hospital transport. Health care would include dental care and free choice of doctor.[80] Income support would apply to gainfully employed people with a minimum income or full-time housewives during part of the duration of an illness.[81] The law limited cash benefits following hospitalization to 730 days following a waiting period of 3 days.[82]

The revised cost of the program was 738 million Crowns.[83] Workers would contribute 44 percent, employers 27 percent and the state 29 percent to the financing of the program. Employers could contribute to both sickness insurance and workmen's compensation. Employers would deduct their employees' contributions at source together with income taxes for non-pensioners earning a minimum of 1,200 Crowns. The Director General of the Swedish Sickness Funds Federation, Erik Malm, welcomed this simplification: "Under the [new] system it will be much easier to control the registration of members in the proper sickness funds."[84]

The Sickness Insurance Law was only one of several reforms in health insurance introduced between 1947 and 1953.[85] A separate compulsory workmen's compensation insurance was passed on May 14, 1954, coming into effect on January 1, 1955.[86] Additional voluntary insurance became available to the self-employed, housewives and students.[87] On May 21, 1954, a separate law integrated maternity benefits and general sickness insurance under the same program.[88] Finally, on June 4, 1954, the cost of medications became subsidized if prescribed by a doctor or dentist.[89]

In 1958, the new Minister of Social Affairs, Torsten Nilsson, established a working Commission under Axel Strand to examine the whole area of pensions, sickness insurance and invalidity benefits. The Commission, reporting in 1961, recommended that pensions and sickness insurance should be integrated into a single plan.

On January 1, 1963, the National Insurance Act unified the National Health Insurance Act with other social insurance programs to complete the long process of integration. The new act converted the sickness funds into new social insurance offices. Each county council would have an insurance office with its own local branches[90] under supervision of a National Insurance Board.

C. CONTINUED POLICY REFORM PROCESS

Two interrelated circumstances prevented the sickness insurance system from providing truly universal entitlement to health care in Sweden. First, there was an overemphasis on the unevenly distributed institutional sector. Second, there was persistent shortage of medical doctors in the primary care. The Seven Crowns Reform, which created a salaried doctor service, was intended to correct some of the barriers to universal entitlement created by the financing of health care through sickness insurance.

1. Regional Hospital Plan of 1958

The institutional sector flourished when Dr. Arthur Engel, an internist and Chief Medical Officer of Health with liberal political views, became Director General of the Board of Health in 1952, replacing Höjer who became Director of the Board of Social Welfare. Following the controversy created by the Höjer Report, Engel tried to reassure Prime Minister Tage Erlander that he envisaged his role as an "unpolitical adviser."[91] In the same breath, he quickly tabled the blueprint for a regionalized hospital system which gained him a reputation as the "father" of the Swedish regional health care system.[92]

While Engel was planning his regional health care system, Erlander appointed Richard Sterner as Chairman of a Commission on Regionalism. Its terms of reference were to examine the broad direction of the Swedish health care system. In his report of 1958, Sterner recommended an expansion in ambulatory care by increasing the number of salaried district and regional medical officers, increasing the facilities for medical education, stimulating the hospital sector and focusing on prevention.[93]

The recommendations affecting the institutional sector were quickly put into place with the county councils forming new hospital management regions.[94] Fridolf Thapper, Chairman of the County Councils Federation, felt that such reforms would optimize coordination of health services and thereby lead to greater cost efficiency. The personal links between the Engel and Thapper guaranteed success for Engel's plans: "I have for many years had the pleasure and the privilege of counting myself as one of Arthur Engel's good friends."[95] Engel presented his regional plan as a national program for combating the "rising costs of hospital care and shortage of medical personnel and especially doctors and nurses."[96]

He felt that local health centers should "integrate their activities as closely as possible with the nearest district hospital" so that the hospital districts would become the core of the Swedish health care system.[97] "I nourish the hope of having our health centers staffed, in the future, with physicians who are specialists (in internal medicine, pediatrics, obstetrics, gynecology and psychiatry)."[98]

By 1963, the county councils had assumed full responsibility for the financing, organization and administration of both in-patient and out-patient care in hospitals.[99] This fulfilled the recommendations of Dr. C. J. Ekströmer, Director General of the National Health Services in 1846, who had advocated that the county councils should be given full control of local state hospitals: "The State should be responsible for the over-all planning only and fulfill an advisory and supervising function."[100]

Dr. Bror Rexed, Engel's successor, continued the emphasis on institutional care following his appointment in 1965: "In principle everybody working in the health system should be exposed to a successively more specialized, continued training throughout his whole working life."[101] Rexed's skill as a negotiator led to an expansion in the budget for the Ministry of Social Affairs until it consumed 25 percent of the national budget: "The value placed on health and medical care is generally very high and it is my opinion that politicians have a duty to encourage citizens to pay for what they want and need."[102]

Instead of controlling cost as initially intended, there was a rapid rise in cost of the Swedish health care system during the 1960s.[103] "Every self-respecting central hospital included in its plans new clinics for thoracic surgery, neuro-surgery ... concerned with fairly uncommon diseases."[104] The hope of controlling costs through economies of scale such as institutional care had backfired.

Gunnar Sträng, the Minister of Finance, felt that the county councils had reached their financial limits.[105] Thapper, who had previously had great faith in the Engel Regional Plan, now shared this concern: "From an economic point of view, the late 1950s and early 1960s were record-breaking years. The growth rate was higher than ever before."[106] Health expenditure grew 231 percent in a decade from 1950 to 1960 and 346 percent from 1960 to 1968.[107]

In 1967, Sven Aspling, the new Minister of Social Affairs, emphasized that preventive care was "at least as important as care in the case of illness.... [requiring] a more intimate collaboration between hospitals, home care and social care."[108] Universal entitlement had become increasingly limited by lack of access to the highly specialized institutional facilities which were often the sole providers of health care.

2. Swedish Younger Doctors' Association

Although the belligerent posture of the Swedish Medical Association under the leadership of Knutson lasted until 1962, the Swedish Younger Doctors' Association had by then become impatient with the practice of patronage in hospitals and the poor opportunities for future advancement. With no advancement in sight, the younger doctors' fear of displeasing senior consultants disappeared. From then on, they simply bypassed the Swedish Medical Association in their collective negotiations with the Government.

This revolt happened at a time when both local governments and the state were experiencing problems with the senior hospital consultants. The county councils had become acutely aware that the hospital sector was a costly way to provide ambulatory care and the Social Democratic Party Government was embarrassed by consultants who flaunted their high incomes.[109]

Hospital consultants continued to overcharge patients under the insurance reimbursement system, resulting in in-patient care being cheaper than out-patient care. Hospital appointments remained more highly honored than work as district medical officers or clinic doctor. This discouraged the younger doctors from pursuing training in primary care and seeking non-institutional posts. Although, ambulatory care was thought to offer a cheap alternative to institutional care, available posts were nearly impossible to fill.

Both the county councils and the Government felt that abuses under the fee-for-service insurance system in the out-patient departments were responsible for many of their problems: "One way to improve the chances for other sectors within the health care system to compete for physicians would be to deny physicians additional incomes from out-patient work, in other words to integrate out-patient work into those service duties that are compensated for by salaries."[110]

Dr. Bo Hjern, the Chairman of the Younger Doctors' Association (later Director of the Swedish Medical Association), had long advocated that the Association abandon its free medical profession model and adopt a collective bargaining role which would give greater recognition to the plight of the younger doctors.[111] Other influential leaders, such as Åke Lindgren and Nils Terner, supported this view.[112] "Without embarrassment, we call ourselves a trade union."[113] By infiltrating both the general assembly and the executive of the Association, the Younger Doctors' Association slowly succeeded in its goals. "We... wanted to turn the association into something more like a modern trade union. When Knutson realized that there were many members of the Association who wanted a new Chairman, he resigned."[114]

3. Seven Crowns Reform of 1969

Over the years, the Social Democratic Party had promoted several distinct policy platforms. During the early years, it focused on political democracy. Later, during the 1940s and 1950s, it built the Swedish welfare state.

In the 1960s, a new platform based on employment equality led to the Seven Crowns Reform. Under this reform Swedish doctors became salaried state employees.

The Social Democratic Party's margin for exercising power had continued to decrease following World War II. After the 1956 general election, the Coalition Government, composed of Social Democrats and Agrarians, continued to lose popular support. In the 1966 local elections, the Social Democrats suffered the worst setback since the war, winning only 42 percent of the popular vote. They badly needed a new political platform to boost their popularity. Further increases in the cost of the health care system and hostility from the powerful county councils worsened their political position.

Finding a stimulating election platform formed the basis for the Party Congress in 1967.[115] "They needed a new issue that could rekindle the enthusiasm of the labor movement and encourage a new belief in change."[116] To make matters worse, just before the 1968 general elections, the county councils decided to increase in-patient fees to draw public attention to their plight — an awkward event for the Government.

The post-war economic boom had allowed the Swedish welfare state to develop without radical challenges to private industry. This had been an affront to the more radical factions of the Social Democratic Party. To regain its more radical constituents, the party decided to focus on equality among workers as its new political platform.[117] "Its most important purpose was to generate enthusiasm among Social Democratic precinct workers and to draw a clear line between their party and the non-socialists."[118]

The September 1968 elections witnessed a voter turnout of 89 percent and led the Social Democratic Party gain over 50 percent of the popular the vote, a rare event in a multi-party political system.[119] The Party's income equality platform, the personal popularity of Tage Erlander, who had become a cult father figure, and the economic success of two decades of growth contributed to the landslide election victory.

Following the elections, the Ministry of Social Affairs and County Council Federation met to discuss the necessary measures to implement the Government's election promises. Both felt that eliminating the disproportionately high incomes of some doctors would serve as a symbolic showpiece of their commitment to income equality. By December, an *ad hoc* working committee rushed through an analysis of various proposals, which they "presented as a binding agreement to the respective parties ... passed and implemented virtually unchanged" in what would become the Seven Crowns Reform.[120]

The Government informed the medical profession in February that the county council hospitals would take over the full responsibility of collecting patient fees, thereby eliminating all direct financial transactions between doctors and patients. The executive of the Swedish Medical Association, agreeing with the principles of the reform, advised its membership that the Association had no jurisdiction over the determination of the mode of remuneration of doctors.[121]

When the Government introduced its memorandum containing the Seven Crowns Reform in March 1969, the Association accepted what they understood as the principles of the reform. Their main objection was the rushed manner in which the Government introduced the proposal: "The proposals should be improved considerably and backed with documentations and data on the important issues."[122]

Bo Hjern then hosted a dinner for members of the Government during which he proposed that the medical profession negotiate the terms of its involvement through collective bargaining. During this and other closed meetings, he and the leaders of the Medical Association became aware of the Government's underlying intentions to create a salaried service. The executive decided, however, not to inform the membership, fearing that this would give opponents time to mount a protest. Instead they "allowed the reform to progress unhindered."[123]

This course of action reflected the deep division that existed within the Swedish medical profession at the time. Junior doctors resented how a few privileged consultants enjoyed great financial advantages over them, usually at their expense. Doctors with comfortable incomes found that long hours of work often made little difference in terms of real income. When the general membership realized the full extent of the reform during the October and November parliamentary debates, many doctors were well on the road to accepting the notion of salaries if they were "combined with regulation of working hours."[124]

The Seven Crowns Reform succeeded in equalizing the incomes of medical doctors who became salaried employees of the state. In return, doctors gained normal working hours, and the Swedish Medical Association took on a new role as a professional trade union. The Reform abolished the fee-for-service system of remuneration and established a new flat-rate user fee of 7 Crowns collected by the county councils. This excluded doctors from all direct financial transactions with patients. The nominal in-patient users-fees was doubled to discourage overuse of hospitalization where adequate ambulatory care was available.[125]

The decrease in patient contributions led to an annual out-of-pocket saving of 4 million Crowns. The corresponding increase in the cost of out-patient care to the county councils was 121 million Crowns.[126] Employer contributions on wages were increased from 2.6 to 2.9 percent to provide the additional finances required by the National Insurance Fund. This allowed the Government to eliminate entirely all employee contributions.

4. Public Health Service Act of 1981

In Sweden, the introduction of public financing for universal entitlement to health care occurred slowly. There were no major milestones transforming the system through a single radical piece of legislation. The evolving public system of hospitals, financed and run by the county councils, has remained the backbone of its health care system.

Swedes slowly realized the shortcomings of the social insurance system for the financing of ambulatory care. The reimbursement system of sickness insurance, doctors over-charging patients and the over-emphasis on the institutional care all created barriers to universal access. The Seven Crowns Reform, which created a salaried health service, attempted to correct these shortcomings by encouraging a more even distribution of primary care services.

The Public Health Service Act of 1981 obliged the county councils to provide a full range of health care services. It completed the health-related responsibilities of local authorities. Under the act, the county councils became responsible for general health care, public health services, hospital care, public dental care, care for the mentally retarded, family counseling and children's homes. The local municipalities became responsible for social welfare, housing, sanitation, environment and health protection and emergency and fire protection.

Today the county councils spend 75 percent of their budget on health care. Taxation revenues finance 60 percent of this outlay, while state grants-in-aid and direct charges account for an additional 15 percent each.[127] The municipalities have powers to levy their own taxes to finance their expenses.[128] Following further reforms in 1986, contributory social insurance was eliminated as one of the sources of financing for health care.[129]

Höjer envisaged the present primary health care system in 1948.[130] His supporters had waited with impatience: "To my joy, I find modern scholars studying Höjer's vision of how the health care system should evolve.[131] This completed a process that he had begun thirty-five years earlier, which aimed not only at equal health care for all, but good health for all as well."[132]

5. Entry into the European Union

Sweden joined the European Economic Community with Finland and Austria on January 1, 1995. Although this did not change the fundamental character of the Danish health system, the fiscal constraints on deficit funding under the Acquis, and accompanying requirements of freedom of movement of people, goods, services and financing opened up the Danish health service to completion in both the provision of services and the health labor market.[133]

6. Major Policy Updates in Sweden Since the 1980s

Since the latter part of the 1980s, the National Health Service in the Sweden has continued to evolve. Starting with what was originally a mixed insurance-based system and then fully publicly funded and publicly owned national health service post World War II, recent reforms have reintroduced more market based approaches to both funding and delivery of health care, but preserving its predominant public tax funded and public National Health Service character.[134]

As described above, by the late 1970s, the county councils had become responsible for most health care services in Sweden. Even the Karolinska Hospital in Stockholm and the Academic Hospital in Uppsala, which were previously under responsibility of the national government, were transferred to their respective county councils in the early 1980s. In 1985, they expanded their responsibility to include payment private practitioners. And finally, in 1998, became responsible for prescription drugs.

During the early 1990s, a new trend started with a transfer responsibility for additional services to municipalities, with the objective of integrating those services that needed coordinating between social and health care. In 1992, under the ÄDEL reform, responsibility for long-term inpatient and geriatric care was transferred from the county councils to the municipalities. Similarly, the Handicap Reform of 1994 and Psychiatric Care Reform of 1995 made the municipalities responsible for the physically disabled and those with serious mental illness.

During the 1990s, Sweden also embraced the "new public sector" management approaches that were first pioneered in New Zealand, with a focus on greater managerial accountability, market-based economic incentives and greater competition among providers, including a purchaser–provider split, diagnosis-related groups (DRGs) payment systems and increased choice for patients.[135] The corporatization of hospital management that was given prominence in the UK were originally piloted during the late 1980s in Gothenburg, Sweden.[136]

Ironically, having started the early experiments, Sweden did not fully embrace the market based reforms like the UK and New Zealand. Instead, most of the 1990s were preoccupied with administrative county council and municipality balance. Many returned to traditional planning and control mechanisms. For example, in 1999, the Region Skåne and the Västra Götaland Region were established by merging county councils. In recent years, discussion about such administrative realignments have dominated the reform discussion in Sweden.

Two exceptions were to allow new owners to operate pharmacies from 2009. And giving patients the choice to select their provider following an amendment to the Health and Medical Services Act in 2010, that made choice of primary care provider and freedom of to establish accredited private care providers by the local county councils mandatory. This formally abandoned the previous responsibility for a geographical population coverage requirements. These reforms essentially re-established the prevailing conditions before the "seven-crown reform" and the socialization of pharmacies in the early 1970s and there was a new focus on cutting waiting times and waiting lists. Patients that could not be treated within these time limits were allowed to go elsewhere for care within Finland and EU.

As in the other Scandinavian countries, the consensual system of government in Sweden, avoided the ideological swings that were observed since the 1980s in Australia, Canada, New Zealand and the UK. Prime Minister Stefan Löfven, who took office on October 3, 2014, leads a Social Democrat Coalition government. Having dominated Swedish politics for several decades, the Social Democrat party has allowed a continuation of a mix of administrative reforms and experimentation with market based approaches without any major radical reforms.

ENDNOTES

1. Sweden, Inrikesdepartementet (I), "Den oppna Lakarvarden i Riket: Utredning och forslag av Medieinalstyrelsen," *Statens Offentliga Utredningar*, 14 (Sweden: Iduns Tryckeriaktiebolag, 1948): 14, translated by U. Serner, "Swedish health legislation: Milestones in reorganization," in *The Shaping of the Swedish Health System*, by A. J. Heidenheimer and N. Elvender, eds. (London: Croom Helm, 1980): 101.
2. A. Gustafsson, *Local Government in Sweden*, Sweden Books (Stockholm: The Swedish Institute, 1983): 11.
3. Sweden, "The Instrument of Government Act," (Stockholm: Parliament, 1974): Art. 1.1.
4. Three years later, in 1866, a bicameral parliamentary system replaced the old parliamentary system of four estates: nobility, clergy, burghers and peasants. In 1871, the system became unicameral with the King acting as an official figurehead with no powers. See E. Lindstrom, *The Swedish Parliamentary System: How Responsibilities are Divided and Decisions are Made* (Stockholm: The Swedish Institute, 1983): 12.
5. G. Heckscher, *The Welfare State and Beyond: Success and Problems in Scandinavia* (London: Croom Helm, 1980): 23.
6. E. Borgenhammar, *Halsans Pris: En Hatsokontroll av Sjukvarden* (Stockholm: Studieforbundet Naringsliv och Samhalle, 1982): 14.
7. Their original function was to prevent the spread of venereal disease among soldiers. See *Borgenhammar, Halsans Pris*, p. 13
8. State pensions were especially attractive to the Medical Officers of Health. See G. Tornell, *Svenska Provinsiallakareforenings Historia 1906–1930* (Stockholm: Svenska Tryckcriektiebolaget, 1930); and H. Ito, "Health

insurance and medieval services in Sweden and Denmark 1850–1950," in *The Shaping of the Swedish Health System*, A. J. Heidenheimer and N. Elvander, eds. (London: Croom Helm, 1980): 63.

9. The population for 1900 is based on United Nations (UN), Statistics Office (SO), Department of Economic and Social Affairs (DESA), *Demographic Yearbook* 1962, 14th Edition (New York: UN, 1962): 280 and the area is based on J. Paxton, ed., *The Statesman's Year-Book: Statistical and Historical Annual of the States of the World for the Year 1986–1987*, 123rd Edition (London: MacMillan Press, 1986): 1132.
10. G. Lindeberg, *Den Svenska Sjukkasserorelsens Historia* (Lund: Carl Bloms Boktryckeri, 1949): 7.
11. *Ibid.*, p. 26.
12. Norway, *Social Insurance in Norway* (Stockholm: National Insurance Administration, 1984): 5
13. The Government appointed the Commission in 1885. See E. Tegendal, "Den Svenska sjukkasselagstiftningen 1891–1931," in *Den Svenska Sjukkasserorelsens Historia*, by G. Lindeberg, ed. (Lund: Carl Bloms Boktryckeri, 1949): 286.
14. E. Michanek, *Sukforsakring for Alla* (Stockholm: Tidens Forlag, 1953): 12.
15. Limited workmen's compensation was introduced in 1901. See Tegendal, "Sjukkasselagstiftningen 1891–1931," pp. 286–7.
16. R. Broberg, *Sa Formades Tryggheten: Socialforsakringens Historia 1946–1972* (Stockholm: Forsakringkasseforbundet, 1973): 12.
17. Hjalmar Branting, quoted by Michanek, *Sukforsakring*, p. 12.
18. Tegendal, "Sjukkasselagstiftningen 1891–1931," p. 315.
19. Tegendal, "Sjukkasselagstiftningen 1891–1931," pp. 310–13.
20. Up until 1930, benefits in kind comprised less than 3 percent of total benefits covered by the sickness funds. See Ito, "Health Insurance," p. 61.
21. Later, on January 1, 1938, the Board of Pensions assumed the administrative responsibility for the sickness funds and other social insurance programmes, except for unemployment insurance. See Tegendal, "Sjukkasselagstiftningen 1891–1931," p. 373, 1982.
22. The Accidents Insurance Law was passed in 1916. Cash support during incapacity due to short-term injuries would be paid through ordinary sickness insurance.
23. Tegendal, "Sjukkasselagstiftningen 1891–1931," p. 317.
24. *Ibid.*, p. 319; and Michanek, *Sukförsäkring*, pp. 13–14.
25. M. W. Childs, *Sweden: The Middle Way on Trial* (New Haven: Yale University Press, 1980): 15.

26. Tegendal, "Sjukkasselagstiftningen 1891–1931," p. 330; and Broberg, *Tryggheten*, p. 3.
27. The Sickness Fund Federation and its Chairman G. Lindeberg supported such an extension in sickness insurance. See Lindeberg, *Sjukkasserorelsens Historia*, pp. 218–31.
28. Tegendal, "Sjukkasselagstiftningen 1891–1931," p. 358.
29. Negotiations over the fee schedule and interference with the doctor-patient relationship, however, caused recurrent conflicts between the doctors and the sickness funds.
30. Personal communication with Professor O. Johansson, President of the Younger Doctors' Association from 1951–1960 and later Chairman of the Swedish Medical Association from 1966–1968. SYLF was created in 1921.
31. Lindeberg, *Sjukkasserorelsens Historia*, p. 257.
32. Before 1930, 65 percent of the sickness funds incurred deficits on a regular basis. See Ito, "Health Insurance," p. 65.
33. By the mid-1940s, only 30 percent of the population were members of a sickness fund. See Lindeberg, *Sjukkasserorelsens Historia*, p. 257. Personal communication with R. Broberg, former Director General of the Swedish National Social Insurance Board.
34. Branting and Hansson, both journalists, supplemented their incomes by acting as parliamentary correspondents for *The Daily News* during the early days. See A. L. Berkling, *Fran Fram till Folkhemmet: Per Albin Hansson som Tidningsman och Talare* (Falköping: Metodica Press, 1982): 23.
35. Childs, *Sweden 1980*, p. 19; and M.W. Childs, *Sweden: The Middle Way* (New Haven: Yale University Press, 1935).
36. The following name changes occurred in the Swedish political parties: the Conservative Party became the Moderate Party in 1969, the Liberal Party became the People's Party in 1934, the Agrarian Party became the Centre Party in 1958, the Communist Party became the Left Party Communists in 1963. The Christian Democrats appeared in 1964.
37. P. A. Hansson, "Sverige at Svenskarna," Valbroschyr [1926], quoted in A. L. Berkling, *Från Fram till Folkhemmet: Per Albin Hansson som Tidningsman och Talare* (Falköping: Metodica Press, 1982).
38. Childs, *Sweden 1980*, p. 16.
39. Wigforss was the Minister of Finance from 1932 to 1949. See Childs, *Sweden 1980*, p. 16.
40. E. Wigforss, *Frihet och Gemenskap: Essayer*, Socialistisk Bokklubb (Stockholm: Tidens Förslag, 1962): 52.

41. This was the Swedish forerunner of Beveridge's "From the Cradle to the Grave." See S. Hadenius, *Swedish Politics During the 20th Century* (Stockholm: The Swedish Institute, 1985): 41; and T. Erlander, *Tage Erlander 1901–1939* (Stockholm: Tidens Forlag, 1972): 273. On October 1, 1937, at Möller's request, Tage Erlander (later Prime Minister) joined the Department of Social Affairs to help him with this task. See Erlander, 1901–1939, p. 231.
42. Hadenius, *Swedish Politics*, p. 41.
43. Childs, *Sweden 1980*, p. 3.
44. B. Eriksson, who was Minister of Social Affairs in the early 1920s, later served as a County Governor.
45. Wigforss wanted to refuse Germany the right to send German troops through Sweden to Finland which had retained close ties to Sweden since its independence in 1909.
46. T. Erlander, *Tage Edander 1940-1949* (Stockholm: Tidens Förlag, 1973): 109.
47. Childs, *Sweden 1980*, p. 120.
48. A. J. Heidenhelmer, "The debate over 'surplus or shortage'," in *The Shaping of the Swedish Health System*, by A. J. Heidenheimer and N. Elvander, eds. (London: Croom Helm, 1980): 71.
49. A. J. Heidenheimer, "Conflict and compromises," in *The Shaping of the Swedish Health System*, by A. J. Heidenheimer and N. Elvander, eds. (London: Croom Helm, 1980): 121. At the time of the address, Dr. K. Evang was head of the Norwegian Socialist Doctors' Association (later Director General of the Norwegian Board of Health).
50. Sweden, Inrikesdepartementet (I), "Utredning och förslag ang, Lag om Allmäm Sjukförsakring," *Statens Offentliga Utredningar* 15 (Sweden: Iduns Tryckeriaktiebolag, 1944); and Sweden, Inrikesdepartementet (I), "Kostnadsberäknlngar ang, Lag om Allman Sjukförsakring," *Statens Offelltliga Utredningar* 16 (Sweden: Iduns Tryckeriaktiebolag, 1944).
51. Broberg, *Tryggheten*, p. 3.
52. Cash benefits excluded civil servants, pensioners, those already on social assistance and those with inherited wealth.
53. Broberg, *Tryggheten*, p. 4.
54. K. Persson was the Director General of the Board of Pension in 1944.
55. Broberg, *Tryggheten*, p. 34.
56. *Ibid.*, p. 39.
57. In 1945, there were only six articles on sickness insurance in the *Svenska Läkanidningen*, the journal published by the Swedish Medical Association, and in 1946, there were none. See Ito, "Health Insurance," p. 63.

58. S. Läkartidningen, "Lagen om Allmän Sjukförsälkring: Sveriges Lakeferbunds yttrande över sociälvardskommittëns betänkande," *Svenska Läkattidningen*, 40(1944), 2372. The voluntary insurance system had attained a membership of only 53 percent of the population by 1945.
59. Erlander, *1901–1939*, pp. 266–7.
60. G. Hedlund, a lawyer and farmer, led the Agrarian Party. See T. Erlander, *Tage Erlander 1949–1954* (Stockholm: Tidens Förlag, 1974): 267–72.
61. Sweden, Allmänna *Sjukförslikringen* No. 1 (Sweden: Svenska Sjukkasse-förbundet, 1947).
62. In 1962 a further reform created new economic, geographic and cultural units with populations of at least 8,000. By 1983 most of these municipalities had populations of at least 20,000.
63. Erlander, *1949–1954*, p. 287.
64. Childs, *Sweden 1980*, p. 43.
65. Dr. A. Höjer occupied the post as Director-General of the Swedish Board of Health between 1935 and 1952.
66. Serner, "Swedish health legislation," p. 101.
67. Sweden, I, "Den öppna lakarvarden," p. 14.
68. *Ibid.*, p. 316.
69. Sweden, I, "Den öppna lakarvarden."
70. Sweden, National Board of Health and Welfare (NBHW), *The Swedish Health Services in the 1990s* (Stockholm: National Board of Health and Welfare, 1985): 64–67.
71. Ito, "Health Insurance," p. 57.
72. *Ibid.*, p. 63.
73. Dr. D. Knutson, quoted by B. Hjern, "Commentary on part three," in *The Shaping of the Swedish Health System*, A. J. Heidenheimer and N. Elvander, eds. (London: Croom Helm, 1980): 174. Personal communication with Dr. Hjern, the present Director General of the Swedish Medical Association.
74. Borgenhammar, *Halsans Pris*, p. 15. The Socialist Doctors Federation was one of the few organizations to support Höjer's proposed reforms in 1948.
75. Höjer describing Knutson's reaction to their meeting in 1937. See A. Höjer, *En Läkares Väg* (Stockholm: Bonniers, 1976): 192. Translated by Heidenheimer, "Conflict and compromises," p. 122.
76. Heidenheimer, "Conflict and compromises," p. 121.
77. Sweden, Riksdag Propositionnen Nr. 569 of 19 June 1953, quoted in R. Broberg, I. Lindell and Y. Samuelsson, *Den Allmänna Sjukförsäkringen: RedgiJrelse för den År* 1955 *Genomförda Sjukförsäkringsreformen* (Stockholm: Norstedt & Söners Förlag, 1956): 13.
78. Erlander, *1949–1954*, p. 289.

79. Broberg, Lindell and Samuelsson, *Almänna Sjukförsäkringen*, p. 22.
80. General health care comprised only 15 percent of the expenditure of sickness funds by 1950. See Ito, "Health Insurance," p. 54.
81. Eligibility for cash benefits continued to be means-tested.
82. For recipients of old-age pensions the duration would be 90 days.
83. A review of the actual cost of the programme for 1955 was 800 million Crowns, very close to the original estimate.
84. E. Malrn, "En översikt över Sjukförsäkringenslagens huvudbestämmelsen," in *Föredrag I Sjukkassefrogor 1953–56*, by Svenska Sjukkasseferbundet, ed. (Stockholm: Svenska Sjukkasseforbundct, 1957): 9.
85. Broberg, Lindell and Samuelsson, *Almänna Sjukförsäkringen*, pp. 11–15.
86. Sweden, *Lag om Yrkesskadeförsäkring*, No. 243 (Stockholm: Svenska Sjukkasseförbundet, 1954).
87. Sweden, *Lag med Särskilda Bestämmelser om Frivillig Sjukpenningförsäkring* i *Allmän Sjukkassa*, No. 774 (Stockholm: Svenska Sjukkasseförbundet, 1954).
88. Sweden, *Lag om Moderskapshjälp*, No. 266 (Stockholm: Svenska Sjukkasseförbundet, 1954).
89. Sweden, *KF Angäende Kostnadsfria eller Prisnedsatta Lakemedel*, No. 519 (Stockholm: Svenska Sjukkasseförbundet, 1954).
90. Broberg, *Tryggheten*, pp. 49–52. R. Broberg was the first General Director.
91. Heidenheimer, "Conflict and compromises," p. 125. Personal communication with Dr. A. Engel.
92. His plan was based on the existing French regional system. See Borgenhammar, *Hälsans Pris*, p. 14. A similar proposal had been suggested by a Swedish Commission in 1930. A. G. W. Engel, "Planning and spontaneity in the development of the Swedish health system," Paper presented at the 1968 M. M. Davis Lecture at the Chicago Centre for Health Administration Studies, Graduate School of Business, University of Chicago, 1968, p. 6.
93. Sweden, Inrikesdepartementet (I), "Regionsiukvarden," Statens Offentliga Utredningar 26 (Sweden: Iduns Tryckeriaktiebolag, 1958): 15. It led to the Hospital Law of 1959.
94. Sweden, I, "Hälsovard och öppen sjukvärd."
95. Fridolf Thapper speaking about Dr. A. Engel. See F. Thapper, "The regional plan," in *Regional Hospital Planning*, by M. Tottie and B. Janzon, eds. (Stockholm: National Board of Health, 1967): 13.
96. A. Engel, "The Swedish regionalized hospital system," in *Regional Hospital Planning*, by M. Tottie and B. Janzon, eds. (Stockholm: National Board of Health, 1967): 14.

97. Engel, "Planning and spontaneity," p. 10.
98. *Ibid.*, p. 11.
99. They financed a significant part of the cost through autonomous taxation. Responsibility for psychiatric hospitals was transferred from the state to the county councils in 1967.
100. Dr. C. J. Ekströmer, Director-General of Swedish Hospital Services in 1846, quoted by Dr. A. Engel , "Planning and spontaneity," p. 1.
101. B. Rexed, "Public policy and medicine," in *The Swedish Health Services System: Lectures from the A. C. H.'s Twenty-Second Fellows Seminar Stockholm 1969*, by the American College of Hospital Administrators, eds. (Chicago: ACHA, 1969): 34. The Board of Health became part of the Board of Social Welfare in 1968.
102. Rexed, "Public policy and medicine," p. 217.
103. Borgenhammar, *Hälsans Pris*, pp. 14–15. Personal communication with Professor E. Borgenhammar, Economist and Professor of Health Administration.
104. Thapper, "Regional Plan," p. 10.
105. He was responsible for introducing a sales tax (later transformed into a value-added tax, VAT). This trend has continued until today when the Swedish VAT accounts for 25 percent of the central government income.
106. Hadenius, *Swedish Politics*, p. 93.
107. M. Carder and B. Klingeberg, "Towards a salaried medical profession: How 'Swedish' was the Seven Crowns Reform," in *The Shaping of the Swedish Health System*, by A. J. Heidenheimer and N. Elvander, eds. (London: Croom Helm, 1980): 148.
108. S. Aspling, "Forward," in *Regional Hospital Planning*, by M. Tottie and B. Janzen, eds. (Stockholm: National Board of Health, 1967): 9.
109. Such out-patient departments handled 40 percent of medical consultations in 1963.
110. Sweden, Inrikesdepartementet (I), "Sjukhus och öppna värd," Statens Offentliga Utredningar 21 (Sweden: Iduns Tryckeriaktiebolag, 1963): 165; and Carder and Klingeberg, "Salaried medical profession," p. 147.
111. Personal communication with Dr. B. Hjern, present Director General of the Swedish Medical Association.
112. Personal communication with Dr. Å. Lindgren.
113. B. Hjern, "The Swedish Medical Association and its role in Swedish health care," in *Scandinavian Health Care: Report of an Estes Park Conference*, by R. C. Bates, ed. (Englewood, Colorado: Estes Park Institute, 1983): 55.
114. Hjern, "Commentary," p. 1975. Personal communication with Dr. B. Hjern.

115. T. Erlander, *Tage Erlander 1955–1960* (Stockholm: Tidens Förlag, 1976): 256–62.
116. Hadenius, *Swedish Politics*, p. 125.
117. A. Myrdal, *Towards Equality: The Alva Myrdal Report to the Swedish Social Democratic Party* (Stockholm: Prisma, 1971): 24; and T. Erlander, *Tage Erlander 1960-talet* (Stockholm: Tidens Förlag, 1982): 218. Such wage equality *was* the terms of reference for the Low Income Commission that had just reported.
118. Hadenius, *Swedish Politics*, p. 126.
119. *Ibid.*, 128.
120. Carder and Klingeberg. "Salaried medical profession," p. 149.
121. *Ibid.*, p. 160, quoting the *Svenska Läkartidningen* 66(1969): 978.
122. Swedish Medical Association Brief to the Seven Crowns Reform Memorandum from the Ministry of Social Affairs, U 91/69, (20 April 1969): 17, Mimeograph. The idea of a salaried health service was far from new: Höjer proposed it in 1948, and the Royal Commission on Health Insurance debated its merits in 1963.
123. Carder and Klingeberg, "Salaried medical profession," p. 169.
124. Hjern, "Commentary," p. 175.
125. The Royal Commission on Insurance in 1967 had recommended the introduction of free health care with an abolition of all in-patient fees.
126. Patients contributed 7 Crowns, while the sickness funds contributed 31 crowns. Under the previous system, patients often contributed more than 7 Crowns, depending on what the doctors charged.
127. Figures based on data for 1981. See Gustaffson, *Local Government*, p. 110.
128. Sweden, "The Instrument of Government Act," Art. 1, p. 7.
129. Since 1986 the county councils no longer receive a contribution from the National Insurance Board toward the finance of health care.
130. Sweden, National Board of Health and Welfare (NBHW), *The Swedish Health Services in the 1980s* (Stockholm: National Swedish Board of Health and Welfare, 1976); Sweden, Ministry of Health and Social Affairs (MHSA), *Health in Sweden HS 90: Swedish Health Service in the 1990s* (Stockholm: Swedish Ministry of Health and Social Affairs, 1982); and Sweden, NBHW, *Health Services in the 1990s.*
131. Erlander, *1960-talet*, p. 275.
132. B. Westerholm, "The Swedish National Health Services: Goals, organization and problems," in *Scandinavian Health Care: Report of an Estes Park Conference*, by R. C. Bates, ed. (Englewood, Colorado: Estes Park Institute, 1983): 51.

133. The term acquis is also used to describe laws adopted under the Schengen Agreement, prior to its integration into the European Union legal order by the Treaty of Amsterdam, in which case one speaks of the Schengen acquis. The term acquis has been borrowed by the World Trade Organization Appellate Body, in the case Japan — Taxes on Alcoholic Beverages, to refer to the accumulation of General Agreement on Tariffs and Trade (GATT) and WTO law ("acquis gattien"), though this usage is not well established.
134. A. Anell, A. H. Glenngård, and S. Merkur, *Sweden: Health system review in Health Systems in Transition* 14(5)(2012):1–159. http://www.euro.who.int/__data/assets/pdf_file/0008/164096/e96455.pdf. Accessed July 25, 2017
135. G. Scott, L. McKenzie and J. Webster, "Maladjustments in the Corporatization Model: Hospital Reform in New Zealand, in *Innovations in Health Service Delivery*: *The Corporatization of Public Hospitals*, by A. S. Preker and A. Harding, eds. (2003, Washington, DC: World Bank). https://openknowledge.worldbank.org/handle/10986/15145. Accessed August 17, 2017; pp. 205–345.
136. C. Ham, "Betwixt and Between: Autonomization and Centralization of UK Hospitals, in *Innovations in Health Service Delivery*: *The Corporatization of Public Hospitals*, A. S. Preker and A. Harding, eds. (2003, Washington, DC: World Bank). https://openknowledge.worldbank.org/handle/10986/15145. Accessed August 17, 2017; pp. 265–297.

CHAPTER 10

FINLAND

Social legislation in our country has come a long way in many fields but still suffers from shortcomings [in health care] that are not worthy of a modern welfare state.[1]

Carl Olof Tallgren, 1962

A. HISTORICAL CONTEXT

1. Early Health Provisions

Ravaged by wars and civil strife, "Finns lived for centuries in the shadow of other nations."[2] The early organization of health care services reflected 800 years of Swedish and Russian domination which ended when Finland finally gained its full independence in the wake of the Russian civil war which followed the 1917 Bolshevik Revolution.[3] "Being Nordic is more than a matter of will to us Finns: it is an inseparable part of our history."[4]

During the early years of the nineteenth century, the Finnish Lutheran Church provided some outdoor relief to the poor. The communes assumed this responsibility when the administration of parishes and secular communes separated into two branches in 1836. From this stage onward, provision of medical care was seen as an "obligation of the society and their utilization as a natural right of the citizen."[5]

Institutional care followed the same course. Hospices for lepers and those suffering from infectious diseases date back to the fourteenth century, while asylums or Holy Spirit houses, under parish supervision, remained available for containment, isolation and social control of the undesirable. Later, as the running costs of the parish hospitals rose, the state assumed their financing. With the growth of local government, the communes slowly took over this task.[6]

Early forms of sickness insurance started with the trade guilds in the eighteenth century.[7] The Crafts Order Act of 1720 established the basic rules for these organizations: "If some master of a trade, not through his own fault, becomes poor or ill he should receive help from the 'Craft Box.'"[8] When a member regained his working capacity, he had to pay back what he received during the period of his illness.

The Royal Order on the Foundries Act of 1766 established the practice of "iron boxes" for foundry workers. Under the provisions of this act, blacksmiths who were unable to work for a week received a cash benefit from his employer and the foundry "benefit box,"[9] Later, Finlayson and Co., a cotton factory, established the first sickness fund in 1846. Under the plan, the employers offered medical treatment at work and paid a cash benefit to workers during illness.[10]

The provision of sickness funds were rudimentary during the nineteenth century. Since they were not under public supervision, their standards varied and their benefits were often inadequate. Furthermore, since there were few doctors, benefits aimed at economic support during illness, not medical treatment or health care.[11]

2. Finnish Medical Association

During the nineteenth and early twentieth centuries, most Finnish doctors worked in hospitals as public employees on a salary.[12] As in Sweden, fee-for-service private practice offered little financial security and was less honored than hospital work. The few doctors who kept such private practices worked in isolation with little collaboration from their colleagues.[13]

From the 1750s onwards, the local communes, which became responsible for the provision of health care, employed district doctors to carry out both public health and clinical duties.[14] These doctors supplemented their basic salary with fee-for-service for clinical work.[15] While the number of district doctors did grow slowly, the increase was too small to provide adequate health care for the Finnish population of 2,712,562 which, at the turn of the century, was scattered over 304,623 square kilometers of lake-covered northern regions.[16]

Finland's doctors created the Finnish Medical Association as a professional syndicate and political lobby in 1910.[17] "The founding of the Finnish Medical Association was based on the idea of a common professional association, which would take care of the physicians' economic interests and numerous obligations to society, such as expertise in developing health care and turning in reports to the legislator."[18]

Of the country's 523 doctors, 500 immediately joined the association. Meetings often focused on "health policy and the improvement of health care ... government bills and reformatory measures."[19] Through their Association, Finnish doctors began influencing policy through "quiet diplomacy," much as they did in the other Nordic countries.[20]

3. Public Involvement

In 1888, the Finnish Diet appointed Senator A. L. Gripenberg as Chairman of a Sickness Insurance Committee to examine the function, organization and shortcomings of the existing sickness funds. This ended the *laisser-faire* period during which the voluntary sickness funds had escaped public supervision and regulation.[21] The committee, which reported in 1892, recommended the creation of a Medical Supervisory Board to oversee the activities of the sickness funds.

Based on the recommendations of the committee, Parliament introduced a Workers' Benefit Fund Act in 1897, which offered specific groups of workers cash support during times of incapacity due to industrial accidents. Although the Law recognized the sickness funds, it did not call for means-tested compulsory sickness insurance as recommended by a minority report of the Gripenberg Committee.[22]

The Senate and Governor General assumed the responsibility of establishing "pensions and sickness funds for certain groups of workers... and ratifying their rules, directives and regulations."[23] The sickness funds which applied for official registration with the County Council Boards were eligible for small public subsidies.

Public subsidies were too low, however, to entice a significant number of the sickness funds to seek official registration. As a result, a new committee was created to examine the role of the sickness insurance system. This committee concurred with the minority opinion of the first committee, calling for a means-tested compulsory sickness insurance for all workers.[24] The Senate, feeling that such a program would be too expensive, ignored its recommendations.[25]

4. Multi-party Politics

In Finland, both social class structure and politics determine the popularity of political parties. The tradition of proportional representation, characteristic of all Nordic countries, has led to a multi-party system of five major parties: the Conservatives, Liberals, Agrarian/Centre, Social Democrat and Left Socialist/Communists.[26]

Among the Nordic countries, Denmark led the way in the evolution of political parties. Norway and Sweden were next with Finland was last. The Finnish working class felt less threatened by external Russian rulers than by threats of cultural assimilation from the Swedish-speaking upper class.[27] Finland was, therefore, the last Nordic country to shed the four-estate political structure of the Diet — the nobility, the clergy, the burghers and the peasants. Although enfranchisement and a unicameral representative assembly were finally introduced in 1906, the Russian Tsar, who dominated its Government and Senate, continued to maintain the power of veto.

During the latter part of the nineteenth century, the conservative bourgeois parties at the right, the liberal parties in the center and the Labor Party at the left appeared. The agrarian/center parties, Communist Party and socialist parties appeared later during the early twentieth century.[28]

Since many doctors in Finland at the turn of the twentieth century were Swedish, the medical profession was more sympathetic to Swedish-speaking, right-wing bourgeois conservative parties than Finnish-speaking counterparts. The Finnish-speaking division of the Medical Association supported the more complex central political parties.[29] Evolution in social policy and health care appeared only after further political reforms had taken place.

5. First Parliamentary Proposal

In 1917, the Government appointed a new Sickness Insurance Committee with Onni Hallstenin as Chairman. Its terms of reference were once again to review the existing sickness insurance system. Before the committee reported, however, a faction of the Finnish labor movement formed the "Red Guards" and unsuccessfully attempted a military *coup d'etat*.

The Finnish Social Democratic Party (SDP), founded on a belief in peaceful social and economic reform, rejected calls for armed uprising.[30] Their leader, Väinö Tanner, ousted the communists who continued to support violent insurrection. This action won him strong popular support, resulting in a gain by the Social Democratic Party of 80 of the 200 seats in the 1919 parliamentary elections.[31]

Despite this strong showing by the SDP, the Conservative Government rejected the Sickness Insurance Committee's proposal for a means-tested old-age pension and compulsory sickness insurance in 1921.[32] When Väinö Tanner formed a short-lived Social Democratic Party Minority Government in 1926, he was equally unsuccessful in introducing the legislation. The Conservatives, now in the Opposition, had convinced Parliament that the introduction of old-age pensions took precedence over sickness Insurance.[33]

In 1934, the Conservatives, who now formed another Coalition Government, appointed a Sickness Benefit Fund Committee with Councilor Niilo A. Mannion as Chairman. This committee recommended that old-age pensions should be introduced before sickness insurance. The National Pensions Act of 1937 followed these recommendations.[34] The committee also recommended that means-tested compulsory sickness insurance should cover urban workers, while a voluntary programs should be made available for the rest of the country.

After the defeat of the Social Democratic Party Minority Government during the 1920s, the party was forced to accept more gradual social reforms as partners in Conservative and Central Party dominated Governments. As a result, prior to World War II, the Finnish Social Democratic Party failed to pursue "the principles of [Keynesian] anti-depression fiscal policies, for which its Nordic sister parties would become so famous."[35]

B. LANDMARK LEGISLATIVE REFORMS

1. Governmental Proposal to Parliament of 1954

After World War II, the Social Democratic Party called for a major social reconstruction similar to that of the other Nordic countries: "There would be a planned economy, full employment, a general social insurance scheme, redistribution of income via tax reform, industrial democracy, wage bargaining on a basis of equality with the employers, etc."[36] Its political platform, passed at the Party Conference of 1945, stressed such welfare programs.[37]

The war had, however, left Finland in economic ruins. "Wars had sucked the country's economy dry, foreign trade had come to a standstill, and there were shortages of everything. Lapland lay in ruins and had to be reconstructed. The war indemnity which we were required to pay under the terms of the armistice agreement was so large that economists considered it impossible to accomplish."[38]

Niilo A. Mannion was once again appointed Chairman of a Sickness Insurance Committee whose terms of reference were to enquire into compulsory sickness insurance. Its majority report of 1949 proposed a gradual introduction of compulsory sickness insurance in larger factories, a recommendation similar to that made in the reports during the 1930s. The committee also felt that a more extensive program was impossible, given Finland's scarce economic resources and limited health care facilities.[39] Two minority reports were notable. First, Tyyne Leivo-Larsson proposed universal entitlement under compulsory plan.[40] At the same time, Mauri Ryömä proposed financing sickness insurance entirely through employer contributions and a state subsidy.[41]

The Social Democratic Party supported the recommendations of the minority reports, while the Conservative Party favored the recommendations of the majority report. A new balance of political power, however, had emerged in Parliament. The new Agrarian Coalition Government had banned the right-wing Fascist Party, while allowing the Finnish Communist

Party to re-enter the political arena. Finland had become acutely aware of its delicate position between the East and West.

As a result of these changes, the conservative policies which had dominated the political scene before the war were soon dropped. This allowed Finnish social reformers to become more aggressive in rebuilding the country's economic base and finally establishing a comprehensive social security infrastructure.

2. Sickness Insurance Committees

The seemingly endless proposals for expanding the Finnish sickness insurance system continued. On April 15, 1955, the Government appointed another Sickness Insurance Committee "to work on a proposal for a sickness insurance law, taking into account that the insurance must cover the whole population except possibly those which already benefit from some other type of social insurance."[42]

Tauno Jylhä, a department head at the National Pensions Board, became the Chairman of the committee. Erkki Mäkelä, Senior Government Secretary at the Ministry of Social Affairs, became its secretary. Other prominent members included Niilo Pesonen, Director of the National Medical Board; Erkki Jäämeri, representing the Finnish Medical Association; Erkki Canth, representing the Ministry of Finance; and Martti Vihma, representing the Ministry of Social Affairs. Many other organizations also had members on the committee: trade unions, employer's union, agricultural unions, benefit funds association, town and city associations, rural boroughs and professional unions.

When the committee reported in 1959, its majority report outlined the sorry state of collective financing of health care in Finland. Apart from state- and commune-owned hospitals, which received public financing at an early stage, collective provisions for both financial support and treatment during illness remained minimal. By 1957, after 60 years of debate, sickness insurance remained voluntary and restricted to industrial employment. The 254 sickness funds covered only 145,000 of the country's 4 million citizens.[43]

In comparison to social security programs throughout the world, the committee felt that the existing lack of comparable provisions in Finland was an embarrassment to the country.[44] To correct these shortcomings, the majority report recommended that the Government should introduce a Compulsory Sickness Insurance Law as soon as possible.

The committee prepared a draft legislation calling for universal entitlement under compulsory sickness insurance.[45] Benefits would include health care, maternity care, drugs, transportation to hospital, cash support during illness and maternity benefits. Every person in Finland, including those who for one reason or another did not contribute, would enjoy the benefits of the new insurance system. Workers' and employers' contributions as well as subsidies from the local communes and the state would jointly finance the program. Membership contributions would depend on taxable income. A new central insurance organization would oversee the program, while local authorities, using the private sickness funds as agents, would administer the benefits.

Several members of the committee, once again, submitted important minority reports. Uuno Hiironen and Niilo Jerninen, representing the trade unions, felt that the majority report had placed the financial burden of the program directly on workers: "In our view the insured's proportion is too high in comparison with that of other contributors."[46] They therefore recommended that state financing be increased.

Dr. Niilo Pesonen warned that despite the laudable recommendations of the committee, it would be difficult to implement the proposed sickness insurance program because "at the moment there are few doctors in comparison with the populations, and they [are] inequitably distributed throughout the country."[47]

The infrastructure of Finland's health care system had been slow to develop. In 1961, the country had 12 hospital beds per 10,000 population and one doctor per 1,516 people.[48] This compared poorly with Sweden's 15.1 beds per 10,000 and one doctor per 1,000 population.[49] In the northern regions, the dearth of health care services was even more pronounced.

Pesonen therefore recommended that the new Sickness Insurance Law initially be restricted to the workers and only later be extended to cover the whole population: "In my view the law should be put into operation in two stages, during the first stage it would cover only those in employment and in the second stage it would cover the whole population."[50] This would give the country time to expand its health care services and sickness insurance slowly in parallel.

Others, such as Mäkinen, also felt that the committee had gone too far in its recommendations for universal entitlement: "The committee has included less important support which will increase the total cost too rapidly for the total program to be put into force." He feared that this would "delay the realization of support given to those suffering from long-term illness."[51]

The Government appointed a Legislative Committee to prepare the Sickness Insurance Law on October 26, 1961. Erkki Mäkelä, who had submitted a minority report in 1959, became the Chairman of the Committee. Dr. Niilo Pesonen, who submitted a minority report, and Jaakkco Pajula, later Director General of the National Pensions Institution, were members of the committee.

The Legislative Committee reported on November 28, 1961.[52] Relying heavily on the majority report of the 1959 committee, the Legislative Committee warned that the program needed to be economically feasible: "None can be of a different opinion that sickness insurance is needed quickly.... When this question is examined, however, the society as a whole needs to be considered and how it would affect its economic development."[53] It nevertheless recommended that the new law "should include [the] whole population."[54]

The committee also reminded the Government that social expenditures were taking up an increasing proportion of the country's GDP. It therefore recommended that the sickness insurance should be introduced gradually and that the proposed law should apply primarily to ambulatory care, since institutional care was already financed by the state and local governments. The committee concluded by warning the Government against overloading existing services which might compromise treatment of the seriously ill.[55]

3. Social and Political Transformation

Several new circumstances finally broke the vicious circle of aborted attempts to expand coverage under sickness insurance from the 1920s to 1950s. First, Finland transformed from an agricultural to an industrial community during the late 1950s and early 1960s.[56] People who moved into the cities could no longer rely on the security of the land and family networks during times of unemployment and illness. The social hardships and needs created by this industrialization were similar to those experienced by other countries during the nineteenth and early twentieth centuries.

Second, despite the absence of a national health care system during the 1950s, social legislators had begun to expand health care facilities in a piecemeal fashion.[57] Within a few years, the public sector built 19,000 new general hospital beds and 11,000 mental hospital beds. Three new medical school appeared, and educational grants encouraged the training of doctors abroad.[58] These events countered some of the fears expressed by Dr. Niilo Pesonen in his minority report of 1959.

Third, although the public sector had financed hospitals since the nineteenth century, treatment by doctors and ambulatory care were still outside the means of most people.[59] The wealth generated through increased industrialization and completion of the repayment of war-time debts allowed the Finnish economy to improve. As resources became more visible, there was increasing political pressure to bring health care services within the reach of the ordinary person.

Finally, as a result of weak Coalition Governments and internal power struggles within the political parties during the 1950s, the bureaucracy of the administrative branches of the Government controlled much of Finnish policy-making. To influence this bureaucratic process, political parties had tried to be represented on administrative boards and committees of inquiry. Even parliamentary committees now had such party representation: "Institutions and organizations which had traditionally remained outside the domain of party politics were also affected by this development."[60] The 1959 majority and minority committee reports reflected this trend.

The multi-party system had led to a process of convergence and revisionism. The series of unstable and short-lived Coalition Governments that had existed up until the 1960s, had polarized the five major parties into two camps: the center coalition (Centre, Liberal and Swedish People's Parties) and the left (Social Democratic Party and Finnish People's Democratic League — communist offspring).

Only policies that were acceptable to all the parties in a Coalition Government could be implemented. Lack of unanimous support for a given policy within a political party often led to internal strife. Fragile coalitions, therefore, avoided introducing radical social reforms for fear not only of provoking a conflict which would lead to a defeat of the Government but also a breakup of parties themselves. Although this made achieving radical reforms difficult to impossible, it engendered a "middle-of-the-road" political process similar to that which had evolved in Sweden.

The Social Democratic Party, although a firm supporter of an expanded social security system, had on repeated occasions compromised its principles in exchange for remaining a partner in Coalition Governments. Unlike its Scandinavian counterparts, the Finnish Social Democratic Party had to compete with a strong Communist Party. Anti-communist sentiments engendered by the Cold War were especially pronounced in Finland. This complicated a reconciliation among the left-wing political parties and forced the Social Democratic Party into a close alliance with the Agrarian Party (later Center). With the right holding a majority in Parliament and the Agrarian Party holding balance of power in the Government, the range of movement for the Social Democratic Party was restricted.[61]

The subordinate position of the Social Democratic Party, moreover, excluded it from important decision-making. In 1952, the party finally dropped its emphasis on class conflict, replacing it with a new "Principles Program." This program followed the guidelines of the 1951 Socialist International Program which sought a planned economy and opposed communism. The adoption of the compromise stance led to a split between the Parliamentary representatives of the Social Democratic Party and the non-elected trade unionists who supported more radical reforms.

When Tanner won the election as Party Chairman in 1957, the faction headed by the previous Party Chairman, Emil Skog, walked out in protest. The result was a complete breakdown in party unity. In defiance of the party leadership, the "Skogite" minority proposed its own candidates to become members of the Agrarian-led Government of V. J. Sukselainen in 1957. The expulsion of the "Skogites" led to a near total disintegration of the Social Democratic Party.[62]

The Agrarian Party, which dominated the Coalition Governments following the war, was also experiencing internal discord. Although the party consolidated its power in 1950 when Urho Kekkonen became Prime Minister (later President), this did not prevent it from suffering the political repercussions of the social upheaval of industrialization. It had previously represented the rural center in Finnish politics. It stood for "a mixed economy, small and medium-scale industry, intensive regional policies, decentralization, promotion of the rural way of life and an anti-bureaucratic, humane environment."[63] As Finland industrialized and urbanized during the 1960s, the younger generation which moved from the country into the cities voted for other parties.[64]

In 1962, to adapt to the realities of the times, the Agrarian Party moved away from its previous emphasis on agrarianism toward a more central platform.[65] At the Party Conference of 1965, it changed its name to the Centre Party. Although this secured some support from the political center in urban areas, the change also estranged the party's traditional rural constituencies.

President Kekkonen, nevertheless, became a strong national figurehead who believed that cooperation among the political parties was crucial for Finnish society. He encouraged the partners of Coalition Governments to cooperate with each other in an attempt to increase their period in office. He also managed to improve Finland's relations sufficiently with the Soviet Union: "Thus our geographical location makes it essential for us to arrange our relations with our neighbours in a satisfactory manner."[66] Kekkonen shared this feeling with his predecessor, President J. K. Paasikivi: "The most important thing for Finland is and will always be the preservation of good relations with Russia. Geography and history dictate that so it must be."[67]

All these circumstances broke the long deadlock caused by political instability that had prevented previous Governments from introducing significant social reforms necessary to public financing of health care.

4. Sickness Insurance Act of 1963

On March 6, 1962, Carl Olof Tallgren set the legislative machinery in motion in Parliament: "Social legislation in our country has come a long way in many fields but still suffers from shortcomings that are not worthy of a modern welfare state."[68] He described how Governments since 1927 had unsuccessfully presented repeated proposals for improved sickness insurance.

During the same debate, the Government insisted that Finland's social security system had evolved into a near comprehensive system, comparable with those found in other Western developed nations. Others supported this opinion: "Particularly as a result of developments over the past 20 years, Finnish social security is of a standard comparable to that of the other industrialized countries of Europe."[69]

The Government, however, conceded that despite general improvements in other areas of social insurance, sickness insurance had lagged behind; the voluntary sickness funds offered inadequate protection for those who needed help the most. The explosive increase in the cost of institutional care during the late 1950s and early 1960s was of added concern to the Government: "The introduction of sickness insurance is, therefore, of the most immediate importance to us, and the most pressing socio-political task."[70]

Kyllikki Pohjala, the Minister of Social Affairs, had the Secretary-General of the Ministry, Aarne Tarasti, initiate negotiations with the Finnish Medical Association, the trade unions and other interest groups. Public opinion was indirectly reflected through extensive coverage in the press.[71] "The establishment of the [Sickness Insurance] scheme in 1964, followed a typical Finnish pattern, in which a social reform, on the basis of prior political negotiations, was considered necessary and a parliamentary committee was formed for the preparation of the draft legislation."[72]

As a result, by the time Pohjala presented the Sickness Insurance Bill to Parliament on December 9, 1962, negotiations were well on the road to securing full support for the reform, despite compromises along the way. The Government notably had little difficulty obtaining the collaboration from the medical profession. "The Finnish Medical Association is delighted about the recent action for sickness insurance. General sickness insurance which covers the whole population will greatly increase the possibilities for health care for the whole population, but particularly for the poorest members of the society who live in the countryside."[73]

The medical profession regarded the proposals for out-patient care as important because "being sick at home is so expensive that people chose hospital care to avoid such treatment even when it was possible."[74] Furthermore, they recommended that the new sickness insurance program should support prevention and rehabilitation: "Doctors in Finland are ready to give their assistance in planning a good sickness benefit system"[75]

The doctors, however, did object to several of the specific issues raised by the proposed legislation. Fearing abuses, they felt that it was important to start the new system in stages, allowing for a simultaneous growth in the health care system and the training of new doctors. They also supported a continuation of the sickness funds which they felt would allow them to carry on in private practice.[76]

The universal compulsory Sickness Insurance Act was passed in Parliament on July 4, 1963, and would be implemented on April 1, 1964: "Every person resident in Finland [would] be insured against sickness under this Act."[77] Persons between the ages of 16 and 65 years were eligible for the specified cash benefits during illness or incapacity due to maternity, based on their previous income.[78]

The new program offered benefits in cash, not kind: "An insured person shall be entitled on the grounds of sickness to compensation for expenses on necessary health care to a daily allowance on account of incapacity for work due to sickness and on the grounds of pregnancy and confinement."[79] Such reimbursable health care included treatment from doctors, laboratory investigations, radiology exams, drugs, dental treatment and travel expenses during illness.[80]

The program would reimburse 60 percent of doctors' fees based on an established fee-schedule.[81] A similar fee-schedule would likewise determine the rate of reimbursement for other services that were prescribed by doctors.[82] This "60 percent solution" was the result of the political compromises that had taken place during the process of negotiations.[83]

The program divided the country into sickness insurance administrative districts and areas. Each district would have a board of five members who were familiar with the insured person's conditions, consisting of the Chairman appointed by the National Pensions Institution, a doctor appointed by the county and three others, at least one of which had to be a woman. The National Pensions Institution would "supervise the determination, the assessment, the collection and the rendering of accounts of the insured persons' sickness contributions."[84]

Workers and employers as well as a state subsidy would finance the program. All insured persons would pay a sickness insurance contribution based on income. Employers would be responsible for submitting their employees' contributions.[85] The same rule applied to the self-employed. Those receiving national pensions or who did not pay taxes for lack of an income, would make no contributions but would still benefit from the program.[86]

The state would cover any deficit incurred through the program through general revenues, therefore, guaranteeing the solvency of the sickness funds.[87] The estimated income from all sources was 7.9 billion Marks from the insured, 7.9 billion Marks from employers and 3.9 billion Marks from the state.[88]

The cost of the resulting sickness insurance program compared favorably with the estimated costs, "There were some 'experts' who believed … it would lead to escalating cost of health care but no such phenomenon was found."[89] The reform succeeded in stimulating private practice in the urban setting; its shortcomings in the rural regions and the erosion in coverage under the reimbursement system soon became apparent.

C. CONTINUED POLICY REFORM PROCESS

Several interrelated circumstances prevented universal entitlement under sickness insurance from providing truly universal health care. As in Sweden, there was an overemphasis on an unevenly distributed institutional sector; the growth of private practices was mainly in urban areas; and medical doctors in the primary care sector refused to respect the established fee schedules. Instead, the Public Health Act of 1972, which established a network of multi-disciplinary health centers with salaried doctors, paved the way for true universal entitlement in Finland, where the social insurance model had failed.

1. Beyond Social Insurance

To examine and evaluate the successes and failures of the new Sickness Insurance Act, the Social Insurance Institution established a Research Institute for Social Security in 1964.[90] The legislators who formulated the Sickness Insurance Law of 1963 sought to advance two major social reforms: compensate for economic losses during illness and increase the use of ambulatory health services.[91] Following a review of the outcome of the reform, the Institute concluded the following: "The Scheme contributes to social security through economic means only, [that is], by lowering the price for health services and by compensating for the loss of income. The scheme does not directly affect the supply of health services and their distribution over various population groups."[92]

A nationwide survey showed that the gap between stated needs and care obtained had narrowed, with only a small increase in general utilization following introduction of the 1963 Sickness Insurance Law: "However, the results suggest that financial arrangements, [that is], health insurance, must be accompanied by other measures (in Finland an increase in the supply of ambulatory health services) if the objectives of health policy are to be obtained on a more satisfactory scale."[93]

The first policy objective of the Social Insurance Law was to compensate people for their direct financial losses because of illness. Such financial barriers were partially removed by the new sickness insurance: "The purpose of social insurance is to protect the population against loss of income in the event of sickness, invalidity, old age, the death of the family provider, maternity and unemployment. It also aims at alleviating the burden of medical expenses incurred as a result of sickness."[94]

The program, however, failed to equalize the burden of expense between the sick and healthy, and between the rich and poor: "Since the supply of physician services in ambulatory care did not increase markedly between 1964 and 1968, the impact of sickness insurance could only mean a redistribution of the services among the population groups. After this redistribution, acutely ill respondents in the lower-income categories visited a physician more often than previously, whereas older chronically ill persons decreased their use."[95]

The second policy objective of the Sickness Insurance Law was to increase the use of ambulatory health services by making such services more available to the public, thereby making institutional services less important. Although the 1963 Sickness Insurance Law represented "the most important measure in Finnish health policy in the 1960s," it failed to affect the geographic distribution of health care resources.[96] "It became clear … that the use of health services was decisively dependent on the supply of health services."[97]

From 1960 to 1967, Finland had a 17 percent growth in health care expenditures. The main reason for this growth was the cost of the hospital sector. The institutional sector comprised 85 percent of total cost of health care and was financed through the state and local communes, not sickness insurance. Increases in hospital construction which had occurred during the 1950s was largely responsible for this trend.[98] The original decision to postpone the introduction of sickness insurance for ambulatory care in favor of increased public expenditure on institutional care made it difficult for the former to catch up even when financing became available through the new program.[99]

Finally, the reimbursement principle of paying for services stimulated private out-patient care: "It was argued that the development of out-patient care would reduce the use of hospital services and that in fact the increased costs of out-patient care could be covered by savings in hospital expenditure."[100] In practice, this failed to occur, and institutional care continued to increase. Moreover, the real level of reimbursement dropped as doctors charged above the official fee-schedule on which the reimbursements were based.

The Sickness Insurance Law, therefore, eliminated only some of the financial hardship associated with illness. The cost of medical treatment was not the only expense for those unable to lead productive lives because of chronic illnesses. Uneven geographic distribution of resources among subgroups of the population remained a problem.[101] "In 1968, an average of six families out of 100 had been obliged to finance some of their sickness expenses from loans or monetary aid from relatives or social welfare authorities."[102]

When the socialists gained a majority in Parliament during the mid- to late-1960s, the shortcomings of the sickness insurance system became politically intolerable: "As the SDP and the labour movement began to resolve their internal conflicts and to rise to a dominant position in the new industrial society, the Centre Party found itself increasingly on the defensive and hard-pressed to develop a program in tune with the rapid changes Finnish society was undergoing."[103]

2. Public Health Act of 1972

Under the leadership of Prime Minister Rafael Paasio, the Social Democratic Party overcame its disarray and internal strife, improving both its relations with President Kekkonen and the Soviet Union. A new era in Finnish politics began in 1966 with the election of a left-wing majority to Parliament.[104] The Sickness Insurance Law became a clear target for reform.

The new socialist-dominated Coalition Cabinet, called the "Popular Front," included the Social Democratic Party, the People's Democratic League (Communists), the Social Democratic League (Social Democratic Party splinter group) and the Centre Party (Former Agrarians). Rafael Paasio was Prime Minister from 1966 to 1968. Mauno Koivisto, who succeeded him from 1968 to 1970, later became President.

Finland's new political stability and economic prosperity led the Social Democratic Party to initiate several overdue social reforms. The expansion of health care, introduction of a comprehensive education system and guarantee of employment security became priority issues: "The reforms in the educational and health care systems were introduced, however, only after overcoming resistance from a majority of teachers and medical doctors who have traditionally identified with the political Right."[105]

The work of the two earlier sickness insurance committees had already paved the way for the health care reforms. On October 11, 1960, the Ministry of Social Affairs appointed Dr. Niilo Pesonen as Chairman of a committee on public health. The terms of reference of the committee, which reported on October 5, 1965, were "to examine the possibility of improving the effectiveness of public health services," within the context existing legislation and regulations.[106]

Later, on January 18, 1967, the Ministry of Social Affairs appointed O. Blomqvist as Chairman of another Committee on Public Health. The terms of reference of this second committee were "to study the [previous] 1965 report compiled by the Public Health Committee ... with the aim to ... recommend ways to introduce the proposal ..., to put forward its own proposal ..., [and] to examine the basis for a new Public Health and Hospital network."[107] Its report of May 21, 1969, formed the basis for the Public Health Act of 1972.[108]

Both committees emphasized the failings of the Sickness Insurance Law in meeting growing manpower shortages, and expressed a loss of confidence in the capacity of the institutional sector as the basis for solving all health care problems. The committee recommended the establishment of a new health system to serve the whole population with a network of publicly financed health centers. Such centers would offer general practitioner services, public health nurses, dentists, physiotherapists, dieticians, psychologists and social workers.

The team of public health nurses, midwives and communal doctors aimed to "strengthen primary health care services, and to shift the point of gravity from hospital-oriented secondary and tertiary health care into ambulatory services."[109] Local governments would be responsible for administering the new system, reflecting the Nordic countries' tradition for local self-government: "The responsibility of the local health care in the public sector is based on the responsibility of local authorities to organize the delivery of services."[110]

On October 23, 1971, the Minister of Social Affairs and Health, Pekka Kuusi, introduced a Public Health Bill. He relied heavily on the work of Aarne Tarasti, the Secretary-General of the Ministry (1964) in preparing the new legislation.[111] The reform finally passed into law on January 28, 1972, under a new Minister, Alli Lahtinen, following extensive debates and conflicts with the Finnish Medical Association.[112]

"[What is meant] by primary care is ... health care directed at the individual and his or her environment, and the health care of the individual as well as activities associated with these and having the object of maintaining and promoting the state of health of the population."[113] The new law hoped to improve the coordination between the institutional sector and primary care sectors through joint five-year resource allocation and strategic planning cycles.[114] "The National Board of Health shall draw up each year a national plan for the arrangement for the following five calendar years of the primary care referred to in this Act."[115]

The communes became responsible for both the financing and administration of the new program, providing the following services: health education including family planning, health care supervised by a doctor, transport, dental treatment and school health.[116] "The commune shall have a health center for the functions referred to above."[117] Such health centers, depending on their size, included hospital beds. A medical doctor determined the level of treatment needed at the health centers and decided which patients to refer to larger centers for more advanced treatment.

The communes, in turn, depended on local taxation powers, including income tax and state grants, to finance the services which they offered. State grants ranging from 39 to 70 percent of the total cost of the program supplemented the communes' finances.[118] Only curative treatment would have a user-fee, while "services devolving [from] the commune and referred to above ... shall be free of charge to their consumers."[119]

Unlike the Seven Crowns Reform in Sweden, doctors in Finland who participated in the Public Health Act of 1972 were still allowed to maintain private offices. The National Pensions Institution continued to reimburse 60 percent of doctors' fees as established in 1963. Any monies collected directly from a patient living in a commune or through the Sickness Insurance Act were, however, deducted from the amount that the commune could use in the calculations for state subsidies. This gave the communes a powerful incentive to establish effective health centers.[120]

To prevent abuse and control costs, the state demanded the right to approve the plans for all new health centers before offering financing through the public sector. Only costs arising out of activities carried out by the health centers were eligible for subsidies.[121] The popularity of the health centers allowed them to become a successful alternative to the private sector.[122] Demand for services unfortunately increased more rapidly than anticipated: "This led to queuing in the public sector and presumably also to underutilization of resources in the private sector."[123]

The estimated cost of the previous system for the year 1972 was 170 million Marks. The estimated increase in state expenditure was 62 million Marks.[124] Eliminating direct charges to patients cost the state an additional 25–30 million Marks. The reformers hoped, however, to make savings through a reduced need for curative services.[125]

Even the Public Health Act of 1972, therefore, did not solve all the problems in the Finnish health care system since it led to a skewed growth in health care services at the expense of the social services. This hampered the development of services for the elderly, chronic care patients and those with physical problems stemming from social maladjustment such as alcoholics.[126] These imbalances led to a call for further reforms during the 1980s.

3. Finnish "Health for All" of the 1970s

Through the construction of health centers, out-patient care expanded rapidly during the 1970s. By the mid-1970s, the use of the ambulatory sector had increased, while that of the hospital sector decreased.[127] The personnel employed in health centers doubled, and there was less disparity among population subgroups groups.[128] The national sickness legislation of 1963 had aimed to alleviate the financial burden of illness. The Public Health Act of 1972 tried to improve coordination of such health care and to promote regional equalization.[129]

To complete the process of public sector financing for universal entitlement to health care, Finland has gone one step beyond that of most other countries by fully embracing the World Health Organization's "Health for all by the year 2000." Through this program, Finland has tried to shift the emphasis from secondary and tertiary hospital care to primary care:[130] "Exchange of information and experience, especially in the World Health Organization, is particularly important for a small country like Finland."[131]

The basic aim of Finnish health policy today is to promote both the health and welfare of its citizens:

- Adding years to life: This means that premature death rates will be reduced and the mean life expectancy thus increased.
- Adding health to life: This means that, in the future, people will have more healthy and active years. People will have fewer illnesses and accidents than before.
- Adding life to years: This means promotion of health so that as many people as possible will feel healthy in every way throughout their lives, will manage their everyday activities well and will experience their life as rich and varied.

Finland, which views itself as a developing country, continues to emphasize the importance of primary care.[132] "Health can only be attained if the basic needs of life are satisfied."[133] Since the activities of the individual determine his lifestyle, the program encourages active consumer participation. To achieve the above goals, the country has continued to set aside an increase in funds for programs in the social sector.[134] It has pledged to double the commitment of public financing in this area in the coming years.

To achieve its goals within affordable limits, Finland's health policies also attempt to focus its attention on the target groups needing medical attention the most: "Primary attention must be given to the needs of underprivileged individuals and population groups and to equality among citizens so that financial considerations do not prevent appropriate use of health services."[135] Today, the country claims to have achieved many of these objectives. It uses fewer financial resources than most other industrialized countries, yet has managed to increase life expectancy and quality of treatment more rapidly than most.

4. Entry into the European Union

Finland joined the European Economic Community with Sweden and Austria on January 1, 1995. Although this did not change the fundamental character of the Finnish health system, the fiscal constraints on deficit funding under the Acquis, and accompanying requirements of freedom of movement of people, goods, services and financing opened up the Finnish health service to completion in both the provision of services and the health labor market.[136]

5. Major Policy Updates in Finland Since the 1980s

Since the 1980s, the National Health Service in the Finland has continued to evolve. Starting with what was originally a mixed insurance-based system and then fully publicly funded and publicly owned national health service post World War II, recent reforms have reintroduced more market based approaches to both funding and delivery of health care, but preserving its predominant public tax funded and public National Health Service character. [137]

The Primary Health Care Act of 1972, discussed above, led to a major expansion in both health centers and staff during the 1980s and early 1990s. Dental care was also added during this period. For about 10 years, a small out-of-pocket user fee was introduced for curative services

(services not focused on health promotion and prevention). Later during the recession during the 1990s, the level of the user-fees were increased leading to extensive debate and protest.

Following introduction of the Occupational Health Care Act in 1979, all employers had to provide occupational health services to their employees, with special attention to preventive measures and eventually also curative health services.

By the mid-1980s, there was an effort to improve coordination between social and health care at both local and national levels. There was also an effort to address regional differences in both the supply and quality of services. Municipalities were given the option to offer a "personal doctor", by assigning families to a doctor at a specific health center. Mental health care shifted towards outpatient care, with a reduction in the number psychiatric hospital beds.

In 1991, the Specialized Medical Care Act, created multi-purpose hospital districts, owned and operated by federations of municipalities. This led to an integration of general hospitals, psychiatric hospitals and tuberculosis hospitals, which previously had been fragmented. Every municipality was required to be a member of one of the hospital districts. The objective was to provide economic incentives for municipalities to improve the efficiency of services.

Through these reforms in the 1990s, Finland also embraced the "new public sector" management approaches that were first pioneered in New Zealand, with a focus on greater managerial accountability, market-based economic incentives and greater competition among providers, including a purchaser–provider split, diagnosis-related groups (DRGs) payment systems and increased choice for patients.[138]

These reforms led to a dismantling of the historical role of the National Board of Health in directly administering health and social welfare services. New state agencies and institutions were set up, subordinate to the Ministry and Social Affairs and Health, to oversee pharmaceutical products, quality of care and research and development to promote health and social care planning. The reforms were also accompanied by numerous cuts in resources and staff layoffs, with later shortages emerging.

In 2001, the Government initiated "the National Project to Ensure the Future of Health Care" to address some of problems with access, waiting times, waiting lists, staff shortages and other deteriorations that occurred following the budget and resource cuts of the 1990s. The new focus was on cutting waiting times and waiting lists. Patients that could not be treated within these time limits were allowed to go elsewhere for care within Finland and EU.

As in the Scandinavian countries, the consensual system of government in Finland, avoided the ideological swings that were observed since the 1980s in Australia, Canada, New Zealand and the UK. Prime Minister Lars Løkke Rasmussen, who took office on May 29, 2015, leads the Center Party in a center-right coalition government. So far his government has followed previous trends of slow incremental improvements in access and quality of care.

ENDNOTES

1. Finland, "Yleistä sairausvakuutusta koskevan esitykdsen antamisesta," *Valtiopäivät Liitteet*, IX-XII A. Toiv. al. No 678 (Helsinki: Government of Finland, 1867).
2. Finnish Medical Association, *Finnish Medical Association and Medical Profession in Finland, Monograph* (Helsinki: Finnish Medical Association, 1986): 3.
3. Although Finland became an autonomous Grand Duchy under the Russian Empire in 1809, Finnish did not become the official language until towards the end of the nineteenth century.
4. U. Kekkonen, *A President's View* (London: Heinemann, 1982): 84.
5. Finland, National Board of Health (NBH), Department of Planning and Evaluation (DPE), "The health services system of Finland: Description," *Memorandum* (Helsinki: NBH, DPE, 1972): Sec. 1.1.
6. Unlike in other Nordic countries, this did not occur until the early 1950s. See E. Kalimo, "The relationship between trends in health expenditure and the type of organization of health care: National Monograph of Finland," *Research Institute for Social Security Publication* M:31 (Helsinki: Social Insurance Institution, 1979): 4.
7. Finland, "Sairausvakuutuskomitean mietintö," *Valtioneuvostolle*, by Helle Satälä, trans. (Helsinki: 15 April 1959): 7.
8. From the Crafts Order Act quoted in Finland, "Sairausvakuutuskomitean 1959," p. 7.

9. The foundry benefit funds ceased to exist in 1854. In 1868, Parliament abolished the other trade guilds, replacing them with workers' and craftsmen's funds. See Finland, "Sairausvakuutuskomitean 1959," p. 7.
10. Employers also supplied the personnel for the secretariat of the sickness funds. See Finland, "Sairausvakuutuskomitean 1959," p. 7.
11. The first hospital with nine beds was established in Turku in 1759. See Finland, "Sairausvakuutuskomitean 1959," p. 8.
12. The first Finnish Collegium Medicum was similar to its counterpart in Stockholm, and the first Professor in the Faculty of Medicine at the University of Turku was Swedish.
13. The wealthy upper class used foreign doctors for their medical needs. See Finland, "Sairausvakuutuskomitean 1959," p. 3.
14. The first district doctor post was established in 1749.
15. Kalimo, "Trends in health expenditure," p. 4.
16. The population for 1900 is based on United Nations (UN), Statistics Office (SO), Department of Economic and Social Affairs (DESA), *Demographic Yearbook 1962*, 14th Edition (New York: UN, 1962): 277 and the area is based on J. Paxton, ed., *The Statesman's Year-Book: Statistical and Historical Annual of the Stales of the World for the Year 1986–1987*, 123rd Edition (London: MacMillan Press, 1986): 464.
17. Swedish doctors had earlier established a Finnish Medical Society in 1835 whose members were mainly Swedish. Finnish-speaking doctors later established the Finnish Medical Society Duodecim to promote their own language.
18. Finnish Medical Association, "Medical Profession," p. 5.
19. *Ibid.*, p. 6.
20. The number of communal doctors never rose beyond 1,000. See Finnish Medical Association, "Medical Profession," p. 6.
21. Finland, "Sairausvakuutuskomitean 1959," p. 8.
22. J. Pajula and E. Kalimo, "Social security in Finland," *International Social Security Review* 32(1979): 161.
23. A Senate directive of 1892 quoted in Finland, "Sairausvakuutuskomitean 1959," p. 8.
24. A. Ramsayn was appointed its Chairman.
25. Finland, "Sairausvakuutuskomitean 1959," p. 9.
26. J. Mylly, "The emergence of the Finnish multi-party system: A comparison with developments in Scandinavia, 1870–1920," in *Political Parties in Finland: Essays in History and Politics*, by J. Mylly and R. M. Berry, eds. Series C:21 (Turku: University of Turku, 1984): 9.

27. *Ibid.*, p. 13.
28. *Ibid.*, p. 10.
29. The Finnish Party split into the Young Finnish Party (later Liberal Party) which joined the Centre Party during the 1980s) and the Old Finnish Party (later Conservative Party). The Agrarian Party became a Centre Party, while the Finnish Labour Party split into a Social Democratic Party and a Communist Party.
30. The Finnish Labour Party, formed in 1899, changed its name to the Social Democratic Party in 1903. See T. Paavonen, "The Finnish Social Democratic Party since 1918," in *Political Parties in Finland: Essays in History and Politics*, by J. Mylly and R. M. Berry, eds., Series C:21 (Turku: University of Turku, 1984): 137; and Mylly, "Finnish multi-party system," p. 17.
31. The Conservatives wanted to create a constitutional monarchy while the centre and left wanted a Republican-Democratic Constitution. See Paavonen, "Finnish Social Democratic Party," p. 138.
32. Finland, "Sairausvakuutuskomitean 1959," p. 9.
33. *Ibid.*
34. *Ibid.*, p. 10.
35. Paavonen, "Finnish Social Democratic Party," p. 140.
36. *Ibid.*, p. 141.
37. T. Soikkanen, "Changing bourgeois parties in a changing Finnish society," in *Political Parties in Finland: Essays in History and Politics*, by J. Mylly and R. M. Berry, eds. Series C:21 (Turku: University of Turku, 1984): 83.
38. Kekkonen, *President's View*, p. 37.
39. Finland, "Sairausvakuutuskomitean 1959," p. 10.
40. This was the first proposal to include contributions from the self-employed.
41. Finland, "Sairausvakuutuskomitean 1959," p. 11.
42. *Ibid.*, Forward.
43. Ninety percent of the existing 36,794 beds were already under state or local authority ownership, financed through the public sector. See Finland, "Sairausvakuutuskomitean 1959," pp. 11–14.
44. Finland, "Sairausvakuutuskomitean 1959," pp. 116–27.
45. *Ibid.*, pp. 71–92.
46. *Ibid.*, p. 131.
47. *Ibid.*, pp. 135–6. Personal communication with Professor N. Pesonen, Director-General of the Finnish National Board of Health in the late 1950s and early 1960s. He was a member of the Sickness Insurance Committee of 1955 and Chairman of another committee in 1961.

48. There was 1 doctor per 755 people in the large cities, and 1 per 4,290 people in the country.
49. Finland, "Regeringens proposition till Riksdagen med förslag till Sjukförsätkringslag och Vissa Därtill Anslutna Lagar," *Handlingar* Part 3 (Helsinki: Statsrådets Tryckeri, 1962): 2. By today's standards, both would be considered high.
50. Finland, "Sairausvakuutuskomitean 1959," p. 136.
51. Finland, "Sairausvakuutuskomitean 1959," p. 133.
52. Tallgren in parliamentary debates during the introduction of the Sickness Insurance Law. Finland, "Yleistä sairausvakuutusta," p. 1867; Personal communication with Professor Niilo Pesonen and Jaakko Pajula, members of the 1961 Sickness Insurance Legislative Committee.
53. Finland, "Hallituksen esitys eduskunnalles sairausvakuutuslaiksi ja eräiksi siihen liittyviksi laeiksi," *Valtioneuvostolie*, Helle Satälä, trans. (Helsinki: 15 November 1961): 1–3.
54. Finland, "Yleistä sairausvakuutusta," p. 1867.
55. Finland, "Hallituksen esitys," p. 3.
56. E. Kalimo, "Planning and evaluation of national health insurance in Finland," *Research Institute for Social Security Publication* M: 32 (Helsinki: Social Insurance Institution, 1979): 2.
57. Kalimo, "Planning and evaluation," p. 5.
58. Finland, Ministry of Social Affairs and Health (MSAH), "Health policy report by the Government to Parliament," *Report*, by Medical Translation Office, ed. (Helsinki: Ministry of Social Affairs and Health, 1985): 10. By 1966, 90 percent of financial resources used for health care were spent on hospital care, while only 10 percent was spent on ambulatory care. See Kalimo, "Trends in health expenditure," p. 4.
59. Kalimo, "Planning and evaluation," p. 2.
60. O. Rantala, "Changing features in the Finnish party system from the 1960s to the present: An overview," in *Political Parties in Finland: Essays in History and Politics*, by J. Mylly and R. M. Berry, eds., Series C:21 (Turku: University of Turku, 1984): 35.
61. Paavonen, "Finnish Social Democratic Party," p. 144.
62. *Ibid.*, p. 145.
63. J. Mylly, "The Agrarian/Centre Party in Finnish politics," in *Political Parties in Finland: Essays in History and Politics*, by J. Mylly and R. M. Berry, eds., Series C:21 (Turku: University of Turku, 1984): 114–5.
64. A similar phenomenon had occurred in the Scandinavian countries at an earlier stage.

65. In 1950, 50 percent of the labor force was still engaged in agricultural activities; in 1980, only 13 percent remained in this sector. See M. Vienonen, "How to plan the resource allocation," HEDC 86 Section 3, Paper presented by the Working Group on primary, secondary and tertiary health care, National Board of Health, Helsinki, August 28, 1986, p. 2.
66. Kekkonen, *President's View*, p. 17.
67. J. K. Paasikivi quoting the present President Mauno Koivisto in *Landmarks: Finland in the World* (Helsinki: Kirjayhtymä, 1985): 39. The original quote appeared in a 1955 summer edition of a Swedish daily, *Dagens Nyheter.* "Finlandization" is a term used to describe a country that has "fared badly by cultivating such a friendly relations with the Soviet Union." Finns would argue, however, that they have not sacrificed their "independence in order to appease a large neighbour." See Koivisto, *Landmarks*, p. 20, 138.
68. Tallgren during parliamentary debates on the Sickness Insurance Law. See Finland, "Yleistä sairausvakuutusta," p. 1867.
69. Pajula and Kalimo, "Social security," p. 160.
70. Finland, "Regeringens proposition," p. 1.
71. Kalimo, "Planning and evaluation," p. 5.
72. *Ibid.*
73. Finland, "Eduskunnan sosiaalivaliokunnalle," *Hallituksem Pöytäkirja Liite D* S 13 ptk 3, H. Satälä, trans. (Helsinki: 1963): 1.
74. *Ibid.*, p. 2.
75. *Ibid.*, p. 3.
76. Personal Communication with Professor M. J. Karvonen, Secretary General of the Finnish Medical Association in 1963.
77. Finns serving overseas and seamen would also be covered. See Finland, "Sickness Insurance Act," Law No. 364, National Pensions Institute, trans., (Helsinki: Parliament, 1963): sec. 1.1.
78. Finland, "Sickness Insurance Act," sec. 2.16.
79. *Ibid.*, sec. 2.4.
80. *Ibid.*, sec. 2.5.
81. The law delayed the financing of doctor services by two years, and excluded medical prosthesis, dressings and other medical accessories. *Ibid.*, sec. 2.7.
82. *Ibid.*, sec. 2.8.
83. If doctors charged above the recommended schedule, the reimbursed portion would fall below the 60 percent coverage. This became a major cause of erosion in the original principles of the reform.
84. Since 1937, the National Pensions Institution (later called the Social Insurance Institution) serves as an autonomous public institution for the

administration of national pension benefits. See Finland, "Sickness Insurance Act," sec. 2.39.

85. *Ibid.*, sec. 3.32.
86. *Ibid.*, secs. 3.34 and 3.35.
87. *Ibid.*, secs. 6.58 and 6.59.
88. Finland, "Regeringens proposition," p. 6.
89. Personal communication with Dr. E. Kalimo, Director of the Research Institute for Social Security of the National Insurance Institution.
90. It has later expanded its function to include the pensions plan and health-related studies. See Kalimo, "Planning and evaluation," p. 10.
91. Kalimo, "Planning and evaluation," p. 12.
92. *Ibid.*, p. 2.
93. T. Purola *et al.*, "National health insurance in Finland: Its impact and evaluation," *International Journal of Health Services* 3(1973): 69.
94. V. Kopra, "Social insurance in Finland," *Bank of Finland Monthly Bulletin* 11(1981): 1.
95. Purola *et al.*, "National health insurance," p. 7.
96. *Ibid.*, p. 70.
97. Kalimo, "Planning and evaluation," p. 13.
98. The Central Hospital Construction Act No 337/50 initiated this building programme.
99. T. Purola, E. Kalimo, and K. Nyman, "Health services use and health status under national sickness insurance: An evaluative resurvey [sic] of Finland," Research Institute for Social Security Publication A:11 (Helsinki: Social Insurance Institution, 1974): 247.
100. P. Sirén, "The growth of health expenditure in Finland 1960–80 and prospects for curbing its future growth," in *Improving Cost Effectiveness in Health Care*, Studies and Research No. 19 (Geneva: International Social Security Association, 1983): 32.
101. E. Kalimo, "Determinants of health care utilization," Research Institute for Social Security Publication, E:11 (Helsinki: Social Insurance Institution, 1969); and Purola *et al.*, "National health insurance."
102. Purola, Kalimo and Nyman, "Health services use," p. 235. In rural regions this rate was 1 out of 10, and it was even higher for low-income groups.
103. Mylly, "The Agrarian/Centre Party," p. 115.
104. After 1966, with minor exceptions, the same Coalition Government ruled Finland up until 1987. See Rantala, "Changing features," p. 52.
105. Paavonen, "Finnish Social Democratic Party," p. 148.

106. Finland, "Kansanterveyskomitean mietintö," *Valtioneuvostolle*, Helle Satälä, trans. (Helsinki: Government of Finland, 1965).
107. *Ibid.*
108. *Ibid.*
109. Vienonen, "Resource allocation," p. 6.
110. A. Niemi, "Community involvement in primary health care in Finland." Paper presented at the Interregional Meeting on Community Involvement for Health in Brioni, Yugoslavia, June 9–14, 1985, p. 1.
111. Personal communication with E. Tainio, Budget Officer, Ministry of Social Affairs and Health. The Public Health Act of 1972, the Public Health Act of 1972 and the National Health Act 1972, all refer to the same Act.
112. Personal communication with Dr. M. Kvist, Assistant Secretary General of the Finnish Medical Association. See M. Kvist, "Presentation of the Nordic countries and their primary health care: Part 2. Finland," *Scandinavian Journal of Primary Health Care* 1(1983): 88–92.
113. Finland, "Primary Health Care Act" (Helsinki: Parliament, 1972): sec. 1.1. Personal communication with Dr. M. Vienonen, Acting Deputy Director of the Department of Primary Health Care, Finnish National Board of Health.
114. The two sectors operate under different legislation, different managements and different financial systems.
115. Finland, "Primary Health Care Act," sec. 2.3. The plans originally covered only the primary care sector, expanded in 1974 to include secondary and tertiary care and in 1984, to include the social sector.
116. Finland, "Primary Health Care Act," sec. 2.
117. *Ibid.*, sec. 3.15.
118. The level of state subsidies was based on a solvency classification. See Finland, "Primary Health Care Act," sec. 4.27.
119. Finland, "Primary Health Care Act," sec. 4.21.
120. Forty percent of the medical profession, nevertheless, still engage in part-time private practice in 1986. Personal communication with Dr. M. Kvist.
121. Finland, "Primary Health Care Act," sec. 4.36.
122. P. Kekki, "Analysis of relationships between the availability of resources and the use of health services in Finland: A cross-sectional study," *Medical Care* 18(1980): 1238.
123. Sirén "Growth of health expenditure," p. 33.
124. Finland, National Board of Health (NBH), Department of Planning and Evaluation (DPE), "Government's general argumentation," *Memorandum* (Helsinki: NBH, DPE, 1972): 8.
125. Finland, "Primary Health Care Act," p. 9.

126. Finland, Ministry of Social Affairs and Health (MSAH), "The national 5-year planning system for social welfare and health care: Its main principles and its role in the management of national health policies," Report (Helsinki: MSAH, 1985): 2.
127. Some public health centres are, however, in reality small hospitals, have as many as 120 beds.
128. E. Kalimo *et al.*, "Need, use and expenses of health services in Finland 1964–1976," English summary, *Research Institute for Social Security Publication* A:18 (Helsinki: Social Insurance Institution, 1982): 476.
129. Finland, National Board of Health (NBH), Department of Planning and Evaluation (DPE), "Development of primary care services in Finland," *Memorandum* (Helsinki: NBH, DPE, 1972): 1.
130. Vienonen, "Resource allocation," p. 1.
131. Finland, MSAH, "Health policy report," p. 58.
132. Today primary care receives 40 percent of the funds allocated to health care. See Finland, MSAH, "Health policy report," p. 11.
133. Finland, MSAH, "Health policy report," p. 7.
134. *Ibid.*, p. 58.
135. Finland, MSAH, "Health policy report," p. 9.
136. The term acquis is also used to describe laws adopted under the Schengen Agreement, prior to its integration into the European Union legal order by the Treaty of Amsterdam, in which case one speaks of the Schengen acquis. The term acquis has been borrowed by the World Trade Organization Appellate Body, in the case Japan — Taxes on Alcoholic Beverages, to refer to the accumulation of General Agreement on Tariffs and Trade (GATT) and WTO law ("acquis gattien"), though this usage is not well established.
137. L. Vuorenkoski, P. Mladovsky, and E. Mossialos, *Finland: Health System Review Health Systems in Transition*, 2008; 10(4): 1–168. http://www.euro.who.int/__data/assets/pdf_file/0007/80692/E91937.pdf. Accessed July 25, 2017.
138. G. Scott, L. McKenzie, and J. Webster, "Maladjustments in the Corporatization Model: Hospital Reform in New Zealand, in A. S. Preker and A. Harding, eds. *Innovations in Health Service Delivery: The Corporatization of Public Hospitals* (2003, Washington, DC: World Bank). https://openknowledge.worldbank.org/handle/10986/15145. Accessed August 17, 2017; pp. 205–345.

PART III

DISCUSSION

In Chapter 11, this section of the book provides an analysis of the experience of the eight countries in the OECD that introduced landmark legislative health care financing reforms to achieve universal access to health care that were examined in this volume in Chapter 12, it provides an evaluation of the performance of these countries in achieving various health care policy and health financing targets through this reform using a Performance Evaluation Log-frame and in Chapter 13, it provides a summary of lessons learned that may be useful to other countries attempting similar reforms.

CHAPTER 11

ANALYSIS

The public sectors of all western developed countries have become increasingly involved in financing health care during the past century through regulations, subsidies and direct provision of services. In 1938, New Zealand became the first country with a market economy to introduce compulsory participation and universal entitlement to a comprehensive range of health services, financed largely through general revenues. By now, 13 OECD countries have passed landmark legislation offering similar coverage for their population.[1] The discussion that follows will first attempt to clarify some of the issues relating to the various complex concepts in health care financing. A descriptive analysis of the historical profiles of eight of these countries and subsequent quantitative analysis of all OECD countries give rich insights into *why, how* and *to what effect* their governments introduced such policies, while the others restrict compulsory participation and entitlement to a targeted sub-group of the population.[2] Finally, theories will be proposed about processes that have occurred in health care financing over the past decades. See Table 11.1.

A. CLARIFICATION OF CONCEPTS

Western countries were separated into two groups in this study based on similarities in policies relating to health care financing: Group I is characterized largely by compulsory participation and universal entitlement to comprehensive services, while the countries in Group II lack several of these characteristic. This is represented schematically in Table 11.2,

Table 11.1 Issues, Policies and Hypotheses

Objective	Clarification of Issues and Policy Options in Health Care Financing
Mechanisms	Direct charges versus prepayment
Participation	Voluntary versus compulsory
Entitlement	Restricted versus universal
Services	Basic versus comprehensive
Linkages	Risk rated versus open-ended
Hypotheses	**Government Involvement in Health Care Financing**
Why	Socio-economic, political processes, bureaucratic structures, market failure
How	Allocation, redistribution and stabilization
Effects	Growth, debt, opportunity, displacement, backlash, expenditure, equity

Source: Adapted from Preker (1989).

Table 11.2 Groups of Countries and Clusters of Policy Options

Domain characteristics based on cluster analysis				
Participation:	1. Voluntary		3. Compulsory	
Entitlement:	2. Restricted		4. Universal	
	Group I		*Group II*	
Clustering		1 2 3 4		1 2 3 4
Present (+)				
Absent (––)				
	Australia	– – + +	Austria	+ + – –
	Canada	– – + +	Belgium	+ + – –
	Denmark	– – + +	France	+ + – –
	Finland	– – + +	Germany	+ + – –
	Greece	– – + +	Ireland	+ + – –
	Iceland	– – + +	Japan	+ + – –
	Italy	– – + +	Luxembourg	+ + – –
	New Zealand	– – + +	Netherlands	+ + – –
	Norway	– – + +	Switzerland	+ + – –
	Portugal	– – + +	Turkey	+ + – –
	Spain	– – + +	United States	+ + – –
	Sweden	– – + +		
	UK	– – + +		

Source: Adapted from Preker (1989).

where the presence of a dominant trait is indicated by a plus and its absence by a minus. Although these issues and policy options were not readily quantifiable in their historical context, scaling ratios could be constructed from the degree of voluntary versus compulsory participation and restricted versus universal entitlement with data on the OECD dating from the early 1980s, Subsequent cluster analysis confirmed that there is a dichotomy in policies relating to these key issues in health care financing and that western countries can be divided into two groups based on this information. See Table 11.2.

Detailed narrative and linguistic analysis of the eight case studies indicated that there is a great deal of confusion about basic concepts relating to health care financing.[3] Despite similarities within each of the two groups of countries noted above, a number of significant differences and transformations occurred over time in the terminology, content, scope, boundaries and units-of-measurement in a perfectly uniform situation, policy options 1 and 2 would be absent, while 3 and 4 would be present for Group I countries, and the opposite would be true for Group II countries. This was not the case. Instead, there was an overlap of some characteristics between the two groups. Similarly, if all definitions had been identical everywhere and well polarized, Group I countries would have fallen into the anterior part of the upper-right quadrant in Figure 11.1, and Group II countries would have fallen into the posterior part of the lower-left quadrant. Once again, this was not the case. Definitions differed from country to country, so there was no true dichotomy between opposing policy options and no homogeneity in the formulation of any one concept. To avoid the classification of countries into two groups being misconstrued as an oversimplification, these inconsistencies will be explored in detail before shedding light on possible determinants, program features and outcomes of compulsory participation and universal entitlement to health services.

1. Financing Mechanisms

Elimination of financial barriers to health care and financial protection against the risks of illness were key objectives of the reforms leading to compulsory participation and universal entitlement in each of the eight countries examined. Although many countries portrayed it as "free"

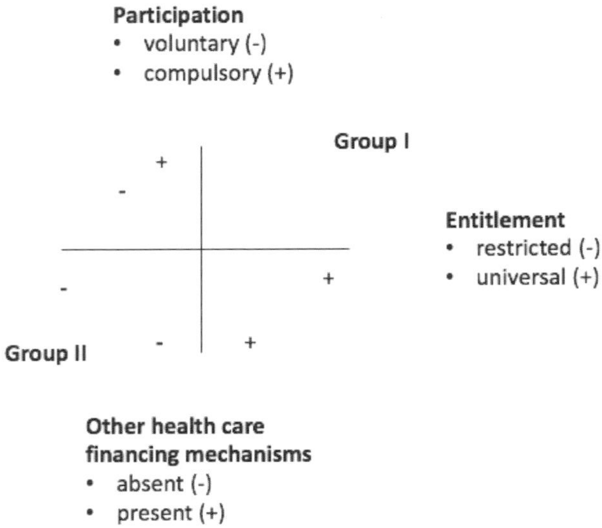

Figure 11.1 Axes of Key Issues in Health Care Financing

Source: Adapted from Preker (1989).

services, direct charges continued to exist everywhere.[4] New Zealand has never achieved complete prepayment for its general practitioner services because reimbursements to patients cover only a small part of the fee charged by doctors. Incomplete reimbursements exist in Australia, Norway and Finland. In Sweden, official co-payments were introduced on standard services under the Seven Crowns Reform in the belief that this would discourage excessive utilization. In Canada, where such user charges are illegal, more than 25 percent of total health care expenditure involves the private purchase of medical goods and services that are not provided by the public sector.[5] In the UK, symbolic charges for pharmaceuticals, private pay beds in public hospitals and an extensive range of private services have existed throughout the history of the British NHS. The debate on direct charges versus prepayment continues to plague all health care financing reforms currently taking place in western countries. Arguments in favor or against such charges, and their impact on efficiency and equity, will be discussed later in greater detail.

Health care has come to rely increasingly on general revenues, social insurance and various combinations of public and private health insurance for financing rather than on direct charges in all western countries. Unfortunately, the term health insurance is poorly differentiated and used generically to describe almost all forms of prepayment, including general revenues. In New Zealand, while political reformers talked specifically about "health insurance" prior to 1938, bureaucrats made plans to finance the National Health Service (NHS) through general revenues. In Britain, Winston Churchill's "magic of insurance" also turned out to be primarily general revenues, although national insurance did eventually play a small role in financing the British NHS. In Canada and Australia, Medicare and Medibank were both referred to as health insurance even though financing came mainly from earmarked tax levies and general revenues. Universal compulsory sickness insurance was transformed into a mixture of social insurance and general revenues, and since the early 1980s, the social insurance contribution toward health care financing has been dropped in Norway and Sweden. True risk-rated insurance is not used as a major source of revenue for health care financing in any western country, with the exception of the US. Instead, contributions to most health insurance schemes are non-risk-rated and benefits are open-ended for at least part of the population.

Confusion in the use of the term insurance is compounded by a number of false premises. Health insurance is used almost synonymously with fee-for-services remuneration for doctors and retrospective reimbursements for hospitals. The idea of general revenues, on the other hand, immediately triggers an image of the British NHS with salaried doctors and global prospective hospital budgets. Closer analysis of the eight case histories, as well as of other western countries, indicates that these associations are excessively stereotyped. Countries such as Austria, Belgium, France, Germany, Japan and the Netherlands depend on social insurance for health care financing. They rely on fee-for-service to pay their doctors in private offices, but use salaries to pay hospital doctors. In Australia, Canada, Finland, Norway and New Zealand, where general revenues play a larger role, doctors in private offices still receive a fee-for-service. Only in the UK, Sweden and Finland, are non–hospital-based doctors paid a capitation payment or salary.[6] Doctors working in public hospitals are almost always paid a salary, with the exception of the US, Canada and Australia where they continue to be paid a fee-for-service. Countries with a dominant general revenues component in health care financing are more prone to use global budgets to pay for hospitals; those with a dominant insurance component more frequently use itemized charges, per diem rates or Diagnostic Related Group (DRG) activity reimbursements.[7]

The central issues in health care financing were even more confusing because at times they referred to activities involving revenue collection, at other times, to budget processes or resource allocation and at still other times, to costs and expenditures. These processes are connected, but often not linked directly. Most prepayments through general revenues, social insurance and health insurance are pooled before they are spent on hospitals, doctors and other health care goods and services, or used to reimburse patients for their outlay. This gives the budget process some control over the flux in revenues through the system and the remuneration of health care providers. The flow of financial resources from direct charges is much more complex. Sometimes they are pooled with funds collected from prepayment schemes and are under budgetary control. At other times, they are paid directly to health care providers and are therefore outside budgetary control. In the latter case, patients are sometimes, but not always, given full or partial reimbursement for their outlay. Because these differences are in degree only, both Group I and Group II countries can be fitted into this schema. See Figure 11.2.

Much of the striking variability in the health systems of western countries can be explained by the public/private mix in the financing, administration and ownership of the institutions that produce health care goods and services. They may produce public, private, mixed and merit goods.[8] Just as the public sector may participate to varying degrees in the financing of health care through regulations, subsidies and the direct provision of services, so the production of health care in terms of its administration and ownership is often a mixture of public and private concerns. Private services may receive some of their revenue from public sources through subsidies or direct charges for services rendered. Public services may receive some of their revenue from private sources through direct user-fees and co-payments. Likewise, the allocation of the health care goods that are produced may occur through either the public or private sector.

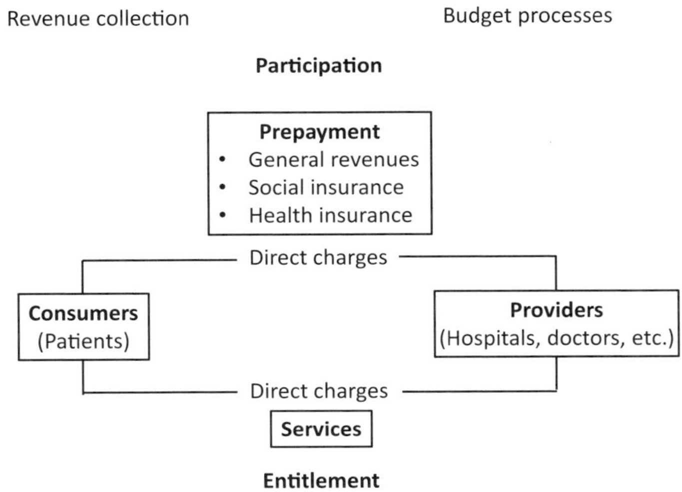

Figure 11.2 Flux in Health Care Financing in all Western Countries

Source: Adapted from Preker (1989).

Most western countries have adopted an approach somewhere between pure market-oriented and centrally planned health care. The optimal, acceptable and feasible balance between these extremes remains the subject of endless disagreement.[9] See Table 11.3.

As a result of the overlaps that occur between direct charges and various forms of prepayment, and between private and public involvement in financing, production and allocation of health services, none of these criteria provided a good way to differentiate between possible policy options in health care financing. Table 11.4 gives a typology of health care financing mechanisms.[10] Most western countries have sub components that fall into several cells at the same time. For example, the UK., New Zealand and the Nordic countries are dominant in cell A, but also have components of B and C, and J to L in their public sectors. Their private sectors include a range from D to L. Canada and Australia are dominant in B and C, but likewise include D to L in their private sectors. In Canada, J to L are prohibited by law for standard services in the public sector, but there are direct charges for above standard-services, pharmaceuticals and many

Table 11.3 Public/Private Mix

		Private	
	Public	Non-profit	For-profit
Financing	100%	< 50 >	100%
Production and delivery	100%	< 50 >	100%
Allocation	100%	< 50 >	100%

Source: Adapted from Preker (1989).

Table 11.4 Typology of Health Care Financing

Production	Prepayment in health care financing			Direct charges
Ownership & delivery	Government Taxes	Statutory Social Insurance	Regulated Private Insurance	Competitive User-fees
Purely public	A	D	G	J
Private non-profit	B	E	H	K
Private for-profit	C	F	I	L

Source: Adapted from Preker (1989).

other goods and services provided through ambulatory care. Some continental European countries dominate in cells D to F, but include A to C through the public sector for targeted services and populations. The comparative literature on health care financing does not make these distinctions clear. There are many studies that compare and contrast countries such as Australia, Canada, the US, France and Germany because they use health insurance. This approach is not helpful in clarifying the complex issues that arise relating to health care financing. See Table 11.4.

2. Participation

The dispute over voluntary versus compulsory participation is a good example of how notions about individual rights and collective responsibilities were manipulated to suit the purposes of vested interest groups such as the medical profession, health insurance organizations and private hospitals as well as the governments in question and their oppositions.

When doctors and hospitals had a difficult time making ends meet, or when local communities did not want to foot the bill for Poor Law provisions, there was little debate about compulsory membership in friendly societies or sickness funds to ensure participation of low-income earners. Later, when compulsory participation was extended to the whole population, there were claims that it represented state interference in the doctor-patient relationship, an individual sense of responsibility for health care, the just treatment of doctors and so on. The extreme example was in Australia where the medical profession challenged the government and won a legal test case on the grounds that forcing doctors to make prescriptions on official paper was unconstitutional, being a form of civil conscription. Objections to compulsory participation were much more pronounced in English-speaking countries prior to the introduction of universal entitlement than in the Nordic countries, where there was almost no protest.[11] Arguments for and against individualism and collectivism were, therefore, different in different countries and at different times.

The meaning of voluntary and compulsory participation is open to interpretation. Denmark was credited with having achieved a remarkably high membership in the so-called voluntary sickness funds prior to the 1970s. However, only the upper echelons of a means-tested population could afford to opt out. Medium- to low-income workers were not offered a choice, because failure to be a member in good standing in a sickness fund meant automatic loss of eligibility for a number of other social benefits such as pensions, unemployment benefits and so on. Canadian participation depends largely on provincial compliance because the federal government has no direct jurisdiction over most aspects of health care. When the government introduced its Medical Care Act in the late 1960s, Ontario was allowed to qualify for federal co-financing once it had achieved 90 percent rate of voluntary participation even though the law called for 100 percent participation. All other countries that have been classified as having compulsory participation offer some voluntary programs through supplemental or private health insurance to cover above-standard services provided by both the private and public sectors. Only Australia and Denmark have in the past allowed those who participate in these programs to opt out of their public programs. Likewise, all the countries that have been classified in Group II have compulsory participation for part of their populations. Compulsory participation in this study therefore means compulsory for everyone.

3. Entitlement

Universal entitlement implies that the whole population is eligible for benefits irrespective of income, health status, membership in good-standing or other constraints. All Group I countries offer such benefits, while Group II countries restrict entitlement to a targeted portion of the population such as low-income earners, children, pensioners and other groups of the non-employed. Higher income groups may participate on a voluntary basis in a variety of ways that would give them similar entitlement. Many Group II countries that do not have legislative provisions for universal entitlement, such as France, Germany, Japan and the Netherlands, achieve extensive coverage through non-statutory arrangements.[12] Belgium achieves virtual universal entitlement through various pieces of legislation that require extensive compulsory membership in sickness funds and other insurance organizations. Most of the Nordic countries and the United Kingdom passed through a similar historical phase before extending coverage to the whole population. Because most western countries offer supplemental health insurance to cover higher standards of care, private accommodations in hospitals and so on, entitlement is a question of degree and open to interpretation as in the case of participation. The dates of the legislative reforms that introduced universal entitlement as interpreted in the eight case studies are given in Table 11.5.

Furthermore, universal entitlement was meaningful only to the extent that access to services matched legal provisions. In practice, a lag occurs between the time that policies are formulated, legislation prepared and laws passed, and the date that programs are implemented, services offered and entitlement exercised. Examination of resource allocation and access to services therefore provides a more subtle interpretation of restricted versus universal entitlement. Access to health care is difficult, and sometimes impossible, to achieve in all countries. Where geographical, financial, cultural and functional barriers exist, legal entitlement to health care has little meaning. This has remained a topic of heated debate in all

Table 11.5 Legislative Reforms for Universal Entitlement

Country	Date	Passed	Date	Implemented
New Zealand	1938	(September 8)	1939	(April 1)
England/Wales	1946	(November 6)	1948	(July 5)
Sweden	1953	(June 19)	1955	(January 1)
Norway	1956	(March 2)	1956	(July 2)
Finland	1963	(July 4)	1964	(April 1)
Canada	1966	(December 21)	1968	(July 1)
Denmark	1971	(May 28)	1973	(April 1)
Australia	1974	(August 7)	1975	(July 1)

Source: Adapted from Preker (1989).

countries that claim to offer universal entitlement. Additional reforms were required in many of the eight countries to deal with this problem following the legal provisions for universal entitlement. For example, compulsory universal health insurance in Sweden led to universal entitlement to health services in 1955. But it was the Seven Crowns Reform of 1969 that expanded and reorganized health services to permit universal access. Likewise, compulsory universal health insurance was introduced in Finland in 1964, but it was the Public Health Act of 1972 that extended access to the whole population.

The services offered through various forms of entitlement have changed greatly over time, and vary from one country to another.[13] The minimum standards of health care provided through social security advocated by the ILO in 1952[14] were much more limited than the more comprehensive requirements needed to satisfy the WHO.[15] Even the core contents, such as health promotion, prevention, curative treatment, rehabilitation and chronic care, have changed over time. Each of the eight countries defined health services differently. The most clear-cut segmentation into limited and comprehensive services occurred in Canada. The National Hospital and Diagnostic Services Act of 1957 called for compulsory participation and universal entitlement to hospital care only. Treatment by doctors was not included until 1967 under the Medical Care Act.[16]

A full range of services exists in all western countries today, but only some provide them for the whole population. Populations that do not qualify for such benefits under the limited compulsory programs in Group II countries have access to services through voluntary schemes, private insurance, direct out-of-pocket payment or simply by using them when seriously ill. In the US, where 30 million people still do not have adequate protection through any form of prepayment, the problems associated with restricted entitlement are much more dramatic.

B. HYPOTHESES (WHY, HOW AND TO WHAT EFFECT)

1. Determinants of Health Policy (Why)

The best way to establish causal relationships is through combined regression and path analysis. Group II countries, unfortunately, do not have historical legislative landmarks that could be used as points of reference for comparison with Group I countries. Instead, to understand more fully *why* governments introduced compulsory participation and universal entitlement to health services, these policies will be analyzed against existing theories on the determinants of the welfare effort: socio-economic development, political processes, bureaucratic structures and market failure. Chronological sequencing, historical breaks, thresholds and other developments in social policy will be used as supplementary, indirect evidence to support or contest hypotheses about various reforms that have occurred in health care financing. Determinants that have been identified by comparative studies in the social policy literature are relevant to developments in health care financing, but not directly transferable without prior empirical validation. Health care is a benefit in kind with many features that are different from most social security cash benefits. Furthermore, the relative significance of determinants changes over time. Factors that were significant during the early growth of infrastructures for the prepayment of health care were different to those that played a significant role in extending participation and entitlement to larger segments of the population.

(a) Socio-economic Development

Socio-economic development, along with its bureaucratic and demographic correlates — the number of years that social security systems have been in existence and the age structure of the population — has been considered to be the most significant determinant of the welfare effort in the comparative literature on social policy.[17] Many authors have convincingly demonstrated that there is a high correlation between a country's level of socio-economic development, urbanization and accumulation of national wealth, and its expenditure on social security programs.[18] Similar observations have been made about the correlation between GDP as a measure of national wealth, and expenditure on health care, life expectancy and infant mortality rates.[19] Vulnerable populations benefit when industrialization and urbanization provide the state with the economic means to pay for social security benefits or health care.[20] Yet aggregate data on GDP and expenditure trends in the social sectors clearly does not tell the full story. Scholars have found it much more difficult to unravel the complex interplay between historical, political and bureaucratic factors, and socio-economic development, industrialization and urbanization.

The links between socio-economic development and the growth of infrastructures for prepayment of health care are clearest during the late nineteenth and early twentieth centuries. The displaced populations, unemployment, unsanitary dwellings and unsafe working conditions that often mark the early years of industrialization heightened the risks of poverty, illness and neglect of the needy. Urbanization broke down the traditional network of care provided by families and rural communities, leaving urban populations unprotected during times of unemployment, poor health and old age. The countries that were first to industrialize were also the first to introduce collective provisions for financing social benefits through charitable organizations, guilds, friendly societies, sickness funds and so on. They were established not only to protect individuals from the uncertainties of urban life but also to relieve local authorities, rate-payers and doctors of the welfare burden of caring for the sick and the poor. Great Britain and northern continental Europe were the first to industrialize and urbanize. The rural Nordic countries, southern Europe and the English-speaking New World were much later to industrialize and to introduce similar structures for health care financing. The sickness funds and friendly societies never took hold in countries such as Finland and Sweden, or Australia, Canada, New Zealand and the US.

Beyond these early developments, evidence in favor of a correlation between socio-economic development and extensions in coverage through prepayment of health care becomes progressively weaker. By the twentieth century, cash benefits were slowly supplemented by rudimentary entitlement to medical treatment as a benefits in kind in many of the countries that had such programs. Voluntary participation was replaced by compulsory membership for a means-tested portion of the population to ensure participation by low-income groups. Incremental growth in participation and entitlement was interspersed with the occasional rapid extension in coverage. Increased health benefits often occurred at the same time as other significant reforms in social security, but there are no convincing correlations between these events and socio-economic development. New Zealand and the US were both pioneers and leaders in social security reforms during the 1930s. The US did not include health care as a benefit under the Social Security Act of 1935.[21] New Zealand not only included health care in 1938 but also took a quantum leap by introducing compulsory participation and universal entitlement as a separate benefit. The US has become one of the richest countries in the world, but remains a welfare laggard, while New Zealand has maintained its extensive provisions despite a much lower national income.

Based on the timing that OECD countries introduced compulsory participation and universal entitlement to health care, the empirical evidence against the significance of socio-economic development as a significant determinant becomes overwhelming. New Zealand was a poor rural country, recovering from the Great Depression and entering World War II when it implemented its National Health Service in 1938. Great Britain, Sweden and Norway introduced their reforms during the post-war reconstruction, while Canada, Denmark and Australia introduced theirs during the economic expansion of the late 1960s and early 1970s. Although this may suggest that social transformations and economic growth were significant factors, this was neither the case in Finland during the early 1960s nor in Spain and Greece during the economic slowdown of the early 1980s. Furthermore, the governments of Group II countries did not introduce coverage for health care financing during their periods of economic expansion or when they had reached a similar level of socio-economic development. Among the seven richest western countries, Canada, Italy and the UK have introduced compulsory participation and universal entitlement, while France, Germany, Japan and the US do not offer such provisions. Regression analysis of all OECD countries shows no significant correlation between national wealth as measured by GDP per capita and compulsory participation with universal entitlement in health care financing.[22]

The comparative literature on social policy indicates that some level of socio-economic development, industrialization and urbanization may be a necessary pre-condition to the welfare effort, which in turn provides the means for growth in physical, human and financial resources in the health sector. No western country introduced comprehensive coverage for health care financing without prior or parallel growth in social security provisions. In settings where these prerequisites are met, an interplay of other factors, such as political processes, bureaucratic structures and the pressures of market failure, may enhance the emergence of more refined provisions such as compulsory participation and universal entitlement. Socio-economic development may be necessary for these factors to play a role in defining health policy, but it was not sufficient as the only causal factor.

(b) Political Processes

The legislative reforms that introduced compulsory participation and universal entitlement occurred during the mid-twentieth century, but the debates that accompanied then portray a complex mosaic of unresolved concerns about natural rights, freedom, justice, social contracts and state absolutism that arose out of seventeenth to nineteenth century political philosophy.[23] The tensions that existed between individualist and collectivist points of view during previous centuries were repeated, and often distorted, in the arguments about various aspects of health care financing. These observations lend support to a second school of thought that claims that the welfare effort is due to not only socio-economic factors but also a complex interplay between different political processes: ideology, democratization and political party formation.[24] The eight case studies demonstrated that, although these political processes may not be as significant to expenditure on social security and health care as socio-economic development, they were the key elements in shaping the more refined characteristics of the associated benefits. Ideology provided the direction for politically motivated reforms to take place, democratization the means, and political parties the continuity and timing.

(i) *Ideology*

The eight case histories on the evolution of health care financing revealed two intertwined ideological processes that were difficult to separate. First, the choice between voluntary versus compulsory participation and between restricted versus universal entitlement reflected differences between individualistic and collectivist beliefs. The decisions that governments made in terms of taxation policies and public expenditure policies when faced with these options in health care financing represented complex ideological trade-offs between opposing political platforms that were not apparent from aggregate expenditure data of either the welfare effort or health care itself.[25] Second, the choice between fee-for-service versus salaries, private practice versus public clinics, specialists versus generalists, hospitals versus primary care, private versus public ownership, health insurance versus tax-funding and so on included underlying meritocratic and egalitarian arguments that went beyond the political arena of the societies in question. Studies that lump these factors under a single heading, or try to measure them by one indicator, confuse the subtle differences between *individualist* and *elite* ideology.[26] In an attempt to avoid falling into this trap, these two processes will be treated separately.

It was left-wing-oriented governments (socialist, labor, social democratic and liberal in the case of Canada) that passed the legislative reforms for compulsory participation and universal entitlement in all 13 OECD countries.[27] This supports similar observations made in the comparative literature on social policy that when left-wing ideologies dominate, governments are more likely to introduce compulsory programs (Norway and Sweden), and when liberal ideologies dominate (Denmark), they are more likely to introduce subsidized voluntary schemes.[28] In countries where left-wing political groups enjoyed many consecutive years in power, public policy reflected a conscious effort to redistribute income and to restrain bourgeois privileges that went beyond simple social security provisions.[29] Social democratic parties in the Nordic countries focused on income redistribution and social reforms through taxation in mixed-market economies, while the more left-wing labor parties in New Zealand and the UK emphasized the elimination of the reward system of capitalism through government ownership, publicly run clinics and salaried doctors. Liberal and more right-wing parties impeded progressive social security legislation which was felt to interfere with competitive markets.[30] Policies on participation and entitlement to health services reflected the choices governments had made based on these ideologies.[31] See Table 11.6.

Both of the ideological camps used arguments about efficiency and equity to support their stance. Left-wing-oriented groups claimed that

Table 11.6 Party Dominance of Governments that Introduced Reforms

Country	Party Dominance
Australia	Labor
Canada	Liberal
Denmark	Social democratic
Finland	Social democratic
Greece	Social democratic
Iceland	Social democratic
Italy	Socialist
New Zealand	Labor
Norway	Labor
Portugal	Socialist
Spain	Socialist
Sweden	Social democratic
United Kingdom	Labor
Reform: Compulsory participation and universal entitlement	

Source: Adapted from Preker (1989).

compulsory prepayment and universal access to health care was the most efficient way to ensure maximum participation in revenue collection and equitable entitlement to benefits. They feared that high-income groups would not voluntarily contribute their share to public programs and considered means-testing a distasteful way to stigmatize the social groups targeted by this practice. General revenues were favored over contributory social insurance and direct charges because the latter two were believed to put an unfair share of the financial burden of health care on the shoulders of workers. In direct contrast, liberal and more right-wing groups argued that compulsory participation was unnecessary except to ensure that those below an income determined by a means-test carried their own weight. Those earning above this level of income should be allowed to join voluntary programs that would also provide them with above standard services. Financing through social insurance was favored over general revenues because it allowed those who contributed to voluntary schemes to opt out of public programs and made participation more visible to those who contributed to the financing of health care. These groups felt that universal entitlement was unnecessary and even wasteful because it did not target the populations that needed publicly funded services.

The final mix in financing between prepayment through general revenues, social insurance and direct charges reflected the many compromises that occurred along the way. Debates on the relative merit of tax-funding versus health insurance occurred in all of these countries. Left-wing labor groups in New Zealand and Norway argued for universal access to health services provided by the state and financed through general revenues as early as the late nineteenth century.[32] Similar proposals were made in the UK during the early twentieth century. Likewise, proposals for national health insurance were presented in New Zealand in 1924, Australia in 1927, South Africa in 1928, the UK in 1930 and Canada in 1932.[33] New Zealand and the UK introduced a tax-funded National Health Service in 1938 and 1946, although it was labeled as health insurance in New Zealand. Sweden, Norway and Finland consolidated compulsory membership with their sickness insurance funds in 1953, 1956 and 1963, while Denmark continued to rely on subsidized voluntary membership until 1971. Canada and Australia introduced health insurance levies to supplement tax-funding in 1966 and 1974. During the negotiations leading up to the final compromises, the English-speaking countries were more successful in introducing radical reforms than were the Nordic countries.[34]

Conflicts about fee-for-service, salaries, private practice, public clinics, specialists, generalists, institutional care, primary care, ownership and so on occurred concurrent to the debates on revenue collection, and continue today in most of the countries examined. Clashes over these issues between the medical profession and other health professionals, unionized health professionals, and between generalists and specialists, are usually presented in the literature as part of an underlying class struggle.[35] The medical profession and other health providers were divided into three competing camps in all the countries examined: specialists working in hospitals, general practitioners and public health officers. All exerted an iron-clad influence over their respective systems and maintained an organizational division which authorities were unsuccessful in breaking, even through the most radical reforms. These struggles were most apparent during the reform period in the UK before 1946, in Canada between 1966 and 1972 and in Sweden before 1969 when there was an overt split between specialists and generalists.

The eight case studies, however, provided clear evidence that these conflicts reflected not only class struggles but also elite ideology which cut across classes.[36] The scientific approach to medicine valorized health care and the medical profession during the past century in a way that was previously unknown. Public health programs led to the first significant relief from the scourges of communicable diseases that had plagued populations prior to the latter part of the nineteenth century. Technical advances led to cures for conditions that had been left to prayer and quarantine. As medical science became more complex, the gap in information between providers and patients also grew. Knowledge about the course of illness, options for treatment and likely outcome remains largely a mystery even when consumers have access to information. Elite ideology contributed to making this gap in knowledge even larger. Calls for clinical freedom, confidentiality and preservation of the doctor-patient relationship prevented public authorities from gaining the control over financing and provision of health services that they had hoped for through some of the reforms. Despite fears by doctors that compulsory participation and universal entitlement would lead to socialized medicine, the profession retained control of health care in most of the countries examined.

The resulting elite ideology was used in pressure politics to influence the reform process.[37] In the English-speaking countries, doctors, voluntary hospitals, friendly societies and other vested-interest groups influenced the opinion of commissions of enquiry and departments of health through open confrontation.[38] They fought against the introduction of compulsory prepayment and universal entitlement with obstructive publicity campaigns and threats of civil disobedience. In New Zealand, Canada and Australia, doctors, private hospitals and insurance organizations succeeded in frustrating the legislative process on several occasions by having doctors refuse to work in salaried clinics, by billing patients directly and by supporting private insurance plans. In the Nordic countries, the vested-interest groups were much more subtle, but equally, if not more, successful in influencing the reforms. Instead of public confrontations, they exerted their authority strategically by infiltrating the policy-making machinery of the government.[39] Unpopular proposals, such as the Norwegian Civil Defense Health Plan and the Swedish Höjer Plan, were blocked long before going to Parliament.[40] Differences in financing mechanisms, remuneration of doctors and ownership were due as much to these ideological undercurrents as to overt political platforms of the governments that introduced the final reforms.

(ii) *Democratization*

If democracy is taken to mean government by the people, this factor had an indirect rather than direct impact of the reform process. In modern states, the acts of government are performed by representatives of the people, elected on a free and equal basis, not the population itself. In an ideal democracy, the actions of government are always in perfect accordance with public preference. This rarely happens. Direct democracy, such as by referendums, only takes place on rare occasions.[41] Instead, governments try to respond in relative *degrees,* for a relative period of *time* and in relative *correspondence* with preferences of the elected representatives of citizens.[42] The infrastructures needed to collect the funds to pay for health care are complex and require time to develop and the participation of the public. A strengthening of the democratic process was critical in enhancing this development because it allowed populations to influence governments through the electoral process without having to resort to bloody uprisings,[43] but there was little evidence in this study to suggest that democratization played a role beyond that of a facilitator in the introduction of prepaid health care.

Modern democracy is a recent phenomenon. There were no true democratic governments during the nineteenth century.[44] Older parliamentary systems, such as in the UK and Belgium, were slower to extend franchise than were Denmark, Norway and Finland where, by contrast, democratization was late to develop. By the twentieth century, statism and the divine right monarchies gave way to democracy, but it was not until the end of World War II that most western countries enjoyed a continuous period of democratic regime. New Zealand and Australia were among the first countries to have fully democratic regimes with firm popular control of government institutions and universal adult suffrage.[45] New Zealand was the first to introduce compulsory participation and universal entailment; Australia was among the last. Greece, Portugal and Spain have recently introduced similar legislation but have not enjoyed continuous democratic regimes since World War II. All other OECD countries have had continuous democratic governments since World War II, but the countries classified in Group II in this study did not introduce compulsory participation and universal entitlement in health care financing.

Furthermore, responsive democracy requires that eight institutional guarantees be fulfilled: freedom to form and join organizations; freedom of expression; right to vote; eligibility for public office; right of political leaders to compete for support and votes; alternative sources of information; free and fair elections; and institutions for making government policies that depend on voter preference.[46] These principles embody the classic, but often conflicting democratic principles of liberty and equality. The governments that introduced policies to enforce compulsory participation and universal entitlement often had to defend themselves against accusations of anti-democratic behavior. This has led some authors to conclude that the parliamentary monarchies lacking some of these ideological restraints felt a more pressing need to control the bureaucratic machinery and appease militant labor movements at the turn of the century. These same countries later supported more paternalistic policies through the introduction of extensive social security programs than their liberal continental counterparts.[47] The strong growth of sickness funds in Denmark and Norway at the turn of the century would support this theory, but the late development of sickness funds in Sweden and Finland and the later introduction of extensive provisions in Denmark and Finland, contradict it.

Majoritarian[48] or consensual[49] regime type did not seem to influence the outcome either; countries in both Group I and Group II have these regimes. Among the countries with majoritarian democratic regimes, New Zealand, the UK, Canada and Australia have introduced the reforms in question, while the US has notably resisted similar legislation. Among the countries with consensual regimes, the Nordic countries have introduced these reforms, while most continental northern European countries have not taken this step.

Several other factors were also examined for their possible impact on the reform process leading to compulsory participation and universal entitlement. The extent of pluralism and religious-linguistic homogeneity worked against such reforms: Denmark, Iceland, Ireland, Japan, New Zealand, Norway, Sweden, the UK and Australia have been classified as non-plural societies; Finland, France, Italy, Canada, Germany and the US have been classified as semi-plural societies; and Austria, Israel, Luxembourg, Belgium, the Netherlands and Switzerland have been classified as plural societies.[50] Group I countries belong primarily to the non- and semi-plural societies, while Group II countries tend to belong to the semi-plural and plural societies. Plural societies may be more likely to offer greater choice to their populations, including choice in health care financing. Most of the countries in Group I are classified as having weak executive power (Finland being an exception), but some Group II countries also belong in this category.[51] The following other key characteristics of democratic regimes did not correlate with the classification of countries into Group I and Group II according to this study: majority rule versus power sharing, unicameral versus bicameral parliaments, two-party versus multiple party systems, majority versus proportional representation, unitary versus federal states and majority versus minority constitutional rights.

Public choice, as expressed through the electoral process, is an imperfect substitute for consumer choice.[52] Some authors have tried to construct theoretical models to approximate the classical consumer-demand relationship based on median-voter preferences.[53] Rules that offer incentives for voters to reveal their economic preferences could be developed,[54] but are often not politically desirable. Representative democracy is therefore not a reliable way to reflect the balance between a politician's objective to maximize votes to stay in power and the voters' objective to maximize their net benefit from public policies.[55] The delegation of choice to elected representatives, sub-maximal voter turnout, lack of accurate information, silent majorities, government monopolies and so on are all unavoidable imperfections of even the most idealized democratic process. For citizens, to have a significant effect on health policy, the electorate must be offered distinct platforms, voters must make identified, well-informed choices, and governments must have a concrete mandate to implement these choices. During most of the reform period leading up to the introduction of compulsory participation and universal entitlement, parties offered generalities, voters responded to distorted images of platforms and the media created its own political agenda.[56] Health care financing was only a stirring campaign issue during elections in New Zealand in 1935 and Australia in 1969.

Evidence for the significance of democratization as a determinant of health policy is therefore weak and marked by contradictions. It probably played its most significant role in the introduction of compulsory participation and universal entitlement as a precursor to other political processes such political party formation and in allowing social transformations to take place peacefully. This in itself was a significant achievement.

(iii) *Political Party Formation and Vested Interests*

Most political parties have evolved since World War I and II.[57] The key groups are liberals, conservatives, socialists, Christian democrats and communists.[58] Because older equivalents have changed their names and ideological orientation, it is difficult to classify them under one ideological family, and their functional equivalents are more significant than their names.[59] In modern societies, interest groups *articulate,* while parties *aggregate* public interest and choice, but the boundaries between these distinctions are not clear. In earlier societies, these functions were performed by different classes, estates or the bureaucracy. The ideological unity of parties is frequently undermined by interest groups that existed before policies and political platforms were formulated. In party typology, the ideology of multi-party systems (Nordic and other European)[60] are more likely to coexist with interest groups than in two-party systems (Anglo-American).[61] Parties work through competition, while interest groups avoid competition by penetrating and infiltrating the committees and ministries that are significant to them.[62] The eight case studies gave clear evidence that doctors, insurance organizations and, to a lesser extent, private hospitals formed three powerful lobbies that influenced party platforms throughout the many health care financing reforms that have taken place during the past century.

Hypotheses that the formation of modern political parties provided continuity in regime and timing for the introduction of significant peaceful reforms in social policy[63] need to be seen in this context and were supported by observations in the case study countries. At the turn of the twentieth century, during the early growth of the trade guilds, sickness funds, friendly societies and so on, the process of political party formation was still in its infancy in most western countries.[64] The forerunners to both left-wing and right-wing political parties supported these organizations for different reasons. Parties with right-wing platforms hoped that contributory programs would lead to greater self-reliance, less money spent on various forms of social assistance and decreased taxes. Parties with left-wing platforms hoped that public subsidies would act as a vehicle for income transfers from the rich to the poor. Countries that were early to democratize, such as the UK, Canada, Australia and New Zealand, had time for nineteenth-century liberal free-market and *laissez-faire* ideologies to take hold. They resisted government-subsidized social security programs. Countries that were late to democratize, such as the Nordic countries, had small and splintered right-wing political parties that were divided among conservative, agrarian, Christian Democratic and liberal parties. The united left provided strong support for working class welfare-oriented ideologies.[65]

In the Nordic countries, proportional representation led to many small and diversified political parties. This resulted in multi-party consensual political systems with fragile coalition governments whose survival depended on political compromises.[66] At the turn of the century, the monarch, supported by an appointed government, a conservative bureaucracy and a conservative bourgeois minority, was pitted against an emerging liberal-peasant majority in the Lower House of Parliament.[67] As industrialization and urbanization spread, socialist and communist parties gained strength and demanded social reforms. An increase in sickness funds and social security provisions occurred parallel to these events. As urbanization progressed, rural political factions lost popular support, and cleavages occurred between conservative and socialist coalitions. Right-wing conservative governments backed contributory social insurance, while left-wing opposition parties called for tax-based financing as early as the 1890s. Compromises between these two opposing political groups led to extensive expansion in the financial infrastructures needed to pay for health care through government-subsidized sickness insurance.[68] According to this political scenario, Denmark led the way, followed by Norway, Sweden and Finland. Finland's evolution was delayed by slower industrialization, Finnish-Swedish language conflicts and violent battles of secession with Sweden and Russia.

In the Anglo-American countries, majoritarian rule led to two-party adversarial systems that were radically different from the Nordic multiparty consensual systems.[69] Coalition governments were an exception and compromise discouraged. At the turn of the century, liberal *laissez-faire* ideologies dominated with much weaker left-wing oppositions. Socialist and communist parties existed, but were never able to secure a strong foothold. In Australia, Canada and New Zealand, these political tendencies were accentuated by a strong reaction against any government intervention brought on by memories of their colonial past. During the development of the early infrastructures for health care financing, the UK therefore led the way in terms of the evolution of friendly societies and the former English-speaking colonies lagged far behind, although some public services were initially financed by the British Treasury and later, the state budget when the colonies gained their independence. Direct out-of-pocket payments and private insurance played a much more significant role. The dominant liberal political mood kept state-run programs and subsidies for the friendly societies to a minimum in an attempt to encourage self-reliance and thrift.

At the time of the introduction of compulsory participation and universal entitlement, the relative advantages and disadvantages of these political models had changed. The consensual model had enhanced public subsidies for the sickness funds and the majoritarian model had discouraged such left-wing compromises during the right-wing or liberal party dominance of the early twentieth century. Policies calling for compulsory membership and universality were more radical reforms that had all the potential elements needed to evoke strong protest from opponents — political parties and vested interests. Policies calling for salaries, public clinics, major organizational reforms, public ownership and funding through taxes required not only ideological commitment but also party strength. Parties also had to have sufficiently clear political platforms that their policies were not diluted by the time the legislative phase was reached, and they had to stay in power long enough to prepare, pass and implement these policies. Labor parties in New Zealand, Australia, the UK and Norway were committed to such radical social reforms as were the Social Democratic parties in Sweden, Denmark and Finland as well as the Liberal Party in Canada. As is often the case in representative democracies,[70] the electorate was not presented with a clear choice. Many of these policies, therefore, became hidden agendas that were often lost along the way during the battle with opposition parties and vested interest groups.

Labor governments in New Zealand and Britain relied on their majority to introduce tax-funded and salaried National Health Services in 1938 and 1946. The Liberal government in Canada and Labor government in Australia introduced their reforms despite strong protest from the opposition in 1966 and 1973, but their weaker position as federal states and strong opposition from vested interest groups diluted the more radical elements such as tax-funding, salaries and state ownership. The multiparty consensual political systems of the Nordic countries had a distinct disadvantage during the introduction of radical reforms. The universal sickness insurance programs introduced by Sweden and Norway in 1953 and 1955 were filled with the remnants of compromises that grew out of the consensual model.[71] The late arrival of political parties in Finland delayed expansion of its sickness insurance program until 1963. Some of the more radical elements, such as salaried doctors and public clinics, were not introduced until later.[72] Denmark was much more complex. Although political parties were early to develop, liberal ideologies played a dominant role for a much longer period. When the Social Democratic Party did come to power, it was plagued by a series of weak coalitions. Furthermore, generous subsidies for voluntary membership in the sickness insurance funds had achieved virtual universal adhesion by 1960, making further extension a weak political platform.

Regime stability can be viewed as constitutional continuity and peaceful transfer of power through electoral decisions; political stability can be looked at as the length of time that a particular party is in power. The social policy literature suggests that party continuity is a significant determinant of early progressive reforms because it increases the likelihood of successful enactment of legislation and of fiscal commitment.[73] Evidence for this hypothesis comes mainly from Norway and Sweden where Labor and Social Democratic governments enjoyed long periods in power and were successful in introducing progressive reforms in health care financing during the 1950s. Denmark and Finland may have been retarded by frequent changes in weak coalition governments. Evidence from the English-speaking countries is less conclusive. In New Zealand, the UK and Australia, it was newly elected Labor governments that introduced compulsory prepayment and universal entitlement. In Canada, it was when the Liberal party regained power after a period of Conservative rule.[74] In the UK and Australia, the reform governments lost to the opposition in subsequent general elections, while in the other six countries, there was no change in power. Lack of political durability compromised health care reforms that had been carefully planned during the late 1920s and 1940s in Canada and Australia.[75] This would indicate that political stability does not guarantee reforms, but instability might compromise it.

It is necessary to balance the significance of political parties in the introduction of compulsory participation and universal entitlement to health care with that of leadership and personalities. The latter have been described by a number of scholars as key factors in public policy.[76] It is surprising that the comparative literature on social policy has given so little attention to this potentially significant determinant of the welfare effort.[77] The case studies gave clear evidence that it was the leadership and personalities of government ministers and other senior officials that, more often than not, played a key role in formulating policies, making political parties stick to their election platforms and implementing reforms. Advocacy and tenacious opposition from the medical profession and other vested interest groups was equally a determinant. The machinations that occurred behind the scene in shaping the final policy during the consensus-making process in the Nordic countries, is in direct contradiction to the usual stereotyped view of their lifeless party platforms, inanimate bureaucracies and faceless political characters. The bureaucratic process itself was headed by individuals who, in many cases, had a decided impact on the policy-making process. Some authors maintain that bureaucrats engage in empire building to increase their budgets, raise their salaries and extend their power. This study provides no evidence, however, to substantiate this hypothesis.

(c) Bureaucratic Structures[78–80]

Proponents of a third school of thought claim that it is the ageing of bureaucratic infrastructures or the length of time that a program has been in existence and the consensus-making machine of corporatism — the interplay of highly organized interest groups and governments — that was principally responsible for a flourishing of social security provisions such as pensions, unemployment benefits, sick pay, accident insurance and family allowances.[81] These observations are not strictly transferable to some aspects of health policy. For example, Group I and Group II countries are interspersed over the spectrum of corporatism: Norway, Sweden, Finland and Austria ranked among the most corporatist countries by the late 1970s, followed by the Netherlands, Denmark, Belgium and West Germany, and trailed by Britain, the US, Canada, Australia, New Zealand, Japan, France and Italy. Although the Nordic countries are more corporatist than the English-speaking ones, this factor fails to correlate with degree of participation and entitlement in health care financing, or timing of the introduction of significant reforms.

Links between the ageing of bureaucratic infrastructures and the growth of prepaid health care were clearest during the late nineteenth and early twentieth centuries.[82] From the Middle Ages to the nineteenth century, care for the sick and the poor was largely the business of the church and charitable organizations. Venerable institutions were financed by the church and quarantine hospitals by the state. Later, private and voluntary hospitals were financed by a hodgepodge of bazaars, lotteries, tea parties, private patrons, charitable organizations, provident funds and user-fees. Like the workhouse infirmaries, hospitals served primarily to isolate the undesirable and dangerous from society. Loss of income was a greater threat during illness than the cost of medical care which, during the nineteenth century, was still regarded as ineffective, if not dangerous. Accident, disability and sick pay were among the earliest cash benefits provided by mutual cooperatives, trade guilds, sickness funds, friendly societies and so on; treatment by doctors and hospitals as a benefit in kind was introduced much later. Uncoordinated benefits were introduced in a sporadic manner, interspersed with the occasional significant reform. These were later unified at local levels, then at regional/provincial/state levels and finally at the national level. The financial infrastructures needed to collect funds were complex and required time to develop. No country introduced health care benefits in total isolation from other social benefits.

The first infrastructures for collective financing of health care were established by the private sector. Public authorities, however, soon realized that it was in their interest to support this development because one way or another, they also ended up providing part of the financing through social assistance, or subsidies for public health programs and hospitalization. During the latter part of the nineteenth century, at the same time as the early infrastructures for health insurance were developing in northern Europe, medical officers of health provided some treatment in addition to their public health duties in the Nordic countries and the UK. Similar provisions in English-speaking colonies came from a totally different direction. European settlers in Australia, Canada and New Zealand began their colonial history with centrally organized medical services, financed through the Exchequer in London, and delivered through military outposts and by naval surgeons.

These public provisions were, however, short-lived. When the colonies became independent, Britain cut off its financial support. An ongoing revolt against European-styled bureaucracies, which reminded many settlers of the conditions they had fled from, made further public sector involvement through social insurance objectionable and unwelcomed overseas. In Australia, Canada and New Zealand, out-of-pocket payment and private insurance remained the rule long after most European countries had turned to social insurance to finance health care.

Support for the significance of bureaucratic structures in influencing the timing, scope and content of these events comes primarily from detailed analysis of Denmark, Norway, Sweden and Finland from the 1880s onward.[83] The Nordic countries and the UK followed the lead in social insurance set by Bismarck in Germany during the late nineteenth century. Instead of introducing a means-tested compulsory national insurance, however, Denmark offered generous public subsidies for the officially recognized sickness funds which successfully stimulated extensive growth in membership. In Sweden, public subsidies were more modest, failing to stimulate a similar growth beyond the mandatory means-tested compulsory membership. Norway, with its complex historical links to Denmark and Sweden, introduced a mixed voluntary-compulsory model. Held back by Swedish, Russian and German occupations, Finland did not develop a sickness insurance system until after the 1950s. The Lloyd George Plan of 1911 in England extended the coverage and benefits provided by the already existing friendly societies. It is difficult to isolate the significance of this evolution from other socio-economic and political determinants because they all have the same rank order. It is entirely possible that the evolution in collective provisions for prepayment of health care was a direct result of underlying socio-economic growth and political forces rather than bureaucratic infrastructures.

There were both advantages and disadvantages to the depolarized policy-making of corporatism during the period of reform leading up to the introduction of compulsory participation and universal entitlement. In the eight case studies, there was clear evidence of the role of corporatism in reforms relating to health care financing. As has been observed in the comparative literature on social policy, the corporatist Nordic countries forced working groups, committees and commissions into a long consensus-making process.[84] Interest groups, such as the medical profession and the sickness funds, were consulted early in the policy-making process. This led to extensive contact between adversaries and an opportunity for these groups to infiltrate the policy-making machinery.[85] Radical options, such as the nationalization of hospitals, salaried doctors and tax-based financing, were eliminated through bargaining and trade-offs long before legislation was presented to parliament. Governments, political parties and interest groups were forced begrudgingly to seek consensus to stay in power, not just in the planning of policies but also in their implementation: "The politics of compromise was forced by the electoral situation, not by the fact that the Swedes loved compromise."[86]

Although the consensus-making machine of corporatism in the Nordic countries prevented long and drawn-out deadlocks ill parliament, there was a price attached to the concessions that were made in the process. In Sweden and Norway, there was hardly any debate in parliament when the government tabled legislation to introduce compulsory and universal sickness insurance. There was surprisingly no mention in the press or medical journals that other committees had already developed much more radical proposals for the introduction of British- and New Zealand-styled National Health Services.[87] The hidden compromises of corporatism failed to present voters with these clear-cut alternatives: "No politician worth his salt ... voluntarily seeks consensus: consensus has to be forced upon him."[88] In Finland and Denmark, there was some debate, but little protest.[89] The broadly defined statutes that resulted from the consensus-making process left considerable room for real policy to be defined by administrators and interest groups after the legislative phase. Both Sweden and Finland subsequently had to introduce additional legislation to cover the inadequacies of compulsory universal sickness insurance and independent private medical doctors.

In contrast, the confrontational and polarized policy-making process of the noncorporatist English-speaking countries exaggerated and sensationalized many of the key issues that were debated during the period of reform leading up to the introduction of compulsory participation and universal entitlement. In the more polarized political arena of these countries, there were no corporatist pressures to prevent executives, legislatures and regulatory agencies from introducing partisan policies. Media presentations and mass political leverage often took priority over the findings of working groups, committees and commissions. As a result, labor governments in New Zealand and the UK successfully introduced compulsory participation and universal entitlement to comprehensive health services in 1938 and 1946, which was earlier than most other countries.

The Labor and Liberal governments of Australia and Canada attempted to introduce similar legislation during the late 1940s, but changes in government and objections to interference in the market economy from a conservative-oriented opposition prevented the reforms from proceeding. The administrators working behind the scenes in these countries were more successful in isolating their work from the medical profession, insurance organizations and other interest groups than were their Nordic counterparts.

Socio-economic development and political processes appear to have been prerequisites for subsequent expansion in bureaucratic structures for prepayment of health care. Over time, as these infrastructures grew, the public became conditioned to paying taxes and making social insurance contributions toward plans that offered collective benefits. In this respect, the early experience with the friendly societies, sickness funds and other prepayment schemes may have acted as a social conditioning for popular acceptance of the higher taxes and broader tax-bases that would later be necessary to finance ambitious national programs. Similar tax burdens would have cause popular revolts in earlier times and in different cultural settings.[90] The great variability in membership rates in these schemes prior to the reforms is an argument against there being a threshold in contributory insurance before governments can introduce compulsory participation and universal entitlement.[91] See Table 11.7.

Table 11.7 Membership with Prepayment Schemes Prior to Reforms

Country	Date	Membership as % or population
New Zealand	1938	20
England	1946	50
Sweden	1953	30
Norway	1956	90
Finland	1963	10
Canada	1966	68 (different in each province)
Denmark	1971	90
Australia	1974	83 (different in each state)

Source: Adapted from Preker (1989).

(d) Market Failure

There are three standard requirements before a market economy can reach equilibrium and function efficiently in the allocation of economic goods in response to the expression of consumer preferences: perfect competition, a full set of markets and perfect information.[92] If all of these conditions are met, a Pareto-efficient allocation of resources can be expected with state intervention being limited to taxes and lump-sum transfers. Any restrictions in these criteria require additional state intervention to ensure Pareto improvements. Analysis of market failure in health care has come to the forefront in the literature only during recent years and there have been no systematic attempts to identify its existence in a cross-national or historical context.[93] A review of the history of medicine and the eight case histories presented in this study give clear evidence that market failure existed in health care long before the nineteenth century, that it occurred in all of the countries examined and that it was a significant reason for public sector involvement in health care financing.

Codes governing the conduct of healers date to antiquity when the medical profession consisted of a tightly controlled guild.[94] A clear distinction can be made between the legal responsibilities that were enforceable by law (intervention of the state), and supra-legal or ethical responsibilities that were left to the profession itself (self-regulation and exclusion from the guild). The guild approach to medicine restricted competition and markets. The doctrine of secrecy restricted information. Fee schedules influenced prices. Early laws pertaining to healers were mainly concerned with the transition from blood revenge to the principle of monetary compensation for injury. One of the earliest evidence of these duties is the *Code of Ur-nammu* (2112–2095 BC). Statute 15 reads as follows: "If a man ... cut off the foot of [another man ...] he shall pay ten shekels of silver."[95] The *Code of Hammurabi* (1792–-1750 BC) establishes a system of direct fee-for-service payment based on the nature of services rendered and the ability of the patient to pay. For two millennia, this fundamental balance between healers and patients remained essentially unchanged.

Public revenues provided the financing at an early stage for quarantine hospitals, health-related provisions under poor law relief and the public health movement in all the countries examined. In the Nordic countries, local authorities became responsible *de facto* for financing hospitals long before the end of the last century. In the English-speaking countries, private revenues played a more significant role. Australia, Canada and New Zealand had only a small landed gentry to establish voluntary, charitable and venerable institutions. As in the Nordic countries, this forced public authorities to provide financing and build public hospitals at an early stage. In this respect, Australia and Canada built more of these institutions than New Zealand, which was a much poorer country. In England, they were even more numerous. As antiseptic techniques improved and medical science advanced, hospitalization became an increasingly standard part of health care. Direct out-of-pocket payments, bazaars, lotteries, tea parties, private patrons and so on became insufficient as the main source of financing for most hospitals. With time, many of the private and non-profit institutions that were chronically underfinanced came to depend on public subsidies to stave off bankruptcy. In all eight countries, governments that provided financing for hospitals also demanded control over the institutions that they were bankrolling, even when the ownership remained in private hands. In this context, competition was far from perfect and markets severely restricted, giving rise to further government regulations, subsidies and direct provision of services.

Parallel to these developments in institutional care and public health, the trade guilds, sickness funds, friendly societies, providence funds and other health insurance organizations provided cash benefits at times of illness for groups of workers and their families. All of these organizations were established to respond to the uncertainties of urban living (unemployment, old age, illness and so on) by pooling risks and resources — a standard market technique for dealing with risk though insurance. During their early existence, the staple revenue for these organizations was provided by contributions from workers and employers. The state did not interfere with their activities. With time, however, they experienced many of the same problems that are associated with market failure in health insurance today: inconsistent contribution schedules, exclusion criteria, disclaimers, waiting periods, time limits, skim-creaming, unjustified retention rates, reserves, diversion of funds, corrupt administration, bankruptcies, low adhesion, freeriders, moral hazards and so on. When treatment by medical doctors became a benefit in kind, the various prepayment organizations of all of these countries experienced additional problems due to conflicts with doctors who accused them of interfering with the practice of medicine. Collusion among doctors against the funds, and among funds against doctors, *only* contributed to market imperfections.

Governments initially became indirectly involved in financing ambulatory care in response to these market failures.[96] In the Nordic countries, they offered public subsidies on a voluntary basis to the sickness funds that observed standardized criteria for membership and benefits.[97] When the net gains of these subsidies offset the additional benefits that they had to provide to comply with regulations, these funds had a competitive edge over those that did not receive subsidies. This was especially true when the subsidies were generous, as in Denmark and Norway, where they led to a quick rise in membership rates; when they were less generous or non-existent, as in Sweden, Finland and the English-speaking countries, the subsidies were less effective in attracting new memberships. A firm conviction that voluntary participation failed to attract adequate members, especially among low-income earners and their families, led most of the Group I countries to introduce compulsory participation for a means-tested portion of their population.[98] In Denmark, where entitlement to other social benefits was made conditional on active membership in voluntary funds, this rule had the same effect as compulsory membership for most of the population. With time, as the means-test and regulations changed, a greater percentage of the population was covered by these provisions, but this varied greatly from country to country, as was seen in Table 11.7.

At the time of the introduction of legislation calling for compulsory participation and universal entitlement, a continued failure of the competitive market to provide adequate health care for at least part of the population through prepayment schemes served as a powerful argument for additional government intervention on the basis of both efficiency and equity. As institutional care — the most expensive component of health services — became increasingly financed through public funds, reformers argued that an extension of coverage to ambulatory care would represent only a minor additional financial outlay to the public sector. This argument certainly had merit in the case of the Nordic countries, New Zealand and Canada, where universal access to hospital care was already financed largely through public funds before the reforms. In Canada, universal access to hospitals was introduced under the National Hospital and Diagnostic Services Act of 1957, nine years before the Medical Care Act of 1966.[99] In Australia, access to treatment on public wards was introduced temporarily under the Hospital Benefits Act of 1946, years before entitlement was extended to ambulatory care in 1973.[100] In Great Britain, treatment of war casualties during World War I and World War II exposed the population to universal entitlement to hospital care prior to the creation of the National Health Service in 1948, although this entitlement was retracted following the wars.

In the Nordic countries, the free-rider problem was extensively used to argue in favor of extending compulsory sickness insurance to the whole population. Low membership in the sickness funds in Sweden in the early 1950s provided additional ammunition for those who claimed that the potential gains from introducing compulsory participation in revenue collection outweighed the risk of increased expenditure due to universal entitlement. The low membership in the friendly societies in New Zealand prior to 1938 provided a similar argument. The restriction of ambulatory care to members of the sickness funds and those who could afford to pay cash in Norway in the early 1950s was thought to contribute to an inappropriate use of free institutional care by those who had no other coverage.[101] In Denmark and Canada, the reforms were originally proposed by conservative political groups who believed that centralized control over public expenditure would enhance administrative efficiency, and eliminate the misappropriation of public funds through high retention rates and reserves of some private insurance organizations. In New Zealand and the UK, the reformers feared that disability payments, sickness pay and illness-related unemployment benefits would reach astronomic levels if universal access to state-controlled health services were not created to monitor these potential abuses. See Table 11.8.

A caveat is necessary when discussing market failure in health care in the context of this study. Given that all the governments that introduced compulsory participation and universal entitlement had left-wing

Table 11.8 Government Responses to Market Failure

Market Failure in Health Care Financing	Government Responses
Risks, uncertainty, asymmetric information	Prepayment
Cost of health care, need	Prepayment
Moral hazards, free riders	Co-payments
Supplier induced demand, congestion	Co-payments
Monopolies, monopsonies,	Regulations
Endowments, insolvency	Subsidies
Rivalness, excludability, externalities	Public services
Free riders	Compulsory participation
Adverse selection	Universal entitlement

Source: Adapted from Preker (1989).

ideologies, there is a risk that market failure was specifically highlighted in these countries in defense of these reforms. There is also a possibility that extensive government regulations, subsidies and direct provision of services distort imperfect markets more in these countries than in those where there is less government intervention, leading to a vicious circle of escalating imbalances. The international literature on market failure in health care comes almost exclusively from the UK, Canada, New Zealand, Australia and the Nordic countries, especially Sweden. There is much less literature on this subject from the US, Germany and France, where one would assume that market failure in health care is even more pronounced due to the less direct involvement of governments in correcting these imperfections. There is plenty of evidence that the phenomena described in the English and Scandinavian literature on market failure also exists in other countries. One possibility is that, in countries where governments have not tried to introduce compulsory and universal policies, state intervention may be viewed as a normal regulatory activity in response to market imperfections rather than as a socialist political agenda. Future work is needed to validate this hypothesis.

2. Normative Functions of Governments (How and What)

Whatever the reasons for the introduction various of degrees of participation in and entitlement to health services, the state needs the financial means to carry out its business, and policies on *how* and on *what* to spend them. Many of the differences that are observed in health care financing in the OECD can be explained by the choices that governments have made when faced with conflicts between their role in resource allocation, income distribution and stabilization of economic activity.[102] These three activities have come to be viewed as normative functions of government in all western societies, irrespective of their political inclination: all use regulations, subsidies and direct provision of services as a way to allocate social goods; all use various forms of taxation (social insurance) and social security benefits (cash and in kind) as a way to redistribute income; and all use fiscal and monetary policies as a way to influence employment, prices and economic growth. Each plays an important role in addressing various market failures in the health sector. This study gave rich insights into how and what governments did to use health care financing as an instrument for performing these functions.[103] The introduction of legislation for compulsory participation and universal entitlement was part of this process. See Table 11.9.

(a) Allocation Function

A distinction needs to be made in how several categories of goods and services are allocated in mixed-market economies.[104] Some goods can be classified as private goods. These are marketable in that they can be sold at a price that is based on their market value and are allocated efficiently

Table 11.9 Health Care Financing as Instrument of Public Policy

Functions	Allocation	Distribution	Stabilization
Instruments	Regulations	Revenue collection	Employment
	Subsidies	Reimbursements	Cost controls
	Services	Benefits in kind	Production

Source: Adapted from Preker (1989).

through a competitive market mechanism. Both private firms and public enterprises may produce marketable goods. Private goods produced by public enterprises include transportation, postal services, energy and so on. Other goods can be classified as public goods. They are non-marketable because they lack rivalness and excludability, and often have externalities that make it difficult to limit their consumption to any individual user.[105] Examples of these goods include military services, courts, police and fire departments. Everyone in society can share their collective benefit. **Merit goods** are marketable but given away free-of-charge because governments judge it desirable that they be available without exclusion due to non-payment. Examples of these goods include food, housing and education.[106] Finally, governments can choose to tax **demerit goods** such as tobacco and alcohol because of their undesirable effects.[107] Through their allocation function, governments use regulations, subsidies and direct provision of goods and services as instruments to correct failures that occur in the allocation of social goods in a competitive market, as well as to achieve a desired balance between them.[108]

Health care is not a homogeneous activity and cannot be fitted into any one of these categories in either Group I or Group II countries. Most health care goods and services are mixed goods because they have some rivalness and some excludability.[109] For example, the benefits of immunization are not only externalized like public goods by preventing the spread of disease in the community but are also internalized like private goods by preventing personal illness which leads to rivalness and excludability if the supply of vaccine is limited. Yet, public health services, such as disease control, prevention and health promotion are usually provided as public goods. Hospital care and physician services, although marketable, are increasingly provided as merit goods, free-of-charge or with modest co-payments. Long-term residential care for those who are dependent on the rest of society at either extreme of the life cycle is often still regarded a private good. Institutions for this kind of care usually require payments by residents or their families. Their ownership and management is shared between the private and public sectors. Most countries also make a limited number of these institutions available as merit goods through public subsidies for patients who could not afford to pay. Ambulatory care not provided by doctors, pharmaceuticals, medical appliances and so on is more

Health Care Functions
- Financing
- Clinical and non-clinical services
- Manufacturing of inputs

Public goods
- policy making
- prevention
- health promotion

Private goods
- most financing
- most services
- most manufacturing

Merit goods
- depends on policy choice
- extensive in OECD
- Increases over time

Figure 11.3 Public, Private and Merit Goods

Source: Adapted from Preker (1989).

difficult to place. Sometimes it is sold as private goods; at other times they are provided as merit goods. See Figure 11.3.

The principal difference between health care financing in Group I and Group II countries is the place that the boundaries are draw to account for some of these differences in the allocation of health care as an economic good. When they introduced compulsory prepayment and universal entitlement, countries in Group I choose to treat most health services as merit goods, irrespective of whether or not sub-components behave more as public, mixed or private economic goods. The intention was to eliminate the elements of excludability and rivalness based on the ability to pay. Previous restrictions to access based on market forces and ability to pay were replaced by professional control and limits in the supply of public resources.[110] Direct charges were maintained on some excluded goods and services, and as symbolic co-payments on others. In Canada, only hospital care and services provided by doctors were initially treated as merit goods. All other ambulatory care continued to be treated as private goods. In New Zealand, Norway, Sweden and Finland, general practitioners continued to charge a fee, while patients received a partial reimbursement from the state or insurance fund. In the UK, above-standard care continued to be provided through a small private sector. Direct charges and co-payments were continued on pharmaceuticals and medical supplies in almost all countries.

Although the classification of most health care as a merit good helped Group I countries overcomes some of the problems created by market failure, it created others. The nature of the economic good determines its efficient and equitable allocation, not its production function or arbitrary classification as a merit good by governments. Components that behaved as private goods continued to be allocated more efficiently and equitably through a decentralized market mechanism based on consumer preference and some out-of-pocket payment. Components that behaved as public goods were better allocated through centralized planning. When these classifications were wrong, social goods became congested and began to behave increasingly like private goods. By offering doctors and other health care providers gratuities or "black money" to jump the queue, an underground market environment was sometimes created that undermined the official policy on how *to* treat the involved goods and services.[111] This phenomenon was observed to some extent in each of the eight case studies and many introduced subsequent reforms to deal with the resulting barriers to universal entitlement. More research is required *to* identify the threshold at which congestion takes place and the type of health care goods that are most vulnerable to this phenomenon.

Apart from the problems that were created by underground markets, no western country can claim to have found the ideal solution to the planned allocation of social goods.[112] In practice, national resource allocation is usually carried out in a haphazard manner, based on a combination of historical trends, influenced by public choice (voters), pressure groups, political parties and the power of various ministries.[113] As a result of these force, the regional budgets (B_r) of most western countries remain historical and resource-driven. The previous year's regional budget (B_{t-1}) is increased incrementally to accommodate approved requests from individual institutions ($B_{i \ldots n}$).

$$B_r = (B_{t-1} + \Sigma B_{i \ldots n})$$

The UK and Nordic countries were among the first to try to improve the planned allocation process by basing their regional budgets on a baseline adjusted budget that was determined by the population structure of the region (B_b) and adjusted for morbidity (M), socio-economic factors (S), resource levels (R) and cross-boundary flows (F) as well as other factors (K).[114] Canada and Australia tried similar techniques at the regional level within individual provinces and states. These techniques have reduced but not eliminated inequities because even the most sophisticated statistical analysis[115] cannot address the fundamental question of the relationship between need and provision of health care.[116]

$$B_r = B_b[M,S,R,F \ldots K]$$

A variety of methods have been tried to improve the planned allocation of resources to local institutions ($B_{t'}$). Retrospective reimbursements may be based on price (P) and services rendered (Q) such as admissions, length-of-stay or individual services ($B_t = \Sigma P_i\, Q_i$). This leads to a maximization of output and expenditure without any guarantee of improved efficiency, effectiveness or equity. Diagnosis Related Group (DRG) reimbursements are a variation on retrospective systems.[117] They also lead to maximization of price (P_{DRG}) and services rendered (Q_{DRG}). However, they encourage internal efficiency because hospitals are paid the same for each episode of illness regardless of the length-of-stay or the level of resources used. They also potentially lead to increased costs as institutions and health professionals maximize revenues ($B_t = P_{DRG}Q_{DRG}$) by manipulating volumes and diagnostic groups. Global prospective reimbursements may be based on planned allocation formulas. Health Management Organizations (HMOs) or Preferred Provider Organizations (PPOs) are local variations on prospective reimbursements.[118] The key variables needed to establish an equitable budget in all of these cases are often missing: population, case-mix, socio-economic factors and so on ($B_{t'}$ = (B_b[M,S,R,F ... K])). All lead to some inequity as better performing institutions grow stronger and laggards fall further behind. Group I countries use the prospective model more than the retrospective model, and vice versa for Group II countries. But this is not a hard fast rule.

The planned allocation of scarce resources requires a trade-off between two conflicting concepts — Pareto efficiency and social justice or equity. These issues were not resolved through the introduction of compulsory prepayment and universal entitlement. Central strategies often failed to be transmitted to the local level.[119] Because of incremental changes over time, political pressure tactics, practice styles, ideology and class struggles,[120] the resources of local institutions within a given region continued to vary greatly. The definition of catchment populations, cross-boundary flows, centers of excellence, the balance between capital and recurrent expenditure, limited resources, unbalanced demands and so on all created the same problems following the reforms as they do today.[121] Local institutions, departments and individual health care providers were able to remain unresponsive to central strategies. What was intended as a rational top-down approach to resource allocation often ended up as a bottom-up utilization drive system because of retrospective reimbursements or manipulation of global budgets at the institutional level.[122] The resulting imperfections in planning were at times as inefficient and inequitable as the market failures they were intended to replace. These issues, which remain largely unresolved, are at the center of the health care financing reforms taking place today in both Group I and Group II countries.

(b) Distribution Function

A distinction can be made in how income and wealth is distributed and how resources are allocated in market economies.[123] Efficient use of resources requires that factors of production equal the value of their marginal product. But distribution of income is rarely equal to the proceeds from the sale of factor products in either capitalist or socialist societies. Instead, distribution of income is based on a number of imperfect factor endowments. Labor endowments depend on the ability and desire to sell personal services. These are influenced by variables such as education, professional skills, salary structure, family connections, social status, personality, race, sex, age and so forth. Capital endowments depend on inheritance, marriage and lifetime savings. These are also influenced by variables similar to those described for labor income. Health status can be seen as both a natural and acquired endowment. In contrast to the allocation of resources, Pareto efficiency and social welfare functions fail to provide a satisfactory or fair mechanism for the distribution of income. This has led some authors to claim that "just and equitable distribution is not within the purview of economics but should be left to philosophers, poets and politicians."[124] Natural law philosophers such as Hobbes and Locke would support endowment-based criteria. Bentham and Mills would support utilitarian criteria. Rousseau, Marx and Rawls would support different variations on egalitarian criteria.

Through their distribution function, governments try to correct some of the inefficiencies and injustices that occur in the natural distribution of income and accumulation of wealth. They use two sets of instruments for this purpose — revenue collection and income redistribution. A gross overview of the current accounts of most western countries indicates that the main instruments used for revenue collection are taxation, social insurance, grants, interest, loans and other miscellaneous categories.[125] The balance between these categories, and between central and local levels of government, varies greatly from one country to another.[126] On the expenditure side, outlays are made on goods and services, transfer payments, grants-in-aid, interest and other miscellaneous categories. A distinction once again needs to be made between central and local government spending as well as between capital and current expenditure. Because funds are usually pooled rather than earmarked, the revenue collection process is rarely directly linked to the distribution process (pensions and unemployment benefits. The instruments used to achieve efficiency and equity in the two processes are likewise different.

Much of the literature on the welfare state deals with various aspects of efficiency and equity relative to the income distribution function of governments. Revenue collection for health care is clearly part of this process, but with rare exceptions,[127] it is usually treated as part of the resource allocation function or a pooling of risk through insurance.[128] Health care provided through the public sector is a benefit in kind, and patient reimbursements are a form of transfer payment or cash benefit. The governments of the eight countries examined in this study intended compulsory and universal entitlement to serve as an instrument for income redistribution, and not only to protect the population against the uncertainties of illness.

Two issues and their associated policy options were at the center of the debates on revenue collection during the reform period — direct versus prepaid financing mechanisms and voluntary versus compulsory participation. As described earlier, the cornerstone of revenue collection in most western counties is prepayment, which falls into one of three broad categories: general revenues characterized by the British National Health Service, social insurance characterized by Bismarckian sickness funds and private insurance characterized by American consumer sovereignty.[129]

Each of these was used to some extent by the eight countries at the time of their reforms. When faced with a choice between progressive, proportional or regressive contribution schemes, advocates of Pareto efficiency choose a progressive tax (social insurance) based on income and collected at source.[130] They argued that the coercive power of the poor needed to be exercised through the democratic political process to enforce income redistribution.[131] The continued use of direct charges and co-payments was defended and accused on the basis of both efficiency and equity criteria, as well as on broader socio-economic, political and bureaucratic grounds. In Sweden they were seen as an economic incentive to encourage the efficient use of scarce resources. In Canada they were seen as an ineffective way to influence efficiency and a regressive way to distribute the welfare burden illness. These issues remained unresolved in Group I countries.

Government redistribution strategies invariably require that significant efficiency/equity tradeoffs be made. First, as tax rates rise, a point is reached beyond which revenues and funds available for redistribution actually decline because individuals work less.[132] Second, it lowers disposable income which might be spent on food, housing and so on, which have a significant indirect impact on health. The limits to acceptable loss in efficiency in exchange for equity gains are not clear in health care and the cutoff-point at which this occurs is open to considerable debate.[133]

Detailed analysis of equity in health care financing is complex because the source of revenues is diverse and pooled.[134] Although Gini coefficients and Lorenz curves have been used as indicators of income inequality,[135] they are less useful in the analysis of health care financing.[136] Analysis of equity in revenue collection for the health care can nevertheless be separated into vertical and horizontal components.[137] Vertical equity requires that contributions be related to ability to pay, and that unequals be treated in an appropriately dissimilar way. Several models have been developed for measuring vertical equity,[138] which is determined by the progressivity of the contribution scheme.[139] Horizontal equity requires that contributions be similar among those with comparable income or wealth, and that equals be treated equally. Methodologies for measuring this in terms of family size, pre-tax versus post-tax income, capital assets and inherited wealth are much more complex.[140] Combining the collection and benefit processes through risk-rated contributions and membership-dependent access works against both of these components of equity.

These techniques were not well developed at the time most countries in Group I introduced their legislative reforms. Instead, their governments believed that compulsory participation by those who were able to pay was the most efficient and equitable way to collect revenues for universal entitlement to health care. No quantitative analysis was conducted to calculate the progressivity of the proposed financing mechanisms. The main concern was to extend and enforce the contribution base as broadly as possible.

Two issues and their associated policy options were also at the center of the debates on the distribution of health care as a benefit in kind — restricted versus universal entitlement and basic versus comprehensive services. The efficiency and equity of health care as an instrument of income redistribution need to be distinguished from similar issues in revenue collection and resource allocation. Based on the law of diminishing marginal utility, inequalities are inefficient in that they satisfy less urgent needs of the rich at the expense of the more urgent needs of the poor.[141] The transfer of income from the rich to the poor can therefore be justified from a utilitarian point of view because it would satisfy more intense wants at the expense of less intense wants.[142] Scholars during the 1940s used egalitarian arguments to justify dividing income equally.[143] Others since then claim that, because people's tastes differ, the marginal utility of income differs and the maximization of minimum standards may be preferable over equality.[144]

Applying these arguments to health care as a benefit in kind, some countries maintain that entitlement should be equal for the whole population while others favor targeting needy populations. Some offer comprehensive services while others limit benefits to a minimal set of basic services. Countries in Group I adhere to the former view, while those in Group II adhere to the latter. The introduction of compulsory prepayment and universal entitlement to comprehensive health services were the policies chosen by the countries of the eight case studies.

Conceptually, the role health care plays as an instrument of redistribution need to be analyzed in terms that are different from those for the allocation of public and social goods in response to market failure. Conflicts often exist between the most efficient and equitable redistribution of health care as a benefit in kind and the allocation of health care as goods and services.[145] Each function can and should be evaluated on its own merit so that the compromises that are made along the way are clear.

The transfer of income from the "relatively well to the relatively sick" can be carried out effectively through the various forms of prepayment of health care.[146] Central planning may be an effective way to respond to market failures in the efficient and equitable allocation of health care goods and services, but insufficient as instruments for redistributing endowments unless policies are designed to achieve this objective. Natural and acquired health, and the resulting requirements for health care, is influenced by both labor and capital, as well as by the many variables that influence these endowments.[147] The lower down the socio-economic scale, the greater the prevalence of illness and potential benefit from health care. Observed increases in reported illness among lower social groups are rarely matched by the rate of increase in utilization of health care.[148] Resource allocation mechanisms therefore do not fulfill the requirements for additional redistribution.[149] Universal entitlement as a resource allocation mechanism may not achieve this objective. Additional targeting for the needy populations may be necessary. See Table 11.10.

Table 11.10 Health Care as a Benefit in Kind

Issues	Policy Options
Revenue collection	
Mechanisms	Direct charges versus prepayment
Participation	Voluntary versus compulsory
Benefits in kind	
Entitlement	Restricted versus universal
Services	Basic versus comprehensive
Linkages	
Contributions	Risk-rated versus non-rated
Access	Membership-dependent versus open-ended

Source: Adapted from Preker (1989).

(c) Stabilization Function

The stabilization function of government can be achieved through two mechanisms — fiscal policy and monetary policy.[150] At first glance, health care does not appear to be directly involved in either of these processes. This is a false impression. When health care financing depends on public funds, as it did in all the countries examined in this study as well as in most other western countries, activities in the health sector have a significant impact on economic stabilization and vice versa. The usual targets of Keynesian policies are employment, prices and economic growth. Monetarist concerns with the adverse effects of deliberate manipulation of these factors ignore the indirect effects that government involvement in resource allocation and income distribution has on stabilization. Health care expenditure, which continues to increase in most western countries, influences not only growth but also employment, aggregate demand and prices. Cost containment policies to counteract this trend have filled the health care literature during the 1980s,[151] but they are seldom referred to as stabilization policies.[152] Although public sector deficits are making these strategies seem all the more urgent in recent years,[153] this study did not find a significant correlation between indicators of socio-economic development (GDP per capita, economic growth and national debt) and the introduction of compulsory participation and universal entitlement.[154]

The potential economic impact of public involvement in health care financing was a subject of considerable debate during the period leading up to the reforms. Two different points of view were expressed in the eight case histories. There were those that warned that universal entitlement to health care would lead to a cost explosion and increased public expenditure on health care to the point where it would damage economic stability and public expenditure on other social benefits. Opponents to this point of view claimed that because the public sector already financed hospitals, the most expensive part of health care, it would be advantageous to also have greater control over these expenditures. It was felt that compulsory participation would not only increase revenues but also give authorities more control over the services that it already financed.

Longitudinal analysis of health care expenditure trends, opportunity costs and displacement effects indicated that both of these divergent points of view had some merit. In nominal values, public expenditure on health care increased rapidly both before and after the introduction of compulsory participation and universal entitlement in each of the eight countries. (See the example below and the Appendix for the remaining countries). Similar increases have, however, occurred in all OECD countries, and the rate of growth in Group I has not been significantly greater than that in Group II.[155] Health care expenditure represented in this way is deceptive because it ignores a number of important hidden features that were difficult to measure in their historical context: demographic growth, health care price increases, changes in utilization per capita and growth in GDP.[156] Information on health care price indexes, GDP deflators and utilization rates was unreliable during the period of the early reforms, making it impossible to represent these trends in real values. Relative to GDP, health care expenditure stabilized during the decade that followed the reforms in most of these countries.[157] In most cases, GDP elasticity of health care expenditure was less than 1.0 during this period, which indicates that relative changes in health care expenditure per GDP did not distort the trends.[158] The mean elasticity for the OECD group was 1.7 from 1960–1975 and 1.3 from 1975–1987 in real values.[159] Both are higher than what was observed following the reforms. (See Appendix for the expenditure pattern for all eight countries during the decade the followed the landmark legislative reforms).

Health care expenditure relative to total government expenditure and government consumption expenditure also stabilized during the decade that followed the reform. This indicates that the reform was not associated with a significant opportunity cost or displacement effect in terms of money that could have been spent on other economic activities or public works. Government total expenditure and government consumption expenditure increased relative to GDP, which indicated that the public sector continued to consume an increasing part of these economic resources of these countries and that there was both a willingness and capacity to pay. Following this initial decade of stability, public expenditure on health care increased compared with GDP and rose in an erratic manner until the early 1980s, as did expenditure on other social benefits financed through the public sector. It rose more slowly, than total government expenditure. (See Appendix for the expenditure pattern for all eight countries during the decade the followed the landmark legislative reforms).

There are several compelling arguments in favor of cost containment in health care, but each has its shortcomings. First, since consumer preferences for social goods are concealed, cost containment may be seen as a way to set limits. But arguments that public opinion is expressed through the election process are unconvincing because cost containment is rarely a central issue. Second, it is often presented as a way to force institutions to become more efficient and effective. But in practice, repairs, maintenance and the quality of services deteriorate without eliminating waste. Third, it offers the possibility of stability in health care expenditure relative to the state budget and GDP. But in practice, this only occurs when the budget and GDP also remain stable. Fourth, it is a way to limit health care expenditure according to the capacity to pay. But there is no evidence that the health sector can contract as rapidly as restrictive fiscal policies are introduced during periods of economic hardship. Instead, it leads to health sector deficits and a destabilization of service delivery. Finally, advocates of cost containment claim that expenditure on health care encroaches on other social sectors that have a significant impact on health and that it may have a "crowding-out" effect on the private sector. There was no evidence for this in the study. Nor is there any evidence in the literature that more meritorious alternatives are chosen when public sector spending on health care is curtailed or that saving leads to more productive re-investments in other areas of the economy.

This leads to equally compelling counter-arguments against cost containment which also have serious failings. First, if medical care confers benefits in terms of health, the opportunity cost of cost containment may be higher that the savings gained. But cost benefit and cost-effectiveness studies are not yet advanced enough to establish convincing evidence to support this claim and treatments that lead to increased life-expectancy adds the cost of caring for the more fragile elderly. Furthermore, the human desire to avoid illness and death outstrips the capacity to pay even in the richest countries. Second, health care is a production function in itself that is hurt by aimless cost containment. It employs workers and provides income that is recycled through the economy. Such growth may, however, be undesirable when restrictive fiscal policies are being used to stabilize prices and economic growth. Third, because unemployment is associated with deteriorating health status, cost containment at the time of economic hardship weakens the social infrastructures needed to respond to the potentially increased demand for services. Critics of health care would, of course, say that the focus is wrong. Food, housing and income support may be more meritorious at such times and have a greater impact on health than health care itself. Finally, in mixed systems, cost containment in the public sector does not stop expenditure in the private sector, but it may hurt equity at a time when this is needed the most.

In addition to the unresolved debate described above, there are also several conceptual problems associated with the generic term cost containment, which is sometimes interchanged inappropriately with the notions of cost recovery and co payments. The term may refer to either aggregate expenditure trends at the national level or specific institutional responses at the local level. It may refer to public expenditure and leave private expenditure uncontrolled. It may refer to direct costs and ignore indirect costs such as waiting time, lost work and the value of good health. Some authors even question whether cost containment by itself is a valid health care policy option. Because most health care goods and services are not allocated by a market mechanism, the optimal and desired level of spending from the point of view of the consumer is largely unknown. When spending caps are set too low, congestion occurs and black markets develop which defeats the normative function of governments in the resource allocation process.

The most serious flaw in analyses of expenditure and cost containment policies in the health sector is therefore the lack of positioning of these policies in relation to the three normative functions of government that have been described in this section —allocation, distribution and stabilization. The role that health care plays as an instrument of stabilization can and should be analyzed in conceptual terms that are different from those for resource allocation and income redistribution because the objectives are different. When each is evaluated on its own merit, some of the contradictions become apparent. At a time of restrictive fiscal policies, cost containment may be correct from a stabilization point of view. But it implies significant trade-offs in the redistribution of benefits in kind and the balance in resource allocation between different public and merit goods that should be accounted for in the final analysis. These issues were not properly analyzed by the reformers who introduced compulsory participation and universal entitlement as a way to gain greater public control over the allocation of health care goods and services. They remain poorly analyzed today.

3. Outcome from Public Financing of Health Care (To What Effect)

An attempt was made to not only look at the determinants of policies relating to health care financing but also establish correlations between these policies and other aspects of modern societies. With rare exceptions, virtually no studies have turned the usual questions about causal factors around and looked at the impact of health policy and expenditure on economic development, political processes, bureaucratic structures and responses to market failure. The few studies that have looked at these issues have left many questions unanswered and hypotheses on the impact of the welfare effort need to be validated before they are transferred to health care as a specific program feature. Because macro-aggregates never describe reality perfectly, this analysis was supplemented by information from descriptive analysis. Standard indicators were developed to quantify a number of possible long-term effects of the reforms: economic performance, national debt, opportunity costs, displacement effects on social security, political backlash, public sector activity, health care expenditure and equity.[160]

The following section looks at proxy performance measures that can be derived from the specific research done in this study. A broader, discussion on the overall impact of universal health care coverage is provided in Chapter 12, using secondary sources that were not part of the specific research done for this volume. Table 11.11 provides a summary of proxy measure of performance in terms of their domain, effects and indicators used for this study.

In Table 11.12, Group I countries were assigned the "dummy" variable $\tau = 1$, while Group II countries were assigned $\tau = 0$. When the landmark legislation in Greece, Italy and Spain occurred too close to the date of the outcome indicators, these countries were assigned $r = 0$. Lack of consistent date made it necessary to omit some of the OECD counties, such as Portugal, Iceland, Switzerland and Turkey from this part of the analysis.

Table 11.11 Proxy Measures of Performance

Domain	Effect	Indicator
Socio-economic development	Growth	GDP_{cap} and GDP_{gwt}
	Debt	GGD/GDP
	Opportunity cost	GCE/GDP
Political processes	Displacement	GSE/GDP
	Backlash	HCE_{ela}
Administrative structures	Expenditure	GTE/GDP and HCE_{ppp}/GDP_{cap}
Market failure responses	Equity	Pub/Tot

Source: Adapted from Preker (1989).

The variables used were GDP per capita (GDP_{cap}), average real GDP growth rates (GDP_{gwt}), general government debt (GGD), government consumption expenditure (GCE/GDP), government social expenditure (GSE), GDP elasticity of health care expenditure (HCE_{ela}), general government total expenditure (GTE), purchase-power-parity-adjusted health care expenditure (HCE_{ppp}) and the ratio of public to total health care expenditure (Pub/Tot).[161] This representation allowed some of the abstract ideas described in the discussion on determinants to be translated into concrete concepts that could be measured and validated in a consistent way. See Table 11.12.

In Table 11.13, the "dummy" variable τ became the independent variable which was used to validate hypotheses about correlations between the introduction of legislation for compulsory participation and universal entitlement to various aspects of socio-economic development, political processes, administrative structures and market failure through regression techniques.[162] Much as positive correlations do not imply causality, when there was no correlation, it disproved hypotheses on determinant relationships and popular myths. The negative findings were therefore, in many respects, more significant than the positive ones. The analysis was performed with and without countries such as Greece, Italy and Spain to rule out the possibility that late entrants might distort the findings. See Table 11.13.

The most striking observation made in this study was the lack of a significant correlation between the introduction of landmark legislative

Table 11.12 Outcome Indicators for Effects of Legislative Reforms

Group I and Group II Countries	τ	GDP_{cap}	GDP_{gwt}	GGD/GDP	GCE/GDP	GSE/GDP	GTE/GDP	HCE_{ppp}	HCE/GDP	HCE_{ela}	Pub/Tot
			%	%	%	%	%		%	%	%
		$US 87	65–87	85	87	87	87	$US	87	75–87	87
Aus	1	12612	1.8	25.2	18.0	10.8	28.8	939	7.4	0.9	70.5
Aut	0	11664	3.1	48.5	19.0	21.3	40.3	982	8.4	0.8	67.1
Bel	0	11802	2.6	126.6	16.0	36.9	52.9	879	7.4	1.6	76.9
Can	1	17211	2.7	69.2	20.0	4.2	24.2	1483	8.6	0.9	73.9
Den	1	13329	1.9	68.6	25.0	14.8	39.8	792	5.9	0.9	85.5
Fin	1	12838	3.2	20.2	21.0	10.9	31.9	949	7.4	0.9	78.6
Fra	0	12803	2.7	34.0	19.0	26.1	45.1	1105	8.6	3.1	74.8
Ger	0	13323	2.5	42.2	20.0	10.1	30.1	1093	8.2	0.9	78.4
Gre	1	6363	3.1	53.2	20.0	30.9	50.9	337	5.3	2.5	75.3
Ire	0	7541	2.0	128.3	18.0	42.4	60.4	561	7.4	1.5	87.0
Ita	1	12254	2.7	99.4	17.0	35.0	52.0	841	6.9	1.7	79.2
Jap	0	13182	4.2	69.4	10.0	7.4	17.4	915	6.9	1.4	73.0
Net	0	12252	2.1	70.3	16.0	41.7	57.7	1041	8.5	1.1	73.9
New	1	10680	0.9	45.0	15.0	32.1	47.1	733	6.9	0.9	82.5
Nor	1	15405	3.5	31.4	21.0	19.6	40.6	1149	7.5	2.0	97.6
Spa	1	8681	2.3	41.7	14.0	20.8	34.8	521	6.0	1.1	71.5
Swe	1	13771	1.8	71.4	27.0	15.9	42.9	1233	9.0	1.0	90.8
UK	1	12340	1.7	56.5	21.0	17.9	38.9	758	6.1	1.0	86.4
US	0	18338	1.5	48.3	21.0	2.3	23.3	2051	11.2	1.1	41.4

Source: Adapted from Preker (1989).

Table 11.13 Regression Analysis Using τ as the Independent Variable

Independent Variable	R^2 with Changes in $\tau = 0$		
Dependent Variables Below	Full list	Spain Greece	Spain Greece Italy
GDP_{cap}	0.00	0.10	0.11
GDP_{gwt}	0.03	0.06	0.07
GGD	0.02	0.04	0.012
GCE/GDP	0.11	0.19	0.24
GSE/GDP	0.03	0.06	0.14
HCE_{ela}	0.02	0.07	0.14
GTE/GDP	0.01	0.01	0.05
HCE_{ppp}/ GDP_{cap}	0.26	0.04	0.02
HCE_{ppp}	0.07	0.00	0.01
Pub/Tot	0.17	0.23	0.22
No. of observations		19	
Degrees of freedom		17	

Source: Adapted from Preker (1989).

reforms in Group I compared with Group II and most of the outcome indicators. Perhaps most significantly, there was no correlation between these reforms and most of the indicators for socio-economic development. The reform policies introduced by the countries in Group I did not correlate with problems in national wealth, economic growth or national debt. This contradicts claims by some critics who have argued that public expenditure increases the cost of production, lowers demand, displaces the productive labor force and makes industries less competitive.[163] The indicators in this category are highly standardized and well-recognized measures of economic performance and therefore least likely to suffer from distortions due to misinterpretation. Opportunity costs in terms of government consumption expenditure were, however, greater for Group I countries than for Group II when Greece, Italy and Spain were reclassified as $\tau = 0$. There was, therefore, weak evidence that these policies were associated with governments that had greater consumption expenditure, which might imply less private sector activity. Furthermore, this correlation does not imply causality because public sector activities, such as wages, are spent and recycled through the private sector in western countries.

The introduction of the reforms in Group I countries compared with those in Group II did not show any correlation with a displacement of revenues away from government social expenditure such as social security benefits or slow the expansion of the health sector: correlations with social expenditure and GDP elasticity of health care were both insignificant. The indicators used for political processes and backlash are less standardized than those use for socio-economic development. It is therefore necessary to supplement these findings with observations from the descriptive analysis. There has been a backlash against "free" entitlement to health care in both western and eastern European countries during the late 1980s. Financing through "painfully visible" general revenues is the frequently cited cause of discontent. Some recent reforms may therefore represent a tax revolt and anti-government sentiment rather than a backlash against prepayment of health care. But the proposals for reform often include a call for a return to direct charges rather than prepayment which, in the long run, will have a significant negative impact on equity and financial protection against the risk of illness. It is too early to know if the countries in Group I are more prone to this trend than those of Group II.

Correlations between the introduction of compulsory participation and universal entitlement with administrative infrastructures were less clear. The reforms were not associated with larger public sectors than in countries that had not introduced these policies, but it did show a weak correlation with higher total health care expenditure per GDP. This observation is surprising because it contradicts most of the current anecdotal evidence in the literature that public sector involvement in health care is an effective way to control costs: "the general conclusion [is] that centralized cash-limited budgets have a significant negative impact on the total and that public finance also reduces total expenditure,"[164] because governments are more likely to impose expenditure caps and global budgets than insurance funds. This negative observation is highly significant, because it may indicate that there are some serious problems in existing cost containment theories that need to be re-examined. It merits much more detailed work than was possible during the study. The fact that the observation only holds true when Greece, Italy and Spain were classified as $\tau = 1$ indicates that these countries contribute positively to the correlation. The eight case studies demonstrated that there was always a transient increase before health care expenditure per GDP finally stabilized and decreased during the decade after the reform. This may be the effect observed in the regression analysis.

Finally, the introduction of compulsory participation and universal entitlement was associated with a greater degree of public financing for health care than in countries that do not have these provisions, irrespective of whether the prepayment is made through general taxation, social insurance or health insurance. This observation was most significant when the late entrants, Greece, Spain and Italy, were excluded. Taxes, cash transfer payments, indirect benefits in kind and other publicly financed programs all lead to income redistribution and greater economic equality for the non-working poor — the aged, single mothers, older workers and other unemployed.[165] In this respect, the reforms were associated *with* greater equity than in countries that rely more on privately financed health care. Once again, however, the quantitative indicator used for this variable does not guarantee that other qualitative aspects of equity, such as access and comprehensiveness, will also be met. The impact of increased health care expenditure and increase public financing could be offset by inefficient, ineffective and poor quality treatment. This study did not clarify hypotheses about these issues.

Because HCE_{ppp}/GDP_{cap} appeared to have a significant correlation with the introduction of compulsory participation and universal entitlement, this indicator was checked for cross-correlations against several of the other variables. The strongest cross-correlation was between HCE_{ppp} and GDP_{gwt} ($R^2 = 0.83$). This is similar to the observations that have been made by other authors who have carried out such analysis.[166] The temptation to conclude that a determinant relationship exist when statistical analysis reveals the presence of strong correlations should be resisted, Without concomitant path analysis, even a strong correlation like this fails to give unequivocal evidence of a causal relationship. The weak correlation between HCE_{ppp}/GDP_{cap} and the other variables, such as GSE/GDP,

Table 11.14 Regression Analysis Using HCE_{ppp} as Dependent Variable

Dependent Variable = HCE_{ppp} Independent Variables Below	R^2
GDP_{cap}	0.83
GDP_{gwt}	0.01
GGO	0.03
GCE/GDP	0.09
GSE/GDP	0.32
HCE_{ela}	0.03
GTE/GDP	0.24
Pub/Tot	0.25
No. of observations	19
Degrees of freedom	17

Source: Adapted from Preker (1989).

GTE/GDP and Pub/Tot, is not surprising because they are all cross-linked. See Table 11.14.

There are clear limits to relative growth in health care expenditure and the social sectors cannot continue forever to consume an increasing part of GDP.[167] At one point or another, growth in relative expenditure has to cease. As we approach 2020, this point has not yet been reached in western societies. The slow-down that was observed in some European countries during the fiscal contraction of the 1990s and later following the financial crisis in 2008 did not last. Health expenditure has continued to increase in all the eight case study countries as in all other OECD countries up until the latest comparable data point available in 2015.[168]

ENDNOTES

1. The eastern European countries, Albania, Bulgaria, Czechoslovakia, Hungary, Poland, Romania and the USSR, as well as many developing countries, have passed similar legislation. See Table A.2 in the Appendix.
2. The eight case studies were Australia, Canada, Denmark, Finland, New Zealand, Norway, Sweden and the UK.

3. Past comparative analysis of health care financing has suffered greatly because authors have not examined the key issues being investigated in the language of the country in question.
4. The terms user charges, fees, out-of-pocket payments, co-payments, cost recovery and *ticket moderateur* are used interchangeably and inconsistently for direct payments.
5. Public health, hospital care, doctors, medical education and capital investments are the main services provided by the public sector and financed through prepayment mechanisms; dentists, pharmaceuticals, medical supplies, chronic care institutions and different kinds of ambulatory services such as physiotherapy, laboratory services, home care and so on continue to be paid for largely with direct charges or voluntary supplemental insurance.
6. Some doctors working in public clinics are paid a *vacation* (based on time) in Quebec.
7. The private sector generally relies more on fee-for-service for doctors and retrospective reimbursements for hospitals, but even this is not a hard fast rule. Some American Health Maintenance Organizations (HMOs) have salaried doctors and global budgets for their hospitals.
8. The distinction between these types of economic goods will be described in greater detail in the section on normative functions of governments.
9. G. McLachlan and A. Maynard, *The Public/Private Mix for Health* (London: Nuffield Provincial Hospital Trust, 1982); and A. J. Culyer and B. Jönsson, eds., *Public and Private Health Services: Complementarities and Conflicts* (Oxford: Basil Blackwell, 1986); C. Propper and A. Maynard, "Whither the private health care sector?" in *Competition in Health Care: Reforming the NHS*, by A. J. Culyer, A. K. Maynard, and J. W. Posnett, eds. (London: Macmillan, 1990): 48–66.
10. Adapted from U.E. Reinhardt, "Health Insurance," Working Paper, Princeton University, Princeton, 1989.
11. The sickness funds did argue against a compulsory scheme when Denmark threatened to abolish them in the 1970s.
12. The Netherlands is planning to introduce compulsory participation and universal entitlement in 1993.
13. See the discussion on methodology.
14. International Labor Office (ILO), Social Security (Minimum Standards) Convention, No. 102 (Geneva: ILO, 1952).
15. World Health Organization (WHO), Regional Office for Europe (ROE), *Targets for Health for All: Targets in Support of the European Regional Strategy for Health for All* (Copenhagen: WHO, ROE, 1985): 23.

16. Most other ambulatory services, dental care, chronic care, pharmaceuticals and so on were included under either piece of legislation.
17. See the discussion on theoretical framework. H. L. Wilensky, G. M. Luebbert, S. R. Hahn, and A. M. Jamieson, "Comparative social policy: Theories, methods, findings," in *Comparative Policy Research: Learning from Experience*, by M. Dierkes, H. N. Weiler and A. B. Antal, eds., WZB-Publications (Rants: Gower, 1987): 384; H. L. Wilensky, *The Welfare State and Equality: Structural and Ideological Roots of Public Expenditures* (Berkeley: University of California Press, 1975); F. Pryor, *Public Expenditure in Capitalist and Communist Nations* (Homewood, I.L.: Irwin, 1968): 179–80, 205, 219.
18. P. Cutright, "Political structure, economic development and national social security programs," *American Journal of Sociology*, 70(March 1965): 537–50; P. Cutright, "Income redistribution: A cross-national analysis," *Social Forces* 46(1967): 180–90; H. J. Aaron, "Social security: International comparisons," in *Studies in the Economics of Income Maintenance*, by O. Eckstein, ed. (Washington, D. C.: The Brookings Institution 1967); and J. A. Pechman, H. J. Aaron, and M. K. Taussing, *Social Security: Perspectives for Reform* (Washington, D.C.: The Brookings Institution 1968).
19. J. P. Newhouse, "Development and allocation of medical care resources: Medico-economic approach," in *Development and Allocation of Medical Care Resources*, Proceedings of the 29th World Medical Assembly, Tokyo, Japan Medical Association, 1975; J. P. Newhouse, "Medical care expenditure: A cross-national survey," *Journal of Human Resources* 12(1)(1977): 115–25; R. J. Maxwell, *Health and Wealth: An International Study of Health-Care Spending* (Lexington, M. A.: Lexington Books, 1981); OECD, *Measuring Health Care 1960–1983: Expenditure, Costs and Performance*, OECD Social Policy Studies (Paris: OECD, 1985); OECD, *Financing and Delivering Health Care: A Comparative Analysis of OECD Countries*, OECD Social Policy Studies No. 2 (Paris: OECD, 1987); G. J. Schieber and J-P. Poullier, "International health spending and utilization trends," *Health Affairs* 7(4)(1988): 105–12.
20. J. Rage and R. Hanneman, *The Growth of the Welfare State in Four Western European Societies: A Comparison of Three Paradigms* (Madison, W.I.: Institute for Research on Poverty, 1977).
21. The U.S. Social Security Act of 1935 was one of the attempts to introduce a comprehensive old age, death, disability and unemployment program.
22. The same observation holds true for the 10 countries with the highest GDP per capita, where the rank order is different from the 7 richest countries. See the discussion on outcome in the section below ($R^2 = 0.00$).

23. See the introduction on the historical role of the state for a more detailed overview of these concepts.
24. J. Alber, G. Esping-Andersen, and L. Rainwater, "Studying the welfare state: issues and queries," in *Comparative Policy Research: Learning from Experience*, by M. Dierkes, H. N. Weiler and A. B. Antal, eds., WZB-Publications (Hants: Gower, 1987): 458–68; P. Flora and J. Alber, "Modernization, democratization and the development of welfare states in Western Europe," in *The Development of Welfare States in Europe and America*, by P. Flora and A. J. Heidenheimer, eds. (New Brunswich, N.J.: Transaction Books and the HIWED Project, 1981): 37–80; and P. Flora, "The growth of mass democracies and the welfare states," in *State, Economy and Society in Western Europe 1815–1975: A Data Handbook*, Volume I (Frankfurt: Campus, 1983); G. Espling-Andersen and W. Korpi, "From poor relief to institutional welfare states," in *The Scandinavian Model*, by R. Eriksson *et al.*, eds. (New York: M. E. Sharpe, 1985).
25. R. M. Coughlin, *Ideology, Public Opinion, and Welfare Policy: Attitudes Towards Taxing and Spending in Industrialized Societies*, Monograph Series No. 42 (Berkeley: Institute of International Studies, University of California, 1980).
26. M. M. Czudnowski, *Political Elites and Social Change* (DeKalb: NIU Press, 1983); G. Lowell Field and J. Higley, *Elitism* (London: Routledge and Kegan Paul, 1980); H. L. Wilensky, *The Welfare State and Equality: Structural and Ideological Roots of Public Expenditures* (Berkeley: University of California Press, 1975).
27. In the case of Denmark and Canada, the proposal for these reforms was made under conservative governments, while the legislation was subsequently introduced by liberal governments.
28. J. Alber, "Government responses to the challenge of unemployment: The development of unemployment insurance in Western Europe," and S. Kuhnle, "The growth of social insurance programs in Scandinavia: Outside influences and internal forces," in *The Development of Welfare States in Europe and America*, by P. F1ora and A. J. Heidenheimer, eds. (New Brunswich, N. J.: Transaction Books and the HIWED Project, 1981): 125–83.
29. H. L. Wilensky, G. M. Luebbert, S. R. Hahn, and A. M. Jamieson, "Comparative social policy: Theories, methods, findings," in *Comparative Policy Research: Learning from Experience*, by M. Dierkes, H. N. Weiler and A. B. Antal, eds., WZB-Publications (Hants: Gower, 1987): 404; and E. Einhorn and J. Logue, *Welfare States in Hard Times: Denmark and Sweden in the 1970s* (Kent O. H.: Kent Popular Press, 1979).

30. S. B. Wolinetz, ed., *Parties and Party Systems in Liberal Democracies The Canadian Liberal Party* (London: Routledge, 1988); and S. Henig, *Political Parties in the European Community* (London: George Allen & Unwin, 1979). The Canadian Liberal Party, which until recently was center-left on the Canadian political spectrum, introduced many progressive social security reforms and should not be equated with other European liberal parties whose political orientation would fall to the right of the Canadian counterpart.
31. It fails to explain why left-wing-oriented governments of other countries did not introduce similar policies. Left-wing orientation may have been a necessary but not sufficient criterion.
32. Left-wing political groups argued a similar case during the early twentieth century in Britain.
33. British Medical Journal "British Medical Association's proposals for a general medical service for the nation," Supplement, *British Medical Journal*, (April 26, 1930). The *British Medical Journal* published a similar proposal in 1938.
34. Possible reasons for these differences will be described in greater detail in the section on bureaucratic structures.
35. H. Eckstein, *Pressure Group Politics: The Case of the British Medical Association* (London: Allen & Unwin, 1960); R. F. Badgley, "Health worker strikes: Social and economic bases of conflict," *International Journal of Health Services* 5(1)(1975): 9–17; B. Ehrenreich and J. H. Ehrenreich, "Hospital workers: Class conflicts in the making," *International Journal of Health Services* 5(1)(1975): 43–51; T. R. Marmor and D. Thomas, "Doctors, polities and pay disputes: 'Pressure group politics' revisited," *British Journal of Political Science* 2(4)(1972): 421–42; V. Navarro, *Class Struggle, The State and Medicine: A Historical and Contemporary Analysis of the Medical Sector in Great Britain* (London: Martin Rovertson, 1978); V. Navarro, "Social class, political power and the state and their implications in medicine," *Social Science and Medicine*, 10(9/10)(1976); R. Klein, *Ideology, Class and the National Health Service*, Project Paper No. RC4 (London: Kings Fund, 1980).
36. Specialists are accorded greater esteem than generalists, and there is a distinct pecking order even among the specialities, starting with geriatrics and psychiatry at the bottom ranging through general surgery and internal medicine and peaking with specialties such as cardiology and neurosurgery.
37. A. R. Ball and F. Millard, *Pressure Politics in Industrial Societies: A Comparative Introduction* (London: Macmillan, 1986); and S. Sax, *A Strife*

of Interests: Politics and Policies in Australian Health Services (Sydney; George Allen & Unwin, 1984).

38. Doctors who played a significant role in advancing the cause for universal access to medical care were punished by excommunication from the medical community.
39. In Denmark, the Medical Association deliberately refused to participate in the consultation process since it did not want to support the dying sickness funds.
40. Later, during the Swedish Seven Crowns Reform and Finnish Public Health Reform, Nordic doctors raised the same protest that their English-speaking counterparts had raised during earlier battles.
41. Switzerland, which has developed the theory and practice of referendum to perfection, is an exception. See D. Butler and A. Ranney, eds., *Referendums: A Comparative Study of Practice and Theory* (Washington: American Enterprise Institute, 1978).
42. A. Lijphart, *Democracies: Patterns of Majoritarian and Consensus Government in Twenty-One Countries* (New Haven: Yale University Press, 1984): 2.
43. Social insurance legislation increased after a "suffrage threshold" of 50 percent of the male population had been reached. See P. Flora and J. Alber, "Modernization, democratization and the development of welfare states in Western Europe," in *The Development of Welfare States in Europe and America*, by P. Flora and A. J. Heidenheimer, eds. (New Brunswich, N.J.: Transaction Books and the HIWED Project, 1981): 37–80.
44. A. Lijphart, *Democracies: Patterns of Majoritarian and Consensus Government in Twenty-One Countries* (New Haven: Yale University Press, 1984): 37; D. Arter, *The Nordic Parliaments: A Comparative Analysis* (London: Hurst, 1984).
45. G. Therborn, "The rule of capital and the rise of democracy," *New Left Review* 103(May–June 1977): 11–17.
46. R. A. Dahl, *Polyarchy: Participation and Opposition* (New Haven: Yale University Press, 1971); and J. D. May, "Defining democracy: A bid for coherence and consensus," *Political Studies* 26(1)(1978): 1–14.
47. J. Alber, "Government responses to the challenge of unemployment: The development of unemployment insurance in Western Europe," and S. Kuhnle, "The growth of social insurance programs in Scandinavia: Outside influences and internal forces," in *The Development of Welfare States in Europe and America*, by P. Flora and A. J. Heidenheimer, eds. (New Brunswich, N. J.: Transaction Books and the HIWED Project, 1981): 125–83.

48. Government by the majority in accordance with the wishes of the majority is the essence of the majoritarian model.
49. Government by and responsive to a minority or as many people as possible is the essence of the consensual model.
50. V. R. Lorwin, "Segmented pluralism: Ideological cleavages and political cohesion in the smaller European democracies," *Comparative Politics* 3(2) (1971): 148.
51. A. Lijphart, *Democracies: Patterns of Majoritarian and Consensus Government in Twenty-One Countries* (New Haven: Yale University Press, 1984): 88.
52. D. Muller, *Public Choice* (Cambridge, Cambridge University Press, 1979).
53. R. P. Inman, "The fiscal performance of local governments: An interpretative review," in P. Mieszkowski and M. Straszheim, eds., *Current Issues in Urban Economics* (Baltimore: Johns Hopkins, 1978).
54. G. Tullock and N. Tiedeman, "A new and superior principle of public choice," *Journal of Political Economy* 84(6)1976: 1145–1159.
55. J. A. Schumpeter, *Capitalism, Socialism and Democracy* (New York: Harper, 1950): 282; A. Downs, *An Economic Theory of Democracy* (New York: Harper & Row, 1956).
56. N. W. Polsby, "Party realignment in the 1980 election," *Yale Review*, 72(1982): 42–54.
57. The US Democratic Party (1828) and British Conservative Party (1832) were two early exceptions. The Anglo-American and Scandinavian are two of the most extensively studied systems.
58. K. von Beyme, *Political Parties in Western Democracies* (Aldershot: Gower, 1985); and K. Lawson, *The Comparative Study of political parties* (New York: St. Martin's Press, 1976): 4.
59. Theories on the determinants of modern political parties include the following: they derive from developments in parliamentary systems; they derive from new states and the collapse of constitutional systems; and they are part of political modernization. See J. La Palombara and M. Weiner, eds., *Political Parties and Political Development* (Princeton: Princeton University Press, 1966): 7.
60. L. D. Epstein, *Political Parties in Western Democracies* (London: Pall Mall, 1967).
61. H. D. Clark and M. M. Czudnowski, *Political Elites in Anglo-American Democracies: Changes in Stable Regimes* (DeKalb, Illinois: Northern Illinois University Press, 1987).
62. G. Alderman, *Pressure Groups and Government in Great Britain* (London: Longman, 1984); H. Eckstein, *Pressure Group Politics* (London: Allen &

Unwin, 1960); D. Marsh, ed., *Interest Groups in Britain* (London: Junction Books, 1983); B. Pym, *Pressure Groups and the Permissive Society* (London: David & Charles, 1974); and J. La Palombara and M. Weiner, eds., *Political Parties and Political Development* (Princeton: Princeton University Press, 1966): 7.

63. F. Castles, *The Social Democratic Image of Society* (London: Routledge and Kegan Paul, 1978): 76; C. Hewitt, "The effects of political democracy and social democracy on equality in industrial societies: A cross-national comparison," *American Sociological Review* 42(1977): 450–64.
64. J. Blondel, *Political Parties: A Genuine Case for Discontent?* (London: Wildwood House, 1978); K. Janda, *A Conceptual Framework for the Comparative Analysis of Political Parties* (Sage: Beverly Hills, 1980); and G. Sartori, *Parties and Party Systems* (Cambridge: Cambridge University Press, 1976).
65. Among the eight case studies, the English-speaking countries that were early to democratize also had majoritarian rule, while the Nordic countries had consensual rule. In other European countries, these cleavages do not occur so closely.
66. N. Elder, A. H. Thomas and D. Arter, *The Consensual Democracies? The Government and Politics of the Scandinavian States* (Oxford: Martin Robertson, 1982).
67. D. D. Selskab, *Nordic Democracy* (Copenhagen: Det Danske Selskab, 1981).
68. It was easier for the Nordic countries to expand coverage through the sickness insurance funds than for the English-speaking countries to extend their tax bases.
69. The majority rules with no concern for unanimity or minority concerns.
70. M. Harrop and W. L. Miller, *Elections and Voters: A Comparative Introduction* (London: Macmillan, 1987); A. M. Carstairs, *A Short History of Electoral Systems in Western Europe* (London: George Allen & Unwin, 1980); R. C. Macridis and B. E. Brown, *Comparative Politics: Notes and Readings* (Homewood, Illinois: Dorsey Press, 1977); and G. Smith, *Politics in Western Europe: A Comparative Analysis*, 5th Edition (London: Gower, 1989).
71. In Sweden, the Höjer Report of 1948 presented a radical alternative to the Sickness Insurance Law of 1953, and in Norway, the health care component of the Civil Defense Law of 1953 presented a radical alternative to the Compulsory Universal Sickness Insurance Law of 1956.
72. Seven Crowns Reform of 1969 in Sweden and the Public Health Act of 1972 in Finland.

73. J. Alber, "Government responses to the challenge of unemployment: The development of unemployment insurance in Western Europe," and S. Kuhnle, "The growth of social insurance programs in Scandinavia: Outside influences and internal forces," in *The Development of Welfare States in Europe and America*, by P. Flora and A. J. Heidenheimer, eds. (New Brunswich, N. J.: Transaction Books and the HIWED Project, 1981): 125–83.
74. Denmark and Finland also introduced their reforms shortly after changes in government.
75. Legislation was prepared for extensive expansion in health insurance in the 1920s and for the introduction of British-styled National Health Service in the late 1940s. New governments either ignored or reversed policies introduced by previous governments.
76. J. Blondel, *Government Ministers in the Contemporary World* (London: Sage, 1985); J. Blondel, *Political Leadership: Towards a General Analysis* (London: Sage, 1987); R. M. Stogdill, *Handbook of Leadership: A Survey of Theory and Research* (New York: Free Press, 1974); and J. McGregor Burns, *Leadership* (New York: Harper and Row, 1978).
77. G. D. Paige, *The Scientific Study of Political Leadership* (New York: Free Press, 1977); and B. Kellerman, *Leadership: A Multidisciplinary Perspective* (Englewood Cliffs, NJ.: Prentice-Hall, 1984).
78. H. Helco, *A Government of Strangers* (Washington: Brookings Institution, 1977); and P. Kellner and L. Crowther-Hunt, *The Civil Servants* (London: Macdonald, 1980).
79. The civil service was crucial to the health care reforms examined in this study. See H. H. Gerth and C. Wright Mills, *From Max Weber* (New York: Oxford University Press, 1972): 196–245; G. Colm, *Essays in Public Finance and Fiscal Policy* (New York: Oxford University Press, 1955).
80. W. A. Niskanen, *Bureaucracy and Representative Government* (Chicago: Aldine, 1974), Chapter 5.
81. G. Lembruch and P. C. Schmitter, eds., *Patterns of Corporatist Policy-making* (Beverly Hills: Sage, 1982); P. C. Schmitter "Interest intermediation and regime governability in contemporary Western Europe and North America," in *Organising Interests in Western Europe: Pluralism, Corporatism and the Transformation of Politics*, by S. Berger, ed. (Cambridge: Cambridge University Press, 1981).
82. Public bureaucracies have been a relatively neglected area of comparative studies. With a few exceptions, most focus on one or two countries. See G. Peters, *Comparing Public Bureaucracies: Problems and Methods* (Tuscaloosa: University of Alabama, 1988).

83. J. Alber, "Government responses to the challenge of unemployment: The development of unemployment insurance in Western Europe," and S. Kuhnle, "The growth of social insurance programs in Scandinavia: Outside influences and internal forces," in *The Development of Welfare States in Europe and America*, by P. Flora and A. J. Heidenheimer, eds. (New Brunswich, N. J.: Transaction Books and the HIWED Project, 1981):125–83.
84. F. Castles, *The Social Democratic Image of Society: A Study of the Achievements and Origins of Scandinavian Social Democracy in Comparative Perspective* (London: Routledge & Kegan Paul, 1978); and F. Castles, "Scandinavia: The politics of stability," in *Modern Political Systems: Europe*, by R. C. Macridis, ed. (Englewood Cliffs, N. J.: Prentice-Hall, 1978).
85. G. Heckscher, "Interest groups in Sweden: Their political role," in Ehrmann H. W. (ed.), *Interest Groups on Four Continents* (Pittsburgh: University of Pittsburgh Press, 1958).
86. F. R. Scott, *Sweden: The Nation's History* (Minneapolis: University of Minneapolis, 1977): 476.
87. The Höjer Plan of 1948 in Sweden and the Civil Defense Law of 1953 in Norway.
88. N. Elder, A. H. Thomas, and D. Arter, *The Consensual Democracies: The Government and Politics of the Scandinavian States* (Oxford: Basil Blackwell, 1982): 159.
89. In Denmark, the Medical Association refused to be represented on the Social Reform Commission of 1969, wanting to remain neutral during what it felt would be a fight-to-the-finish between the government and the sickness funds.
90. V. Tanzi, "Public expenditure and public debt: An international and historical perspective," in *Public Expenditure: The Key Issues*, by J. Bristow and D. McDonagh, eds. (Dublin: Institute of Public Administration 1986): 6–37.
91. Those without financial protection to pay for health care prior to the introduction of universal entitlement were also those most likely to need these services and those who made the greatest claims on other social security benefits: the sick, disabled, elderly, unemployed, women, children and so on.
92. K. J. Arrow and F. H. Hahn, *General Competitive Analysis* (Edinburgh: Oliver and Boyd, 1971); E. Malinvaud, *Lectures on Microeconomic Theory* (Amsterdam: North-Holland, 1972); and A. B. Atkinson and J. E. Stiglitz, *Lectures on Public Economics* (London: McGraw-Hill, 1980).

93. The literature on market failure in the health sector was reviewed in the introduction on determinants. Parallels will be drawn with the literature on public sector economics in the following section on normative functions of government in health care.
94. See the *Hippocratic Oath.* British Medical Association (BMA), *Handbook of Medical Ethics*, (London: BMA, 1984): 6.
95. C. B. Chapman, *Physicians, Law, and Ethics* (New York: New York University Press, 1984): 3–5.
96. In Britain and the Nordic countries, they also became directly involved in financing ambulatory care through the clinical services provide by the state-employed Medical Officers of Health.
97. Subsidies were also introduced to prevent the bankruptcy of some funds.
98. Many Group II countries introduced similar legislation.
99. Individual provinces, such as Saskatchewan and British Columbia, had previously introduced similar coverage.
100. Queensland maintained this system after the other states reverted to a means-tested system.
101. Advocates of reforms in the other Nordic countries made a similar claim prior to introducing universal sickness insurance, but it is impossible to validate this claim because of the many other factors that may have influenced ambulatory/institutional utilization ratios.
102. R. A. Musgrave and P. B. Musgrave, *Public Finance in Theory and Practice*, 4th Edition (New York: McGraw-Hill, 1984): 6–19.
103. There is a danger of a tautological circle in the analysis of normative functions of governments. It is easy to postulate the functions that institutions fulfill and then rediscover these through empirical validation. The following analysis therefore has an unfortunate, but unavoidable, fatalistic flavor. It is necessary for a fuller understanding of how, and not just why, governments became involved in the financing of health care.
104. R. Rose, "Public employment and public expenditure," in *Public Expenditure: The Key Issues*, by J. Bristow and D. McDonagh, eds. (Dublin: Institute of Public Administration, 1986), 81–82.
105. P. A. Samuelson, "The pure theory of public expenditures," *Review of Economics and Statistics*, (1954): 386–89; P. A Samuelson, "Diagrammatic exposition of a theory of public expenditures," *Review of Economics and Statistics* (1955): 350–56; H. Aaron and M. C. McGuire: "Efficiency, equity and optimal supply of a public good," *Review of Economics and Statistics*, (1969); J. M. Buchanan, *The Demand and Supply of Public Goods* (Chicago: Rand McNally, 1968); M. Peston, *Public Goods and the Public*

Sector (London: Macmillan, 1972); J. M. Buchanan, *The Demand and Supply of Public Goods* (New York: Rand McNally, 1968); J. G. Head, *Public Goods and Public Welfare* (Durham: N. C., Duke University Press, 1974).

106. A. Sandmo, "*Ex post* welfare economics and the theory of merit goods," *Economica* 50(1983): 19–33; K. J. Arrow and F. H. Hahn, *General Competitive Analysis* (Edinburgh: Oliver and Boyd, 1971); B. Malinvaud, *Lectures on Microeconomic Theory* (Amsterdam: North-Holland, 1972); and H. R. Varian, *Microeconomic Analysis* (New York: Norton, 1978).
107. W. Baumol, "On taxation and the control of externalities," *American Economic Review* (1972): 307–22.
108. The term social goods will be used generically to refer to public goods, mixed goods and merit goods.
109. J. G. Cullis and P. A. West, *The Economics of Health: An Introduction* (Oxford: Martin Robertson, 1979): 36–38; R. A. Musgrave and P. B. Musgrave, *Public Finance in Theory and Practice*, 4th Edition (New York: McGraw-Hill, 1984): 71–73; C. S. Shoup and J. Head, "Public goods, private goods and ambiguous goods," *Economic Journal* (1969): 1119–28; J. M. Buchanan, "An economic theory of clubs," *Economica* (1965): 1–14.
110. Doctors and other health care providers act as gate-keepers to access in even the most highly planned systems.
111. In recent years, this has become especially apparent in the former Eastern European communist countries. Patients make significant co-payments due to gratuities despite universal entitlement to all health care as a merit.
112. R. Klein, "Priorities and the problems of planning," *British Medical Journal* 22(1977):1076–7; B.-A. Kaminsky, "Rational planning models for resource allocation in health care," *Health Management Forum* (1984): 43–57; A. B. Atkinson, *The Economics of Inequality*, 2nd Edition (Oxford: Clarendon Press, 1983); J. Le Grand, *The Strategy of Equality Redistribution and the Social Services* (London: George Allen and Unwin, 1982); N. Mays and G. Bevan, *Resource Allocation in the Health Service: A Review of the Methods of Resource Allocation Working Party* (RAWP) (London: Bedford Square Press/NCVO, 1987); A. McGuire, "Ethics and resource allocation: An economist's view," *Social Science and Medicine* 22(1986):1167–74; G. H. Mooney and A. McGuire, eds., *Medical Ethics and Economics in Health Care* (Oxford: Oxford University Press, 1988).
113. K. Arrow, *Social Choice and Individual Values*, 2nd Edition (New York: Wiley, 1951); and D. Mueller, *Public Choice* (Cambridge: Cambridge University Press, 1979); and A. R. Ball and F. Millard, *Pressure Politics in*

Industrial Societies: A Comparative Introduction (London: MacMillan, 1986).

114. United Kingdom, Department of Health and Social Security, "Sharing Resources for Health Care," in *England: Report of the Resource Allocation Working Party* (RAWP) (London: HMSO, 1976); M. Butts, D. Irving and C. Whitt, *From Principles to Practice* (London: Nuffield Provincial Hospital Trust, 1981); M. J. Buxton and R. E. Klein, *Allocating Health Resources: A Commentary on the Report of the Resources Allocation Working Party* (London: HMSO, 1978).
115. Coopers and Lybrand, *Integrated Analysis for the Review of RAWP* (London: Coopers and Lybrand, 1988).
116. R. Carr-Hill, "RAWP is dead: Long live RAWP," in *Competition in Health Care: Reforming the NHS*, by A. J. Culyer, A. K. Maynard, and J. W. Posnett, eds. (London: Macmillan, 1990): 192–200; United Kingdom, Department of Health and Social Security (DHSS), *Review of the Resource Allocation Working Party Formula* (London: HMSO, 1988).
117. R. R. Arons, *The New Economics of Health Care: DRGs Case Mix, and Length of Stay* (New York: Praeger, 1984); R. B. Fetter, Y. Shin, J. L. Freeman, R. F. Averill, and J. D. Thompson "Case mix definition by Diagnosis Related Groups," Supplement, *Medical Care* 18(20)(1980): 1–53.
118. P. Boland, *The New Healthcare Market: A Guide to PPOs for Purchasers, Payers and Providers* (Homewood, Illinois: Dow Jones-Irwin, 1985).
119. R. E. Klein and J. Lewis, *The Politics of Consumer Representation: A Study of Community Health Councils* (London: Center for Studies in Social Policy, 1976).
120. R. Klein, *Ideology, Class and the National Health Service*, Project Paper No. RC4 (London: Kings Fund, 1980).
121. Princeton University and Bristol-Myers Squibb Company, *The Economics of Health Care: Challenges for the Nineties* (London: MEDIQ, 1990).
122. M. Ellman, *Socialist Planning*, 2nd Edition (Cambridge: Cambridge University Press, 1989).
123. R. A. Musgrave and P. B. Musgrave, *Public Finance in Theory and Practice*, 4th Edition (New York: McGraw-Hill, 1984): 82–101.
124. *Ibid.*, p. 83.
125. For a detailed taxonomy of the different modalities of revenue collection, see R. A. Musgrave and P. B. Musgrave, *Public Finance in Theory and Practice*, 4th Edition (New York McGraw-Hill, 1984); and A. R. Prest and N. A. Barr, *Public Finance: In Theory and Practice* (London: Weidenfeld

and Nicolson, 1985). In developing countries, grants in the form of foreign aid may be a significant component of revenues. See A. R. Prest, *Public Finance in Developing Countries*, 3rd Edition (London: Weidenfeld and Nicholson, 1985).

126. OECD, *Revenue Statistics of the OECD Member Countries, 1965–1985* (Paris: OECD, 1986).
127. R. Klein, J. Barnes, M. Buxton and E. Caven, *Social Policy and Public Expenditure* (London: Centre for Studies in Social Policy, 1974); J. I. Grand, "The distribution of public expenditure: The case of health care," *Economica*, 45(1978): 125–42; P. Gottschalk, B. Wolfe and R. Haveman, "Health care financing in the US, UK and the Netherlands: Distributional consequences," 42nd Congress of the International Institute of Public Finance, Athens, 1986.
128. K. J. Arrow, "Uncertainty and the welfare economics of medical care," *American Economic Review*, 53(1963):941–73. See the discussion on health insurance under the section on market failure in health care.
129. J. Hurst, *Financing Health Care in the US, Canada and Britain* (London: King's Fund, 1985).
130. H. M. Hochman and J. D. Rodgers, "Pareto optimal redistribution," *American Economic Review*, 59(1957); J. M. Buchanan and G. Tullock, *The Calculus of Consent* (Ann Arbor: University of Michigan Press, 1965); and W. J. Blum and H. Kalven, *The Uneasy Case for Progressive Taxation* (Chicago: Diversity Press, 1953).
131. A. Downs, *An Economic Theory of Democracy* (New York: Harper, 1957).
132. This point can be calculated using the Laffer curve. See D. Fullerton, "On the possibility of an inverse relationship between tax rates and government revenues," *Journal of Public Economics*, 19(1)(1982): 3–22.
133. R. Klein, R. Pinker, P. Collison and A. J. Culyer, *Acceptable Inequalities? Essays on the Pursuit of Equality in Health Care*, by D. G. Green, ed. (London: IEA Health Unit, 1988).
134. A. Wagstaff, "Progressivity and horizontal equity in the finance of health care: Some tentative cross-country comparisons," Second World Congress on Health Economics, University of Zurich, Switzerland, September 10–14, 1990.
135. A. B. Atkinson, "On the measurement of inequality," *Journal of Economic Theory* 2(1970): 244–63; A. B. Atkinson, *The Economics of Inequality* (Oxford: Clarendon Press, 1975); F. A. Crowell, *Measuring Inequality* (Oxford: Philip Allan, 1977); and A. K. Sen, *On Economic Inequality* (Oxford: Clarendon Press, 1973).

136. M. Sawyer, "Income distribution in OECD countries," *OECD Economic Outlook Occasional Studies* (Paris: OECD, 1976).
137. M. C. Berliant and R. P. Strauss, "The horizontal and vertical equity characteristics of the federal individual income tax 1966–1977," in *Horizontal Equity, Uncertainty and Economic Well-Being*, by M. David and T. M. Smeeding, eds. (Chicago: Chicago University Press, 1985).
138. N. C. Kawani, "Measurement of tax progressivity: An international comparison," *Economic Journal* 87(1977):71–80; N. C. Kawani and N. Podder, "Efficient estimation of the Lorenz curve and associated inequality measures from grouped observations," *Econometrica* 44(1976): 137–48; D. Suits, "Measurement of tax progressivity," *American Economic Review* 67(1977): 747–52; W. J. Smith, "A comparison of two new measures of tax progressivity," *Economic Journal* 91(1981): 1015–9.
139. P. J. Lambert, "Tax progressivity: A survey of the literature," *Working Paper* (London: Institute of Fiscal Studies, 1985); J. P. Formby, T. G. Seaks, R. Hemming, and M. J. Keen, "Single-crossing conditions in comparisons of tax progressivity," *Journal of Public Economics* 20(1983): 373–80.
140. R. D. Plotnik, "A measure of horizontal inequity," *Review of Economics and Statistics* 63(1981): 283–8; R. D. Plotnick, "The concept and measurement of horizontal inequity," *Journal of Public Economics* 17(1982): 283–8; and L. Kaplow, "Horizontal equity: measures in search of a principle," *National Tax Journal* 42(2)(1989): 139–152.; A. B. Atkinson, "Horizontal equity and the distribution of the tax burden," in *The Economics of Taxation*, by H. Aaron and M. Boskin, eds. (Washington, D.C.: Brookings Institution, 1980).
141. H. Dalton, *Some Aspects of Inequality of Incomes in Modern Communities* (London: Routledge, 1920): 10.
142. A. C. Pigou, *The Economics of Welfare* (London: Macmillan, 1932): 89.
143. A. P. Lerner, *The Economics of Control* (London: Macmillan, 1944).
144. A. K. Sen, *On Economic Inequality* (Oxford: Clarendon Press, 1973).
145. R. A. Musgrave and P. B. Musgrave, *Public Finance in Theory and Practice*, 4th Edition (New York: McGraw-Hill, 1984): 18.
146. A. J. Culyer, *The Political Economy of Social Policy* (Oxford: Martin Robertson, 1980): 124–127.
147. E. Collins and R. Klein, "Equity and the NHS: Self-reported morbidity, access and primary care," *British Medical Journal* 281(1980): 1111–5; B. Buhmann, L. Rainwater, G. Schmaus, and T. M. Smeeding, "Equivalence scales, well-being, inequality and poverty: Sensitivity estimates across ten countries using the Luxembourg Income Study Database," *Review of*

Income and Wealth (1988): 115–42; M. A. King, "An index of inequality: With applications to horizontal equity and social morbidity," *Econometrica* 51(1983): 99–115.

148. J. LeGrand, "The distribution of public expenditure: The case of health care," *Econometrica* 45(1978): 125–42.
149. It could be argued that this is a failure of the allocation function, but equitable allocation may still fall short of the need for additional redistribution.
150. R. A. Musgrave and P. B. Musgrave, *Public Finance in Theory and Practice*, 4th Edition (New York McGraw-Hill, 1984): 14–16.
151. K.-D. Henke, "Cost containment in health care: Justification and consequences," in *Health Economics Worldwide*, by P. Zweifel and H. E. French, eds. (Netherlands: Kluwer, 1991); A. S. Preker, "Expenditure control through public financing in the OECD," Second World Congress on Health Economics, University of Zurich, Switzerland, September 10–14, 1990; A. J. Culyer, "Cost containment in Europe," Annual Supplement, *Health Care Financing Review* (1989): 31; and B. Abel-Smith, "Cost containment in health care," Occasional Papers on Social Administration (London: Bedford Square Press, NCVO, 1984).
152. M. Huber and M. Schneider, "Evaluation of the Health Care Reform Act of 1989 on economic growth, employment and prices in the FRG," Second World Congress on Health Economics, University of Zurich, Switzerland, September 10–14, 1990.
153. H. Cavanna, ed., *Public Sector Deficits in OECD Countries: Causes, Consequences and Remedies* (London: Macmillan, 1988).
154. See discussion on outcome in the section below.
155. F. Champagne, A.-P. Contandriopoulos, A. Lemay, and A. S. Preker, "Evaluation of health care performance in the OECD," Second World Congress on Health Economics, University of Zurich, Switzerland, September 10–14, 1990.
156. G. J. Schieber and J. P. Poullier, "Overview of international comparisons of health care expenditures," Annual Supplement, *Health Care Financing Review* (1989): 1–9.
157. In each of the countries, the reform was associated with an initial increase in health care expenditure per GDP, which then stabilized during the decade that followed. In Finland, stabilization of health care expenditure did not occur until after introduction of the Public Health Act of 1972; in New Zealand, there was a modest increase throughout the early reform period.

158. GDP elasticity of health care expenditure is defined as the percentage change in per capita health care expenditure divided by the percentage change in per capita GDP.
159. A. J. Culyer, "Cost containment in Europe," Annual Supplement, *Health Care Financing Review* (1989): 31.
160. The rationale for these indicators was described in the section on methodology. It was felt to be premature to include health status as one of these indicators.
161. See Table A.11 in the Appendix for the references for the data used in the following tables.
162. The statistical significance and reliability of these observations are demonstrated in greater detail in Tables A.12 and A.13 in the Appendix.
163. D. Cameron, "On the limits of the public economy," *Annals of the American Academy of Political and Social Science* 459(1982): 46–62; M. G. Schmidt, "Does corporatism matter? Economic crisis, politics and rates of unemployment in capitalist democracies in the 1970s," in *Patterns of Corporatist Policy-Making*, by G. Lehmbruch and P. C. Schmitter, eds. (Beverly Hills: Sage, 1982); R. Rose, ed., *The Dynamics of Public Policy: A Comparative Analysis* (Beverly Hills: Sage, 1976); R. Rose and G. Peters, *Can Governments Go Bankrupt?* (New York: Basic Books 1978); and H. Cavanna, ed., *Public Sector Deficits in OECD Countries: Causes, Consequences and Remedies* (London: Macmillan, 1988).
164. A. J. Culyer, "Cost containment in Europe," Annual Supplement, *Health Care Financing Review* (1989): 31.
165. H. L. Wilensky, *The Welfare State and Equality: Structural and Ideological Roots of Public Expenditures* (Berkeley: University of California Press, 1975); R. Rubinson and D. Quinlam, "The world economy and the distribution of incomes within states: A cross-national study," *American Sociological Review* 41(1976):638–9; R. Robinson and D. Quinlam, "Democracy and social inequality: A reanalysis," *American Sociological Review* 42(1977): 611–23; and D. Cameron, "The expansion of the public economy: A comparative analysis," *American Political Science Review* 72(4)(1978): 1243–61.
166. Newhouse (1975 and 1977) found an $R^2 = 0.92$; Kleiman (1974), $R^2 = 0.92$; Culyer (1988), $R^2 = 0.91$; OECD, $R^2 = 0.81$; and Parkin, McGuire and Yule (1987), $R^2 = 0.87$. J. P. Newhouse, "Development and allocation of medical care resources: Medico-economic approach," in *Development and Allocation of Medical Care Resources*, Proceedings of the 29th World Medical Assembly, Tokyo, Japan Medical Association, 1975; J. P. Newhouse,

"Medical care expenditure: A cross-national survey," *Journal of Human Resources* 12(1)(Winter 1977): 115–25; E. Kleiman, "The determinants of national outlay on health," in *The Economics of Health and Medical Care*, by M. Periman (London: Macmillan, 1974); D. Parkin, A. McGuire and B. Yule, "Aggregate health care expenditures and national income: Is health care a luxury good?" *Journal of Health Economics* 6(2)(1987); A. J. Culyer, *Health Care Expenditure in Canada: Myth and Reality: Past and Future*, Canadian Tax Paper No. 82 (Toronto: Canadian Tax Foundation, 1988).

167. J. Alber "Germany," in *Growth to Limits: The Western European Welfare States since World War II*, by P. Flora, ed. (New York: de Gruyter, 1988).
168. See latest WHO NHA data. http://apps.who.int/nha/database. Accessed, July 25, 2017.

CHAPTER 12

PERFORMANCE EVALUATION

This chapter provides an evaluation of the performance of the eight countries in the OECD that introduced landmark legislative health financing reforms to achieve universal access to health care in achieving various health care policies and health financing targets through this reform.

A. PERFORMANCE EVALUATION LOG-FRAME

Comparisons are made for key indicators between the 8 countries reviewed in this volume and the full dataset of 28 OECD countries that have achieve universal access to health care.[1] Performance is assessed using the Performance Evaluation Log-frame (see Table 1.4) presented under the discussion on methodologies in Chapter 1. The Performance Evaluation Log-frame identifies various levels of independent and dependent variables, along a causal path. See Figure 12.1.

The Performance Evaluation Log-frame follows a value for money approach for assessing the performance of the key health care functions under universal health care.[2–7]

- Inputs in terms of the financing (money), health training (people), research (information), manufacturing (drugs, medical technology, supplies and consumables) and construction (infrastructure)
- Processes in terms of the role of the state (stewardship, governance, management, monitoring and evaluation) and the role of markets (supply, demand, prices and market equilibrium);

Figure 12.1 Causal Pathway Under Performance Evaluation Log-frame

Source: Author (2017).

- Outputs in terms of services provided (hospital care, rehabilitation, chronic care, primary care, diagnostic services, dental care, health promotion and prevention).
- Proxy measures in terms of efficiency, effectiveness, equity, access, productivity and quality and universal health care (population coverage, service depth and level of prepayment)
- Impact indicators in terms of health status, financial protection and patient experience

B. COUNTRY PERFORMANCE

1. New Zealand

This section will apply the performance evaluation log-frame to data on inputs, process, outputs, proxy measures and impact indicators to recent data on New Zealand.

(a) Inputs

In terms of financial resources mobilized, cost and public affordability, after the initial period of stable spending following introduction of universal access, health care spending in New Zealand like in all other OECD countries, has increased over time but at a rate that is lower than the OECD average and much lower than in the USA. Age-adjusted total expenditure on health in 2012 was 10.5 percent of GDP. Health Expenditure per GDP in New Zealand has remained in the range of 10–11 percent of GDP over the past decade, varying slightly from year to year.[8]

As a result, health care expenditure in New Zealand is among the highest among OECD countries that have a universal health care system. It is the 4th highest in age-adjusted expenditure per GDP but 15th highest in expenditure per capita, reflecting the lower GDP in New Zealand.[9] See Table 12.1.

Table 12.1 Age-adjusted Spending Per GDP and Per Capita Spending 2012

	Spending as Percentage of GDP		Spending Per Capita	
	Percentage	Rank	US$PPP	Rank
New Zealand	10.5	4	3,446.2	15

Source: Barua *et al.* (2016), Database for New Zealand.

Table 12.2 Resources, Age-adjusted, Per 1000 Population in 2012

	Physicians		Nurses		Acute Beds		Psychiatric Beds	
	Per'000	Rank	Per'000	Rank	Per'000	Rank	Per'000	Rank
New Zealand	2.9	20	10.7	11	2.8	15	0.2	26

Source: Barua *et al.* (2016), Database for New Zealand.

New Zealand has a modest network of training. The admission to its medical and dental schools is tightly regulated to control the total number of doctors and dentists that are trained. As a result of such controls, New Zealand is in the lower third in terms of the number of doctors, compared with other OECD countries. The building of new hospital and public clinics is also tight. In terms of human and capital resources, New Zealand ranks 20th for doctors, 11th for nurses, 15th acute care beds, and 26th for psychiatric care beds per thousand population, the latter is low for the OECD.[10] See Table 12.2.

In terms of medical technology, there are a wide range or indicators that could be used. New Zealand ranks 15th (out of 26) for MRI units per million population, 17th for CT scanners, 16th for PET scanners, 21st for Gamma cameras, 17th for Digital Subtraction Angiography units, 7th for Mammographs, and 15th for Lithotriptors.[11] For most of these high-end diagnostic techniques, New Zealand is in the mid-range of the OECD. See Table 12.3.

(b) Process

Strong stewardship, policy making, governance, management, monitoring and evaluation is one of the fundamental features of universal health care and has been a major focus of the New Zealand health sector.

Table 12.3 Availability of Diagnostic Technology in 2012

	MRI Units		CT Scanners		PET Scanners	
	Per Million	Rank	Per Million	Rank	Per Million	Rank
New Zealand	11.1	15	15.3	17	1.1	16

Gamma Cameras		Digital Subtraction Angiography Units		Mammographs		Lithotriptors	
Per Million	Rank	Per Million	Rank	Per Million	Rank	Per Million	Rank
3.4	21	5.0	17	24.8	7	0.7	15

Source: Barua *et al.* (2016), Database for New Zealand.

Although New Zealand is not Federal State, there is significant devolution of responsibly for health care from the national level to the regions and local governments.[12–14]

Since passage of the Social Security Act in 1938, the governmental has played a pivotal role in providing health care for New Zealanders. It sets the policy agenda, provides an annual budget for publicly funded providers and regulates the sector.[15–17]

At the national level, the Ministry of Health (MOH) has oversight responsibility for the whole system. Below that, 20 geographically defined District Health Boards (DHBs), are responsible for planning, commissioning, and providing health services and disability benefits for the population over 65. The DHBs are semi-autonomous, in that they follow the overall directives of the MOH, but have considerable decision rights in how public hospitals and community services are run and financed. They can also contract nongovernment and private providers.

In addition, there is a National Health Board (NHB) that has oversight responsibility for the quality, safety, and sustainability of the health care system. It also oversees capital investment and infrastructure in public facilities as well as the implementation and use of integrated health information systems. Some of its roles and responsibilities were delegated to the New Zealand Health Partnerships in July 2015.

A Pharmaceutical Management Agency of New Zealand has oversight responsibility for the effective use of drugs, prescription guidelines, and the drugs that are listed on a national formulary. A Health Quality and Safety Commission has oversight responsibility for improved quality, safety, patient experience, equity and value for money spent on health care. And finally, a National Health Committee (NHC) has oversight responsibility for health technology assessment.

Over time, a small but important private sector has emerged that provides New Zealanders with some choice of care outside the public sector.

(c) Outputs

The utilization of health care resources can be used as a high-level proxy indicator for the output of a health system. Below are four key utilization indicators, in areas linked to the resource levels described above, that indicate the function of the New Zealand health system compared with other OECD countries that have universal coverage.[18] New Zealand ranks 24th for doctor consultations per 100 population, 17th for hospital discharge rates per 100,000 population, 23rd for MRI exams per thousand population, and 22nd for CT scans per thousand population. On these indicators, New Zealand is among lower third.[19] See Table 12.4.

(d) Proxy Measures

OECD conducts detailed reviews of proxy outcome indicators related to proxy indicators like efficiency, equity, access, productivity and quality.[20,21] A detailed review of these indicators for New Zealand and the other countries is beyond the scope of this volume.

Table 12.4 Use of Resources, Age-adjusted in 2012

	Doctor Consultations		Discharge Rates		MRI Exams		CT Exams	
	Per 100	Rank	Per 100,000	Rank	Per 1,000	Rank	Per 1,000	Rank
New Zealand	4.0	2.4	15,992.1	17	4.4	23	28.5	22

Source: Barua *et al*. (2016), Database for New Zealand.

(e) Impact Indicators

(i) *Financial Protection*

All citizens and permanent residents are eligible for free access to health care under the New Zealand health system. Temporary visitors and illegal aliens pay the full cost of services except for the cost of treatment for accidents, which is covered by the national no-fault accident compensation scheme. [22]

Estimating the relative share of impoverishment which is attributable to health expenditure is difficult because there are many other causes of financial hardship. For example, in a given year when a person becomes impoverished, there may be other sources of unexpected expenditure such as education, food, unexpected housing costs, etc. And there may be loss of income from a change or loss of employment by one or more household members.

Out-of-pocket expenditure, as an indirect indicator of financial protection, is among the lowest in the OECD and has decreased over the past 20 years, indicating the progress made by New Zealand during the past two decades in protecting the population against the impoverishing effects of illness. See Table 12.5.

(ii) *Health Outcomes*

As seen in the methodology chapter, at the aggregate level, health status does not have a strong correlation with the financing of health care such as health insurance or health care interventions. Centre for International

Table 12.5 Financial Protection in 2014: Public and Private Health Expenditure (% of THE)

	1995	2000	2005	2010	2013	2014
General government expenditure on health (GGHE) as % of THE	77.2	78.0	79.7	83.1	82.6	82.3
Private expenditure on health (PvtHE) as % of THE	22.8	22.0	20.3	16.9	17.4	17.7

Source: Knoema (2017), Database for New Zealand.

Table 12.6 Health Outcomes and Ranks in 2012

	Life Expectancy at Birth (Le)		Healthy-Age Life Expectancy (HALE)		Infant Mortality Rate		Perinatal Mortality		Mortality Amenable to Health Care (MAH), 2011	
	Years	Rank	Years	Rank	Deaths Per 1,000 Live Births	Rank	Deaths Per 1,000 Total Births	Rank	SDRs Per 100,000	Rank
New Zealand	81.2	14	71.8	9	5.2	26	6.1	20	82.1	15

Source: Barua *et al.* (2016), Database for New Zealand.

Statistics, 1998. It has a stronger correlation with socioeconomic and other non-medical factors. So, no direct attribution to universal health care should be implied in the following section.

Nevertheless, the following 5 indicators can be used to get a rough sense of how well a country is doing in health, irrespective of any direct attribution to health care spending or the underlying health care system: life expectancy [LE] at birth, healthy-age life expectancy [HALE], infant mortality, perinatal mortality, and mortality amenable to health care [MAH]. The last two are the most sensitive to health care interventions.

New Zealand ranks 14th for life expectancy, 9th for healthy-age life expectancy, 26th for infant mortality, 20th for perinatal mortality and 15th for mortality amenable to health care. In these terms, health outcomes in New Zealand across a large range of variables remain among of the top third in the OECD for some but bottom third on infant mortality and perinatal mortality.[23] See Table 12.6.

(iii) *Patient Experience*

Although the level of health care resources that are available to the population may influence how they are used, in addition to the need for care, the experience that patients have when accessing a health care system will influence demand and the use of appropriate care. The timeliness of care, as measured by waiting lists, is an important indicator of the patient experience which affects accessibility.

Murray and Frenk propose that individuals value prompt attention for two reasons: "it may lead to better health outcomes" and "it can allay fears and concerns that come with waiting for diagnosis or treatment."[24]

A frequent criticism of state-funded health care systems is that they use waiting time to ration care. Life-threatening cases in New Zealand are dealt with immediately while non-urgent cases are forced to wait. [25] New Zealand ranks 2nd (out of 9) on ability to make a same-day appointment when sick, 5th (out of 10) on ease of finding care after hours, 8th (out of 14) on waiting more than four weeks for an appointment with a specialist, 8th (out of 10) on waiting two months or more for a specialist appointment, 7th (out of 9) on waiting four months or more for elective surgery and 9th (out of 10) on experiencing a barrier to access in the past year. Compared with other OECD countries, New Zealand does not do well on any of the indicators other being able to make an appointment quickly with a generalist and ease of finding care after hours.[26] See Table 12.7.

Although such waiting time is not necessarily related to patient satisfaction with or dissatisfaction with their health care system, it is often credited to or blamed on the system used to finance health care. This is equally true for health care providers, politicians, and many other groups in society. Reinforcing this criticism of universal access to health care in New Zealand, in recent years, many people feel very strongly about being able to access the parallel private health care system and are even willing to carry duplicative health insurance to cover part of the cost.

Table 12.7 Patient Experience Interacting With the Health System in 2013

	Able to Make Same-Day Appointment When Sick		Very or Somewhat Easy to Find Care after Hours		Waiting Time of More than Four Weeks for Getting an Appointment with a Specialist		Waited 2 Months or More for Specialist Appointment		Waited 4 Months or More for Elective Surgery		Found Cost a Barrier to Access in Past Year	
	%	Rank	%	Rank	%	Rank	%	Rank	%	Rank	%	Rank
New Zealand	72	2	54	5	44.1	8	19	8	15	7	21	9

Source: Barua *et al.* (2016), Database for New Zealand.

2. United Kingdom

(a) Inputs

In terms of financial resources mobilized, cost and public affordability, after the initial period of stable spending following introduction of universal access, health care spending in United Kingdom like in all other OECD countries, has increased over time but at a rate that is lower than the OECD average and much lower than in the USA. Age-adjusted total expenditure on health in 2012 was 8.3 percent of GDP. Health Expenditure per GDP in United Kingdom has increased in recent years from a very low starting point during the 1990s.[27]

As a result, health care expenditure in United Kingdom is among the lowest in the OECD countries that have a universal health care system. It is the 21st highest in age-adjusted expenditure per GDP but 17th highest in expenditure per capita, making it one of the lowest spenders in the OECD.[28] See Table 12.8.

United Kingdom has one of the most extensive medical training programs in the world. The admission to its medical and dental schools is less tightly controlled than in other countries because working positions are fixed after graduation through fixed slots with the Royal Colleges and National Health Service. This attracts a lot of foreign students. As a result of the latter, United Kingdom is in the lower third in terms of the number of doctors, compared with other OECD countries despite the large number of student admitted to medical, dental and nursing school programs. The building of new hospital and public clinics is also very tightly regulated. In terms of human and capital resources, United Kingdom ranks 23rd for doctors, 17th for nurses,

Table 12.8 Age-adjusted Spending Per GDP and Per Capita Spending in 2012

	Spending as Percentage of GDP		Spending Per Capita	
	Percentage	Rank	US$ PPP	Rank
United Kingdom	8.3	21	3,116.9	17

Source: Barua *et al.* (2016), Database for United Kingdom.

Table 12.9 Human and Capital Resources, Age-adjusted, Per Thousand Population in 2012

	Physicians		Nurses		Acute Beds		Psychiatric Beds	
	Per'000	Rank	Per'000	Rank	Per'000	Rank	Per'000	Rank
United Kingdom	2.7	23	8.1	17	2.3	24	0.5	20

Source: Barua *et al.* (2016), Database for United Kingdom.

Table 12.10 Availability of Diagnostic Technology in 2012

	MRI Units		CT Scanners		PET Scanners	
	Per Million	Rank	Per Million	Rank	Per Million	Rank
United Kingdom	6.0	24	7.7	26	0.5	22

Gamma Cameras		Digital Subtraction Angiography Units		Mammographs		Lithotriptors	
Per Million	Rank	Per Million	Rank	Per Million	Rank	Per Million	Rank
		1.0	20	8.6	19	NA	NA

Source: Barua *et al.* (2016), Database for United Kingdom.

24th acute care beds, and 20th for psychiatric care beds per thousand population, all low for OECD.[29] See Table 12.9.

In terms of medical technology, there are a wide range or indicators that could be used. United Kingdom ranks 24th (out of 26) for MRI units per million population, 26th for CT scanners, 22nd for PET scanners, 20th for Digital Subtraction Angiography units, 19th for Mammographs. Data in this analysis was not available for Gamma cameras and lithotripters.[30] For most of these high-end diagnostic techniques, the United Kingdom is in the lower third of the OECD. See Table 12.10.

The United Kingdom has one of the strongest research-based pharmaceutical manufacturing industries in the OECD.

(b) Process

Strong stewardship, policy making, governance, management, monitoring and evaluation have been a major focus of the health sector in the United Kingdom.[31–33]

Although the United Kingdom is not considered a Federal State, the governance of health care is devolved, with England, Northern Ireland, Scotland and Wales each having their own system of publicly owned, funded and managed health care. Each has its own policies and specific characteristics. Despite this devolution, each of the four systems is similar, and so the performance of the National Health Service (NHS) across the UK can be measured for the purpose of making international comparisons.[34–36]

In England, the Secretary of State for Health, and the Department of Health have responsibility for policy development and health legislation. The Department of Health (DOH) and Secretary of State for Health provide stewardship for the English system. The National Health Service (NHS) manages the budget, provides oversight for 209 local Clinical Commissioning Groups (CCGs), and monitors and enforces laws and regulations. Local government authorities hold the budget, manage "health and well-being boards" to coordinate with local services and to reduce health disparities. The English NHS also commissions some specialized low-volume services, national immunization and screening programs, primary care and standardization of health information technology.

The National Institute for Health and Clinical Excellence (NICE) conducts reviews and sets standards for clinical efficacy and cost-effectiveness as well as medical technology assessments. The Care Quality Commission (CQC) ensures basic standards of safety and quality. It has the authority to close down services that have serious quality problems. The Office of Fair Trading and the Competition Commission oversee the economic behavior of both public and private providers. Healthwatch England promotes patient interests. NHS Choices provides online information about health conditions, quality of care and other consumer information.

Over time, an important private sector has emerged that provides Britons with some choice of care outside the public sector.[37] Under the EU membership, UK citizens also have access to continental European health care systems, especially for conditions where there are long waiting lists in the UK.

(c) Outputs

The utilization of health care resources can be used as a high-level proxy indicator for the output of a health system. Below are four key utilization

Table 12.11 Use of Resources, Age-adjusted, 2012

	Doctor Consultations		Discharge Rates		MRI Exams		CT Exams	
	Per 100	Rank	Per 100,000	Rank	Per 1,000	Rank	Per 1,000	Rank
United Kingdom	4.9	19	12,758.4	21	39.7	14	74.3	19

Source: Barua *et al.* (2016), Database for United Kingdom.

indicators, in areas linked to the resource levels described above, that indicate the function of the United Kingdom health system compared with other OECD countries that have universal coverage.[38] United Kingdom ranks 19th for doctor consultations per 100 population, 21st for hospital discharge rates per 100,000 population, 14th for MRI exams per thousand population, and 19th for CT scans per thousand population. On these indicators, United Kingdom is among lower third. See Table 12.11.

(d) Proxy Measures

OECD conducts detailed reviews of proxy outcome indicators related to proxy indicators like efficiency, equity, access, productivity and quality.[39,40] A detailed review of these indicators for United Kingdom and the other countries is beyond the scope of this volume.

(e) Impact Indicators

(i) *Financial Protection*

All citizens and permanent residents as well as non-residents from the European Union with a European Health Insurance Card are eligible for free access to health care under the UK health system. Temporary visitors and illegal aliens pay the full cost of services except for the cost of treatment for accidents and some reportable infectious diseases.[41]

Estimating the relative share of impoverishment which is attributable to health expenditure is difficult because there are many other causes of financial hardship. For example, in a given year when a person becomes impoverished, there may be other sources of unexpected expenditure such

Table 12.12 Financial Protection in 2014: Public and Private Health Expenditure (% of THE)

	1995	2000	2005	2010	2013	2014
General government expenditure on health (GGHE) as % of THE	83.9	79.6	80.9	83.5	83.3	83.1
Private expenditure on health (PvtHE) as % of THE	15.0	20.4	19.1	16.5	16.7	16.9

Source: Knoema (2017), Database for United Kingdom.

as education, food, unexpected housing costs, etc. And there may be loss of income from a change or loss of employment by one or more household members.

Out-of-pocket expenditure, as an indirect indicator of financial protection, increased during the 1990s and a few years following 2000, but then decreased again during the past 10 years to reach a level which is among the lowest in the OECD, indicating the commitment made by the United Kingdom to protecting the population against the impoverishing effects of illness. See Table 12.12.

(ii) *Health Outcomes*

As seen in the methodology chapter, at the aggregate level, health status does not have a strong correlation with the financing of health care such as health insurance or health care interventions. Centre for International Statistics, 1998. It has a stronger correlation with socioeconomic and other non-medical factors. So, no direct attribution to universal health care should be implied in the following section.

Nevertheless, the following five indicators can be used to get a rough sense of how well a country is doing in health, irrespective of any direct attribution to health care spending or the underlying health care system: life expectancy [LE] at birth, healthy-age life expectancy [HALE], infant mortality, perinatal mortality, and mortality amenable to health care [MAH]. The last two are the most sensitive to health care interventions.

United Kingdom ranks 16th for life expectancy, 21st for healthy-age life expectancy, 24th for infant mortality, 25th for perinatal mortality and

Table 12.13 Health Outcomes and Ranks in 2012

	Life Expectancy at Birth (LE)		Healthy-age Life Expectancy (HALE)		Infant Mortality Rate		Perinatal Mortality		Mortality Amenable to Health Care (MAH), 2011	
	Years	Rank	Years	Rank	Deaths Per 1,000 Live Births	Rank	Deaths Per 1,000 Total Births	Rank	SDRs Per 100,000	Rank
United Kingdom	81.0	16	70.4	21	4.1	24	7	25	87.9	17

Source: Barua *et al.* (2016), Database for United Kingdom.

17th for mortality amenable to health care. In these terms, health outcomes in United Kingdom across a large range of variables remain among the top third in the OECD for some but bottom third on infant mortality and perinatal mortality.[42] See Table 12.13.

(iii) *Patient Experience*

Although the level of health care resources that are available to the population may influence how they are used, in addition to the need for care, the experience that patients have when accessing a health care system will influence demand and the use of appropriate care. The timeliness of care, as measured by waiting lists, is an important indicator of the patient experience which affects accessibility.

Murray and Frenk propose that individuals value prompt attention for two reasons: "it may lead to better health outcomes" and "it can allay fears and concerns that come with waiting for diagnosis or treatment."[43]

A frequent criticism of state-funded health care systems is that they use waiting time to ration care. Life-threatening cases in the United Kingdom are dealt with immediately, while non-urgent cases are forced to wait.[44] United Kingdom ranks 7th (out of 9) on ability to make a same-day appointment when sick, 1st (out of 10) on ease of finding care after hours, 2nd (out of 14) on waiting more than four weeks for an appointment with a specialist, 3rd (out of 10) on waiting two months or more for a specialist appointment, and 1st (out of 10) on experiencing a barrier to

Table 12.14 Patient Experience Interacting With the Health System in 2013

	Able to Make Same-Day Appointment when Sick		Very or Somewhat Easy to Find Care After Hours		Waiting Time of More than Four Weeks for Getting an Appointment with a Specialist		Waited 2 Months or More for Specialist Appointment		Waited 4 Months or More for Elective Surgery		Found Cost a Barrier to Access in Past Year	
	%	Rank	%	Rank	%	Rank	%	Rank	%	Rank	%	Rank
United Kingdom	52	7	69	1	18.3[b]	2	7	3	NA	NA	4	1

Source: Barua *et al.* (2016), Database for United Kingdom.

access in the past year. Compared with other OECD countries, United Kingdom does very well on most of these indicators, except being able to make an appointment on the same day when sick.[45] See Table 12.14.

Although such waiting time is not necessarily related to patient satisfaction with or dissatisfaction with their health care system, it is often credited to or blamed on the system used to finance health care. This is equally true for health care providers, politicians, and many other groups in society. In recent years, the United Kingdom has worked very hard to improve the patient experience in the NHS. Based on the above indicators, these efforts seem to have paid off.

3. Canada

(a) Inputs

In terms of financial resources mobilized, cost and public affordability, after the initial period of stable spending following introduction of universal access, health care spending in Canada, like in all other OECD countries, has increased over time at a rate slightly higher than the OECD average but much lower than in the USA. Age-adjusted total expenditure on health in 2012 was 10.6 percent of GDP. Health Expenditure per GDP in Canada has remained in the range of 10–11 percent of GDP over the past decade, varying slightly from year to year.[46]

As a result, health care expenditure in Canada is among the highest among OECD countries that have a universal health care system. It is the

Table 12.15 Age-adjusted Spending Per GDP and Per Capita Spending in 2012

	Spending as Percentage of GDP		Spending Per Capita	
	Percentage	Rank	US$ PPP	Rank
Canada	10.6	3	4,463.5	5

Source: Barua *et al.* (2016), Database for Canada.

Table 12.16 Resources, Age-adjusted, Per Thousand Population in 2012

	Physicians		Nurses		Acute Beds		Psychiatric Beds	
	Per '000	Rank	Per '000	Rank	Per '000	Rank	Per '000	Rank
Canada	2.6	2.4	9.7	13	1.8	28	0.4	24

Source: Barua *et al.* (2016), Database for Canada.

3rd highest in age-adjusted expenditure per GDP and 5th highest in expenditure per capita.[47] See Table 12.15.

Canada has an extensive network of training facilities in each Province and the Territories. The admission to its medical and dental schools is tightly regulated to control the total number of doctors and dentists that are trained. As a result of such controls, Canada is in the lower third in terms of the number of doctors, compared with other OECD countries. The building of new hospital and public clinics is also tightly. In terms of human and capital resources, Canada ranks 25th for doctors, 15th for nurses, 28th acute care beds, and 25th for psychiatric care beds per thousand population, the latter is low for the OECD.[48] See Table 12.16.

In terms of medical technology, there are a wide range or indicators that could be used. Canada ranks 19th (out of 26) for MRI units per million population, 19th for CT scanners, 15th for PET scanners, 1st for Gamma cameras, 15th for Digital Subtraction Angiography units, 11th for Mammographs, and 18th for Lithotriptors.[49] For most of these high-end diagnostic techniques, Canada is in the lower third of the OECD. See Table 12.17.

Canada does not have a strong research-based pharmaceutical manufacturing industry.

Table 12.17 Availability of Diagnostic Technology in 2012

	MRI Units		CT Scanners		PET Scanners	
	Per Million	Rank	Per Million	Rank	Per Million	Rank
Canada	8.8	19	14.6	19	1.2	15

Gamma Cameras		Digital Subtraction Angiography Units		Mammographs		Lithotriptors	
Per Million	Rank	Per Million	Rank	Per Million	Rank	Per Million	Rank
20.6	1	5.4	15	15.9	11	0.4	18

Source: Barua *et al.* (2016), Database for Canada.

(b) Process

Strong stewardship, policy making, governance, management, monitoring and evaluation have been a major focus of Canadian researchers.

Canada is a Federal State with significant devolution of responsibly for health care from the Federal Government to the Provinces and Territories.[50–52]

The Federal–Provincial division, which is defined under the Canadian constitution, has remained relatively constant over time with the transfer of much of the financial responsibly for health care from the Federal to Provincial level and the use of block grants rather than earmarked transfers (the provinces receive their Federal transfers as a single payment that is not earmarked for subsectors like health).

The Federal government also regulates the safety and efficacy of medical devices, pharmaceuticals, and natural health products; funds health research; administers a range of services for certain populations, including First Nations, Inuit, Métis, and inmates in federal penitentiaries; and administers several public health functions.

The Provinces and Territories continue to have responsibility for new policy development, legislative and regulatory changes, and oversight for organizing and delivering health services. In many Provinces, regional health authorities are responsible for both planning and delivery of services. In respect to the latter, the pendulum has swung back and forth several times from greater to lesser regionalization. Currently, there is a trend across Canada to merge and eliminate many of the regional authorities.

Canada and Australia are among the few countries where medical doctors still wield significant power being independent contractors with practice privileges rather employees of the hospital answerable to the medical director. This continues to create tension and sometimes conflicting interests between the medical profession and the management of health care facilities in which they work.

(c) Outputs

The utilization of health care resources can be used as a high-level proxy indicator for the output of a health system. Below are four key utilization indicators, in areas linked to the resource levels described above, that indicate the function of the Canadian health system compared with other OECD countries that have universal coverage.[53] Canada ranks 6th for doctor consultations per 100 population, 28th for hospital discharge rates per 100,000 population, 8th for MRI exams per thousand population, and 11th for CT scans per thousand population. On these indicators, Canada is among the top ten.[54] See Table 12.18.

(d) Proxy Measures

OECD conducts detailed reviews of proxy outcome indicators related to proxy indicators like efficiency, equity, access, productivity and quality.[55,56] A detailed review of these indicators for Canada and the other countries is beyond the scope of this volume.

Table 12.18 Use of Resources, Age-adjusted in 2012

	Doctor Consultations		Discharge Rates		MRI Exams		CT Exams	
	Per 100	Rank	Per 100,000	Rank	Per 1,000	Rank	Per 1,000	Rank
Canada	8.0	6	8,628.3	28	52.9	8	131.4	8

Source: Barua *et al.* (2016), Database for Canada.

(e) Impact Indicators

(i) *Financial Protection*

All citizens and permanent residents are eligible for free access to health care under the Canadian health system. Temporary legal visitors, undocumented refugees and those who stay in Canada beyond the duration of a legal permit, are not covered, although the provinces and territories do provide some limited treatment for special situations.[57]

Estimating the relative share of impoverishment which is attributable to health expenditure is difficult because there are many other causes of financial hardship. For example, in a given year when a person becomes impoverished, there may be other sources of unexpected expenditure such as education, food, unexpected housing costs, etc. And there may be loss of income from a change or loss of employment by one or more household members.

Out-of-pocket expenditure, as an indirect indicator of financial protection, is relatively high compared with other OECD countries that offer universal health care and has increased over the past 20 years, indicating the challenge that Canada faces in protecting the population against the impoverishing effects of illness.[58–60] See Table 12.19.

(ii) *Health Outcomes*

As seen in the methodology chapter, at the aggregate level, health status does not have a strong correlation with the financing of health care such

Table 12.19 Financial Protection in 2014: Public and Private Health Expenditure (% of THE)

	1995	2000	2005	2010	2013	2014
General government expenditure on health (GGHE) as % of THE	71.2	70.4	70.2	70.4	71.0	70.9
Private expenditure on health (PvtHE) as % of THE	28.8	29.6	29.8	29.6	29.0	29.1

Source: Knoema (2017), Database for Canada.

Table 12.20 Health Outcomes and Ranks in 2012

	Life Expectancy at Birth (LE)		Healthy-Age Life Expectancy (HALE)		Infant mortality rate		Perinatal Mortality		Mortality Amenable to Health Care (MAH), 2011	
	Years	Rank	Years	Rank	Deaths Per 1,000 Live Births	Rank	Deaths Per 1,000 Total Births	Rank	SDRs Per 100,000	Rank
Canada	81.5	10	71.8	9	4.8	25	6	18	70.5	8

Source: Barua *et al.* (2016), Database for Canada.

as health insurance or health care interventions. Centre for International Statistics, 1998. It has a stronger correlation with socioeconomic and other non-medical factors. So, no direct attribution to universal health care should be implied in the following section.

Nevertheless, the following five indicators can be used to get a rough sense of how well a country is doing in health, irrespective of any direct attribution to health care spending or the underlying health care system: life expectancy [LE] at birth, healthy-age life expectancy [HALE], infant mortality, perinatal mortality, and mortality amenable to health care [MAH]. The last two are the most sensitive to health care interventions.

Canada ranks 10th for life expectancy, 9th for healthy-age life expectancy, 25th for infant mortality, 18th for perinatal mortality and 8th for mortality amenable to health care. In these terms, health outcomes in Canada across a large range of variables remain among of the top third in the OECD for some but bottom third on infant mortality and perinatal mortality.[61] See Table 12.20.

(iii) *Patient Experience*

Although the level of health care resources that are available to the population may influence how they are used, in addition to the need for care, the experience that patients have when accessing a health care system will influence demand and the use of appropriate care. The timeliness of care, as measured by waiting lists, is an important indicator of the patient experience which affects accessibility.

Murray and Frenk propose that individuals value prompt attention for two reasons: "it may lead to better health outcomes" and "it can allay fears and concerns that come with waiting for diagnosis or treatment."[62]

A frequent criticism of state-funded health care systems is that they use waiting time to ration care. Life-threatening cases in are dealt with immediately, while non-urgent cases are forced to wait.[63] Canada ranks 9th or worst (out of 9) on ability to make a same-day appointment when sick, 8th (out of 10) on ease of finding care after hours, 14th or worst (out of 14) on waiting more than four weeks for an appointment with a specialist, 10th or worst (out of 10) on waiting two months or more for a specialist appointment, 8th or worst (out of 9) on waiting four months or more for elective surgery and 4th (out of 10) on experiencing a barrier to access in the past year. Compared with other OECD countries, Canada does not do well on any of the indicators other than there not being any serious perceived financial barrier to entry.[64] This perception, however, may be false because household spending in Canada (out-of-pocket and private health insurance) has now reached 30 percent of total spending. See Table 12.21.

Although such waiting time is not necessarily related to patient satisfaction with or dissatisfaction with their health care system, it is often credited to or blamed on the system used to finance health care. This is equally true for health care providers, politicians, and many other groups in society. Despite this criticism of universal access to health care in

Table 12.21 Patient Experience Interacting With the Health System in 2013

	Able to Make Same-Day Appointment when Sick		Very or Somewhat Easy to Find Care After Hours		Waiting Time of More than Four Weeks for Getting an Appointment With a Specialist		Waited 2 Months or More for Specialist Appointment		Waited 4 Months or More for Elective Surgery		Found Cost a Barrier to Access in Past Year	
	%	Rank	%	Rank	%	Rank	%	Rank	%	Rank	%	Rank
Canada	41	9	38	8	62.1	14	29	10	18	8	13	4

Source: Barua *et al.* (2016), Database for Canada.

Canada, people still prefer public rather than a for-profit private nature of their health care system. A 2003 Gallup poll found 25 percent of Americans are either "very" or "somewhat" satisfied with "the availability of affordable health care in the nation," versus 50 percent of those in the UK and 57 percent of Canadians.[65] Those "very dissatisfied" made up 44 percent of Americans, 25 percent of respondents of Britons, and 17 percent of Canadians. Regarding quality, 48 percent of Americans, 52 percent of Canadians, and 42 percent of Britons say they are satisfied. Later in 2009 a Harris-Decima poll found 82% of Canadians preferred their health care system to the one in the United States.[66]

4. Australia

(a) Inputs

In terms of financial resources mobilized, cost and public affordability, after the initial period of stable spending following introduction of universal access, health care spending in Australia, like in all other OECD countries, has increased over time at a rate slightly higher than the OECD average but much lower than in the USA. Age-adjusted total expenditure on health in 2012 was 9.3 percent of GDP. Health Expenditure per GDP in Australia has remained in the range of 10–11 percent of GDP over the past decade, varying slightly from year to year.[67]

As a result, health care expenditure in Australia is in the upper third of the OECD countries that have a universal health care system. It is the 11th highest in age-adjusted expenditure per GDP and 10th highest in expenditure per capita.[68] See Table 12.22.

Table 12.22 Age-adjusted Spending Per GDP and Per Capita Spending in 2012

	Spending as Percentage of GDP		Spending Per Capita	
	Percentage	Rank	US$ PPP	Rank
Australia	9.3	11	4,095.1	10

Source: Barua *et al.* (2016), Database for Australia.

Table 12.23 Resources, Age-adjusted, Per Thousand Population in 2012

	Physicians		Nurses		Acute Beds		Psychiatric Beds	
	Per '000	Rank	Per '000	Rank	Per '000	Rank	Per '000	Rank
Australia	3.5	11	10.8	10	3.6	9	0.4	23

Source: Barua *et al.* (2016), Database for Australia.

Table 12.24 Availability of Diagnostic Technology 2012

		MRI Units		CT Scanners		PET Scanners	
		Per Million	Rank	Per Million	Rank	Per Million	Rank
Australia		15.0	9	50.5	2	1.9	10
Gamma Cameras		Digital Subtraction Angiography Units		Mammographs		Lithotriptors	
Per Million	Rank	Per Million	Rank	Per Million	Rank	Per Million	Rank
20.1	2	16.6	3	22.8	8	NA	NA

Source: Barua *et al.* (2016), Database for Australia.

Australia has an extensive network of training facilities in each State and the territories. The admission to its medical and dental schools is tightly regulated to control the total number of doctors and dentists that are trained. Despite such controls, Australia is in the upper third in terms of the number of doctors, compared with other OECD countries. The building of new hospital and public clinics is also tightly regulated, but there is an active private hospital sector. Australia ranks 11th for doctors, 10th for nurses, 9th acute care beds, and 23rd for psychiatric care beds per thousand population, the latter is low for the OECD.[69] See Table 12.23.

In terms of medical technology, there are a wide range of indicators that could be used. Australia ranks 9th (out of 26) for MRI units per million population, 2nd for CT scanners, 10th for PET scanners, 2nd for Gamma cameras, 3rd for Digital Subtraction Angiography units, and 8th for Mammographs.[70] For most of these high-end diagnostic techniques, Australia is in the upper third of the OECD. See Table 12.24.

Australia does not have a strong research-based pharmaceutical manufacturing industry.

(b) Process

Strong stewardship, policy making, governance, management, monitoring and evaluation have been a major focus of the Australian health sector.

Australia is a Federal State with significant devolution of responsibly for health care from the Federal Government to the States and Territories.[71–74]

Three levels of government, Federal, State/Territory and Local, are responsible for the stewardship of the Australian health care system. Although the division of responsibility, which is defined under the Australian constitution, has remained relatively constant, the pendulum has swung back and forth over time in terms of the balance of power.

The Federal Government has a very limited role in the direct provision of health. It focusses on governance, management, monitoring and evaluation as well as providing funding and support to the States. It also subsidizes primary care providers through the Medicare Benefits Scheme (MBS) and the Pharmaceutical Benefits Scheme (PBS) and it provides some funds for state services. The Federal Department of Health (DH) oversees these programs, and financing is administered by the Department of Human Services.

Several national agencies have oversight responsibility for areas of national interest. For example, the Council of Australian Governments (COAG), with representation from the Prime Minister and First Ministers of each state, are responsible for intergovernmental collaboration and decision-making at the federal level. The COAG deals mainly with priority issues, such as major policy and funding discussions. It is supported by the Australian Health Ministers Advisory Council.

Regulatory oversight is provided by a number of agencies that oversee supply, imports, exports, manufacturing, advertisement and harmonization of data. The Australian Competition and Consumer Commission is one of the most active in the OECD in enforcing anti-trust regulation and ensuring that there is a level playing field not just in the private sector but also between the private and the public sector. The AIHW and the Australian Bureau of Statistics (ABS) provide national information on health data.

The States and the Territories have their own State- and Territory-level Departments of Health. They are responsible for public hospitals, ambulance services, public dental care, community health services, and mental health care. And even the States they have devolved management of hospitals and many other services to Local Health Networks. In many States, the Local Health Networks are responsible for both planning and delivery of day-to-day services. The pendulum has swung back and forth over time from greater to lesser decentralization.

Although significant funding for the States and the Territories comes from the Federal Government and Australian Health Insurance system, the States, Territory and Local governments contribute their own. Local governments play a particular role in the delivery of community health and preventive health programs, such as immunization and regulation of food. This split funding system, with the Federal, State, Territory, Local government, and health insurance program causes budget shifting and endless negotiation back and forth between the States and the Federal levels of government.

Australia is among the few countries where medical doctors still wield significant power, being independent contractors with practice privileges rather than employees of the hospital answerable to the medical director. This continues to create tension and sometimes conflicting interests between the medical profession and the management of health care facilities such as hospital where they work.

(c) Outputs

The utilization of health care resources can be used as a high-level proxy indicator for the output of a health system. Below are four key utilization indicators, in areas linked to the resource levels described above, that indicate the function of the Australian health system compared with other OECD countries that have universal coverage.[75] Australia ranks 8th for doctor consultations per 100 population, 6th for hospital discharge rates per 100,000 population, 18th for MRI exams per thousand population, and 13th for CT scans per thousand population. In terms of medical visits and discharges, Australia is among the top 10.[76] See Table 12.25.

Table 12.25 Use of Resources, Age-adjusted in 2012

	Doctor Consultations		Discharge Rates		MRI Exams		CT Exams	
	Per 100	Rank	Per 100,000	Rank	Per 1,000	Rank	Per 1,000	Rank
Australia	7.3	8	18,287.9	6	27.5	18	110.3	13

Source: Barua *et al.* (2016), Database for Australia.

(d) Proxy Measures

OECD conducts detailed reviews of proxy performance indicators related to proxy indicators like efficiency, effectiveness, equity, access, productivity and quality.[77,78] A detailed review of these indicators for Australia and the other countries is beyond the scope of this volume.

(e) Impact Indicators

(i) *Financial Protection*

All citizens and residents with a permanent visa are eligible for free access to health care under the Australian health system. Citizens of some other countries with formal agreements may also have access under these arrangements. Temporary visitors and illegal aliens pay the full cost of services except for the cost of treatment for accidents, which is covered by the national no-fault accident compensation scheme.[79]

Estimating the relative share of impoverishment which is attributable to health expenditure is difficult because there are many other causes of financial hardship. For example, in a given year when a person becomes impoverished, there may be other sources of unexpected expenditure such as education, food, unexpected housing costs, etc. And there may be loss of income from a change or loss of employment by one or more household members.

Out-of-pocket expenditure, as an indirect indicator of financial protection, is relatively high compared with other OECD countries that offer universal health care and has remained around the same level over the past 20 years, indicating the challenge that Australia faces in protecting the population against the impoverishing effects of illness. See Table 12.26.

(ii) *Health Outcomes*

As seen in the methodology chapter, at the aggregate level, health status does not have a strong correlation with the financing of health care such as health insurance or health care interventions. Centre for International Statistics, 1998. It has a stronger correlation with socioeconomic and other non-medical factors. So, no direct attribution to universal health care should be implied in the following section.

Table 12.26 Financial Protection in 2014: Public and Private Health Expenditure (% of THE)

	1995	2000	2005	2010	2013	2014
General government Expenditure on health (GGHE) as % of THE	65.8	66.8	67.0	68.0	67.0	67.0
Private expenditure on health (PvtHE) as % of THE	34.2	33.2	33.0	32.0	33.0	33.0

Source: Knoema (2017), Database for Australia.

Table 12.27 Health Outcomes and Ranks in 2012

	Life Expectancy at Birth (LE)		Healthy-age Life Expectancy (HALE)		Infant Mortality Rate		Perinatal Mortality		Mortality Amenable to Health Care (MAH), 2011	
	Years	Rank	Years	Rank	Deaths Per 1,000 Live Births	Rank	Deaths Per 1,000 Total Births	Rank	SDRs Per 100,000	Rank
Australia	82.1	6	72.5	4	3.3	13	8.2	27	61.4	2

Source: Barua *et al.* (2016), Database for Australia.

Nevertheless, the following five indicators can be used to get a rough sense of how well a country is doing in health, irrespective of any direct attribution to health care spending or the underlying health care system: life expectancy (LE) at birth, healthy-age life expectancy (HALE), infant mortality, perinatal mortality, and mortality amenable to health care (MAH). The last two are the most sensitive to health care interventions.

Australia ranks 6th for life expectancy, 4th for healthy-age life expectancy, 13th for infant mortality, 27th for perinatal mortality and 2nd for mortality amenable to health care. In these terms, health outcomes in Australia across a large range of variables remain among of the best in the world.[80] See Table 12.27.

(iii) *Patient Experience*

Although the level of health care resources that are available to the population may influence how they are used, in addition to the need for care, the experience that patients have when accessing a health care system will influence demand and the use of appropriate care. The timeliness of care, as measured by waiting lists, is an important indicator of the patient experience which affects accessibility.

Murray and Frenk propose that individuals value prompt attention for two reasons: "it may lead to better health outcomes" and "it can allay fears and concerns that come with waiting for diagnosis or treatment."[81]

A frequent criticism of state-funded health care systems is that they use waiting time to ration care. Life-threatening cases in Australia are dealt with immediately while non-urgent cases are forced to wait.[82] Australia ranks 4th (out of 9) for ability to make a same-day appointment when sick, 7th (out of 10) on ease of finding care after hours, 9th (out of 14) waiting more than four weeks for an appointment with a specialist, 6th (out of 10) on waiting two months or more for a specialist appointment), 6th (out of 9) on waiting four months or more for elective surgery and 7th (out of 10) on experiencing a barrier to access in the past year. Compared with other OECD countries, Australia does not do well on any of the indicators other than the lack of any serious financial barrier to entry.[83] See Table 12.28.

Although such waiting time is not necessarily related to patient satisfaction with or dissatisfaction with their health care system, it is often credited to or blamed on the system used to finance health care. This is equally true for health care providers, politicians, and many other groups in society. Reinforcing this criticism of universal access to health care in Australia, many people feel very strongly about being able to access the

Table 12.28 Patient Experience Interacting With the Health System in 2013

	Able to Make Same-day Appointment When Sick		Very or Somewhat Easy to Find Care After Hours		Waiting Time of More than Four Weeks for Getting an Appointment With a Specialist		Waited 2 Months or More for Specialist Appointment		Waited 4 Months or More for Elective Surgery		Found Cost a Barrier to Access in Past Year	
	%	Rank	%	Rank	%	Rank	%	Rank	%	Rank	%	Rank
Australia	58	4	46	7	46.2	9	18	6	10	6	16	7

Source: Barua *et al.* (2016), Database for Australia.

parallel private health care system and are even willing to carry duplicative health insurance to cover part of the cost.

5. Denmark

(a) Inputs

In terms of financial resources mobilized, cost and public affordability, after the initial period of stable spending following introduction of universal access, health care spending in Denmark like in all other OECD countries has increased over time, but at a rate that is lower than the OECD average and much lower than in the USA. Age-adjusted total expenditure on health in 2012 was 10.0 percent of GDP. Health Expenditure per GDP in Denmark has remained in the range of 10–11 percent of GDP over the past decade, varying slightly from year to year.[84]

As a result, health care expenditure in Denmark is among the highest in the OECD countries that have a universal health care system. It is the 7th highest in age-adjusted expenditure per GDP but 7th highest in expenditure per capita, reflecting the lower GDP in Denmark.[85] See Table 12.29.

Denmark has an aggressive training of primary care doctors and nurses. The admission to its medical and nursing schools focusses on these two areas. As a result, Denmark is in the upper third in terms of the number of doctors and nurses, compared with other OECD countries. The building of new hospital and public clinics is more tightly controlled. In terms of human and capital resources, Denmark ranks 12th for doctors, 4th for nurses, 19th acute care beds, and 19th for psychiatric care beds per thousand population, the latter is low for the OECD.[86] See Table 12.30.

Table 12.29 Age-adjusted Spending Per GDP and Per Capita Spending in 2012

	Spending as Percentage of GDP		Spending Per Capita	
	Percentage	Rank	US$ PPP	Rank
Denmark	10.0	7	4,348.7	7

Source: Barua *et al.* (2016), Database for Denmark.

Table 12.30 Resources, Age-adjusted, Per Thousand Population in 2012

	Physicians		Nurses		Acute Beds		Psychiatric Beds	
	Per'000	Rank	Per'000	Rank	Per'000	Rank	Per'000	Rank
Denmark	3.5	12	15.7	4	2.4	19	0.5	19

Source: Barua *et al.* 2016, Database for Denmark.

Table 12.31 Availability of Diagnostic Technology in 2012

		MRI Units		CT Scanners		PET Scanners	
		Per Million	Rank	Per Million	Rank	Per Million	Rank
Denmark		15.4	8	33.1	7	5.0	1
Gamma Cameras		Digital Subtraction Angiography Units		Mammographs		Lithotriptors	
Per Million	Rank	Per Million	Rank	Per Million	Rank	Per Million	Rank
17.4	3	NA	NA	18.5	9	NA	NA

Source: Barua *et al.* 2016, Database for Denmark.

In terms of medical technology, there are a wide range or indicators that could be used. Denmark ranks 8th (out of 26) for MRI units per million population, 7th for CT scanners, 1st for PET scanners, 3rd for Gamma cameras, and 9th for Mammographs.[87] Data for this series was not available for Digital Subtraction Angiography and Lithotriptors. For all of these high-end diagnostic techniques for which data was available, Denmark is in the upper third of the OECD. See Table 12.31.

Denmark does not have a strong research-based pharmaceutical manufacturing industry other than for insulin and a couple of other products.

(b) Process

Strong stewardship, policy making, governance, management, monitoring and evaluation have been a major focus of the Denmark health sector.

Although Denmark is not Federal State, there is significant devolution of responsibly for health care from the national level to the Regions and Local Municipalities.[88–90] Denmark's Health Law sets out the government's responsibility for health promotion and prevention of illness, curative care, relief of suffering, and measures to address functional limitations. There is also a focus on access, quality, service integration, choice, information to provide transparency and short waiting times.

The Health Law defines the balance in responsibility for health care between the National Government, the Regions and the Municipalities. The Danish Ministry of Health and the Danish Health Authority, Danish Medicines Agency, and Danish Patient Safety Authority are responsible for policy making, planning and the regulatory framework of health services, including cost control mechanisms. General supervision of health personnel and quality management is shared between the national level bodies and medical societies, including the skill mix and geographic deployment. The national level also pays a role in health technology assessments and comparative productivity and cost-effectiveness studies.

Responsibility for the planning and delivery of specialized services is delegated to five elected Administrative Regions. The Regions own, finance and manage hospitals, specialized rehabilitation and most services provided by general practitioners (GPs), specialists and other health workers like physiotherapists, dentists, and pharmacists. Municipalities finance and provide nursing home care, health visitors, home care, dental care, and school health. They also provide programs for the prevention, treatment for drug and alcohol abuse and rehabilitation.

In Denmark, organized patient groups play a strong role in policymaking at all levels of the system — national, regional, and municipal levels. Complaints and compensation claims are handled by a patient ombudsman.

The Danish have a strong orientation towards primary care. General practitioners are independent contractors that play a strong role both as coordinators of care and for appropriate referrals.

(c) Outputs

The utilization of health care resources can be used as a high-level proxy indicator for the output of a health system. Below are four key utilization indicators, in areas linked to the resource levels described above, that indicate the function of the Denmark health system compared with other OECD countries that have universal coverage.[91] Denmark ranks 20th for doctor consultations per 100 population, 11th for hospital discharge rates

Table 12.32 Use of Resources, Age-adjusted in 2012

	Doctor Consultations		Discharge Rates		MRI Exams		CT Exams	
	Per 100	Rank	Per 100,000	Rank	Per 1,000	Rank	Per 1,000	Rank
Denmark	4.5	20	16,531.6	11	64.6	6	125.4	10

Source: Barua *et al.* (2016), Database for Denmark.

per 100,000 population, 6th for MRI exams per thousand population, and 10th for CT scans per thousand population. On these indicators, Denmark is among upper third, with the exception of doctor consultation where it is in the lower 3rd. See Table 12.32.

(d) Proxy Measures

OECD conducts detailed reviews of proxy outcome indicators related to proxy indicators like efficiency, equity, access, productivity and quality.[92,93] A detailed review of these indicators for Denmark and the other countries is beyond the scope of this volume.

(e) Impact Indicators

(i) *Financial Protection*

All citizens and permanent residents as well as non-residents from the European Union with a European Health Insurance Card are eligible for free access to health care under the Danish Health system. Temporary visitors and illegal immigrants are partially covered through a voluntary, privately funded initiative by Danish doctors, supported by the Danish Red Cross and Danish Refugee Aid.[94]

Estimating the relative share of impoverishment which is attributable to health expenditure is difficult because there are many other causes of financial hardship. For example, in a given year when a person becomes impoverished, there may be other sources of unexpected expenditure such as education, food, unexpected housing costs, etc. And there may be loss of income from a change or loss of employment by one or more household members.

Out-of-pocket expenditure, as an indirect indicator of financial protection, is among the lowest in the OECD and has decreased over the past

Table 12.33 Financial Protection in 2014: Public and Private Health Expenditure (% of THE)

	1995	2000	2005	2010	2013	2014
General government expenditure on health (GGHE) as % of THE	82.5	83.9	84.5	85.1	85.3	84.8
Private expenditure on health (PvtHE) as % of THE	17.5	16.1	15.5	14.9	14.7	15.2

Source: Knoema (2017), Database for Denmark.

20 years, indicating the continued progress made by Denmark during the past two decades in protecting the population against the impoverishing effects of illness. See Table 12.33.

(ii) *Health Outcomes*

As seen in the methodology chapter, at the aggregate level, health status does not have a strong correlation with the financing of health care such as health insurance or health care interventions. Centre for International Statistics, 1998. It has a stronger correlation with socioeconomic and other non-medical factors. So, no direct attribution to universal health care should be implied in the following section.

Nevertheless, the following five indicators can be used to get a rough sense of how well a country is doing in health, irrespective of any direct attribution to health care spending or the underlying health care system: LE at birth, HALE, infant mortality, perinatal mortality, and MAH. The last two are the most sensitive to health care interventions.

Denmark ranks 24th for life expectancy, 23rd for healthy-age life expectancy, 15th for infant mortality, 18th for perinatal mortality and 12th for mortality amenable to health care. In these terms, health outcomes in Denmark across a large range of variables is in the mid-range to lower third in the OECD.[95] See Table 12.34.

(iii) *Patient Experience*

Although the level of health care resources that are available to the population may influence how they are used, in addition to the need for care,

Table 12.34 Health Outcomes and Ranks in 2012

	Life Expectancy at Birth (LE)		Healthy-age Life Expectancy (HALE)		Infant Mortality Rate		Perinatal Mortality		Mortality Amenable to Health Care (MAH), 2011	
	Years	Rank	Years	Rank	Deaths Per 1,000 Live Births	Rank	Deaths Per 1,000 Total Births	Rank	SDRs Per 100,000	Rank
Denmark	80.1	24	70.0	23	3.4	15	6	18	79.9	12

Source: Barua *et al.* (2016), Database for Denmark.

Table 12.35 Patient Experience Interacting With the Health System in 2013

Able to Make Same-day Appointment When Sick		Very or Somewhat Easy to Find Care After Hours		Waiting Time of More than Four Weeks for Getting an Appointment With a Specialist		Waited 2 Months or More for Specialist Appointment		Waited 4 Months or More for Elective Surgery		Found Cost a Barrier to Access in Past Year	
%	Rank	%	Rank	%	Rank	%	Rank	%	Rank	%	Rank

Note: No comparable data available through the analysis by Barua *et al.* (2016).
Source: Barua *et al.* (2016), Database for Denmark.

the experience that patients have when accessing a health care system will influence demand and the use of appropriate care. The timeliness of care, as measured by waiting lists, is an important indicator of the patient experience which affects accessibility.

Murray and Frenk propose that individuals value prompt attention for two reasons: "it may lead to better health outcomes" and "it can allay fears and concerns that come with waiting for diagnosis or treatment."[96]

A frequent criticism of state-funded health care systems is that they use waiting time to ration care. Life-threatening cases in Denmark are dealt with immediately while non-urgent cases are forced to wait. [97] Comparable data for these indicators were unfortunately not available for Denmark. Anecdotally, based on discussions with people who know Scandinavian systems, on these indicators Denmark seems to be similar to Norway and Sweden, that is, in the mid- to lower third of the OECD.[98] See Table 12.35.

Although such waiting time is not necessarily related to patient satisfaction with or dissatisfaction with their health care system, it is often credited to or blamed on the system used to finance health care. This is equally true for health care providers, politicians, and many other groups in society. Reinforcing this criticism of universal access to health care in Denmark, in recent years, many people feel very strongly about being able to access the parallel private health care system and are even willing to carry duplicative health insurance to cover part of the cost.

6. Norway

(a) Inputs

In terms of financial resources mobilized, cost and public affordability, after the initial period of stable spending following introduction of universal access, health care spending in Norway, like in all other OECD countries, has increased over time but at a rate that is lower than the OECD average and much lower than in the USA. Age-adjusted total expenditure on health in 2012 was 9 percent of GDP. Health Expenditure per GDP in Norway has remained in the mid-range for the OECD, varying slightly from year to year.[99]

As a result, health care expenditure in Norway is in the mid-range in the OECD countries that have a universal health care system. It is the 14th highest in age-adjusted expenditure per GDP but 15th highest in expenditure per capita.[100] See Table 12.36.

Norway has an aggressive training of primary care doctors and nurses. The admission to its medical and nursing schools focusses on these two areas. As a result, Norway is in the upper third in terms of the number of doctors and nurses, compared with other OECD countries. The building of new hospital and public clinics is more tightly controlled, although

Table 12.36 Age-adjusted Spending Per GDP and Per Capita Spending in 2012

	Spending as Percentage of GDP		Spending Per Capita	
	Percentage	Rank	US$ PPP	Rank
Norway	9.0	14	5,965.0	1

Source: Barua *et al.* (2016), Database for Norway.

Table 12.37 Resources, Age-adjusted, Per Thousand Population in 2012

	Physicians		Nurses		Acute Beds		Psychiatric Beds	
	Per'000	Rank	Per'000	Rank	Per'000	Rank	Per'000	Rank
Norway	4.3	2	16.9	1	2.4	20	1.2	4

Source: Barua *et al.* (2016), Database for Norway.

Table 12.38 Availability of Diagnostic Technology in 2012

	MRI Units		CT Scanners		PET Scanners	
Norway	Per Million	Rank	Per Million	Rank	Per Million	Rank

Gamma Cameras		Digital Subtraction Angiography Units		Mammographs		Lithotriptors	
Per Million	Rank	Per Million	Rank	Per Million	Rank	Per Million	Rank

Note: No comparable data available through the analysis by Barua *et al.* (2016).
Source: Barua *et al.* (2016), Database for Norway.

there has been a focus on psychiatry. In terms of human and capital resources, Norway ranks 2nd for doctors, 1st for nurses, 20th acute care beds, and 4th for psychiatric care beds per thousand population, the latter is very high for the OECD.[101] See Table 12.37.

In terms of medical technology, there are a wide range of indicators that could be used. Comparable data for these indicators were unfortunately not available for Norway. Anecdotally, based on discussions with people who know Scandinavian systems, these indicators for Norway seem to be similar to those in Denmark and Finland, in the upper third of the OECD. [102] See Table 12.38.

Norway does not have a strong research-based pharmaceutical manufacturing industry.

(b) Process

Strong stewardship, policy making, governance, management, monitoring and evaluation have been a major focus of the Norwegian health sector.

Although Norway is not Federal State, there is significant devolution of responsibly for health care to the Regional Health Care Authorities (RHAs) and 428 Local Municipalities that are responsible for primary and social care.[103–106]

The Norwegian Ministry of Health is responsible for policy making, planning and the regulatory framework for health services. It is also responsible for a range of funding functions such as establishing the health budget at the national level, setting the budget allocation to the RHAs, Municipalities, and negotiating provider fees, the level of out-of-pocket payments, and cost containment measures, like ceilings. The Ministry of Health is the owner of most hospitals and responsible for specialist care. It provides guidance to the RHAs, Municipalities and sub-ordinate agencies on their priorities and activities.

The Directorate for Health sets clinical guidelines, it coordinates 18 patient ombudsmen and is responsibility for health promotion and prevention of illness as well as a new National Patient Safety Program. It sets the standards and participates in the development and implementation of health information technology. It sets guidelines and applies recommendations on health technology assessments (HTAs) established by the Norwegian Knowledge Center for Health Services. Finally, the Directorate for Health is responsible establishing Diagnostic Related Groups (DRGs) fees for hospitals.

Other agencies play important roles. The Medicines Agency selects which drugs to reimburse and sets reference prices. The Norwegian Knowledge Center for Health Services conducts cost-effectiveness studies and surveys on quality, patient safety, and patient experience. Its Health Technology Assessments (HTAs) are used by the Norwegian Council for Priority Setting in Health Care and the National System for the Introduction of New Health Technologies.

The Board of Health Supervision audits the different components of the health care system. When problems are identified, the institution involved is notified so that corrective measures can be taken. Sanctions include warnings, fines and revoking the right to practice for personnel or institution involved. The Norwegian Institute of Public Health provides advice on public health such as infection control and infectious disease surveillance. And it participates in issues relating to forensic medicine.

(c) Outputs

The utilization of health care resources can be used as a high-level proxy indicator for the output of a health system. Below are four key utilization

Table 12.39 Use of Resources, Age-adjusted in 2012

	Doctor Consultations		Discharge Rates		MRI Exams		CT Exams	
	Per 100	Rank	Per 100,000	Rank	Per 1,000	Rank	Per 1,000	Rank
Norway	4.5	21	17,952.8	7	NA	NA	NA	NA

Source: Barua *et al.* (2016), Database for Norway.

indicators, in areas linked to the resource levels described above, that indicate the function of the Norway health system compared with other OECD countries that have universal coverage.[107] Norway ranks 21st for doctor consultations per 100 population and 7th for hospital discharge rates per 100,000 population. Although data is missing for Norway on MRI exams per thousand population and CT scans per thousand population, anecdotally, based on discussions with people who know Scandinavian systems, on these indicators Norway seems to be similar to Denmark, in the upper third of the OECD.[108] On these indicators, Norway is among lower third. See Table 12.39.

(d) Proxy Measures

OECD conducts detailed reviews of proxy outcome indicators related to proxy indicators like efficiency, equity, access, productivity and quality.[109,110] A detailed review of these indicators for Norway and the other countries is beyond the scope of this volume.

(e) Impact Indicators

(i) *Financial Protection*

Although Norway is not a member of the EU, through mutual agreement all citizens and permanent residents as well as some non-residents from the European Union with a European Health Insurance Card are eligible for free access to health care under the Norwegian health system. Temporary visitors and illegal immigrants are partially covered only for emergency acute care.[111]

Estimating the relative share of impoverishment which is attributable to health expenditure is difficult because there are many other causes of

Table 12.40 Financial Protection in 2014: Public and Private Health Expenditure (% of THE)

	1995	2000	2005	2010	2013	2014
General government expenditure on health (GGHE) as % of THE	84.2	82.5	83.5	84.7	85.2	85.5
Private expenditure on health (PvtHE) as % of THE	15.8	17.5	16.5	15.3	14.8	14.5

Source: Knoema (2017).

financial hardship. For example, in a given year when a person becomes impoverished, there may be other sources of unexpected expenditure such as education, food, unexpected housing costs, etc. And there may be loss of income from a change or loss of employment by one or more household members.

Out-of-pocket expenditure, as an indirect indicator of financial protection, is among the lowest in the OECD and has decreased over the past 20 years, indicating the continued progress made by Norway during the past two decades in protecting the population against the impoverishing effects of illness. See Table 12.40.

(ii) *Health Outcomes*

As seen in the methodology chapter, at the aggregate level, health status does not have a strong correlation with the financing of health care such as health insurance or health care interventions. Centre for International Statistics, 1998. It has a stronger correlation with socioeconomic and other non-medical factors. So, no direct attribution to universal health care should be implied in the following section.

Nevertheless, the following 5 indicators can be used to get a rough sense of how well a country is doing in health, irrespective of any direct attribution to health care spending or the underlying health care system: LE at birth, HALE, infant mortality, perinatal mortality, and MAH. The last two are the most sensitive to health care interventions.

Norway ranks 10th for life expectancy, 19th for healthy-age life expectancy, 5th for infant mortality, 9th for perinatal mortality and 5th for mortality amenable to health care. In these terms, health outcomes in Norway

Table 12.41 Health Outcomes and Ranks in 2012

	Life Expectancy at Birth (LE)		Health-age Life Expectancy (HALE)		Infant Mortality Rate		Perinatal Mortality		Mortality Amenable to Health Care (MAH), 2011	
	Years	Rank	Years	Rank	Deaths Per 1,000 Live Births	Rank	Deaths Per 1,000 Total Births	Rank	SDRs Per 100, 000	Rank
Norway	81.5	10	70.5	19	2.5	5	4.2	9	68.2	5

Source: Barua *et al.* (2016), Database for Norway.

across a large range of variables remains among the top third and mid-range in the OECD.[112] See Table 12.41.

(iii) *Patient Experience*

Although the level of health care resources that are available to the population may influence how they are used, in addition to the need for care, the experience that patients have when accessing a health care system will influence demand and the use of appropriate care. The timeliness of care, as measured by waiting lists, is an important indicator of the patient experience which affects accessibility.

Murray and Frenk propose that individuals value prompt attention for two reasons: "it may lead to better health outcomes" and "it can allay fears and concerns that come with waiting for diagnosis or treatment."[113]

A frequent criticism of state-funded health care systems is that they use waiting time to ration care. Life-threatening cases in Norway are dealt with immediately while non-urgent cases are forced to wait.[114] Norway ranks 7th (out of 9) on ability to make a same-day appointment when sick, 2nd (out of 10) on ease of finding care after hours, 13th (out of 14) on waiting more than four weeks for an appointment with a specialist, 9th (out of 10) on waiting two months or more for a specialist appointment, 9th (out of 9) on waiting four months or more for elective surgery and 3rd (out of 10) on experiencing a barrier to access in the past year. Compared with other OECD countries, Norway does not do well on many of these

Table 12.42 Patient Experience Interacting With the Health System in 2013

	Able to Make Same-day Appointment When Sick		Very or Somewhat Easy to Find Care After Hours		Waiting Time of More than Four Weeks for Getting an Appointment With a Specialist		Waited 2 Months or More for Specialist Appointment		Waited 4 Months or More for Elective Surgery		Found Cost a Barrier to Access in Past Year	
	%	Rank	%	Rank	%	Rank	%	Rank	%	Rank	%	Rank
Norway	52	7	58	2	55.3	13	26	9	22	9	10	3

Source: Barua *et al.* (2016), Database for Norway.

indicators other than ease of finding care after hours and the lack of any serious financial barrier to entry.[115] See Table 12.42.

Although such waiting time is not necessarily related to patient satisfaction with or dissatisfaction with their health care system, it is often credited to or blamed on the system used to finance health care. This is equally true for health care providers, politicians, and many other groups in society. Reinforcing this criticism of universal access to health care in Norway, in recent years, many people feel very strongly about being able to access the parallel private health care system and are even willing to carry duplicative health insurance to cover part of the cost.

7. Sweden

(a) Inputs

In terms of financial resources mobilized, cost and public affordability, after the initial period of stable spending following introduction of universal access, health care spending in Sweden like in all other OECD countries, has increased over time but at a rate that is lower than the OECD average and much lower than in the USA. Age-adjusted total expenditure on health in 2012 was 10.0 percent of GDP. Health Expenditure per GDP in Sweden has remained in the range of 10 percent of GDP over the past decade, varying slightly from year to year.[116]

Table 12.43 Age-adjusted Spending Per GDP and Per Capita Spending in 2012

	Spending as Percentage of GDP		Spending Per Capita	
	Percentage	Rank	US$ PPP	Rank
Sweden	10.0	6	4,380.0	6

Source: Barua *et al.* (2016), Database for Sweden.

Table 12.44 Resources, Age-adjusted, Per Thousand Population in 2012

	Physicians		Nurses		Acute Beds		Psychiatric Beds	
	Per'000	Rank	Per'000	Rank	Per'000	Rank	Per'000	Rank
Sweden	3.7	8	10.3	12	1.8	27	0.4	22

Source: Barua *et al.* (2016), Database for Sweden.

As a result, health care expenditure in Sweden is among the highest among OECD countries that have a universal health care system. It is the 6th highest in age-adjusted expenditure per GDP and also 6th highest in expenditure per capita.[117] See Table 12.43.

Sweden has an aggressive training of primary care doctors and nurses. The admission to its medical and nursing schools focusses on these two areas. As a result, Sweden is in the upper third in terms of the number of doctors and nurses, compared with other OECD countries. The building of new hospital and public clinics is more tightly controlled. In terms of human and capital resources, Sweden ranks 8th for doctors, 12th for nurses, 27th acute care beds, and 22nd for psychiatric care beds per thousand population, the latter is among the lowest for the OECD.[118] See Table 12.44.

In terms of medical technology, there are a wide range or indicators that could be used. Comparable data for these indicators were unfortunately not available for Sweden. Anecdotally, based on discussions with people who know Scandinavian systems, on these indicators Sweden seems to be similar to Denmark and Finland, in the upper third of the OECD.[119] See Table 12.45.

Sweden has a modest research-based pharmaceutical manufacturing industry.

Table 12.45 Availability of Diagnostic Technology in 2012

		MRI Units		CT Scanners		PET Scanners	
		Per Million	Rank	Per Million	Rank	Per Million	Rank
Gamma Cameras		Digital Subtraction Angiography Units		Mammographs		Lithotriptors	
Per Million	Rank	Per Million	Rank	Per Million	Rank	Per Million	Rank

Note: No comparable data available through the analysis by Barua *et al.* (2016).
Source: Barua *et al.* (2016), Database for Sweden.

(b) Process

Strong stewardship, policy making, governance, management, monitoring and evaluation have been a major focus of the Swedish health sector.

Although Sweden is not federal state, there is significant devolution of responsibly for health care from the national level of government to the Regions, County Councils and Local levels of government.[120–122]

At the national level, the Ministry of Health and Social Affairs is responsible for overall health and health care policy, regulation and sectoral oversight. It performs this function through eight national agencies. Below the national level, there are 12 County Councils and Regional Authorities that provide financing and direct delivering health services. At the local level, there are 290 Municipalities that are responsible for elderly care and the disabled. The Swedish Association of Local Authorities and Regions (SALAR) represents the Regions, Counties and Municipalities.

At the primary care level, both public and private providers can compete for patients that are on their list but not on pricing. Fixed fees are set to avoid price competition. The County Councils regulate the entry, accreditation and payment of new doctors (public and private) that enter the marketplace. They also have a mandate to review new technologies and treatments to ensure that they are cost-effective. The results from these reviews are widely disseminated with an aim to improve the decision-making process in delivering health care in Sweden.

The Dental and Pharmaceutical Benefits Agency determines which drugs will be included in the National Drug Benefit Scheme, while the Medical Products Agency provides regulatory oversight for the development, manufacture, and sale of drugs and other medicinal products.

(c) Outputs

The utilization of health care resources can be used as a high-level proxy indicator for the output of a health system. Below are four key utilization indicators, in areas linked to the resource levels described above, that indicate the function of the Sweden health system compared with other OECD countries that have universal coverage.[123] Sweden ranks 27th for doctor consultations per 100 population and 20th for hospital discharge rates per 100,000 population.[124]

Although data is missing for Sweden on MRI exams per thousand population and CT scans per thousand population, anecdotally, based on discussions with people who know Scandinavian systems, on these indicators Norway seems to be similar to Denmark, in the upper third of the OECD. See Table 12.46.

(d) Proxy Measures

OECD conducts detailed reviews of proxy outcome indicators related to proxy indicators like efficiency, equity, access, productivity and quality.[125,126] A detailed review of these indicators for Sweden and the other countries is beyond the scope of this volume.

(e) Impact Indicators

(i) *Financial Protection*

All citizens and permanent residents as well as some non-residents from the European Union with a European Health Insurance Card are eligible for free access to health care under the Swedish health system. Temporary

Table 12.46 Use of Resources, Age-adjusted in 2012

	Doctor Consultations		Discharge Rates		MRI Exams		CT Exams	
	Per 100	Rank	Per 100,000	Rank	Per 1,000	Rank	Per 1,000	Rank
Sweden	2.7	27	15,006.3	20	NA	NA	NA	NA

Source: Barua *et al.* (2016), Database for Sweden.

Table 12.47 Financial Protection in 2014: Public and Private Health Expenditure (% of THE)

	1995	2000	2005	2010	2013	2014
General government expenditure on health (GGHE) as % of THE	86.6	84.9	81.2	81.5	84.0	84.0
Private expenditure on health (PvtHE) as % of THE	13.4	15.1	18.8	18.5	16.0	16.0

Source: Knoema (2017), Database for Sweden.

visitors and illegal immigrants are partially covered only for emergency acute care. [127]

Estimating the relative share of impoverishment which is attributable to health expenditure is difficult because there are many other causes of financial hardship. For example, in a given year when a person becomes impoverished, there may be other sources of unexpected expenditure such as education, food, unexpected housing costs, etc. And there may be loss of income from a change or loss of employment by one or more household members.

Out-of-pocket expenditure, as an indirect indicator of financial protection, is among the lowest in the OECD and has decreased over the past 20 years, indicating the continued progress made by Sweden during the past two decades in protecting the population against the impoverishing effects of illness. See Table 12.47.

(ii) *Health Outcomes*

As seen in the methodology chapter, at the aggregate level, health status does not have a strong correlation with the financing of health care such as health insurance or health care interventions. Centre for International Statistics, 1998. It has a stronger correlation with socioeconomic and other non-medical factors. So, no direct attribution to universal health care should be implied in the following section.[128]

Nevertheless, the following 5 indicators can be used to get a rough sense of how well a country is doing in health, irrespective of any direct attribution to health care spending or the underlying health care system:

Table 12.48 Health Outcomes and Ranks in 2012

	Life Expectancy at Birth (LE)		Healthy-age Life Expectancy (HALE)		Infant Mortality Rate		Perinatal Mortality		Mortality Amenable to Health Care (MAH), 2011	
	Years	Rank	Years	Rank	Deaths Per 1,000 Live Births	Rank	Deaths Per 1,000 Total Births	Rank	SDRs Per 100,000	Rank
Sweden	81.8	8	71.6	11	2.6	7	5.1	14	67.1	4

Source: Barua *et al.* (2016), Database for Sweden.

LE at birth, HALE, infant mortality, perinatal mortality, and MAH. The last two are the most sensitive to health care interventions.

Sweden ranks 8th for life expectancy, 11th for healthy-age life expectancy, 7th for infant mortality, 14th for perinatal mortality and 4th for mortality amenable to health care. In these terms, health outcomes in Sweden across a large range of variables remains among of the top third and mid-range in the OECD.[129] See Table 12.48.

(iii) *Patient Experience*

Although the level of health care resources that are available to the population may influence how they are used, in addition to the need for care, the experience that patients have when accessing a health care system will influence demand and the use of appropriate care. The timeliness of care, as measured by waiting lists, is an important indicator of the patient experience which affects accessibility.

Murray and Frenk propose that individuals value prompt attention for two reasons: "it may lead to better health outcomes" and "it can allay fears and concerns that come with waiting for diagnosis or treatment."[130]

A frequent criticism of state-funded health care systems is that they use waiting time to ration care. Life-threatening cases in Sweden are dealt with immediately while non-urgent cases are forced to wait.[131] Sweden ranks 4th (out of 9) on ability to make a same-day appointment when sick, 10th (out of 10) on ease of finding care after hours, 10th (out of 14) on waiting more than four weeks for an appointment with a specialist, 5th

Table 12.49 Patient Experience Interacting With the Health System in 2013

	Able to Make Same-day Appointment When Sick		Very or Somewhat Easy to Find Care After Hours		Waiting Time of More than Four Weeks for Getting an Appointment With a Specialist		Waited 2 Months or More for Specialist Appointment		Waited 4 Months or More for Elective Surgery		Found Cost a Barrier to Access in Past Year	
	%	Rank	%	Rank	%	Rank	%	Rank	%	Rank	%	Rank
Sweden	58	4	35	10	48.7	10	17	5	6	5	6	2

Source: Barua *et al.* (2016), Database for Sweden.

(out of 10) on waiting two months or more for a specialist appointment, 5th (out of 9) on waiting four months or more for elective surgery and 2nd (out of 10) on experiencing a barrier to access in the past year. Compared with other OECD countries, Sweden does not do well on most of these indicators other than the lack of any serious financial barrier to entry.[132] See Table 12.49.

Although such waiting time is not necessarily related to patient satisfaction with or dissatisfaction with their health care system, it is often credited to or blamed on the system used to finance health care. This is equally true for health care providers, politicians, and many other groups in society. Reinforcing this criticism of universal access to health care in Sweden, in recent years, many people feel very strongly about being able to access the parallel private health care system and are even willing to carry duplicative health insurance to cover part of the cost.

8. Finland

(a) Inputs

In terms of financial resources mobilized, cost and public affordability, after the initial period of stable spending following introduction of universal access, health care spending in Finland, like in all other OECD countries, has increased over time but at a rate that is lower than the OECD average and much lower than in the USA. Age-adjusted total expenditure on health in 2012 was 8.0 percent of GDP. Health Expenditure per GDP

Table 12.50 Age-adjusted Spending Per GDP and Per Capita Spending in 2012

	Spending as Percentage of GDP		Spending Per Capita	
	Percentage	Rank	US$ PPP	Rank
Finland	8.0	22	3,200.2	16

Source: Barua *et al.* (2016), Database for Finland.

Table 12.51 Resources, Age-adjusted, Per Thousand Population in 2012

	Physicians		Nurses		Acute Beds		Psychiatric Beds	
	Per'000	Rank	Per'000	Rank	Per'000	Rank	Per'000	Rank
Finland	2.8	21	13.3	6	2.7	16	0.6	13

Source: Barua *et al.* (2016), Database for Finland.

in Finland has increased slowly over time from a very low starting point during the 1990s.[133]

As a result, health care expenditure in Finland is among the lowest in the OECD countries that have a universal health care system. It is the 22nd highest in age-adjusted expenditure per GDP but 16th highest in expenditure per capita. See Table 12.50.

Finland has a modest network of training for doctors but a stronger one for nurses. The admission to its medical and dental schools is tightly regulated to control the total number of doctors and dentists that are trained. As a result of such controls, Finland is in the lower third in terms of the number of doctors, compared with other OECD countries. The building of new hospital and public clinics is also tightly controlled. In terms of human and capital resources, Finland ranks 21st for doctors, 6th for nurses, 16th acute care beds, and 13th for psychiatric care beds per thousand population, the latter being mid-range for the OECD.[134] See Table 12.51.

In terms of medical technology, there are a wide range of indicators that could be used. Finland ranks 5th (out of 26) for MRI units per million population, 11th for CT scanners, 7th for PET scanners, 12th for Gamma cameras, 2nd for Digital Subtraction Angiography units, 6th for Mammographs, and 16th for Lithotriptors.[135] For most of these high-end diagnostic techniques, Finland is in the upper third of the OECD. See Table 12.52.

Table 12.52 Availability of Diagnostic Technology in 2012

	MRI Units		CT Scanners		PET Scanners	
	Per Million	Rank	Per Million	Rank	Per Million	Rank
Finland	21.6	5	21.8	11	2.2	7

Gamma Cameras		Digital Subtraction Angiography Units		Mammographs		Lithotriptors	
Per Million	Rank	Per Million	Rank	Per Million	Rank	Per Million	Rank
8.5	12	19.6	2	29.2	6	0.6	16

Source: Barua *et al.* (2016), Database for Finland.

Finland does not have a strong research-based pharmaceutical manufacturing industry.

(b) Process

Strong stewardship, policy making, governance, management, monitoring and evaluation have been a major focus of the Finnish health sector. Although Finland is not Federal State, like the Scandinavian countries, there is significant devolution of responsibly for health care to the Regions and Local Municipalities.[136–138]

At the national level, the Ministry of Health and Social Affairs is responsible for overall health and health care policy, regulation and sectoral oversight. It performs this function through several national agencies.

The National Institute for Health and Welfare is particularly well known for its research on public health and statistical function. Five University Teaching Hospitals provide tertiary care. Below the national level, the Finnish health system is highly decentralized. Secondary care is provided through regional hospitals. And municipalities have extensive control over the district hospitals and local services provided (health and social services).

Primary care is still provided largely through doctors and nursed who are employed in the health care centers that were set up during the 1970s. These centers provide both personal care to families and public health activities like health promotion and prevention. General practitioners act as gatekeepers to the more specialized secondary and tertiary services that require a referral before patients can access them.

(c) Outputs

The utilization of health care resources can be used as a high-level proxy indicator for the output of a health system. Below are four key utilization indicators, in areas linked to the resource levels described above, that indicate the function of the Finland health system compared with other OECD countries that have universal coverage.[139] Finland ranks 28th for doctor consultations per 100 population, 10th for hospital discharge rates per 100,000 population, 15th for MRI exams per thousand population, and 23rd for CT scans per thousand population. On most of these indicators, Finland is in the mid-range to lower third of the OECD. See Table 12.53.

(d) Proxy Measures

OECD conducts detailed reviews of proxy outcome indicators related to proxy indicators like efficiency, equity, access, productivity and quality.[140,141] A detailed review of these indicators for Finland and the other countries is beyond the scope of this volume.

(e) Impact Indicators

(i) *Financial Protection*

All citizens and permanent residents as well as some non-residents from the European Union with a European Health Insurance Card are eligible for free access to health care under the Finnish health system. Temporary

Table 12.53 Use of Resources, Age-adjusted in 2012

	Doctor Consultations		Discharge Rates		MRI Exams		CT Exams	
	Per 100	Rank	Per 100,000	Rank	Per 1,000	Rank	Per 1,000	Rank
Finland	2.5	28	16,691.5	10	39.6	15	27.4	23

Source: Barua *et al.* (2016), Database for Finland.

Table 12.54 Financial Protection in 2014: Public and Private Health Expenditure (% of THE)

	1995	2000	2005	2010	2013	2014
General government expenditure on health (GGHE) as % of THE	71.7	71.3	73.8	74.5	75.5	75.3
Private expenditure on health (PvtHE) as % of THE	28.3	28.7	26.2	25.5	24.5	24.7

Source: Knoema (2017), Database for Finland.

visitors and illegal immigrants are partially covered only for emergency acute care.

Estimating the relative share of impoverishment which is attributable to health expenditure is difficult because there are many other causes of financial hardship. For example, in a given year when a person becomes impoverished, there may be other sources of unexpected expenditure such as education, food, unexpected housing costs, etc. And there may be loss of income from a change or loss of employment by one or more household members.

Out-of-pocket expenditure, as an indirect indicator of financial protection, has decreased over the past 20 years, starting from a level that was relatively high for an OECD country with universal health care, indicating the progress made by Finland over the past two decades in protecting the population against the impoverishing effects of illness. See Table 12.54.

(ii) *Health Outcomes*

As seen in the methodology chapter, at the aggregate level, health status does not have a strong correlation with the financing of health care such as health insurance or health care interventions. Centre for International Statistics, 1998. It has a stronger correlation with socioeconomic and other non-medical factors. So, no direct attribution to universal health care should be implied in the following section.

Nevertheless, the following five indicators can be used to get a rough sense of how well a country is doing in health, irrespective of any direct attribution to health care spending or the underlying health care system:

Table 12.55 Health Outcomes and Ranks in 2012

	Life Expectancy at Birth (LE)		Healthy-age Life Expectancy (HALE)		Infant Mortality Rate		Perinatal Mortality		Mortality Amenable to Health Care (MAH), 2011	
	Years	Rank	Years	Rank	Deaths Per 1,000 Live Births	Rank	Deaths Per 1,000 Total Births	Rank	SDRs Per 100,000	Rank
Finland	80.7	20	70.8	17	2.4	4	3.1	3	82.0	14

Source: Barua *et al.* (2016), Database for Finland.

LE at birth, HALE, infant mortality, perinatal mortality, and MAH. The last two are the most sensitive to health care interventions.

Finland ranks 20th for life expectancy, 17th for healthy-age life expectancy, 4th for infant mortality, 3rd for perinatal mortality and 14th for mortality amenable to health care. In these terms, health outcomes in Finland across a large range of variables remain among of the top third to mid-range in the OECD, with the exception of life-expectancy which is not strongly correlated to health systems performance.[142] See Table 12.55.

(iii) *Patient Experience*

Although the level of health care resources that are available to the population may influence how they are used, in addition to the need for care, the experience that patients have when accessing a health care system will influence demand and the use of appropriate care. The timeliness of care, as measured by waiting lists, is an important indicator of the patient experience which affects accessibility.

Murray and Frenk propose that individuals value prompt attention for two reasons: "it may lead to better health outcomes" and "it can allay fears and concerns that come with waiting for diagnosis or treatment."[143]

A frequent criticism of state-funded health care systems is that they use waiting time to ration care. Life-threatening cases in Finland are dealt with immediately while non-urgent cases are forced to wait.[144] Anecdotally, based on discussions with people who know Scandinavian systems, on these indicators Denmark seems to be similar to Norway and Sweden, in the mid- to lower third of the OECD.[145] See Table 12.56.

Table 12.56 Patient Experience Interacting With the Health System in 2013

Able to Make Same-day Appointment When Sick		Very or Somewhat Easy to Find Care After Hours		Waiting Time of More than Four Weeks for Getting an Appointment With a Specialist		Waited 2 Months or More for Specialist Appointment		Waited 4 Months or More for Elective Surgery		Found Cost a Barrier to Access in Past Year	
%	Rank	%	Rank	%	Rank	%	Rank	%	Rank	%	Rank

Note: No comparable data available through the analysis by Barua *et al.* (2016).
Source: Barua *et al.* (2016), Database for Finland.

Although such waiting time is not necessarily related to patient satisfaction with or dissatisfaction with their health care system, it is often credited to or blamed on the system used to finance health care. This is equally true for health care providers, politicians, and many other groups in society. Reinforcing this criticism of universal access to health care in Finland, in recent years, many people feel very strongly about being able to access the parallel private health care system and are even willing to carry duplicative health insurance to cover part of the cost.

C. CONCLUSIONS

In all the eight countries, achieving universal coverage and access to health care did not end with the introduction of a landmark legislative reform. It has been an ongoing process that took many years before passing a major legislative reform and it has continued up until today, with many unfinished agendas. In most of the countries reviewed, universal coverage and access "health (care) for all" remains an elusive target that has not yet translated into good "health for all" or a high satisfaction in terms of patient experience accessing care when needed.

The initial stabilization in health expenditure during the decade following the introduction of landmark legislation for universal health coverage did not last. Eventually, spending in all of the 8 countries increased, both as spending per capita and as a percentage of GDP, like most other OECD countries that also offer universal health coverage. Spending in the USA, which is an outlier, is provided as a comparator. See Figures 12.2 and 12.3.

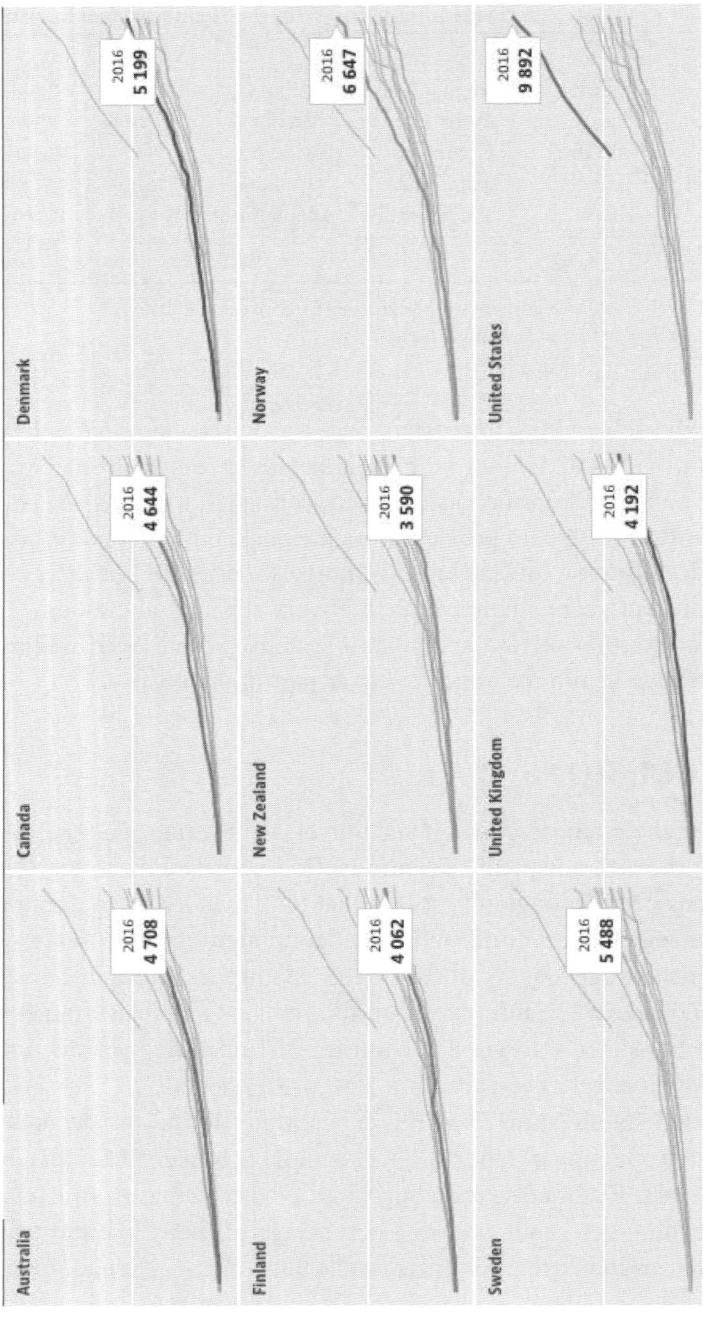

Figure 12.2 Health Spending Per Capital in the OECD from 1970 to 2016

Source: Author calculations using OECD Health Expenditure database.

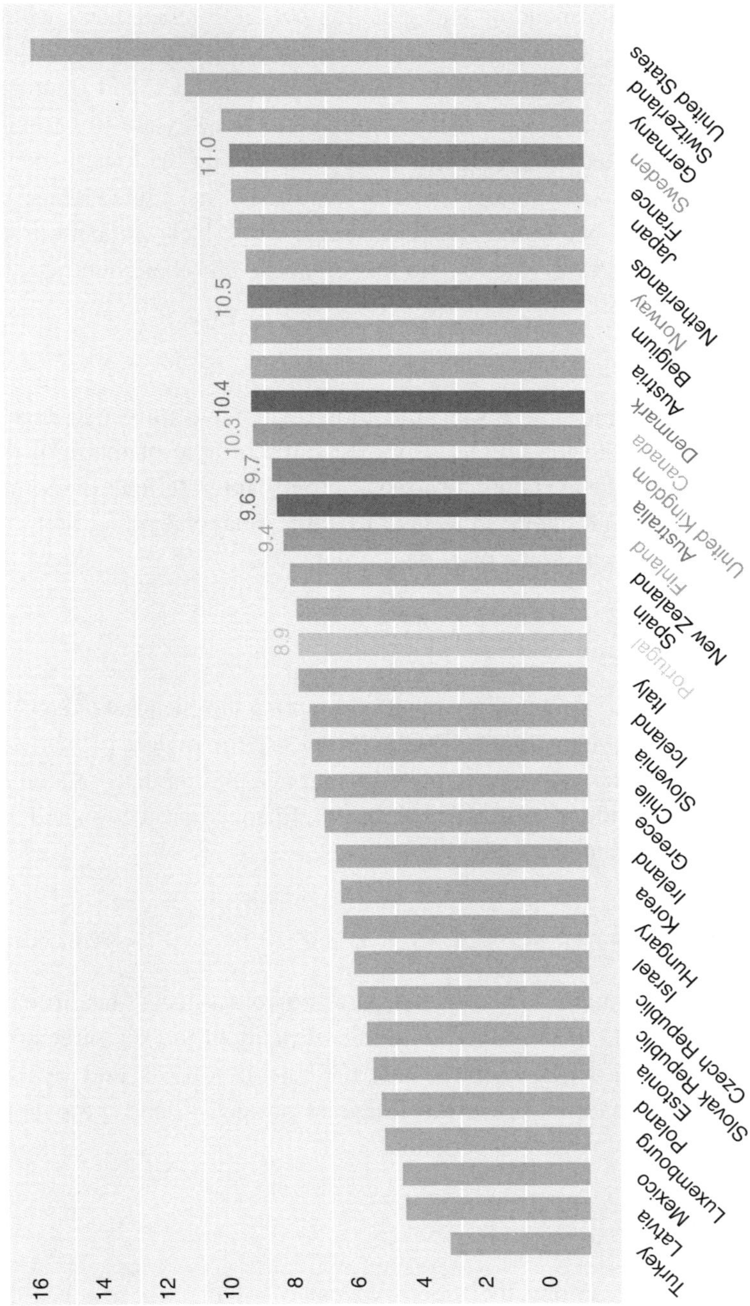

Figure 12.3 Health Spending Per GDP in the OECD in 2016

Source: Author calculations using OECD Health Expenditure database for 2016.

Straight per capita spending and spending per GDP hides many subtleties. Notably, using age-adjusted health expenditure, Canada and New Zealand are today among the highest spenders, with Sweden and Denmark also being among the high spenders. Australia and Norway are in the mid-range, while the United Kingdom and Finland are among the lowest spenders using an age-adjusted ranking. On a PPP-adjusted basis, United Kingdom and Finland are still below the OECD average, while New Zealand drops below the average and Norway rises to the top above all other countries.[146]

1. New Zealand

Overall, New Zealand's is among the most expensive universal-access health-care systems in the OECD. It ranks in the middle of many of the key indicators related to inputs, process, outputs, intermediate outcomes and overall impact indicators in terms of health, financial protection and the overall patient experience provided to patients.

2. United Kingdom

Overall, United Kingdom, like Finland, is also among the cheapest universal-access health-care systems in the OECD. It ranks in the middle of many of the key indicators related to inputs, process, outputs, intermediate outcomes and overall impact indicators in terms of health, financial protection and the overall patient experience provided to patients.

3. Canada

Overall, Canada is among the most expensive universal-access health-care systems in the OECD. It ranks in the middle of many of the key indicators related to inputs, process, outputs, intermediate outcomes and overall impact indicators in terms of health, financial protection and the overall patient experience provided to patients.

4. Australia

Overall, Australia is among the more expensive universal-access health-care systems in the OECD. It ranks well on many key performance related to inputs, process, outputs, intermediate outcomes and overall impact indicators in terms of health, financial protection and the overall patient experience provided to patients.

5. Denmark

Overall, Denmark is among the more expensive universal-access health-care systems in the OECD. It ranks in the middle of many of the key indicators related to inputs, process, outputs, intermediate outcomes and overall impact indicators in terms of health, financial protection and the overall patient experience provided to patients.

6. Norway

Overall, Norway is in the average range of spending for universal-access health care systems in the OECD. It ranks in the middle of many of the key indicators related to inputs, process, outputs, intermediate outcomes and overall impact indicators in terms of health, financial protection and the overall patient experience provided to patients.

7. Sweden

Overall, Sweden is among the more expensive universal-access health care systems in the OECD. It ranks in the middle of many of the key indicators related to inputs, process, outputs, intermediate outcomes and overall impact indicators in terms of health, financial protection and the overall patient experience provided to patients.

8. Finland

Overall, Finland, like United Kingdom, is also among the cheapest universal-access health-care systems in the OECD. It ranks in the middle of many of the key indicators related to inputs, process, outputs, intermediate outcomes and overall impact indicators in terms of health, financial protection and the overall patient experience provided to patients.

ENDNOTES

1. OECD countries that have not achieved Universal Access such as Mexico, Turkey and the USA are not included in the rankings or comparisons made in this section, which draws heavily from a publication by the Fraser Institute. OECD Health Expenditure Database. https://data.oecd.org/healthres/health-spending.htm Accessed July 17, 2017.
2. B. Barua, I. Timmermans, I. Nason, and N. Esmail, *Comparing Performance of Universal Health Care Countries, 2016,* Report (Vancouver: Fraser Institute, October 2016). https://www.fraserinstitute.org/sites/default/files/comparing-performance-of-universal-health-care-countries-2016.pdf. Accessed July 17, 2010.
3. N. Esmail and M. Walker, *How Good Is Canadian Healthcare? 2008 Report: An International Comparison of Healthcare Systems* (Vancouver: Fraser Institute, 2016). https://pdfs.semanticscholar.org/c4a0/5d20fa32a624c40729023292fc316662684e.pdf?_ga=2.8718645.1044595675.1499713218-4413199.1499713218. Accessed July 10.
4. M. Rovere and B. J. Skinner, *Value for Money on Health Insurance Systems in New Zealand and the OECD, 2012 edition,* Fraser Institute (Vancouver: Fraser Institute, October 2013). https://www.fraserinstitute.org/sites/default/files/value-for-money-from-health-insurance-systems-2012.pdf. Accessed July 10, 2017.
5. B. Barua, *Provincial Healthcare Index 2013* (Vancouver: Fraser Institute, 2013). https://www.fraserinstitute.org/sites/default/files/provincial-healthcare-index-2013-rev.pdf. Accessed July 10, 2017.
6. C. J. Murray and J. Frenk, A Framework for Assessing the Performance of Health Systems. *Bulletin of the World Health Organization* (2000)(78)6: 717–731.
7. A. Onyebuchi, G. P. Westert, J. Hurst, and N. S. Klazinga (2006). A Conceptual Framework for the OECD Healthcare Quality Indicators Project. *International Journal for Quality in Healthcare* (September): 5–13.
8. World Health Organization (WHO), *National Health Accounts*, (Geneva: WHO, 2015).
9. Barua *et al.*, *Comparing Performance*, 2016: 9.
10. *Ibid.*: 13.
11. Barua *et al.*, *Comparing Performance*, 2016: 44–45.
12. E. Mossialos, M. Wenzl, R. Osborn, and D. Sarnak, *2015 International Profiles of Health Care Systems* (New York: Commonwealth Fund, January 2016):123–133. http://www.commonwealthfund.org/~/media/files/publications/

fund-report/2016/jan/1857_mossialos_intl_profiles_2015_v7.pdf. Accessed July 17, 2017.

13. K. Davis, C. Schoen *et al.*, *Mirror, Mirror on the Wall: An International Update on the Comparative Performance of American Health Care* (New York: Commonwealth Fund, May 15, 2007). http://www.commonwealthfund.org/usr_doc/1027_Davis_mirror_mirror_international_update_final.pdf. Accessed May 28, 2017.
14. J. Cumming, J. McDonald, C. Barr, G. Martin, Z. Gerring, and J. Daubé, *New Zealand: Health System Review in Health Systems in Transition*, 2014, 4(2): 1–272. http://www.wpro.who.int/asia_pacific_observatory/hits/series/Nez_Health_Systems_Review.pdf. Accessed July 25, 2017.
15. R. Gauld, "Questions About New Zealand's Health System in 2013, Its 75th Anniversary Year," *New Zealand Medical Journal* 126(1380)(2013): 1–7.
16. R. Gauld, "What Should Governance for Integrated Care Look Like? New Zealand's Alliances Provide Some Pointers." *Medical Journal of Australia* 201(3)(2014): s67–s68.
17. Ministry of Health, *Annual Report for the Year Ended 30 June 2013, Including the Director-General of Health's Annual Report on the State of Public Health* (Wellington: Ministry of Health, 2013).
18. It is worth noting that many researchers would categorize utilization indicators under the Proxy Outcome indicator category rather than outputs. But for the purpose of the performance log frame, we are using in this book it utilization fits better under the output category.
19. Barua *et al.*, *Comparing Performance*, 2016: 22.
20. Organisation for Economic Co-operation and Development [OECD], *OECD Health Statistics 2017* (Paris: OECD, 2016a). http://www.oecd.org/els/health-systems/health-data.htm. Accessed July 10, 2017.
21. Organisation for Economic Co-operation and Development [OECD]. *Health at a Glance 2016: OECD Indicators*. (Paris: OECD, 2016b).
22. Davis *et al.*, *Mirror*, 2007.
23. Barua *et al.*, *Comparing Performance*, 2016: 35.
24. Murray and Frenk, *Performance of Health Systems*, 2000: 717–731.
25. Davis *et al.*, *Mirror*, 2007.
26. Barua *et al.*, *Comparing Performance*, 2016: 25.
27. WHO, *National Health Accounts*, 2015.
28. Barua *et al.*, *Comparing Performance*, 2016: 9.
29. Barua *et al.*, *Comparing Performance*, 2016: 13.
30. Barua *et al.*, *Comparing Performance*, 2016: 44–45.
31. Mossialos *et al.*, *International Profiles*, 2016: 49–59.

32. Davis *et al.*, *Mirror*, 2007.
33. J. Cylus, E. Richardson, L. Findley, M. Longley, C. O'Neill, and D. Steel, *United Kingdom: Health System Review in Health Systems in Transition* 17(5) (2015): 1–125. http://www.euro.who.int/__data/assets/pdf_file/0006/302001/UK-HiT.pdf?ua=1. Accessed July 25, 2017.
34. The King's Fund, *Commission on the Future of Health and Social Care in England: Final Report*, (London: King's Fund, 2014). https://www.kingsfund.org.uk/sites/files/kf/field/field_publication_file/Commission%20Final%20%20interactive.pdf. Accessed July 17, 2017.
35. The King's Fund, *The NHS Under the Coalition Government. Part Two: NHS Reform,* (London: King's Fund, February 2015). https://www.kingsfund.org.uk/sites/files/kf/field/field_publication_file/the-nhs-under-the-coalition-government-part-one-nhs-reform.pdf. Accessed July 17, 2017.
36. The King's Fund, *The NHS Under the Coalition Government. Part Two: NHS Performance, (London: King's Fund,* March 2015). https://www.kingsfund.org.uk/sites/files/kf/field/field_publication_file/the-nhs-under-the-coalition-government-nhs-performance-kings-fund-mar15.pdf. Accessed July 17, 2017.
37. The King's Fund, "The UK Private Healthcare Market", Appendix to the *Commission on the Future of Health and Social Care in England: Final Report*, (London: King's Fund, 2014). https://www.kingsfund.org.uk/sites/files/kf/field/field_publication_file/Commission%20Final%20%20interactive.pdf. Accessed July 17, 2017.
38. It is worth noting that many researchers would categorize utilization indicators under the Proxy Outcome indicator category rather than outputs. But for the purpose of the performance log frame, we are using in this book it utilization fits better under the output category.
39. OECD, *Health Statistics*, 2016a.
40. OECD, *Health at a Glance*, 2016b.
41. Davis *et al.*, *Mirror*, 2007.
42. Barua *et al.*, *Comparing Performance*, 2016: 35.
43. Murray and Frenk, *Performance of Health Systems*, 2000: 717–731.
44. Davis *et al.*, *Mirror*, 2007.
45. Barua *et al.*, *Comparing Performance*, 2016: 25.
46. WHO, *National Health Accounts*, 2015.
47. Barua *et al.*, *Comparing Performance*, 2016: 9.
48. Barua *et al.*, *Comparing Performance*, 2016: 13.
49. Barua *et al.*, *Comparing Performance*, 2016: 44–45.
50. Mossialos *et al.*, *International Profiles*, 2016: 21–31.

51. Davis *et al.*, *Mirror*, 2007.
52. G. P. Marchildon. *Canada: Health System Review, Health Systems in Transition* 15(1) (2013): 1–179. http://www.euro.who.int/__data/assets/pdf_file/0009/80568/E87954.pdf. Accessed July 25, 2017.
53. It is worth noting that many researchers would categorize utilization indicators under the Proxy Outcome indicator category rather than outputs. But for the purpose of the performance log frame we are using in this book it utilization fits better under the output category.
54. Barua *et al.*, *Comparing Performance*, 2016: 22.
55. OECD, *Health Statistics*, 2016a.
56. OECD, *Health at a Glance*, 2016b.
57. Davis *et al.*, *Mirror*, 2007.
58. Canadian Institute for Health Information (CIHI), *National Health Expenditure Trends 1975–2015* (Ottawa: CIHI, 2015a).
59. Canadian Institute for Health Information (CIHI), Supply, *Distribution and Migration of Canadian Physicians* (Ottawa: CIHI, 2015b).
60. Canadian Life and Health Insurance Association (CLHIA) Inc., *Canadian Life and Health Insurance Facts* (Toronto: CLHIA, 2014). http://clhia.uberflip. com/i/369328-canadian-life-and-health-insurance-facts-2014-edition. Accessed August 27, 2015.
61. Barua *et al.*, *Comparing Performance*, 2016: 35.
62. Murray and Frenk, *Performance of Health Systems*, 2000: 717–731.
63. Davis *et al.*, *Mirror*, 2007.
64. Barua *et al.*, *Comparing Performance*, 2016: 25.
65. Gallup, "Healthcare System Ratings: U.S., Great Britain, Canada," March 25, 2003. http://www.gallup.com/poll/8056/healthcare-system-ratings-us-great-britain-canada.aspx. Accessed May 28, 2017.
66. E. Zorn, "Never mind the anecdotes: Do Canadians like their health-care system?," Chicago Tribune, August 06, 2009. http://blogs.chicagotribune.com/news_columnists_ezorn/2009/08/never-mind-the-anecdotes-do-canadians-like-their-health-care-system.html. Accessed May 28, 2017.
67. WHO, *National Health Accounts*, 2015.
68. Barua *et al.*, *Comparing Performance*, 2016: 9.
69. Barua *et al.*, *Comparing Performance*, 2016: 13.
70. Barua *et al.*, *Comparing Performance*, 2016: 44–45.
71. Mossialos *et al.*, *International Profiles*, 2016, 11–21.
72. Department of the Prime Minister and Cabinet, Australian Government (2015), *Reform of the Federation White Paper: Roles and Responsibilities in Health. Issues Paper 3* (Canberra, DPMC, 2015).

73. Davis *et al.*, *Mirror*, 2007.
74. J. Healy, E. Sharman, and B. Lokuge, *Australia: Health System Review in Health Systems in Transition* 8(5)(2006):1–158. http://www.euro.who.int/__data/assets/pdf_file/0007/96433/E89731.pdf. Accessed July 25, 2017.
75. It is worth noting that many researchers would categorize utilization indicators under the Proxy Outcome indicator category rather than outputs. But for the purpose of the performance log frame we are using in this book it utilization fits better under the output category.
76. Barua *et al.*, *Comparing Performance*, 2016: 22.
77. OECD, *Health Statistics*, 2016a.
78. OECD, *Health at a Glance*, 2016b.
79. Davis *et al.*, *Mirror*, 2007.
80. Barua *et al.*, *Comparing Performance*, 2016: 35.
81. Murray and Frenk, *Performance of Health Systems*, 2000: 717–731.
82. Davis *et al.*, *Mirror*, 2007.
83. Barua *et al.*, *Comparing Performance*, 2016: 25.
84. WHO, *National Health Accounts*, 2015.
85. Barua *et al.*, *Comparing Performance*, 2016: 9.
86. Barua *et al.*, *Comparing Performance*, 2016: 13.
87. Barua *et al.*, *Comparing Performance*, 2016: 44–45.
88. Mossialos *et al.*, *International Profiles*, 2016: 39–49.
89. Davis *et al.*, *Mirror*, 2007.
90. M. Olejaz, A. Juul Nielsen, A. Rudkjøbing, H. Okkels Birk, A. Krasnik, and C. Hernández-Quevedo. *Denmark: Health System Review in Health Systems in Transition* 14(2)(2012):1–192. http://www.euro.who.int/__data/assets/pdf_file/0004/160519/e96442.pdf. Accessed July 10, 2017.
91. It is worth noting that many researchers would categorize utilization indicators under the Proxy Outcome indicator category rather than outputs. But for the purpose of the performance log frame we are using in this book it utilization fits better under the output category.
92. OECD, *Health Statistics*, 2016a.
93. OECD, *Health at a Glance*, 2016b.
94. Davis *et al.*, *Mirror*, 2007.
95. Barua *et al.*, *Comparing Performance*, 2016: 35.
96. Murray and Frenk, *Performance of Health Systems*, 2000: 717–731.
97. Davis *et al.*, *Mirror*, 2007.
98. Barua *et al.*, *Comparing Performance*, 2016: 25.
99. WHO, *National Health Accounts*, 2015.
100. Barua *et al.*, *Comparing Performance*, 2016: 9.

101. Barua *et al.*, *Comparing Performance*, 2016: 13.
102. Barua *et al.*, *Comparing Performance*, 2016: 44-45.
103. Mossialos *et al.*, *International Profiles*, 2016: 133–143.
104. Davis *et al.*, *Mirror*, 2007.
105. Ministry of Health and Care Services (MHCS), *Helse-og omsorgstjenest-eloven, Translated: The New Law for Health and Care Services*, (Oslo: MHCS, 2011).
106. Å. Ringard, A. Sagan, I. Sperre Saunes, and A. K. Lindahl, *Norway: Health System Review in Health Systems in Transition* 15(8)(2013): 1–162. http://www.euro.who.int/__data/assets/pdf_file/0018/237204/HiT-Norway.pdf. Accessed July 25, 2017.
107. It is worth noting that many researchers would categorize utilization indicators under the Proxy Outcome indicator category rather than outputs. But for the purpose of the performance log frame we are using in this book it utilization fits better under the output category.
108. Barua *et al.*, *Comparing Performance*, 2016: 22.
109. OECD, *Health Statistics*, 2016a.
110. OECD, *Health at a Glance*, 2016b.
111. Davis *et al.*, *Mirror*, 2007.
112. Barua *et al.*, *Comparing Performance*, 2016: 35.
113. Murray and Frenk, *Performance of Health Systems*, 2000: 717–731.
114. Davis *et al.*, *Mirror*, 2007.
115. Barua *et al.*, *Comparing Performance*, 2016: 25.
116. WHO, *National Health Accounts*, 2015.
117. Barua *et al.*, *Comparing Performance*, 2016: 9.
118. Barua *et al.*, *Comparing Performance*, 2016: 13.
119. Barua *et al.*, *Comparing Performance*, 2016: 44–45.
120. Mossialos *et al.*, *International Profiles*, 2016: 153–161.
121. Davis *et al.*, *Mirror*, 2007.
122. A. Anell, A. H. Glenngård, and S. Merkur, *Sweden: Health system review in Health Systems in Transition*, 2012, 14(5):1–159. http://www.euro.who.int/__data/assets/pdf_file/0008/164096/e96455.pdf. Accessed July 25, 2017.
123. It is worth noting that many researchers would categorize utilization indicators under the Proxy Outcome indicator category rather than outputs. But for the purpose of the performance log frame we are using in this book it utilization fits better under the output category.
124. Barua *et al.*, *Comparing Performance*, 2016: 22.
125. OECD, *Health Statistics*, 2016a.

126. OECD, *Health at a Glance*, 2016b.
127. Davis *et al.*, *Mirror*, 2007.
128. Davis *et al.*, *Mirror*, 2007.
129. Barua *et al.*, *Comparing Performance*, 2016: 35.
130. Murray and Frenk, *Performance of Health Systems*, 2000: 717–731.
131. Davis *et al.*, *Mirror*, 2007.
132. Barua *et al.*, *Comparing Performance*, 2016: 25.
133. WHO, *National Health Accounts*, 2015.
134. Barua *et al.*, *Comparing Performance*, 2016: 13.
135. Barua *et al.*, *Comparing Performance*, 2016: 44–45.
136. Data for Finland was not available through the Commonwealth 2016 database. Mossialos *et al.*, *International Profiles*, 2016.
137. Davis *et al.*, *Mirror*, 2007.
138. L. Vuorenkoski, P. Mladovsky, and E. Mossialos, *Finland: Health System Review*. Health Systems in Transition. 2008; 10(4): 1–168. http://www.euro.who.int/__data/assets/pdf_file/0007/80692/E91937.pdf. Accessed July 25, 2017.
139. It is worth noting that many researchers would categorize utilization indicators under the Proxy Outcome indicator category rather than outputs. But for the purpose of the performance log frame we are using in this book it utilization fits better under the output category.
140. OECD, *Health Statistics*, 2016a.
141. OECD, *Health at a Glance*, 2016b.
142. Barua *et al.*, *Comparing Performance*, 2016: 35.
143. Murray and Frenk, *Performance of Health Systems*, 2000: 717–731.
144. Davis *et al.*, *Mirror*, 2007.
145. Barua *et al.*, *Comparing Performance*, 2016: 25.
146. Barua *et al.* (2016): 18.

CHAPTER 13

LESSONS LEARNED

The Chapter looks at the lessons learned from the experience of the 8 countries in the OECD that introduced landmark legislative health care financing reforms to expand access to health care for their whole population.

A. DEVELOPMENT PROCESSES IN HEALTH CARE FINANCING REFORMS

By tracing the developments in health care financing over more than a century, the research conducted in this study provided several important clues that convergence, divergence, interdependence and evolution processes do occur in health policy. Although it may still be too early for a synthesis and the construction of a comprehensive worldwide grand theory on health care financing, the time is ripe for some mid-range theories about OECD countries.

1. Convergence

Proponents of convergence theories maintain that countries have common collective responses to similar socio-economic, political, bureaucratic and other forces such as market failure. This study demonstrated that prepayment of health care has increased steadily over the past century in all western countries in response to the uncertainties of illness and their concomitant financial hardships. State intervention in the health sector increased parallel to this process through the normative functions of modern government:

resource allocation, income distribution and stabilization of economic activity. The allocation function was performed through regulations, subsidies and direct provision of services; the distribution function was performed through revenue collection (taxes and social insurance), reimbursements and benefits in kind; and the stabilization function was performed through employment in the health sector, cost controls and production of services. The introduction of compulsory participation and universal entitlement has been part of a long continuum toward providing more efficient and equitable access to health services. Although there still appears to be a dichotomy in the cluster of policies advocated by Group I and Group II countries, there has been a progressive trend toward greater participation in the financing and extensive entitlement to health care in all OECD countries over the past 50 years, with a decreasing number of countries relying on means-testing and access restricted by ability to pay. See Table 13.1.

Convergence processes can take several forms. See Figure 13.1. This may explain some of the variability and differentiation that occurred within Group I and Group II countries. Similar issues may provoke an identical response each time. Market failure leading to various types of government intervention would be an example of this type of centripetal convergence process. On the other hand, issues may develop into increasingly similar, but still not identical, responses that continue to evolve over time. The standardization of the criteria for membership and benefits provided by the early sickness funds, friendly societies and health insurance schemes would be an example of this type of focused convergence process. Finally, issues may develop in the same direction, but into policies that are differentiating and continually evolving. Revenue collection for prepayment of health care through different financing mechanisms (general taxation, social insurance, health insurance and some direct charges) would be an example of this type of parallel convergence process.

2. Divergence

Proponents of divergence theories maintain that industrial societies and policy-makers imitate the time-proven policies of more advanced

Table 13.1 Landmark and Other Major Health Care Legislation

	Means-tested	Landmark Universal Entitlement
Australia	1944/47/48/53	1973/84
Austria	1888/19/60/74/79	
Belgium	1894/63	
Canada		1957/68
Denmark	1892/21/33/60	1971/73
Finland		1963/72
France	1928/45/67/71/74/78	
Germany	1883/11/27	
Greece	1922/51	1983/86
Iceland	1936	1971
Ireland	1911/81	
Italy	1912/27/43/50/62/70/71	1978
Japan	1922/38/58	
Luxembourg	1901/51/74/80	
Netherlands	1913/64/66/68	
New Zealand		1938/41
Norway	1909	1953/55
Portugal	1919/35	1977
Spain	1929/42/74	1986
Sweden	1891/1931	1947/53
Switzerland	1911	
Turkey	1945/50/64	
United Kingdom	1911	1946/48
United States	1965/72	

countries regardless of their socio-economic, political, bureaucratic or other contexts such as market failure. See Figure 13.2. This study demonstrated that as prepayment of health care increased over time, geographic proximity, hierarchical transmission from leaders to followers and spread along historical, social, cultural, economic, political, bureaucratic and scientific geographic links influenced the divergence of ideas and policies.

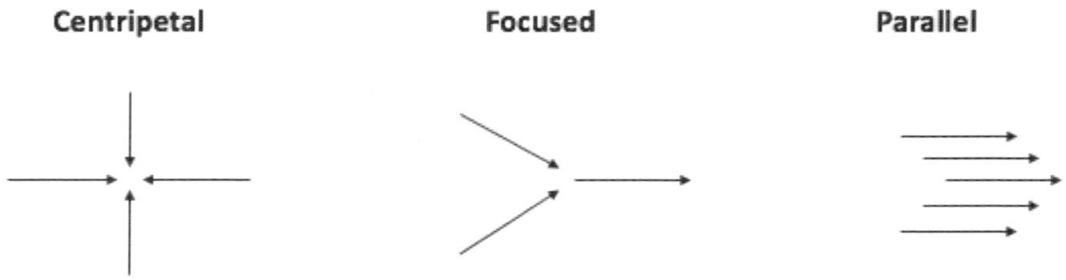

Figure 13.1 Convergence Processes

Source: Adapted from Preker (1989).

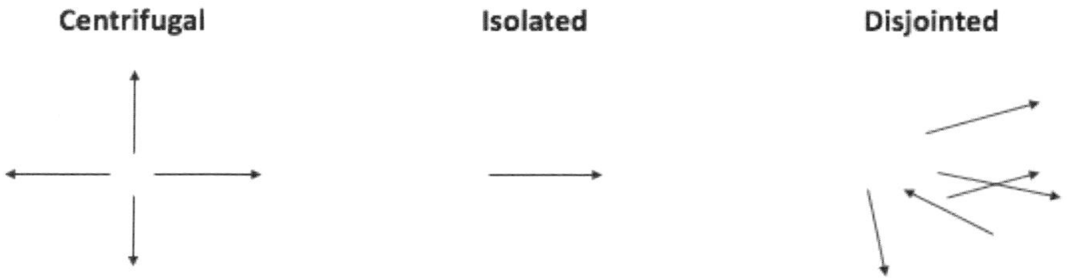

Figure 13.2 Divergence Processes

Source: Author.

Many of these links existed between the Nordic countries as one close knit group of countries with geographic proximity, and between the UK and her English-speaking former colonies despite their lack of such geographic closeness. The sickness funds which developed in the Nordic countries and the friendly societies in the English-speaking countries are only some of the many examples of this process. The Nordic consensual policy-making machine and the English-speaking majoritarian confrontational legislative style is another. Continental Europe was divided from these two groups of countries by geographic barriers, culture, language and the absence of many other key links.

Countries that had reached the most advanced stage of socio-economic development were not always the first to introduce innovative reforms. The United Kingdom, although more industrially developed, was later than Germany in introducing social security and health insurance reforms. New Zealand and the US were geographically detached from

Europe, but nevertheless leaders in introducing welfare legislation during the 1930s.

Divergence processes, like convergence, can take several forms. This may once again explain some of the variability and differentiation that occurred within Group I and Group II countries. Policies may scatter in several directions from a central point. Germany provided a bridge between continental Europe, the Nordic countries and the UK during the early development of social insurance, while the English language, as an international means of communication, was determinant in spreading ideas about the British NHS in a centrifugal-type divergence process. Isolated events were much more likely to encounter barriers, preventing ideas about these policies from spreading to other countries or other levels of abstraction. Few people heard about the 133-day history of the Hungarian National Health Service of Bela Kun in 1919. By contrast, divergence from multiple sources was even more likely to have an impact and to overcome different barriers than single experiences and single policies. Few countries were aware of New Zealand's NHS after 1938. But by the end of the 1940s, when the UK had introduced its NHS, and Canada and Australia had gone through the early legislative motions to introduce similar policies, most western countries were aware of these experiences. Awareness was not, however, sufficient for action, and although both Sweden and Norway were aware of the English-speaking experience during the late 1940s, they introduced compulsory sickness insurance instead of national health services.

3. Interdependence

The study also demonstrated the distinction between functional interdependence and divergence. See Figure 13.3. Often socio-economic developments provided the physical means for reforms, political processes, their direction, bureaucratic structures, the tools and market failures, the motives for change. These factors were interdependent, with no single one being sufficient. Cross-national links clearly existed during the late 1930s to early 1950s. Officials from New Zealand had visited Russia prior to 1938 and were aware of socialist experiences in health care provision. Norway's wartime shadow cabinet in London during World War II was

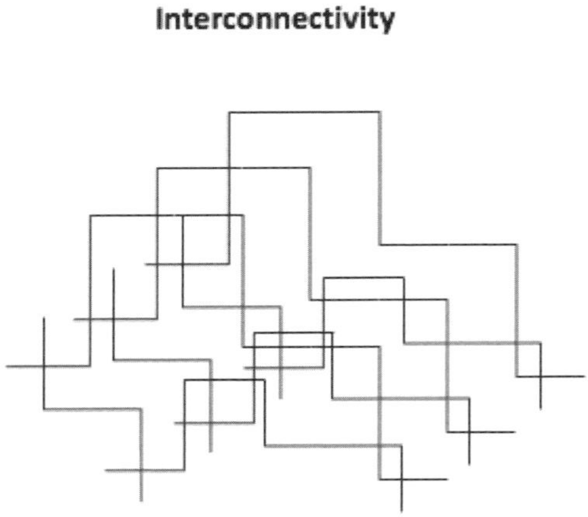

Figure 13.3 Interdependence Processes

Source: Adapted from Preker (1989).

aware of plans to create a British NHS. The allies fought together during the war and were therefore in close contact with each other. Yet proposals for compulsory participation and universal entitlement progressed as much along the direction of other social security reforms taking place in each country as according to developments taking place in other countries. Australia and Canada had the same motives to correct some of the observed market failure in the provision of health care through the private sector as the UK had during the late 1940s, and they went through much of the same motion to prepare reforms. They never introduced national health services because of different political and bureaucratic factors. Denmark, Norway and Sweden were in much the same position, but it was easier both politically and administratively to expand their sickness insurance systems to provide universal compulsory coverage than to create national health services.

4. Evolution

Socio-economic development, political processes, bureaucratic structures and market failures present themselves in different ways in different societies. Even if convergence, divergence, interdependence and other factors

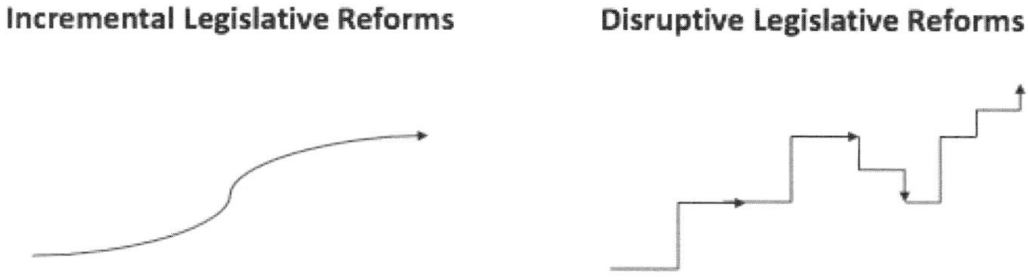

Figure 13.4 Evolution in Policies

Source: Adapted from Preker (1989).

act as forces to drive health care systems in a similar direction, there is still great scope for differentiation and changes over time. This was observed repeatedly during the case studies. See Figure 13.4. Many of the transformations that occurred over time in the terminology, content, scope, boundaries and units-of-measurement were due to disruptive rather than incremental changes in the evolution in concepts, issues and policies. Public expenditure at 10 percent of the GDP at the turn of the century was considered a threat to the economic stability of the state. Today it ranges from 23 to 60 percent of GDP. The social order among highly industrialized states was thought to be polarized into two camps — communism and capitalism — before the early 1980s. By early 1990 and following the Millennium, this view is already challenged. During the past century, the threshold for health care expenditure has been pushed upward continually. But today, some of the Nordic countries are experiencing a decrease in the portion of GDP devoted to health care in recent years. Recent health care reforms in western countries are beginning to challenge some of the elements of compulsory prepayment and universal entitlement that have been taken for granted over the past 50 years in many Group I countries.

Public and social policy appears to evolve over time and not always in the same direction. Health policy may be marked by the same long-term uncertainty as has been observed in social policy,[1] while punctuated by short periods of predictable patterns according to convergence, divergence and interdependence processes.[2] The literature on historical, economic and political theory has multiple references to cyclical or repeating patterns appear to evolve in a precarious way over time. Even the long time-span used for this study may have been too short to accurately portray trends in health care financing. Does health policy eventually double up on its historical path or do new options become available just at the moment when a return to the starting point appears inevitable? Does health care face an unavoidable and impending crisis due to a loss of momentum in historical commitments, self-damaging tendencies or political whims? Although it is too early to decide whether or not recent reversals are due to cyclical variations, "backlash" phenomena or a positive evolution in policies: "systematic investigation [continues to be] needed to establish the extent to which public commitments to the health sector reflect or diverge from commitments to other policy areas and to expansive social policy in general."[3]

B. IMPLICATIONS FOR OTHER COUNTRIES

Each country is unique so one should always exercise caution in applying lessons learned from one country to another country. Nevertheless, there are four major lessons learned from the cross-country reviews of major landmark legislative reforms in the OECD that led to the introduction of universal health care coverage in the OECD. This highlighted the importance of politics, timing, institutions and implementation.

1. Politics Reigns

No matter how long the policy planning process or how much attention was given to the design of a reform, the health financing reforms needed to introduce universal health coverage are intrinsically politically by nature.

In any reform where the poor, the disadvantaged, the elderly and sick get benefits which they would otherwise not be a le to afford, there will be winner and losers. The perceived winners will be those that will get something they did not otherwise have. Often they will be happy. The perceived losers are those who will have to pay not only for themselves but also for others. And they may also have to compete scares services that will have to be spread more widely across the population. Often they will be unhappy.

Reforms that introduce universal health coverage will be more popular at times when the political ideology of the majority of people is favorable to redistributive reforms and less popular during times when the going political ethos is not favorable to social spending and collective benefits to the population as a whole.

2. Timing is Critical

Sometimes a confluence of factors make things just right. Examples would include the World War II emergency service paving the way for the British NHS, the fiscal conservatism paving the way for compulsory members ship to address free-riders that did not pay their fair share in Denmark and citizens feeling ripped off by abusive private health insurance schemes in Canada and Australia.

Striking when the "iron is hot" may be more important than getting preparation "just right." A less-than-perfect reform that may need to be improved over time is better than an over-planned reform that is never gets off the ground.

3. The Devil in the Details of Implementation

Conversely, a badly implemented reform can cause immense damage even when the intent and design is good. There could be no better example than the recent health care reform in the US, which offered a unique opportunity for expanded coverage for millions of needy people but where technical difficulties in signing up for the government sponsored plans caused immense reputational damage for the program from the onset of implementation.

4. Institutions Matter

The latter are a reminder that institutions really do matter in the introduction of universal health coverage. Lofty international slogans about health care for everyone, and constitutional guarantees on the right to health care, are meaningless without a strong political will and institutions at the national and sub national level to implement such programs. The eight countries reviewed in this book, had both: a clear vision on what needed to be done to expand health coverage to their whole population and strengthening of the institutions needed to implement this vision.

ENDNOTES

1. R. Klein and M. O'Higgins, eds., *The Future of the Welfare* (Oxford: Basil Blackwell, 1985).
2. T. E. Getzen and J.-P. Poullier, "International Health Spending Forecasts: Concepts and Evaluation," Second World Congress on Health Economics, University of Zurich, Switzerland, September 13, 1990.
3. H. L. Wilensky, G. M. Luebbert, S. R. Hahn, and A. M. Jamieson, "Comparative social policy: Theories, methods, findings," in *Comparative Policy Research: Learning from Experience,* by M. Dierkes, H. N. Weiler and A. B. Antal, eds., WZB-Publications (Hants: Gower, 1987): 417.

APPENDIX A

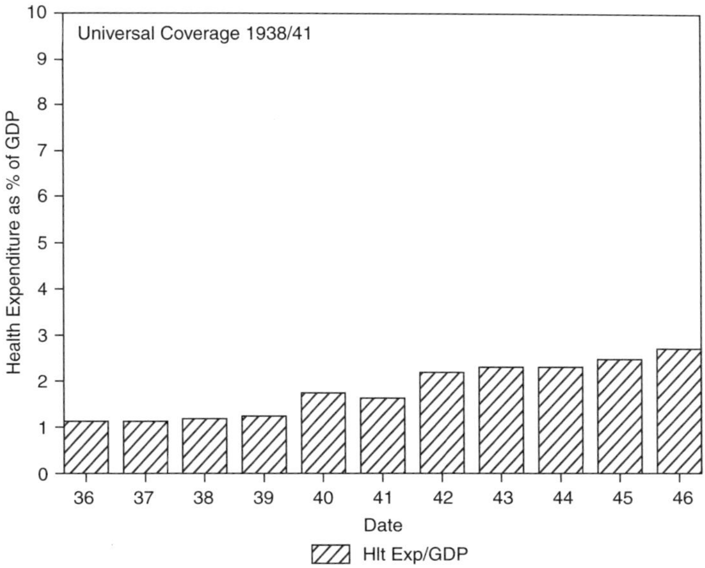

Figure A.1.1 Public Expenditure on Health Care in New Zealand

Source: Preker (1989).

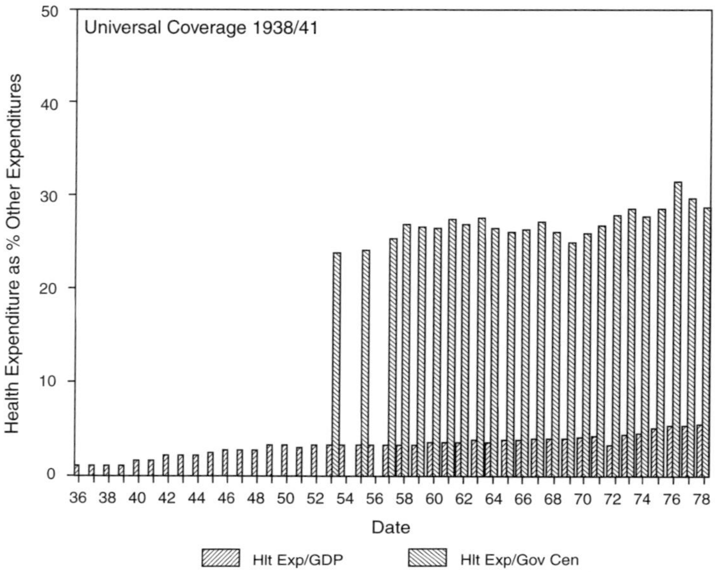

Figure A.1.2 Public Expenditure on Health Care in New Zealand

Source: Preker (1989).

Note: Expenditure on health care includes cash reimbursements for medical treatment but not maintenance payment during illness. See Table A.3 for sources. Hlt Exp = Health Expenditure; Gov Con = Government Consumption Expenditure; Gov Tot = Government Total Expenditure.

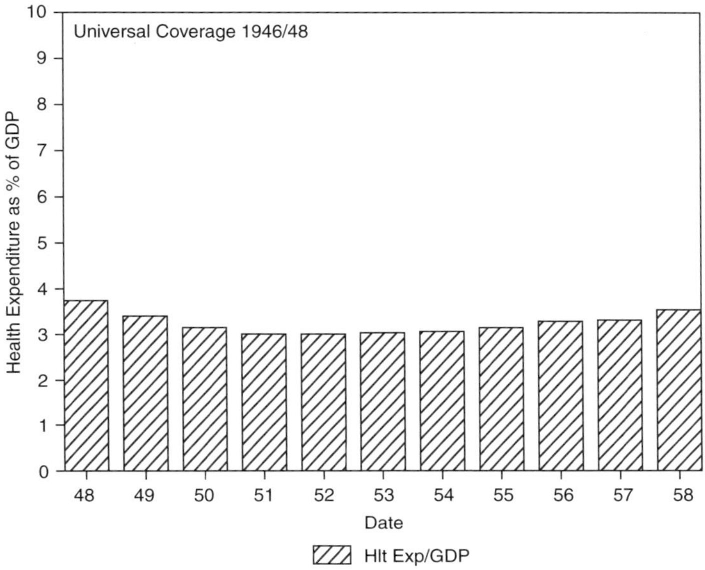

Figure A.2.1 Public Expenditure on Health Care in the United Kingdom

Source: Preker (1989).

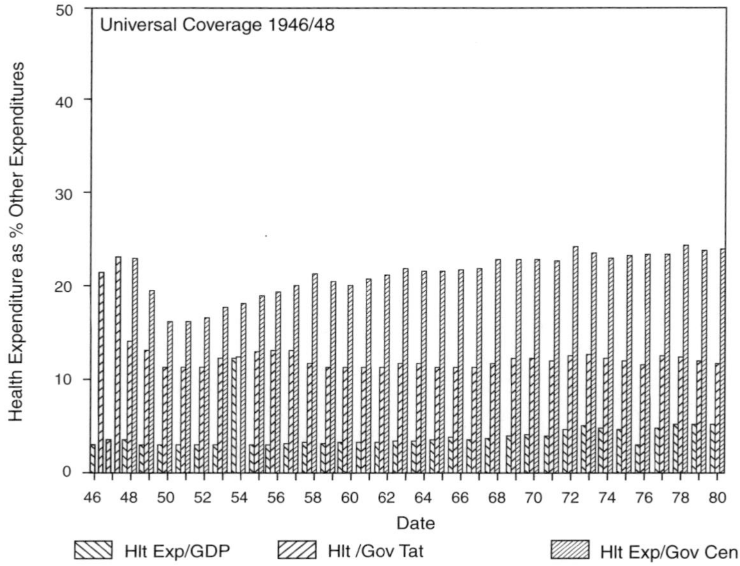

Figure A.2.2 Public Expenditure on Health Care in the United Kingdom

Source: Preker (1989).

Note: Expenditure on health care as recorded by the Department of Health and Social Security is lower than the data reported in the 1985 OECD publication on health care expenditure. See Table A.4 for sources. Hlt Exp = Health Expenditure; Gov Con = Government Consumption Expenditure; Gov Tot = Government Total Expenditure.

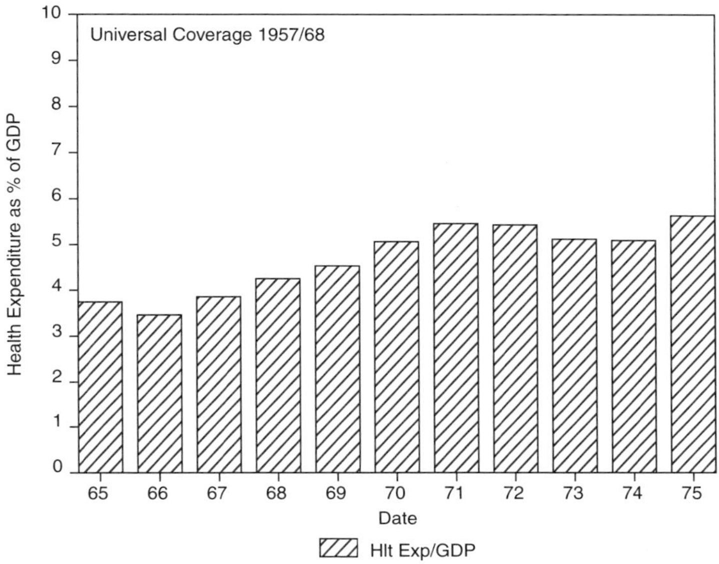

Figure A.3.1 Public Expenditure on Health Care in Canada

Source: Preker (1989).

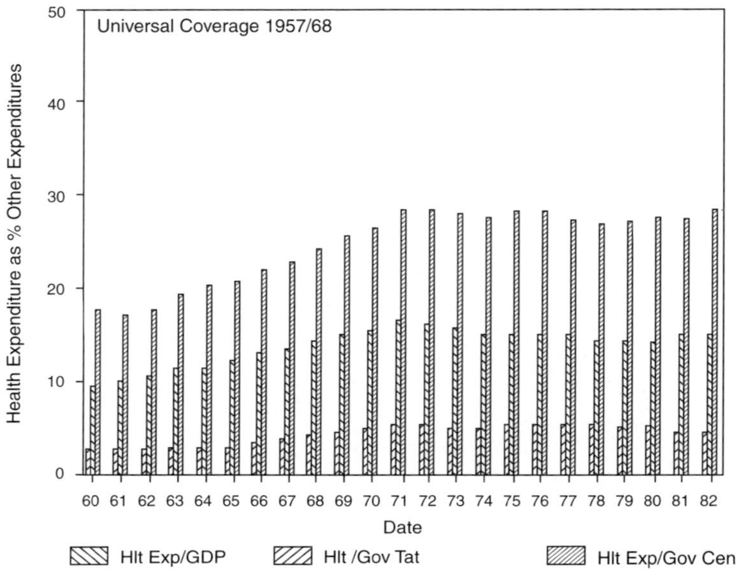

Figure A.3.2 Public Expenditure on Health Care in Canada

Source: Preker (1989).

Note: Expenditure on such "welfare services" was not included in the aggregates for expenditure on health care. Aggregates for public expenditure on health care include expenditure on nursing homes and other forms of long term institutional care. See Table A.5 for sources. Hlt Exp = Health Expenditure; Gov Con = Government Consumption Expenditure; Gov Tot = Government Total Expenditure.

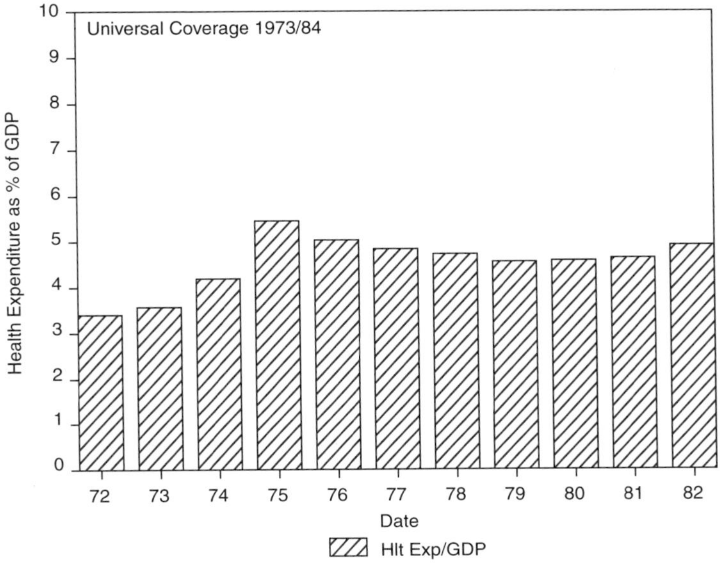

Figure A.4.1 Public Expenditure on Health Care in Australia

Source: Preker (1989).

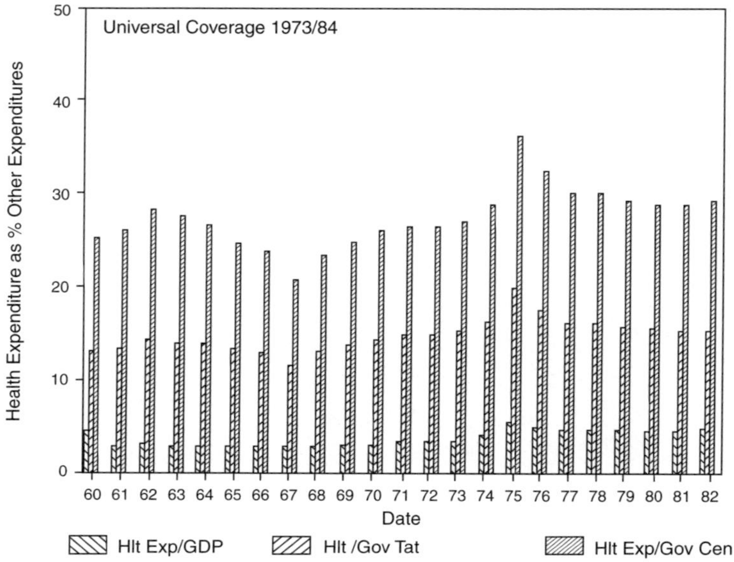

Figure A.4.2 Public Expenditure on Health Care in Australia

Source: Preker (1989).

Note: Expenditure on health care includes cash reimbursements for medical treatment but not maintenance payment during illness. See Table A.6 for sources. Hlt Exp = Health Expenditure; Gov Con = Government Consumption Expenditure; Gov Tot = Government Total Expenditure.

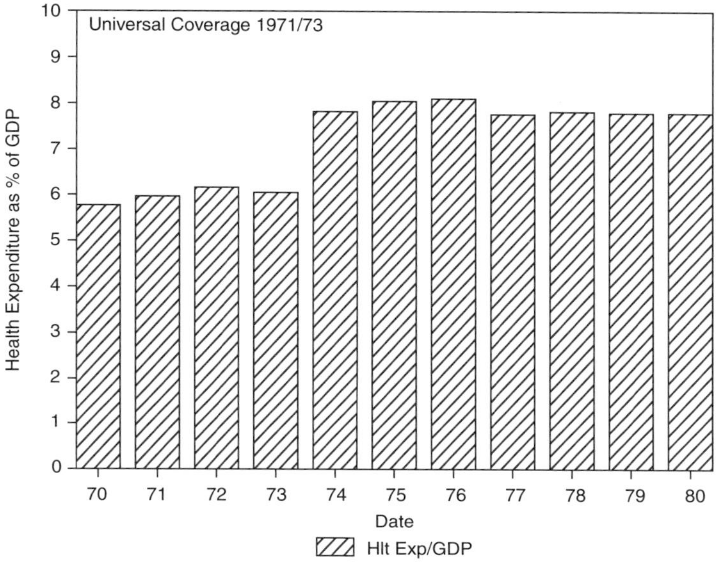

Figure A.5.1 Public Expenditure on Health Care in Denmark

Source: Preker (1989).

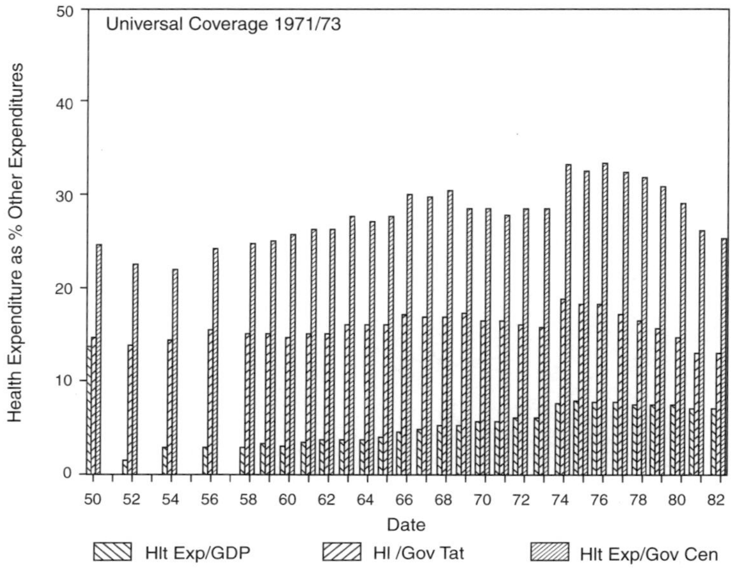

Figure A.5.2 Public Expenditure on Health Care in Denmark

Source: Preker (1989).

Note: Expenditure on health care includes cash reimbursements for medical treatment but not maintenance payment during illness. Total expenditure includes outlays on sickness insurance, hospital care, outpatient care, care of the mentally retarded, care of special groups such as alcoholics and dental care. See Table A.7 for sources. Hlt Exp = Health Expenditure; Gov Con = Government Consumption Expenditure; Gov Tot = Government Total Expenditure.

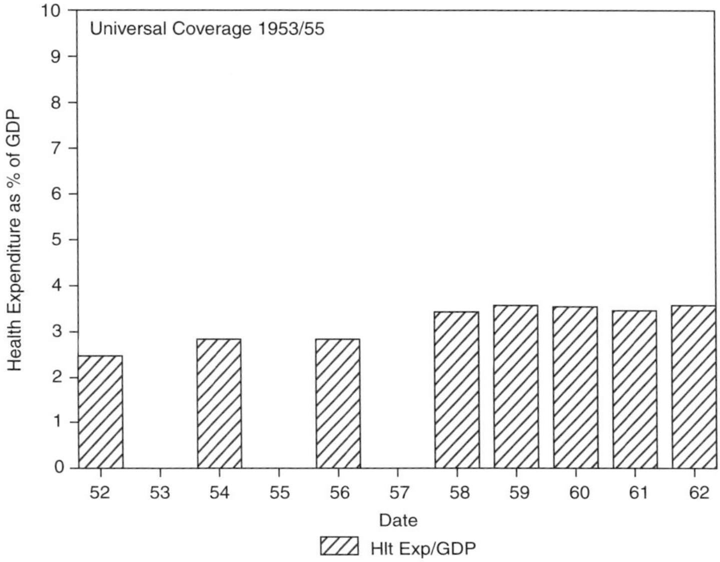

Figure A.6.1 Public Expenditure on Health Care in Norway

Source: Preker (1989).

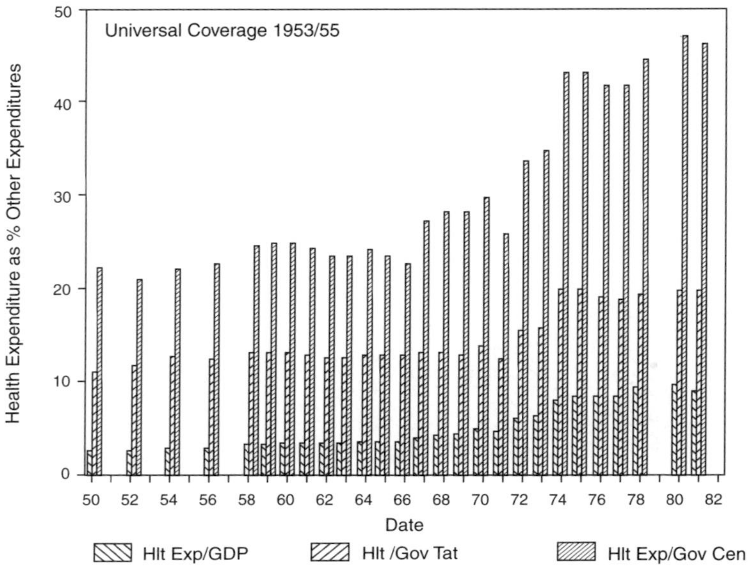

Figure A.6.2 Public Expenditure on Health Care in Norway

Source: Preker (1989).

Note: Expenditure on health care includes cash reimbursements for medical treatment but not maintenance payment during illness. Total expenditure includes outlays on sickness insurance, hospital care, outpatient care, care of the mentally retarded, care of special groups such as alcoholics and dental care. The values for 1953, 1955 and 1957 were interpolated from the series. See Table A.8 for sources. Hlt Exp = Health Expenditure; Gov Con = Government Consumption Expenditure; Gov Tot = Government Total Expenditure.

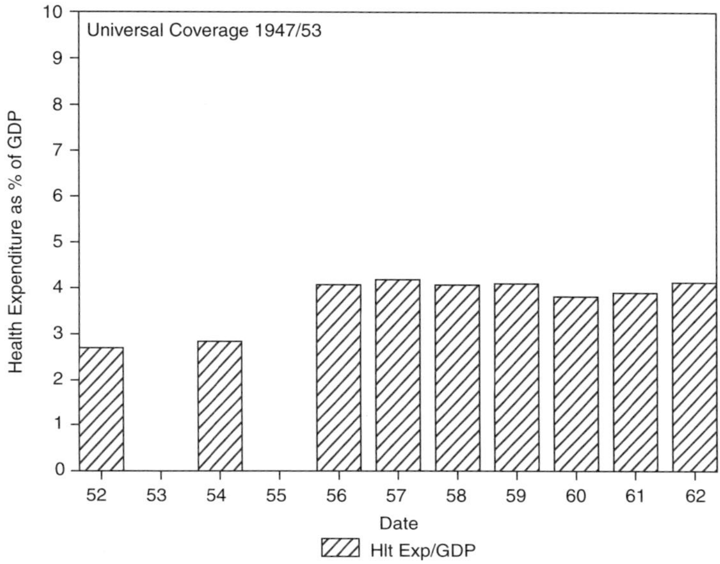

Figure A.7.1 Public Expenditure on Health Care in Sweden

Source: Preker (1989).

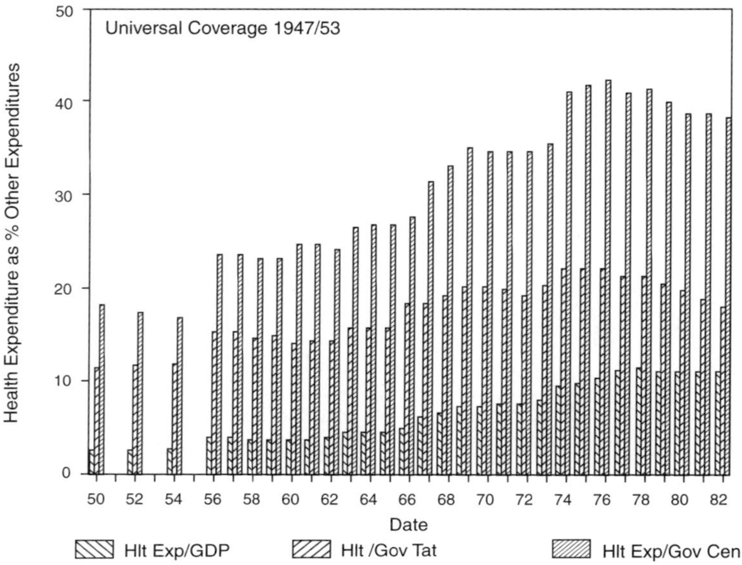

Figure A.7.2 Public Expenditure on Health Care in Sweden

Source: Preker (1989).

Note: Expenditure on health care includes cash reimbursements for medical treatment but not maintenance payment during illness. Total expenditure includes outlays on sickness insurance, hospital care, outpatient care, care of the mentally retarded, care of special groups such as alcoholics and dental care. The values for 1953 and 1955 were interpolated from the series. See Table A.9 for sources. Hlt Exp = Health Expenditure; Gov Con = Government Consumption Expenditure; Gov Tot = Government Total Expenditure.

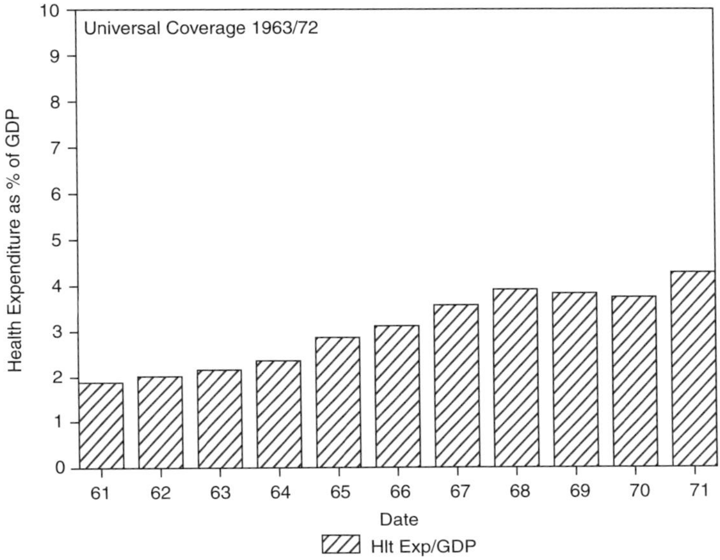

Figure A.8.1 Public Expenditure on Health Care in Finland

Source: Preker (1989).

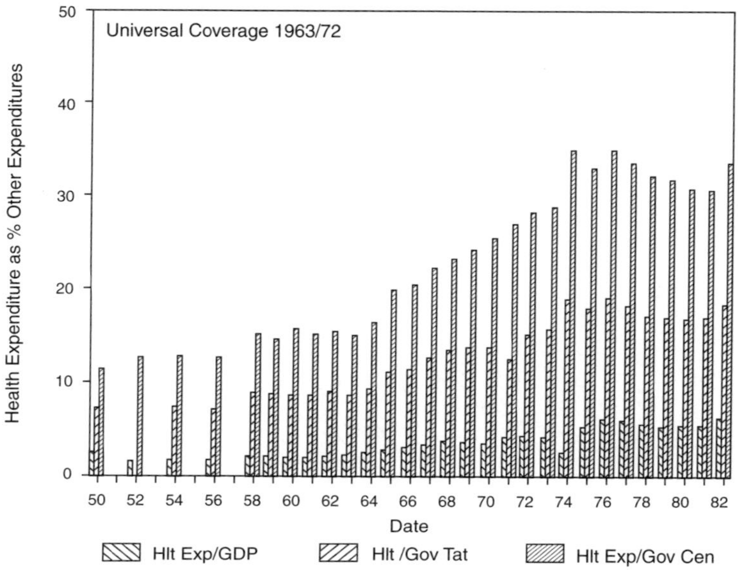

Figure A.8.2 Public Expenditure on Health Care in Finland

Source: Preker (1989).

Note: Expenditure on health care includes cash reimbursements for medical treatment but not maintenance payment during illness. Total expenditure includes outlays on sickness insurance, hospital care, outpatient care, care of the mentally retarded, care of special groups such as alcoholics and dental care. See Table A.10 for sources. Hlt Exp = Health Expenditure; Gov Con = Government Consumption Expenditure; Gov Tot = Government Total Expenditure.

Table A.1 Universal Coverage: Worldwide

Countries with Legislative Provisions for Universal Coverage[1]			
OECD member countries[2]			
Australia	Greece	New Zealand	Sweden
Australia	Iceland	Norway	UK
Denmark	Ireland[3]	Portugal	
Finland	Italy	Spain	
CMEA member countries[4]			
Albania	Cuba	Hungary	USSR
Bulgaria	Czechoslovakia	Romania	
Developing countries[5]			
Algeria	Malawi	Seychelles	Tanzania
Bermuda	Malaysia	Singapore	Zambia
Costa Rica[6]	Mauritius	Somalia	Uganda
Cyprus	Nauru	Sri Lanka	
Kuwait	Papua New Guinea	Swaziland	

Source: Preker (1989).

[1]Adapted from Kaser, *Health Care*, p. 272; and United States, DHHS, *Social Security Programs.*

[2]OECD is the acronym for the Organization for Economic Co-Operation and Development. Other countries include Austria, Belgium, Federal Republic of Germany, France, Ireland, Japan, Luxembourg, the Netherlands, Switzerland, Turkey and USA. Yugoslavia participates with special status. See Paxton, *Statesman's Year-Book 1986–1987*, p. 34.

[3]Universal coverage of health care, although provided for in the constitution, is not implemented in practice.

[4]CMEA is the acronym for Council for Mutual Economic Assistance (COMECON). The seven founding members were later joined by Albania (1949–1961), German Democratic Republic (1950), Mongolia (1962), Cuba (1972), Vietnam (1978). Yugoslavia, Afghanistan, Angola, Ethiopia, Laos, Mexico, Mozambique, Nicaragua and the People's Democratic Republic of Yemen attend as observers. Paxton, *Statesman's Year-Book 1986–1987*, p. 48.

[5]Barriers to access limit true universal coverage.

[6]Costa Rica is in the process of introducing universal coverage.

Table A.2 Health Care Legislation: CMEA Countries

Country[1]	Coverage Through Social Insurance	Coverage as Civic Right
Albania		1947/66
Bulgaria[2]	1905/18/51	1973
Cuba	1934	1974/79
Czechoslovakia[3]	1888	1966/68/71
Germany GDR[4]	1883	1968
Hungary[5]	1891	1919/75
Poland[6]	1920/33	1971
Romania[7]	1912/33	1965/68
USSR[8]	1912/19/36/55	1969

Source: Preker (1989).

[1]The data in this table is based on Kaser, *Health Care;* and US, DHHS, *Social Security Programs.* Data for Mongolia and Vietnam were not available through this series.

[2]Compulsory means-tested social insurance was introduced for wage-earners and civil servants in 1905. Universal coverage was provided as civil right under the Constitution of 1971.

[3]Compulsory means-tested social insurance was introduced for workers in 1888 under the Austro-Hungarian Empire. Universal coverage was provided as civic right by law on the Health Care of the People on March 17, 1966.

[4]Compulsory means-tested social insurance was introduced for workers in 1883. Universal coverage was provided as civic right under the Constitution of 1961.

[5]Compulsory means-tested social insurance was introduced for wage-earners in 1888. Universal coverage was granted in theory to all wage and salary earners in 1919 during the 133 days of the Hungarian Soviet Republic of Bela Kun; the medical profession boycotted the program. Universal coverage was provided as a civic right under the Health Law of 1975. See Balog, *Hungary*, p. 10.

[6]Compulsory means-tested sickness and maternity insurance was introduced for workers in 1919. Universal coverage was provided as civic right after December 1971.

[7]Compulsory means-tested social insurance was introduced for employees in 1912 (extended and unified in 1933). Universal coverage was provided as civic right included under Article 79 of the Constitution of 1952.

[8]Comprehensive means-tested insurance was introduced for workers in 1912. Universal coverage was granted in theory through the revolution of 1919. It was only confirmed in principle as a civil right under the 1936 Constitution and finally implemented through the Health Law of 1969.

Table A.3 New Zealand: Public Expenditure on Health Care

Universal Coverage Implemented in 1939			
Year	1938	1939	1940
Population in thousands[1]	1,604	1,627	1,636
Current expenditure in Millions of New Zealand Dollars[2]			
Gov consumption[3]	—	—	—
Gov total	—	—	—
GDP	—	—	—
Total Hlt Exp[4]	5.17	5.94	8.83
GDP[5]	427	467	503
Relative expenditure in New Zealand Dollars			
Hlt Exp/Capita	3.20	3.60	5.40
Ratio in per cent			
Hlt Exp/GDP	1.2	1.3	1.8
Gov Con/GDP	—	—	—
Gov Tot/GDP	—	—	—
Hlt Exp/GDP	1.2	1.3	1.8
Hlt Exp/Gov Tot	—	—	—
Hlt Exp/Gov Con	—	—	—

Source: Preker (1989).

[1]United Nations, DESA, SO, *Demographic Yearbook*, 1950–1983.

[2]Early values for New Zealand Pounds have been converted into New Zealand Dollars.

[3]Government Consumption Expenditure, Government Total Expenditure and GDP are based on the latest adjusted data available through the United Nations records. United Nations, DESA, SO, *National Accounts Statistics*, 1957–1983; and United Nations, DESA, SO, *Statistical Papers*, 1952–1957.

[4]New Zealand, DH, *Health Expenditure*, 41, Table I.1.

[5]New Zealand, DH, *Health Expenditure*, 41, Table I.1.

Table A.4 United Kingdom: Public Expenditure on Health Care

Universal Coverage Implemented in 1948			
Year	1948	1949	1950
Population in thousands[1]	50,026	50,324	50,616
Current expenditure in millions of Pounds Sterling[2]			
Gov Consumption[3]	1,761	1,977	2,103
Gov total[4]			3,382
GDP	11,533	12,261	12,872
Total Hlt Exp[5]	380	460	484
Relative expenditure in Pounds Sterling			
Hlt Exp/Capita	7.60	9.10	9.50
Ratio in per cent			
Hlt Exp/GDP	3.3	3.8	3.8
Gov Con/GDP	15.3	16.1	16.3
Gov Tot/GDP	—	—	26.3
Hlt Exp/GDP	3.3	3.8	3.8
Hlt Exp/Gov Tot	—	—	14.3
Hlt Exp/Gov Con	21.6	23.3	23.0

Source: Preker (1989).

[1]United Nations, DESA, SO, *Demographic Yearbook*, 1950–83.

[2]Data for the United Kingdom represents aggregates for England, Wales, Scotland and Northern Ireland.

[3]Government consumption expenditure, government total Expenditure, and GDP based on latest adjusted data in United Nations, DESA, SO, *National Accounts Statistics*, 1957–1983; and United Nations, DESA, SO, *Statistical Papers*, 1952–1957.

[4]Data for Government total expenditure was not available through the United Nations records prior to 1948–1949.

[5]United Kingdom, CSO, *Annual Abstract of Statistics*, 1955–1986. Values for 1948 were extrapolated to a full year from the nine-month data available for the incomplete 1948 fiscal year.

Table A.5 Canada: Public Expenditure on Health Care

Universal Coverage Implemented in 1968–1972			
Year	1968	1970	1972
Population in thousands[1]	20,744	21,324	21,822
Current expenditure in millions of Canadian Dollars			
Gov consumption[2]	12,652	16,587	20,249
Gov total	21,327	27,822	35,467
GDP	73,325	86,454	106,005
Total Hlt Exp[3]	3,074	4,392	5,786
Relative expenditure in Canadian Dollars			
Hlt Exp/Capita	148	206	265
Ratio in per cent			
Hlt Exp/GDP	4.2	5.1	5.5
Gov Con/GDP	17.3	19.2	19.1
Gov Tot/GDP	29.1	32.2	33.5
Hlt Exp/GDP	4.2	5.1	5.5
Hlt Exp/Gov Tot	14.4	15.8	16.3
Hlt Exp/Gov Con	24.3	26.5	28.6

Source: Preker (1989).

[1]United Nations, DESA, SO, *Demographic Yearbook*, 1950–1983.

[2]Government consumption expenditure, Government total expenditure and GDP are based on the latest adjusted data available through the United Nations records. United Nations, DESA, SO, *National Accounts Statistics*, 1957–1983; and United Nations, DESA, SO, *Statistical Papers*, 1952–1957.

[3]OECD, *Measuring Health Care 1960–1983*, based on data from Canada: HWC, IFB, *National Health Expenditures in Canada 1960–1975*; and Canada HWC, *National Health Expenditures in Canada 1970–1982*.

Table A.6 Australia: Public Expenditure on Health Care

Universal Coverage Implemented in 1975			
Year	1974	1975	1976
Population in thousands[1]	13,599	13,771	13,916
Current expenditure in millions of Australian Dollars			
Gov consumption[2]	9,012	11,193	13,085
Gov total	16,009	20,291	24,269
GDP	63,191	74,616	85,281
Total Hlt Exp[3]	2,612	4,052	4,266
Relative Expenditure in Australian Dollars			
Hlt Exp/Capita	192	294	307
Ratio in Per Cent			
Hlt Exp/GDP	4.1	5.4	5.0
Gov Con/GDP	14.3	15.0	15.3
Gov Tot/GDP	25.3	27.2	28.5
Hlt Exp/GDP	4.1	5.4	5.0
Hlt Exp/Gov Tot	16.3	20.0	17.6
Hlt Exp/Gov Con	29.0	36.2	32.6

Source: Preker (1989).

[1]United Nations, DESA, SO, *Demographic Yearbook*, 1950–1983.

[2]Government Consumption Expenditure, Government Total Expenditure and GDP are based on the latest adjusted data available through the United Nations records. United Nations, DESA, SO, *National Accounts Statistics*, 1957–1983; and United Nations, DESA, SO, *Statistical Papers*, 1952–1957.

[3]OECD, *Measuring Health Care 1960–1983*, based on data from OECD National Accounts up to 1967; and Australia, CDH, *Health Expenditure 1975–76 to 1979–80.*

Table A.7 Denmark: Public Expenditure on Health Care

Universal Coverage Implemented in 1973			
Year	1972	1973	1974
Population in thousands[1]	4,992	5,022	5,045
Current expenditure in millions of Danish Crowns			
Gov consumption[2]	32,075	36,808	45,254
Gov total	56,716	65,312	79,708
GDP	150,725	172,859	193,629
Total Hlt Exp[3]	9,305	10,493	15,198
Insurance	3,061	3,133	3,384
Medical	5,059	6,030	10,058
Mental	712	807	961
Dental	473	523	795
Cash	1,105	1,312	1,786
Relative expenditure in Danish Crowns			
Hlt Exp/Capita	1,864	2,089	3,012
Ratio in per cent			
Hlt Exp/GDP	6.2	6.1	7.8
Gov Con/GDP	21.3	21.3	23.4
Gov Tot/GDP	37.6	37.8	41.2
Hlt Exp/GDP	6.2	6.1	7.8
Hlt Exp/Gov Tot	16.4	16.1	19.1
Hlt Exp/Gov Con	29.0	28.5	33.6

Source: Preker (1989).

[1]United Nations, DESA, SO, *Demographic Yearbook*, 1950–1983.

[2]Government consumption expenditure, Government total expenditure and GDP are based on the latest adjusted data available through the United Nations records. United Nations, DESA, SO, *National Accounts Statistics*, 1957–1983; and United Nations, DESA, SO, *Statistical Papers*, 1952–1957.

[3]Cash benefits were excluded from the calculations for total expenditure on health care. See Nordic Statistical Secretariat, *Social Security*, 1953–1987; and *Yearbook of Nordic Statistics*, 1962–984.

Table A.8 Norway: Public Expenditure on Health Care

Universal Coverage Implemented in 1956			
Year	1954	1956	1958
Population in thousands[1]	3,394	3,460	3,523
Current expenditure in millions of Norwegian Crowns			
Gov consumption[2]	2,915	3,425	3,990
Gov total	5,072	6,318	7,460
GDP	22,559	27,306	28,924
Total Hlt Exp[3]	643	775	988
Insurance	380	461	618
Medical	226	268	307
Mental	14	19	28
Dental	23	27	35
Cash	105	123	179
Relative expenditure in Norwegian Crowns			
Hlt Exp/Capita	189	224	280
Ratio in per cent			
Hlt Exp/GDP	2.9	2.8	3.4
Gov Con/GDP	12.9	12.5	13.8
Gov Tot/GDP	22.5	23.1	25.8
Hlt Exp/GDP	2.9	2.8	3.4
Hlt Exp/Gov Tot	12.7	12.3	13.2
Hlt Exp/Gov Con	22.1	22.6	24.8

Source: Preker (1989).

[1]United Nations, DESA, SO, *Demographic Yearbook*, 1950–1983.

[2]Government consumption expenditure, Government total expenditure and GDP are based on the latest adjusted data available through the United Nations records. See United Nations, DESA, SO, *National Accounts Statistics*, 1957–1983; and United Nations, DESA, SO, *Statistical Papers*, 1952–1957.

[3]Cash benefits were excluded from the calculations for total expenditure on health care. See Nordic Statistical Secretariat, *Social Security*, 1953–1987; and *Yearbook of Nordic Statistics*, 1962–1984.

Table A.9 Sweden: Public Expenditure on Health Care

Universal Coverage Implemented in 1955			
Year	1954	1956	1957
Population in thousands[1]	7,235	7,316	7,367
Current expenditure in millions of Swedish Crowns			
Gov consumption[2]	6,989	8,301	9,477
Gov total	10,080	12,673	14,407
GDP	42,051	49,102	53,793
Total Hlt Exp[3]	1,186	1,995	2,246
Insurance	231	811	942
Medical	888	1,091	2,198
Mental	27	41	46
Dental	40	52	60
Cash	105	NA	NA
Relative expenditure in Swedish Crowns			
Hlt Exp/Capita	164	273	319
Ratio in per cent			
Hlt Exp/GDP	2.8	4.1	4.2
Gov Con/GDP	16.6	16.9	17.6
Gov Tot/GDP	24.0	25.8	26.8
Hlt Exp/GDP	2.8	4.1	4.2
Hlt Exp/Gov Tot	11.8	15.7	15.6
Hlt Exp/Gov Con	17.0	24.0	23.7

Source: Preker (1989).

[1]United Nations, DESA, SO, *Demographic Yearbook*, 1950–1983.

[2]Government consumption expenditure, Government total expenditure and GDP are based on the latest adjusted data available through the United Nations records. United Nations, DESA, SO, *National Accounts Statistics*, 1957–1983; United Nations, DESA, SO, *Statistical Papers*, 1952–1957; and *Yearbook of Nordic Statistics*, 1962–1984.

[3]Cash benefits were excluded from the calculations for total expenditure on health care. See Nordic Statistical Secretariat, *Social Security*, 1953–87; and *Yearbook of Nordic Statistics*, 1962–1984.

Table A.10 Finland: Public Expenditure on Health Care

Universal Coverage Implemented in 1964			
Year	1963	1964	1965
Population in thousands[1]	4,523	4,549	4,564
Expenditure in millions of Finnish Marks			
Gov consumption[2]	2,925	3,349	3,759
Gov total	5,114	5,865	6,662
GDP	20,541	23,553	25,828
Total Hlt Exp[3]	438	552	742
Insurance	19	56	156
Medical	399	471	555
Mental	10	14	16
Dental	10	11	15
Cash	9	17	68
Relative expenditure in Finnish Marks			
Hlt Exp/Capita	97	121	163
Ratio in per cent			
Hlt Exp/GDP	2.1	2.3	2.9
Gov Con/GDP	14.2	14.2	14.6
Gov Tot/GDP	24.9	24.9	25.8
Hlt Exp/GDP	2.1	2.3	2.9
Hlt Exp/Gov Tot	8.6	9.4	11.1
Hlt Exp/Gov Con	15.0	16.5	19.7

Source: Preker (1989).

[1]United Nations, DESA, SO, *Demographic Yearbook*, 1950–1983.

[2]Government consumption expenditure, Government total expenditure and GDP are based on the latest adjusted data available through the United Nations records. United Nations, DESA, SO, *National Accounts Statistics*, 1957–1983; and United Nations, DESA, SO, *Statistical Papers*, 1952–1957.

[3]Cash benefits were excluded from the calculations for total expenditure on health care. See Nordic Statistical Secretariat, *Social Security*, 1953–1987; and *Yearbook of Nordic Statistics*, 1962–1984.

Table A.11 Economic Outcome Indicators and Their Sources

	τ	HCE_{ppp}	GDP_{cap}	GDP_{gwt}	GGD/ GDP	GTE/ GDP	GCE/ GDP	GSE/ GDP	HCE/ GDP	Pub/ Tot	HCE_{ela}
Years		SUS 1987	SUS 87	% 65–87	% 85	% 87	% 87	% 87	% 87	% 87	% 75–87
Aus	1	939	12612	1.8	25.2	28.8	18.0	10.8	7.4	70.5	0.9
Aut	0	982	11664	3.1	48.5	40.3	19.0	21.3	8.4	67.1	0.8
Bel	0	879	11802	2.6	126.6	52.9	16.0	36.9	7.4	76.9	1.6
Can	1	1483	17211	2.7	69.2	24.2	20.0	4.2	8.6	73.9	0.9
Den	1	792	13329	1.9	68.6	39.8	25.0	14.8	5.9	85.5	0.9
Fin	1	949	12838	3.2	20.2	31.9	21.0	10.9	7.4	78.6	0.9
Fra	0	1105	12803	2.7	34.0	45.1	19.0	26.1	8.6	74.8	3.1
Ger	0	1093	13323	2.5	42.2	30.1	20.0	10.1	8.2	78.4	0.9
Gre	1	337	6363	3.1	53.2	50.9	20.0	30.9	5.3	75.3	2.5
Ire	0	561	7541	2.0	128.3	60.4	18.0	42.4	7.4	87.0	1.5
Ita	1	841	12254	2.7	99.4	52.0	17.0	35.0	6.9	79.2	1.7
Jap	0	915	13182	4.2	69.4	17.4	10.0	7.4	6.9	73.0	1.4
Net	0	1041	12252	2.1	70.3	57.7	16.0	41.7	8.5	73.9	1.1
New	1	733	10680	0.9	45.0	47.1	15.0	32.1	6.9	82.5	0.9
Nor	1	1149	15405	3.5	31.4	40.6	21.0	19.6	7.5	97.6	2.0
Spa	1	521	8681	2.3	41.7	34.8	14.0	20.8	6.0	71.5	1.1
Swe	1	1233	13n1	1.8	71.4	42.9	27.0	15.9	9.0	90.8	1.0
UK	1	758	12340	1.7	56.5	38.9	21.0	17.9	6.1	86.4	1
US	0	2051	18338	1.5	48.3	23.3	21.0	2.3	11.2	41.4	1.1

Source: Preker (1989). Calculated from World Bank, *World Development Report 1989: Financial Systems and Development, World Development Indicators* (Washington: World Bank 1989); OECD, *Health Care Systems in Transition: The Search for Efficiency* (Paris: OECD, 1990); United Nations, DESA, SO, *National Accounts Statistics*, 1989.

Abbreviations Used for Outcome Indicators: GDP_{cap}: GDP per capita; GDP_{gwt}: Average real GDP growth rates; GGD: General government debt; GCE/GDP: Government consumption expenditure per GDP; GSE: Government social expenditure; HCE_{ela}: GDP elasticity of health care expenditure; GTE: General government total expenditure; HCE_{ppp}:

Purchase-power-parity-adjusted health care expenditure; Pub/Tot: Ratio of public to total health care expenditure.

Table A.12 Statistical Analysis Using an Independent Variable

Independent Variable τ		Change in τ = 0		
Dependent Variables Below		No Change	Spain Greece	Spain Greece Italy
HCE_{ppp}				
	Constant	1078.38	948.5	938.73
	Std Err of Y Est	370.20	383.19	382.17
	R^2	0.07	0.00	0.01
	X Coefficient(s)	–193.38	37.83	65.77
	Std Err of Coef.	172.02	176.06	177.58
GDP_{cap}				
	Constant	12613.12	11594.9	11654.81
	Std Err of Y Est	2964.42	2814.53	2803.67
	R^2	0.00	0.10	0.11
	X Coefficient(s)	–296.40	1787.32	1868.43
	Std Err of Coef.	1377.45	1293.19	1302.76
GDP_{gwt}				
	Constant	2.59	2.61	2.62
	Std Err of Y Est	0.80	0.79	0.78
	R^2	0.03	0.06	0.07
	X Coefficient(s)	–0.26	–0.37	–0.43
	Std Err of Coef.	0.37	0.36	0.36
GGD	Constant	1.44	66.25	69.26
	Std Err of Y Est	0.63	30.61	29.32
	R^2	0.02	0.04	0.12
	X Coefficient(s)	–0.18	–12.15	–20.83
	Std Err of Coef.	0.29	14.06	13.62
GTE/GDP				
	Constant	40.9	41.29	42.26
	Std Err of Y Est	12.34	12.28	12.03

(*Continued*)

Table A.12 (*Continued*)

Independent Variable τ		Change in τ = 0		
Dependent Variables Below		No Change	Spain Greece	Spain Greece Italy
	R^2	0.01	0.01	0.05
	X Coefficient(s)	−1.64	−2.82	−5.49
	Std Err of Coef.	5.73	5.64	5.59
GCE/GDP				
	Constant	17.38	17.3	17.27
	Std Err of Y Est	3.72	3.55	3.43
	R^2	0.11	0.19	0.24
	X Coefficient(s)	2.53	3.26	3.73
	Std Err of Coef.	1.73	1.63	1.59
GSE/GDP				
	Constant	23.53	23.99	24.99
	Std Err of Y Est	12.65	12.43	11.90
	R^2	0.03	0.06	0.14
	X Coefficient(s)	−4.17	−6.08	−9.22
	Std Err of Coef.	5.88	5.71	5.53
HCE/GDP				
	Constant	8.35	7.81	7.72
	Std Err of Y Est	1.20	1.37	1.38
	R^2	0.26	0.04	0.02
	X Coefficient(s)	−1.35	−0.51	−0.37
	Std Err of Coef.	0.56	0.63	0.64
Pub/tot				
	Constant	71.56	71.93	72.59
	Std Err of Y Est	10.78	10.40	10.49
	R^2	0.17	0.23	0.22
	X Coefficient(s)	9.51	10.85	10.63
	Std Err of Coef.	5.01	4.78	4.88

(*Continued*)

Table A.12 (*Continued*)

Independent Variable τ		Change in τ = 0	
Dependent Variables Below	No Change	Spain Greece	Spain Greece Italy
HCE_{ela}			
Constant	1.44	1.5	1.53
Std Err of Y Est	0.63	0.62	0.59
R^2	0.02	0.07	0.14
X Coefficient(s)	–0.18	–0.32	–0.46
Std Err of Coef.	0.29	0.28	0.28
No. of Observations	19		
Degrees of Freedom	17		

Source: Preker (1989).

Note: See previous table for glossary to abbreviations.

Table A.13 Statistical Analysis Using a Dependent Variable

Dependent Variable = HCE_{ppp}		
Independent Variables Below		
GDP_{cap}		
	Constant	–502.40
	Std Err of Y Est	156.26
	R^2	0.83
	X Coefficient(s)	0.12
	Std Err of Coef.	0.01
GDP_{gwt}		
	Constant	1083.03
	Std Err of Y Est	381.75
	R^2	0.01
	X Coefficient(s)	–47.85
	Std Err of Coef.	114.35
GGD		
	Constant	1102.93
	Std Err of Y Est	377.16
	R^2	0.03
	X Coefficient(s)	–2.26
	Std Err of Coef.	2.93
GTE/GDP		
	Constant	1578.55
	Std Err of Y Est	333.65
	R^2	0.24
	X Coefficient(s)	–15.32
	Std Err of Coef.	6.54
GCE/GDP		
	Constant	430.19
	Std Err of Y Est	366.92
	R^2	0.09

(*Continued*)

Table A.13 (*Continued*)

Dependent Variable = HCE_{ppp}		
Independent Variables Below		
	X Coefficient(s)	28.46
	Std Err of Coef.	22.56
GSE/GDP		
	Constant	1323.56
	Std Err of Y Est	316.37
	R^2	0.32
	X Coefficient(s)	–16.92
	Std Err of Coef.	5.98
HCE/GDP		
	Constant	–911.17
	Std Err of Y Est	166.49
	R^2	0.81
	X Coefficient(s)	248.19
	Std Err of Coef.	28.99
Pub/Tot		
	Constant	2203.52
	Std Err of Y Est	333.05
	R^2	0.25
	X Coefficient(s)	–16.05
	Std Err of Coef.	6.80
HCE_{ela}		
	Constant	1116.56
	Std Err of Y Est	376.86
	R^2	0.03
	X Coefficient(s)	–112.75
	Std Err of Coef.	142.84
No. of Observations		19
Degrees of Freedom		17

Source: Preker (1989).

Note: See previous table for glossary to abbreviations

APPENDIX B

COMPENDIUM OF HEALTH INSURANCE TERMS*

Alexander S. Preker
Columbia University, Icahn School of Medicine at Mt. Sinai, and Health Investment & Financing, New York, USA

Mark V. Pauly
Wharton School, University of Pennsylvania, Philadelphia, USA

David M. Dror
Micro Insurance Academy, New Delhi, India

Ability to pay (ATP). A subjective social judgment usually based on a comparison of a proposed payment amount and a household's income or wealth. ATP for health insurance must be considered in the context of copayments and transaction costs. Reflects a value judgment about whether the household can obtain socially acceptable levels of other goods after paying for care or insurance. This concept of fairness may be

---

* This Appendix originally appeared in the book, *Scalling Up Affordable Health Insurance: Staying the Course*, edited by A. S. Preker, M. E. Linder, D. Chernichovsky, and O. P. Schellekens, The World Bank, Washington, D. C. (2013).

an important consideration in designing a micro-insurance scheme and setting premiums.

Accountability. Result of the process that ensures that decision makers at all levels actually carry out their designated responsibilities and that they are held accountable for their actions.

Actual premium. The premium arrived at by estimating the average benefit payout, insurer administrative expenses, a safety margin for contingencies, and profits. If profits are at the competitive level the actual premium will be the lowest premium sustainable in the long run.

Actuarially fair premium. A premium equal to average or expected benefit payouts.

Actuary. A professional trained in evaluating the financial implications of contingency events. Actuaries require an understanding of the stochastic nature of insurance and other financial services, the risks inherent in assets, and the use of statistical models. In the context of insurance, these skills are often used, for example, in establishing premiums, technical provisions, and capital levels.

Adverse selection. Also called *antiselection.* Occurs when insurers are unable or are not permitted to charge premiums based on risk levels known to buyers of insurance; can arise either from asymmetric information (buyer knows risk and insurer does not) or regulation (buyer is not allowed to use information it knows in setting premiums). Adverse selection disturbs the operation of the insurance market. The lower-risk insured, knowing the likelihood of events but facing a price higher than that which reflects that risk, chooses not to insure; high risks facing a premium lower than one which reflects risk choose to overinsure. The insurer, having less information, accepts a contract that does not include premiums for low-risk events. Insured temporarily gain from the insurer's inability to distinguish "good" and "bad" risks. In the longer run, adverse selection results in low risks' exiting the insurance market. Providing asymmetric information incentivizes only people who expect to use above-average amounts of care to seek health insurance coverage. Constitutes a key concern for insurers that can lead to higher losses or premiums, which is countered by medical underwriting, which minimizes insuring high-risk individuals.

Affordability. See *Ability to pay.*

Agent, general. Another term for insurer.

Agent, insurer. Someone who assists in the sale of insurance in return for a commission or salary.

Ambulatory care. Outpatient medical care provided in any health care setting except as a stay overnight in a hospital.

Arbitrage. The simultaneous buying and selling of securities, currency, or commodities in different markets or in derivative forms in order to take advantage of differing prices for the same asset.

Asymmetrical information. Parties to a transaction have uneven access to relevant information that governs an informed choice. Such asymmetry can result in an inequitable transaction in favor of the party with the most information, or it can result in the abandonment of the exchange.

Balance sheet. Statement showing the financial position at a particular point in time (for example, at the end of the financial year), listing all assets and liabilities at that time.

Bayesian method. A method (originally enunciated in 1763) for revising the probability of an event's occurrence by taking into account data as they come to hand. The usefulness of this approach depends on the relevance and power of the additional data.

Beneficiary. The person designated to receive payouts from the scheme. This is typically the policyholder or a family member, but it may be an employer.

Benefit exclusion. Refusal of insurer payment for a specific service for an insured. Because this exclusion could be subject to abuse if it is based on arbitrary decisions made at the time of claim rather than as set out in the contract, it tends to be regulated. Reasons for exclusion that are typically allowed include a qualifying period and preexisting illness.

Benefits package. A list of specific benefits agreed upon in the health insurance contract. While private insurance typically offers modules of benefits from which to choose, microinsurers may offer a standard package for simplicity and fairness.

Beta distribution. Beta is a distribution (first used by Gini, 1911) for a real random variable whose density function is null outside the interval [0, 1] and depends on two strictly real parameters. The shape of this distribution depends on the values of the parameters: it can be U-shaped, or J-shaped, or hat-shaped. For this reason, this distribution is very often used for modeling proportions or probabilities.

Bifurcated oversight responsibility. A specialized regulation system in which the supervisory and regulatory functions are broken into a financial component and a health component.

Binomial distribution. A statistical method for understanding the probability of events that have only two possible outcomes — "success" or "failure." These probabilities are constant. In insurance, the binomial distribution is applied to estimate the number of persons in a community who will seek (ambulatory) care in a given period.

Bottom-up. See *Top-down global* strategy.

Broker. An intermediary who sells on behalf of a number of different insurance companies or plans.

Capacity. Has two meanings:

- Insurers' ability to underwrite and pay claims on a large amount of risk on a single loss exposure or many contracts on one line of event. Reinsurance enables a greater capacity among primary insurers.
- Organizational and individual skills. Organizational capacity implies appropriate systems for information and management and adequate resources for handling operations.

Capacity building. Increasing organizational and individual skills and establishing frameworks for that increase to continue.

Capitation payment. Under a capitation payment, the provider receives a fixed fee per individual per month regardless of how many services are provided to any of the individuals covered.

Central limit theorem. States that, as the sample size increases, the characteristics of a sample (e.g., average loss) will more closely approximate those of the population from which that sample was drawn. This theorem is valuable in health insurance as it enables estimates of risk in a population to be based on sample data.

Claim load. The amount of benefits paid to the insured in a period. Fluctuations in claim load in the short term are covered by contingency reserves and in the long run by contribution or premium increases.

Coefficient of variation. The ratio of the sample *standard deviation* to the *sample mean.* It measures the spread of a set of data as a proportion of its mean. It is often expressed as a percentage. This coefficient enables, for example, estimation and comparison of ranges of likely expenses for various risk portfolios or communities.

Coinsurance. An insurance policy provision under which the insurer and the insured share costs incurred after the deductible is met, according to a specific percentage formula. Used to share risk and control moral hazard.

Collection rate or compliance rate. The proportion of possible subscriptions from members that the microinsurer collects. Lack of complete compliance can result from cultural as well as economic factors. It may be used as a measure of a micro-insurer's efficiency/commercial orientation. Members are more likely to pay contributions if their perceived risk is higher.

Community. A group of people with a common characteristic. Often implies locality, but can be occupation-, leisure-, or religion-based.

Community-based health insurance (CBHI) scheme. A voluntary community prepayment health insurance scheme for pooling and averaging risks. The community's policyholders ideally share social values, are involved in the management of health plans, and elect a group of their members to act as managers. CBHIs are common in many low-income countries, where options are unavailable.

Community financing scheme. See *Community-based health insurance scheme.*

Community participation. Sharing by citizens in any kind of community in communal decision-making processes and definitions of problems.

Community rating. A method for determining insurance rates on the basis of the average cost across all insured regardless of risk level for providing health services in a specific geographic area. This method ignores the individual's medical history or the likelihood of the individual's using the services. All members of a community pay the same premium without considering individual health status or other determinants of expected demand. *Modified* or *adjusted community rating* allows premiums to vary with some characteristics relevant to risk (like age, gender, price levels in the locality, or family size) but not with health indicators or any other characteristics that affect demand.

Compensation. Benefit payout.

Complementary private insurance. Insurance that provides coverage for all or part of the costs not covered under a public program.

Compliance. Payment of contribution owed by members.

Compliance gap. Difference between contributions due and contributions collected.

Compliance rate. The ratio of actual contributions over potential contributions. See *Collection rate.*

Compulsory insurance. Any form of insurance the purchase of which is required by law and subject to a penalty for nonpurchase. Governments typically require the purchase of liability insurance with respect to events associated with losses to others than the insured, such as damage due to negligence. Health insurance against noncontagious diseases is often compulsory because of the desire to provide financial protection to the individual and avoid the need for charity care paid by others.

Confidence interval. A range of values estimated to contain the population parameter. To be 95 percent confident that a range contains the parameter requires a larger range than to be 90 percent confident. For example, analysis of data from a community might suggest a 90 percent chance that the number of people seeking hospitalization in a year will be between 1,100 and 1,500, but the confidence interval for 95 percent confidence is 978 and 1,747.

Conglomerate risk. Insurance companies that are participants in financial groups can be exposed to some additional sources of risk, such as (but not limited to) intragroup exposures, contagion, and risk concentration.

Contingency reserves or equalization reserves. Funds held by the insurer in excess of expected benefit payouts in order to cover unexpected events (contingencies) that cause fluctuations in benefit payouts. They are typically regulated to ensure the insurer's continued solvency and ability to pay claims.

Contribution. Payment of an agreed sum of money by a member to a social insurance system in return for specified benefits. The implied assumption is that any other sources of income complement members' payments. See also *Premium.*

Contribution base. The amount that would be available to the insurer if all members contributed fully. When contributions are set as a percentage of income, this base relies on full disclosure of income (disclosure rate).

Contribution rate. The percentage of contribution base actually, or expected to be, collected.

Cooperative. A group of people who have united voluntarily to realize a common goal by establishing predetermined shares of the necessary capital. Any surpluses above some target amount of reserve capital are distributed to members, and any shortfalls because of large losses are assessed on members. Management is selected by the members of the organization based of prespecified voting rules. Members often also take an active part in its operation, but participation is not always required as a condition of continued membership.

Copayment. An insurance policy provision requiring the insured to pay a fixed monetary amount per unit of service of the type of care insured (e.g., $20 per doctor office visit).

Corporate governance. Set of relationships between an organization's management, its board, its shareholders (if organized as a joint-stock company), and other stakeholders. Corporate governance also provides the structure through which the objectives of the company are set, and the means of attaining those objectives and monitoring performance are determined. It also includes compliance with legal and regulatory requirements.

Cost sharing. See *Copayment* and *Coinsurance.*

Covariance. A measure of the relationship between two variables. Covariance does not specifically imply a cause-and-effect relationship ("causation"), although it may intuitively be inferred to exist, as can its direction. For example, if health problems vary with housing density, it may be possible to infer that density affects health, but the observed covariance of the frequency of schizophrenia with social status may not have a simple unidirectional explanation.

Covariant risk. When events are not independent, the occurrence of one may affect the occurrence of another. For example, the risk of one family member's catching influenza is covariant with that of another family member. Disasters and shocks are classic cases in which proximity influences covariation. When insuring against risk of events, the actuary must consider the covariation between those risks.

Cream skimming (preferred risk selection). An exercise whereby an insurer charging identical premiums to different risks which it can identify selects only a part of a larger heterogeneous risk group ("preferred risks"). When the insurer reduces its loss ratio but continues to charge the same premium as when higher risks were covered, the insurer can retain a profit from cream skimming. This profit depends on the insurer's ability to distinguish several subgroups with different expected costs within the larger group and to predict the (lower) future health care expenditure of individuals in the preferred group. Basing insurance premiums on risk prevents cream skimming.

Creditable coverage. Credit for any prior insurance coverage that provides for a reduction of the length of the waiting or preexisting condition exclusion period by the amount of time an individual already had continuous coverage before enrolment.

Credit risk. Most commonly, the risk of financial loss incurred by an insurer when a vendor or service provider ultimately does not provide the services they have agreed upon and have been paid to provide under a binding contract between the two parties. Credit risk may also result from default or movements in the credit rating assignment of issuers of securities (in the company's investment portfolio), debtors (e.g., mortgagors), or counterparties (e.g., on reinsurance contracts, derivative contracts, or deposits) and intermediaries to whom the company has an exposure. Sources of credit risk include investment counterparties, policyholders (through outstanding premiums), reinsurers, and derivative counterparties.

Cross-subsidies. Amounts effectively paid when some insurance buyers pay more than others relative to expected benefits. The wealthy members may pay higher premiums than the poor, but not use higher benefits, or the healthy may pay the same as the sick for lower expected benefits. The poor and the sick are said to receive cross-subsidies from the wealthy and the healthy.

Crude birth rate. A summary measurement of the total number of live births in a specified population at the end of a specific time period (generally one year), divided by the midyear total population count. Expressed as the number of births per 1,000 people within that population.

Crude death rate. A summary measurement of the total number of deaths in a specified population at the end of a specific time period (generally one year), divided by the midyear total population count. Expressed as the number of deaths per 1,000 people within that population.

Declaration rate. See *Contribution base.*

Deductible. A provision requiring the insured to pay part of the loss before the insurer makes any payment under the terms of the policy. Deductibles typically are found in property, health, and automobile insurance contracts. The purpose of establishing deductibles is to eliminate small claims and reduce the average pure premium and administrative costs associated with claims handling. Deductibles can also reduce moral hazard by encouraging persons to be more careful with respect to the protection of their property and prevention of loss. Annual deductibles and waiting periods are the most common forms of deductibles in health insurance contracts.

Defined benefit pension. The amount, usually formula-based, guaranteed to each person who meets defined entitlement conditions. The formula usually takes into account the individual number of contribution or insurance years and the individual amount of earnings during the same period.

Delphi method or nominal group technique. A method of business forecasting that consists of panels of experts expressing their opinions on the future and then revising them in light of their colleagues' views so that bias and extreme opinions can be eliminated.

Demand. The amounts of a good or service that consumers seek to buy at different prices. *Solvent demand* implies the ability to pay (socially determined sufficient resources left over after payment for the good in question) as well as the willingness to pay. *Elasticity of demand* is a measure of the responsiveness of quantity demanded of a particular good or service to a change in its price. *Elastic demand* implies that as the price goes up the total expenditure falls. *Inelastic demand* implies that as the price goes up total expenditure also goes up. Necessities typically have inelastic demand (given an adequate income base). For example, the imperative to have an aching tooth removed means that the dentist is in a position of power to charge a high price; such dental services have inelastic demand, and it is unlikely that a lower price would attract people not suffering from toothache to have a tooth removed. The concept of "necessity" and therefore of what has an inelastic demand is cultural. In some cultures prenatal care may not be considered a necessity. Demand for some procedures may be truncated in poor communities. *Truncated demand* means that, although the demand for surgery (for example) is inelastic and does not change with price, above a certain price it becomes zero. As half an operation is not an option, the demand is truncated because of poverty.

Derivative. A derivative is a financial asset or liability whose value depends on (or is derived from) other assets, liabilities, or indexes (the "underlying asset"). Derivatives are financial contracts and include a wide assortment of instruments, such as forwards, futures, options, warrants, swaps, and composites.

Derivative contract. A contract whose value derives from an underlying financial instrument like a stock, commodity, or index.

Dual theory of risk. The theory that describes the attitudes of individuals toward insuring themselves, by weighing on the one hand their wealth and on the other hand their aversion to risk. Three possible modifications could swing the balance in favor of insurance: decreasing the premium, increasing the loss probability, or increasing aversion to risk. Even with identical feelings toward monetary loss, individuals would likely adopt different attitudes toward insurance because their feeling is different toward the probability of monetary loss; the higher that assessment, the more attractive insurance is. Two individuals sharing the same utility index for certain wealth cannot have a different degree of aversion to risk (and the converse), but they can have different demands for insurance if they face different premia or risk levels.

Dumping. Termination or transfer of membership (though rules, incentives or marketing) of the higher-risk people by an insurer. Will only happen if the insurer cannot risk-adjust premiums precisely.

Duplicate private insurance. A policy that offers coverage for health services that are already included under a public program. The individual remains covered by the public program but opts to buy and use private health insurance instead in order to obtain broader access or better quality. Individuals are not exempted from making their required contribution towards the public program.

Endemic disease. A sickness habitually present in an area or population.

Epidemic. The occurrence of any disease, infectious or chronic, at a frequency greater than expected, based on prior patterns of disease incidence and prevalence.

Epidemiological transition. The changing pattern of health and disease within a specified population from a predominantly infectious disease pattern of low life expectancy and high mortality, to a predominantly chronic disease pattern of high life expectancy with high morbidity. In the intermediate stage of transition, high survival rates from endemic infectious disease combined with high rates of chronic illness in survivors results in a "double burden of disease." The latter is typical of many developing countries.

Epidemiology. The study of any and all health-related issues in specified populations at specified times, including but not limited to the occurrence and frequency of medical conditions, diseases, or other health-related events; identification of the determinants of medical conditions, diseases, health-related events, and health status; the evaluation of medical procedures and diagnostic tests; the evaluation of a health care system; the evaluation of a population's demand and use of health care services; evaluation of the safety and efficacy of a pharmaceutical product; post-market surveillance of pharmaceuticals to determine product effectiveness and occurrence of side effects or adverse events; and the evaluation of quality of life, access to care, and health status in general.

Equalization reserves. See *Contingency reserves.*

Escrow account management. Implies the use of a special account for managing payments of various obligations. For example, an escrow account may be set up as a savings account to set aside funds for paying insurance premiums and loan repayments.

Estimation. The process by which sample data are used to indicate the value of an unknown quantity in a population. Results of estimation can be expressed as a single value, known as a point estimate, or a range of values, known as a confidence interval. The outcome of estimation is the *estimator.*

Excluded population or excluded communities. Typically agricultural, self-employed, or poor people who have neither formal employers nor steady wages as the basis for access to government-run or commercial health insurance. They may also be excluded from housing, education, disaster relief, and other social services. They may also be unable to access financial services or to secure formal recognition of property they control or own, including property obtained under traditional (tribal) law.

Experience rating. A system in which the insurance company evaluates the risk of individuals or groups by examining their health history and past claims experience when setting premium rates. *Modified experience rating* places limits on the extent to which rates may vary based on claims experience or health status.

Externalities. Benefits or costs with an impact beyond the parties to a transaction. That impact is not considered in the buy/sell decision and so is not reflected in the price. Pollution is an example of an external cost; safe waste disposal has external benefits.

Fairness. See *Ability to pay.*

Fertility rate. A measure of the total number of live births in a specified population during a specific time period (generally one year) in relation to the midyear total number of women in the specified population. Expressed as the number of live births per 1,000 women within that population.

Fiduciary. A person who holds something in trust for another.

First-line insurer. See *Insurer.*

Fit-and-proper requirements. Rules that reduce the risk of failure of regulated institutions due to incompetent, reckless, or improper risk management by responsible persons and ensure that beneficiaries are protected under legislation and regulations. Such necessary qualities must be exhibited by a person performing the duties and carrying out the responsibilities of his/her position with an insurer. Depending on the position or legal form, these qualities could relate to a proper degree of integrity in attitude, personal behavior and business conduct, soundness of judgment, degree of knowledge, experience, and professional qualifications and financial soundness.

Formal sector. The part of the economy/society that is registered with authorities and that is subject to taxation, regulations, and standards.

Free-riding. Exists in health care when persons can benefit from a health care system without contributing to the system.

Gatekeeper. A primary care physician responsible for overseeing and coordinating all of a patient's medical needs. The gatekeeper must authorize any referral of the patient to a specialist or hospital. Except in cases of emergency, the authorization must be given prior to care.

Government failure. Occurs where government does not provide goods and services or an adequate regulatory or support framework for the private sector to provide them.

Gross domestic product (GDP). The annual total value of goods and services produced in a country for use in that country.

Guaranteed access provisions. Rules that can help ensure that any eligible person can purchase health insurance and cannot be refused coverage by a private voluntary health insurance (PVHI) entity on the grounds of bad health status and/ or high likelihood for health services utilization. Legal remedies are provided in many developed countries against improper discrimination for a new member, which address discrimination based upon age, frequency of health service use, existence of chronic disease, illness or medical conditions, or health insurance benefits claiming history.

Guaranteed renew ability. Insurers subject to guaranteed renewability standards must renew the policy when it expires for all insured regardless of changes in risk.

Health maintenance organization (HMO). See *Managed care plan.*

Imperfect competition. Occurs in markets or industries with free entry that do not match the criteria for perfect competition. The key characteristics of perfect competition are a large number of small firms; identical products sold by all firms; freedom of entry into and exit out of the industry; and perfect knowledge of prices and technology. These four criteria are essentially impossible to reach in the real world. Product differentiation (e.g., automobile service stations in different locations) often result in imperfect competition but not pure monopoly.

Income effect. The effect on demand for a product arising from changes in real income. A price reduction that gives buyers more real income, or greater purchasing power for their income, even though money or nominal income remains the same, can cause income effects.

Incurred but not reported (IBNR) provision. Provision for claims incurred but not reported by the balance-sheet date. That is, it is anticipated that there would be a number of policies that have, but for the advice of the claim to the insurer, occurred and therefore are likely to result in a liability on the insurer. The magnitude of this provision can be expected to reduce as the time since the insurance risk on the contract expired extends. The magnitude is also likely to vary depending on the type of insurance risk covered by any particular class of insurance contract.

Independence. Two events are independent if the occurrence of one of the events gives no information about whether or not the other event will occur; that is, the events have no influence on each other. For example, having a stroke may be independent of being injured in a cyclone.

Induced demand. Demand created by physicians who are able and willing to change information provided to patients for economic reasons. This allows them to affect both the price and the level of care. This ability to determine their own income is difficult to control when it is present and may have impacts on efforts to control medical spending.

Informal risk-protection mechanism. See *Informal sector.*

Informal sector. The part of the society/economy that is not registered with authorities and, whether with legal exclusion or without it (de jure or de facto), is not subject to public regulation and does not benefit from public services or goods. For example, support given by family, friends, and members of a community in times of loss or illness effectively forms an informal risk-protection mechanism. Despite the presumption that such care is voluntarily given, in some cases (for example, providing care to foster children), payment may in fact be given.

Initial capital requirement. Minimum initial capital that is required to obtain a license and must be provided before an insurer commences business, and cannot be used to finance start-up costs.

Inpatient. Individual admitted to a hospital for health care and allocated a bed for the duration of that admission.

Insolvency. Inability to meet current expenses and contractual obligations from current income plus reserves, leading, in the long run, to bankruptcy.

Institution. Social constructs that contain "rules of the games" and thereby both constrain behavior and enable behavior within those rules. By enabling the individual and organization to understand and predict behavior, the social constructs facilitate economic and social interaction. Institutions include regulations and policies of organizations and governments. They also include community-based traditional patterns of behavior and those that have developed in the face of modernization.

Insurability. A risk is insurable if it is independent and outside the control of the insured. If there is a party willing to accept the risk for an agreed premium and another party is prepared to pay that premium, insurance will be furnished by a profit-seeking firm. This situation implies that the probability is known, it is not subject to very serious moral hazard and adverse selection problems, that it is a legal proposition, and that the premium is affordable. Practical problems associated with information availability may render otherwise insurable risks uninsurable.

Insurance. Insurance is any activity in which a set of agents (members of a mutual plan, stockholders of a company) assumes risk by taking payments (premiums) from individuals or companies and contractually agreeing to pay a stipulated benefit or compensation if certain contingencies specified by contract (death, accident, illness) occur during a defined period.

Insurance threshold. Insurers typically request that the insured pay the first part of any claim. This cost-sharing is a form of deductible, used to simplify administration and reduce administrative costs by reducing the number of small claims.

Insured. Also called *principal;* the end user contracting with an insurer for insurance coverage.

Insured unit. See *Subscription unit.*

Insurer (first-line, primary, or ultimate). The company that contracts with the end user for insurance. The first-line insurer may be the ceding insurer if it chooses to reinsure.

Internal rate of return. The discount rate that makes the net present value of an investment project equal to zero. This is a widely used method of investment appraisal as it takes into account the timing of cash flows.

Late-joiner penalties. Payments, often in the form of higher premiums, imposed on consumers who purchase private voluntary health insurance (PVHI) after they reach an older age, become sick, or do not enroll in a scheme once their coverage by another policy ceases. Protects insurers from adverse selection and encourages consumers to purchase PVHI early.

Law of large numbers. The concept that the greater the number of exposures, the more closely will actual results approach the probable results expected from an infinite number of exposures.

Load. The cost of insurance (administration, finance, and so on) as distinct from payouts (benefits). The difference between premiums and benefits. Efficient competitive companies have a low load relative to benefits. Often expressed as a percentage of premiums or claims.

Local government unit (LGU). The term used in the Philippines to describe public authorities at a lower-than-national level (region, province, municipality, barangay).

Macroeconomic. Refers to factors that operate at the national and global levels, for example, exchange rates, inflation rates, and interest rates. The origins of any factors operating at the local level are large scale. Macroeconomic shocks are changes in the large-scale factors that affect the economy and society.

Managed care plan. A scheme that pools risks and directly provides or arranges for health care services. Use is controlled by mechanisms other than patient cost sharing.

Mandated benefits. Minimum coverage standards imposed by government in order to ensure that certain benefits are covered, especially when coverage serves a primary or more extensive role. They provide a protection against insurer's risk selection that is discriminatory toward high-risk individuals.

Mandatory private insurance. A system in which individuals or employers are required by law to purchase some minimum amount of private or public health insurance.

Market failure. A condition in which a market does not efficiently allocate resources to achieve the greatest possible consumer and producer welfare. The four main market failures are public good, market control, externality, and imperfect information. In each case, a market acting without any government-imposed direction does not direct an efficient amount of resources into the production, distribution, or consumption of the good.

Maximum likelihood estimate (MLE). Provides the best estimate of a population value that makes the sample data most likely. For example, given that a survey of 50 households in a community indicates that 5 percent of individuals have tuberculosis, what is the proportion of tuberculosis sufferers in the community that is most likely to have given rise to this statistic? The MLE techniques enable such calculation.

Mean. Average. It is equal to the sum of the observed values divided by the total number of observations.

Medical underwriting. A process of detailed medical scrutiny of health status, medical history, and other information used by insurers to counter adverse selection and accomplish four specific goals: ascertain the level of risk associated with the person or group applying for insurance, decide if a policy should be sold, decide the terms of the policy, and decide the premium level for the policy.

Members. See *Subscription unit.*

Microfinance institution (MFI). Provides financial services to the poor on a sustained basis. The services include saving and credit societies, agricultural insurance, property insurance schemes, and, more recently, health insurance schemes.

Microinsurance. A mechanism for pooling a whole community's risks and resources to protect all its participating members against the financial consequences of mutually determined health risks.

Microinsurance unit (MIU). A very small finance institution specifically designed to offer health insurance to the poor by pooling risks across a community.

Monte Carlo simulation. A statistical technique in which an uncertain value is calculated repeatedly using randomly selected "what-if" scenarios for each calculation. The simulation calculates hundreds and often thousands of scenarios of a model. Uncertain quantities in the model are replaced with fuzzy numbers to see how that uncertainty affects results. Ideally, the simulation aids in choosing the most attractive course of action, providing information about the range of outcomes such as best- and worst-case, and the probability of reaching specific targets.

Moral hazard. An insurance-prompted change in behavior that affects the probability of a loss-producing event or the amount of benefits conditional on occurrence of an event. For example, an insured's demanding tests that would not be demanded in the absence of insurance (demand-side moral hazard). Provider-induced moral hazards include overservicing (supply-side moral hazard).

Morbidity. Refers to illness from a specified disease or cause or from all diseases. It is a change in health status (short of death) from a state of well-being to disease occurrence and thereby a state of illness.

Mortality. Refers to death from a specified disease or cause or from all diseases.

Multilateral utility. See *Utility.*

Nominal group technique. See *Delphi method or nominal group technique.*

Nongovernmental organization (NGO). Generally refers to a not-for-profit or community organization.

Normal distribution. Statistically speaking, values of events fall in a pattern around the average value with known frequencies. For instance, if the average stay in a hospital after childbirth is three days, the values of each stay would be distributed around three, some more, some less, approximately symmetrically, with greater concentration around three than around any other number. The normal distribution is a particular distribution of this kind that is rigorously defined mathematically and gives the typical bell-shaped curve when graphed. This distribution is very powerful in enabling insurers to calculate costs and utilization.

Off-site monitoring. Review not involving physical visits to the regulated entities that evaluates the financial condition and performance of these entities, including checking assets and liabilities valuation, off-balance sheet exposures, and outsourcing.

Ombudsperson. An official appointed to investigate individuals' complaints against maladministration, especially that of public authorities.

On-site inspection. A physical examination of a regulated entity to examine if it meets the required contractual standards of all involved parties. This procedure supplements information needed for analysis of the reports submitted to the supervisory authorities. Inspectors can be staff of the supervisory authority, or the task can be outsourced to specialists certified and supervised by the authority. On-site inspections can be conducted on a full-scale basis or be focused on investigating areas of specific concern.

Outlier. Denotes events that fall outside the norm. For example, in a "review of utilization" a provider who uses far fewer or far more services than the average is called an "outlier."

Outpatient. Person receiving health care in a hospital without admission to the hospital or accommodation in it. The length of stay is less than 24 hours. The care may be a consultation or a technical act (diagnosis or therapeutic procedure).

Pandemic. A disease that is prevalent throughout a locality or population.

Parameter. A number that describes a characteristic of a population. For example, the life expectancy of men in a community might be 56 years. Health insurance uses statistical techniques to estimate the parameter, and the estimation of the parameter is called the statistic. One sample of 50 men taken from the community might estimate the average age statistic to be 54 years while another sample might estimate it to be 57.5 years.

Pay-as-you-go. Refers to a system of insurance financing under which total expenditure (benefit expenditure plus administrative expenditure) in a given period is met by income (contributions and other sources) from the same period. Pay-as-you-go financed insurance schemes do not accumulate reserves, except contingency reserves; surpluses and deficits translate into increases or decreases in the premium.

Per capita premium. The practice of applying a single premium per head across the population. A form of community rating.

Point estimation. An estimate of a parameter of a population that is given by one number.

Poisson distribution. Typically, a Poisson random variable is a count of the number of events that occur in a certain time interval or spatial area. For example, the number of people seeking critical care for malaria in a wet season month in a particular village. The Poisson distribution can sometimes be used to approximate the binomial distribution when the number of observations is large and the probability of success is small (that is, a fairly rare event). This is useful since the computations involved in calculating binomial probabilities are greatly reduced.

Population density. A measure of the size of the population in comparison to the size of a specified geographic area (region, country, province, city). Typically, it is a count of the number of residents per square kilometer.

Preexisting condition exclusion period. A mechanism that protects the insurer against adverse selection by delaying coverage for health expenses incurred by an individual that are related to a condition the individual had prior to applying for health insurance. The rules governing exclusion period vary, but often can limit coverage to conditions which received medical attention, or conditions for which the person arguably should have been aware of, sought treatment for, or for which there were clear signs or symptoms. Premiums are still due during this exclusion period and pay for coverage of care for conditions other than those excluded.

Preferred risk selection. See *Cream skimming.*

Premium. Fee paid by an insured to an insurance company in return for specified benefits. Under social insurance the premium is called *contribution.* See also *Contribution.*

Premium deficiency reserve. Amount set aside on the balance sheet in addition to unearned premiums with respect to risks to be borne by the insurer after the end of the reporting period, in order to provide for all claims and expenses in connection with insurance contracts in force in excess of the related unearned premiums and any premiums receivable on those contracts. Also called *provision for unexpired risks.*

Prevalence. The total number of cases or people who have a specified disease, health condition, attribute, or risk factor within a specified population at a specific point in time.

Preventive health care. Medical care directed primarily toward early detection and treatment or prevention of disease or ill health (for example, immunizations, prenatal care).

Primary health care. The first level of contact by individuals, families, and communities with the health system, bringing health care as close as possible to where people work and live. The organization of primary health care depends upon the socioeconomic and political characteristics of the country, but should address prevention, curative, and rehabilitation services and include education of the population about major health problems and their prevention and control. Such care may be provided by a variety of health workers, acting together as a team, in partnership with the local community.

Primary insurer. See *Insurer.*

Primary private health insurance. Term is used when private health insurance is the only form of health insurance available to an individual because there is no public option available or one is ineligible for it.

Principal. Denotes the client, in the relationship between an insurer (agent) and the insured (principal). See *Insured.*

Probability. The expected relative frequency of occurrence of a particular event with a large number of tries or exposures. Probability is conventionally expressed on a scale from 0 to 1; a rare event has a probability close to 0, a very common event has a probability close to 1. The probability of occurrence of heads in multiple flips of a fair coin is 0.5.

Probability distribution. The probability distribution of a discrete random variable is a list of probabilities associated with each of its possible values. It is also sometimes called the probability function or the probability mass function. For example, the probability of a woman's delivering a single live baby might be 98 percent, twins 1.78 percent, triplets 0.218 percent, more than triplets 0.002 percent.

Providers. Doctors, nurses, hospitals, clinics, laboratories, imaging facilities, pharmacies, and other deliverers of medical services. The insurer or regulating body typically requires that a provider be qualified and/or registered in order to be included in a health insurance scheme.

Prudential regulation system. Standards that facilitate proper functioning of insurers through licensing, reporting, financial standards, capital adequacy, and product regulation, which limit risk-taking of insurance institutions, ensure the safety of depositors' funds, and keep the stability of the financial system.

Public goods. There are two aspects to public goods: it is difficult to prevent non-payers from consuming them (nonexcludable), and their consumption by one party does not affect their consumption by others (nonrival). Vaccination is an example—those who do not pay and are not vaccinated cannot be excluded from enjoying the lower prevalence of disease; and the fact that they are healthy as a result does not affect another's ability to be healthier as a result of the program. Government usually provides public goods, because private businesses do so profitably.

Pure premium. The pure premium can be defined as the average loss per exposure unit for a specific coverage or, more specifically, the product of the average severity and the average frequency of loss. The result is the amount, which the insurance company should collect to cover all the losses to be met under the predefined types of coverage in a setting with a very large number of exposures. See *Law of large numbers.*

Qualifying conditions. Requirements for acceptance into an insurance plan; also describes the provisions that must be met before a benefit is payable.

Random variable. A function that provides a single numerical value to a particular event or outcome. The value of the random variable will vary from trial to trial as the experiment is repeated. For example, if 10 people visit a hospital as outpatients in a morning, and 7 of them have injuries rather than disease, the random variable for that event is 0.7. Another example: if the life span of a particular baby born 10 weeks premature in a community is 2 days, 4 hours, and 7 minutes, the random variable of that event is that duration.

Rating. See *Risk rating.*

Reciprocating arrangements. Agreements existing between primary insurers to coinsure, the objective being to stabilize funds. These arrangements are sometimes considered an alternative to reinsurance in that they enlarge the pool and reduce risk variance.

Recovery gap. An excess of benefit payouts over income, when the *compliance gap* is assumed to be zero. The recovery gap is not random and so cannot be solved by reinsurance.

Reinsurance. The transfer of liability from the primary insurer, the company that issued the contract, to another insurer, the reinsurance company. This mechanism allows a diversification of the risk and enlarges the risk-pooling base, thereby reducing the risk of insolvency for the reinsuring firm. However, reinsurance extends only to risk defined in the cession contract (called *treaty).* For example, a treaty to cede fluctuations in payouts will not cover the primary insurer against the financial risk of insolvency, for example, because of poorly run or unviable insurance.

Reinsurance premium. The amount charged by the reinsurer to accept an agreed amount of risk.

Reinsurance threshold. Reinsurers typically require that the insurer retains the first proportion of risk for any event. That proportion is the threshold as it is equivalent to the deductible or excess borne by the insured when making a claim against property insurance.

Reinsurer. An insurance company for insurers. A reinsurer offers protection through the sale of a reinsurance contract to a risk-transferring policyholder who is an insurer. If the risk-transferring policyholder is a (re)insurer itself, the risk-assuming insurer is called the reinsurer, and the risk transfer is known as (retro) cession. Usually used to deal with low probability risks that are large relative to the initial insurer's capital or revenues, such as total claims exceeding expected claims by a large amount.

Renewability. See *Guaranteed renewability.*

Reserves. Funds set aside to meet unforeseeable liabilities (i.e., obligations that have not yet materialized) or statutory requirements, and stemming either from shareholders' capital or, in the case of mutuals, members' contributions and from accumulated surplus. Reserves are part of the own funds (in contrast to provisions that support liabilities to parties other than shareholders or other owners). A major financial management goal is to minimize reserves and thus maximize funds available for current use.

Risk. The probability or likelihood that a specified health event (for example, the occurrence of a disease or death) will occur to an individual or population group within a specific period of time.

Risk-based capital model. Applying ongoing solvency standards based on the level of risk assumed by an insurer (including investment, credit, insurance, and operational risks), and weighing out uncorrelated factors to calculate the minimum capital level.

Risk equalization. Provisions under which insurers with higher risk profiles receive a transfer of funds from insurers with lower risk profiles. Used in many countries with community rating schemes.

Risk factor. An attribute (for example, a lifestyle factor or a personal characteristic) or an exposure to an environmental factor associated with an increase in the probability that a specified health event (for example, onset of disease) will occur.

Risk pooling. A health system function in which collected health revenues are transferred to purchasing organizations, and the pooled risk of bearing the financial burden of future unexpected health services is shared and dispersed over large numbers of heterogeneous contributors. Insurers pool risk through reinsurance.

Risk rating. Calculation of health insurance premiums based on the risk of each client. When the premium is calculated based on the risk not of a single individual but of a group, this is called *community rating* or *group rating.* When the premium is set in relation to the client's income, this is called *income rating.*

Risk segregation. Each individual or member of an individual risk class faces a premium based only on that risk class and is not averaged with other distinctive risk classes.

Risk selection. A practice of excluding those who may present a higher risk for the insurer by making more, or more costly, claims.

Risk sharing. Individuals agree to split the cost of future risky events. Insurers share risk through reciprocal relationships and reinsurance. Loan guarantees and insurance are among the many ways of sharing risks.

Safety coefficient. A measure of the difference between the expected annual result of an insurance scheme and the worst possible loss that can be borne. Information on the safety coefficient enables management to make decisions about reserve levels.

Self insurance. A group pays all claims out of its own resources without sharing risk with an outside insurer. For example, a large employer providing coverage to workers under an arrangement in which it pays total claims regardless of their magnitude is self-insuring.

Self-protection. Refers to all the arrangements made by an individual or group to protect themselves from risk. It includes not only saving and establishing contingency reserves but also changing behavior to diminish or avoid risk.

Simulation. The technique of imitating behavior and events during an experimental process. Typically involves a computer.

Small-country [financial system] rationale. Establishing one centralized, integrated supervisory body due to scarce human resources necessary to administer regulation. Common in many transition and developing economies based on a desire to achieve economies of scale in regulation.

Social capital. Refers to the multidimensional "glue" that binds community members together. While concepts of social capital vary from culture to culture, in "Social Capital and Institutional Success" Robert Putnam (1993) defined it as including trust, community involvement, tolerance of diversity, value of life, and extent of connectivity (social and professional).

Social exclusion. Inadequate or unequal participation in social life, or exclusion from a place in the consumer society, often linked to the social role of employment or work.

Social insurance. A compulsory insurance program that is shaped by broader collectively chosen objectives than just interest of each individual principal or agent, while retaining insurance principles that persons are insured against a definite risk.

Social protection. Policies and programs designed to reduce poverty and financial vulnerability. Social protection policies typically focus on labor market policies, social insurance, social assistance, community-based schemes, and child protection.

Social reinsurance. Reinsurance undertaken in pursuit of social goals rather than profit.

Social utility. The alleged gain to society from, in this case, insurance, as distinct from the sum of the gains to the individual members of the society. Where insurance has zero or negative social utility it may be banned; where it has high social utility but low private utility it may be mandated. The choice of rendering a public utility mandatory or not depends on political will or the power of authorities, including community leaders.

Soft budget. A budget with a flexible limit.

Solidarity principle. Applying rules that spread risks and resources across members of a group in a way that provides both insurance coverage and egalitarian distribution. *Risk solidarity* would imply that high-risk individuals receive a subsidy from low-risk individuals, allowing all risk levels to pay the same price for health care coverage. Solidarity between high- and low-income individuals, or *income solidarity,* implies income redistribution through organized transfers. In insurance, the solidarity principle is juxtaposed to the *equivalence principle,* which implies that the insurer seeks to break even on each insurance contract, by applying *risk rating.*

Solvable. An insurance transaction is said to be solvable if the risk is observable, there is no antiselection (adverse selection), and the premium is acceptable to both parties.

Solvency margin. Surplus of assets over liabilities.

Solvency requirements. The whole set of statutory requirements or rules as regards the required solvency margin and eligible capital elements to cover the margin; includes the performance of the solvency test to prove compliance with these requirements.

Solvent demand. See *Demand.*

Spot market transactions. The "spot market" implies transactions for immediate delivery of services as distinct from the insurance requirement of prepayment against (possible) future delivery of services. Populations that are excluded from health insurance rely on spot payments to access health care.

Standard deviation. A statistical term for a measure of the variability in a population or sample.

Subscription unit. Refers to the people covered by a single membership. This may be the individual (usually in developed economies) or the household (usually in developing economies).

Supervisor. An administrator of insurance laws responsible for supervision of the management of an insurer or intermediary. Also supervisory agency/regulator.

Supplementary private health insurance. Provides coverage for health services that are not fully covered by a public program, such as luxury care, elective care, long-term care, dental care, pharmaceuticals, rehabilitation, alternative or complementary medicine, or superior amenity services in the hospital (differs per country).

Swaps. See *Derivative.*

Target group. Refers to both current and future beneficiaries of the insurance system. The target group can comprise several subgroups of people with similar characteristics (for example, income, economic sector).

Technical provisions. Funds for outstanding claims or unearned premiums, required by supervisors. Also called *reserves.*

Top-down global strategy. Implies that a public policy, for instance the approach to improving access to health care or health insurance, was directed by a powerful global body to national governments and down through the rank and file to the community. This contrasts with the "bottom-up" approach based on the empowerment of communities.

Transaction costs. The costs additional to the price of a good or service, arising, for example, from search costs, travel costs, marketing and distribution, or transfer of ownership costs.

Ultimate insurer. See *Insurer.*

Underwriter. A company that receives the premiums and accepts responsibility for the fulfillment of the policy contract; also the company employee who decides whether or not the company should assume a particular risk at a particular premium; also the agent who sells the policy.

Underwriting. The process by which the insurer decides what risks to cover and what premiums to charge. The profit objectives may conflict with what some regard as social obligation. For the reinsurer, underwriting considerations determine the risks of the primary insurer that can be accepted for reinsurance, and which the insurer will retain.

Underwriting assistance. Reinsurance companies gather extensive data on the insured and events. They can share this information with insurers to improve the performance of insurers.

Unearned premiums. A type of technical provision for premiums received but not yet earned. Amount figure on the balance sheet representing that part of premiums written which is to be allocated to the following financial year or to subsequent financial years.

Unilateral utility. See *Utility.*

Uninsurable. See *Insurability.*

Unit cost. The average cost of particular health care treatments. These costs are negotiated between a microinsurance unit and providers. Insurance enables a move away from fee-for-service toward averaging out of unit costs.

Universal coverage. Implies that all members of a country (or a community) have health insurance that covers all or almost all of the cost of all services.

User fees. Charges payable by users, usually at the point of service. See *Spot market transactions.*

Utility. The satisfaction gained from having the desire for goods and services met. *Multilateral utility* means that several parties benefit from outcomes. These parties can be a group of insured or the insurer and the insured. *Unilateral utility* means that only one party gains. The balance between group and individual utility is a delicate component of relations within a community, between insurer/insured, or between insurer/reinsurer.

Utilization. Refers to utilization patterns of medical services in a location over a period. Data on recent utilization, collected at the national and community levels, are valuable in predicting future patterns.

Variation coefficient. See *Coefficient of variation.*

Vector-home infectious disease. Infections caused by human contact with an infectious agent; transmitted from an infected individual by an insect or other live carrier. For example, malaria is biologically transmitted from an infected individual to a noninfected person by the same mosquito (the vector) biting both people.

Waiting period. A mechanism that protects the insurer against adverse selection by delaying the period before an individual will be covered for any services he or she receives after the effective date of coverage. Access is restricted during the period of delay but not afterward. Policy premiums are still paid during this time.

Willingness to pay (WTP). Willingness to pay for health care or health insurance is affected by a household's income, tastes, and culture and measures the perceived benefit from the good or service. It differs from "ability to pay." There are commonly two ways to estimate WTP:

- Using data on past health care utilization and prices (demand). The price a person pays for the last unit of care purchased equals that person's subjective benefit from that unit. The total amount a consumer would be willing to pay for an amount of a product rather than go without (usually much more than what is actually charged) is a measure of the benefit from that amount of the product compared to none at all.
- Using contingent valuation methods based on surveys.

Working capital. Current assets minus current liabilities. It is the capital available for an organization's short-term financing.

NOTE

This glossary was adapted from "Glossary of Terms," Appendix C in *Social Reinsurance: A New Approach to Sustainable Community Health Financing,* David M. Dror and Alexander S. Preker, eds., 465–485, World Bank, Washington, DC, and International Labour Office, Geneva, Switzerland, 2002. Other sources consulted were WebFinance Inc., http://webfinanceinc.com, 2007; and International Association of Insurance Supervisors, *Glossary of Terms,* Basel, 2007.

GLOSSARY

STANDARD ABBREVIATIONS

DHSS	Department of Health and Social Services
GDP	Gross Domestic Product
OECD	Organisation for Economic Co-Operation and Development
UK	United Kingdom
UN	United Nations
WHO	World Health Organization

ABBREVIATIONS USED FOR OECD MEMBER COUNTRIES IN FIGURES

Aus	Australia	Jap	Japan
Aut	Austria	Lux	Luxembourg
Bel	Belgium	Net	Netherlands
Can	Canada	New	New Zealand
Den	Denmark	Nor	Norway
Ger	Germany	Por	Portugal
Fin	Finland	Spa	Spain
Fra	France	Swe	Sweden
Gre	Greece	Swi	Switzerland

Ice	Iceland	Tur	Turkey
Ire	Ireland	UK	UK
Ita	Italy	USA	USA

ABBREVIATIONS USED IN FIGURES AND TABLES

Com	Commonwealth Government of Australia
Con	Consumption Expenditure
Ela	Elasticity
Emp	Employers
Exp	Expenditure
Fed	Federal Government of Canada
GOP	Gross Domestic Product
Gov	Government
Hlt	Health
Ind	Individuals
Ins	Insured
Loc	Local Government
Med	Medical
Mun	Municipal Government
Prov	Provincial Government
Tot	Total Expenditure

SELECT BIBLIOGRAPHY

Many of the references that are cited in the footnotes are not repeated in this Select Bibliography, which lists only major references dealing with Financing of Health Care, Health Economics, Statutes and Statistical Sources.

MAJOR HEALTH FINANCING PUBLICATIONS BY THE AUTHOR

G. Carrin, R. Zeramdini, P. Musgrove, N. Valentine, and K. Xu, "The impact of the degree of risk-sharing in health financing on health system attainment." *HNP Discussion Paper*. Preker A. S., Series Editor. (Washington: World Bank, 2001).

G. Chellaraj, O. Adeyi, A. S. Preker, and E. Goldstein, "Trends in health status, services and finance: The transition in Central and Eastern Europe." *World Bank Technical Paper Series*. (Washington, World Bank. Volume II, No. 348, 1996).

D. Chinitz, J. Wasem, and A. S. Preker, "Balancing competition and solidarity in health care financing." In Europe R. B. Saltman, J. Figueras and C. Sakallarides, eds., *Critical Challenges for Health Care Reform* (Copenhagen: World Health Organization/European Observatory on Health Care Reform, 1997).

M. Cichon, W. Newbrander, H. Yamabana, A. Weber, C. Normand, D. Dror, and A. S. Preker, *Modelling in Health Care Finance: A Compendium of Quantitative Techniques for Health Care Financing. Financial Modeling in Health Care* (Geneva: ILO/ISSA, 1999).

D. Dror and A. S. Preker, eds., *Social Re-Insurance: A New Approach to Sustainable Community Health Financing*. Technical Issues in Health, Nutrition and Population. (Washington: World Bank/ILO, 2002).

E. Goldstein, A. S. Preker, O. Adeyi, and G. Chellaraj, "Trends in health status, services and finance: The transition in Central and Eastern Europe." *World Bank Technical Paper Series* (Washington, World Bank. Volume I, No. 341, 1996).

A. Harding and A. S. Preker, eds., *Private Participation in Health Services*. Health, Nutrition, and Population Series (Washington: World Bank, 2003).

C.D. James, K. Hanson, B. McPake, D. Balabanova, D. Knippenberg, B. Meessen, S.S. Morris, A. Preker, Villeneuve, and K. Xu, "To retain or remove user in low- and middle-income countries," *Applied Health Review* 5(3) (2006): 137–153.

J. M. Kirigia, A. S. Preker, G. Carrin, C. Mwikisa, and A. J. Diarra-Nama, "An overview of health financing patterns and the way forward in the WHO African region," *East Africa Medical Journal* 83 (2006): 1–28.

H. Maarse, T. A. Rathwell, *et al.*, "Responding to purchasing: Provider perspectives." In J. Figueras, R. Robinson, and E. Jakubowski, eds., *Purchasing to Improve Health Systems Performance* (London: Buckingham, Open University Press, 2005): 265–287.

M. V. Pauly, P. Zweifel, R. M. Scheffler, A. S. Preker, and M. Bassett, "Private health insurance in developing countries," *Health Affairs (Millwood)* 25(2) (2006): 369–379.

A. S. Preker, M. E. Lindner, D. Chernichovsky, and O. P. Schellekens, eds., *Scaling Up Affordable Health Insurance*: *Staying the Course* (Washington: World Bank, 2013).

A. S. Preker, P. Zweifel, and O. P. Schellekens, eds., *Global Marketplace for Private Health Insurance: Strength in Numbers* (Washington: World Bank, 2010).

A. S. Preker, X. Liu, *et al.*, eds., *Public Ends, Private Means: Strategic Purchasing of Value for Money in Health Care.* Health, Nutrition and Population Series (Washington: World Bank, 2006).

A. S. Preker and R. Scheffler, eds., *Friend or Foe: Private Health Insurance in Development*. Health, Nutrition and Population Series (Washington: World Bank, 2007).

A. S. Preker and J. C. Langenbrunner, eds., *Spending Wisely: Buying Health Services for the Poor*. Health, Nutrition and Population Series (Washington: World Bank, 2005).

A. S. Preker and G. Carrin, eds., *Health Financing for Poor People: Resource Mobilization and Risk Sharing*. Health, Nutrition and Population Series (Washington: World Bank/ILO/World Bank, 2004).

A. S. Preker and A. Harding, eds., *Innovations in Health Service Delivery: The Corporatization of Public Hospitals*. Health, Nutrition, and Population Series (Washington: World Bank, 2003).

A. S. Preker, M. Jakab, and M. Schneider, "Health financing reform in Central and Eastern Europe and the Former Soviet Union." In E. Mossialos,

J. Figueras, and A. Dixon, *Funding Health Care: Options for Europe*. Volume No 4. London: Buckingham, (Open University Press/WHO, Funding Health Care: Options for Europe): 80–108.

A. S. Preker, J. Langenbrunner, M. Jakab, and C. Baeza, "Resource allocation and purchasing (RAP) arrangements that benefit the poor and excluded groups," *HNP Discussion Paper Series Editor* (Washington: World Bank 2001).

A. S. Preker, A. Harding, and N. Girishankar, "Private participation in supporting the social contract in health: New insights from institutional economics." In A. Ron and X. Scheil-Adlung. *Recent Health Policy Innovations in Social Security.* Volume No. 5 (London:Transaction Publishers, 2001): 209–252.

A. S. Preker, G. Carrrin, D. Dror, M. Jakab, W. S. Hsiao, and D. Arhin-Tenkorang, "Role of communities in resource mobilization and risk sharing: A Synthesis Report." *HNP Discussion Paper Series* (Washington: World Bank, 2001).

A. S. Preker and A. Harding, "The economics of public and private roles in health care: Insights from institutional economics and organizational theory," *HNP Discussion Paper Series* (Washington: World Bank, 2000).

A. S. Preker, "The introduction of universal access to health care in the OECD: Lessons for development countries." In S. Nitayarumphongand A. Mills *Achieving Universal Coverage of Health Care* (Bangkok: Ministry of Public Health, 1998): 103–124.

A. S. Preker and R. G. A. Feachem, "Market mechanisms and the health sector in Central and Eastern Europe." *Technical Paper Series* No. 293 (Washington: World Bank, 1996).

A. S. Preker, "The introduction of universal health care in the OECD". Report (London: International Institute of Health Services (IHHS), 1987).

P. C. Smith, A. P. Preker, *et al.*, "Role of markets and competition." In J. Figueras, R. Robinson, and E. Jakubowski. eds., *Purchasing to Improve Health Systems Performance* (London: Buckingham, Open University Press, 2005): 102–121.

COMPARATIVE STUDIES ON PERFORMANCE OF HEALTH SYSTEMS

B. Barua, *Provincial Healthcare Index 2013,* (Vancouver: Fraser Institute, 2013). https://www.fraserinstitute.org/sites/default/files/provincial-healthcare-index-2013-rev.pdf. Accessed July 10, 2017.

B. Barua, I. Timmermans, I. Nason, and N. Esmail, *Comparing Performance of Universal Health Care Countries, 2016,* Report (Vancouver: Fraser

Institute, October 2016). https://www.fraserinstitute.org/sites/default/files/comparing-performance-of-universal-health-care-countries-2016.pdf. Accessed July 17, 2010.

K. Davis, C. Schoen *et al.*, *Mirror, Mirror on the Wall: An International Update on the Comparative Performance of American Health Care* (New York: Commonwealth Fund, May 15, 2007). http://www.commonwealthfund.org/usr_doc/1027_Davis_mirror_mirror_international_update_final.pdf. Accessed May 28, 2017.

N. Esmail and M. Walker, *How Good Is Canadian Healthcare? An International Comparison of Healthcare Systems, 2008,* Report (Vancouver: Fraser Institute, 2016). https://pdfs.semanticscholar.org/c4a0/5d20fa32a624c4072 9023292fc316662684e.pdf?_ga=2.8718645.1044595675.1499713218-4413199.1499713218. Accessed July 10.

E. Mossialos, M. Wenzl, R. Osborn, and D. Sarnak, *2015 International Profiles of Health Care Systems* (New York: Commonwealth Fund, January 2016): 123–133. http://www.commonwealthfund.org/~/media/files/publications/fund-report/2016/jan/1857_mossialos_intl_profiles_2015_v7.pdf. Accessed July 17, 2017.

C. J. Murray and J. Frenk, "A framework for assessing the performance of health systems." *Bulletin of the World Health Organization* 78(6) (2000): 717–731.

A. Onyebuchi, G. P. Westert, J. Hurst, and N. S. Klazinga, Healthcare quality indicators project. International 2006 Sep;18 Suppl 1:5–13.

M. Rovere and B. J. Skinner, *Value for Money om Health Insurance Systems in New Zealand and the OECD, 2012 Edition,* Fraser Institute (Vancouver: Fraser Institute, October 2013). https://www.fraserinstitute.org/sites/default/files/value-for-money-from-health-insurance-systems-2012.pdf. Accessed July 10, 2017.

J. Wang, D. T. Jamison, E. Bos, A. S. Preker, and J. Peabody, *Measuring Country Performance on Health: Selected Indicators for 115 Countries*. (Washington: World Bank, 1999).

COMPARATIVE STUDIES ON FINANCING AND COST OF HEALTH CARE

B. Abel-Smith and A. Maynard, *The Organisation, Financing and Cost of Health Care in the European Community*, Social Policy Series No. 36 (Brussels: European Community Commission, 1978).

B. Abel-Smith, *An International Study of Health Expenditure and its Relevance for Health Planning*, Public Health Papers No. 32 (Geneva: WHO, 1967).

B. Abel-Smith, *Paying for Health Services: A Study of the Costs and Sources of Finance in Six Countries*, Public Health Papers No. 17 (Geneva: WHO, 1963).

B. Abel-Smith, *Value for Money in Health Services: A Comparative Study* (London: Heinemann, 1976).

J. Balog, ed., *30 Years of Public Health in Hungary* (Budapest: Ministry of Public Health, 1976).

J. de Kervasdoué, J. R. Kimberly, and V. G. Rodwin, *The End of an Illusion: The Future of Health Policy in Western Industrialized Nations* (Berkley: University of California Press, 1984).

M. Dierkes, H. N. Weiler, and A. B. Antal, eds., *Comparative Policy Research: Learning from Experience* (Hants: Gower, WZB-Publications, 1987).

J. Fry and J. Hasler, *Primary Health Care 2000* (Edinburgh: Churchill Livingstone, 1986).

S. B. Halstead, J. A. Walsh, and K. S. Warren, *Good Health at Low Cost*, Proceedings of a Conference held at the Bellagio Conference Center, Bellagio, Italy, April 29–May 3, 1985 (New York: Rockefeller Foundation, 1985).

A. J. Heidenheimer, H. Heclo, and C. T. Adams, *Comparative Public Policy: The Politics of Social Choice in Europe and America*, 2nd Edition (New York: St. Martin's Press, 1983).

I. Illich, *Limits to Medicine, Medical Nemesis: The Expropriation of Health* (Harmondsworth: Penguin, 1976).

M. Kaser, *Health Care in the Soviet Union and Eastern Europe* (London: Croon Helm, 1976).

A. Mannard, *Health Care in the European Community* (London: Croom Helm, 1975).

R. J. Maxwell, *Health and Wealth: An International Study of Health-Care Spending* (Lexington, M. A.: Lexington Books, 1981).

T. McKeown, *The Role of Medicine: Dream, Mirage or Nemesis*? (Oxford: Basil Blackwell, 1979).

D. Morley, J. Rohde, and G. Williams, eds., *Practicing Health for All* (Oxford: Oxford University Press, 1983).

A. S. Preker, *Public Finance and Provision of Health Care Services in Québec: An International Perspective.* Brief Presented to the Commission of Enquiry into the Health and Social Services of Québec [Chairman Jean Rochon] (London: IIHS, 1986).

M. W. Raffel, ed., *Comparative Health Systems: Descriptive Analyses of Fourteen National Health Systems* (University Park, P. A.: The Pennsylvania State University Press, 1984).

M. I. Roemer, *Health Care Systems in World Perspective* (Ann Arbor, M. I.: Health Administration Press, 1976).

P. Townsend and N. Davidson, eds., *Inequalities in Health: The Black Report* (Harmondsworth: Penguin Books, 1982).

World Health Organization and United Nations Children's Fund, *Alma-ATA 1978: Primary Health Care* (Geneva: WHO and UNICEF, 1978).

World Health Organization, *Global Strategy for Health for All by the Year 2000* (Geneva: World Health Organization, 1981).

World Health Organization, Regional Office for Europe (ROE), *Health Services in Europe: Volume 1 Regional Analysis and Volume 2 Country Reviews and Statistics*, 3rd Edition (Copenhagen: WHO Regional Office for Europe, 1981).

World Health Organization, Regional Office for Europe (ROE), *Targets for Health for All* (Copenhagen: WHO Regional Office for Europe, 1985).

PUBLIC FINANCING AND HEALTH ECONOMICS

A. B. Atkinson and J. E. Stiglitz, *Lectures on Public Economics* (London: McGraw-Hill, 1980).

A. B. Atkinson, *The Economics of Inequality*, Second Edition (Oxford: Oxford University Press, 1983).

A. B. Atkinson, ed., *Wealth, Income and Inequality*, Second Edition (Oxford: Oxford University Press, 1973).

British Medical Association, *Health Services Financing: Chairman Ivory M. Jones* (London: British Medical Association, 1969).

B. E. Coates, R. J. Johnston, and P. L. Knox, *Geography and Inequality* (Oxford: Oxford University Press. 1977).

J. Creedy and R. Disney, *Social Insurance in Transition: An Economic Analysis* (Oxford: Clarendon Press, 1985).

J. G. Cullis and P. A. West, *The Economics of Health: An Introduction* (Oxford: Martin Robertson, 1979).

A. J. Culyer and B. Jönsson, eds., *Public and Private Health Services: Complementarities and Conflict* (Oxford: Basil Blackwell, 1986).

G. Cumper, *Health Sector Financing: Estimating Health Expenditure in Developing Countries*, Discussion Paper, EPC Publication No. 9 (London: London School of Hygiene and Tropical Medicine, 1986).

R. G. Evans, *Strained Mercy: The Economics of Canadian Health Care* (Toronto: Butterworths, 1984).

P. J. Feldstein, *Health Care Economics*, 2nd Edition (New York: John Wiley & Sons, 1983).

V. R. Fuchs, *The Health Economy* (Cambridge, M.A.: Harvard University Press, 1986).

W. A. Glaser, *Health Insurance Bargaining: Foreign Lessons for Americans* (New York: Gardner Press, Inc., 1978).

H. S. E. Granvelle and A. Williams, *Health Service Finance and Resource Management* (London: King's Fund Centre, 1980).

A. Griffiths and M. Mills, *Money for Health: A Manual for Surveys in Developing Countries* (Geneva: Sandoz Institute, 1982).

G. Hoare and A. Mills, *Paying for the Health Sector: A Review and Annotated Bibliography of the Literature on Developing Countries*, EPC Publication No. 12 (London: London School of Hygiene and Tropical Medicine, 1986).

International Labour Office, *Introduction to Social Security* (Geneva: ILO, 1984).

T. Jones and M. Prowle, *Health Service Finance: An Introduction* (London: Certified Accountants Education Trust, 1982).

J. LeGrand and R. Robinson, *The Economics of Social Problems: The Market Versus the State*, 2nd Edition (London: Macmillan Press, 1984).

A. McGuire, J. Henderson, and G. Mooney, *The Economics of Health Care: An Introductory Text* (London: Routledge & Kegan Paul, 1988).

G. McLachlan and A. Maynard, eds., *The Public/Private Mix for Health: The Relevance and Effects of Change* (London: Nuffield Provincial Hospitals Trust, 1982).

R. A. Musgrave and P. B. Musgrave, *Public Finance in Theory and Practice*, 4th Edition (New York: McGraw-Hill, 1984).

A. S. Preker, "Financing Health Care: Beyond Social Insurance." Paper presented to the London School of Economics and Political Science, London, 1987.

A. S. Preker, "The Introduction of Universal Health Care in the OECD". Report (London: International Institute of Health Services (IHHS), 1987).

A. R. Prest and N. A. Barr, *Public Finance: In Theory and Practice* (London: Weidenfeld and Nicolson, 1985).

A. R. Prest, *Public Finance in Developing Countries*, 3rd Edition (London: Weidenfeld and Nicolson, 1985).

A. Walker, ed., *Public Expenditure and Social Policy: An Examination of Social Spending and Social Priorities* (London: Heinemann Educational Books, 1982).

A. Walker, ed., *Public Expenditure and Social Policy: An Examination of Social Spending and Social Priorities* (London: Heinemann Educational Books, 1982).

WHO, *Economic Support for National Health for All Strategies: Background Document, Fortieth World Health Assembly.* A40/Technical Discussions/2 (Geneva: WHO, 1987).

WHO, *Financing Health Development: Economic Strategies in Support of Health for All with Options* (Geneva: WHO, 1987).

WHO, *Health Care — Who Pays? Selected Articles from World Health Forum* (Geneva: WHO, 1987).

Williams, A. ed., *Health and Economics* (London: MacMillan Press, 1985).

World Bank, *Financing Health Services in Developing Countries: An Agenda for Reform.* A World Bank Policy Study (Washington: World Bank, 1987).

COUNTRY REVIEWS FOR UNIVERSAL COVERAGE OF HEALTH CARE

Australia

S. J. Duckett, "Chopping and changing Medibank, Part I," *Australian Journal of Social Issues* 14(1979): 230–43.

S. J. Duckett, "Chopping and changing Medibank, Part II," *Australian Journal of Social Issues* 15(1980): 79–90.

J. Healy, E. Sharman, and B. Lokuge, *Australia: Health System Review in Health Systems in Transition*, 2006; 8(5): 1–158. http://www.euro.who.int/__data/assets/pdf_file/0007/96433/E89731.pdf. Accessed July 25, 2017.

R. Hicks, *Rum Regulations and Riches* (Sydney: Australian Hospital Association, 1981).

G. R. Palmer, "Health," in *From Whitlam to Fraser: Reform and Reaction in Australian Politics*, by A. Patience and B. Head, eds. (Melbourne: Oxford University Press, 1979).

S. Sax, *A Strife of Interests: Politics and Policies in Australian Health Services* (Sydney: George Allen & Unwin, 1984).

C. Thame, "Health and the state: The development of collective responsibility for health care in the first half of the twentieth century," Ph.D. Dissertation (Canberra: Australian National University, 1974).

Canada

R. F. Badgley and S. Wolf, *Doctors' Strike: Medical Care and Conflict in Saskatchewan* (New York: Atherton Press, 1967).

D. Gruending, *Emmett Hall* (Toronto: Macmillan, 1985).

G. P. Marchildon, *Canada: Health System Review, Health Systems in Transition*, 2013; 15(1): 1–179. http://www.euro.who.int/__data/assets/pdf_file/0009/80568/E87954.pdf. Accessed July 25, 2017.

C. H. Shillington, *The Road to Medicare in Canada* (Toronto: Del Graphics, 1972).

L. Soderstrom, *The Canadian Health System* (London: Croom Helm, 1978).

M. G. Taylor, *Health Insurance and Canadian Public Policy: The Seven Decisions that Created the Canadian Health Insurance System* (Montréal: McGill-Queen's University Press, 1978).

E. A. Tollefson, *Bitter Medicine: The Saskatchewan Medicare Feud*, Prairie Books (Saskatoon: Modern Press, 1964).

Denmark

Denmark, Ministry of Social Affairs (MSA), National Board of Social Welfare (NBSW), *Social and Health Planning: Administrative Organization and Decentralization* (Copenhagen: MSA, NBSW, 1982).

Denmark, Socialministeriet (S), "Socialreformkommissionens 1, det sociale tryghedssystem: Struktur og dagpenge," Betaenkning No. 543 (Copenhagen: Statens Trykningskontor, 1969).

D. Gannik, E. Holst, and M. Wagner, "The national health system in Denmark: A descriptive analysis," Department of Health, Education and Welfare (DHEW) and National Institute for Health (NIH), Monograph, Publication No. 77–673 (Washington: John E. Fogarty International Center for Advanced Study in Health Sciences, 1976).

H. C. Hansen, *Historien om Sygekasserne* (Copenhagen: De Samvirkende Centralforeninger af Sygekasser i Denmark, 1974).

H. Ito, "Health insurance and medical services in Sweden and Denmark 1850–1950," in *The Shaping of the Swedish Health System*, by A. J. Heidenheimer and N. Elvander, eds. (London: Croom Helm, 1980).

M. Olejaz, A. Juul Nielsen, A. Rudkjøbing, H. Okkels Birk, A. Krasnik, and C. Hernández-Quevedo. *Denmark: Health System Review in Health Systems in Transition*, 2012, 14(2): 1–192. http://www.euro.who.int/__data/assets/pdf_file/0004/160519/e96442.pdf. Accessed July 10, 2017.

O. Rasmussen, *Sygesikringsloven med Kommentarer* (Copenhagen: Juristforbundets Forlag, 1961).

Finland

Finland, "Sairausvakuutuskomitean mietintö," *Valtioneuvostolle*, by H. Satälä, trans. (Helsinki: Government of Finland, April 15, 1959).

Finland, "Hallituksen esitys eduskunnalles sairausvakuutuslaiksi ja eräiksi siihen liittyviksi laeiksi," *Valtioneuvostolle*, by H. Satälä, trans. (Helsinki: Government of Finland, November 15, 1961).

Finland, "Eduskunnan sosiaalivaliokunnalle," *Hallituksem Pöytäkirja Liite* D S 13 ptk 3, by H. Satälä, trans. (Helsinki: Government of Finland, 1963).

Finland, National Board of Health (NBH), Department of Planning and Evaluation (DPE), "The health services system of Finland: Description," *Memorandum* (Helsinki: NBH, DPE, 1972).

J. Pajula and E. Kalimo, "Social security in Finland," *International Social Security Review* 32 (1979): 160–173.

L. Vuorenkoski, P. Mladovsky, and E. Mossialos, *Finland: Health System Review.* Health Systems in Transition (2008) 10(4): 1–168. http://www.euro.who.int/__data/assets/pdf_file/0007/80692/E91937.pdf. Accessed July 25, 2017.

New Zealand

J. Cumming, J. McDonald, C. Barr, G. Martin, Z. Gerring, and J. Daubé, *New Zealand: Health System Review in Health Systems in Transition* (2014) 4(2): 1–272. http://www.wpro.who.int/asia_pacific_observatory/hits/series/Nez_Health_Systems_Review.pdf. Accessed July 25, 2017.

E. A. Hanson, "The social security story: A study of the political origins of the 1938 Social Security Act," Master's thesis (Auckland: University of Auckland, 1975).

J. B. Lovell-Smith, *The New Zealand Doctor and the Welfare State* (Auckland: Blackwood & Janet Paul, 1966).

D. Robb, *Health Reform in New Zealand* (Christchurch: Whitcombe & Tombs, 1947).

K. Sinclair, *Walter Nash* (Auckland: Auckland University Press, 1976).

Norway

O. Berg, "Verdier og interesser: Den Norske Laegeforenings fremvekst og utvikling," In *Legerne of Samfunnet*, O. Larsen, O. Berg and F. Hodne, eds. (Oslo: Den Norske Laegeforening, 1986).

S. E. Ekeid, "Health services in Norway: Commitment to decentralization," *Monograph* (Oslo: Directorate of Health, n.d.).

K. Evang, *Health Services in Norway*, 4th Edition (Oslo: Universitetsforlaget, 1976).

F. W. Ohldieck, I. Litleré, and H. Rygh, *Lov om Syketrygd: Av 2 Mars 1956 med Senere Endringer of Tillegg, Sist ved Low av 22 Januar 1960* (Oslo: Sem & Stenersen, 1960).

Å. Ringard, A. Sagan, I. Sperre Saunes, and A. K. Lindahl, *Norway: Health System Review in Health Systems in Transition*, (2013) 15(8): 1–162. http://www.euro.who.int/__data/assets/pdf_file/0018/237204/HiT-Norway.pdf. Accessed July 25, 2017.

K. Salvesen, *Norwegian Health Administration: Past and Present*, Monograph (Oslo: Royal Norwegian Ministry of Health and Social Affairs, 1985).

H. Siem, *Choices for Health: An Introduction to the Health Services in Norway* (Oslo: Universitetsforlaget, 1985).

N. Urdal, *Syketrygden i Femti År: Historien om en Grunnleggende Social Reform* (Oslo: Norges Trygdekasselag, 1961).

Sweden

A. Anell, A. H. Glenngård, and S. Merkur, *Sweden: Health System Review in Health Systems in Transition* (2012) 14(5):1–159. http://www.euro.who.int/__data/assets/pdf_file/0008/164096/e96455.pdf. Accessed July 25, 2017.

E. Borgenhammar, *Hälsans Pris: En Hälsokontroll av Sjukvården* (Stockholm: Studieförbundet Näringsliv och Samhälle, 1982).

R. Broberg, *Så Formades Tryggheten: Socialförsäkringens Historia 1946–1972* (Stockholm: Försäkringkasseförbundet, 1973).

A. J. Heidenheimer and N. Elvander, *The Shaping of the Swedish Health System* (London: Croom Helm, 1980).

G. Lindeberg, *Den Svenska Sjukkasserrörelsens Historia* (Lund: Carl Bloms Boktryckeri, 1949).

Svenska Sjukkasseförbundet, *Föredrag I Sjukkassefrågor 1953–1956* (Stockholm: Svenska Sjukkasseförbundet, 1957).

Sweden, Inrikesdepartementet (I), "Den öppna läkarvården i Riket: Utredning och förslag av Medicinalstyrelsen," *Statens Offentliga Utredningar*, 14 (1948).

United Kingdom

B. Abel-Smith, *The Hospitals 1800–1948*, Heinemann Books on Sociology, by D. G. MacRae, ed. (London: Heinemann, 1964).

British Medical Association, *Health Services Financing: Chairman Ivory M. Jones* (London: British Medical Association, 1969).

J. Cylus, E. Richardson, L. Findley, M. Longley, C. O'Neill, and D. Steel, *United Kingdom: Health System Review in Health Systems in Transition* (2015)

17(5): 1–125. http://www.euro.who.int/__data/assets/pdf_file/0006/302001/UK-HiT.pdf?ua=1. Accessed July 25, 2017.

D. S. Murray, *Health for All* (London: Victor Gallancz, 1942).

J. E. Pater, *The Making of the National Health Service.* King's Fund Historical Series No. 1 (London: King Edward's Hospital Fund, 1981).

J. S. Ross, *The National Health Service in Great Britain: An Historical and Descriptive Study* (London: Oxford University Press, 1952).

C. Webster, *The Health Services Since the War: Problems of Health Care — The National Health Service Before 1957*, Volume 1 (London: HMSO, 1988).

A. J. Willcocks, *The Creation of the Health Service: A Study of Pressure Groups and a Major Social Policy Decision* (London: Routledge and Kegan Paul, 1967).

STATUTES INTRODUCING UNIVERSAL COVERAGE OF HEALTH CARE

Australia — National Health and Pensions Insurance Act, 1938.

Australia — National Health Services Act, 1948.

Australia — Health Insurance Act, 1973.

Australia — Medicare Act, 1984.

Canada — National Hospital and Diagnostic Services Act, 1957.

Canada — National Medicare Act, 1968.

Denmark — Sickness Insurance Law, 1971.

Finland — Sickness Insurance Act, 1963.

Finland — Public Health Act, 1972.

New Zealand — Social Security Act, 1938.

New Zealand — Social Security Amendment Bill, 1941.

Norway — Compulsory Universal Sickness Insurance, 1955.

Sweden — Sickness Insurance Law, 1947.

Sweden — Sickness Insurance Law, 1953.

Sweden — Seven Crowns Reform, 1969.

United Kingdom — National Health Service Act for England and Wales, 1946.

United Kingdom — An Act to Provide for the Establishment of a Comprehensive Health Service for Scotland, and for Purposes Connected Therewith, 1947.

United Kingdom — Northern Ireland Health Services Act, 1948.

STATISTICAL SOURCES FOR UNIVERSAL COVERAGE OF HEALTH CARE

Australia, Commonwealth Department of Health (CDH), *Australian Health Expenditure 1975–1976 to 1979–1980: An Analysis* (Wooden: CDH, 1983).

Australia, Australian Institute of Health (AIH), *Australian Health Expenditure 1979–1980 to 1981–1982: Parliamentary Papers* (Canberra: AIH, 1986).

Canada, Health and Welfare Canada (HWC), Information Systems Branch (IFB), *National Health Expenditures in Canada 1960–1975* (Canada: HWC, ISB, 1979).

Canada, Health and Welfare Canada (HWC), *National Health Expenditures in Canada 1970–1982: With Comparative Data for the United States, Provincial Data and Sectoral Analysis* (Ottawa: Minister of Supply and Services Canada, n.d.).

New Zealand, Department of Health (DH), *Health Expenditure in New Zealand: Trends and Growth Patterns*, Special Report No. 53, by A. G. Smith and P. M. Tatchell, eds. (Wellington: Government Printer, DH, 1979).

Nordic Statistical Secretariat (NSS), *Social Security in the Nordic Countries* (Copenhagen: NSS, 1953–1987).

Nordic Statistical Secretariat (NSS), *Yearbook of Nordic Statistics* (Copenhagen: Nordic Statistical Secretariat, 1962–1984).

OECD, *OECD Health Statistics 2017* (Paris: OECD, 2016a). http://www.oecd.org/els/health-systems/health-data.htm. Accessed July 10, 2017.

OECD, *Health at a Glance 2016: OECD Indicators* (Paris: OECD, 2016b).

OECD, *Health Care Systems in Transition: The Search for Efficiency* (Paris: OECD, 1990).

OECD, *Financing and Delivering Health Care: A Comparative Analysis of OECD Countries*, OECD Social Policy Studies No. 2 (Paris: OECD, 1987).

OECD, *Measuring Health Care 1960–1983: Expenditure, Costs and Performance*, OECD Social Policy Studies (Paris: OECD, 1985).

OECD, *Social Expenditure 1960–1990: Problems of Growth and Control*, OECD Social Policy Studies (Paris: OECD, 1985).

J. Paxton, ed., *The Statesman's Year-Book: Statistical and Historical Annual of the States of the World for the Year 1986–1987*, 123rd Edition (London: MacMillan Press, 1986).

United Kingdom, Central Statistical Office (CSO), *National Income and Expenditure 1968* (London: CSO, 1968).

United Kingdom, Department of Health and Social Services (DHSS), *Digest of Health Statistics for England and Wales* (London: HMSO, 1969–1971).

United Kingdom, Department of Health and Social Services (DHSS), *Health and Personal Social Services Statistics for England and Wales* (London: HMSO, 1972–1985).

United Kingdom, Department of Health and Social Services Welsh Office (DHSSWO), *Health and Personal Social Services Statistics for Wales* (London: HMSO, 1974–1986).

United Kingdom, Ministry of Health (MH), "Report of the Ministry of Health," *Accounts and Record* (London: HMSO, 1950–1959).

United Kingdom. Central Statistical Office (CSO), *Annual Abstract of Statistics* (London: HMSO, COS, 1955–1986).

United Nations, Department of Economic and Social Affairs (DESA), Statistical Office (SO), *Demographic Yearbook* (New York: United Nations, DESA, SO, 1950–1983).

United Nations, Department of Economic and Social Affairs (DESA), Statistical Office (SO), *Yearbook of National Accounts Statistics* (New York: United Nations, DESA, SO, 1957–1983).

United Nations, Department of Economic and Social Affairs (DESA), Statistical Office (SO), *Statistical Papers Series H* (New York: United Nations, DESA, SO, 1952–57): No. 1–10.

United States, Department of Health and Human Services (DHHS), *Social Security Programs Throughout the World — 1983*, Research Report No. 59 (Washington D.C.: Government Printing Office, 1984).

World Bank, *World Development Report 1989: Financial Systems and Development, World Development Indicators* (Washington: World Bank, 1989).

NAME INDEX

SUBJECT INDEX

COUNTRY INDEX